Asia Pacific Derivative Markets

Asia Pacific Derivative Markets

Erik Banks

MACMILLAN
Business

First published in the United Kingdom by
MACMILLAN PRESS LTD, 1996
Companies and representatives throughout the world.

Distributed by Macmillan Direct
Brunel Road, Houndmills,
Basingstoke, Hants RG21 6XS.

ISBN 0-333-65464-1

A catalogue record for this book is available from the British Library.

10 9 8 7 6 5 4 3 2
05 04 03 02 01 00 99 98

Typeset by Lorraine Hodghton
Printed in Great Britain by Antony Rowe Ltd, Chippenham.

Contents

Acknowledgements

Various individuals deserve thanks and recognition for their contribution to this text. I would like to express my gratitude to the following for their valuable assistance and helpful comments: T.S. Cheah at Goldman, Sachs in Hong Kong; John Bautista at Liberty Patriot in Hong Kong; Mohan Kohli at Price Waterhouse in Hong Kong; and, Dr. K. Sriram at BIM in India. Yukiko Kubo deserves thanks for helping obtain and translate Japanese source material. I would also like to thank the organizations listed below for their assistance in providing important data and information on a timely basis:

ASX Derivatives
Hong Kong Futures Exchange
Indonesian Commodity Exchange Board
Kansai Agricultural Commodity Exchange
Korea Stock Exchange
Kuala Lumpur Commodity Exchange
Kuala Lumpur Options and Financial Futures Exchange
Manila International Futures Exchange
New Zealand Futures and Options Exchange
New Zealand Stock Exchange
Rating Agency of Malaysia
Singapore Commodity Exchange
Singapore International Monetary Exchange
Stock Exchange of Singapore
Sydney Futures Exchange
Taipei Securities Dealers' Association
Thai Rating and Information Service
Tokyo Commodity Exchange
Tokyo Grain Exchange
Tokyo International Financial Futures Exchange
Tokyo Stock Exchange

Tremendous thanks are due to Andrea Hartill at Macmillan Press for being supportive of this project and permitting me to write under the Finance and Capital Markets Series once again. Sophie Lawrence and Penelope Allport deserve thanks for their great editorial assistance.

And to my wife, Milena, the greatest thanks of all...

Erik Banks
September 1995, Hong Kong

Abbreviations

Exchanges

ASX	Australian Stock Exchange
ASXD	ASX Derivatives
BCE	Beijing Commodity Exchange
BSE	Bombay Stock Exchange
CBOE	Chicago Board Options Exchange
CBOT	Chicago Board of Trade
CCFEH	China Commodity Futures Exchange of Hainan
CME	Chicago Mercantile Exchange
CUFE	Changchun United Futures Exchange
CZCE	China Zhengzhou Commodity Exchange
DCE	Dalian Commodity Exchange
GUFE	Guangdong United Futures Exchange
HGE	Hokkaido Grain Exchange
HKFE	Hong Kong Futures Exchange
ICEB	Indonesian Commodity Exchange Board
IMM	International Monetary Market
IPE	International Petroleum Exchange
JSE	Jakarta Stock Exchange
KANEX	Kansai Agricultural Commodity Exchange
KCE	Kanmon Commodity Exchange
KLCE	Kuala Lumpur Commodity Exchange
KLOFFE	Kuala Lumpur Options and Financial Futures Exchange
KLSE	Kuala Lumpur Stock Exchange
KRE	Kobe Rubber Exchange
KRSE	Kobe Raw Silk Exchange
KSE	Korea Stock Exchange
LIFFE	London International Financial Futures Exchange
MDCE	Maebashi Dried Cocoon Exchange
MIFE	Manila International Futures Exchange
MME	Malaysia Monetary Exchange
NANPEX	Nanjing Petroleum Exchange
NGSE	Nagoya Grain and Sugar Exchange

NSE	Nagoya Stock Exchange
NTE	Nagoya Textile Exchange
NYMEX	New York Mercantile Exchange
NZFOE	New Zealand Futures and Options Exchange
NZSE	New Zealand Stock Exchange
OSE	Osaka Stock Exchange
OTE	Osaka Textile Exchange
PHLX	Philadelphia Stock Exchange
PSE	Philippine Stock Exchange
SCE	Shanghai Commodity Exchange
SCOE	Shanghai Cereals and Oils Exchange
SEHK	Stock Exchange of Hong Kong
SES	Stock Exchange of Singapore
SET	Stock Exchange of Thailand
SFE	Sydney Futures Exchange
ShCE	Shenyang Commodity Exchange
SHSE	Shenzhen Stock Exchange
SICOM	Singapore Commodity Exchange
SIMEX	Singapore International Monetary Exchange
SME	Shanghai Metals Exchange
SMUFE	Shenzhen Metal and United Futures Exchange
SSE	Shanghai Stock Exchange
SuCE	Suzhou Commodity Exchange
TDCE	Toyohashi Dried Cocoon Exchange
TGE	Tokyo Grain Exchange
TIFFE	Tokyo International Financial Futures Exchange
TOCOM	Tokyo Commodity Exchange
TSE	Tokyo Stock Exchange
TwSE	Taiwan Stock Exchange
TUFE	Tianjin United Futures Exchange
WSEC	Wuhan Securities Exchange Centre
YRSE	Yokohama Raw Silk Exchange

Currencies		**FX rates used in this text**
A$	Australian dollar	US$0.74/US$
HK$	Hong Kong dollar	HK$7.74/US$
IDR	Indonesian rupiah	IDR2230/US$
IRP	Indian rupee	IRP31.70/US$
JPY	Japanese yen	JPY90.0/US$
KRW	Korean won	KRW770/US$
MYR	Malaysian ringgit	MYR2.50/US$
NT$	New Taiwan dollar	NTD27.40/US$
NZ$	New Zealand dollar	US$0.65/NZ$
PHP	Philippine peso	PHP25.50/US$
RMB	Chinese renminbi	RMB8.30/US$
SGD	Singapore dollar	SGD1.40/US$
THB	Thai baht	THB24.60/US$

Miscellaneous

CCS	Cross currency swap
bps	basis points
FRA	Forward rate agreement
FX	Foreign exchange
IRS	Interest rate swap

1: Asia Pacific Derivatives in the Global Financial Markets

INTRODUCTION

The Asia Pacific financial markets have developed as a vital component of the global financial system during the past decade. The expansion of regional economies and the growth in domestic equity, fixed income, currency and commodity markets have created increasingly stable and mature financial systems in countries throughout the Pacific. Development of regional financial infrastructure has, in turn, generated investment and risk management opportunities for domestic and foreign institutions. Such institutions increasingly utilize the local markets for investing, funding, hedging, speculating and arbitraging strategies; these strategies are often executed using derivatives.

The ability to attract domestic and international institutions to the Asia Pacific financial markets suggests regional derivatives, exchanges, intermediaries and regulatory infrastructure are sufficiently developed and sophisticated to provide the necessary opportunities. As we discuss at length in this text, significant market developments have occurred in each of 13 Asia Pacific nations (Australia, China, Hong Kong, India, Indonesia, Japan, Malaysia, New Zealand, Philippines, Singapore, South Korea, Taiwan and Thailand) over the past decade which have assisted in making the region an effective arena for derivatives activity. Advancements and innovation in listed and over-the-counter (OTC) derivatives, growth in liquidity of such products, development of derivative pricing tools and hedging instruments, and creation of appropriate regulations and laws permit local, regional and global institutions to utilize the Asia Pacific derivative markets to execute risk management, investment, or funding strategies. While a great deal of work remains to be done to advance regional products and markets to the most developed stages possible, such work is already underway.

To emphasize briefly the extent of progress in the Pacific derivative markets we highlight certain examples of risk protection or speculative opportunity which can already be executed through the regional markets. Within the category of listed derivatives, an institution can create or manage:

- Japanese equity exposures through Tokyo Stock Exchange (TSE) Topix futures/options and warrants, Osaka Stock Exchange (OSE) Nikkei 225/300 futures/options, Nagoya Stock Exchange (NSE) Nagoya 25 options or Singapore International Monetary Exchange (SIMEX) Nikkei 225/300 futures/options;

- Australian equity exposures through Sydney Futures Exchange (SFE) All Ordinaries futures/options, ASX Derivatives (ASXD) All Ordinaries, Twenty Leaders or Gold Index options, or Australian Stock Exchange (ASX) warrants;
- Hong Kong equity exposures via Hong Kong Futures Exchange (HKFE) Hang Seng futures/options, Stock Exchange of Hong Kong (SEHK) equity options and warrants or SIMEX MSCI HKI futures/options;
- short- or long-term US interest rate exposures through SIMEX Eurodollar futures/options, Tokyo International Financial Futures Exchange (TIFFE) Eurodollar futures/options or TSE US Treasury bond futures;
- short- or long-term Japanese interest rate exposures via TSE Japanese Government Bond futures/options, TIFFE Euroyen futures/options, or SIMEX Japanese Government Bond futures/options and Euroyen futures/options;
- short- or long-term Southeast Asian interest rate exposures through Malaysia Monetary Exchange (MME) KLIBOR futures, HKFE HIBOR futures, or Manila International Futures Exchange (MIFE) Philippine Treasury bill futures;
- US dollar/Japanese yen currency exposures through SIMEX deferred currency futures, HKFE rolling spot currency futures, TIFFE currency futures, or MIFE currency futures;
- benchmark grade crude exposures through SIMEX/International Petroleum Exchange (IPE) Brent crude futures or SFE/New York Mercantile Exchange (NYMEX) light sweet crude futures;
- benchmark grade rubber exposures via Singapore International Commodity Exchange (SICOM) rubber futures, Kuala Lumpur Commodity Exchange (KLCE) rubber futures, Tokyo Commodity Exchange (TOCOM) rubber futures, Kobe Rubber Exchange (KRE) rubber futures, or Indonesian Commodity Exchange Board (ICEB) rubber forwards;
- gold exposures through SIMEX gold futures, HKFE gold futures or TOCOM gold futures; and so on.

Many of the same exposure management profiles can be obtained through over-the-counter derivatives. An institution can create or manage:

- Japanese equity exposures through OTC equity forwards, swaps and options, basket forwards, swaps and options, and index forwards, swaps and options, or via OTC equity, basket and index warrants;
- Australian equity exposures through OTC equity forwards, swaps and options, basket forwards, swaps and options, and index forwards, swaps and options, or via OTC equity, basket and index warrants;

- Hong Kong equity exposures through OTC equity forwards, swaps and options, basket forwards, swaps and options and index forwards, swaps and options, or via OTC equity, basket and index warrants;
- short- or long-term US interest rate exposures through US dollar interest rate forwards, swaps and options (executed during Asia Pacific hours);
- short- or long-term Japanese interest rate exposures through yen interest rate forwards, swaps and options;
- short- or long-term Southeast Asian interest rate exposures (e.g. Malaysia, Hong Kong, Philippines) through OTC Southeast Asian interest rate forwards, swaps and options;
- US dollar/Japanese yen currency exposures through OTC currency forwards, swaps and options;
- benchmark grade crudes through OTC oil forwards, swaps and options;
- benchmark grade rubber exposures through OTC commodity forwards and swaps;
- gold exposures through OTC commodity forwards, swaps and options; and so on.

As indicated above, this is but a small sample of derivatives which can already be executed in the Pacific region.

One fundamental reason for the significant growth in regional listed and OTC derivatives is related to growth in the underlying cash markets which such derivatives reference. With expansion of the regional equity, debt, currency and commodity markets there has been increased need for derivatives geared specifically to the regional markets; as we discuss at greater length below, more than 90% of listed derivatives and virtually 100% of OTC derivatives in Asia Pacific (excepting those executed by financial institutions in the Asian time zone as part of their global book-running process) target specific local or regional equity/index, fixed income, currency or commodity indicators.

Growth in Asia Pacific equity markets has been substantial since 1990. Though the Japanese market continues to dominate the region in terms of market capitalization, it is the Southeast Asian and North Asian equity markets which have experienced the greatest growth and provided investors with the most significant returns. Market capitalization for the entire region increased from US$3.5 tln in 1990 to US$5.5 tln at the end of 1994; Japan's share of the total market declined from a peak of 82% in 1990 to a low of 63% in 1993 (with a slight rebound to 67% in 1994, primarily as a result of the massive Japan Tobacco privatization and initial public offering).

Growth in market capitalization has come from four primary sources: outright price increases due to significant foreign and domestic investment in regional equities (which was especially pronounced during 1993); privatizations of state-owned companies in the region (e.g. Indosat in Indonesia, Telecom Asia in Thailand, JR East and the aforementioned Japan Tobacco in Japan, Telecom in Australia, Singapore Telecom in Singapore, STM in Malaysia, and so on); initial public offerings for hundreds of new local companies; and, secondary equity flotations for hundreds of established companies. The growth in equity activity in the Pacific has led to increased regional and global demand for equity-related derivatives, including listed equity options, index futures, index options and equity warrants, as well as OTC equity warrants, equity/basket/index forwards, swaps and options. Such instruments provide local, regional and global institutions with protection against price risk or participation in market appreciation. Table 1.1 highlights the growth in Asia Pacific equity market capitalization since 1990.

Country	**1990**	**1991**	**1992**	**1993**	**1994**
Australia	140.9	186.9	281.0	342.2	323.6
China	0.0	2.0	18.3	40.6	43.5
Hong Kong	83.4	122.0	172.1	385.2	269.5
India	38.6	47.7	65.1	98.0	127.5
Indonesia	8.1	6.8	12.0	33.0	47.2
Japan	2917.7	3130.9	2399.0	2999.8	3719.9
Malaysia	48.6	58.6	94.0	220.3	199.3
New Zealand	8.8	14.3	15.3	25.6	27.2
Philippines	5.9	10.2	13.8	40.3	55.5
Singapore	34.3	47.6	48.8	132.7	134.5
South Korea	110.6	96.4	107.4	139.4	191.8
Taiwan	100.7	124.8	101.1	195.1	247.3
Thailand	23.9	35.8	58.3	130.5	131.5
Total (US$ bln)	3521.5	3884.0	3386.2	4782.7	5518.3

Sources: World Bank, 1995; ASX, 1995; IFC, 1995

Table 1.1 Asia Pacific Equity Market Capitalization

While regional equity markets have been expanding rather dramatically for several years, local currency fixed income markets have begun growing at a rapid pace as well. The outlook for further growth is extremely strong as most nations in Asia Pacific have substantial development and infrastructure plans which will be funded partly through the issuance of local currency debt. Although Japan continues to dominate local currency fixed income issuance, nations such as Korea, Taiwan and Australia already feature substantial domestic debt markets while nations such as Malaysia, Singapore and India are experiencing rapid growth in their markets. At the end of 1994 total outstanding local currency fixed income instruments (sovereign and private sector money and bond market securities) amounted to US$4.14 tln (with Japan accounting for 83% of the total). In addition to providing a mechanism to meet local funding requirements, most Asia Pacific central banks and financial authorities recognize that further expansion of debt programmes is necessary in order to provide price benchmarks for future bond issues and promote development of local fixed income derivatives. While certain countries (e.g. Japan, Australia, New Zealand, Hong Kong) already feature liquid listed and/or OTC fixed income derivatives, most other nations are in the process of developing such capabilities. Priorities in the region include the establishment, or enhancement, of short-term benchmark instruments which can help promote use of a standard short-term interest rate; such rates are vital in the development of OTC forwards and swaps. A second priority is to foster additional primary and secondary activity in medium- and long-term fixed income securities in order to strengthen local yield curves and provide institutions with hedging tools for swaps. As we discuss at length in this text development of fixed income derivatives in emerging Pacific nations, and expansion of fixed income derivatives in developed Pacific nations, is well underway. Table 1.2 highlights local currency fixed income outstandings for Asia Pacific at the end of 1994. Table 1.3 illustrates the composition of debt and equity within the capital markets of each Asia Pacific nation, while Figure 1.1 highlights the same information in graphical form.

Country	**1994**
Australia	121.7
China	33.3
Hong Kong	24.9
India	83.6
Indonesia	15.2
Japan	3442.7
Malaysia	42.3
New Zealand	24.0
Philippines	39.8
Singapore	44.9
South Korea	161.0
Taiwan	78.8
Thailand	25.0
Total US$ bln	4137.2

Sources: World Bank, 1995; Banks, 1994; CBC, 1995; HKMA, 1995; Paisley, 1995

Table 1.2 Asia Pacific Debt Market Capitalization, 1994

Country	Equity US$ bln	Debt US$ bln	Equity (%)	Debt (%)
Australia	323.6	121.7	72.7	27.3
China	43.5	33.3	56.6	43.4
Hong Kong	269.5	24.9	91.5	8.5
India	127.5	83.6	60.4	39.6
Indonesia	47.2	15.2	75.6	24.4
Japan	3719.9	3442.7	51.9	48.1
Malaysia	199.3	42.3	82.5	17.5
New Zealand	27.2	24.0	52.8	47.2
Philippines	55.5	39.8	58.2	41.8
Singapore	134.5	44.9	74.9	25.1
South Korea	191.8	161.0	54.4	45.6
Taiwan	247.3	78.8	75.8	24.2
Thailand	131.5	25.0	84.3	15.7
Total	5523.0	4137.2	57.2	42.8

Table 1.3 Asia Pacific Debt and Equity Market Capitalization

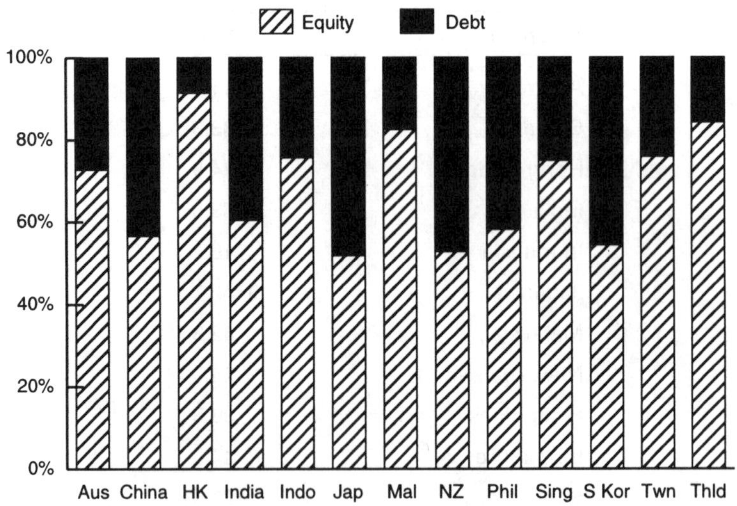

Figure 1.1 Asia Pacific Debt and Equity Market Capitalization

Currency trading has increased significantly in Asia Pacific, with Tokyo, Singapore and Hong Kong now accounting for a considerable portion of global turnover in Group of 10 (G10) currencies; the three centres rank as the third, fourth and fifth most active global currency trading centres (respectively), recording average daily turnover of US$ 1.4 tln in 1994 (Hastings, 1995). While established currencies such as the Japanese yen and Australian dollar have been actively traded for many years, attention has been drawn more recently to the exotic currencies of Asia. Singapore and Hong Kong dominate regional spot and forward trading of Thai baht, Singapore dollars, Hong Kong dollars, Malaysian ringgit and Indonesian rupiah, and have experienced dramatic increases in turnover over the past five years. Regional trading has been fuelled by global institutions investing in Asia Pacific equity markets (and requiring FX to effect such investment); issuers, importers and exporters hedging liabilities or currency receipts; and institutions speculating on the direction or volatility of particular currencies (or domestic interest rates, which can often be accessed through the local forward FX markets). The most active segment of the Pacific currency derivative market is in OTC structures (options, swaps, forwards) targeting Southeast Asian currencies (plus the yen and Australian dollar). Exotic options (e.g. average rate or Asian options, barrier options, outperformance options, digital options, and so on) are also utilized in the region, primarily against the yen and Australian dollar, but increasingly against Southeast Asian currencies as well. While regional OTC currency derivative activity is on the rise, interest in listed currency derivatives appears to be on the decline; several of the region's listed currency futures, based on G10 currencies, are either dormant (e.g. TIFFE's JPY/US$ futures) or have been delisted (e.g. NZFOE's NZ$/US$ future, SIMEX's conventional currency contracts); futures have proven unsuccessful primarily because participants have regional access to very liquid spot and forward trading in most global currencies (note: not to be deterred, some exchanges, such as HKFE, are undertaking significant expansion in listed currency derivatives).

Commodity markets have been fundamental to the development of economies in virtually every country considered in this text; continued expansion in regional agricultural, energy and base metal commodities is generating ever-increasing derivatives activity (particularly in listed futures). Countries in Asia Pacific are major producers and exporters of commodities such as coffee, sugar, soybeans, red beans, rice, rubber, palm oil, copper, aluminium, crude oil and natural gas; in addition, many nations are major consumers, or importers, of raw materials or finished goods such as crude oil (and products obtained from crude oil), aluminium, copper, gold and steel. Prior to trading of equities, bonds and currencies, most countries were buying and selling physical commodities on a spot basis; forward trading of physical commodities soon followed and the creation of futures developed in the final stage. Development of futures created specifically for local commodities made it possible for commodity price risk to be managed in an efficient fashion; rather than rely on international commodity contracts geared towards general hedgers and speculators (and being forced to assume basis risks in the process), the Pacific nations created contracts which suited their markets more specifically. Countries such as Japan, Malaysia, Philippines, Australia, Hong Kong, Indonesia, Singapore and China began their listed derivative programmes with commodity contracts. While most have added financial contracts over time, virtually all continue to list and trade commodity futures and many are seeking to expand listed product offerings. For some, such as the Philippines, Indonesia, Malaysia and China, commodity futures remain the focal point of local listed derivatives trading. Note that in contrast to listed derivatives, the market for regional OTC commodity derivatives has been far less active and remains comparatively underdeveloped. This is primarily true because the global commodity derivative market is still small, and hedgers and speculators prefer to utilize more familiar listed products; in many instances local institutions have been using listed Asia Pacific commodity derivatives for 20 or 30 years (e.g. Japan, Australia and Malaysia have each featured vibrant commodity exchanges for several decades) and have gained substantial experience using such instruments. With the exception of certain OTC energy derivatives traded through Singapore, the regional OTC commodity derivative market is relatively inactive.

LISTED DERIVATIVES

The emergence of the Asia Pacific listed derivative markets (based primarily on exchange-traded futures and options) has been impressive. In 1985 Asian exchanges accounted for approximately 0.5% of total global contract volume, with only the Sydney Futures Exchange (SFE) and Tokyo Grain Exchange (TGE) particularly active (Park and Schoenfeld, 1993); key contracts such as Nikkei 225 Index futures, Hang Seng Index futures and Japanese Government Bond futures had not yet been created or were in their first months of trading. During the course of the past decade, increased liquidity in individual cash markets, development of innovative derivative products and heightened need for speculative and hedge instruments in the Pacific region have propelled a number of regional exchanges into the list of the world's most active trading forums. Six of the top 20 most active futures and options exchanges are now located in Asia Pacific; these six accounted for almost 12% of global contract volume in 1994 (FI, 1995). Featured on these exchanges are several of the world's most liquid contracts, including TIFFE's three-month Euroyen future (ranked as the fifth most active derivative with 1994 volume of 37.4 mln contracts) and the TSE's Japanese Government Bond (JGB) future (ranked as the 20th most active derivative with 1994 volume of 13 mln contracts). The prospect for additional expansion in turnover appears favourable, as four of the region's exchanges ranked among the fastest growing in the world in 1994, including TIFFE (58% increase in turnover over 1993), SIMEX (53%), SFE (47%), and Tokyo Commodity Exchange (TOCOM) (41%) (FI, 1995).

There are currently 49 listed futures/options exchanges in Asia Pacific trading a total of 251 futures contracts and 34 futures options/ options contracts. The importance of regional exchanges and regional derivatives is evident in the current product availability; excluding offshore contracts accessible on regional exchanges via global links (discussed at length below), 259 of 285 futures and options contracts listed as of mid-1995 relate specifically to Asia Pacific markets while just 26 are based on offshore markets (e.g. contracts which reference international prices, rates or indexes, or accept only international deliverables). Table 1.4 highlights the 20 most active global exchanges in 1994.

Rank	**Exchange**	**Country**	**Contracts Traded (mln)**
1	Chicago Board of Trade	US	219.5
2	Chicago Mercantile Exchange	US	205.2
3	London International Financial Futures Exchange	UK	148.7
4	Chicago Board Options Exchange	US	115.0
5	Bolsa de Mercadorias e Futuros	Brazil	103.0
6	Marche a Terme Int. de France	France	93.4
7	NY Mercantile Exchange	US	78.7
8	Deutsche Terminborse	Germany	49.3
9	London Metals Exchange	UK	47.7
10	Tokyo International Financial Futures Exchange	Japan	38.0
11	Meff Renta Variable	Spain	34.6
12	Sydney Futures Exchange	Australia	31.6
13	Tokyo Commodities Exchange	Japan	30.5
14	Singapore International Monetary Exchange	Singapore	24.1
15	OM Stockholm	Sweden	21.7
16	Meff Renta Fija	Spain	19.7
17	Tokyo Stock Exchange	Japan	17.5
18	Osaka Stock Exchange	Japan	14.9
19	International Petroleum Exchange	UK	14.5
20	Coffee, Sugar and Cocoa Exchange	US	12.7

Source: Futures Industry Association, 1995

Table 1.4 Twenty Most Active Global Futures/Options Exchanges, 1994

(Note: several other Asia Pacific exchanges are included in the world's top 50, including Tokyo Grain Exchange (22), Kansai Agricultural Commodity Exchange (26), Hong Kong Futures Exchange (27), Osaka Textile Exchange (34), Manila International Futures Exchange (35), Kobe Rubber Exchange (37), ASX Derivatives (40), Nagoya Textile Exchange (44), Yokohama Raw Silk Exchange (47) and New Zealand Futures and Options Exchange (50)).

With the emergence of the Asia Pacific market as a major centre for listed derivatives trading it has become possible for global, regional and local participants to engage in hedging, speculating or arbitraging in global, regional or local contracts during the Asia Pacific trading day. Tables 1.5 through 1.8 display all listed futures and options contracts traded in Asia Pacific as of mid-1995 (including several contracts in the final stages of launch); all contracts listed are discussed in greater detail in relevant country chapters.

Country	Exchange	Product
Australia	• ASX Derivatives	• Equity Options • Share Ratios • Low Exercise Price Options • All Ordinaries Index Options • Twenty Leaders Index Options • Gold Index Options
	• Sydney Futures Exchange	• Share Futures • All Ordinaries Index Futures and Options
China		None Currently Available
Hong Kong	• Hong Kong Futures Exchange	• Share Futures • Hang Seng Index Futures and Options • Hang Seng Sub-index Futures
	• Stock Exchange of Hong Kong	• Equity Options
India		None Currently Available
Indonesia		None Currently Available
Japan	• Nagoya Stock Exchange	• Nagoya 25 Index Options
	• Osaka Stock Exchange	• Nikkei 225 Index Futures and Options • Nikkei 300 Index Futures and Options
	• Tokyo Stock Exchange	• Topix Futures and Options
Malaysia	• Kuala Lumpur Options and Financial Futures Exchange	• Equity Options (proposed) • KLC Index Futures and Options (latter proposed)
New Zealand	• New Zealand Futures and Options Exchange	• Equity Options • NZSE Ten Index Futures and Options
Philippines		None Currently Available
Singapore	• Singapore International Monetary Exchange	• Nikkei 225 Index Futures and Options • Nikkei 300 Index Futures and Options • MSCI Hong Kong Index Futures
	• Stock Exchange of Singapore	• Equity Options
South Korea	• Korea Stock Exchange	• KOSPI 200 Index Futures (proposed)
Taiwan		None Currently Available
Thailand		None Currently Available

Table 1.5 Listed Equity/Index Futures/Options in Asia Pacific

Country	Exchange	Product
Australia	• Sydney Futures Exchange	• 90-Day Bank Bill Futures and Options • Three-Year Australian Commonwealth Government Bond Futures and Options • Ten-Year Australian Commonwealth Government Bond Futures and Options
China	• Beijing Commodity Exchange	• Two-Year Treasury Bond Futures • Three-Year Treasury Bond Futures • Five-Year Treasury Bond Futures
	• China Commodity Futures Exchange of Hainan	• Three-Year Treasury Bond Futures •Five-Year Treasury Bond Futures
	• China Zhegzhou Commodity Exchange	• Two-Year Treasury Bond Futures • Three-Year Treasury Bond Futures • Five-Year Treasury Bond Futures
	• Guangdong United Futures Exchange	• Three-Year Treasury Bond Futures • Five-Year Treasury Bond Futures
	• Shanghai Stock Exchange	• Two-Year Treasury Bond Futures • Three-Year Treasury Bond Futures • Five-Year Treasury Bond Futures
	• Shenyang Commodity Exchange	• Two-Year Treasury Bond Futures • Three-Year Treasury Bond Futures • Five-Year Treasury Bond Futures
	• Shenzhen Metal and United Futures Exchange	• Three-Year Treasury Bond Futures
	• Shenzhen Stock Exchange	• Two-Year Treasury Bond Futures • Three-Year Treasury Bond Futures • Five-Year Treasury Bond Futures
	• Wuhan Securities Exchange Centre	• Two-Year Treasury Bond Futures • Three-Year Treasury Bond Futures • Five-Year Treasury Bond Futures
Hong Kong	• Hong Kong Futures Exchange	• Three-Month HIBOR Futures
India		None Currently Available
Indonesia		None Currently Available
Japan	• Tokyo International Financial Futures Exchange	• Three-Month Euroyen Futures and Options • 12-Month Euroyen Futures • Three-Month Eurodollar Futures
	• Tokyo Stock Exchange	• 10-Year Japanese Government Bond Futures and Options • 20-Year Japanese Government Bond Futures • 20-Year US Treasury Bond Futures

Table 1.6 Listed Fixed Income Futures/Options in Asia Pacific

Country	Exchange	Product
Malaysia	• Malaysia Monetary Exchange	• Three-Month KLIBOR Futures (proposed) • Five-Year Malaysian Government Securities Futures (proposed)
New Zealand	• New Zealand Futures and Options Exchange	• 90-Day Bank Bill Futures and Options • Three-Year New Zealand Government Bond Futures and Options • Ten-Year New Zealand Government Bond Futures and Options
Philippines	• Manila International Futures Exchange	• 91-Day Treasury Bill Futures
Singapore	• Singapore International Monetary Exchange	• Three-Month Eurodollar Futures and Options • Three-Month Euroyen Futures and Options • Three-Month Euromark Futures • Ten-Year Japanese Government Bond Futures and Options
South Korea		None Currently Available
Taiwan		None Currently Available
Thailand		None Currently Available

Table 1.6 Listed Fixed Income Futures/Options in Asia Pacific (continued)

Country	Exchange	Product
Australia		None Currently Available
China		None Currently Available
Hong Kong	• Hong Kong Futures Exchange	• JPY/US$, DM/US$, CHF/US$, US$/C$ One Day Rolling Currency Futures • US$/JPY, US$/DM, GBP/US$, A$/US$, US$/CHF,C$/US$, US$/FFR, ECU/US$ Currency Options#
India		None Currently Available
Indonesia		None Currently Available

Table 1.7 Listed Currency Futures/Options in Asia Pacific

Country	Exchange	Product
Japan	• Tokyo International Financial Futures Exchange	• JPY/US$ Currency Futures
Malaysia		None Currently Available
New Zealand		None Currently Available
Philippines	• Manila International Futures Exchange	• JPY/US$, CHF/US$, US$/GBP, DM/US$, PHP/US$ Currency Futures
Singapore	• Singapore International Monetary Exchange	• US$/JPY, US$/DM Deferred Currency Futures
South Korea		None Currently Available
Taiwan		None Currently Available
Thailand		None Currently Available

via the PHLX link

Table 1.7 Listed Currency Futures/Options in Asia Pacific (continued)

Country	Exchange	Product
Australia	• Sydney Futures Exchange	• Wool Futures • Heating Oil Futures# • Gulf Unleaded Gas Futures# • NY Unleaded Gas Futures# • Natural Gas Futures# • Propane Gas Futures# • Sweet Crude Oil Futures# • Sour Crude Oil Futures#
China	• Beijing Commodity Exchange	• Corn Futures • Red Bean Futures • Soybean Futures • Soybean Meal Futures • Vegetable Oil Futures • Domestic Wheat Futures • Domestic Rice Futures • Peanut Kernel Futures • White Sugar Futures • Plywood Futures • Rubber Futures • Polyvinyl Chloride Futures • Polypropylene Futures • Sodium Carbonate Futures • Copper BJ Futures • Copper #1 Futures • Aluminium BJ Futures • Graded Aluminium Futures • Wire Rod Futures

Table 1.8 Listed Commodity Futures/Options in Asia Pacific

Country	Exchange	Product
	• Changchun United Futures Exchange	• Corn Futures • Soybean Futures • Soybean Meal Futures • Red Bean Futures • Green Bean Futures • White Wheat Futures • Dalian Freight Futures • Shanghai Freight Futures
	• China Commodity Futures Exchange of Hainan	• Sugar Forwards • RBD Palm Olein Futures • Red Bean Futures • Barley Futures • Coffee Futures • Cocoa Futures • Rubber Futures • Plywood Futures
	• China Zhengzhou Commodity Exchange	• Wheat Futures • Corn Futures • Soybean Futures • Soybean Meal Futures • Green Bean Futures • Hard Rice Futures • Peanut Kernel Futures • Red Bean Futures • Cotton Yarn Futures • Aluminium Futures
	• Dalian Commodity Exchange	• Corn Futures • Green Bean Futures • Red Bean Futures • Rice Futures • Soybean Futures • Soybean Meal Futures • Soybean Oil Futures • Wheat Futures
	• Guangdong United Futures Exchange	• Sugar Forwards • Soybean Futures • Soybean Meal Futures • Corn Futures • Rice Futures • 70 octane Gasoline Futures • 90 octane Gasoline Futures • Gasoil Futures • Aluminium Futures • Copper Futures • Guangzhou Copper Futures
	• Nanfang Non-ferrous Metals Exchange	• Aluminium Forwards • Shanghai Copper Forwards • Guangzhou Copper Forwards
	• Nanjing Petroleum Exchange	• Gasoil Futures • Gasoline Futures

Table 1.8 Listed Commodity Futures/Options in Asia Pacific (continued)

Country	Exchange	Product
	• Shanghai Cereals and Oils Exchange	• Corn Futures • Green Bean Futures • Red Bean Futures • Rice Futures • Soybean Futures • Wheat Futures
	• Shanghai Commodity Exchange	• Plywood Futures • Rubber Futures • Polyvinyl Chloride Futures
	• Shanghai Metals Exchange	• Copper Futures • Aluminium Futures • Lead Futures • Nickel Futures • Tin Futures • Zinc Futures
	• Shenyang Commodity Exchange	• Barley Futures • Sorghum Futures • Peanut Kernel Futures • Plywood Futures • Wood Futures • Aluminium Futures • Copper Futures • Wire Rod Futures
	• Shenzhen Metal and United Futures Exchange	• Aluminium Futures • Copper Futures • Nickel Futures • Tin Futures • Zinc Futures • Antimony Forwards • Lead Forwards • Magnesium Forwards
	• Suzhou Commodity Exchange	• Plywood Futures • Red Bean Futures • Rod Coil Futures
	• Tianjin United Futures Exchange	• Corn Futures • Green Bean Futures • Red Bean Futures • Tianjin Red Bean Futures • Soybean Futures • Soybean Meal Futures
Hong Kong	• Hong Kong Futures Exchange	• Gold Futures
India		None Currently Available
Indonesia	• Indonesian Commodity Exchange Board	• Domestic Robusta Coffee Forwards • Offshore Robusta Coffee Forwards • Domestic SIR Rubber Forwards • Domestic RSS Rubber Forwards • Offshore SIR Rubber Forwards • Offshore RSS Rubber Forwards

Table 1.8 Listed Commodity Futures/Options in Asia Pacific (continued)

Country	Exchange	Product
Japan	• Hokkaido Grain Exchange	• Imported Soybean Futures • Domestic Soybean Futures • Red Bean Futures • White Bean Futures • Potato Starch Futures
	• Kanmon Commodity Exchange	• Red Bean Futures • US Soybean Futures • Yellow Corn Futures • Refined Sugar Futures
	• Kansai Agricultural Commodity Exchange	• Red Bean Futures • Imported Soybean Futures • Raw Sugar Futures and Options • Refined Sugar Futures
	• Kobe Raw Silk Exchange	• Raw Silk Futures
	• Kobe Rubber Exchange	• RSS3 Rubber Futures • Rubber Index Futures
	• Maebashi Dried Cocoon Exchange	• Dried Cocoon Futures
	• Nagoya Grain and Sugar Exchange	• Red Bean Futures • Imported Soybean Futures • Sweet Potato Starch Futures • Refined Sugar Futures
	• Nagoya Textile Exchange	• Cotton Yarn Futures • Woollen Yarn Futures • Staple Fibre Yarn Futures
	• Osaka Textile Exchange	• Cotton Yarn Futures (20S) • Cotton Yarn Futures (30S) • Cotton Yarn Futures (40S) • Woollen Yarn Futures • Staple Fibre Yarn Futures
	• Tokyo Commodity Exchange	• Gold Futures • Silver Futures • Platinum Futures • Palladium Futures • RSS3 Rubber Futures • Cotton Yarn Futures • Woollen Yarn Futures
	• Tokyo Grain Exchange	• US Soybean Futures and Options • Corn Futures • Red Bean Futures • Raw Sugar Futures and Options • Refined Sugar Futures
	• Toyohashi Dried Cocoon Exchange	• Dried Cocoon Futures
	• Yokohama Raw Silk Exchange	• Raw Silk Futures

Table 1.8 Listed Commodity Futures/Options in Asia Pacific (continued)

Country	Exchange	Product
Malaysia	• Kuala Lumpur Commodity Exchange	• Crude Palm Oil Futures • Crude Palm Kernel Oil Futures • RSS1 Rubber Futures • SMR Rubber Futures • Cocoa Futures • Tin Futures
New Zealand	• New Zealand Futures and Options Exchange	• Wool Futures
Philippines	• Manila International Futures Exchange	• Robusta Coffee Futures • Copra Futures • Sugar Futures • Soybean Futures • Dried Cocoon Futures
Singapore	• Singapore Commodity Exchange	• RSS1 Rubber Futures • RSS3 Rubber Futures • TSR20 Rubber Futures • RCS Rubber Index Futures • Robusta Coffee Futures
	• Singapore International Monetary Exchange	• Gold Futures • High Sulphur Fuel Oil Futures • Brent Crude Oil Futures and Options## • Heating Oil Futures# • Gulf Unleaded Gasoline Futures# • NY Unleaded Gasoline Futures# • Natural Gas Futures# • Propane Futures# • Sweet Crude Oil Futures# • Sour Crude Oil Futures#
South Korea		None Currently Available
Taiwan		None Currently Available
Thailand		None Currently Available

via the NYMEX link (established for Australia, proposed for Singapore);
via the IPE link

Table 1.8 Listed Commodity Futures/Options in Asia Pacific (continued)

In additional to growth and liquidity in the underlying cash markets, an important reason for the success of Asia Pacific exchange-traded derivatives is attributable to links developed between Pacific exchanges and those in Europe and North America. Co-operation has generally taken one of three forms: creation of completely fungible contracts which are mutually offsettable on other exchanges (e.g. positions can be opened, closed or transferred between two exchanges); creation of nearly fungible contracts which, though not mutually offsettable, provide users with sufficiently accurate proxies that trading can be extended to a second exchange in the region or a different time zone; and establishment of direct links between exchanges where a 'guest' exchange has access to a 'host' exchange's derivative product line.

Examples of all three linkages are evident in Asia Pacific. In the instance of mutually offsettable contracts, SIMEX's arrangement with the Chicago Mercantile Exchange (CME) permits flexible management of Eurodollar futures between the two exchanges (note that the same arrangement existed with SIMEX conventional currency futures until their recent delisting); positions can be initiated, transferred or closed down on either the CME or SIMEX. The same mutual offset system now also exists between SIMEX and the International Petroleum Exchange (IPE) with the IPE's Brent crude future. TIFFE and London International Financial Futures Exchange (LIFFE) are presently considering a similar arrangement on the three-month Euroyen contract (though it would only be offsettable by LIFFE members on TIFFE, not vice versa).

Very nearly fungible (though not offsettable) trading occurs between the TSE and LIFFE on the ten-year Japanese Government Bond (JGB) future. Though positions are not offsettable, contract specifications are so closely matched (the only difference being LIFFE's non-deliverability) that the LIFFE contract is a suitable substitute for most participants active in JGB futures trading; this lengthens the trading day in JGB futures to 15 hours. SIMEX Euromark, Euroyen and Nikkei 225 contracts settle at the same price and expire on the same day as LIFFE Euromarks, TIFFE Euroyen and CME Nikkei 225/OSE Nikkei 225; though not offsettable these contracts are nearly fungible, providing traders with an extended trading day offshore (e.g. LIFFE and SIMEX, CME and SIMEX) or additional regional trading (e.g. SIMEX and TIFFE, SIMEX and OSE). Although the regional exchanges in particular are fierce competitors, the fact that their contracts are calibrated simply means that derivative traders have greater trading opportunities, perhaps alternating between exchanges depending on current liquidity (note: the identical settlement price and expiry are relevant only when contracts are held until maturity; prior to maturity there are generally small price discrepancies between contracts from which arbitrageurs attempt to profit).

Direct exchange linkages have proven popular in recent years. Such relationships provide participants in Asia Pacific with daylight access to products traded on overnight systems of host exchanges, promoting greater volumes on the host exchanges and providing regional Pacific participants with access to derivatives which might not otherwise be available; in certain instances a guest exchange's overnight system can also access the host exchange's products during the latter's daylight hours, when liquidity is greatest. There are several exchange linkage agreements in place, or under discussion, in Asia Pacific, including: SFE's arrangement with the New York Mercantile Exchange (NYMEX) to trade NYMEX's energy derivatives during Asian daylight hours (through NYMEX ACCESS) and Asian

Regional Exchange	Overseas/ Regional Exchange	Product	Co-operation
HKFE	PHLX	All PHLX FX options	Daylight trading via HKFE
SIMEX	CME	Eurodollar futures	Mutually Offsettable
SIMEX	CME	Nikkei 225 futures	Fungible contract for extended trading day
SIMEX	IPE	Brent futures	Mutually Offsettable
SIMEX	LIFFE	Euromark futures	Fungible contract for extended trading day
SIMEX	NYMEX	All NYMEX energy derivatives	Daylight trading via NYMEX ACCESS*
SIMEX	OSE	Nikkei 225 futures	Fungible contract for additional regional trading
SIMEX	TIFFE	Euroyen futures	Fungible contract for additional regional trading
SFE	NYMEX	All NYMEX energy derivatives	Daylight trading via NYMEX ACCESS, over-night trading via SFE SYCOM
SFE	NZFOE	All NZFOE derivatives	Daylight trading by SFE members
TIFFE	LIFFE	Euroyen futures	Creation of Euroyen contract offsettable by LIFFE members on TIFFE*
TSE	LIFFE	JGB futures	Fungible contract for extended trading day

** proposed*

Table 1.9 Asia Pacific/Global Cooperation

overnight hours (through SFE's SYCOM); SIMEX's proposed arrangement with NYMEX to trade the latter's energy products during Asian daylight hours only (e.g. trading will occur via ACCESS); SFE's arrangement with the NZFOE to trade the latter's derivatives directly from the SFE (this occurred following the SFE's acquisition of the NZFOE in 1992); and HKFE's recently concluded arrangement with the Philadelphia Stock Exchange (PHLX) to trade the latter's currency options during Asian daylight hours, beginning in 1996. Potential linkages are also being negotiated between SFE and Chicago Board of Trade (CBOT) to trade CBOT's US fixed income futures during Sydney hours, and between SFE and TGE, to trade TGE's grain futures via SFE; both are in the preliminary stages of discussion. The co-operative arrangements mentioned above have proven beneficial for regional and offshore exchanges by extending trading days, adding liquidity to existing contracts and providing more effective management of positions. Table 1.9 above highlights the major Asia Pacific global exchange trading agreements.

OVER-THE-COUNTER DERIVATIVES

Not all advances and growth in Asia Pacific derivatives have come from exchange-traded products. Over-the-counter derivatives specific to Asia (based on interest rate forwards, swaps and options, currency forwards, swaps and options, equity/basket/index forwards, swaps and options, and commodity forwards, swaps, and options) have become more comprehensive and liquid than ever before, and virtually all regional markets appear to be preparing for further product development and market expansion. Domestic and international institutions utilize the Asia Pacific OTC markets for a variety of reasons: to generate cost effective funding (often through the use of swaps), to obtain attractive investment or speculative opportunities (particularly among the emerging Asian markets), or to access risk management or hedging tools (particularly in markets not accessible through listed products). In certain cases OTC derivatives are used to synthetically construct instruments not in existence or not available to domestic or foreign institutions.

Certain Asia Pacific OTC markets have already developed into extremely liquid forums used by participants around the world; examples include the Japanese yen swap market, the Japanese yen currency forward and options markets, the Australian dollar swap market and the Hong Kong equity derivative market, among others. These markets feature substantial liquidity and few barriers to participation, and have proven attractive to a broad variety of participants (e.g. financial institutions, corporations, fund managers). Other Asian markets, such as those of Malaysia, Thailand, Indonesia, Singapore, Philippines, Taiwan, China, South Korea and India, are presently developing OTC derivative capabilities, and are not yet as liquid and sophisticated as participants would like. Although we provide a more detailed discussion regarding the nature and availability of OTC derivatives in the Pacific markets throughout the text, Tables 1.10 to 1.12 summarize the current state of OTC derivative availability and liquidity (none, poor, fair, good, excellent) and maximum maturity (one to ten years) by fixed income, currency and equity product; we ignore commodity derivatives for the moment, as such instruments are still not particularly prevalent in the Asian markets.

	Swaps	Caps/Floors	Swaptions*	Bond Options
Australia	Excellent/10 yrs	Good/5 yrs	Good/10 yrs	Good/3 yrs
China#	Poor/1 yr	None	None	None
Hong Kong	Good/10 yrs	Fair/5 yrs	Poor/3 yrs	None
India#	Poor/1 yr	None	None	None
Indonesia	Fair/5 yrs	Poor/3 yrs	None	None
Japan	Excellent/10 yrs	Excellent/10 yrs	Excellent/10 yrs	Excellent/5 yrs@
Malaysia	Fair/10 yrs	Poor/1 yr	None	None
New Zealand	Good/10 yrs	Good/5 yrs	Good/5 yrs	Good/3 yrs
Philippines	Poor/3 yrs	None	None	None
Singapore	Fair/10 yrs	Fair/5 yrs	None	None
South Korea	Poor/5 yrs	None	None	None
Taiwan	Poor/5 yrs	None	None	None
Thailand	Fair/7 yrs	Poor/2 yrs	None	None

no onshore transactions, only offshore transactions
@ offshore OTC; onshore OTC limited to one year
• maximum maturity of the underlying swap

Table 1.10 OTC Fixed Income Derivatives

	Forwards	Swaps	Options
Australia	Excellent/5 yrs	Excellent/10 yrs	Good/5 yrs
China	Poor/1 yr	Poor/1 yr	None
Hong Kong	Good/5 yrs	Good/10 yrs	Good/5 yrs
India	Poor/1 yr	Poor/1 yr	Poor/1 yr
Indonesia	Fair/5 yrs	Fair/5 yrs	Fair/1 yr
Japan	Excellent/5 yrs	Excellent/10 yrs	Excellent/5 yrs
Malaysia	Fair/3 yrs	Fair/7 yrs	Fair/1 yr
New Zealand	Good/5 yrs	Good/10 yrs	Good/5 yrs
Philippines	Poor/3 yrs	Poor/3 yrs	Poor/1 yr
Singapore	Fair/3 yrs	Fair/7 yrs	Fair/2 yrs
South Korea	Poor/6 mos	Poor/3 yrs	Poor/1 yr
Taiwan	Poor/1 yr	Poor/1 yr	Poor/1 yr
Thailand	Fair/5 yrs	Fair/7 yrs	Fair/1 yr

Table 1.11 OTC Currency Derivatives

	Forwards	Swaps	Options
Australia	Good/5 yrs	Good/5 yrs	Good/5 yrs
China	None	None	None
Hong Kong	Good/5 yrs	Good/5 yrs	Good/3 yrs
India	Poor/1 yr	Poor/1 yr	Poor/1 yr
Indonesia	Poor/3 yrs	Poor/3 yrs	Poor/1 yr
Japan	Good/5 yrs	Good/5 yrs	Good/5 yrs
Malaysia	Fair/1 yr	Fair/3 yrs	Fair/3 yrs
New Zealand	Fair/1 yr	Fair/5 yrs	Fair/3 yrs
Philippines	Poor/1 yr	Poor/3 yrs	Poor/1 yr
Singapore	Fair/1 yr	Fair/3 yrs	Fair/3 yrs
South Korea	Poor/1 yr	Poor/3 yrs	Poor/3 yrs
Taiwan	Poor/1 yr	Poor/1 yr	Poor/1 yr
Thailand	Fair/1 yr	Fair/5 yrs	Fair/3 yrs

Table 1.12 OTC Equity/Basket/Index Derivatives

In emerging Asian markets which are not yet sufficiently developed to provide potential participants with a full range of liquid or accessible OTC derivatives, numerous international institutions have developed or applied innovative instruments to generate participation in, and expansion of, local derivatives. Through the creation of instruments which provide access to underlying markets these institutions hope to attract additional activity and enhance overall liquidity and market development. Three ready examples of OTC innovation include the establishment of the Singapore swap offer rate (SOR), the development of non-deliverable currency forward contracts (NDFs) and the creation of regional OTC equity derivative structures.

Many Asian financial markets still lack robust floating rate benchmarks, or feature benchmarks which cannot be readily traded or hedged (e.g. minimum lending rate (MLR) and Bangkok Interbank Offered Rate (BIBOR) in Thailand, Kuala Lumpur Interbank Offered Rate (KLIBOR) in Malaysia, Jakarta Interbank Offered Rate (JIBOR) in Indonesia, Singapore Interbank Offered Rate (SIBOR) in Singapore, and so on). In certain instances offshore institutions are restricted from dealing in the local money markets and cannot, therefore, access short-term instruments or the rates on which such instruments are based. As a result of these hurdles, growth in fixed/floating local currency interest rate swaps, particularly in Southeast Asia, has been slowed. Rather than wait for benchmarks to be established or for complete unrestricted foreign access to develop (processes which could take several years to accomplish), a 'synthetic' floating rate benchmark has been developed through the Singapore-based SOR; the SOR is increasingly used by financial institutions as an offshore floating benchmark for pricing Thai baht, Indonesian rupiah,

Singapore dollar and Malaysian ringgit interest rate swaps. Use of the SOR is equivalent to borrowing in US dollars and converting into an Asian currency of the same maturity through the forward FX market; SOR uses the offer side of the FX forward to swap out of dollars and into the Asian currency. The SOR is derived from the interest rates implied in foreign exchange forwards for each of the four currencies against the US dollar, in maturities of one, three, six and 12 months. The actual calculation is obtained every day at 11 a.m. in Singapore by averaging spot and forward point quotes from 12 domestic and foreign banks operating in Singapore; quotes are carried on Telerate page 44178. By setting an interest rate swap's fixed flows against the SOR's floating flows (typically based on the six month rate), participants are able to generate uniformity and consistency in pricing, and have a simpler task of managing cash rolls. Use of the SOR in domestic interest rate swap markets is discussed at greater length in individual country chapters. Table 1.13 highlights a representative sampling of Singapore SORs from mid-1995.

	1 month	**3 months**	**6 months**	**12 months**
SGD	2.05962	1.91482	2.03629	2.50138
MYR	5.79557	5.70537	5.71953	5.89120
THB	10.48962	10.22701	10.13545	10.19902
IDR	16.04467	16.00146	15.67920	16.03693

Source: Dow Jones Telerate, 6/95

Table 1.13 Singapore Asian Swap Offer Rate Quotes

Another example of regional OTC innovation is the creation of the non-deliverable forward (NDF), also known as the dollar-settled exchange agreement. NDFs have been created to provide institutions exposure to, or protection against, the exchange rate movements of non-convertible, or severely restricted, Asian currencies such as the New Taiwan dollar, Korean won, Philippine peso, Chinese renminbi and Indian rupee. With an NDF an institution enters into a traditional forward (e.g. US dollars against an Asian currency); at maturity the net market value of the forward is settled in US dollars, with no physical exchange of underlying currencies as is common under a conventional forward. This provides an institution with exposure or protection in the local currency, without the need for physical delivery of a restricted currency. The same concept is often applied to currency swaps and options.

A third example of OTC product development is the creation of offshore equity derivatives targeting Asia Pacific stocks, baskets of stocks and broad market indexes. Although numerous countries in the region already feature listed equity options and listed index futures/options, many other countries (e.g. Taiwan, Korea, Thailand, India, Philippines, Indonesia and so on) do not. In order to provide domestic or international investors with exposure to what have been high performing stocks and markets, international financial institutions have applied derivative technologies to the creation of options, forwards and swaps on Asia Pacific equities, baskets and indexes. While such structures are not liquid on a secondary basis (e.g. they are customized to meet specific investor needs and are not traded between third parties) they are flexible with regard to target stock or index, maturity, notional, strike price, and so on. Such derivatives have enabled institutional investors (e.g pension funds, mutual funds and so on) to gain the desired level of exposure to specific regional equity markets; they have also permitted institutions seeking hedging cover to do so on a flexible basis. Virtually every equity market in the countries discussed in this text has been accessed through OTC equity derivative structures.

Despite gains made in the area of regional OTC derivatives, it is clear that a great deal of work remains to be done in order to bring all segments of the Asian market to higher levels of development. Specifically, there must be: (a) increased awareness and education regarding the risks and rewards of derivatives (particularly among local institutions); (b) improvements in pricing and hedging mechanisms; (c) establishment of proper regulations so all participants receive adequate protection; (d) development of legal and accounting frameworks so that derivative exposures are properly reported and appropriately managed; and (e) creation of a 'level playing field' so that foreign institutions, who often carry valuable technical expertise, are permitted to participate in local products; we discuss certain of these points in greater detail below. Advancement in these areas is likely to lead to greater product innovation and liquidity in each of the underlying local derivative markets.

CHALLENGES IN THE DEVELOPMENT OF ASIA PACIFIC DERIVATIVE MARKETS

benefit

As individual countries seek to expand their financial markets, substantial efforts are often placed on developing listed and OTC derivative products. Development of local derivative capabilities is often sought in order to: (a) provide domestic (and offshore) participants with risk management or speculative instruments based on local financial indicators; (b) deepen or expand the underlying local equity, fixed income, currency and commodity markets; (c) establish the local market as a recognized, full-service, regional (and eventually global) financial centre; and (d) promote financial education and sophistication among domestic intermediaries and end-users (including investors and issuers). The benefits derived from achieving these goals, in a properly controlled fashion, are significant.

The countries of Asia Pacific have all realized the importance of developing local derivative markets. As we shall discuss at length in this text, all have attempted, or are in the process of attempting, to develop or expand their derivative markets. As one might expect, development has progressed at an uneven pace. The uneven development is attributable primarily to the diversity of the countries and financial systems in question; those with mature financial markets have, in general, been more successful in expanding their derivative capabilities, while those with developing or immature financial systems have been less successful, though in many cases no less persistent, in developing their markets. Specific factors which influence the degree of derivative market development within Asia Pacific include the demand for derivatives by local (and, often, offshore) participants, the overall size and liquidity of the underlying cash markets (which often impacts demand), the nature of controls and restrictions imposed on the cash markets, and the regulatory perception and treatment of derivatives by financial authorities. Insufficient advancement and/or flexibility in these areas is often cause for slow or improper development of local derivative products.

Though necessarily subjective we define, for our discussion in this chapter, advanced derivative markets as those featuring: (a) an extremely comprehensive range of listed and OTC derivatives, including exotic structures (i.e. second generation derivatives such as barrier options (options which are activated or extinguished once a barrier level is reached), lookback options (options which pay the maximum achieved during the life of the derivative regardless of the ending level of the reference), Asian options (options which payoff based on either an average strike or price), outperformance options (options which payoff based on the performance of one reference against another), quanto options (options which pay a fixed foreign exchange amount), digital options (options which payoff in a binary, rather than continuous, fashion) and so on); (b) good to excellent liquidity in most instruments at most times; (c) active participation by domestic and offshore intermediaries and end-users; and (d) a generally flexible regulatory environment permitting innovation and foreign participation, but with sufficient control to ensure proper protection. Developed derivative markets are defined as those which offer: (a) a reasonable number of derivatives, though perhaps few or none of the exotic variety; (b) fair to good liquidity in most instruments at most times; (c) active participation by domestic and offshore intermediaries and end-users; and (d) a sufficiently flexible regulatory regime which also provides adequate control. Developing derivative markets are characterized by: (a) formative listed and/or OTC derivatives, with a limited range and no exotics; (b) poor to fair liquidity, which is perhaps erratic in nature; (c) limited participation by domestic intermediaries and end-users, with little or no participation by foreign institutions; and (d) a strict, or rigid, regulatory regime, not fully adapted to the concept of derivatives, which imposes undue barriers to product development. Underdeveloped derivative markets are best described as those which feature: (a) few, or perhaps no, listed or OTC derivatives; (b) generally poor liquidity in the few contracts available; (c) narrow participation by intermediaries and end-users, with no participation by foreign institutions; and (d) ill-defined regulations coupled, in certain instances, with inadequate controls. In this text we include Japan and Australia in the advanced category, New Zealand, Hong Kong and Singapore in the developed category, Malaysia, Thailand,

Indonesia and the Philippines in the developing category, and China, Korea, Taiwan and India in the underdeveloped category.

Although we summarize the state of each domestic derivative market later in this chapter and discuss the markets in detail in individual country chapters, we shall briefly discuss select markets according to the definitional framework outlined immediately above. As already indicated, Japan and Australia possess extremely well developed derivative capabilities. Both nations feature very liquid and well-established cash markets for equity, currency and fixed income instruments (and reasonably liquid markets for certain commodities). The presence of deep cash markets, with no restrictions on foreign participation, has fuelled demand and need for derivatives for both risk management and speculative purposes, and has provided participants (especially intermediaries) with sufficient tools to price derivatives and manage the risks inherent in such products. In addition, the regulatory regimes in each country (and particularly in Australia) have proven sufficiently flexible to permit a broad range of derivative products to enter the system and allow offshore institutions to participate in local derivatives. Although Japanese regulators still restrict certain types of structures (e.g. listed and OTC equity options, listed basket/index warrants), the overall regulatory framework has been sufficiently accommodative to permit introduction and use of virtually all other types of derivatives. When a given market is free of onerous regulatory barriers, innovation and participation follow. While regulatory flexibility is vital, adequate control of derivative activity is equally important. Advanced derivative markets, such as those of Japan and Australia, feature sufficient control in the form of derivative regulation, guidelines on permissible derivative activity, clearinghouse security/guarantees, and so on, to ensure market participants are suitably protected.

While Japan and Australia feature advanced derivative markets, other Pacific nations are more accurately described as having developed, developing or underdeveloped derivative markets. As indicated above, in most cases the degree of development is related to the status of underlying demand for derivatives, the size and depth of the cash markets, foreign institutional access to cash and derivative instruments, and the state of the regulatory environment (though other factors, such as the status of legal and accounting conventions, opportunities for credit/funding arbitrage, and so on, also influence the development of a given market).

Countries such as New Zealand, Hong Kong, Malaysia, Indonesia, Singapore, Thailand, Taiwan, Korea, China, India and the Philippines are in the process of developing their local derivatives markets. In virtually all of these countries the underlying cash markets are still modest in size, though all are growing. Absence of well-established and liquid cash markets and cash trading affects derivative development in various ways. First, the need for derivatives may not be present. If the cash markets are dormant or inactive, it is unlikely that intermediaries, investors or issuers will seek to participate in either hedge or speculative derivatives linked to such cash instruments, and demand for local derivative products will be negligible. Examples of this are evident in India and the Philippines, where thinly traded bond markets have resulted in negligible demand for local interest rate swaps and options. Second, still-growing cash markets are often characterized by volatility and outright price gapping. While these characteristics make derivatives ideal instruments for the management of such price behaviour, in practice they may present unacceptable risks for intermediaries or market makers to bear. This presents a "catch 22" situation, where thinly traded cash markets are volatile and require derivatives to help manage risks, but where derivatives cannot be constructed because the markets are too thinly traded and risks of participating (especially as a dealer) are potentially costly. Associated with this is a third point, where limitations of the cash markets may mean an absence of liquid hedge instruments, the inability to short sell and/or the presence of wide bid-offer spreads (all characteristics of various Asia Pacific bond and equity markets); such may make cash hedges impractical, expensive or impossible to execute, once again forcing market makers or dealers to bear an unacceptable level of risk. Fourth, absence of developed cash markets may produce difficulties in pricing OTC derivatives. While in advanced financial systems liquid cash instruments are generally used as pricing references for certain derivatives, absence of liquid cash markets and instruments often means satisfactory pricing references are not available. Derivative pricing may then become subjective and potentially unattractive for participants.

While the absolute size and liquidity of cash markets are significant factors in determining both the demand for derivatives and the liquidity of such derivatives, it is equally true that the nature and degree of foreign investor access to cash markets influences derivative product development. In financial markets where foreign institutions are free to participate in the buying and selling of equity, debt, currency or commodities, there is typically greater derivative product development. The ability to execute hedges in the cash markets is fundamental to the creation of derivatives. If an institution is attempting to create an OTC option, for example, it will need access to the underlying security the option references in order to delta hedge (e.g. remove directional risk); the same is true for an institution attempting to create forwards, swaps, covered warrants, and so on. Inability to freely buy and sell underlying securities or commodities removes an institution's ability to hedge its book, which dampens overall derivative development and activity; very few foreign institutions are willing to forego hedging in the cash market and accept outright risk on derivatives positions (particularly in emerging markets, which may be particularly volatile). In certain countries, such as Korea and Taiwan, which have large and developed bond and equity markets, onerous cash market restrictions placed on foreign institutions have resulted in a relative lack of derivative product development. In countries such as Australia, New Zealand, Japan and Hong Kong, where foreign institutional access to cash instruments is largely unrestricted, foreign participation in derivatives is widespread and derivative development is complete. An associated point relates to the ability of foreign institutions freely and actively to participate in the local derivative markets (e.g. the institution may have access to the cash markets but not to the derivative markets). Failure by foreign institutions to participate most often means that derivative product technology is not transferred into the local markets. Since foreign banks and securities firms are generally the most active and qualified of all global derivative intermediaries, their absence from local participation slows the pace of growth considerably.

In addition to foreign institutional access to the local cash and/or derivative markets, Asia Pacific faces substantial challenges in other areas of regulatory control and restriction. The natural inclination for countries and regulators not familiar with derivatives is either to impose strict regulations on derivatives or users of derivatives, or to prohibit classes of derivatives outright. Such regulations may mean no practical derivative activity is possible, that product innovation is limited, and/or that foreign financial institutions are barred from participation. Equally important is the question of regulatory control. While certain nations may impose strict regulations regarding aspects of their derivative markets (particularly OTC derivatives), they may be unable to control, or enforce control of, more fundamental aspects of the markets (e.g. clearinghouses, protection of participants, and so on); this may lead to losses by clients or abuse of the local financial system.

Strict regulations may exist for perfectly legitimate reasons. Some countries, such as Korea, Singapore and Malaysia, limit the range of permissible domestic derivatives in order that control of local financial matters (e.g. monetary policy) not be jeopardized. Certain countries (e.g. Indonesia, Singapore, Malaysia, Thailand) also restrict the types of permissible domestic derivatives to ensure no speculative abuses occur in the local market; this has become particularly true in the wake of various derivative-related losses affecting institutions in Asia Pacific over the past few years (as discussed below). In certain instances strict regulatory rules or guidelines may exist for historic or *ad hoc* reasons, and may be unrelated to the items mentioned above. The Japanese treatment of listed/OTC equity options appears to fall in this category; the Indian ban on equity options was, until recently, another example (the 38-year-old ban was rescinded in early 1995). In such instances derivative development and growth are almost certainly jeopardized for no sound or justifiable reason. The absence of proper regulatory control, as mentioned above, can also be detrimental. While regulatory flexibility feeds product innovation and participation, too much flexibility (i.e. too little control or oversight) can lead to abuse of the financial markets. China is currently experiencing this problem, as we discuss at length in chapter 3. Lack of strict regulatory control has led to the creation of myriad futures exchanges, many without proper clearinghouse structures, guarantee funds or control mechanisms. This, in turn, has led to rampant speculation in certain contracts on certain exchanges and has resulted in losses for a number of participants.

In order for derivative markets to develop in a sound and orderly fashion, a foundation (e.g. liquid cash markets and appropriate regulatory control) must first be in place. Once a foundation is in place, a sequence must be followed: underlying need for derivatives must develop, derivative product technology must be introduced, suitable pricing and hedging mechanisms must evolve, and so on.

Premature, or forced, development of derivatives in a local setting can be more damaging than not introducing derivatives at all. Forced introduction of derivatives into a local market (e.g. futures in China) or of futures on an exchange (e.g. HKFE's HIBOR contract, OSE's Stock Futures 50 contract, SFE's currency contracts, and so on) before such instruments are in demand may lead to one or more of the following: (a) lack of liquidity and demand, leading to abandonment of the derivative(s); (b) imbalance between hedgers and speculators, or dealers and end-users, again leading to illiquidity in the derivative(s) and their eventual abandonment; (c) unnecessary losses and abuses as a result of uncertain or unsatisfactory controls put in place in a hasty fashion; (d) losses and abuses created by a general lack of education and information; and (e) tarnished reputation in the view of global participants, causing avoidance of the market in the future.

While the Asia Pacific derivative markets have progressed significantly over the past decade, it is clear that various challenges will have to be overcome before the markets are at the most advanced stages of development.

DERIVATIVE LOSSES IN THE ASIA PACIFIC MARKETS

While use of derivatives in a properly controlled fashion is intended to provide institutions with manageable hedging, arbitraging or speculating opportunities, improper use or application can create losses; the global press has reported extensively on such derivative-related losses in recent years. Certain derivative losses have occurred with Asian institutions or with Asian-related derivatives. Fundamental reasons for the losses or difficulties have been various: speculation gone wrong, misunderstanding or miscommunication of structures or products, failed attempts at hedging exposures, or outright internal fraud. In this section we highlight some of the key losses which have occurred in the Pacific derivatives market; our point is to underscore the need continuously to exercise caution and diligence when employing derivatives in any type of hedging, arbitraging or speculating strategy.

Barings (Singapore)

In February 1995 the UK merchant bank Barings was taken over by the Dutch banking group, ING, after rampant, uncontrolled speculation in Nikkei stock index futures, JGB futures, and Euroyen futures by its Singapore office caused a GBP1 bln (US$1.6 bln) loss and forced the bank into technical insolvency. The losses were reportedly due to outright overtrading and lack of internal control.

Berjaya Industrial (Malaysia)

In 1994 Berjaya Industrial, a trading and manufacturing subsidiary in the Berjaya Group, announced that it had lost US$14 mln from dealing in leveraged interest rate swaps. The specific transactions Berjaya had entered into in 1993 and 1994 were related to Australian dollar and Deutschmark interest rate swaps (leveraged up to four times), intended to help defray the negative cost of carry it was facing between interest obligations on a bond issue and interest receipts on a deposit. Berjaya settled the dispute with the arranging banks in late 1995.

China National Metals and Minerals Import and Export Company (Minmetals) (China)

In 1994 Minmetals posted US$52.5 mln in losses on a series of foreign exchange derivatives and was sued by the arranging bank for non-payment under the trades. Minmetals countersued the bank, claiming the trades were unauthorized and unduly complex and should not have been executed by the bank. As of this writing the dispute is in litigation and remains unresolved.

China International Petroleum and Chemical Company (Unipec) (China)

Unipec's losses and actions are virtually identical to those of Minmetals. In 1994 Unipec reportedly posted up to US$44 mln in losses on various foreign exchange-related derivatives and was sued by the arranging bank for non-payment under the trades. As in the Minmetals case, Unipec countersued the bank, claiming the trades were unauthorized and should not have been executed. As of this writing the dispute remains in litigation and is unresolved.

CITIC Shanghai (China)

In 1994 CITIC Shanghai, a subsidiary of CITIC, announced that it had generated losses in excess of US$42MM from trading in LME copper futures; the trades were reportedly unauthorized and conducted fraudulently by several individuals in the firm. Various foreign financial institutions, who had extended credit lines to accommodate the trading, reached a settlement on amounts due from CITIC Shanghai in early 1995.

Dharmala Group (Indonesia)

The Dharmala group announced that it had lost US$5 mln in derivatives in 1994; though no further details were disclosed, Dharmala's losses (along with those experienced by both Indorayon and Sinar Mas, discussed below) caused BAPEPAM, the Indonesian capital markets regulator, to conduct an investigation into use of derivatives by local companies. In addition to the loss described above Dharmala Sakti Sejahtara, a member of the Dharmala Group, is being sued by a US bank for non-payment of US$64 mln generated from early termination of various US dollar swaps booked and restructured in 1994. The transactions were reportedly structured to provide Dharmala with a leveraged position in US rates; subsequent restructurings of the original basis swaps into LIBOR barrier swaps added to the company's liability as US rates rose. The matter is presently in litigation in the UK and is unresolved as of this writing.

Hanwa Corporation (Japan)

Hanwa, a steel trading company, was particularly active during the late 1980s and early 1990s as a speculator in global financial markets and instruments, including various vanilla and exotic derivatives. For the fiscal year to March 1994, the company reported extraordinary losses of JPY120 bln (US$1.33 bln), primarily from failed investments. For the interim period September 1994, at which time it declared it would no longer speculate in the financial markets, the company reported total investment losses, net of reserves, of JPY177 bln (US$1.96 bln) (not all related to derivatives, it should be noted).

Indorayon (Indonesia)

The Indorayon group in Indonesia reportedly lost US$1.3 mln in derivatives trades in 1994; no further details were disclosed by the company. As with the Sinar Mas Group and the Dharmala Group, Indorayon's losses attracted the attention of BAPEPAM.

Kashima Oil (Japan)

In 1994 Kashima Oil, an unlisted company affiliated with Mistubishi Petrochemical, Cosmo Oil and Japan Energy, announced losses of JPY160 bln (US$1.77 bln) from dealing in forward foreign exchange contracts. The losses had been rolled over since the late 1980s through historical rate rollovers (e.g. new forward contracts priced at rates which included the losses, rather than at market), in the same fashion as those executed by Showa Shell and Tokai Corporation (discussed below).

Nippon Sanso (Japan)

In early 1995 Nippon Sanso, the largest Japanese oxygen and pressurized gas maker, announced that it would report an extraordinary loss of JPY11.9 bln (US$132 mln) as a result of interest rate swaps which went against the company. The nature of the transactions called for Nippon Sanso to receive a fixed yen interest coupon of 6.4% and to pay the difference between short rates and ten year Japanese Government Bond yields. The fixed yen coupon was used to service interest due on Nippon Sanso Euroyen bonds; the swap pay leg appears to have been more speculative in nature, with the company betting the spread between the two reference rates would narrow. The spread widened from under 100 basis points to over 250 basis points by the time the company closed out the transactions.

Nippon Steel Chemical (Japan)

In 1993 Nippon Steel Chemical, a subsidiary of Nippon Steel, announced it lost approximately JPY13.9 bln (US$154 mln) through forward foreign exchange agreements and currency futures entered into in 1990, committing the company to purchase nearly US$310 mln at JPY152.75/US$ (with no offsetting gains as would be expected in a legitimate hedge transaction).

Overseas Chinese Bank (Taiwan)

In 1995 Overseas Chinese Bank (OCB), based in Taiwan, announced that it had lost a minimum of US$20 mln (and perhaps as much as US$60 mln) over two years from engaging in five quanto swaps. The transactions involved OCB swapping US dollars for Italian lira and Danish kroner, with the bank believing US dollar rates would not rise.

Showa Shell (Japan)

In 1994 Showa Shell, a Japanese oil refiner, reported losses of JPY125 bln (US$1.39 bln) after it entered into a series of forward foreign exchange contracts which it subsequently rolled through historical rate rollovers. The strategy began in 1989 when the company entered into forwards at JPY145/US$, believing the dollar would appreciate. As the dollar depreciated over the next four years the losses were hidden in historical rate rollovers. The loss in OTC FX forwards was of such magnitude that it prompted the Japanese Ministry of Finance to ban, effective March 1995, the practice of rolling over forwards at historical rates in order to mask foreign exchange losses.

Sinar Mas (Indonesia)

In 1995 Indonesian conglomerate Sinar Mas announced that two of its key subsidiaries, Indah Kiat Pulp & Paper and Pabrik Kertas Tjiwi Kimia lost US$35 mln and US$12.5 mln, respectively, in interest rate swaps; they lost an additional US$21.5 mln in associated foreign exchange derivatives, for a group-wide total of US$69 mln (Halesworth, 1995). The transactions were terminated for total losses of US$32.9 mln (Tjiwi Kimia) and US$36.15 mln (Indah Kiat). A third Sinar Mas subsidiary, Sinar Mas Agro Resources and Technology also posted modest derivatives losses (included in the US$69 mln total). The holding company absorbed the losses and, being a non-public group, made no further disclosure about the precise nature of the transactions (note: Asia Pacific Resources International Limited (APRIL); which holds stakes in both companies and issued equity in 1995, made certain references to the transactions in its disclosure statement but did not provide additional detail).

Tokai Corporation (Japan)

In late 1993, Tokai, a Japanese gas distribution company, announced that it had lost JPY3.87 bln (US$43 mln) from dealing in forward foreign exchange contracts and foreign exchange options of yen against the Australian dollar and the US dollar, and rolling such losses forward over time. The underlying dollar derivative positions amounted to US$200 mln, while the Australian dollar positions totalled A$170 mln.

Tokyo Securities (Japan)

Tokyo Securities, a Japanese securities firm affiliated with Nikko Securities, posted extraordinary losses of JPY32 bln (US$355 mln) for the period ending March 1995. The losses resulted from unauthorized trading in OTC options on US Treasury bonds, UK gilts and various foreign currencies.

TPI Polene (Thailand)

TPI Polene, a Thai petrochemical company, lost up to US$31.3 mln (including the cost of covering previously unhedged exposures) on a derivative in 1994. TPI Polene reportedly had an unhedged Deutschmark exposure of DM143 mln (US$105 mln) related to a loan from the German export credit agency which it attempted to hedge with a currency swap; TPI Polene ostensibly entered into a derivative transaction which did not cover the exposure and sustained a loss in the process. The matter was ultimately resolved between TPI Polene and the original arranging bank, with TPI Polene paying the bank US$31.3 mln over four years.

SUMMARY OF THE CURRENT STATE OF ASIA PACIFIC DERIVATIVE MARKETS

Having reviewed the general state of the Asia Pacific derivative markets, the challenges facing the broader development of local derivatives and the nature of losses which have occurred in the region, we now provide a brief summary of each country's regional derivative market. The summaries draw on information contained in each detailed country chapter (note: throughout this text we will employ abbreviations for certain products, including IRS (interest rate swap), CCS (cross currency swap), FRA (forward rate agreement), FX (foreign exchange)).

Australia: The Australian derivative market is perhaps the most complete, flexible and advanced of those in the Asia Pacific region. Although absolute trading volume for most derivatives ranks second to that of Japan, Australia features a broader range of traditional derivatives and a series of new instruments which are not presently traded in Japan (or other Asia Pacific nations). Australia features three listed derivative exchanges which trade equity futures, equity options, deposit and bond futures/options, index futures/options, wool futures, equity warrants, index warrants and basket warrants. The OTC market features very liquid FRAs, IRSs, CCSs, caps, floors, swaptions, bond options and FX options, as well as a series of equity derivative structures (including basket/index warrants, index-linked notes, index swaps and options, and so on). Maturities on OTC swaps extend as far as ten years. Liquidity in most derivatives is considered good and a broad range of hedge instruments is available for the benefit of market makers. As indicated above, the country features a series of new derivative products made possible in part by a flexible regulatory environment which encourages innovation; these new derivatives include equity futures, share ratios, low exercise price options, overnight options and long-term options, and exotic OTC options and swaps.

China: China's derivative market is confined to listed derivative products at the present time. Since the early 1990s over 40 commodity exchanges (some more accurately characterized as commodity marketing centres focused on physical trading) have been established; most exchanges are centred on spot, forward and futures trading of agricultural, base metal and energy products. Through a series of mergers or outright closures the number of official exchanges dropped to 15 in early 1995. The most active listed futures trading in China is based on agricultural products (red beans, soybeans, green beans, corn, wheat), base metals (copper, aluminium) and energy products (gasoline, gasoil); numerous other futures are also available (e.g. rubber, plywood, polyvinyl chloride, and so on), but turnover is often lower. Within the financial futures sector, various exchanges list multiple maturity bond futures; these contracts have been the focus of rampant speculative activity since late 1994, and trading in all bond futures was temporarily suspended in May 1995. In addition to listed futures, the country also features a very small market for listed equity warrants, and is in the process of introducing forward foreign exchange trading of the Chinese renminbi against the US dollar. Other OTC derivatives (e.g. swaps, equity options, and so on) are not presently in existence in the local market, though a small amount of non-deliverable transactions are executed in the offshore market.

Hong Kong: The local Hong Kong listed and OTC derivative market is the most advanced in Southeast Asia. In the listed market, Hong Kong features two separate exchanges which deal in futures/options and warrants/equity options. Despite the lacklustre performance of commodity futures, deposit futures and sub-index futures, the country has developed liquid trading in index futures and options and, more recently, equity options. In addition to its traditional product line, it introduced currency futures and equity futures in late 1995. Hong Kong's listed covered and non-collateralized equity warrant market is extremely active and efforts have been made to promote local issuance of fixed income, currency and commodity warrants. The presence of a well-developed equity market has led to very active trading in OTC equity, basket and index warrants and options. Additional OTC derivatives are available in the form of Hong Kong dollar IRSs and FRAs, CCSs, and FX options; bond options, caps, floors and swaptions are available but not particularly liquid. Overall liquidity in domestic derivatives is mixed: fixed income derivatives are active primarily in the two- and three-year sector (though quotes are generally available to ten years); FX forwards and options are generally considered liquid, while listed index futures and options are extremely liquid. As indicated, commodity futures and deposit futures (as well as equity sub-index futures) are effectively dormant. The availability of instruments to hedge derivative books is very good; in addition to hedging via local instruments, the currency link to the US dollar provides opportunities to hedge with certain US dollar instruments. The

Hong Kong regulatory regime is flexible (with appropriate controls) and has, in the past, encouraged innovation in derivatives.

India: India's local derivative market is very limited. Listed derivatives are concentrated on certain agricultural forwards and local currency convertible bonds and warrants; the country has no firm plans to expand into financial futures or options contracts at the present time. Listed and OTC equity options, though now permissible under Indian law (following the repeal of a 38-year-ban), have not yet been introduced to the market. In the OTC market the primary focus has been on equity forwards, which have historically added liquidity to the underlying equity market. A suspension of the equity forward system occurred in 1994 (following significant speculative activity) and was followed, in 1995, by the introduction of a more restrictive system. Presence of equity-related derivatives is still negligible and limited to a few offshore basket warrants on Indian equities. IRSs and CCSs are very illiquid and occur only on a very structured basis. FX forwards and options are also inactive, primarily because the local currency is not freely convertible and foreign participants must adhere to very strict currency regulations; certain non-deliverable currency derivatives, however, are executed offshore.

Indonesia: Indonesia's derivative market features modest, though growing, activity in commodity forwards and OTC derivatives. The country's sole commodity exchange lists domestic and offshore forward contracts on rubber and coffee; these instruments are based, not coincidentally, on two of the country's most significant agricultural exports. Indonesia's recent attempts at introducing listed equity warrants have been delayed by the regulatory authorities, but such issues are likely to appear in the near future once regulatory concerns are resolved; the listed market currently only features a modest amount of convertible bonds. OTC activity is centred on FX options and FX forwards, as well as short maturity (one-to-three-year) IRSs and CCSs; overall liquidity in such derivatives, however, is still very modest, and hedging can be challenging. Interest rate options (caps, floors, swaptions) are not presently in use. Equity derivative structures (e.g. forwards, options, basket warrants, and so on) are still limited and occur strictly on an offshore OTC basis.

Japan: Japan boasts the single largest derivative market in Asia Pacific. The country currently features a broad range of commodity derivatives (agricultural and metals futures/options) and financial derivatives (deposit and bond futures/options, index futures/options, and currency futures). There is also an active market for onshore equity warrants and convertibles, though more innovative OTC single stock, basket and index warrants and options have been forced offshore as a result of regulatory restrictions. The OTC market features very liquid, and well established, IRS and CCS markets, as well as active OTC interest rate and FX option markets; exotic swaps and options are also becoming popular. The local swap market features active quotes out to ten years and a significant number of hedge instruments are available to dealers and market makers for risk management purposes; liquidity in most Japanese derivatives is very good and bid-offer spreads are narrow. Despite the availability of a substantial number of listed and OTC products, as well as the significant trading volumes such instruments display, the Japanese market historically has not been the primary innovator of derivative instruments. In many cases strict regulation has prevented the development or introduction of such instruments. For instance, yen FRAs were banned until late 1994, while listed/OTC equity options are still not permissible at all. Even within the listed futures market, Japan has occasionally been a follower, not a leader. The key Nikkei 225 index futures contract, for instance, was introduced on SIMEX and CME several years before being introduced on the home exchange in Osaka. Various other restrictions regarding derivatives are still in place but efforts are underway to continue deregulating local products and markets.

Malaysia: Malaysia's derivative market is presently skewed toward activity in listed products, with the prospect of even greater growth in the months and years ahead. Malaysia's listed commodity futures exchange, which has existed for nearly 20 years, trades a range of agricultural/soft (e.g. crude palm oil, crude palm kernel oil, rubber, cocoa) and base metal (e.g. tin) contracts. In 1991 and 1992 the country created two new futures exchanges designed to list and trade financial futures. One exchange commenced trading of index futures in late 1995 (and will follow with equity and index options in 1996) while the second exchange is expected to begin trading of deposit and interest rate futures in early 1996. The local stock exchange is an active trading forum for convertible bonds as well as issuer and, more recently, third party, equity warrants. While the Malaysian listed derivative market is reasonably well established, the country's OTC derivative capabilities are still developing. Malaysia features modest trading and liquidity in IRSs, CCSs, FX forwards and FX options; FRAs are not widely used in the local market, and interest rate options (caps, floors, swaptions, bond options) are only rarely executed. Swaps are limited in most cases to the short end of the curve, though quotes are available to five and, occasionally, ten years. Certain Malaysian OTC equity derivatives (e.g index swaps, basket options, single stock options) exist as well but are transacted primarily offshore. While hedging of derivative positions has been challenging for dealers, the introduction of index and interest rate futures contracts on the country's new exchanges should prove helpful in the management of risk positions.

New Zealand: New Zealand features developed, though occasionally illiquid, listed and OTC derivative markets. Within the listed market, the country's two primary exchanges list and trade equity warrants, deposit futures/options, bond futures/options, index futures/options and equity options; these contracts feature varying degrees of liquidity, with deposit/interest rate futures and equity options consistently the most active among all products. Currency futures were previously listed on the exchange but were abandoned due to inactivity, while wool futures are still listed but remain dormant; even the key index future was restructured in 1995 in order to attract more participants. The OTC market features a standard range of instruments including FRAs, IRSs, CCSs, FX forwards and FX options; there is also reasonable activity in interest rate options on bills and bonds. Swaps are active primarily in the two- and three-year sector, though quotes are available to five years and transactions are occasionally booked to seven and ten years. Liquidity in swaps (both IRSs and CCSs) is very erratic and can disappear quickly as arbitrage opportunities cease to exist. OTC equity derivatives are reasonably popular, though the small universe of liquid local stocks limits the size of the market to modest volumes. Hedging of fixed income, equity and currency exposures is quite efficient as the domestic market features a range of cash and derivative instruments which are sufficiently active to ensure availability when required.

Philippines: The Philippine derivative market is based almost solely on listed futures. The country has featured a commodities exchange for the past ten years and has achieved reasonable success in the area of agricultural futures. The Exchange's main contracts are based on sugar, soybeans, copra, coffee and dried cocoon; all feature significant, and consistent, turnover. In addition to its active agricultural contracts, the exchange also lists a series of financial contracts based on domestic treasury bills and currencies (including one on the local currency which, not surprisingly, is its least active); liquidity in financial contracts is very modest compared with agricultural contracts. Activity in the OTC market is virtually non-existent, primarily because of restrictive foreign exchange and foreign investment rules. Both have stifled product innovation and have kept participants on the sidelines. There is a very small market for short-term IRSs, CCSs, and FX forwards/options, but liquidity in all products is poor. Non-deliverable currency contracts are transacted on occasion in the offshore market, while equity-related derivatives are limited to periodic basket warrants executed by foreign banks in the offshore market.

Singapore: Singapore features an exceptionally active and liquid derivative market based almost exclusively on listed futures/options referencing offshore prices and indexes. The country's main futures exchange lists and trades index futures/options, deposit futures/options, bond futures/options, gold futures and energy futures, all based on international instruments or commodities. Trading in local listed derivatives is modest and limited to convertibles, equity options and equity warrants. Singapore's secondary futures exchange is focused on both rubber and coffee futures, and is due to list contracts on cocoa, copper, zinc and aluminium in the near future. Activity in OTC derivatives based on local rates and prices is still quite modest; the regulatory authorities discourage derivatives based on such indicators unless used for legitimate hedging purposes. Nonetheless, there is a market for IRSs (to five years), FRAs, and caps/floors; there is also activity in FX forwards and CCSs, once again extending to five years. Liquidity in the IRS/CCS market can be thin and hedging can be challenging. The OTC equity derivative market, based on single stock/basket/index options, swaps and warrants, is reasonably active and exists primarily offshore. The OTC energy forward/swap market is large and active. Singapore's geographic location and its role as a key storage, refining and transhipment point has resulted in the creation of a significant energy derivative capability.

South Korea: South Korea's derivative market is extremely limited at the present time, though the country is in the final stages of introducing its listed futures programme. The programme, slated to become operational in early 1996, will initially focus on stock index futures and will follow, over time, with equity options, interest rate futures and commodity futures. Though futures trading has not yet commenced, the country's stock exchange already trades domestic convertibles and warrants. The OTC derivative market is very narrow and limited primarily to onshore FX forwards and options; non-deliverable currency derivatives are also executed in the offshore market. IRSs and CCSs display minimal liquidity, primarily because certain interest rates are still controlled by the government, no established short-term floating benchmark exists and foreign exchange flows are tightly regulated. Until controls are deregulated (a process which has already begun) and a short-term benchmark is established, overall activity is likely to remain negligible. Equity-related structures are modest in size and scope; foreign investor access to equities is still restrictive and has kept many foreign institutions from engaging in OTC equity derivative transactions.

Taiwan: Taiwan's derivative market is underdeveloped but in the process of gradual expansion. The regulatory authorities and the government are considering the final passage of legislation to create a domestic futures exchange which will list and trade index futures, interest rate futures and currency futures. Though precise timing for the establishment of the exchange is uncertain, a target date of 1996 is expected. While futures trading is not yet established, the stock exchange already lists and trades convertibles and equity warrants. The OTC market remains reasonably inactive, primarily as a result of foreign exchange controls and foreign investor restrictions. Both are in the process of being deregulated, which should spur additional growth in the OTC market. At the present time there is very modest trading in FX forwards, IRSs and CCSs; maturities are concentrated in the short end and turnover is minimal; non-deliverable currency transactions are occasionally executed in both the onshore and offshore market. Equity derivative activity is still modest, primarily because of investment restrictions placed on foreign participants in the equity market (though such restrictions are gradually disappearing).

Thailand: Thailand's derivative market is still in the formative stage. The country features no commodity futures exchange at the present time, though preliminary plans have been drawn up to create an exchange to trade agricultural futures (rice, rubber) and financial futures (stock index futures, currency futures); no date has yet been set for the establishment of such an exchange. The only exchange-traded derivatives presently available are domestic convertible bonds and equity warrants, both of which are listed on the local stock exchange. Trading in warrants is reasonably active, though the absolute number of issues is small (particularly in comparison with other Southeast Asian nations such as Malaysia, Singapore and Hong Kong); issuance of convertibles is on the rise but secondary liquidity is still thin. OTC products are growing in scope and stature. The most active derivatives are FX forwards and options, CCSs, and IRSs. Swap maturities extend to five years though longer term quotes can be obtained. Liquidity in swaps is gradually increasing, primarily because Thailand features active onshore and offshore participation. Hedging, however, is still a complex undertaking, primarily because the country does not feature active government bond issuance and, as indicated above, has no interest rate futures programme. Thailand's equity derivative market is limited but growing; virtually all equity derivatives are structured on an offshore OTC basis.

OVERVIEW OF COUNTRY CHAPTERS

The remainder of this text is devoted to a detailed examination of the derivative markets of Asia Pacific. As indicated above, our specific country coverage includes Australia, China, Hong Kong, India, Indonesia, Japan, Malaysia, New Zealand, Philippines, Singapore, South Korea, Taiwan and Thailand. The general outline for each country chapter is as follows:

(A) Overview of the local financial markets. This section includes a brief discussion of the nature, size and performance of key local equity, fixed income and currency markets. Further to the discussion above, the depth of the local cash markets plays an integral role in the state and development of each local derivative market.

(B) Derivative market and product description. In this section we commence our discussion with a brief description of all listed derivative exchanges in the country (typically one or more futures exchanges and, on occasion, one or more stock exchanges (which often list and trade equity options, warrants and/or convertibles)). This is followed by detailed product description of all local listed and OTC derivatives related to the equity, fixed income, currency and commodity markets. It should be noted that the primary focus of this text is on the nature and development of domestic derivatives (or offshore derivatives traded on domestic exchanges). It is virtually impossible, however, to focus on domestic derivatives without referencing activity which occurs in the offshore market; this is particularly true in the case of offshore OTC equity derivatives and swaps, as well as offshore listed/OTC convertibles and warrants. Our discussion, then, references activity in such markets as well. Although there are various ways of classifying and discussing derivatives, we elect to do so on the following basis:

I. Listed futures and options (e.g. those traded on a formal exchange), divided into the following subcategories:

Equity futures/options
Index futures/options/futures options
Deposit futures/options/futures options
Interest rate futures/options/futures options
Currency futures/options/futures options
Commodity futures/options/futures options

Within our grouping of commodity futures/options we concentrate our discussion by product offering by exchange, rather than sub-categorizing soft, agricultural, metal and energy products across exchanges. This approach is deemed logical since most exchanges in Asia Pacific have a specific product focus and only rarely a generalist approach.

It should be noted that the contract tables on futures and options include a distinction between domestic and offshore contracts. Domestic contracts are defined as those based strictly on domestic rates, prices or indexes accepting only domestic deliverables (when physical settlement is required); offshore contracts are defined as those referencing international (e.g. non-domestic) rates prices or indexes; domestic/offshore contracts are defined as those based on local prices, rates or indexes and denominated in local currency, but which accept deliverables from foreign countries. Although we provide details for every listed contract, we elect not to include specific margin requirements or current maximum position limits, primarily because both are subject to rather frequent change; such details are readily available in the most current form from exchanges themselves, or from real-time data vendors such as Telerate, Reuters, Bloomberg, Quick, Teletext, Bridge, Knight-Ridder, and so on. Contract specification tables for each listed derivative provide relevant Telerate, Reuters and Bloomberg codes for each contract (where such codes exist); readers may consult such codes (or those provided by other services, which we do not cover in this text), for a link into real-time pricing as well as current margin and position limit information.

II. Listed/over-the-counter warrants, convertibles and hybrids. This category includes listed and OTC instruments since there is often little distinction between the structural details of listed and OTC products (such as warrants and convertibles), with the exception of listing and trading forum. Listed warrants, convertibles and hybrids (e.g. index-linked notes) are most often true domestic instruments, which are listed and traded on domestic exchanges. OTC warrants, convertibles and hybrids may be either domestic or offshore instruments; these derivatives are most often unlisted, or listed on overseas exchanges (such as the Luxembourg Stock Exchange, Swiss exchanges, London Stock Exchange, and so on), and traded on an OTC basis. Though these OTC derivatives are based on local prices, rates or indexes, they may be denominated in foreign currencies. Specific sub-categories in this group include:

Equity warrants
Basket/Index warrants
Convertible bonds
Index-linked notes
Fixed income warrants
Currency warrants
Commodity warrants

III. Over-the-counter (OTC) forwards, swaps and options. This category includes the customized derivatives of a given country and focuses on vanilla and exotic structures (where such exist). OTC transactions are not listed on exchanges and are not actively traded (though they may be liquid, and can often be transferred or unwound). Sub-categories in this group include:

Equity forwards/swaps
Equity options
Basket/Index forwards/swaps
Basket/Index options
Fixed income forwards/swaps
Fixed income options
Currency forwards/swaps
Currency options
Commodity forwards/swaps
Commodity options

Within the product categories outlined above, we present relevant details on the instruments, trading volume, pricing, quoting conventions, representative historical price information, and so on.

(C) Regulatory/legal framework governing local derivatives. This section discusses the primary regulators charged with overseeing derivative activities, as well as specific rules and regulations, together with recent changes in such regulations, designed to protect participants and end-users. Where relevant, there is also a discussion on specific laws governing derivatives.

(D) Local accounting treatment of derivatives. In this section we cover relevant accounting principles applied to the valuation and reporting of listed and OTC derivatives. In reviewing this section the reader will discover this is an undeveloped, yet critical, area within local derivative product management.

(E) Prospects for the local derivative product market. This section provides a summary of near- and medium-term prospects for expansion (or contraction) in particular domestic instruments or markets.

Each chapter concludes with a summary of listed futures/options turnover for all contracts, as well as a summary description of instruments in the domestic OTC market.

The Asia Pacific derivative markets are among the most exciting in the world, primarily because they are in the process of development, expansion and change. Since these markets are dynamic, and subject to more interesting changes over the coming months and years, this text simply represents a picture of how the markets appear and function at the present time, with some conjecture on the challenges and prospects which lay ahead.

2: Australia

FINANCIAL MARKET OVERVIEW

Australia's financial markets are among the most developed in the Asia Pacific region. The equity, fixed income and foreign exchange markets have been in existence for many decades and feature significant primary and secondary activity. The presence of liquid and well-established cash markets has led to comprehensive development and use of domestic listed and OTC derivatives; as a result, Australia's domestic derivative market is one of the most vibrant and advanced in the region.

The Australian equity market has been in existence since 1828, although a formal exchange did not exist until the Sydney Stock Exchange (SSE) was founded in 1871. Though the SSE was the country's primary equity trading centre throughout the 1900s, numerous regional exchanges (including those at Hobart, Brisbane, Melbourne, Adelaide and Perth) were created over ensuing decades to promote trading in local stocks. In 1987, after several decades of independent operation, the regional exchanges were merged into a new Sydney-based forum known as the Australian Stock Exchange (ASX); the ASX is the country's sole equity exchange at the present time.

The Australian equity market is very large on a primary basis; at the end of 1994 it featured total market capitalization of US$323 bln, making it the second largest of Asia Pacific's 13 markets. Secondary trading is also substantial, though overall liquidity is still concentrated in 60 to 70 of the country's largest blue-chip companies; since the market lists well over 1,100 firms, trading and liquidity in the shares of smaller capitalization stocks are often non-existent. The vibrant primary and secondary markets have led to very extensive development and use of listed and OTC equity derivatives (as we discuss at length later in this chapter). Figure 2.1 illustrates the historical movement of the benchmark All Ordinaries Share Price Index (All Ords or SPI) while Table 2.1 provides data on key Australian equity market indicators. Note that foreign investors have unrestricted access to local shares, though investors with 'substantial' domestic shareholdings must have such holdings reviewed for appropriateness by the Foreign Investment Review Board.

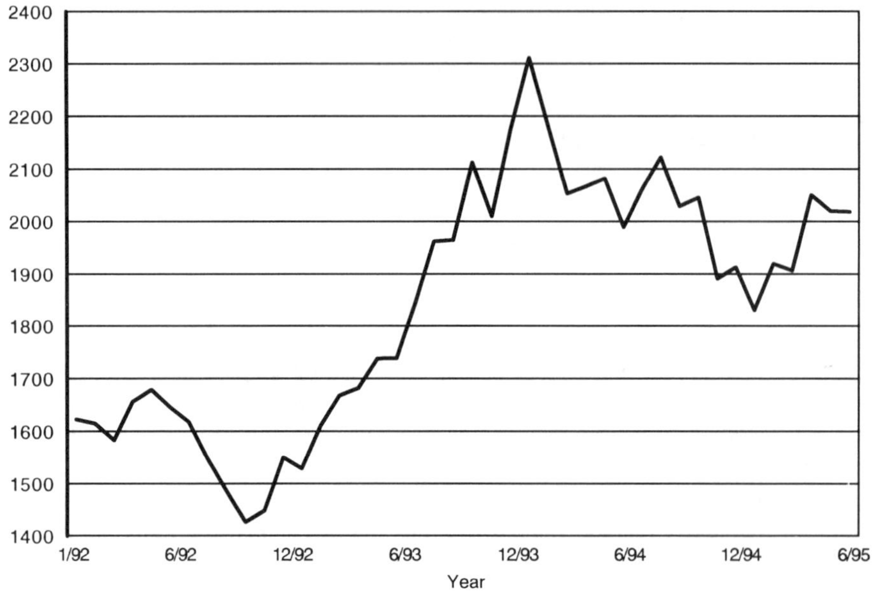

Figure 2.1 Historical Movement of Australian All Ordinaries Share Price Index

Year*	Market Capitalization (US$ bln)**	Trading Value (US$ bln)	Listed Companies (#)
1994	323.6	94.5	1,143
1993	342.2	72.7	1,101
1992	281.0	45.4	1,065
1991	186.9	43.9	994
1990	140.9	37.5	1,122

* to December of each year; Source: ASX, 1994

** includes foreign companies with ordinary share listings

	1/92-6/95 Annualized Return*	1/92-6/95 Total Return*
All Ordinaries	8.62%	31.70%

* dividends reinvested in index

Table 2.1 Domestic Equity Market Indicators

Australia's fixed income market is the third largest in Asia Pacific after Japan and South Korea. The Australian fixed income market consists of bank accepted bills and certificates of deposit (CDs) in the short end of the curve (to one year), and Australian Commonwealth Government Bonds (ACGBs), semi-government authority bonds, and corporate bonds in the intermediate and long end of the curve (primarily one to ten years). ACGBs, which constitute the primary debt obligations of the Commonwealth itself, represent the single largest component of the Australian debt market. From the late 1920s until the early 1950s the Commonwealth was the sole issuer of sovereign bonds in the country, floating debt securities for itself and on behalf of individual states. Since 1953, however, states have issued their own bonds (i.e. semi-government securities) and have become active liability managers in their own right. ACGBs are presently issued in the form of Treasury bills, Treasury notes and Treasury bonds (along with a series of savings bonds and other funded securities), with maturities extending from one to ten years (though longer-term securities are floated on occasion). Only notes and bonds are actively traded, primarily in the OTC market; average daily turnover of ACGBs amounted to A$4.1 bln (US$3 bln) in 1994. Total outstanding Commonwealth securities (bills, notes, bonds) reached A$100 bln (US$74 bln) at the end of 1994 (RBA, 1995). Figure 2.2 illustrates the historical movement of Australian government yield curves while Figure 2.3 traces the movement of benchmark three- and ten-year bond yields. Semi-government bonds are issued by state authorities who retain responsibility for funding the operations of each state (and of major public corporations operating in each state); the three main Australian semi-government authorities include Treasury Corporation of Victoria (TCV), New South Wales Treasury Corporation (TCorp) and Queensland Treasury Corporation (QTC) (though there are numerous other state authorities and state enterprises which raise funds in the semi-government bond market). Average daily turnover in semi-government bonds amounted to A$3 bln (US$2.2 bln) during 1994, while total outstandings reached A$48 bln (US$35.5 bln) at the end of 1994. The private sector market consists of fixed rate bonds, floating rate bonds (pegged to Australian dollar LIBOR or the domestic bank bill rate) and convertible bonds, with maturities ranging from one to ten years (though certain issues are occasionally floated with 15 year maturities); total private sector outstandings amounted to A$21 bln (US$15.5 bln) as at September 1994 (Euromoney, 1994).

The key interest rates in the Australian market include the Australian bank bill rate (BBR) (the short-term borrowing cost for companies in the bank bill market), Australian dollar LIBOR (the short-term borrowing cost for banks in the offshore market), Australian Commonwealth Government Bond yields (the medium- and long-term borrowing costs of the government itself), semi-government bond yields (the medium- and long-term borrowing costs of major state and semi-government authority borrowers), EuroA$ bond rates (the borrowing cost for domestic and foreign issuers in the offshore market), and Australian dollar swap rates (the rate for transacting interest rate swaps in the domestic interbank market). We shall discuss

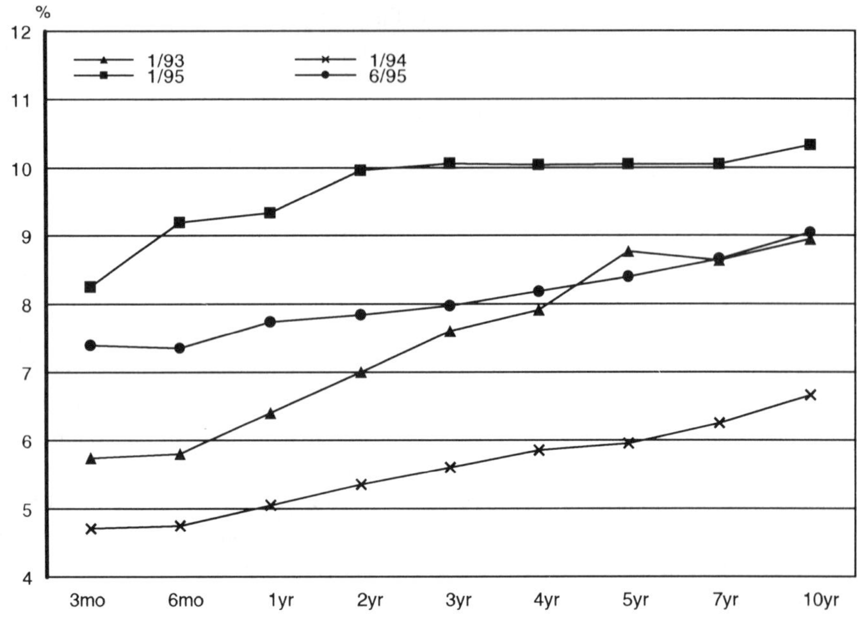

Figure 2.2 Historical Movement of Australian Government Yield Curves

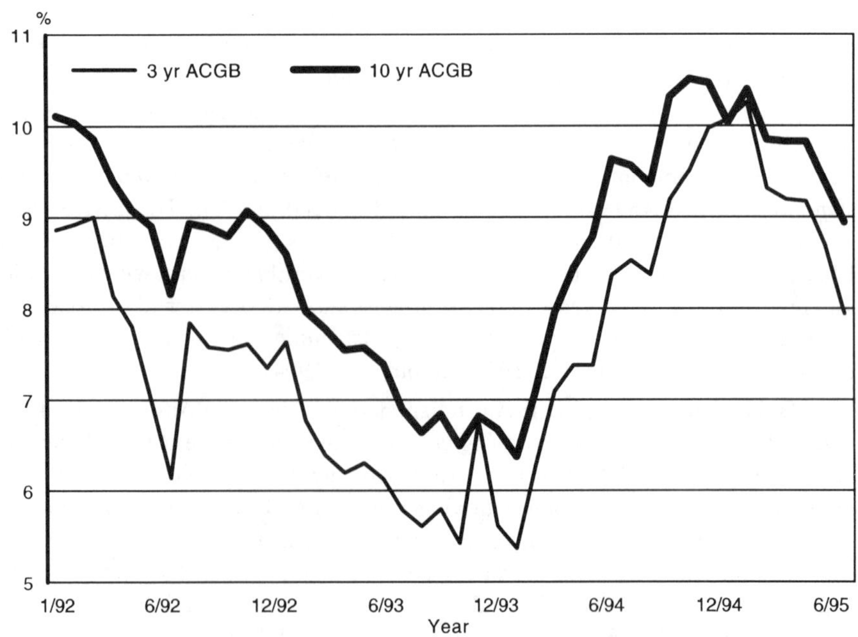

Figure 2.3 Historical Movement of Three- and Ten-year ACGB Yields

Rate	Payment Frequency	Compounding Frequency	Day Count Convention
A$ BBR	–	–	Actual/365
A$ LIBOR	–	–	Actual/360
ACGB	semi- annual	semi- annual	Actual/365
Semigov't Bonds	semi-annual	semi-annual	Actual/365
Euro A$	annual	annual	30/360
Swaps	quarterly (1–3 year), semi-annual (4+ year)	quarterly (1–3 year), semi-annual (4+ year)	Actual/365

Table 2.2 Domestic Interest Rate Summary

these rates in greater detail in our section on fixed income swaps and forwards. Table 2.2 summarizes the payment frequency, compounding frequency and day count convention for each key rate.

The Australian dollar (A$) is a freely convertible currency whose value is determined entirely by market forces; there are no onshore or offshore restrictions imposed on buying or selling spot or forward Australian dollars. While Australia is not generally considered a major global currency trading centre, activity by inter-bank and corporate participants has resulted in significant average trading volumes of both Australian dollars against foreign currencies and foreign currencies against other foreign currencies. During the period June 1993–94, average daily spot

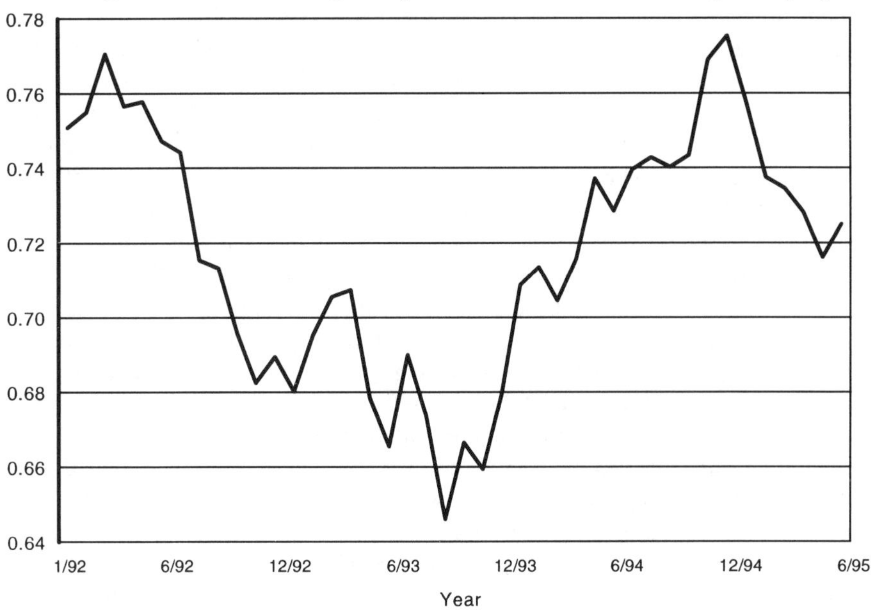

Figure 2.4 Historical Movement of Spot US$/A$

turnover in Australian dollars versus foreign currencies was A$7.2 bln (US$5.3 bln), up from A$6.3 bln (US$4.6 bln) in 1993 (spot turnover in currencies other than the Australian dollar amounted to A$15 bln (US$11.1 bln) in 1994, down from A$15.55 bln (US$11.5 bln) in 1993 (AFMA, 1994)). Standard interbank dealing size in spot Australian dollars is A$10 mln (US$7.4 mln) and bid offer spreads are a very narrow US$0.0005/A$ under normal market conditions. Figure 2.4 traces the historical movement of spot US$/A$.

DERIVATIVE MARKETS AND PRODUCTS

LISTED DERIVATIVE EXCHANGES

Australia features three separate domestic exchanges which list and trade derivatives, including the Sydney Futures Exchange (and its overnight forum, Sydney Overnight Computerized Exchange), ASX Derivatives and the ASX itself; for a brief period the country also featured a fourth exchange known as the Australian Financial Futures Market.

The Australian listed futures market dates back to 1960 when the Sydney Greasy Wool Exchange was created to provide a forum for hedging of wool, Australia's largest export at the time. The original wool exchange eventually became known as the Sydney Futures Exchange (SFE) and expanded from commodity futures (i.e. wool (1960), cattle (1975), and gold (1978)) into financial contracts; financial futures and options are the mainstay of the Exchange today. Over the past two decades the SFE has introduced contracts on 90-day accepted bank bills, three- and ten-year Australian Commonwealth Government Bonds, the All Ordinaries share price index and, most recently, on shares themselves (note that the Exchange also introduced and abandoned Fifty Leaders index futures, five- and ten-year semi-government bond futures and currency futures during the late 1980s/early 1990s; it also delisted its gold and cattle contracts and restructured its wool contract). Based on 1994 trading volume, SFE was the 12th most active exchange in the world, posting total turnover of 31.5 mln contracts (FI, 1995).

Trading of SFE futures occurs via open outcry on the floor of the Exchange. In addition to daylight trading on the floor, the Exchange also trades on an overnight basis through its overnight screen dealing system known as Sydney Overnight Computerized Market (SYCOM). SYCOM, which was established in November 1989, has permitted the Exchange to extend trading hours to cover a 20-hour time span; it has also allowed the creation of overnight options which are traded during the SYCOM evening session (from 4:40 p.m. to 6:00 a.m.) and expire during the next morning's SFE session. Since its creation, SYCOM has grown to account for 10% of SFE's overall trading volume (e.g. SYCOM monthly average turnover in 1994 was 225,000 contracts). Futures and options trades executed on the SFE and SYCOM are cleared through, and guaranteed by, the Sydney Futures Exchange

Clearing House (SFECH), which is constituted as a wholly-owned subsidiary of the SFE. SFECH was created in November 1991 after the SFE opted to self-clear rather than rely on external services provided by the International Commodities Clearing House, which had been its clearer since the 1960s; SFECH has 28 members and is backed by an A$100 mln guarantee. Membership in the Exchange takes one of three forms: floor members (who have direct access to the floor and can deal on their own accounts (and can deal for client accounts when licensed)), local members (who have direct access to the floor and can trade on their own accounts), and associate members (who can trade on behalf of clients or introduce clients to floor members); associate membership is sub-divided into full associate members (who can accept and transact client orders if licensed), introducing broker associate members (who can advise clients and introduce them to floor members) and market associate members (who are simply associated with the SFE, but cannot transact or advise).

In addition to its own product line, SFE expanded geographically in 1992 by acquiring the New Zealand Futures and Options Exchange (NZFOE). The NZFOE, which had existed as an independent entity from its establishment in 1985 until the SFE's acquisition in 1992, presently lists options and futures on the new NZSE Ten stock index (which replaced the traditional NZSE 40 index in 1995), the New Zealand 90-day bank bill, and three- and ten-year New Zealand Government Bonds. It also lists options on individual equities and futures on wool; we discuss the NZFOE and its individual contracts at greater length in chapter 9. Note that SFE members are now permitted to trade the entire range of NZFOE products directly from the SFE. In addition to its link with NZFOE, the SFE has also entered into an agreement with NYMEX which permits SFE members to trade NYMEX energy derivatives via SFE's SYCOM and NYMEX's ACCESS (we discuss this at greater length later in the chapter).

Australia's second major listed exchange is ASX Derivatives (ASXD, a subsidiary of the country's stock exchange), which trades listed equity derivatives. The country's listed equity option market dates back to 1976 when the Australian Options Market (AOM) was established. The AOM was the first listed equity options market created outside the US and was organized as a subsidiary of the Sydney Stock Exchange; the first equity options traded on the AOM were on the shares of BHP, Western Mining, CSR and Woodside Petroleum. Following the 1987 merger of the regional Australian stock exchanges the AOM became part of the Australian Stock Exchange (ASX) (AOM was renamed ASXD in 1994). ASXD's product line has expanded considerably since the mid-1970s; the Exchange now offers options on 49 shares and has introduced a variety of new listed derivatives, such as short- and long-term options, low exercise price options (LEPOs) and share ratios (we discuss these derivatives at length below). Based on 1994 trading volume, ASXD ranked as the 40th most active derivatives exchange in the world (FI, 1995). ASXD is organized as an open outcry forum, where registered traders make continuous two-way markets in listed products. Orders are sent via the Options

Automated Trading System (OATS) to ASXD board brokers for trade execution. Trades are cleared and settled through the Options Clearing House, a separate subsidiary of the ASX.

The country's third listed derivative exchange is ASX, the national stock exchange. As indicated above, ASX has existed in its present form since 1987, when passage of the Australian National Guarantee Fund Act allowed the regional Australian exchanges to be merged into a single national entity. While trading of cash equities, through the electronic Stock Exchange Automated Trading System (SEATS), remains the ASX's primary focus, it is also directly active in the local derivative market through the listing and trading of convertible bonds, issuer equity warrants and third-party covered warrants; within the broad category of covered warrants the ASX currently lists index warrants, equity warrants and basket warrants (though its mandate permits it to list commodity warrants and currency warrants as well). All trading in convertibles and warrants on ASX is effected through the SEATS system. Table 2.3 highlights the listed exchanges and derivatives of Australia.

Exchange	Primary Derivatives
Australian Stock Exchange (ASX)	Convertible bonds; issuer equity warrants; covered equity warrants; index/basket warrants; currency warrants; commodity warrants
ASX Derivatives (ASXD)	Equity options; low exercise price options; share ratios; index options
Sydney Futures Exchange (SFE)	Share futures; index futures, options; deposit futures, options; bond futures, options; wool futures; crude oil futures#; gasoline futures#; heating oil futures#; propane futures#; natural gas futures#
Sydney Overnight Computerized Market (SYCOM)	Share futures; index futures, options; deposit futures, options; bond futures, options; wool futures; overnight options on: index futures, bond futures

via NYMEX link

Table 2.3 Listed Derivative Exchanges

As indicated above, the AFFM existed as a separate listed derivative exchange for approximately six years. AFFM was established in Melbourne in September 1985 (by the then-independent Stock Exchange of Melbourne) to challenge SFE in the futures business; it began by listing and trading equity futures (a product which SFE itself introduced in 1994, as discussed below). Equity futures were initially available on ten stocks, primarily of Melbourne-based companies, namely BHP, CSR, CRA, Santos, Western Mining, Westpac, National Australia Bank, ANZ Bank, Coles Myer and Fosters Brewing. The AFFM achieved only modest success and was dormant by 1991.

LISTED FUTURES AND OPTIONS

Equity

Equity Futures/Options

The Australian derivative market features equity futures (traded via SFE) and equity options (traded via ASXD); Australia is one of only two markets in Asia Pacific (along with Hong Kong) to trade both futures and options on individual equities.

In May 1994 the SFE introduced futures on several Australian blue chip equities, including BHP, National Australia Bank, and News Corp; it followed with additional futures on Westpac, BTR Nylex, MIM, Western Mining, CRA, ANZ, Pacific Dunlop and Foster's Brewing several months later (note: the BTR Nylex contract was delisted in 1995 after its parent company assumed majority control). The SFE share futures, which are cash-settled contracts, command 1,000 shares of underlying equity (except MIM and News Corp which command 1,022 and 1,420 shares, respectively); the contracts are traded to the next two quarter months on SFE and SYCOM (on a standard SFE cycle). Two advantages which SFE share futures offer investors include the ability to obtain a leveraged position in the shares of a company and the ability to obtain lower costs on 'round trip' (buy/sell) transactions; the SFE estimates that transaction costs for share futures on an equivalent amount of the underlying equity equal 10% of the costs incurred in trading shares themselves. The disadvantages of equity futures include the limited number of shares on which contracts are available and the loss of dividends and voting rights which occurs when using futures.

Trading in SFE share futures has gradually gained momentum. During the first six months of trading, total turnover averaged 300 contracts per day (equal to 25–50% of underlying daily cash turnover (depending on the equity being considered)). By the end of 1994 turnover in all share futures reached 72,310 contracts and by May 1995, the first anniversary of the launch of the initial contracts, a total of 150,000 contracts had been traded (SFE, 1995).

Note that the SFE is considering listing share futures on international stocks and is exploring the possibility of making the contract deliverable. Table 2.4 contains contract specifications on SFE/SYCOM share futures.

While SFE trades listed share futures, ASXD trades listed equity options. ASXD has offered listed puts and calls on Australian equities since the Exchange was created in 1976. Conventional American exercise equity options are presently available on 49 stocks, with maturities extending to nine months; unlike share futures, exercise of equity options results in physical delivery of shares. Determination of strike intervals is based on the price of the underlying share; strikes are set at A$0.10 intervals if the share price is under A$1, A$0.25 intervals if the price is between A$1.01 and A$5, A$0.50 intervals if the price is between A$5.01 and A$10, and A$1 intervals if the price is over A$10. In 1991 ASXD sup-

Contract	**Share Futures**
Type	Domestic
Exchange	Sydney Futures Exchange/Sydney Overnight Computerized Market
Months	Next two quarter months on March, June, September, December cycle (BHP, Western Mining, CRA) or January, April, July, October cycle (NAB, Westpac, MIM, Foster's, ANZ) or February, May, August, November cycle (News Corp, Pacific Dunlop)
Contract Size	1,000 shares of underlying equity (except News Corp (1,420 shares), and MIM (1,022 shares))
Tick Value	A$0.01/share
Daily Limit	No limit
Deliverable Instrument	Cash settlement based on average price during last two hours of trading
Last Trading Day	Thursday preceding the last Friday of the contract month
Delivery Day	Business day following the last trading day
Real-time price data	Bloomberg: SFE – BHA <Cmdty>, ANA <Cmdty>, NCA <Cmdty>, WPA <Cmdty>, WNA <Cmdty>, IMA <Cmdty>, PCA <Cmdty>, ECA <Cmdty>, ENA <Cmdty>, EAA <Cmdty>, SYCOM – BTA <Cmdty>, DNA <Cmdty>, DPA <Cmdty>, NSA <Cmdty>, WEA <Cmdty>, WGA <Cmdty>, YIA <Cmdty>, YCA <Cmdty>, YAA <Cmdty>, YTA <Cmdty>; Reuters: SFE – <0#YBH:>, <0#YNA:>, <0#YNX:>, <0#YWB:>, <0#YMI:>, <0#YBT:>, <0#YWM:>, <0#YCR:>, <0#YFB:>, <0#YAN:>, SYCOM – <0#YBP:>, <0#YNB:>, <0#YNP:>, <0#YWC:>, <0#YMM:>, <0#YPC:>, <0#YWQ:>, <0#YCA:>, <0#YFG:>, <<0#YNZ:>; Telerate: SFE – 22602- 3, 6193, SYCOM – 22735- 6, 6194

Table 2.4 Contract Specifications for SFE/SYCOM Share Futures

plemented its conventional options by offering both spot and long-dated options. Spot options, which have 30 day maturities, are currently offered on 32 stocks. Long-term options, which have been available with maturities of two and three years since 1991 and maturities of five years since 1994, are offered on 17 stocks (note: strike intervals for spot and long-term options are established in the same manner as conventional options). Total turnover in all equity options amounted to 9.5 mln contracts in 1993 and 10.2 mln contracts in 1994; within that total, turnover in long-term options increased from 82,639 contracts in 1993 to nearly 257,000 contracts in 1994 (ASXD, 1995). The Exchange's most active equity options during 1994 were on BHP, Western Mining, CRA, MIM and News Corp. Contract specifications for conventional equity options, spot options and long-term options are reflected in Tables 2.5, 2.6 and 2.7. Table 2.8 summarizes the availability of conventional, spot and long-term options.

Contract	**Conventional Equity Options**
Type	Domestic
Exchange	ASX Derivatives
Months	Four per year on February, May, August, November cycle or March, June, September, December cycle or January, April, July, October cycle
Contract Size	1,000 shares
Tick Value	A$0.01
Daily Limit	No limit
Deliverable Instrument	Physical settlement of underlying equity
Last Trading Day	Thursday before the last Friday of settlement month (or the last business day before expiry if a holiday)
Exercise Day	American exercise – any business day up to, and including, the last Friday of settlement month
Real-time price data	Reuters: <0#equity ticker*.AX>

Table 2.5 Contract Specifications for ASXD Conventional Equity Options

Contract	**Spot Equity Options**
Type	Domestic
Exchange	ASX Derivatives
Months	Consecutive spot months
Contract Size	1,000 shares
Tick Value	A$0.01
Daily Limit	No limit
Deliverable Instrument	Physical settlement of underlying equity
Last Trading Day	Thursday before the last Friday of settlement month (or the last business day before expiry if a holiday)
Exercise Day	American exercise – any business day up to, and including, the last Friday of settlement month
Real-time price data	Reuters: <0#equity ticker*.AX>

Table 2.6 Contract Specifications for ASXD Spot Equity Options

Contract	**Long-term Equity Options**
Type	Domestic
Exchange	ASX Derivatives
Months	Four per year on February, May, August, November cycle or March, June, September, December cycle or January, April, July, October cycle for two and three year options; five year options on request
Contract Size	1,000 shares
Tick Value	A$0.01

Contract	Long-term Equity Options
Daily Limit	No limit
Deliverable Instrument	Physical settlement of underlying equity
Last Trading Day	Thursday before the last Friday of settlement month (or the last business day before expiry if a holiday)
Exercise Day	American exercise – any business day up to, and including, the last Friday of settlement month
Real-time price data	Reuters: <0#equity ticker*.AX>

Table 2.7 Contract Specifications for ASXD Long-term Equity Options

Equity	Conventional	Spot	Long-term
Acacia Resources	Yes		
Advance Bank	Yes	Yes	
Amcor	Yes		
Ampolex	Yes	Yes	Yes
ANZ Banking	Yes	Yes	Yes
ANI	Yes	Yes	
Boral	Yes	Yes	
Brambles Industries	Yes		
Brierley Investments	Yes		
BHP Company	Yes	Yes	Yes
BTR Nylex	Yes	Yes	
Carter Holt Harvey	Yes	Yes	
Coles Myer	Yes	Yes	
Commonwealth Bank	Yes	Yes	
CRA	Yes	Yes	Yes
CSR	Yes	Yes	Yes
John Fairfax	Yes		
Fletcher Challenge	Yes	Yes	
Foster's Brewing	Yes	Yes	Yes
GIO Australia	Yes	Yes	
Gold Mines of Kalgoorlie	Yes	Yes	
Goodman Fielder	Yes	Yes	
Lend Lease	Yes		
Lion Nathan	Yes		
Mayne Nickless	Yes		
MIM	Yes	Yes	Yes
National Australia Bank	Yes	Yes	Yes
National Foods	Yes		

Equity	Conventional	Spot	Long-term
Newcrest Mining	Yes	Yes	News
Corporation	Yes	Yes	Yes
North Broken Hill Peko	Yes	Yes	
Pacific Dunlop	Yes	Yes	Yes
Pasminco	Yes	Yes	
Pioneer International	Yes	Yes	
Placer Pacific	Yes	Yes	
Poseidon Gold	Yes	Yes	
Publishing & Broadcasting	Yes	Yes	Yes
QRL Resources	Yes		
QNI	Yes		
Santos	Yes	Yes	
Seven Network	Yes	Yes	
Southcorp	Yes		
St George	Yes		
Telecom NZ	Yes		
TNT	Yes	Yes	Yes
Western Mining	Yes	Yes	Yes
Westpac Banking	Yes	Yes	
Woodside Petroleum	Yes	Yes	
Woolworths	Yes	Yes	Yes

Table 2.8 Availability of ASXD Equity Options

In 1994, in an apparent challenge to the SFE's share futures, the ASXD proposed introduction of equity derivatives known as 'Low Exercise Price Options' or LEPOs. LEPOs are listed, physical delivery, structured call options with strikes set at A$0.01; only one strike price is available for a particular contract month and the options always expire in-the-money. Given the low strike price of the derivative the delta of a LEPO (i.e. the rate of change in the option's price for a small change in the price of the underlying equity) is very close to one, causing the option to behave like a share or a share future. An interesting characteristic of the LEPO is that investors need only pay a small portion of the premium upfront, with the balance payable at maturity if the contract is not closed out; this suggests LEPOs command substantial leverage. Although LEPOs were initially announced in May 1994, legal action by the SFE forced a delay in trading until 1995. The SFE, perhaps sensing encroachment on its territory, claimed that LEPOs were effectively futures and should be regulated as such. The Australian courts, however, rendered a decision in March 1995 which cleared the way for the start-up of LEPO trading. The court's rationale for permitting LEPO trading is that the law on futures applies only to commodities, and shares are not commodities; consequently, share derivatives (such as LEPOs) are not futures contracts and should not be regulated as such.

Trading in LEPOs began in early April 1995 on ten stocks (CRA, Western Mining, Westpac Banking, ANZ, BHP, BTR Nylex, Foster's Brewing, MIM, National Australia Bank and News Corp); additional LEPOs were added in late 1995 (Boral, CSR, Coles Myer, North Broken Hill, Pacific Dunlop, Pioneer, Qantas, Woodside Petroleum and Woolworth's), and more are expected in the future. Table 2.9 contains contract specifications for LEPOs.

Contract	Low Exercise Price Options (LEPOs)
Type	Domestic
Exchange	ASX Derivatives
Months	Four contracts per year on the February, May, August, November cycle or the March, June, September, December cycle, or the January, April, July, October cycle
Contract Size	1,000 shares of underlying equity
Tick Value	A$0.01
Daily Limit	A$0.10 per day
Deliverable Instrument	Physical settlement of underlying equity
Last Trading Day	Thursday preceding the last Friday of settlement month (or the last business day before expiry if a holiday)
Exercise Day	European exercise – on the last Friday of settlement month only
Real-time price data	Reuters: <AXLEPO>; Telerate: 57960

Table 2.9 Contract Specifications for ASXD Low Exercise Price Options

In addition to the products mentioned above ASXD introduced a unique hybrid derivative in 1994 (the first of its kind in the global listed derivatives market) known as the share ratio. Share ratios are contracts designed to allow participants to take a view on a specific stock in relation to the overall equity market. While OTC equity derivative outperformance options are reasonably common in many markets, the ASXD share ratio is the first listed contract to provide a similar payoff profile. With a share ratio contract the share price of a target stock is compared with the underlying index at the time of purchase or sale; as the share price of the individual stock outperforms the index the ratio becomes larger and a long position gains, while a short position loses. As the share price of the individual stock underperforms the index, the ratio becomes smaller and a long position loses, while a short position gains. Share ratios have appealed to investment and fund managers who can target performance of specific equities against the performance of a broad index without being concerned about the overall direction of the market. Share ratios are presently available on eight blue-chip Australian equities, namely ANZ, Westpac, National Australia Bank, BHP, CRA, MIM, Western Mining and News Corp; additional ratios are to be added by the ASXD in the future. Table 2.10 contains relevant details on the share ratio contract while Table 2.11 summarizes, as of mid-1995, the stocks on which share futures, LEPOs and share ratios are available.

Contract	Share Ratio
Type	Domestic
Exchange	ASX Derivatives
Months	2 nearest months of the March, June, September, December cycle
Contract Size	A$10 * calculated ratio
Tick Value	A$10
Daily Limit	No limit
Deliverable Instrument	Cash settlement
Last Trading Day	Last business day of the contract month
Delivery Day	Last business day of the contract month
Ratio calculation	((Average share price weighted by volume during last two trading hours)/Overnight level of index on expiry day) * 1000
Real-time price data	Bloomberg: ZXA <Cmdty>, HXA <Cmdty>, MXA <Cmdty>, CXA <Cmdty>, WXA <Cmdty>, EXA <Cmdty>, XRA <Cmdty>, XIA <Cmdty>; Reuters: <AXRATIO>; Telerate: 57950

Table 2.10 Contract Specifications for ASXD Share Ratios

Stock	Share Futures	LEPOs	Share Ratios
ANZ Banking	Yes	Yes	Yes
BHP	Yes	Yes	Yes
Boral		Yes	
BTR Nylex	Yes	Yes	
Coles Myer		Yes	
CRA	Yes	Yes	Yes
CSR		Yes	
Foster's Brewing	Yes	Yes	
MIM	Yes	Yes	Yes
National Australia Bank	Yes	Yes	Yes
News Corp	Yes	Yes	Yes
North Broken Hill		Yes	
Pacific Dunlop	Yes	Yes	
Pioneer International		Yes	
Qantas		Yes	
Western Mining	Yes	Yes	Yes
Westpac Banking	Yes	Yes	Yes
Woodside Petroleum		Yes	
Woolworth's		Yes	

Table 2.11 Availability of SFE Share Futures and ASXD LEPOs and Share Ratios

Contract	All Ordinaries Share Price Index Futures
Type	Domestic
Exchange	Sydney Futures Exchange/Sydney Overnight Computerized Market
Months	March, June, September, December, up to six quarter months ahead
Contract Size	A$25 * All Ordinaries Index
Tick Value	1 index point
Daily Limit	No limit
Deliverable Instrument	Cash settlement based on the closing level of the All Ords on the last trading day
Last Trading Day	Last business day of the contract month
Delivery Day	2nd to last business day following the last trading day
Real-time price data	Bloomberg: SFE – AOA <Cmdty>, SYCOM – SAA <Cmdty>; Reuters: SFE – <0#YIX:>, SYCOM – <0#YIS:>; Telerate: SFE – 6183, SYCOM – 6195

Table 2.12 Contract Specifications for SFE/SYCOM All Ordinaries Share Price Index Futures

Index Futures/Options/Futures Options

Australia's sole index future is the All Ordinaries Share Price Index contract listed on the SFE. The underlying All Ords index, which was developed in 1979, is a market capitalization-weighted index consisting of 341 stocks. All Ords futures, which are cash-settled contracts traded through the SFE and SYCOM, were originally introduced in 1983 (three years ahead of SIMEX's Nikkei 225 contract and HKFE's Hang Seng Index contract); over the past 15 years the contract has become one of the most popular and actively traded derivatives on the Exchange. Despite its present success, earlier years were characterized by reasonably low turnover. In order to add liquidity to the market the value of the contract was restructured with a multiplier of A$25 (compared with an original multiplier of A$100); interest and liquidity soon increased.

As indicated, activity in All Ords futures has been on the rise over the past few years: total trading volume increased from 980,866 contracts in 1993 to a record 2.55 mln contracts in 1994; year-end open interest amounted to 104,653 contracts in 1993 and 103,232 contracts in 1994 (SFE, 1995). Table 2.12 highlights details on the SFE contract while Figure 2.5 traces the historical price movement of the future.

Although the Australian derivative market lists only a single index futures contract, it lists four distinct index options/futures options contracts. The key Australian index options include SFE's All Ords Index futures options (and overnight futures options) and ASXD's All Ords Index options, Gold Index options, and Twenty Leaders Index options.

SFE's All Ords futures options, introduced in 1985, continue to dominate the domestic market. The option is structured as an American exercise, physical delivery derivative, with strikes set at 25 point intervals (note that SYCOM overnight options are struck at five point intervals). In addition to standard day trading on the SFE, SYCOM currently lists and trades conventional All Ords futures options (on the standard SFE cycle) as well as overnight options expiring at the opening of the next morning's SFE session; the short maturity of the overnight option is intended to give hedgers the ability to cover exposures on a very short-term basis. Note that all overnight SYCOM contracts (including those on fixed income futures, discussed later in the chapter) are settled in cash, not physical. Total turnover in SFE/SYCOM All Ords options increased from 466,896 contracts in 1993 to 833,667 contracts in 1994; despite the sharp increase in turnover, year-end open interest declined from 316,230 contracts in 1993 to 169,240 contracts in 1994 (SFE, 1995). Tables 2.13 and 2.14 contain relevant details on the conventional and overnight SFE and SYCOM All Ords futures options contracts.

The ASXD's product line is presently centred on three distinct indexes, including the popular All Ords Index, the Gold Index (a market capitalization- weighted index comprised of Australia's largest mining companies) and the Twenty Leaders Index (a market capitalization-weighted index comprised of Australia's 20 largest companies). In contrast to the SFE index contracts, the ASXD index options are European exercise, cash-settlement derivatives with strikes set at 25 point intervals. Turnover in all ASXD index options has been lacklustre, primarily because hedgers and speculators have become accustomed to the deep liquidity of the SFE's

Figure 2.5 Historical Movement of SFE All Ordinaries Share Price Index Futures

Contract	**Options on All Ordinaries Share Price Index Futures**
Type	Domestic
Exchange	Sydney Futures Exchange/Sydney Overnight Computerized Market
Months	March, June, September, December, to six quarter months forward
Contract Size	1 All Ordinaries Index future
Tick Value	0.1 point
Daily Limit	No limit
Deliverable Instrument	Physical settlement into underlying futures contract
Last Trading Day	Last business day of the futures contract month
Exercise Day	American exercise – any business day up to, and including, the last trading day in futures
Real-time price data	Bloomberg: SFE – AOA <Cmdty> OMON, SYCOM – SAA <Cmdty> OMON; Reuters: SFE – <0#YIXmy+>, SYCOM – <0#YISmy+>; Telerate: SFE – 22713-16, SYCOM – 22674-77

Table 2.13 Contract Specifications for SFE/SYCOM Options on All Ordinaries Share Price Index Futures

Contract	**Overnight Options on All Ordinaries Share Price Index Futures**
Type	Domestic
Exchange	Sydney Overnight Computerized Market
Months	Next quarter month only
Contract Size	1 All Ordinaries Index future
Tick Value	0.1 point
Daily Limit	No limit
Deliverable Instrument	Cash settlement based on the average price of 10 quotes on futures contract, taken following the SYCOM session
Last Trading Day	End of each SYCOM session
Exercise Day	Business day immediately following the overnight SYCOM session
Real-time price data	Bloomberg: AZA <Cmdty> OMON; Reuters: <0#YAZmy+>; Telerate: 22600-01

Table 2.14 Contract Specifications for SYCOM Overnight Options on All Ordinaries Share Price Index Futures

Contract	All Ordinaries Share Price Index Options
Type	Domestic
Exchange	ASX Derivatives
Months	March, June, September, December, plus spot month
Contract Size	A$10 * All Ordinaries Index
Tick Value	A$1
Daily Limit	No limit
Deliverable Instrument	Cash settlement
Last Trading Day	Last business day of the contract month
Exercise Day	European exercise – on last trading day only
Real-time price data	Bloomberg: AS30 <Cmdty> OMON; Reuters: <0#AOX*.AX>

Table 2.15 Contract Specifications for ASXD All Ordinaries Share Price Index Options

Contract	Gold Index Options
Type	Domestic
Exchange	ASX Derivatives
Months	March, June, September, December
Contract Size	A$10 * Gold Index
Tick Value	A$1
Daily Limit	No limit
Deliverable Instrument	Cash settlement
Last Trading Day	Last business day of the contract month
Exercise Day	European exercise – on last trading day only
Real-time price data	Bloomberg: AS01 <Cmdty> OMON; Reuters: <0#GOL*.AX>

Table 2.16 Contract Specifications for ASXD Gold Index Options

Contract	Twenty Leaders Index Options
Type	Domestic
Exchange	ASX Derivatives
Months	March, June, September, December plus spot month
Contract Size	A$10* Twenty Leaders Index
Tick Value	A$1
Daily Limit	No limit
Deliverable Instrument	Cash Settlement
Last Trading Day	Last business day of the contract month
Delivery Day	European exercise – on last trading day only
Real-time price data	Bloomberg: AS26 <Cmdty> OMON; Reuters: <0#TLX*.AX>

Table 2.17 Contract Specifications for ASXD Twenty Leaders Index Options

contract. The ASXD All Ords option contract (which has a multiplier of A$10, compared with SFE's A$25) traded a mere 119 contracts in 1993 and 9,396 contracts in 1994; year-end open interest amounted to 23 contracts in 1993 and 590 contracts in 1994. Turnover in Gold Index options amounted to 20 contracts in 1993 and 616 contracts in 1994, with year-end open interest of only 14 contracts in 1993 and 16 contracts in 1994. Turnover in Twenty Leaders Index options declined from 2,176 contracts in 1993 to 1,450 contracts in 1994, with year-end open interest falling from 128 contracts in 1993 to 20 contracts in 1994 (ASXD, 1995). Despite the rather lacklustre performance of all three options the Exchange has made no announcement regarding possible restructuring or delisting of the contracts. Tables 2.15, 2.16, and 2.17 contain relevant details on ASXD's index options.

Fixed Income

Deposit Futures/Options/Futures Options

The SFE introduced its physical settlement bank bill futures contract in November 1979. The underlying bill market is based on short-term bank accepted bills arising from the extension of credit to local borrowers. Borrowers issue bills in exchange for funds, with a promise to return the funds on a specified date; banks accept the bills at a discount (based on the creditworthiness of the borrower) and trade them in the secondary market. The SFE contract references the 90-day bank bill rate (BBR), which is Australia's primary short-term interest rate benchmark (note that BBR is also used in pricing OTC derivatives such as FRAs and swaps). A unique feature of the Australian fixed income futures/options market is a variable futures tick value which changes as yields change. Variable ticks are applicable to deposit contracts (such as the bank bill future) and interest rate contracts (such as three- and ten-year bond futures, discussed below); the formula for determining tick values for bills is given immediately following and the formula for three- and ten-year bond futures is described in the section below. For bills, the tick value is determined by comparing the value of the bill future at two different yields and subtracting the difference. The value of a bill future is calculated by the following:

$$P = \frac{365 \times 1{,}000{,}000}{365 + (I \times (90/100)}$$

where $I = 100 -$ quoted bill futures price

At a futures price of 95 (i.e. a yield of 5%), the contract value is A$987,821. At a futures price of 94.99 (i.e. a yield of 5.01%), the contract value is A$987,797; the net differential, A$24, is the tick value for a one basis point move in yield. The tick value from 5.01% to 5.02% can be determined in the same fashion, and so on. As yields increase, tick values decrease, and vice versa.

The bank bill contract (which trades through SFE and SYCOM (on a standard SFE cycle)) has grown to become one of the Exchange's most active derivatives and routinely trades five times the volume of the underlying cash market. Total turnover increased from 6.41 mln contracts in 1993 to a record 9.37 mln contracts in 1994; year-end open interest increased from 253,310 contracts in 1993 to 307,747 contracts in 1994 (SFE, 1995). Liquidity in bank bill futures is sufficiently deep that the SFE routinely quotes an active strip out to 21–24 months.

It should be noted that in 1994 members of the SFE elected to double the notional size of the contract, from A$500,000 to A$1 mln, to bring the contract in line with other deposit futures traded on global exchanges; the notional value of the future was doubled on 1 May 1995. Table 2.18 outlines details of the bank bill future, while Figure 2.6 traces the historical price movement of the contract.

Contract	**90-day Bank Accepted Bill Futures**
Type	Domestic
Exchange	Sydney Futures Exchange/Sydney Overnight Computerized Market
Months	March, June, September, December, up to 12 quarter months
Contract Size	A$1,000,000 face value of bank accepted bills
Tick Value	0.01% of yield (approximately A$24, varies with interest rates)
Daily Limit	No limit
Deliverable Instrument	Physical settlement of ten accepted bills or negotiable certificates of deposit (NCD) with face value A$100,000, or one bill or NCD with face value A$1,000,000, maturing 85 to 95 days from delivery day
Last Trading Day	Business day prior to delivery day
Delivery Day	2nd Friday of the delivery month
Real-time price data	Bloomberg: SFE – IRA <Cmdty>, SYCOM – SRA <Cmdty>; Reuters: SFE – <0#YBA:>, SYCOM – <0#YBS:>; Telerate: SFE – 6181, SYCOM – 6191

Table 2.18 Contract Specifications for SFE/SYCOM 90-day Bank Accepted Bill Futures

The success of the SFE's 90-day bank bill future led, not surprisingly, to the introduction of bank bill futures options on SFE and SYCOM; trading in bill options began in 1985, six years after the introduction of bill futures. The bank bill futures option is an American exercise, physical delivery contract with strikes set at 0.25% intervals. Trading in the contract has grown steadily and is now quite significant; total turnover increased from 663,317 contracts in 1993 to 943,749 contracts in 1994, with year-end open interest of 121,295 contracts in 1993 and 111,677 contracts in 1994 (SFE, 1995). Table 2.19 contains relevant contract details on bank bill futures options.

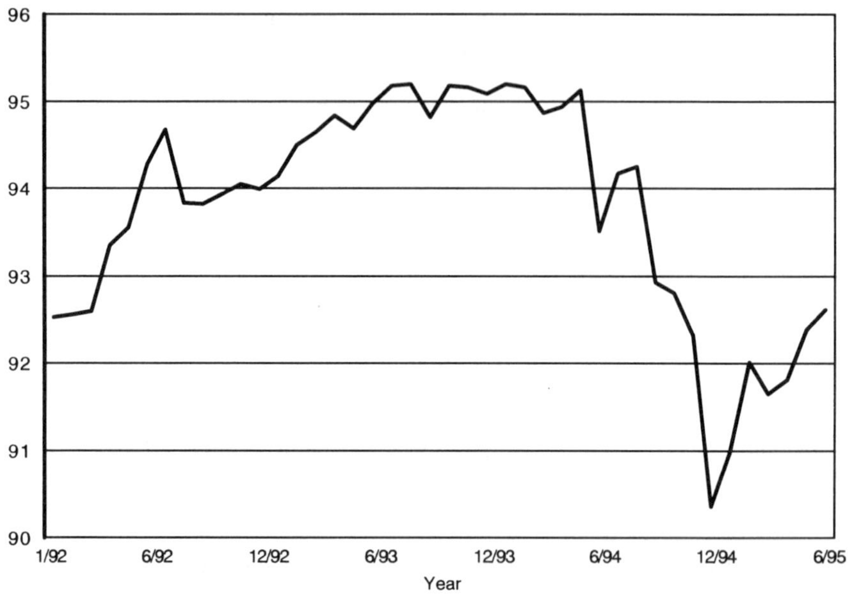

Source: Sydney Futures Exchange

Figure 2.6 Historical Movement of SFE 90-day Bank Accepted Bill Futures

Contract	**Options on 90-day Bank Accepted Bill Futures**
Type	Domestic
Exchange	Sydney Futures Exchange/Sydney Overnight Computerized Market
Months	Same as futures, up to 8 quarter months forward
Contract Size	1 90-day bank accepted bill future
Tick Value	0.01% of yield (approximately A$24, varies with interest rates)
Daily Limit	No limit
Deliverable Instrument	Physical settlement into underlying futures contract
Last Trading Day	Same as exercise day
Exercise Day	American exercise – any business day up to, and including, last trading day in futures
Real-time price data	Bloomberg: SFE – IRA <Cmdty> OMON, SYCOM – SRA <Cmdty> OMON; Reuters: SFE – <0#YBAmy+>, SYCOM – <0#YBSmy+>; Telerate: SFE – 22709-12, 36434-37, SYCOM – 36430-33, 36446-49

Table 2.19 Contract Specifications for SFE/SYCOM Options on 90 day Bank Accepted Bill Futures

Interest Rate Futures/Options/Futures Options

Australian listed interest rate futures are traded through SFE and SYCOM (on a standard SFE cycle). Over the past decade the SFE has introduced a variety of interest rate contracts; some have proven successful, others have required restructuring, and still others have been abandoned. The first bond futures contracts, on two- and ten-year ACGBs, were introduced in 1984. In 1988 a three-year bond future was developed to replace the two-year future, which had become inactive; three- and ten-year ACGB futures are the focal point of the SFE's interest rate futures programme today. In 1989 the Exchange also introduced two bond futures based on a basket of semi-government securities (issued by the three largest semi-government issuers); the five- and ten-year semi-government contracts were restructured in early 1990 but low turnover caused the Exchange to abandon both at the end of 1990.

As indicated in the section on bill futures above, the tick value of bond futures varies with the level of interest rates. In order to determine the tick value at a given yield, the value of the future is first calculated via:

$$P = \text{A\$}1000 \times (6(1 - V^n)/i + 100V^n)$$

where i is the per annum yield/200
V is $1/(1 + i)$, and
n is 6 for three-year bonds, 20 for ten-year bonds

Once the initial price is determined, the yield is moved by one basis point and a new price is recalculated; the differential between the two prices provides the tick value at that particular yield.

SFE bond futures have proven very popular with financial institutions, which utilize the derivatives to manage asset-liability positions and hedge interest rate exposures generated by swap market-making activities; the Exchange estimates that activity in the three- and ten-year contracts is well balanced between hedgers (50% of volume), speculators (40%) and arbitrageurs (10%). The ten-year contract has experienced consistent growth in trading volume over the past decade and reached a new peak in 1994: total volume increased from 4.78 mln contracts in 1993 to 6.84 mln contracts in 1994, while year-end open interest rose from 46,467 contracts in 1993 to 57,553 contracts in 1994. Trading volume in 1994 was equal to 110% of the turnover in the underlying ten-year cash market. The three-year contract has experienced growing volume over the past few years as well: total turnover increased from 6.94 mln contracts in 1993 to a record 9.7 mln contracts in 1994, making it the SFE's single most active derivative; year-end open interest rose from 64,090 contracts in 1993 to 107,204 contracts in 1994 (SFE, 1995). It should be noted that, unlike benchmark bond futures found in other advanced nations (e.g. Japan, US, Germany), the Australian contracts are not currently deliverable. Although a resurgence in ACGB supply over the past few years resulted in repeated proposals to make both contracts deliverable SFE members voted in 1995 to retain the non-deliverable status of the contract for the forseeable future.

Tables 2.20 and 2.21 contain contract specifications for three- and ten-year bond futures contracts traded on SFE and SYCOM. Figures 2.7 and 2.8 trace the price movement of three- and ten-year bond futures since 1992.

Contract	**Three-year Australian Commonwealth Government Bond Futures**
Type	Domestic
Exchange	Sydney Futures Exchange/Sydney Overnight Computerized Market
Months	March, June, September, December
Contract Size	A$100,000 of Three-year Australian Commonwealth Government Bonds
Tick Value	0.01% of yield (approximately A$26, varies with interest rates)
Daily Limit	No limit
Deliverable Instrument	Cash settlement based on arithmetic mean of quotes from 12 random dealers after excluding two highest and lowest quotes
Last Trading Day	15th business day of the contract month
Delivery Day	Business day following the last trading day
Real-time price data	Bloomberg: SFE – YBA <Cmdty>, SYCOM – SYA <Cmdty>; Reuters: SFE – <0#YTT:>, SYCOM – <0#YTU:>; Telerate: SFE – 6182, SYCOM – 6187

Table 2.20 Contract Specifications for SFE/SYCOM Three-year Australian Commonwealth Government Bond Futures

Contract Government	**Ten-year Australian Commonwealth Bond Futures**
Type	Domestic
Exchange	Sydney Futures Exchange/Sydney Overnight Computerized Market
Months	March, June, September, December, up to 12 months forward
Contract Size	A$100,000 of Ten-year Australian Commonwealth Government Bonds
Tick Value	0.005% of yield (approximately A$33, varies with interest rates)
Daily Limit	No limit
Deliverable Instrument	Cash settlement based on arithmetic mean of quotes from 12 random dealers, after excluding two highest and lowest buying quotes and two highest and lowest selling quotes
Last Trading Day	15th business day of the contract month
Delivery Day	Business day following the last trading day
Real-time price data	Bloomberg: SFE – ATA <Cmdty>, SYCOM – SXA <Cmdty>; Reuters: SFE – <0#YTC:>, SYCOM – <0#YTS:>; Telerate: SFE – 6185, SYCOM – 6189

Table 2.21 Contract Specifications for SFE/SYCOM Ten-year Australian Commonwealth Government Bond Futures

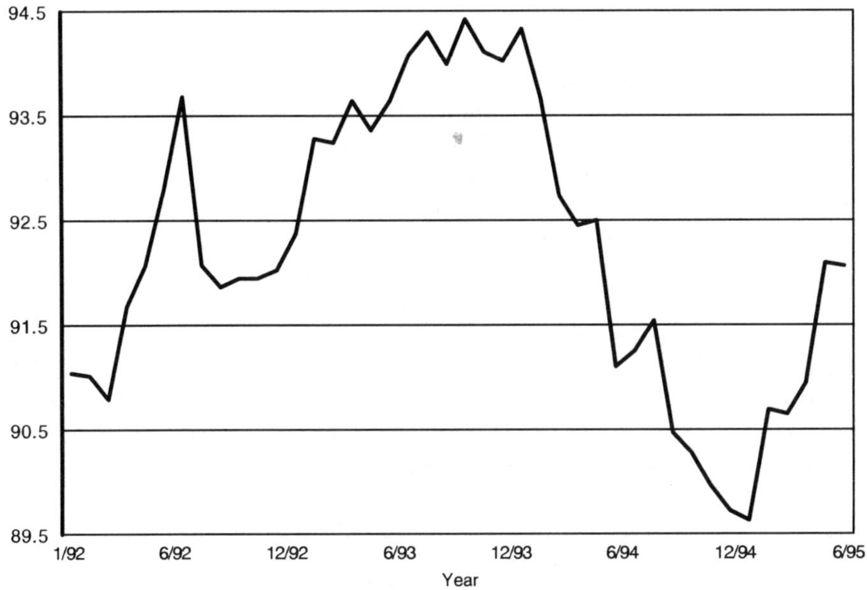

Source: Sydney Futures Exchange

Figure 2.7 Historical Movement of SFE Three-year ACGB Futures

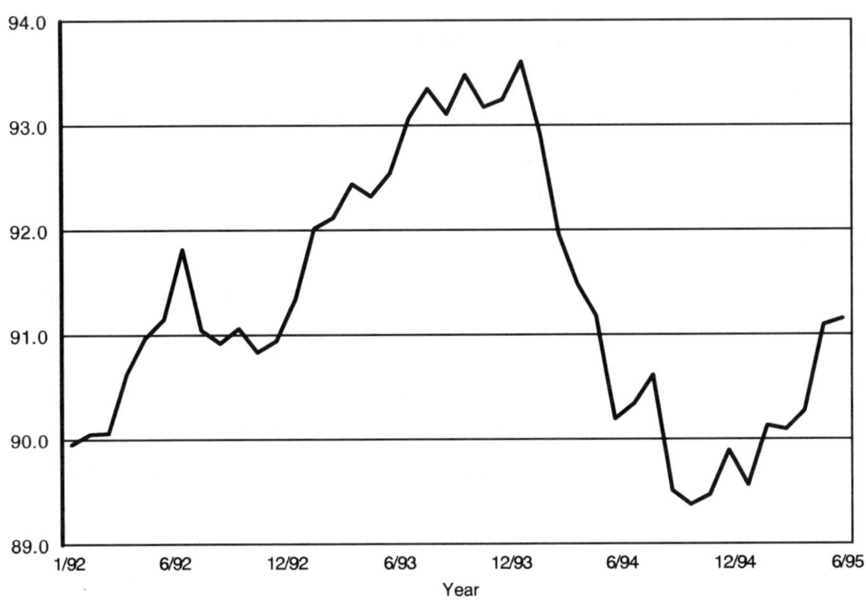

Source: Sydney Futures Exchange

Figure 2.8 Historical Movement of SFE Ten-year ACGB Futures

Futures options are available on both three- and ten-year ACGBs; ten-year bond futures options were introduced in 1985, while three-year contracts were introduced in 1988 (just a month after the underlying futures contract was listed). Conventional bond futures options are American exercise, physical delivery derivatives traded through SFE and SYCOM (on a standard SFE cycle), while overnight bond options are American exercise, cash-settlement derivatives traded on SYCOM; strikes on conventional three- and ten-year options are set at 0.25% intervals, while strikes on three- and ten-year overnight options are set at 0.01% intervals. Total SFE and SYCOM trading volume in three-year options declined from 514,539 contracts in 1993 to 509,330 contracts in 1994; year-end open interest decreased from 12,318 contracts in 1993 to 8,775 contracts in 1994. Trading volume in ten-year bond options increased from 712,686 contracts in 1993 to 818,919 contracts in 1994; year-end open interest decreased from 17,876 contracts in 1993 to 13,748 contracts in 1994 (SFE, 1995). Tables 2.22 through 2.25 contain relevant contract details on all SFE bond options.

Contract	**Options on Three-year Australian Commonwealth Government Bond Futures**
Type	Domestic
Exchange	Sydney Futures Exchange/Sydney Overnight Computerized Market
Months	March, June, September, December
Contract Size	1 Three-year Australian Commonwealth Government Bond future
Tick Value	0.01% of yield (approximately A$26, varies with interest rates)
Daily Limit	No limit
Deliverable Instrument	Physical settlement into underlying futures contract
Last Trading Day	Same day as the last trading day in futures
Exercise Day	American exercise – any business day up to, and including, the last trading day in futures
Real-time price data	Bloomberg: YBA <Cmdty> OMON, SYCOM – SYA <Cmdty> OMON; Reuters: SFE – <0#YTTmy+>, SYCOM – <0#YTUmy+>; Telerate: SFE – 22717-20, SYCOM – 36438-41

Table 2.22 Contract Specifications for SFE/SYCOM Options on Three-year Australian Commonwealth Government Bond Futures

Contract	Overnight Options on Three-year Australian Commonwealth Government Bond Futures
Type	Domestic
Exchange	Sydney Overnight Computerized Market
Months	Near month
Contract Size	1 Three-year Australian Commonwealth Government Bond future
Tick Value	0.01% of yield (approximately A$26, varies with interest rates)
Daily Limit	No limit
Deliverable Instrument	Cash settlement
Last Trading Day	End of each SYCOM session
Exercise Day	Business day immediately following the overnight SYCOM session
Real-time price data	Bloomberg: OOA <Cmdty> OMON; Reuters: <0#YXOmy+>; Telerate: 22933

Table 2.23 Contract Specifications for SYCOM Overnight Options on Three-year Australian Commonwealth Government Bond Futures

Contract	Options on Ten-year Australian Commonwealth Government Bond Futures
Type	Domestic
Exchange	Sydney Futures Exchange/Sydney Overnight Computerized Market
Months	Two nearby months of futures cycle
Contract Size	1 Ten-year Australian Commonwealth Government Bond future
Tick Value	0.005% of yield (approximately A$33, varies with interest rates)
Daily Limit	No limit
Deliverable Instrument	Physical settlement into underlying futures contract
Last Trading Day	Same day as the last trading day in futures
Exercise Day	American exercise – any business day up to, and including, the last trading day
Real-time price data	Bloomberg SFE – ATA <Cmdty> OMON, SYCOM – SXA <Cmdty> OMON; Reuters: SFE – <0#YTCmy+>, SYCOM – <0#YTSmy+>; Telerate: SFE – 22721-24, SYCOM – 36442-45

Table 2.24 Contract Specifications for SFE/SYCOM Options on Ten-year Australian Commonwealth Government Bond Futures

Contract	Overnight Options on Ten-year Australian Commonwealth Government Bond Futures
Type	Domestic
Exchange	Sydney Overnight Computerized Market
Months	Near month
Contract Size	1 Ten-year Australian Commonwealth Government Bond future
Tick Value	0.005% of yield (approximately A$33, varies with interest rates)
Daily Limit	No limit
Deliverable Instrument	Cash settlement
Last Trading Day	End of each SYCOM session
Exercise Day	Business day immediately following the overnight SYCOM session
Real-time price data	Bloomberg: SOA <Cmdty> OMON; Reuters: <0#YOUmy+>; Telerate: 22932

Table 2.25 Contract Specifications for SYCOM Overnight Options on Ten-year Australian Commonwealth Government Bond Futures

Currency

Currency Futures/Options/Futures Options

The SFE introduced currency futures trading to the Australian market in 1980, just after it had successfully launched its 90-day bank accepted bill future. Between 1980 and 1982 the Exchange listed and traded currency futures on JPY/US$, US$/GBP and US$/A$. Despite a promising start volume soon tapered off as most participants preferred the flexibility and liquidity of OTC spot and forward trading, and all three contracts were ultimately delisted. There are presently no plans to reintroduce currency futures or options.

Commodity

Commodity Futures/Options/Futures Options

Although the SFE and its predecessor (the Greasy Wool Exchange) have traded wool futures for 35 years the contract became relatively inactive in the late 1980's and early 1990's, due primarily to government-imposed price floors and an oversupply of wool. The original Sydney exchange traded a very active 22 micron wool contract for 30 years, with volume reaching a peak of 186,000 contracts in 1973. In the 1980s the government introduced a floor price scheme guaranteeing wool producers a basic minimum price of A$7/kg which eliminated the need for price protection through futures; it also had the side effect of causing a buildup of wool stocks, equal to 4.7 mln bales, which caused a price overhang in the market. The price supports were eliminated in 1991 but the oversupply of wool continued to keep futures activity to a minimum. As the wool stock was sold down and price volatility increased, the SFE began designing a new contract, based on 21 micron fibres. In early 1995 the Australian Wool Exchange agreed on the principles of wool appraisal and the quality of wool deliverable into the new contract and trading in the 21 micron contract began in March 1995 (on both SFE and SYCOM); the new physical delivery contract is offered in two month intervals out to 18 months, giving hedgers and speculators more flexible, and longer, maturities than before. Early data already indicates promising turnover and Exchange officials believe that, based on current wool production in the region, turnover of 10,000 contracts per day is a realistic target in the intermediate term. Note that the 22 micron contract was phased out over a period of 20 weeks following the introduction of the 21 micron contract. Table 2.26 contains relevant details on the new SFE wool future while Figure 2.9 illustrates historical Australian wool futures prices based on the original 22 micron contract.

In addition to its own listed derivatives, the SFE finalized negotiations with the New York Mercantile Exchange (NYMEX) in early 1995 permitting SFE members

Contract	**Wool Futures (21 micron)**
Type	Domestic
Exchange	Sydney Futures Exchange/Sydney Overnight Computerized Market
Months	February, April, June, August, October, December, to 18 months
Contract Size	2,500 kg clean weight wool
Tick Value	A$25
Daily Limit	No limit
Deliverable Grade	Physical settlement of 21 micron wool based on Australian Wool Exchange standards
Last Trading Day	Business day following the last day of wool auction sales
Delivery Day	Business day following the last trading day
Real-time price data	Bloomberg – SFE OLA <Cmdty>, SYCOM – LOA <Cmdty>; Reuters: SFE – <0#YGS:>, SYCOM – <0#YSG:>; Telerate: SFE – 6196, SYCOM – 6197

Table 2.26 Contract Specifications for SFE/SYCOM Wool Futures (21 micron)

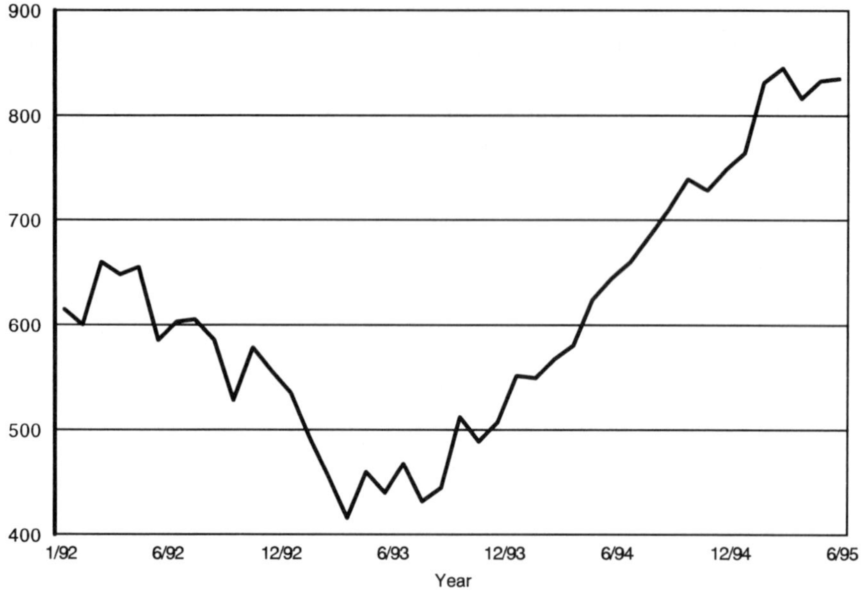

Source: Sydney Futures Exchange

Figure 2.9 Historical Movement of SFE Wool Futures (22 micron)

to trade NYMEX energy products directly through the Australian exchange; the SFE/NYMEX agreement allows trading via each other's overnight system (SYCOM for SFE, ACCESS for NYMEX). During Sydney morning and afternoon hours trading occurs via ACCESS and in the evening it switches to SYCOM; the combination permits participants to trade NYMEX derivatives 16 hours per day. SFE trading of NYMEX's light sweet crude, sour crude, unleaded gasoline, propane, heating oil and natural gas contracts began in late 1995. Discussions are being held on future trading of NYMEX's metal products (e.g. palladium, platinum) as well as its heating oil/gasoline crack spreads. Tables 2.27 through 2.33 contain details on the NYMEX contracts which are presently accessible through the SFE.

(Note: SIMEX and NYMEX are negotiating a similar exchange agreement calling for trading during SIMEX's daylight hours through NYMEX ACCESS; the SIMEX arrangement is likely to create a certain amount of regional competition).

With regard to other commodities the SFE announced in 1995 that it is considering the introduction of the world's first jet fuel and coal contracts. The nature of such contracts, and the potential timetable for listing and trading, is unknown at the present time. The Exchange is also in the process of evaluating the development of grain and beef contracts (the SFE cattle contract introduced in 1975 was abandoned several years after its introduction). In offshore exchange linkages, SFE is exploring possible arrangements with CBOT (to trade CBOT's US fixed income futures) and the TGE (to trade TGE's grain futures); there have been no firm details announced on either arrangement.

Contract	**Light Sweet Crude Oil Futures**
Type	Offshore
Exchange	Sydney Futures Exchange/New York Mercantile Exchange link (via SYCOM and ACCESS)
Months	First 18 consecutive contract months, starting with current nearby contract and four long-dated months to 36 months forward
Contract Size	1,000 US barrels
Tick Value	US$10
Daily Limit	+/– US$15/barrel for first two months, US$1.50 or US$3 in all other months
Deliverable Grade	Physical settlement of deliverable grade crude of the following streams: West Texas Intermediate, Low Sweet Mix, New Mexican Sweet, North Texas Sweet, Oklahoma Sweet, South Texas Sweet, Brent Blend, Bonny Light, Oseberg and Forties, in relevant sulphur weight
Last Trading Day	3rd business day before the 25th calendar day of the month before the delivery month
Delivery Day	By last calendar day of the delivery month
Real-time price data	Bloomberg: CLA <Cmdty>; Reuters: <0#CL:>; Telerate: 8810-11

Table 2.27 Contract Specifications for SFE/NYMEX Light Sweet Crude Oil Futures

Contract	**Sour Crude Oil Futures**
Type	Offshore
Exchange	Sydney Futures Exchange/New York Mercantile Exchange link (via SYCOM and ACCESS)
Months	First 18 consecutive contract months, starting with current nearby contract
Contract Size	1,000 US barrels
Tick Value	US$10
Daily Limit	+/– US$15/barrel for first two months, US$1.50 or US$3 in all other months
Deliverable Grade	Physical settlement of deliverable grade crude of the following streams: New Mexico Sour, West Texas Sour, Iranian Light, Flotta, Dubai, Oman, Oriente, Alaskan North Slope
Last Trading Day	3rd business day before 25th calendar day of the month before the delivery month
Delivery Day	By last calendar day of the delivery month
Real-time price data	Bloomberg: SCA <Cmdty>

Table 2.28 Contract Specifications for SFE/NYMEX Sour Crude Oil Futures

Contract	New York Unleaded Gasoline Futures
Type	Offshore
Exchange	Sydney Futures Exchange/New York Mercantile Exchange link (via SYCOM and ACCESS)
Months	First 18 consecutive contract months, starting with next calendar month
Contract Size	42,000 gallons (1,000 US barrels)
Tick Value	US$4.20
Daily Limit	+/– US$0.40/barrel for first two months, US$0.04 or US$0.06 in all other months
Deliverable Grade	Physical settlement of simple model reformulate gasoline (within industry standards), FOB New York harbor
Last Trading Day	Last business day of the month before the delivery month
Delivery Day	By last business day of the delivery month
Real-time price data	Bloomberg: HUA <Cmdty>; Reuters: <0#HU:>; Telerate: 8807

Table 2.29 Contract Specifications for SFE/NYMEX New York Unleaded Gasoline Futures

Contract	Gulf Coast Unleaded Gasoline Futures
Type	Offshore
Exchange	Sydney Futures Exchange/New York Mercantile Exchange link (via SYCOM and ACCESS)
Months	First 18 consecutive contract months, starting with next calendar month
Contract Size	42,000 gallons (1,000 US barrels)
Tick Value	US$4.20
Daily Limit	+/– US$0.40/barrel for first two months, US$0.04 or US$0.06 in all other months
Deliverable Grade	Physical settlement of Colonial Pipeline fungible Southern Grade 44, 88 octane regular unleaded gasoline, FOB Colonial Pipeline at seller's injection station or at terminals of Amerada Hess, Oil Taking Houston, or GATX Terminals
Last Trading Day	Last business day of the month before the delivery month
Delivery Day	By last business day of the delivery month
Real-time price data	Bloomberg: GGA <Cmdty>

Table 2.30 Contract Specifications for SFE/NYMEX Gulf Coast Unleaded Gasoline Futures

Contract	Propane Futures
Type	Offshore
Exchange	Sydney Futures Exchange/New York Mercantile Exchange link (via SYCOM and ACCESS)
Months	First 15 consecutive contract months, starting with current month
Contract Size	42,000 gallons (1,000 US barrels)
Tick Value	US$4.20
Daily Limit	+/– US$0.40/barrel for first two months, US$0.04 or US$0.06 in all other months
Deliverable Grade	Physical settlement of fungible liquified propane gas conforming to industry standards, FOB seller's pipeline with direct access to Texas Eastern Transmission Pipeline
Last Trading Day	Last business day of the month before the delivery month
Delivery Day	Calendar day prior to the last business day of the delivery month
Real-time price data	Bloomberg: PNA <Cmdty>; Reuters: <0#PN:>; Telerate: 8812

Table 2.31 Contract Specifications for SFE/NYMEX Propane Futures

Contract	Heating Oil Futures
Type	Offshore
Exchange	Sydney Futures Exchange/New York Mercantile Exchange link (via SYCOM and ACCESS)
Months	First 18 consecutive contract months, starting with next calendar month
Contract Size	42,000 gallons (1,000 US barrels)
Tick Value	US$4.20
Daily Limit	+/– US$0.40/barrel for first two months, US$0.04 or US$0.06 in all other months
Deliverable Grade	Physical settlement of deliverable grade No.2 heating oil (or other fungible heating oil within industry standards), FOB New York harbor
Last Trading Day	Last business day of the month before the delivery month
Delivery Day	By last business day of the delivery month
Real-time price data	Bloomberg: HOA <Cmdty>; Reuters: <0#HO:>; Telerate: 8806, 8811

Table 2.32 Contract Specifications for SFE/NYMEX Heating Oil Futures

Contract	Natural Gas Futures
Type	Offshore
Exchange	Sydney Futures Exchange/New York Mercantile Exchange link (via SYCOM and ACCESS)
Months	First 18 consecutive contract months, starting with first nearby month
Contract Size	10,000 mln BTUs (British Thermal Units)
Tick Value	US$10
Daily Limit	+/– US$0.10-US$0.20; no limit on front month contract
Deliverable Grade	Physical settlement of natural gas per pipeline specifications at time of delivery, to Sabine Pipeline, Louisiana
Last Trading Day	Six days prior to the first day of the delivery month
Delivery Day	Last calendar day of the delivery month
Real-time price data	Bloomberg: NGA <Cmdty>; Reuters: <0#NG:>; Telerate: 8813, 9249

Table 2.33 Contract Specifications for SFE/NYMEX Natural Gas Futures

LISTED/OVER-THE-COUNTER WARRANTS, CONVERTIBLES AND HYBRIDS

Equity

Equity Warrants

Australian equity warrants are available in three distinct forms, including listed issuer equity warrants, listed covered equity warrants and OTC covered equity warrants.

The largest segment of the Australian equity warrant market is comprised of warrants issued by domestic companies on their own shares; such derivatives result in the issuance of new equity by the company upon exercise. Issuer equity warrants are American exercise derivatives listed on, and traded through, the ASX, and are virtually always structured in the ratio of one share per warrant; all issues are denominated in Australian dollars and carry maturities ranging from one to five years. As of June 1995 the listed equity warrant market consisted of 232 separate issues; Appendix II contains a listing of all issuer equity warrants traded on the ASX.

In addition to issuer warrants, the domestic market also features a limited number of listed covered equity warrants. Third-party covered warrants were originally introduced on the ASX in early 1991, after the Exchange put forth its warrant issuance guidelines in November 1990 (note: the guidelines set forth for covered equity warrants are also applicable to other categories of covered warrants listed on the ASX, discussed below). Third-party equity warrants are underwritten by domestic or international financial institutions on the stock of Australian companies and result in the reallocation of existing shares, as opposed to the issuance of new shares, upon exercise. The first ASX-listed covered equity warrant was a one year issue underwritten by Macquarie Bank on Boral shares and was followed by several others over the next few years; at the present time the ASX lists covered call warrants on BHP, Qantas and Western Mining. Covered warrants are generally issued in 1,000 share blocks, with maturities extending from 15 months to five years; warrants are available in both American and European exercise and result in either cash or physical settlement.

In addition to domestic listed equity warrants, numerous international banking institutions issue offshore OTC covered warrants on individual Australian equities (primarily larger capitalization blue-chips). As with domestic covered warrants, offshore warrants result in the reallocation of shares from the seller to the buyer of the derivative. Offshore warrants are generally denominated in foreign currencies, and may be unlisted or listed on an offshore exchange and traded OTC; maturities range from one to three years.

Basket/Index Warrants

The Australian basket/index warrant market consists of both domestic listed derivatives and offshore OTC derivatives. Listed basket/index warrants are traded via the ASX, under the guidelines established by the Exchange in 1990. As with listed covered equity warrants, ASX basket/index warrants, which reference baskets of Australian stocks or the broad Australian stock market, are floated by banks or securities firms as American or European exercise derivatives with maturities of one to five years. At present the ASX lists index call warrants on the All Ords, as well as basket call warrants on the Macquarie Base Metals Basket (consisting of stocks of Australian base metal companies); several other baskets have been listed over the past few years.

In addition to listed warrants, international banks actively issue OTC Australian basket and index warrants in the offshore market. Warrants are created on various groupings of Australian equities, including bank baskets, resource baskets, property baskets, and so on. Call and put warrants referencing the All Ords, the Twenty Leaders and other domestic indexes are also floated on a periodic basis. As with OTC equity warrants discussed above, OTC basket/index warrants generally carry maturities of one to three years, and are unlisted or listed on overseas exchanges and traded OTC. Representative issues in this category include Swiss Bank Corporation's Swiss franc basket call warrants on a group of five Australian mining stocks (1994) and Swiss Bank Corporation's Deutschmark put and call index warrants on the All Ords (1994).

Index-linked Notes

Index-linked notes have proven moderately popular in the domestic market and are issued on a public basis (listed on an offshore exchange and traded OTC) or private basis (unlisted and generally held until maturity by investors). The most common structure in this category is the short- to medium-maturity (e.g. one to five year) domestic or offshore issue with an embedded long call on the All Ords, providing investors with either enhanced coupons or principal as the market rises. One example of this structure is the National Australia Bank certificate of deposit programme which provides depositors with upside exposure to the All Ords in the form of enhanced coupons or principal. Index-linked notes may also be structured with embedded long puts (entitling the investor to enhanced returns based on depreciation in an index) or short puts (providing the investor with an enhanced coupon, but reducing principal payout if the market declines). In addition to referencing indexes such as the All Ords or Twenty Leaders, certain notes reference smaller baskets of domestic stocks. Note that more specialized and complex securities are created on occasion by incorporating exotic options such as barriers or digitals; such derivative notes carry unique risk/return profiles.

Convertibles

Australian corporations raise funds in both the domestic and offshore convertible bond markets; in recent years more activity has taken place onshore through the issuance of domestic Australian dollar convertible notes (as they are known locally). Convertible notes are listed on, and traded through, the ASX, and carry maturities ranging from five to ten years. Securities are generally floated with intermediate coupons of 5% to 10% and conversion premiums of 10% to 12%. Total convertible note outstandings have fluctuated from A$1.8 bln (US$1.33 bln) in 1992, to A$2.9 bln (US$1.85 bln) in 1993 and A$2.5 bln (US$2.14 bln) in 1994; representative issuers of such notes include Pacific Dunlop, TNT, BTR Nylex, National Australia Bank, CSR, Lend Lease and Burns Philp.

In addition to funding through the domestic convertible market, certain Australian corporations access the offshore convertible bond market on a periodic basis. While Australian companies were reasonably active issuers of offshore convertibles in the mid- to late-1980s, their overall activity has subsided considerably in the 1990s; the decline in the Australian economy in the early 1990s (along with the fall in the Australian stock market at the same time) and the decreased need for corporate financing have been the primary reasons for the decline in offshore issuance. Deals brought to market by Australian companies to date have been in the Eurodollar market (as opposed to the Swiss franc market, which many other Asia Pacific companies have tapped); the Eurodollar market features issuance of bearer securities which are listed on overseas exchanges and traded on an OTC basis. Australian Eurodollar convertibles have been issued with intermediate coupons of 5% to 7%, high conversion premiums of 15% to 20% and long maturities of ten to

15 years. Appendix III contains details on Australian domestic and offshore convertible issues.

Fixed Income

Fixed Income Warrants

The ASX permits listing and trading of domestic fixed income warrants (characterized by the Exchange as warrants on loan securities), though it maintains no such listings at the present time. ASX fixed income warrants must adhere to all Exchange guidelines and can be issued in varying maturities (e.g. one to five years), exercise styles (e.g. American or European), and denominations. Issuance of offshore OTC warrants has been negligible; only a small number of short-term (e.g. 12 month) call warrants on benchmark ACGBs have been issued to date (one issue was floated as a yield curve warrant, with payoff based on movement in the shape of the curve rather than the direction of rates).

Currency

Currency Warrants

As with fixed income warrants, the ASX also permits the listing and trading of currency warrants. Currency warrants must adhere to all ASX guidelines and can be issued with maturities of 15 months to five years; warrants may be structured with European or American exercise into cash or physical settlement. The Exchange does not list any currency warrants at the present time.

Although the local Exchange does not currently list warrants tied to the Australian dollar, institutions in the offshore market issue such warrants with frequency, particularly when there is evidence of increased volatility in the currency. OTC currency warrants are generally issued with maturities of one to three years and may be unlisted or listed on an overseas exchange. In addition to standard A$ call/US$ put and A$ put/US$ call warrants, there are also periodic issues based on key cross rates such as A$/JPY and A$/GBP.

Commodity

Commodity Warrants

As with other domestic listed warrants, the ASX also permits listing and trading of commodity warrants. Commodity warrants can be issued in American or European form on virtually any underlying commodity (e.g. gold, base metals, and so on), and must carry maturities of 15 months to five years. The ASX does not list any commodity warrants at the present time.

OVER-THE-COUNTER FORWARDS, SWAPS AND OPTIONS

Equity

Equity Forwards/Swaps

OTC equity forwards and swaps based on Australian stocks are available in both the domestic and offshore markets. These derivatives, which call for the purchase or sale of single stocks on a forward basis, or which match flows of a floating index against the appreciation or depreciation of a single stock, are executed primarily on a short- to intermediate-term basis to three years, and are generally structured to reference larger capitalization blue-chip stocks. Despite the existence of equity forwards and swaps the OTC market is more heavily concentrated on OTC equity options and OTC index swaps, as discussed below.

Equity Options

The market for onshore and offshore OTC equity options is very active, with numerous domestic and foreign financial institutions arranging a broad range of options on Australian stocks. Although ASXD features a comprehensive and liquid listing of short-, medium- and long-term equity options on a large number of Australian stocks, the OTC equity market has succeeded because of the additional flexibility it offers. Although any type of option can be created in the OTC market, standard equity options are structured as six to 12 month European or American derivatives exercisable into cash or physical settlement. Note that a certain amount of exotic equity options are also available, including barrier options, outperformance options, digital options, Asian options and others. Unlike listed equity options, OTC structures tend not to be traded among third parties; most transactions are terminated through expiry, exercise or close-out, as opposed to third party resale.

Basket/Index Forwards/Swaps

As with equity forwards and swaps, there is a reasonably active market in Australia for short- to intermediate-term (e.g. one to five year) basket/index forwards and swaps. Index swaps, in particular, have proven popular with investors over the past few years. The conventional index swap exchanges a floating rate flow, such as BBR, for appreciation in an underlying domestic equity index, such as the All Ords. If there is no appreciation in the index the investor receives no incremental return, but is not required to make an additional payment. In this instance the investor is effectively purchasing an All Ords index call and paying premium over time through the BBR flow. Variations on the index swap structure include those where an investor receives index appreciation but pays index depreciation (i.e. purchase of a call swap and sale of a put swap) or those where an investor receives index appreciation but caps potential returns by selling a higher strike call swap; both have the effect of lowering, and in some cases eliminating, premium payable via the BBR flow. Basket swaps based on these concepts are available, though less common. A range of swaps with embedded exotic options, such as barriers, digitals and Asians, are also available.

Basket/Index Options

Despite competition from the listed index option market (primarily through the SFE's contract), the domestic and offshore market for OTC puts and calls on key Australian indexes, such as the All Ords, the Twenty Leaders, the Fifty Leaders and the Gold Index, is active; the market for basket puts and calls on groups of domestic stocks (such as resource companies, financial institutions, retailers and so on) is also quite popular. Though a wide variety of customized strikes, maturities and index/basket references are available, standard structures are centred on cash-settled European or American options maturing in six months to two years. In addition to vanilla options on indexes and baskets, the Australian market features a certain amount of exotic structures. OTC barrier options, Asian options, outperformance options, digital options, quanto options and others are available for institutions seeking very customized risk or payoff profiles; such exotic options are occasionally embedded in notes or swaps. Note that as with OTC equity options there is no secondary market for OTC basket/index options.

Fixed Income

Fixed Income Forwards/Swaps

Australia features very active domestic FRA and IRS markets which have been in existence since the early 1980s. For the period ending December 1994, the International Swap Dealers Association (ISDA) reported total notional Australian dollar IRSs of US$148.5 bln, up from US$131.1 bln at the end of 1993 (Choudhury, 1995); based on these figures, the Australian IRS market is the second largest in Asia Pacific, after the Japanese market.

In the short end of the curve Australian dollar FRAs, which reference BBR, are actively quoted to 12 months and feature very good liquidity; swap market-makers actively use short-term FRAs to manage interest rate risk positions. Nearly two-thirds of deals are executed with maturities under three months (AFMA, 1994); long-term FRAs are available to five years but are far less liquid. Average interbank dealing size is A$50 mln (US$37 mln) and bid-offer spreads range from six to eight basis points under normal market conditions (which is consistent with spreads found on domestic IRSs). Total outstanding Australian dollar FRAs amounted to A$260 bln (US$192 bln) notional at the end of June 1994 (AFMA, 1994) (note: total FRA outstandings in the Australian market, including those related to US dollar, Deutschmark, yen and other interest rates, amounted to A$691 bln (US$511

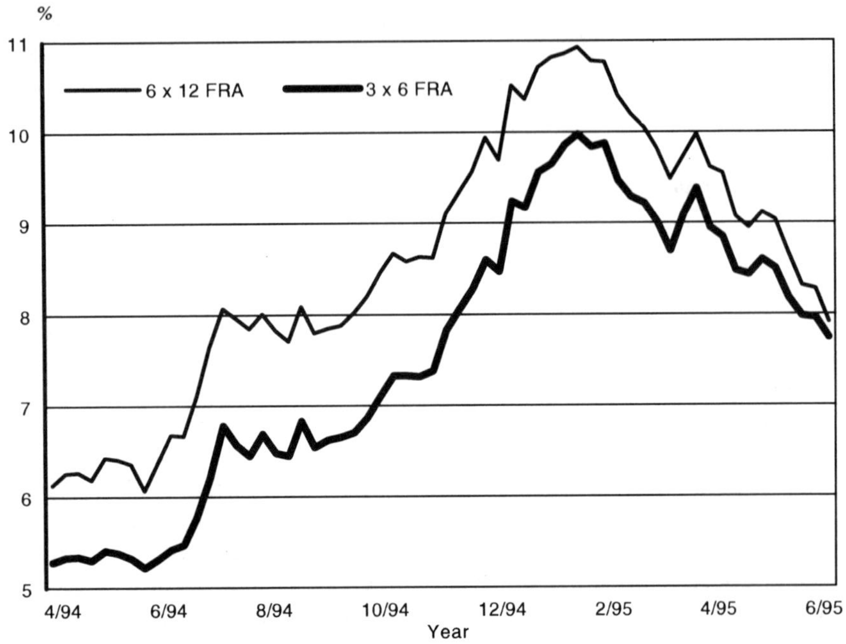

Figure 2.10 Historical Movement of 3 x 6 and 6 x 12 A$ FRAs

bln) in June 1994). Figure 2.10 highlights the historical movement of Australian dollar 3 x 6 and 6 x 12 FRAs.

The Australian interest rate swap market dates back to 1981 when the first 'synthetic' swaps were created through forward sales and purchases of sequential maturity bank bills. The first true IRSs appeared in 1983, when Commonwealth Bank of Australia structured deals with both Australian Investment Development Corporation (AIDC) and Primary Industries Bank of Australia (PIBA); both were five year IRSs converting fixed Australian dollars raised by AIDC and PIBA in the offshore EuroA$ market into floating BBR. The EuroA$ market has historically provided arbitrage opportunities for domestic and offshore issuers (and investors); issuers of EuroA$ are exempt from a 10% withholding tax, while select offshore investors in such securities receive the same exemption. As the expanding market for offshore issues led to swap opportunities, corporates raising funds offshore were active floating rate payers while the central government and larger semi-government institutions were the market's primary fixed rate payers; financial institutions engaged in asset liability management were also seen as frequent fixed rate payers. In addition to EuroA$ issuance by domestic corporations, a number of international issuers (such as IBM, McDonald's and the World Bank) were also active in the market; international investors attracted to the high yield of the Australian dollar (and many being able to take advantage of favourable tax treatment) were eager to purchase issues floated by international, rather than domestic, entities, which prompted issuance from international blue-chip credits. During the mid-1980s swaps were often executed on a brokered basis, where merchant banks or other financial institutions would match two swap counterparties and earn a small fee in the process; widespread positioning or warehousing of swap risk was very uncommon. It was not until 1987–88 that swap market-making (for both IRSs and CCSs) became more common.

In the late 1980s the large funding arbitrages which had existed between the domestic and offshore markets narrowed and became less pronounced; in addition, EuroA$ yields declined and currency volatility increased. As a result of these factors swap opportunities driven by EuroA$ new issue arbitrage disappeared. Swap volumes were aided, however, by increased issuance in the local bond, local CD and matilda bond markets. Domestic issuance of Australian dollar securities expanded, with banks offering fixed rate Australian dollar CDs, corporations and finance companies issuing fixed rate domestic bonds, and offshore issuers (such as Nordic Investment Bank, Swedish Export Credit and others) raising domestic funds via the matilda bond market. Local institutions swapped fixed Australian dollars into BBR, while foreign institutions issuing matilda bonds swapped into BBR or US$ LIBOR. At about this time semi-government institutions were becoming more active fixed and floating payers as they increased control over their own liability and asset management programmes; as the Commonwealth Government shifted more responsibility for both funding and asset allocation directly to the states and the semi-government authorities, these entities became increasingly sophisticated users of swaps. Institutions such as the NSW Treasury Corp (TCorp) and Treasury Corporation of Victoria (TCV) began achieving exceptionally low funding costs as a result of their presence in the market; in recent years semi-governments have enjoyed funding advantages in both the fixed and floating markets, though they typically receive slightly more favourable terms in the fixed rate market. Corporates were also active in the late 1980s as fixed rate receivers through the private placement and dual currency bond markets; we discuss dual currency bond swaps in our section on currency swaps below (and in chapter 7 on Japan). In the early 1990s domestic IRS activity was concentrated in three segments of the market: lower-rated corporations paying fixed Australian dollars and receiving BBR, prime corporates paying BBR and receiving fixed Australian dollars, and sophisticated semi-government authorities converting fixed Australian dollars into sub-BBR funding.

The range of interest rate swap products available in the Australian market has expanded considerably over the past decade and now includes structures common in the world's most advanced swap markets (e.g. US, Japanese and select European markets). In addition to vanilla swaps the domestic market also features zero coupon swaps, amortizing swaps, deferred or forward start swaps, arrears swaps, differential swaps, leveraged swaps, inverse floater swaps, puttable/callable swaps and others. Domestic asset swaps are also popular, where fixed rate Australian dollar bonds issued by finance companies and lower-rated corporates are swapped into floating with banks. Illiquid EuroA$ issues are also used on an asset swap basis, with flows exchanged into either BBR or US$ LIBOR. Exotic swaps incorporating barriers, digitals, Asians and others are also available, though considerably less common than vanilla IRS's. Despite the availability of second generation swaps, most domestic activity remains focused on vanilla transactions.

Although the nature of the domestic swap market has changed over the past decade, fundamental activity in Australian dollar IRSs is ultimately dictated by the credit arbitrage between fixed rate securities of the Commonwealth (and select semi-government authorities such as TCorp and TCV) and floating bank credit levels reflected in the BBR; the relative differentials in borrowing costs between ACGB/TCorp/TCV bonds and BBR drive the domestic swap market. Pricing of Australian dollar swaps is done as a spread to either ACGBs or TCorp/TCV bonds (rather than on an absolute basis). As semi-government authorities have increased their own asset-liability activity and have become frequent and important issuers, their bonds have been used with increasing regularity to provide swap pricing references. One to three year swaps are quoted as fixed quarterly Australian dollars (on an Actual/365 day basis) to BBR flat, while four to ten year swaps are quoted as fixed semi-annual Australian dollars (on an Actual/365 day basis) to BBR flat; the official BBR reference (for 90- or 180-day rates) is Reuters page BBSW. Typical interbank dealing size for Australian dollar IRSs is A$50 mln (US$37 mln); bid-offer spreads range from six to ten basis points across the curve under normal market conditions. Figure 2.11 traces the historical movement of the Australian dollar IRS swap curve while Table 2.34 highlights Australian dollar IRS bid-offer spreads under normal market conditions.

Maturity	**Bid-Offer Spreads**
1 year	6–7 bps
2 years	6–7 bps
3 years	8–10 bps
4 years	8–10 bps
5 years	10 bps
7 years	10 bps
10 years	10 bps

Table 2.34 A$ IRS Bid-Offer Spreads

Figures 2.12 through 2.29 illustrate historical rates and spreads of benchmark maturity Australian dollar IRSs and key pricing securities (i.e. ACGBs, TCorp bonds and TCV bonds). Figures 2.30 to 2.35 highlight the rates and spreads of benchmark maturity Australian dollar IRSs and select AA-rated EuroA$ bonds.

Hedging Australian dollar IRSs can be accomplished in an efficient and cost effective manner with a variety of instruments. Short-end swaps (e.g. those under two years) are hedged primarily through the Australian dollar FRA market (mentioned above) or through bank bill futures traded on the SFE. Though lack of liquidity outside the near months occasionally necessitates use of a stack hedge it is possible, when sufficient liquidity exists, to use the bill strip out to two years to hedge a position or portfolio. Medium term IRSs, to five years, are often hedged with the underlying bonds they reference; if a swap is priced as a spread to ACGBs, the relevant ACGB is utilized and if a swap is priced to either TCorp or TCV, the relevant semi-government bond is used; such hedging removes directional interest rate risk but not spread risk. Note that institutions face no restrictions on short-selling ACGBs or semi-government bonds. In addition to physical bond hedges, the SFE also features three- and ten-year ACGB bond futures, as discussed above. The excellent liquidity of bond futures permits institutions to hedge directional interest rate risk in an efficient manner. Institutions hedging via futures still retain residual basis exposure; the basis between swaps and futures has historically been volatile, so basis risk considerations cannot be ignored. Given substantial liquidity of the IRS market, however, swap dealers are often able to replace temporary bond or futures hedges with back-to-back swaps in a very short time frame, removing spread or basis risks in the process.

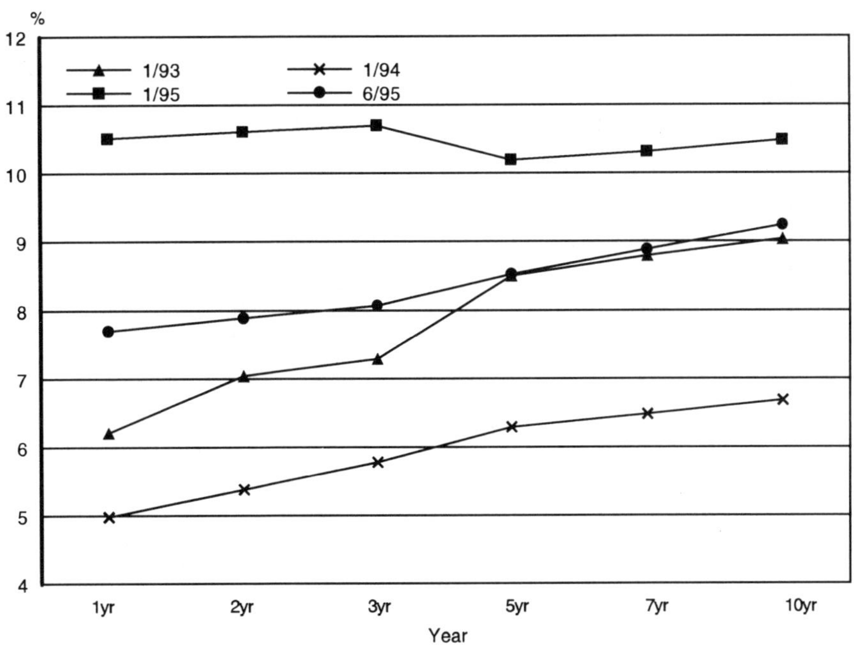

Figure 2.11 Historical Movement of A$ IRS Swap Curves

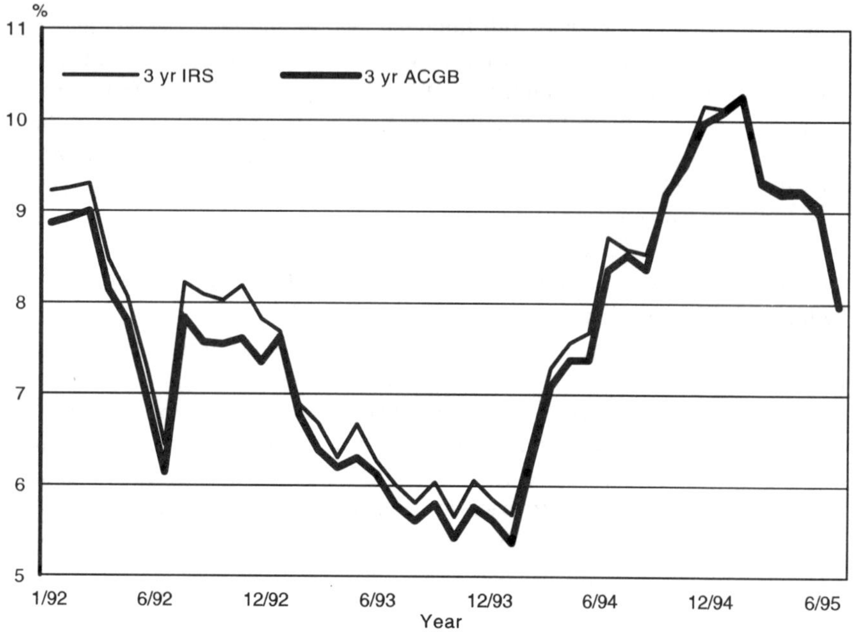

Figure 2.12 Historical Movement of Three-year A$ IRS and Three-year ACGB

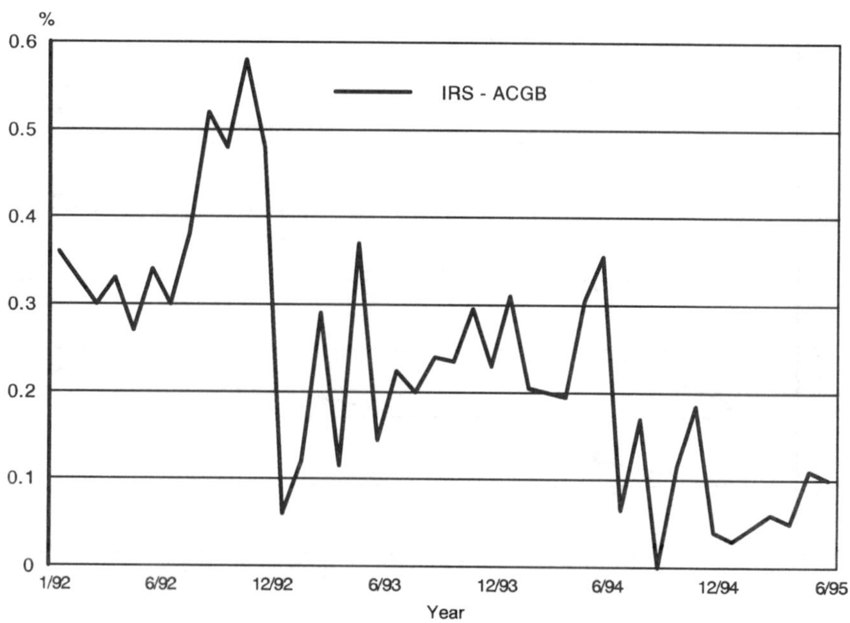

Figure 2.13 Spread of Three-year A$ IRS and ACGB

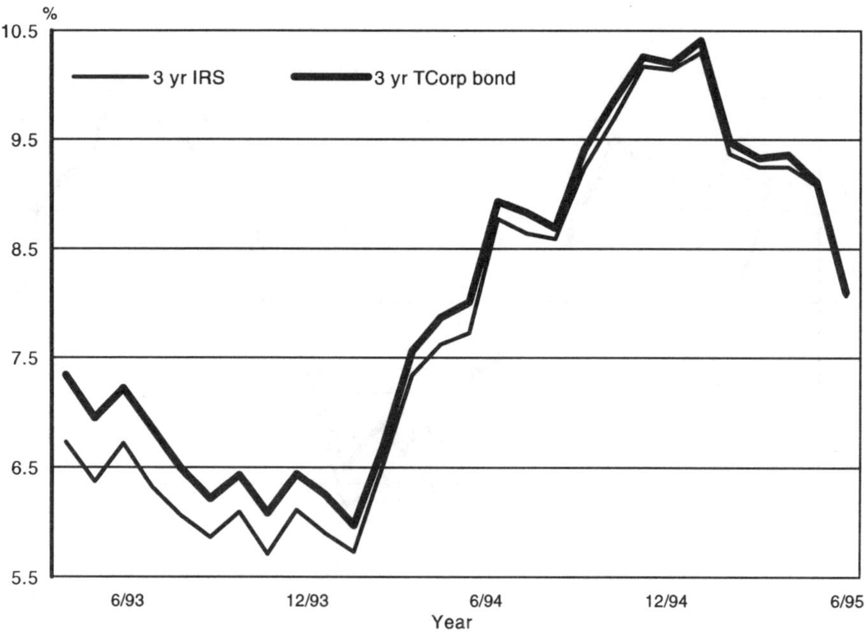

Figure 2.14 Historical Movement of Three-year A$ IRS and Three-year TCorp Bond

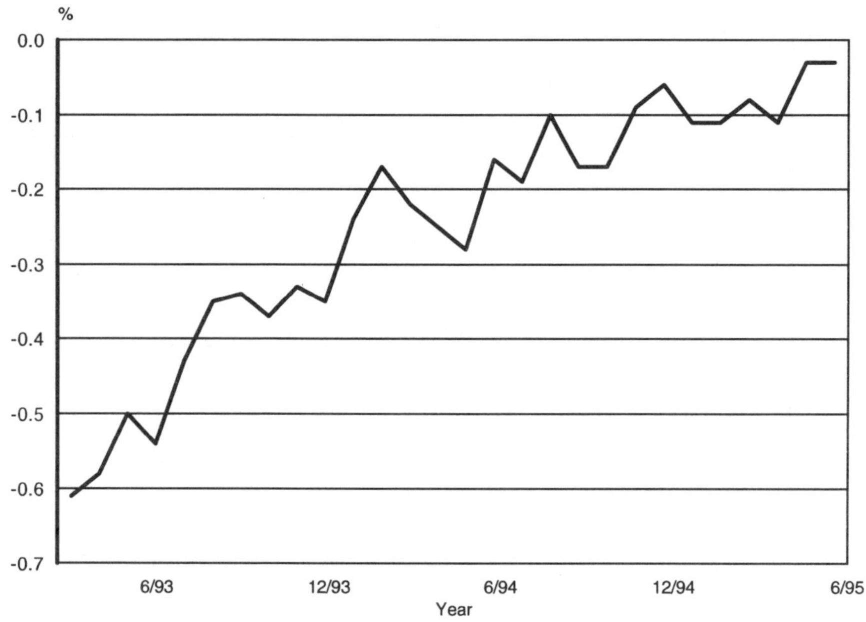

Figure 2.15 Spread of Three-year A$ IRS and TCorp Bond

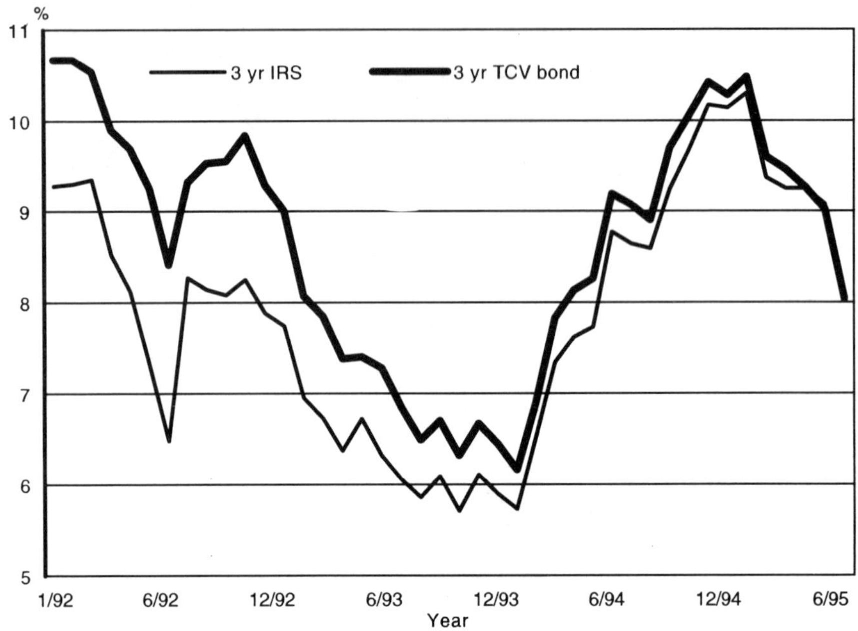

Figure 2.16 Historical Movement of Three-year A$ IRS and Three-year TCV Bond

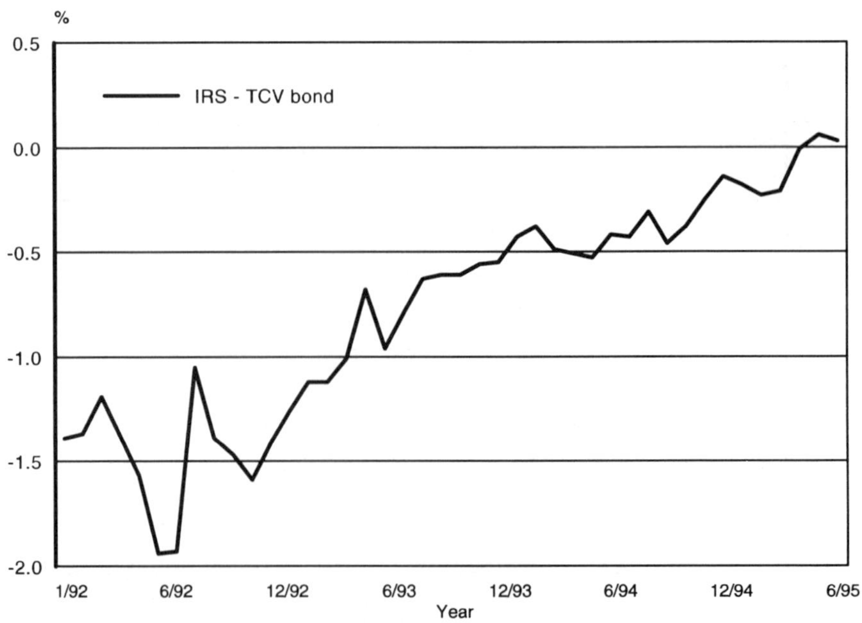

Figure 2.17 Spread of Three-year A$ IRS and TCV Bond

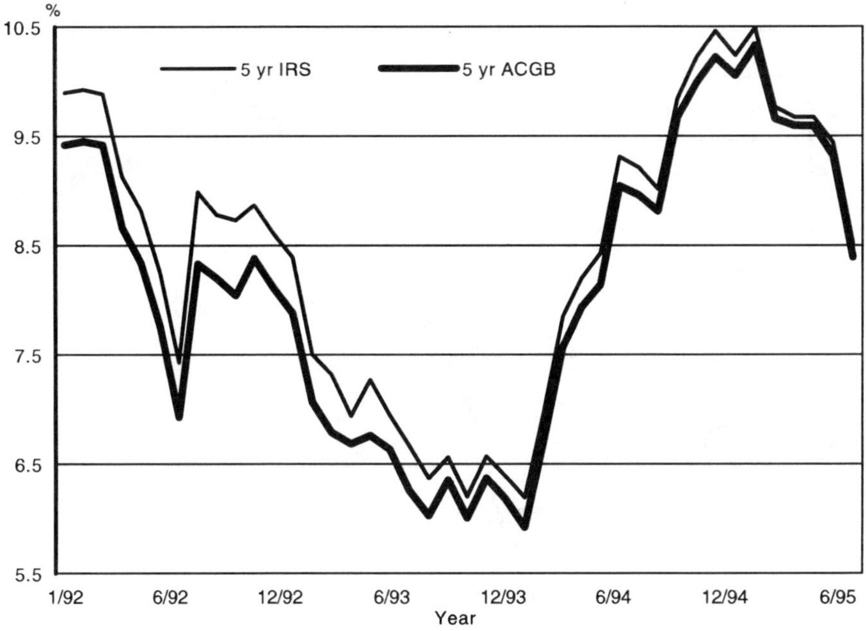

Figure 2.18 Historical Movement of Five-year A$ IRS and Five-year ACGB

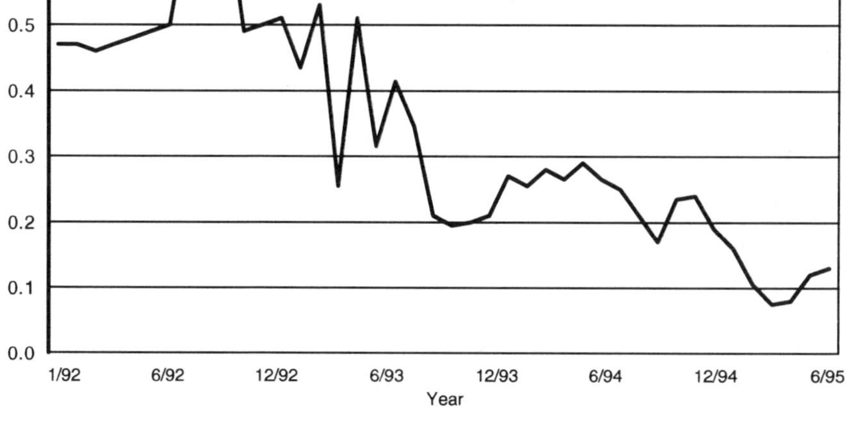

Figure 2.19 Spread of Five-year A$ IRS and ACGB

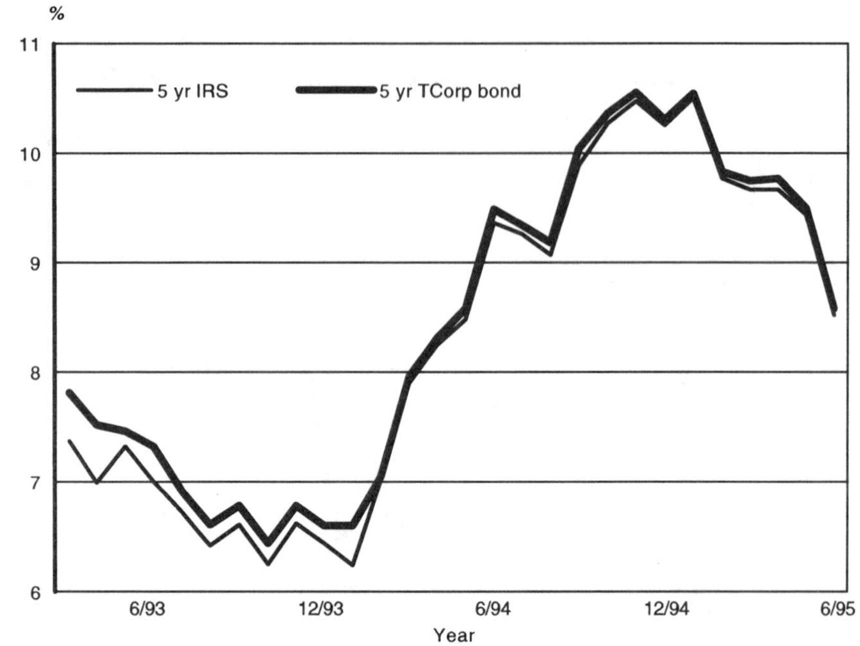

Figure 2.20 Historical Movement of Five-year A$ IRS and Five-year TCorp Bond

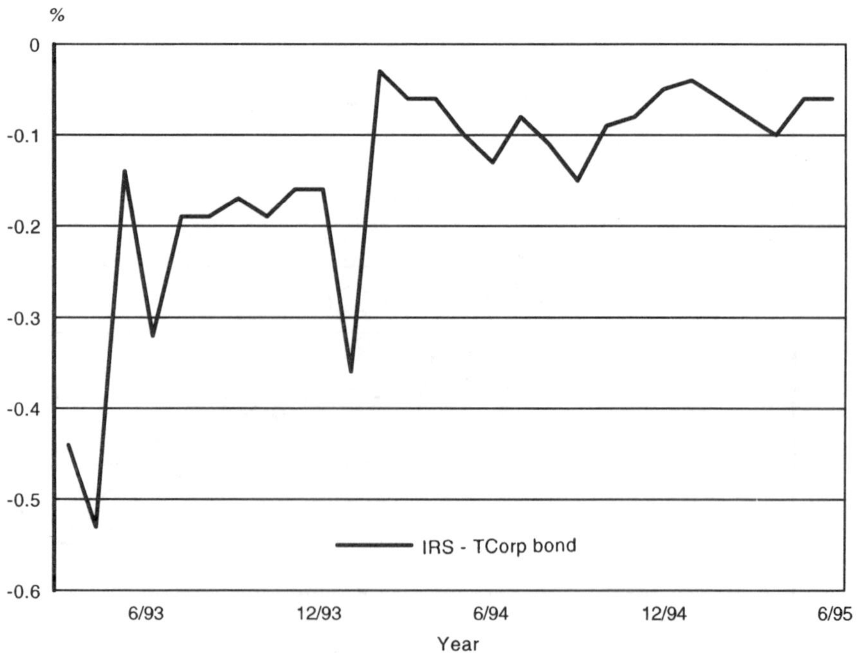

Figure 2.21 Spread of Five-year A$ IRS and TCorp Bond

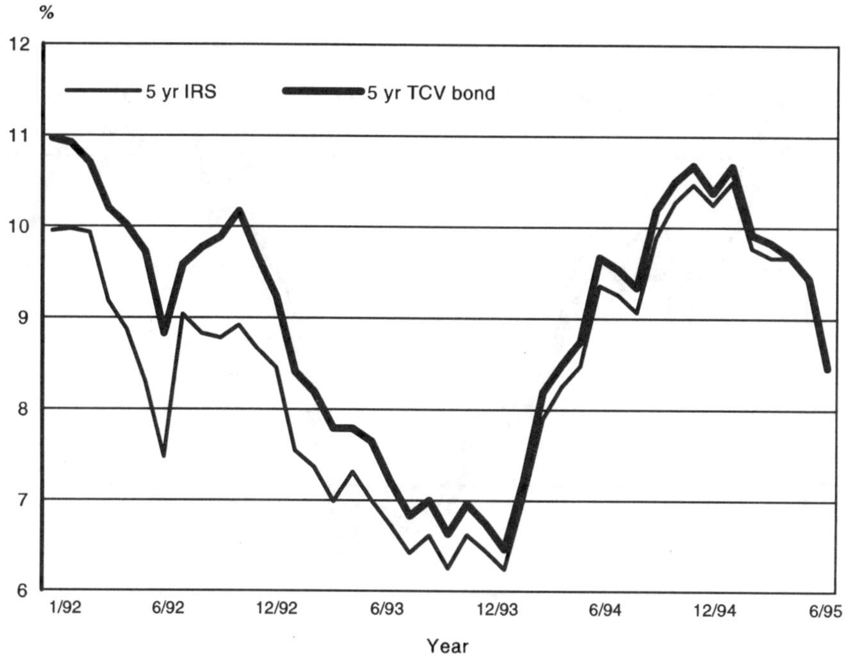

Figure 2.22 Historical Movement of Five-year A$ IRS and Five-year TCV Bond

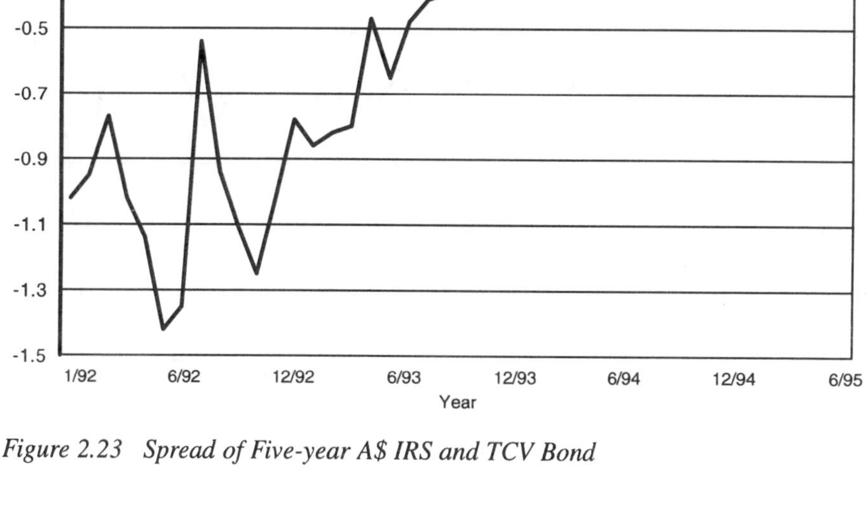

Figure 2.23 Spread of Five-year A$ IRS and TCV Bond

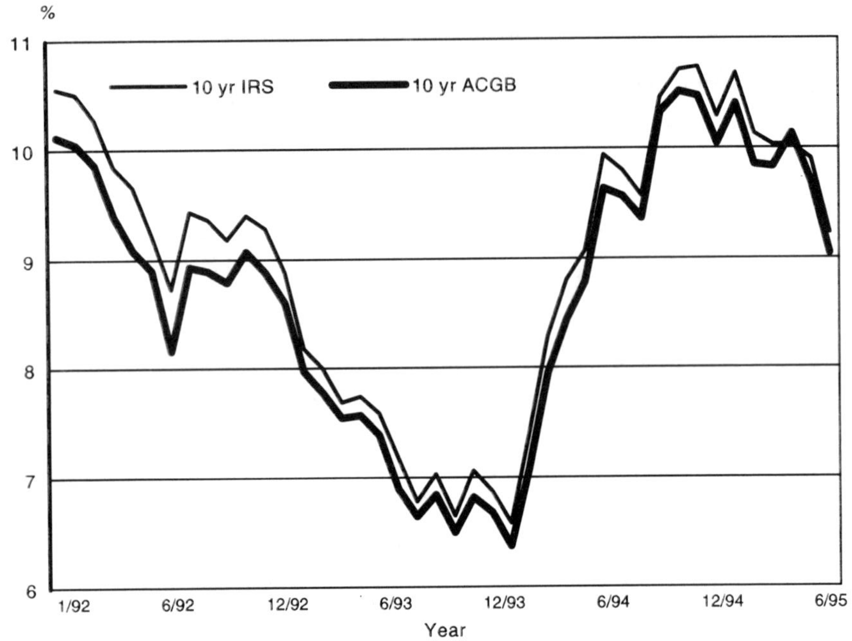

Figure 2.24 Historical Movement of Ten-year A$ IRS and Ten-year ACGB

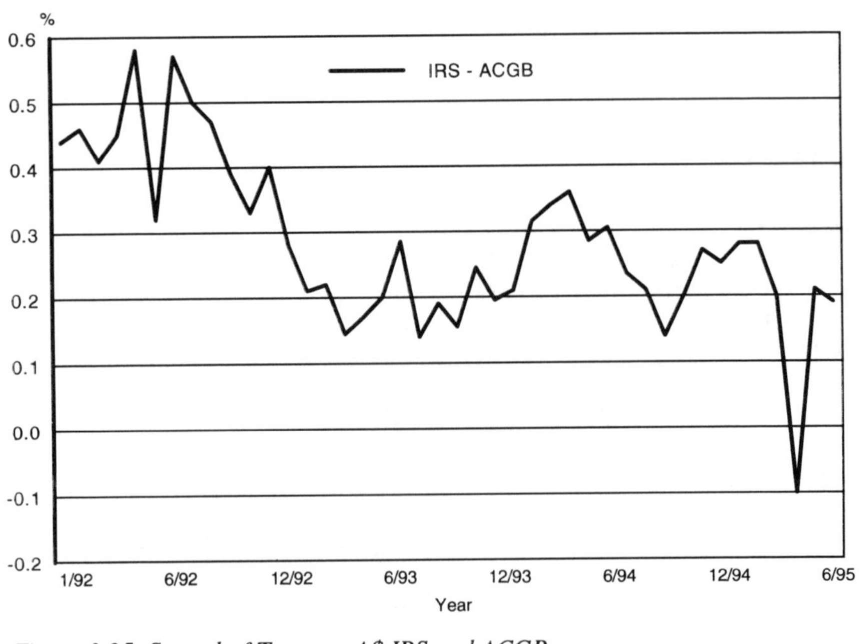

Figure 2.25 Spread of Ten-year A$ IRS and ACGB

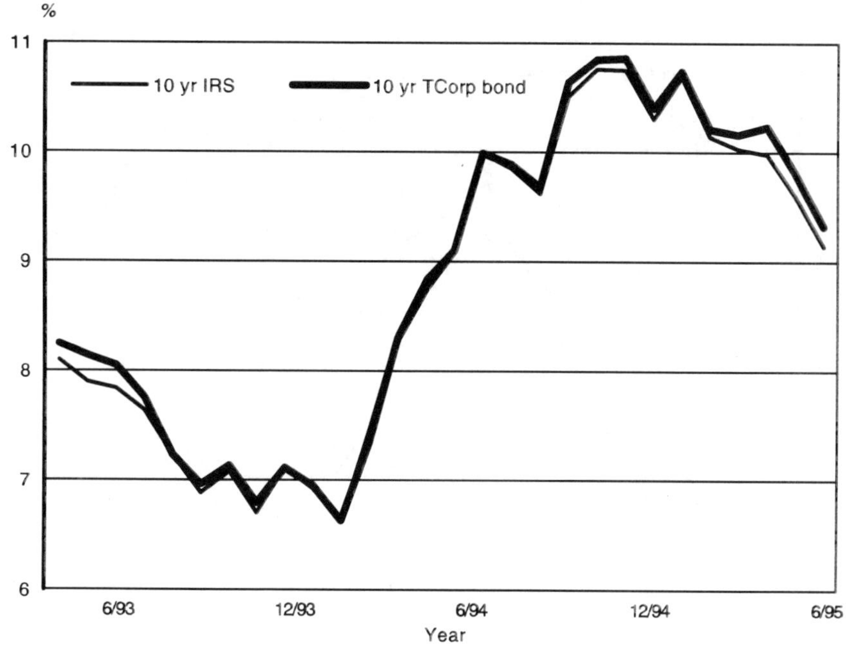

Figure 2.26 Historical Movement of Ten-year A$ IRS and Ten-year TCorp Bond

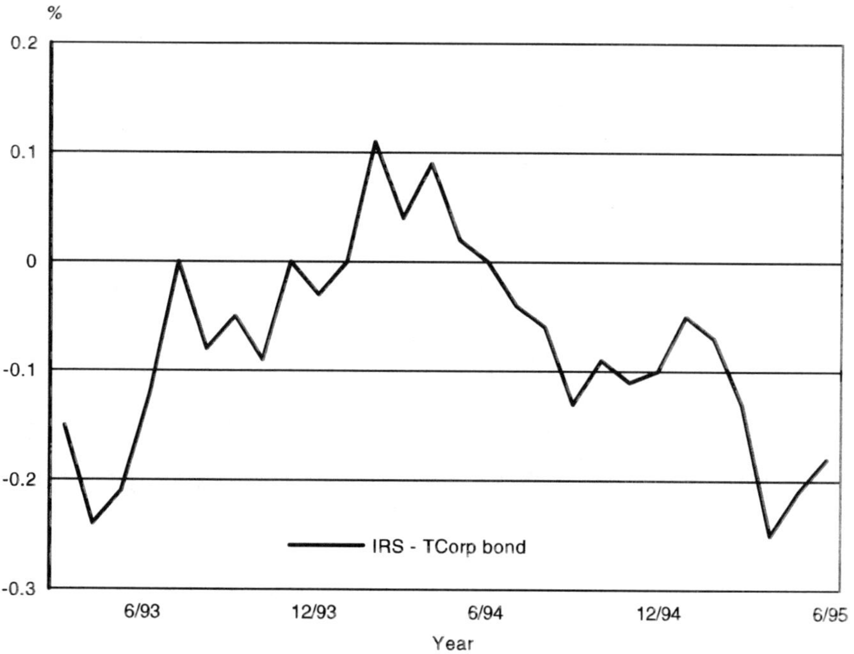

Figure 2.27 Spread of Ten-year A$ IRS and TCorp Bond

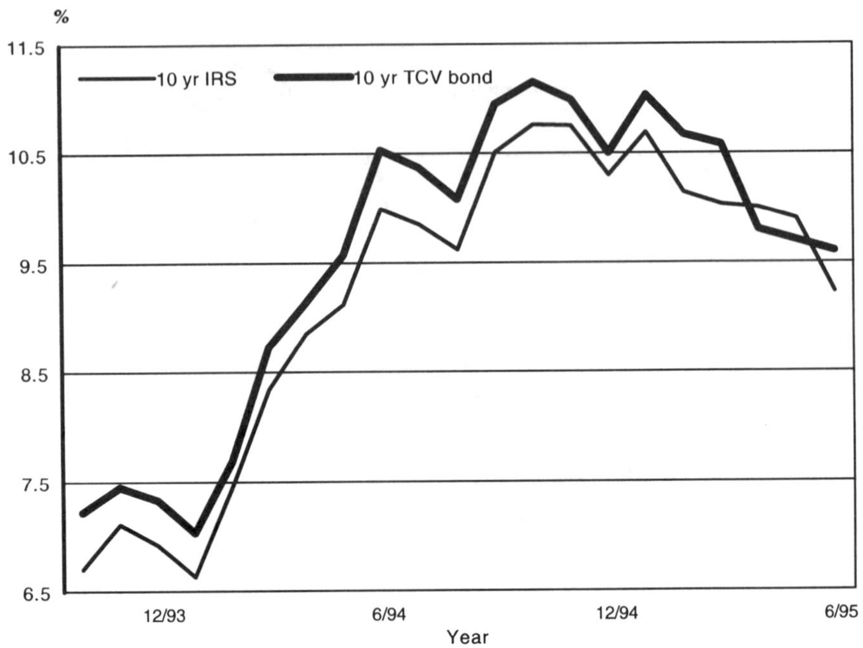

Figure 2.28 Historical Movement of Ten-year A$ IRS and Ten-year TCV Bond

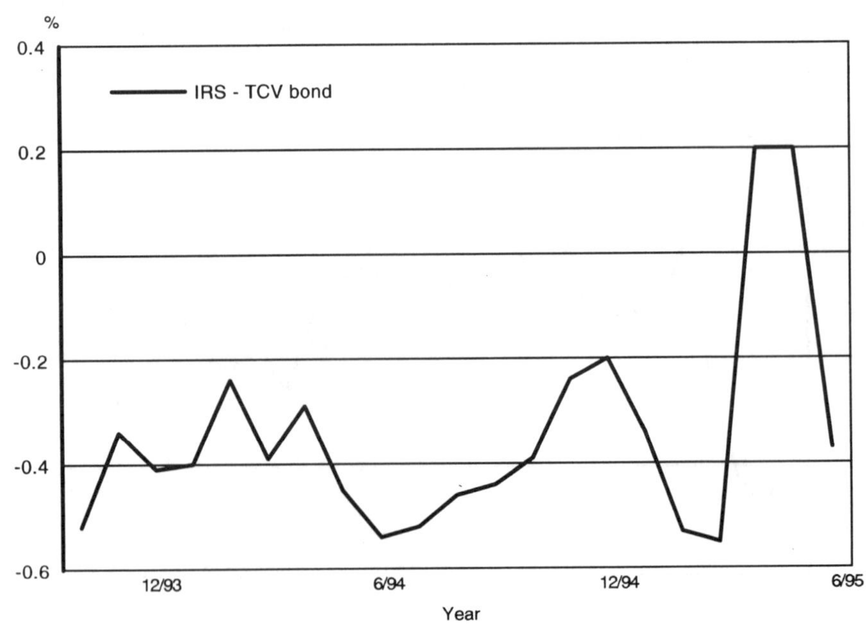

Figure 2.29 Spread of Ten-year A$ IRS and TCV Bond

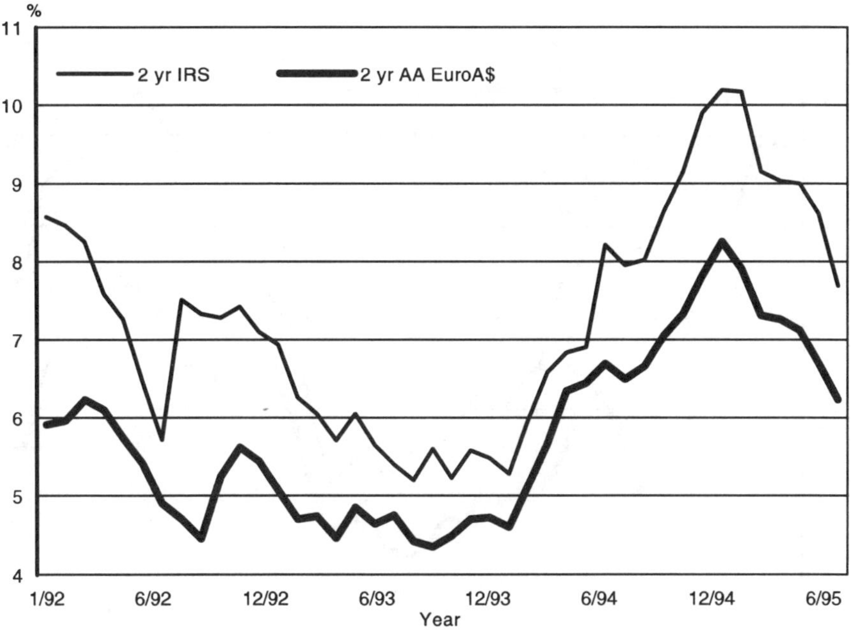

Figure 2.30 Historical Movement of Two-year A$ IRS and Two-year AA EuroA$ Bond

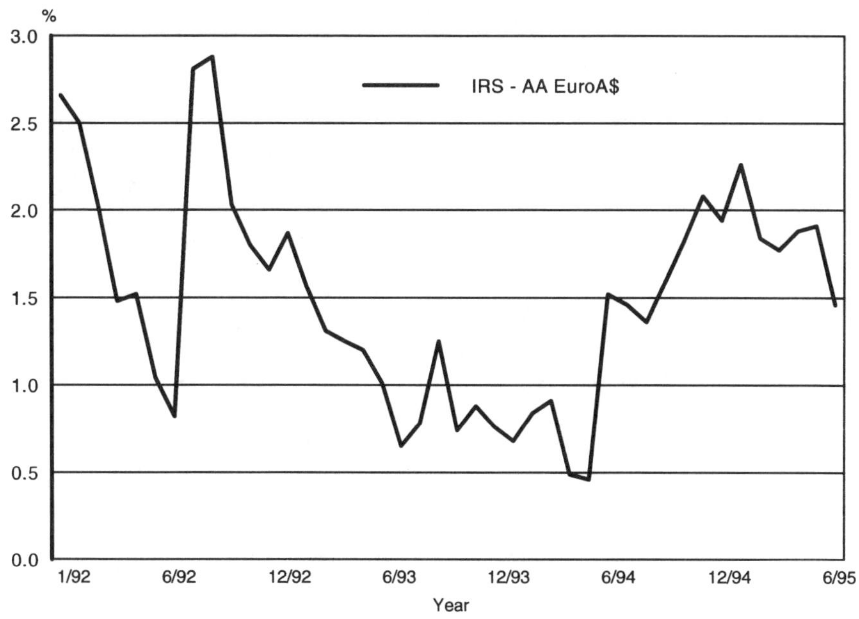

Figure 2.31 Spread of Two-year A$ IRS and AA EuroA$ Bond

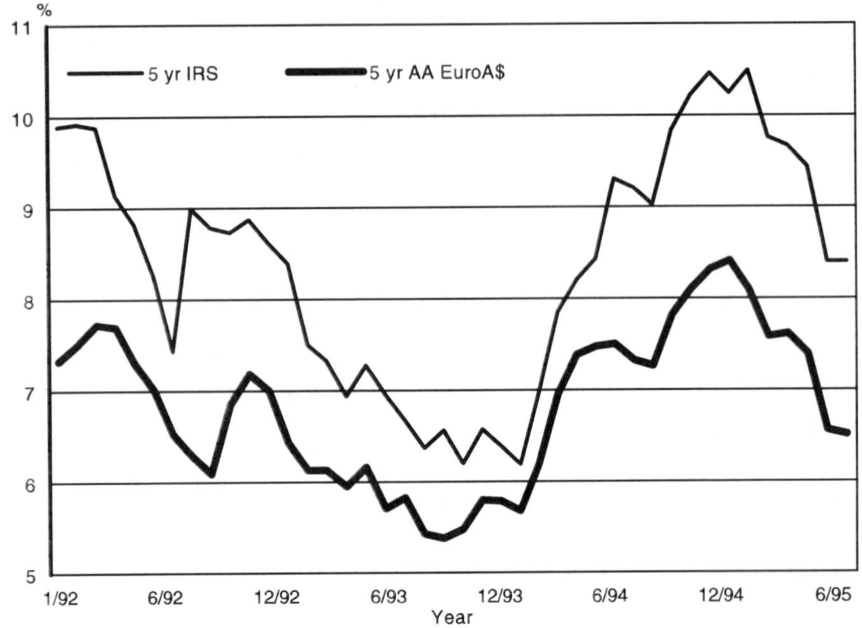

Figure 2.32 Historical Movement of Five-year A$ IRS and Five-year AA EuroA$ Bonds

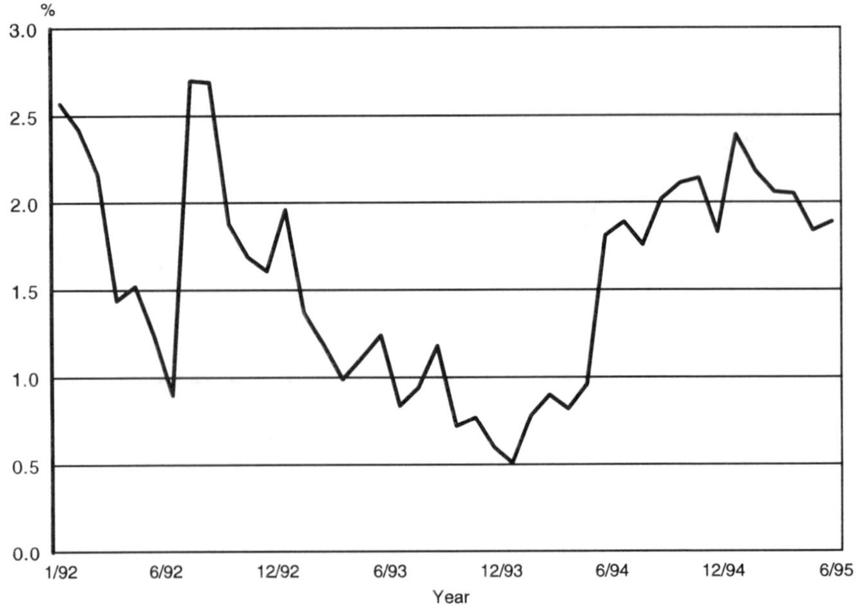

Figure 2.33 Spread of Five-year A$ IRS and AA EuroA$ Bonds

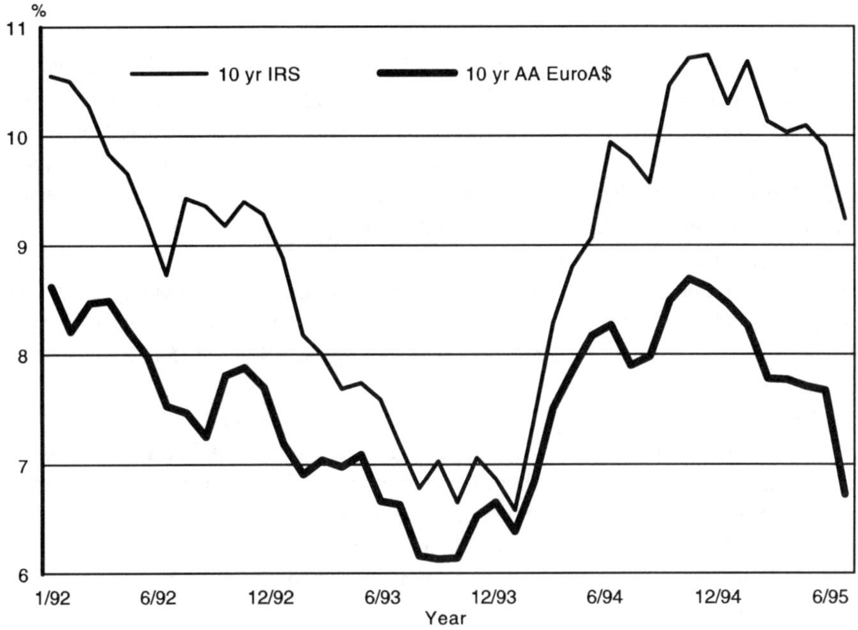

Figure 2.34 Historical Movement of Ten-year A$ IRS and Ten-year AA EuroA$ Bonds

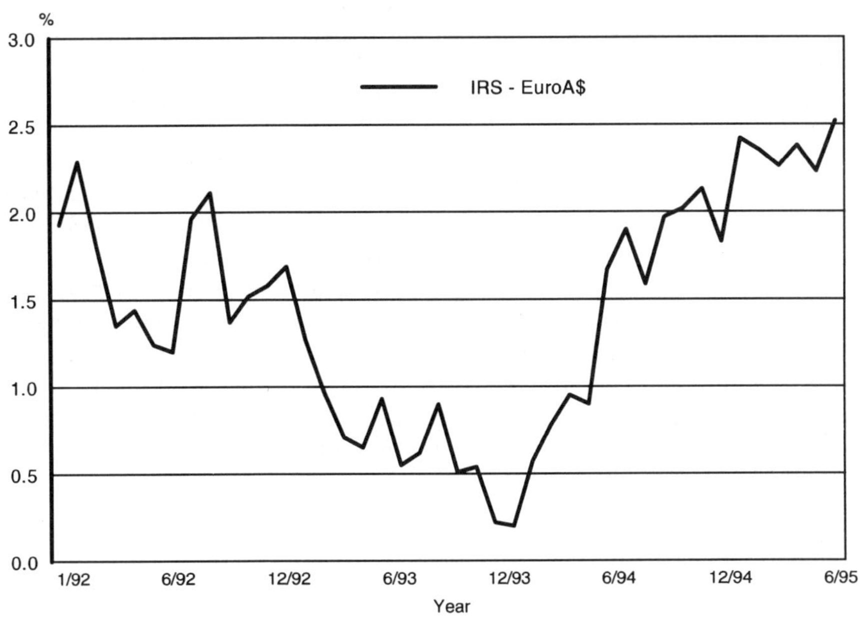

Figure 2.35 Spread of Ten-year A$ IRS and AA EuroA$ Bonds

Fixed Income Options

The Australian fixed income options market (caps, floors, swaptions, and bond options) is still dominated by vanilla structures. Although exotic options, such as spreads, barriers, digitals and compounds are becoming more evident in the domestic market, overall volume in such instruments remains negligible compared with vanilla options. The fixed income option market generally prices to volatility rather than absolute price or premium; interbank dealing size for standard structures ranges from A$10 mln to A$50 mln (US$7.4 mln to US$37 mln) and liquid maturities range from three months to three years (though longer maturity quotes are generally available, particularly for swaptions). Total interest rate options executed in the domestic market in 1994 amounted to A$66.5 bln (US$49.2 bln), a 6% increase over 1993.

European-style bond options remain the single largest component of the domestic fixed income option market. The vast majority of bond options are written on ACGBs (79% in 1994), though options on QTC, TCorp and other semi-government authority bonds are also available. Most options mature in under three months (78%) (though quotes are available to three years) and virtually all result in physical delivery (96%) (AFMA, 1994). For the period ending June 1994 A$28 bln (US$20.7 bln) in bond options were executed, a decline of 6% over 1993 (AFMA, 1994).

Caps and floors, which are most often structured to reference 90- or 180-day BBR, represent the second largest component of the domestic fixed income option market. Though nearly 70% of caps and floors executed in 1994 had maturities under two years, ready quotes are typically available to five years (and longer, in certain special instances). As at June 1994, A$32.6 bln (US$24.1 bln) in caps and floors were dealt, primarily in the interbank market; this represented a 15% increase over 1993 (AMFA, 1994).

Swaptions represent the smallest category of interest rate derivatives in the domestic market, though growth has increased dramatically over the past few years. From June 1992 to 1993 swaption volume increased from A$2.8 bln (US$2.1 bln) to A$4.6 bln (US$3.4 bln), and from June 1993 to 1994 it increased to A$6 bln (US$4.4 bln). The most common domestic swaptions are European options exercisable into Australian dollar fixed/floating swaps; 67% of swaptions written in 1994 had maturities of less than 12 months and 77% were exercisable into swaps with maturities of less than five years (AFMA, 1994). Despite the focus on short-term swaptions, it should be noted that quotes on two and thee year options exercisable into five, seven or ten year swaps can be obtained.

Currency

Currency Forwards/Swaps

The Australian market features well-established FX forward, FX swap and currency swap markets which have been in existence since the early 1980s.

The Australian dollar currency forward and FX swap markets are very active, with ready quotes and substantial liquidity to three years; long-term quotes to five years can be obtained but dealing is far less frequent. Typical interbank dealing size in forwards and FX swaps is A$50 mln (US$37 mln). According to AFMA statistics, turnover in both the FX forward and long-term FX swap market has been on the rise: average daily trading in Australian dollar FX forwards reached A$1.22 bln (US$900 mln) in 1994, up from A$1 bln (US$740 mln) in 1993; average daily turnover in Australian dollar FX swaps amounted to A$13.06 bln (US$9.6 bln) in 1994, up from A$10.75 bln (US$7.9 bln) in 1993. Daily turnover in FX forwards and FX swaps not involving the Australian dollar reached A$1.1 bln (US$810 mln) and A$12.4 bln (US$9.2 bln), respectively, in June 1994. Figure 2.36 traces the historical movement of three and 12 month US$/A$ forwards.

The Australian CCS market developed in tandem with the IRS market in the early 1980s. Numerous EuroA$ issues of the 1980s, which raised fixed Australian dollars for both domestic and foreign borrowers, were swapped into BBR (as described above) or, on a currency basis, into US$ LIBOR. Offshore borrowers often enjoyed a comparative advantage over domestic issuers and were able to raise funds in fixed offshore Australian dollars and swap back to US$ LIBOR at preferential rates. A second segment of the market involved Australian institutions tapping the international capital markets in foreign currencies and swapping flows

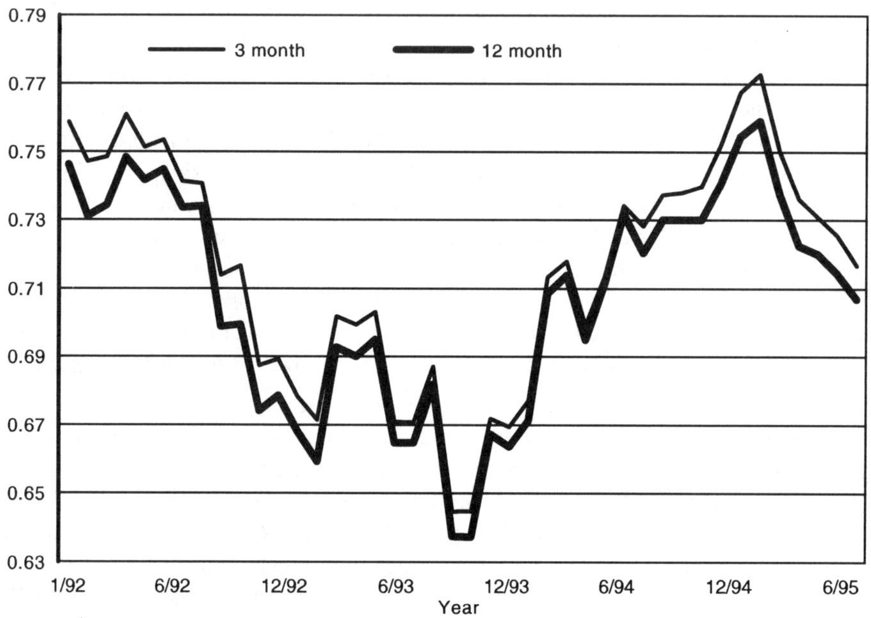

Source: Datastream

Figure 2.36 Historical Movement of Three- and Twelve-month US$/A$ Forwards

back into fixed Australian dollars. The private placement and dual currency bond markets also generated substantial currency swap activity, particularly in fixed Australian dollars against fixed Japanese yen; estimates suggest that nearly 60% of all CCSs transacted in Australia in the late 1980s were related to the dual currency structure (Das, 1994). Under a typical A$/JPY dual currency transaction an institution would issue an Australian dollar bond, raising Australian dollars in the process, and pay an Australian dollar coupon on a periodic basis; at maturity principal would be repaid in yen rather than local currency. Under a reverse dual currency bond an institution would issue and pay coupons in yen and repay principal in Australian dollars. CCSs were often utilized by issuers and/or investors to protect against currency movements and lock in funding costs or investment returns (we discuss dual currency structures and associated currency swaps in greater detail in chapter 7 on Japan).

The CCS market of the 1990s has been focused primarily on semi-government authorities, finance companies and financial institutions exchanging US$ LIBOR for fixed Australian dollars. Finance companies have been able to take advantage of relatively cheap offshore US dollar floating rate funding to lock in fixed Australian dollar rates; likewise, semi-government authorities (who still maintain advantages in fixed and floating rate funding) have utilized overseas funding allocations to raise floating rate foreign currency funds, swapping back to fixed Australian dollars to lock in rates and remove currency exposures; further swaps of fixed Australian dollars into BBR (as discussed above) often give the semi-government authorities exceptionally low funding costs. In addition to standard CCSs Australia also features an active currency basis swap market which exchanges BBR for US$ LIBOR. The basis swap market has historically attracted financial institutions and corporations who have been able to raise US$ LIBOR funds via offshore certificate of deposit (CD) or commercial paper (CP) programmes and swap into BBR to create funding costs lower than those available through the issuance of domestic Australian dollar CDs or CP. Though activity in the Australian dollar CCS market has traditionally been rather buoyant, outstandings decreased between 1993 and 1994. Based on ISDA figures total notional Australian dollar CCS outstandings declined from US$46.4 bln (or 5.2% of the global market) in 1993 to US$37 bln (or 4% of the global market) in 1994 (Choudhury, 1995); 42% of transactions executed had maturities under three years (AFMA, 1994).

The fixed/floating segment of the Australian dollar CCS market is quoted to ten years, though most liquidity is centred in short- and medium-term transactions of two to five years. CCSs to three years are quoted as fixed quarterly Australian dollars (on an Actual/365 day basis) against US$ LIBOR flat; CCSs from four to ten years are quoted as fixed semi-annual Australian dollars (on an Actual/365 day basis) against US$ LIBOR flat. Interbank transaction size is A$50 mln (US$37 mln), though structured asset or liability transactions can result in much larger dealing amounts; bid-offer spreads range from 7 to 10 basis points across the curve under normal market conditions. Quoting convention for currency basis swaps is

BBR plus or minus a spread to three or six month US$ LIBOR flat; standard interbank dealing size is A$50 mln (US$37 mln) and quotes are available to ten years. Table 2.35 below illustrates bid-offer spreads for A$/US$ CCSs and BBR/LIBOR swaps under normal market conditions; Figures 2.37 to 2.40 illustrate the historical movement and spreads of three and six month BBR and US$ LIBOR.

Maturity	A$/US$ CCS Bid-Offer	BBR/US$ LIBOR Bid-Offer
1 year	7–8 bps	7–8 bps
2 years	7–8 bps	7–8 bps
3 years	7–8 bps	7–8 bps
4 years	8–9 bps	8–9 bps
5 years	8–9 bps	8–9 bps
7 years	10 bps	10–12 bps
10 years	10 bps	10–12 bps

Table 2.35 A$/US$ CCS, BBR/LIBOR Bid-Offer Spreads

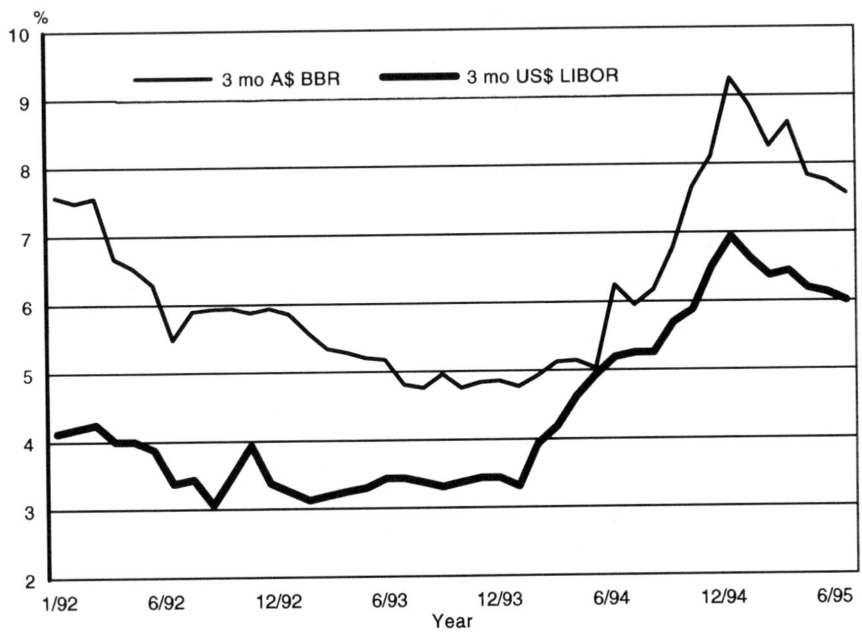

Figure 2.37 Historical Movement of Three-month BBR and US$ LIBOR

Figure 2.38 Spread of Three-month BBR and US$ LIBOR

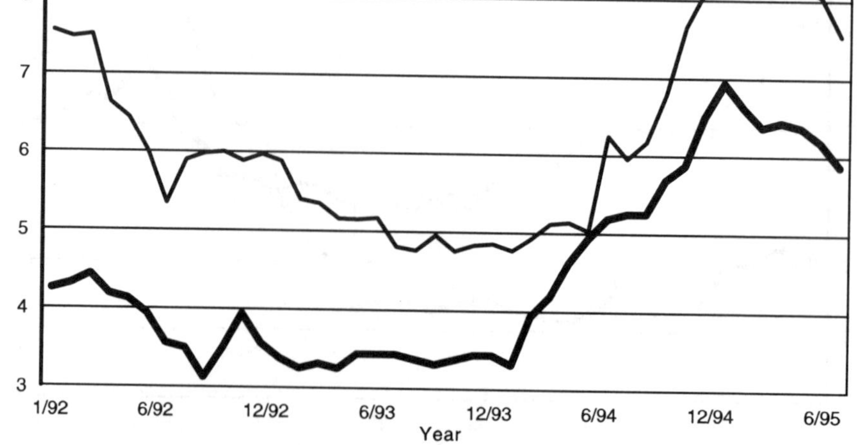

Figure 2.39 Historical Movement of Six-month BBR and US$ LIBOR

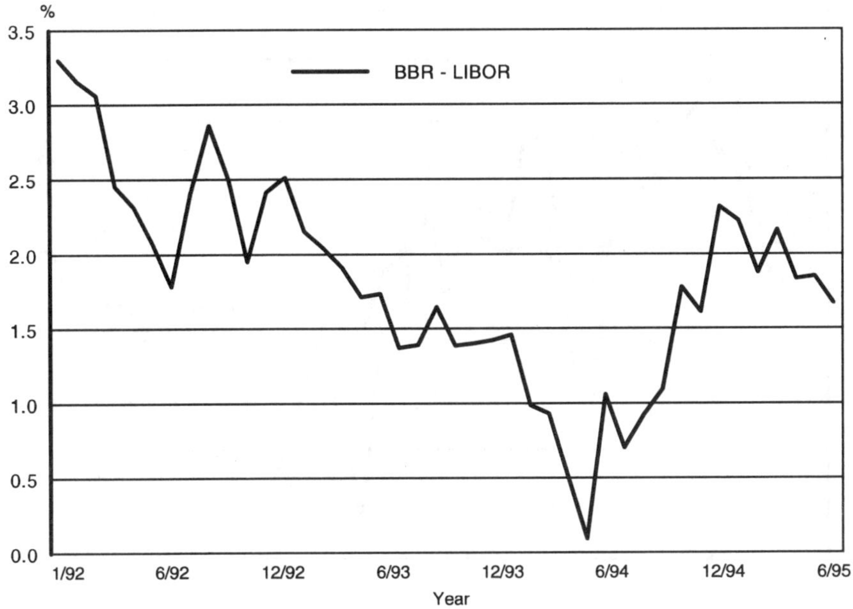

Figure 2.40 Spread of Six-month BBR and US$ LIBOR

Currency Options

The Australian dollar OTC currency option market is based primarily on vanilla structures (though there is a small amount of dealing in exotic options, primarily barriers). Options in the local market are quoted in volatility terms, with short-term options carrying higher volatilities; bid-offer spreads range from 0.40 points for one month options to 0.30 points for 12 month options under normal market conditions. Standard interbank dealing size is A$50 mln (US$37 mln). The most common domestic FX options are European, physical-settlement deals with maturities of three to six months; 78% of transactions executed in 1994 had maturities of less than six months (AFMA, 1994). As at June 1994, total annual FX options turnover (including Australian dollar/foreign currency and foreign currency/foreign currency options) amounted to US$116 bln, down from US$173 bln in 1993 and US$118 bln in 1992 (AFMA, 1994). Total turnover included US$84.8 bln of Australian dollar options (including US$77 bln US$/A$, and US$7.8 bln A$/JPY) and just under US$21 bln of DM/US$ and JPY/US$ options. The Australian FX options market continues to be dominated by interbank institutions (who accounted for 48% of all transactions), followed by local corporations (22%), other financial institutions (12%), and offshore corporations (9%) (AFMA, 1994). Figure 2.41 below traces the historical movement of US$/A$ FX volatilities for one and 12 month European options.

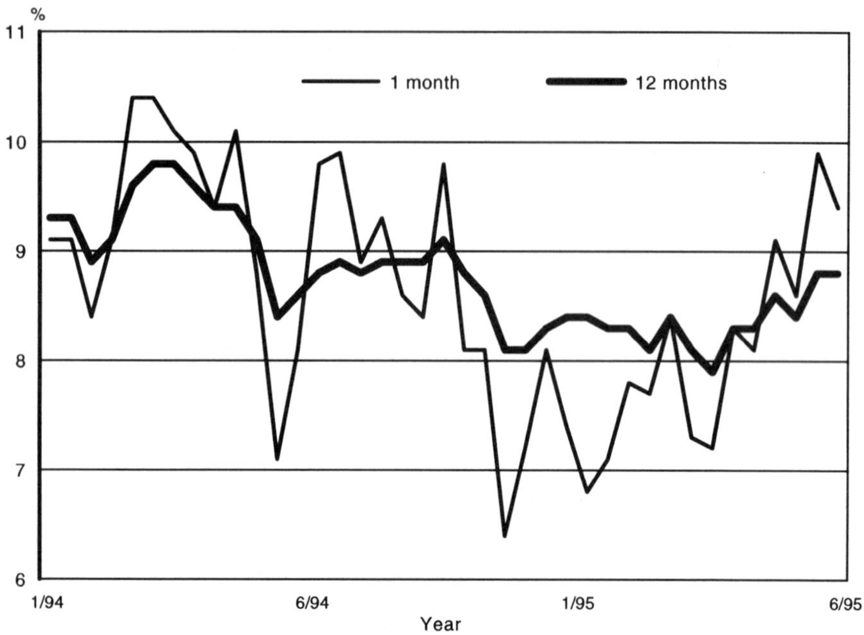

Figure 2.41 Historical Movement of US$/A$ FX Option Volatilities

Commodity

Commodity Forwards/Swaps

Given Australia's role as a key exporter of natural resources (e.g. crude oil, natural gas, precious metals, base metals and so on), it is not surprising to note that OTC commodity forwards and swaps are executed with frequency in the domestic market. Such derivatives are most often arranged by foreign institutions with commodity derivative capabilities and are generally designed to provide hedging cover for producers of commodities (such as resource companies) or consumers of commodities (such as refiners, electricity authorities, and airlines). Since the Australian listed derivative market does not presently feature contracts on base metals or energy products, domestic companies requiring exposure or protection (e.g. resource producers such as BHP, Western Mining, Aluvic, Woodside Petroleum, and others) must use overseas commodity futures exchanges (e.g. the London Metals Exchange, Comex, NYMEX, IPE) or turn to the OTC commodity forward/swap markets. Vanilla commodity forwards (buying or selling commodities on a forward basis at a predetermined price) and swaps (exchanging fixed and floating payments based on international commodity prices or indexes) tend to be the most popular structures; maturities generally range from six months to five years (medium-term transactions are often structured with semi-annual or annual settlement periods, acting, in effect, as strips of forwards). Copper, aluminium, gold, natural gas, and crude oil tend to be the most actively used commodity references.

It should be noted that Australia is a reasonably significant producer of crude oil, including Thevenard, Challis, Jackson Blend, Cooper Basin, Griffin, Jabiru, Gippsland and Skua grades. Australia features no benchmark grade of its own and, as such, often prices against Tapis, the regional benchmark crude. Domestic crude producers often hedge through offshore listed energy contracts (e.g. SIMEX/IPE Brent or SFE/NYMEX light sweet) or on a forward basis through the energy forward/swap markets of Singapore or Japan (chapter 11 on Singapore contains additional details on the regional OTC energy forward/swap markets).

Commodity Options

As with commodity forwards and swaps mentioned above, the market for OTC commodity options (on gold, aluminium, copper, crude, jet fuel and so on) has proven reasonably popular with domestic commodity producers and consumers. Many of the same payoff or protection profiles generated by swaps and forwards can be replicated using commodity options, though often with greater leverage. Exotic commodity options (e.g. barriers, Asians, digitals) are also available but less prevalent.

LOCAL REGULATORY/LEGAL TREATMENT OF DERIVATIVES

The primary regulators of the Australian market are the Australian Securities Commission (ASC) and the Reserve Bank of Australia (RBA). The ASC administers the Corporations Law (discussed at length below) and the Securities Law, while the RBA, as supervisor of banks, monitors all aspects of the banking business, including derivatives. Australia's primary exchanges, the Australian Stock Exchange (ASX) and the Sydney Futures Exchange (SFE), are private exchanges with delegated regulatory functions.

Australian futures contracts and markets were initially regulated by the Futures Industry Code (FIC), which was created in 1986; the FIC was replaced by the more comprehensive Futures Law in 1991, which was eventually consolidated into the Corporations Law (CL), in the form of Chapter 8. The CL was the country's first attempt at implementing a broad-based regulatory framework centred on instruments (including securities and futures), participants (brokers, dealers) and markets (stock market, futures market).

Specific areas related to domestic derivatives activity are contained in Chapter 8 of the CL. Under Sections 1142 and 1143 of the CL, one cannot engage in dealing or broking of futures without a futures broking license. In addition, no futures advisory work is permitted unless one is licensed as an exempt futures advisor. Under Section 72 of the CL the regulators define four distinct types of derivatives, including: (a) eligible commodity agreements; (b) adjustment agreements; (c) futures options; and (d) eligible exchange-traded options. Instruments included in these four categories are governed by standardized agreements which reflect standard quantities and settlement dates. Importantly, the CL exempts futures contracts from gaming or wagering laws (which might otherwise render such contracts legally unenforceable); the exemption was motivated by legislation sponsored by the SFE in 1979.

Providers of derivatives are required to hold a futures dealers license or deal as principal through another licensed member. They must also register under the Financial Corporations Act of 1974 in order to attract exemptions (safe harbors) relating to OTC derivatives such as swaps and FRAs. Interim safe harbors are discussed below. In addition, Section 72(1)(d) of the CL indicates that various OTC derivatives are excluded from futures regulations if an authorized financial institution (such as a registered bank or merchant bank) is a party to the transaction; this is identical to the treatment of OTC derivatives in New Zealand. OTC derivatives which are specifically noted for exemption include interest and currency swaps, FRAs, FRAs with physical delivery of underlying bills, swaptions, FX options, bond options, synthetic FX forwards and repos. It should be noted that as long as an ISDA agreement (or some other standard document) is utilized in an OTC FX derivatives transaction, the RBA does not require separate authority to deal in foreign exchange.

While the regulatory framework originally developed under the CL was adequate for the 1980s, it became apparent to regulators in the early 1990s that the proliferation of OTC derivatives and the expanded use of listed derivatives by retail clients necessitated improvements in the regulatory regime (e.g. alteration of the CL). To that end, the regulators refocused their efforts on three distinct categories of derivatives, including: (a) individually negotiated, or wholesale customized, derivatives; (b) wholesale tradeable derivatives; and (c) retail derivatives. Wholesale customized derivatives, effectively OTC structures between sophisticated institutional counterparties, call for minimal regulation through the use of safe harbors (under an amended CL). The Interim Safe Harbor of 1993 indicates that principal contracts are exempt from futures market regulation if one party is a so-called 'registered facility provider' (an Australian bank, a bank regulated by the BIS, an authorized money market dealer, an entity with a license and an investment grade rating, broker/dealers registered under the US SEC Act of 1934, futures commission merchants registered under the US Commodity Exchange Act and entities eligible to engage in investment business under the Financial Services Act of the UK), the contract is entered into as a principal, the obligation can only be transferred with the consent of the other party and the obligation is not supported by the SFECH or a risk mitigating technique. In short, safe harbor transactions cannot have the characteristics of a tradeable contract and no broking is permitted in the safe harbor market. Instruments not falling under category (a) above (i.e. wholesale tradeable (or listed) derivatives, and those geared for retail participants), do not attract safe harbors and are regulated by the provisions of the CL. Despite the changes undertaken in 1993, the ASC appointed the Companies and Securities Advisory Committee in 1994 to develop a new regulatory regime for derivatives. The new regulatory structure being developed by the Committee is designed to resolve legal uncertainties surrounding derivatives (many generated by the vague 'securities versus futures' definition), eliminate multiple regulation of markets/ institutions/instruments and provide further protection for unsophisticated investors. The ASC has indicated that new Australian regulations should conform with international standards and should not be so restrictive so as to drive business offshore. The Committee's work is underway.

LOCAL ACCOUNTING PRACTICES FOR DERIVATIVES

Although the Australian regulatory authorities have not enforced specific local accounting treatment of derivatives, the largest institutions active in the market (primarily registered banks, foreign banks and merchant banks) tend to adhere to the same general accounting principles. Gains or losses on Australian dollar or foreign currency swaps, futures, forwards/FRAs, bond options, caps, floors, collars and swaptions which are used for legitimate interest or currency rate hedging purposes are recorded on an accrual basis as an adjustment to the yield of the hedged exposure over the period covered by the derivative. If a derivative used as a hedge is terminated early (e.g. the underlying exposure no longer needs to be hedged), the gain or loss is deferred and amortized as an adjustment to the yield of the underlying position over the remaining life of the transaction (based on the original maturity of the transaction). Gains or losses arising from derivatives employed to hedge future anticipated exposures are deferred until the future transaction arises and impacts the financial statements; such treatment is only applied if there is a very likely chance the future exposure will arise. If such exposure does not arise (and the derivative hedge is not required) the deferred gains or losses are recognized immediately in the income statement. Australian dollar or foreign currency derivatives employed as trading or positioning strategies are revalued on a daily basis as the difference between contracted value and market value, with gains or losses posted to the income statement at the time of revaluation (e.g. daily).

PROSPECTS FOR GROWTH IN THE LOCAL DERIVATIVE MARKET

Summarized below are the near-term (one to three year) and medium-term (three to five year) prospects for Australia's domestic derivative markets.

Near-term:

- Further alliances between domestic and international exchanges (e.g. SFE and CBOT, TGE) which will provide regional institutions with greater access to offshore derivatives.
- Introduction of additional commodity futures contracts on the SFE (e.g. energy, agricultural).
- Expansion in the number of reference stocks for LEPOs, share futures and share ratios.
- Restructuring, or potential abandonment, of listed index derivatives which have been unable to generate critical mass (e.g. ASXD's three index option contracts).
- Growth in IRS and CCS volume as domestic and offshore funding opportunities for both local and international companies continue to expand; strengthening of liquidity in intermediate- and long-term transactions as the market continues to mature and deepen.
- Further growth in the domestic fixed income options market as more institutions become accustomed to utilizing such derivatives for risk management or speculative opportunities.
- Greater acceptance of exotic structures in risk management or speculative situations.
- Clarification of accounting treatment for derivatives; completion of new regulatory rules covering OTC derivatives.

Medium-term:

- Growth in OTC commodity derivatives (based on energy, precious metals, base metals) as domestic needs increase and as the global OTC commodity derivative market expands.
- Further expansion of IRSs/CCSs and lengthening of maturities, with more frequent quotes to 10 years and beyond.

Exchange	Contract	1993 Volume (contracts)	1994 Volume (contracts)
ASXD	Equity options	9,500,000	10,200,000
	Low exercise price options	n/l*	n/l*
	Share ratios	n/l*	n/l*
	All Ords Index options	119	9,396
	Gold Index options	20	616
	Twenty Leaders Index options	2,176	1,450
SFE	Share futures	n/l*	72,310
	All Ords Index futures	980,866	2,550,000
	All Ords Index futures options	466,896	833,667
	90-day bank bill futures	6,410,000	9,370,000
	90-day bank bill futures options	663,317	943,749
	Three-year ACGB futures	6,940,000	9,700,000
	Ten-year ACGB futures	4,780,000	6,840,000
	Three-year ACGB futures options	514,539	509,330
	Ten-year ACGB futures options	712,686	818,919
	22 micron wool futures	0	0
	21 micron wool futures	n/l*	n/l*

* n/l: contract not yet listed

Table 2.37 Summary of 1993/1994 Listed Futures and Options Turnover

	Overall Liquidity	Liquid/ Maximum Maturity	Interbank dealing size	Average bid-offer spread
Equity/Index Swaps	good	1–3 yrs/5 yrs	n/a	n/a
Equity/Index Options	good	1–3 yrs/5 yrs	n/a	n/a
Interest Rate Swaps	excellent	1–10 yrs/10 yrs	A$50 mln	6–10 bps
Interest Rate Options	good	3–12 mos/5 yrs	A$50 mln	varies
Currency Swaps	excellent	1–10 yrs/10 yrs	A$50 mln	7–10 bps
Currency Options	good	3–12 mos/5 yrs	A$50 mln	0.4 pts

Table 2.38 Summary of Domestic OTC Derivatives

3: China

FINANCIAL MARKET OVERVIEW

China's equity, fixed income, and currency markets are most accurately characterized as underdeveloped and illiquid at the present time, though certain segments of the market, such as equities and state Treasury bonds, are beginning to develop into increasingly reliable financing mechanisms. The underdeveloped nature of China's financial markets has impacted development of the local derivative market; domestic derivatives are all but non-existent at the present time, with the exception of listed futures and listed equity warrants. Listed futures based on softs, metals and energy have been modestly successful (though very fragmented and the focus of speculative abuse, as discussed at length below), primarily because China features rather deep commodity markets. Domestic futures trading has attracted speculators who have been eager to employ the leverage of futures contracts to increase potential profits; this had led to bouts of speculative activity and price inflation in certain agricultural and energy commodities. The financial authorities are in the process of widespread reform of the local futures market in order to ensure its success and viability over the long term.

China's local equity market has been in existence in its present form since 1990, when both the Shanghai Stock Exchange (SSE) and the Shenzhen Stock Exchange (SHSE) were created. Activity in the local marketplace began on a strong note as domestic investors (investing in A shares) and foreign investors (investing in B shares) were attracted to the potential returns attainable through a gradually opening market. After intense speculative activity in the very early 1990s, when the domestic stock market reached a peak, trading activity in the mid-1990s has returned to more moderate levels. The overall decline in the local market over the past few years has been caused by a slowdown in the economy and the departure of domestic and foreign investors from the market (i.e. domestic investors have exited the market in search of higher returns in alternate domestic instruments (e.g. treasury bonds, bond futures, commodity futures) while offshore investors have left in order to place funds in other Asian equity markets). With the decline in stock returns and the shifting of domestic and offshore funds to alternate investments, liquidity on both the Shanghai and Shenzhen exchanges has dropped considerably. Given the relative infancy of the Chinese equity market overall capitalization is still modest in comparison with other regional markets; total capitalization of US$43.5

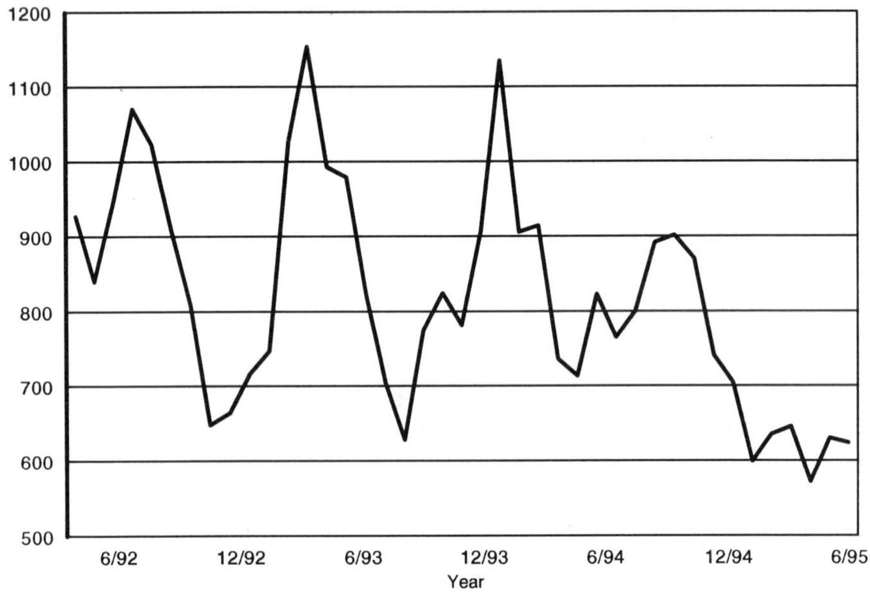

Figure 3.1 Historical Movement of SSE B Share Index

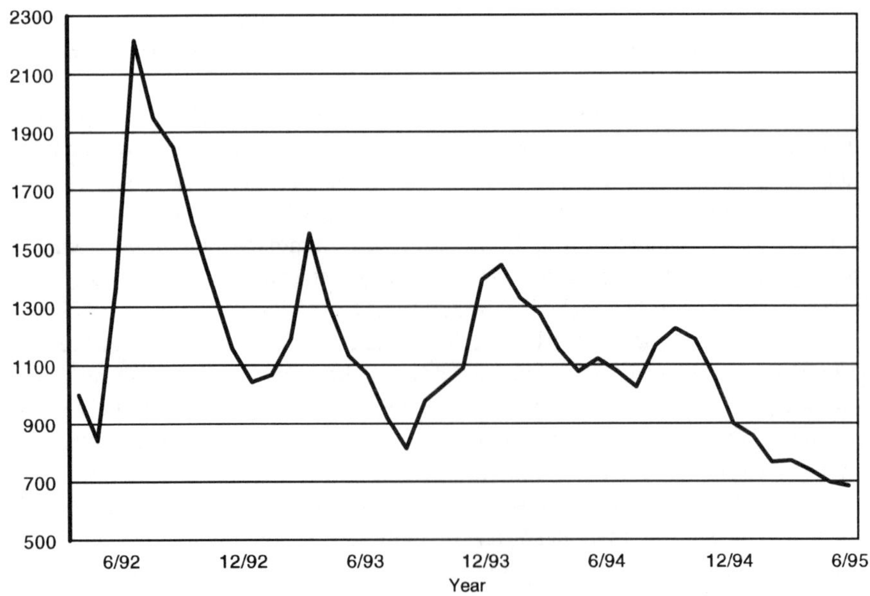

Figure 3.2 Historical Movement of SHSE B Share Index

bln between the two exchanges ranks the Chinese equity market as the 12th largest of Asia Pacific's 13 markets. Figures 3.1 and 3.2 illustrate the historical movement of the two primary Chinese stock markets (based on the B share indexes) while Table 3.1 contains details on relevant equity market indicators.

Foreign investment in domestic equities is very tightly controlled. Offshore investors are only permitted to invest in a company's B shares, with no single investor entitled to purchase more than 5% of a company's outstanding B shares. Purchases in excess of 5% must receive prior approval from the People's Bank of China (PBC)(in the case of Shanghai B shares) or must be reported to the Shenzhen Special Economic Zone Branch of the PBC (in the case of Shenzhen B shares). There is presently discussion regarding a liberalization of the 5% rule, though no decisions have been announced. Note that foreign investment in certain 'national interest' sectors (e.g. banking, communications, defense) is prohibited.

Year*	Market Capitalization (US$ bln)	Trading Value (US$ bln)	Listed Companies (#)
1994	43.5	97.5	291
1993	40.6	43.4	183
1992	18.2	16.7	52
1991	2.0	0.1	14

* to December of each year; Source: IFC, 1995

	1/92–6/95 Annualized Return	1/92–6/95 Total Return
Shanghai B	–11.17%	–31.99%
Shenzhen B	–10.48%	–30.26%

Table 3.1 Domestic Equity Market Indicators: Shanghai/Shenzhen

The Chinese market features very active bond issuance from the central government, which floats periodic, though sizeable, issues of state Treasury bonds. Such bonds have historically carried maturities of one to ten years, though recent issues have been centred in the two through five year sector. Along with Treasury bonds the market also features a range of sovereign-related securities including special construction bonds, fiscal bonds and capital investment bonds; there is also issuance of local and state enterprise bonds and financial bonds. With the exception of Treasury bonds, virtually all local debt instruments are illiquid. Although most Chinese interest rates are not market-determined at the present time, substantial issuance of state Treasury bonds in recent years has forced government authorities issuing bonds to be more responsive to investor demands. As such, yields on state

Treasury bonds are more 'market related' than at any time in the past. Issuance in the local fixed income market during 1994 included RMB102 bln (US$12.3 bln) of Treasury bonds, RMB100 bln (US$12 bln) of financial bonds, and RMB4.5 bln (US$500 mln) of enterprise bonds; total 1994 issuance was five times greater than 1993 issuance (CSB, 12/95). Total outstanding sovereign and sovereign-related bonds amounted to RMB394 bln (US$47.5 bln) in 1994 (and included RMB276 bln (US$33.3 bln) of securities maturing within one year and RMB118 bln (US$14.2 bln) of medium- and long-term securities maturing in more than one year). (Note: unlike other chapters in this text, we choose not to include a chart summarizing benchmark domestic interest rates, primarily because there are no key interest rates in existence which are both widely quoted and market-driven).

China's currency, the renminbi (RMB), or yuan, is not freely convertible at the present time. Prior to 1994 the market value of the renminbi was very tightly controlled through use of an official rate, which set the value of the currency at a fixed RMB5.7/US$. Along with the official rate, a semi-official market-driven rate was also quoted; in January 1994 the authorities elected to devalue the official rate to the swap centre market rate in order to eliminate discrepancies between the two, and to promote use of a single market related rate as a first step towards more flexible management of the currency. The devaluation of January 1994 brought the RMB official rate to approximately RMB8.7/US$; it has since appreciated to RMB8.3/US$, as illustrated in Figure 3.3 below (which depicts the historical movement of the market-related (not official) spot RMB/US$ rate). Between 1994

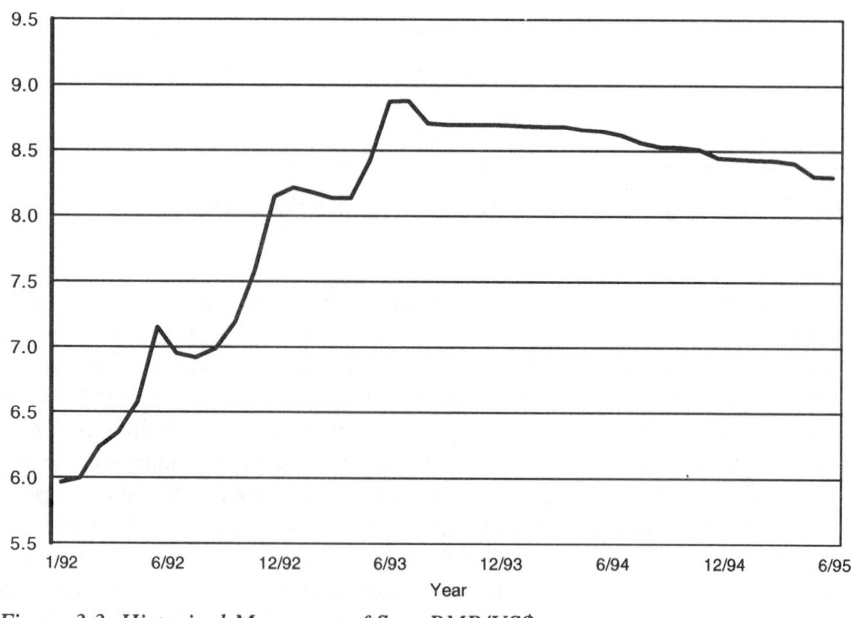

Figure 3.3 Historical Movement of Spot RMB/US$

and 1995 the Chinese authorities increased the number of official foreign currency trading centres (the only entities permitted to deal in foreign exchange) from seven to 24, with plans to add more over the next few years; the increased number of centres has helped expand liquidity in spot renminbi turnover and, between April 1994 and 1995, a total of RMB471 bln (US$56.8 bln) of spot RMB/US$ was traded. An RMB/HK$ crossrate was added in late 1994 and total trading reached RMB 39.8 bln (US$4.8B) by April 1995 (Austin, 1995); note that an RMB/JPY crossrate was introduced in March 1995 and the authorities are presently considering introduction of both Deutschmark and Sterling crosses in 1996.

DERIVATIVE MARKETS AND PRODUCTS

LISTED DERIVATIVE EXCHANGES

Chinese state owned enterprises have dealt in the global listed commodity markets for several decades. Import- or export-oriented institutions such as Ceroilfoods, Minmetals, Sinopec, and others (all associated with the Ministry of Foreign Economic Relations and Trade, MOFERT) have been active commodity hedgers for a number of years, and have gained a certain amount of experience in dealing with derivatives listed on global exchanges. Despite China's involvement in global commodity futures, the country's own listed derivative market traces its formation back as recently as the late 1980s and early 1990s, when decentralization of agricultural distribution and processing led to the formation of regional agricultural wholesale exchanges (or commodity marketing centres) throughout the country. Early trading in spot agricultural commodities paved the way for subsequent trading in agricultural forwards and agricultural futures; trading in metal futures and bond futures has followed in recent years. Overall growth of agricultural, metals and hybrid futures exchanges has been significant. Between 1990 and mid-1994 approximately 40 'futures exchanges' (many actually just commodity marketing centres focused on spot trading) were formed in China, with 2300 members trading over 50 different commodities. The estimated value of trading which took place on these exchanges in 1993 was RMB686 bln (US$82.6B), or RMB4 bln (US$485MM/day); this business flowed through more than 500 futures brokers (only 144 licensed by the State Administration for Industry and Commerce (SAIC)) on behalf of 30,000 clients (Grossman, 1994).

The Chinese listed futures market is not readily comparable to futures markets in other countries. Unlike other global futures markets the Chinese market did not evolve gradually out of uniform, liquid and well-established cash markets, but was created over a short span of time (e.g. five years) based on underlying markets best characterized as illiquid and regionalized. As a result, the domestic futures market carries little depth and many contracts have developed without conforming to the needs or requirements of hedgers and speculators. Given the rapid evolution of the local futures market, it is not surprising to note that it is undergoing rather significant changes at the present time. The changes taking place (many led by the regulatory authorities) are designed to address a variety of problems plaguing the industry, including: overly aggressive creation and expansion of exchanges; lack of uniformity with regard to contract specifications (e.g. deliverable grades, delivery months, delivery points and so on); fragmented and regionalized exchanges trading similar products (with many centres unable to create critical mass in a given contract); abuse of the market by certain participants (e.g. squeezing or ramping the market); unstable and unsophisticated settlement and trading facilities; lack of market-makers; difficulties in arbitraging regional price discrepancies due to transportation and storage problems/costs; inadequate rules regarding open interest, margins and position limits; imbalance between hedgers and speculators, with the latter dominating activity on most exchanges; insufficient clearinghouse facilities or guarantee funds to ensure exchange/member security; and, uncertainty and lack of uniformity regarding regulatory controls. Lack of clarity with regard to property rights, bankruptcy law and the liabilities of state-owned enterprises have also complicated the process. While a great deal of work remains to be done in order to bring the Chinese futures market to a level global participants would consider acceptable, such work has already commenced. In response to both inflationary pressures and the Treasury bond futures scandal (discussed below), the China Securities Regulatory Commission (CSRC) began exercising more authority over exchanges in 1994 and 1995. Our discussion of the regulatory actions enacted since 1993 is included in the regulatory section at the end of this chapter.

The earliest Chinese exchanges, all focused on spot trading of agricultural products, were created in Heilongjiang (grain and edible oils, 1989), Zhengzhou (grain, 1990), Hubei (grain, 1991), Silin (corn, 1991), Anhui (rice, 1991), Jiangsuwuxi (poultry, 1991), Guangdong Yujian (sugar, 1991) and Tianjin (sugar, 1992) (WB, 1994). These commodity trading centres were established by provincial governments as a means of improving the distribution and processing of perishable agricultural commodities. In certain instances the local agricultural exchanges gravitated from being government-controlled centres for the purchase and sale of agricultural goods on a spot basis, to member-owned exchanges offering forward contracts and, in some cases, futures contracts. Following the relative success of trading in agricultural futures contracts, domestic exchanges have turned towards trading futures on base metals, energy products and, more recently, treasury bonds.

Given the large number of exchanges currently operating in China and the fact that some may be closed down or merged over the coming years, we elect to focus our discussion on the officially recognized/sanctioned exchanges which are the primary derivative trading centres of China. Most of the exchanges described below have already received official relicensing from the CSRC; several others are awaiting final relicensing but are expected to gain necessary approvals during 1995 or 1996.

The Beijing Commodity Exchange (BCE) was formally established in May 1993, after receiving approval from the Beijing Municipal Government, and began trading in November 1993. It now features the largest physical trading floor, and the broadest range of futures contracts, in China; average daily turnover across all futures reached RMB10 bln ($1.2 bln) by late 1994 (CSB, 11/94). The Exchange's product listing includes contracts on agricultural commodities, metals, energy, chemicals and bonds. Trading takes place via automated computer matching, with matches prioritized by both price and time. There is some discussion of permitting foreigners direct access to the BCE by 1998; at present, foreigners wanting to participate in the local market must do so through local brokers or joint venture brokers. The BCE has been relicensed by the CSRC.

The Changchun United Commodity Exchange (CUCE) is one of China's newest trading forums. The Exchange was created in late 1994 and licensed in mid-1995, and commenced trading in the third quarter of 1995. CUCE is primarily an agricultural exchange, trading corn, soybean, soybean meal, red bean, green bean and white wheat futures. It also offers China's first, and only, freight index futures, based on the cost of moving 50 tons of corn to Dalian and Shanghai. The Exchange trades via computerized systems and self-clears all trades. Formal relicensing from the CSRC has already been obtained.

The Chengdu United Commodities Futures Exchange (CUCFE) was created through the merger of four separate exchanges, including Sichuan Cereals and Oils Exchange, Chengdu Metals Exchange, Chengdu Meat Products Exchange and Sichuan Commodities Exchange. CUCFE is operating on a trial basis until the end of 1995, at which time it will decide which of its 18 contracts will remain listed. At the present time CUCFE lists contracts from all four previously existing exchanges, including corn, soybean, rapeseed, tung oil, cotton yarn, sorghum, pork, copper, aluminium and nickel futures. The CSRC has already relicensed CUCFE. (Note: given that CUCFE's product listing is expected to change dramatically in the near-term as it abandons or restructures individual derivatives, we have not included specific contract details on any of the Exchange's futures in the section below).

The China Commodity Futures Exchange of Hainan (CCFEH) was established in November 1993 to trade contracts based on sugar, rubber and plywood. During 1994 the Exchange added futures contracts on RBD palm olein, red beans, barley, cocoa, coffee and Treasury bonds, becoming a hybrid exchange in the process. Trading on the CCFEH occurs through a computerized system which matches orders by price. CCFEH has already obtain final relicensing from the CSRC.

The Zhengzhou Grain Wholesale Market was created in 1990, by the Government of Heinan and the Ministry of Commerce, to trade spot and forward contracts on agricultural goods. The market was converted into an exchange in 1993 following approval from the Ministries of Agriculture, Railways and Finance, and the People's Bank of China and was renamed the China Zhengzhou Commodity Exchange (CZCE). CZCE presently trades futures on corn, wheat, soybeans, soybean meal, green beans, red beans, peanut kernel and rice; it recently added futures on aluminium and Treasury bonds to its listing. Trading occurs via automated computer price matching, clearing is contracted to the Bank of Communications (a major Chinese bank), and settlement occurs in physical through the delivery of warehouse bills. In 1994 average daily turnover amounted to 20,000 contracts, with highest one day turnover equal to 50,000 contracts. CZCE has already been relicensed by the CSRC.

The Dalian Commodity Exchange (DCE) is rather unique among domestic futures exchanges in that it began as an agricultural trading centre and has remained such. While other exchanges have added metals, energy or financial futures to become true hybrid exchanges, DCE remains focused solely on agricultural futures trading. Its product listing includes soybean, soybean meal, soybean oil, wheat, rice, corn, green bean and red bean futures. Trading occurs via computerized systems and clearing and settlement is executed by the Exchange itself. DCE has been relicensed by the CSRC.

Guangdong United Futures Exchange (GUFE) was created when the South China Commodities Exchange (SCCE) merged with the Guangzhou Rubber Exchange (GRE) in May 1994; the Exchange was established under the direction of the Ministries of Agriculture and Chemical Industries, the Guangdong Provincial Government and the Guangdong Bureau of Land Reclamation and State Farms. GUFE has evolved into a hybrid exchange, trading softs, base metals, petroleum products and financial contracts; trading is computerized and clearing/settlement occurs through an independent clearing house. GUFE has gained relicensing approval from the CSRC.

Nanfang Non-ferrous Metals Exchange (NNME) is a small regional exchange which trades exclusively in forward contracts on aluminium and copper. The Exchange was founded in 1994 and became operational in 1995; it is currently contemplating conversion of its forwards into futures, though timing of such a change is uncertain. NNME has not yet received final relicensing from the CSRC.

Nanjing Petroleum Exchange (NANPEX) was created in late 1992 and began trading in March 1993. NANPEX's founding members include the Government of Jiangsu Province, China National Chemicals Import and Export Corporation, China National Offshore Oil Corporation and China National Petrochemical Sales Company. The Exchange began trading petroleum-related products on a spot basis in 1993 and followed with futures trading on gasoil and gasoline in 1994. It should be noted that NANPEX's business was curtailed in 1994 when the government announced a temporary ban on trading of certain commodities, including energy products; it is expected, however, that trading will restart once the government eases restrictions. NANPEX has not yet been relicensed by the CSRC.

The Shanghai Cereals and Oils Exchange (SCOE) is one of China's original agricultural futures trading forums and continues to maintain its agricultural focus to this day. SCOE lists and trades futures on corn, green beans, red beans, soybeans, long grain rice and white wheat. Trading occurs by computerized systems and clearing and settling of trades is handled by the Exchange itself. SCOE has already been relicensed by the CSRC.

The Shanghai Commodities Exchange (SCE) was created in April 1995 through the merger of four Shanghai-based exchanges, including Shanghai Petroleum Exchange, Shanghai Chemical Goods Exchange, Shanghai Agricultural Goods Exchange and Shanghai Construction Materials Exchange; the merger was effected in order to permit the smaller Shanghai exchanges to unite and compete more effectively against larger exchanges. The SCE currently trades futures on plywood, rubber and polyvinyl chloride (PVC), and is expected to add other contracts over time. The Exchange trades via a computerized system and trades are cleared and settled by outside banks and financial institutions who are only permitted to deal with approved members. SCE has already been relicensed by the CSRC.

The Shanghai Metals Exchange (SME) was created in early 1992 as the first national metals exchange and began active trading in the same year; SME is currently the third largest metals exchange in the world. The SME was established as a joint venture between the Shanghai Municipal Government and the Ministry of Materials and Equipment; unlike its peer exchange, the open-outcry Shenzhen Metal and United Futures Exchange (previously known as Shenzhen Metals Exchange (ShME)), SME is a screen-based, electronic exchange. The main futures contracts of the SME are based on aluminium and copper, though it also offers contracts on lead, nickel, tin and zinc. SME has not yet been relicensed by the CSRC.

The Shenyang Commodity Exchange (SyCE) developed from a centre trading wood (plywood, Manshurica, Bugeana, Gmelinii) on a spot, forward and futures basis, to a hybrid exchange trading base metal futures (aluminium, copper, wire rod) and, more recently, bond futures. Trading is effected via computerized systems and clearing of trades is executed by the Exchange itself. SyCE has already been relicensed by the CSRC.

The Shenzhen Metal and United Futures Exchange (SMUFE), along with the SME mentioned above, was one of China's two early futures exchanges. SMUFE was originally created as the Shenzhen Metals Exchange (ShME) in June 1991 after receiving approval from the Shenzhen Municipal Government; the exchange opened in mid-1992 and began active trading in 1993. In December 1994 the ShME merged with the Shenzhen United Futures Exchange to become the SMUFE. Though SMUFE has traded various futures in the past (diesel, sugar, grain, bonds) it is now focused primarily on trading of metal futures and forwards (though it retains its bond contract as well). Trading on SMUFE is by open outcry, with trades cleared and settled by the clearing division of the Exchange itself. SMUFE has been relicensed by the CSRC.

The Suzhou Commodity Exchange (SuCE) is a minor regional exchange, though it has good prospects for expanding. At the present time SuCE trades futures on plywood, red beans and rod coils. Trading occurs through computerized systems and clearing/settlement of trades is effected by the Exchange itself. SuCE has already been relicensed by the CSRC.

The Tianjin United Futures Exchange (TUFE) is one of China's newest official exchanges. TUFE was founded in late 1994 and obtained its license in early 1995; trading in corn, soybean, soybean meal, green bean, red bean and Tianjin red bean futures began in mid-1995. All trading on TUFE occurs through its electronic trading system and all clearing/settlement is handled by the Exchange itself. TUFE has been relicensed by the CSRC.

The Wuhan Securities Exchange Centre (WSEC) is focused primarily on trading of government and enterprise bonds; in addition to listing and trading bonds, however, the Exchange also trades in bond futures. Since WSEC is a broad trading forum which is active in cash instruments as well as futures contracts, it does not require specific relicensing by the CSRC.

China's two leading stock exchanges also list and trade derivative securities. The Shanghai Stock Exchange (SSE), which was founded in mid-1990 and began trading in December 1990, is one of the country's two main equity exchanges and has become a leading participant in the bond futures market (as we discuss at length below). The SSE is a non-profit entity owned by more than 500 members, including provinces, municipalities and autonomous regions. Trading on the Exchange is computerized and orders are matched automatically by price and time; securities are cleared through the Shanghai Securities Clearing and Registration Corporation, which was created in May 1993. The Shenzhen Stock Exchange (SHSE) was also founded in mid-1990 and began operations in December 1990. In addition to trading A and B shares, the SHSE also trades bond futures and issuer equity warrants (as well as a single issue of convertible bonds); all trading is via computerized system which matches orders by price and time. As with the WSEC, SSE and SHSE are active traders of cash instruments (as well as futures) and, as such, are not required to be relicensed by the CSRC.

Exchange	**Primary Derivatives**
Beijing Commodity Exchange (BCE)	Bond futures; wheat futures; rice futures; soybean futures; soybean meal futures; red bean futures; corn futures; vegetable oil futures; white sugar futures; green bean futures; peanut kernel futures; polyvinyl chloride futures; rubber futures; plywood futures; polypropylene futures; sodium carbonate futures; copper futures; aluminium futures; wire rod futures;
Changchun United Commodity Exchange (CUCE)	Corn futures; soybean futures; soybean meal futures; red bean futures; green bean futures; white wheat futures; freight index futures
Chengdu United Commodities Futures Exchange (CUCFE)	Corn futures; soybean futures; rapeseed futures; tung oil futures; cotton yarn futures; sorghum futures; pork futures; copper futures; aluminium futures; nickel futures

Table 3.2 Listed Derivative Exchanges

Exchange	Primary Derivatives
China Commodity Futures Exchange of Hainan (CCFEH)	Bond futures; RBD palm olein futures; red bean futures; sugar forwards; coffee futures; cocoa futures; barley futures; plywood futures; rubber futures
China Zhengzhou Commodity Exchange (CZCE)	Bond futures; wheat futures; corn futures; soybean futures; green bean futures; hard rice futures; peanut kernel futures; soybean meal futures; red bean futures; cotton yarn futures; aluminium futures
Dalian Commodity Exchange (DCE)	Corn futures; green bean futures; red bean futures; rice futures; soybean futures; soybean meal futures; soybean oil futures; wheat futures
Guangdong United Futures Exchange (GUFE)	Bond futures; sugar forwards; soybean meal futures; corn futures; soybean futures; long grain rice futures; aluminium futures; copper futures; gasoline futures; gasoil futures
Nanfang Non-ferrous Metals Exchange (NNME)	Copper forwards; aluminium forwards
Nanjing Petroleum Exchange (NANPEX)	Gasoil futures; gasoline futures
Shanghai Cereals and Oils Exchange (SCOE)	Corn futures; green bean futures; red bean futures; long grain rice futures; soybean futures; white wheat futures
Shanghai Commodity Exchange (SCE)	Plywood futures; rubber futures; polyvinyl chloride futures
Shanghai Metals Exchange (SME)	Copper futures; aluminium futures; lead futures; zinc futures; tin futures; nickel futures
Shanghai Stock Exchange (SSE)	Bond futures
Shenyang Commodity Exchange (SyCE)	Bond futures; plywood futures; wood futures; aluminium futures; copper futures; wire rod forwards
Shenzhen Metal and United Futures Exchange (SMUFE)	Bond futures; aluminium futures; copper futures; nickel futures; tin futures; zinc futures; antimony forwards; lead forwards; magnesium forwards
Shenzhen Stock Exchange (SHSE)	Bond futures; equity warrants; convertibles
Suzhou Commodity Exchange (SuCE)	Plywood futures; red bean futures; rod coil futures
Tianjin United Futures Exchange (TUFE)	Corn futures; green bean futures; red bean futures; Tianjin red bean futures; soybean futures, soybean meal futures
Wuhan Securities Exchange Centre (WSEC)	Bond futures

Table 3.2 Listed Derivative Exchanges (continued)

It should be noted that in addition to the exchanges detailed above, the Chongqing Commodities Exchange has obtained a license from the CSRC but has not commenced trading and has not put forth specific contract details on the products it will trade in the future; as such, we have not included the Exchange in our discussion below. Table 3.2 summarizes the main listed exchanges and derivatives of China.

LISTED FUTURES AND OPTIONS

Equity

Equity Futures/Options

The Chinese domestic market does not currently feature listed equity futures or options and there are no immediate plans to introduce such derivatives.

Index Futures/Options/Futures Options

The Chinese futures market has not, to date, introduced stock index futures contracts. The State Council Securities Policies Committee reported, in July 1994, that consideration of stock index futures should be banned for the foreseeable future, in order for local equity markets to gain more time to expand and stabilize and to curb the introduction of further derivative instruments which might fuel financial market speculation. The State Council report has suggested the near-term focus of the market should be on the further development of commodity futures trading (central to the potential hedging activities of producers and end-users), not on financial futures trading.

Despite the findings of the State Council Committee, the Shenzhen Stock Exchange announced in early 1995 its desire to list stock index futures contracts. To date, however, no further announcements regarding timing or possible contract specifications have been put forth.

Fixed Income

Deposit Futures/Options/Futures Options

The Chinese market features no deposit futures at the present time. The local financial system presently has no accepted, market-determined, short-term benchmark deposit rate which could be used as a reference for such a contract; development of deposit futures is likely to take several years.

Interest Rate Futures/Options/Futures Options

China's sole listed interest rate derivative is the futures contract on state Treasury bonds (the derivative is most often referred to as a Treasury note future, though the term bond future is used interchangeably). The contract, which is offered on two-, three- and five-year bonds, is listed on nine domestic exchanges, though the primary trading location has historically been the Shanghai Stock Exchange (accounting for more than two-thirds of all volume); ancillary trading locations include Beijing Commodity Exchange, China Commodity Futures Exchange of Hainan, China Zhengzhou Commodity Exchange, Guangdong United Futures Exchange, Shenyang Commodity Exchange, Shenzhen Metal and United Futures Exchange, Shenzhen Stock Exchange and Wuhan Securities Exchange Centre.

Although bond futures were originally introduced on the SSE in December 1992 trading remained relatively dormant until 1994. Interest and activity in bond futures began increasing in mid- to late-1994 for several fundamental reasons: the SSE reduced margins by one-half (to a modest RMB500 (US$60) per RMB20,000 ($2,380) contract, or 2.5% of face value); the market was opened to retail investors; the Chinese government began actively issuing Treasury bonds, giving the underlying market new supply and increased liquidity; returns on domestic equities were unsatisfactory, causing investors to seek opportunities elsewhere; and investors began expressing views on the payment of enhanced inflation-linked coupons on existing bonds by taking positions in futures (e.g. certain select Chinese Treasury bonds carry special 'inflation adjusted' coupons, which pay a premium over the normal coupon; the announcement of the inflation premium is normally deferred until late in the life of the bond, and is paid at maturity with the balance of the regular coupon). Total bond futures turnover reached RMB2.8 tln (US$333 bln) in 1994, with SSE accounting for more than two-thirds of all trading (CSB, 1995).

In early 1995 bond futures volume, particularly in the 327 contract expiring June 1995, soared in the face of speculative buying and selling (average daily turnover in bond futures between January and March 1995 reached RMB100 bln (US$12 bln). Investor interest in front of the March coupon announcement on the three-year March 1992 issue led to massive buying of the reference futures contract; prices soon reached all-time highs. There was an expectation that new bond issues to be floated in March 1995 would not carry inflation-adjusted coupons (the maturing March 1992 bond, in contrast, was expected to carry an enhanced coupon of nearly 12%); the expectation led to increased purchases by those hoping to profit from the anticipated coupon enhancement on the existing 1992 issue.

At the end of February 1995 one day turnover in Treasury bonds and bond futures reached RMB494 bln (US$59.5 bln), with 90% traded in the form of futures. Several days later turnover reached the RMB 850 bln mark (US$102 bln), as a major securities firm, Shanghai International Securities (SISCO), went short RMB 250 bln (US$30 bln) of futures, in violation of Exchange rules; the massive short brought prices down from RMB152 to RMB147.5 per contract during the trading session. The SSE suspended all trading, cancelled RMB 313 bln (US$37.7 bln) of transactions, raised the closing price back to RMB151.5 and began investigating irregularities in trading. The following day the Exchange suspended the free quotation system (a suspension which lasted several days) and urged buyers and sellers of cancelled transactions to settle trades at negotiated prices. At the conclusion of its investigation the Exchange determined that SISCO, China's largest broker, had gone very short the market, while competing forces were moving in the opposite direction. SISCO's apparent reasons for shorting the market were based on its belief that the March 1992 inflation-adjusted coupon would be small and that new supply of March Treasury bonds would bring prices down. SISCO reportedly lost RMB600 mln (US$72 mln) from its trading and was subjected to severe disciplinary action. As a result of the Treasury bond futures disruption, the authorities issued a special set of regulations designed to bring the market under control; we discuss the measures taken in the regulatory section below.

Despite the imposition of new regulations, overall activity in bond futures remained brisk, particularly in contract 319 (the future on a five-year bond expiring in April 1997) and contract 337 (the future on a three-year bond expiring March 1996). Additional speculative purchases impacted the market again in May/June 1995, forcing more liquidation on certain exchanges and a temporary suspension of bond futures trading nationally. The length of the temporary suspension is unclear though trading is expected to resume in the near term. Tables 3.4 through 3.26 contain contract specifications for the two-, three- and five-year Treasury note futures traded on the BCE, CCFEH, CZCE, GUFE, SSE, SyCE, SMUFE, SHSE and WSEC immediately prior to the temporary suspension, while Figure 3.4 illustrates the recent movement of bond futures prices based on the 327 contract. Table 3.3 summarizes the availability of bond futures contracts on various exchanges.

Exchange	Two-year bond future	Three-year bond future	Five-year bond future
Beijing Commodity Exchange	Yes	Yes	Yes
China Commodity Futures Exchange of Hainan	No	Yes	Yes
China Zhengzhou Commodity Exchange	Yes	Yes	Yes
Guangdong United Futures Exchange	No	Yes	Yes
Shanghai Stock Exchange	Yes	Yes	Yes
Shenyang Commodity Exchange	Yes	Yes	Yes
Shenzhen Metal & United Futures Exchange	No	Yes	No
Shenzhen Stock Exchange	Yes	Yes	Yes
Wuhan Securities Exchange Centre	Yes	Yes	Yes

Table 3.3 Domestic Bond Futures Contract Availability

Contract	Two-year Treasury Note Futures
Type	Domestic
Exchange	Beijing Commodity Exchange
Months	March, June, September, December
Contract Size	RMB10,000 face value of Two-year notes
Tick Value	RMB0.02 per face value RMB100 notes
Daily Limit	+/– RMB2 against previous day's settlement price
Deliverable Instrument	Physical settlement of Two-year Treasury notes in the form of physical commodity certificate or non-physical certificate
Last Trading Day	30th day of the contract month
Delivery Day	6th through 8th business day after the last trading day
Real-time price data	Reuters: <0#BTE:>

Table 3.4 Contract Specifications for BCE Two-year Treasury Note Futures

Contract	Three-year Treasury Note Futures
Type	Domestic
Exchange	Beijing Commodity Exchange
Months	March, June, September, December
Contract Size	RMB10,000 face value of Three-year notes
Tick Value	RMB0.02 per face value RMB100 notes
Daily Limit	+/– RMB2 against previous day's settlement price
Deliverable Instrument	Physical settlement of Three-year Treasury notes in the form of physical commodity certificate or non-physical certificate
Last Trading Day	30th day of the contract month
Delivery Day	6th through 8th business day after the last trading day
Real-time price data	Reuters: <0#BTB:>, <0#BTD:>

Table 3.5 Contract Specifications for BCE Three-year Treasury Note Futures

Contract	Five-year Treasury Note Futures
Type	Domestic
Exchange	Beijing Commodity Exchange
Months	March, June, September, December
Contract Size	RMB10,000 face value of Five-year notes
Tick Value	RMB0.02 per face value RMB100 notes
Daily Limit	+/– RMB2 against previous day's settlement price
Deliverable Instrument	Physical settlement of Five-year Treasury notes in the form of physical commodity certificate or non-physical certificate
Last Trading Day	30th day of the contract month
Delivery Day	6th through 8th business day after the last trading day
Real-time price data	Reuters: <0#BTC:>

Table 3.6 Contract Specifications for BCE Five-year Treasury Note Futures

Contract	Three Year Treasury Note Futures
Type	Domestic
Exchange	China Commodity Futures Exchange of Hainan
Months	March, June, September, December
Contract Size	RMB20,000 face value of Three-year notes
Tick Value	RMB10/contract
Daily Limit	+/– RMB400/contract against previous day's settlement
Deliverable Instrument	Physical settlement of Three-year Treasury notes, at CFFEH
Last Trading Day	On, or before, the 10th business day counting back from last business day of the month
Delivery Day	Day after the last trading day
Real-time price data	Reuters: <0#HTB:>, <0#HTD:>

Table 3.7 Contract Specifications for CCFEH Three-year Treasury Note Futures

Contract	**Five-year Treasury Note Futures**
Type	Domestic
Exchange	China Commodity Futures Exchange of Hainan
Months	March, June, September, December
Contract Size	RMB20,000 face value of Five-year notes
Tick Value	RMB10/contract
Daily Limit	+/– RMB400/contract against previous day's settlement
Deliverable Instrument	Physical settlement of Five-year Treasury notes, at CCFEH
Last Trading Day	On, or before, the 10th business day counting back from last business day of the month
Delivery Day	Day after the last trading day
Real-time price data	Reuters: <0#HTC:>, <0#HTE:>

Table 3.8 Contract Specifications for CCFEH Five-year Treasury Note Futures

Contract	**Two-year Treasury Note Futures**
Type	Domestic
Exchange	China Zhengzhou Commodity Exchange
Months	March, June, September, December
Contract Size	RMB10,000 face value of Two-year notes
Tick Value	RMB1/contract
Daily Limit	+/– RMB100/contract against previous day's settlement
Deliverable Instrument	Cash settlement, or physical settlement of Two-year Treasury notes
Last Trading Day	Seven business days before the last business day of the contract month
Delivery Day	Last business day of the contract month
Real-time price data	Reuters: <0#CTE:>

Table 3.9 Contract Specifications for CZCE Two-year Treasury Note Futures

Contract	**Three-year Treasury Note Futures**
Type	Domestic
Exchange	China Zhengzhou Commodity Exchange
Months	March, June, September, December
Contract Size	RMB10,000 face value of Three-year notes
Tick Value	RMB1/contract
Daily Limit	+/– RMB100/contract against previous day's settlement price
Deliverable Instrument	Cash settlement, or physical settlement of Three-year Treasury notes
Last Trading Day	Seven business days before the last business day of the contract month
Delivery Day	Last business day of the contract month
Real-time price data	Reuters: <0#CTB:>, <0#CTC:>

Table 3.10 Contract Specifications for CZCE Three-year Treasury Note Futures

Contract	**Five-year Treasury Note Futures**
Type	Domestic
Exchange	China Zhengzhou Commodity Exchange
Months	March, June, September, December
Contract Size	RMB10,000 face value of Five-year notes
Tick Value	RMB1/contract
Daily Limit	+/– RMB100/contract against previous day's settlement price
Deliverable Instrument	Cash settlement, or physical settlement of Five-year Treasury notes
Last Trading Day	Seven business days before the last business day of the contract month
Delivery Day	Last business day of the contract month
Real-time price data	Reuters: <0#CTD:>

Table 3.11 Contract Specifications for CZCE Five-year Treasury Note Futures

Contract	Three-year Treasury Note Futures
Type	Domestic
Exchange	Guangdong United Futures Exchange
Months	March, June, September, December
Contract Size	RMB100,000 face value of Three-year notes
Tick Value	RMB10
Daily Limit	+/– 2% against previous day's settlement price
Deliverable Instrument	Physical settlement of Three-year Treasury notes
Last Trading Day	Last business day of the contract month
Delivery Day	Seven business days after the last trading day
Real-time price data	Reuters: <0#UTC:>, <0#UTD:>

Table 3.12 Contract Specifications for GUFE Three-year Treasury Note Futures

Contract	Five-year Treasury Note Futures
Type	Domestic
Exchange	Guangdong United Futures Exchange
Months	March, June, September, December
Contract Size	RMB100,000 face value of Five-year notes
Tick Value	RMB10
Daily Limit	+/– 2% against previous day's settlement price
Deliverable Instrument	Physical settlement of Five-year Treasury notes
Last Trading Day	Last business day of the contract month
Delivery Day	Seven business days after the last trading day
Real-time price data	Reuters: <0#UTE:>, <0#UTF:>

Table 3.13 Contract Specifications for GUFE Five-year Treasury Note Futures

Contract	Two-year Treasury Note Futures
Type	Domestic
Exchange	Shanghai Stock Exchange
Months	March, June, September, December
Contract Size	RMB20,000 face value of Two-year notes
Tick Value	RMB0.05 per RMB100 face value of notes
Daily Limit	+/– RMB200 against previous day's settlement price
Deliverable Instrument	Physical settlement of Two-year Treasury notes via physical certificate or non-physical certificate
Last Trading Day	Last business day of the contract month
Delivery Day	Day after the last trading day
Real-time price data	Reuters: <0#STF:>

Table 3.14 Contract Specifications for SSE Two-year Treasury Note Futures

Contract	Three-year Treasury Note Futures
Type	Domestic
Exchange	Shanghai Stock Exchange
Months	March, June, September, December
Contract Size	RMB20,000 face value of Three-year notes
Tick Value	RMB0.05 per RMB100 face value of notes
Daily Limit	+/– RMB200 against previous day's settlement price
Deliverable Instrument	Physical settlement of Three-year Treasury notes via physical certificate or non-physical certificate
Last Trading Day	Last business day of the contract month
Delivery Day	Day after the last trading day
Real-time price data	Reuters: <0#STC:>, <0#STE:>

Table 3.15 Contract Specifications for SSE Three-year Treasury Note Futures

Contract	Five-year Treasury Note Futures
Type	Domestic
Exchange	Shanghai Stock Exchange
Months	March, June, September, December
Contract Size	RMB20,000 face value of Five-year notes
Tick Value	RMB0.05 per RMB100 face value of notes
Daily Limit	+/– RMB200 against previous day's settlement price
Deliverable Instrument	Physical settlement of Five-year Treasury notes via physical certificate or non-physical certificate
Last Trading Day	Last business day of the contract month
Delivery Day	Day after the last trading day
Real-time price data	Reuters: <0#STD:>, <0#STG:>

Table 3.16 Contract Specifications for SSE Five-year Treasury Note Futures

Contract	Two-year Treasury Note Futures
Type	Domestic
Exchange	Shenyang Commodity Exchange
Months	March, June, September, December
Contract Size	RMB10,000 face value of Two-year notes
Tick Value	RMB0.01 per RMB100 face value of notes
Daily Limit	+/– RMB1 against previous day's settlement price
Deliverable Instrument	Physical settlement of Two-year Treasury notes via physical certificate or non-physical certificate
Last Trading Day	On, or before, the 3rd business day counting back from the last business day of the month
Delivery Day	Day after the last trading day
Real-time price data	Reuters: <0#YTF:>

Table 3.17 Contract Specifications for SyCE Two-year Treasury Note Futures

Contract	**Three-year Treasury Note Futures**
Type	Domestic
Exchange	Shenyang Commodity Exchange
Months	March, June, September, December
Contract Size	RMB10,000 face value of Three-year notes
Tick Value	RMB0.01 per RMB100 face value of notes
Daily Limit	+/– RMB1 against previous day's settlement price
Deliverable Instrument	Physical settlement of Three-year Treasury notes via physical certificate or non-physical certificate
Last Trading Day	On, or before, the 3rd business day counting back from the last business day of the month
Delivery Day	Day after the last trading day
Real-time price data	Reuters: <0#YTB:>, <0#YTE:>

Table 3.18 Contract Specifications for SyCE Three-year Treasury Note Futures

Contract	**Five-year Treasury Note Futures**
Type	Domestic
Exchange	Shenyang Commodity Exchange
Months	March, June, September, December
Contract Size	RMB10,000 face value of Five-year notes
Tick Value	RMB0.01 per RMB100 face value of notes
Daily Limit	+/– RMB1 against previous day's settlement price
Deliverable Instrument	Physical settlement of Five-year Treasury notes via physical certificate or non-physical certificate
Last Trading Day	On, or before, the 3rd business day counting back from the last business day of the month
Delivery Day	Day after the last trading day
Real-time price data	Reuters: <0#YTD:>

Table 3.19 Contract Specifications for SyCE Five-year Treasury Note Futures

Contract	Three-year Treasury Note Futures
Type	Domestic
Exchange	Shenzhen Metal and United Futures Exchange
Months	March, June, September, December
Contract Size	RMB10,000 face value of Three-year notes
Tick Value	RMB0.02 per RMB100 face value of notes
Daily Limit	N/A
Deliverable Instrument	Physical settlement of Three-year Treasury notes
Last Trading Day	Seven business days before the last business day of delivery month
Delivery Day	Day after the last trading day
Real-time price data	None available

Table 3.20 Contract Specifications for SMUFE Three-year Treasury Note Futures

Contract	Two-year Treasury Note Futures
Type	Domestic
Exchange	Shenzhen Stock Exchange
Months	March, June, September, December
Contract Size	RMB20,000 face value of two-year notes
Tick Value	RMB0.05 per RMB100 face value of notes
Daily Limit	+/– RMB200 against previous day's settlement
Deliverable Instrument	Physical settlement of Two-year Treasury notes via physical certificate or non-physical certificate
Last Trading Day	Last business day of the contract month
Delivery Day	Day after the last trading day
Real-time price data	Reuters: <0#ZTF:>

Table 3.21 Contract Specifications for SHSE Two-year Treasury Note Futures

Contract	Three-year Treasury Note Futures
Type	Domestic
Exchange	Shenzhen Stock Exchange
Months	March, June, September, December
Contract Size	RMB20,000 face value of Three-year notes
Tick Value	RMB0.05 per RMB100 face value of notes
Daily Limit	+/– RMB200 against previous day's settlement price
Deliverable Instrument	Physical settlement of Three-year Treasury notes via physical certificate or non-physical certificate
Last Trading Day	Last business day of the contract month
Delivery Day	Day after the last trading day
Real-time price data	Reuters: <0#ZTB:>, <0#ZTD:>

Table 3.22 Contract Specifications for SHSE Three-year Treasury Note Futures

Contract	Five-year Treasury Note Futures
Type	Domestic
Exchange	Shenzhen Stock Exchange
Months	March, June, September, December
Contract Size	RMB20,000 face value of Five-year notes
Tick Value	RMB0.05 per RMB100 face value of notes
Daily Limit	+/– RMB200 against previous day's settlement price
Deliverable Instrument	Physical settlement of Five-year Treasury notes via physical certificate or non-physical certificate
Last Trading Day	Last business day of the contract month
Delivery Day	Day after the last trading day
Real-time price data	Reuters: <0#ZTC:>, <0#ZTE:>

Table 3.23 Contract Specifications for SHSE Five-year Treasury Note Futures

Contract	Two-year Treasury Note Futures
Type	Domestic
Exchange	Wuhan Securities Exchange Centre
Months	March, June, September, December
Contract Size	RMB20,000 face value of Two-year notes
Tick Value	RMB200
Daily Limit	+/– 2% against previous day's settlement price
Deliverable Instrument	Physical settlement of Two-year Treasury notes
Last Trading Day	Last business day of the contract month
Delivery Day	Day after the last trading day
Real-time price data	Reuters: <0#WTF:>

Table 3.24 Contract Specifications for WSEC Two-year Treasury Note Futures

Contract	Three-year Treasury Note Futures
Type	Domestic
Exchange	Wuhan Securities Exchange Centre
Months	March, June, September, December
Contract Size	RMB20,000 face value of Three-year notes
Tick Value	RMB200
Daily Limit	+/– 2% against previous day's settlement price
Deliverable Instrument	Physical settlement of Three-year Treasury notes
Last Trading Day	Last business day of the contract month
Delivery Day	Day after the last trading day
Real-time price data	Reuters: <0#WTB:>, <0#WTD:>

Table 3.25 Contract Specifications for WSEC Three-year Treasury Note Futures

Contract	Five-year Treasury Note Futures
Type	Domestic
Exchange	Wuhan Securities Exchange Centre
Months	March, June, September, December
Contract Size	RMB20,000 face value of Five-year notes
Tick Value	RMB200
Daily Limit	+/– 2% against previous day's settlement price
Deliverable Instrument	Physical settlement of Five-year Treasury notes
Last Trading Day	Last business day of the contract month
Delivery Day	Day after the last trading day
Real-time price data	Reuters: <0#WTC:>

Table 3.26 Contract Specifications for WSEC Five-year Treasury Note Futures

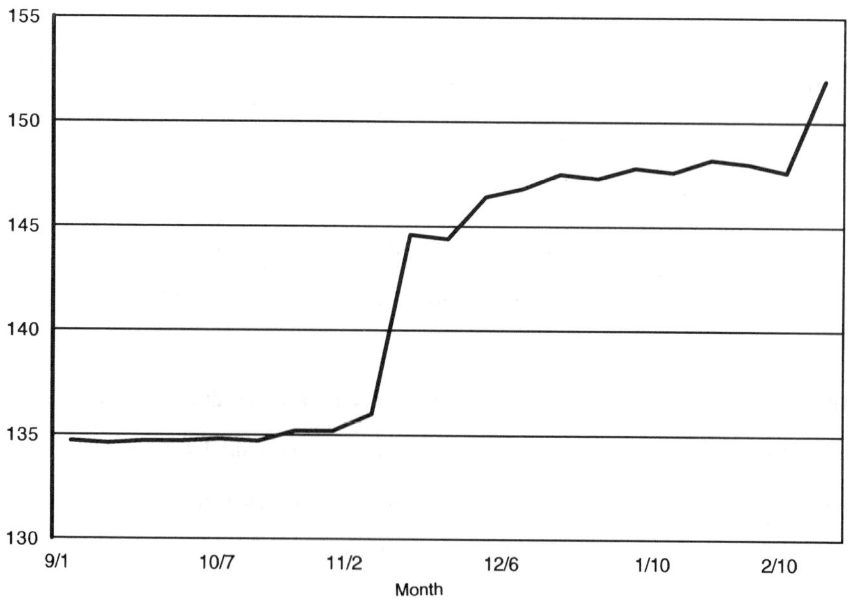

Figure 3.4 Historical Movement of SSE Treasury Bond Futures (Contract 327, 9/94–2/95)

Currency

Currency Futures/Options/Futures Options

The domestic market features no listed currency futures or options, though it is in the process of introducing OTC currency forwards on RMB/US$, RMB/HK$ and RMB/JPY, as discussed later in this chapter.

Commodity

Commodity Futures/Options/Futures Options

As indicated at the beginning of the chapter, the primary thrust of the domestic Chinese derivative market has been in the area of commodity futures (though interest rate futures have attracted most attention of late). We confine our discussion in this section to contracts offered by major exchanges which have been (or are widely expected to be) relicensed by the CSRC. This section focuses on futures offered via the Beijing Commodity Exchange (BCE), Changchun United Commodity Exchange (CUCE), China Commodity Futures Exchange of Hainan (CCFEH), China Zhengzhou Commodity Exchange (CZCE), Dalian Commodity Exchange (DCE), Guandgong United Futures Exchange (GUFE), Nanfang Non-ferrous Metals Exchange (NNME), Nanjing Petroleum Exchange (NANPEX), Shanghai Cereals and Oils Exchange (SCOE), Shanghai Commodity Exchange (SCE), Shanghai Metals Exchange (SME), Shanghai Petroleum Exchange, Shenyang Commodity Exchange (SyCE), Shenzhen Metal and United Futures Exchange (SMUFE), Suzhou Commodity Exchange (SuCE) and Tianjin United Futures Exchange (TUFE) (as indicated above, we have not detailed contract information for Chengdu United Commodities Futures Exchange (CUCFE)).

It should be noted that due to temporary bans enacted by the government to control speculative activity (which has fuelled price inflation in certain commodities), a number of contracts listed below have been temporarily suspended (e.g. diesel, rice, sugar); nonetheless, we present full details on all futures (both active and suspended) under the assumption that the government will lift its ban on restricted commodities in the near term (as it has done in the past) and that trading will resume. It should also be noted that, unlike contracts offered on other Asia Pacific exchanges, direct foreign participation in Chinese futures is not presently permitted.

When reviewing contract details and the similarity of offerings between various domestic exchanges, it is clear why so many contracts have been unable to gain sufficient liquidity to be successful; there is substantial duplication of contracts in many segments of the market (often caused by poor telecommunications or transportation infrastructure which forces exchanges to create their own local/regional contracts) and that duplication has directly impacted liquidity. Elimination of contract duplication is one of China's key challenges and is likely to take several years to accomplish. Table 3.27 details the number of similar or identical contracts available on major domestic exchanges.

The BCE has managed to incorporate three distinct segments of the commodity market into its product range, including agriculture, chemical by-products and metals. Within the agricultural sector BCE trades futures on corn, red bean, soybean, soybean meal, vegetable oil, domestic wheat, rice, green beans, peanut kernel and white sugar; it also trades rubber, plywood and sodium carbonate contracts. Within the chemical by-product sector BCE lists futures on polyvinyl chloride (PVC) and polypropylene, and in metals it lists futures on copper, aluminium and wire rods. Note that BCE's product offering is very similar to that of both CZCE and GUFE. As indicated above, speculative trading in futures, leading to inflationary pressures in the underlying reference commodities, has resulted in temporary suspension of certain BCE contracts in the past. Nonetheless, all the contracts listed below are actively traded on the Exchange when suspensions are not in force. As at June 1995, the green bean future was the BCE's most active contract, with open interest of 255,000 contracts and active quotes in the next six contract months. Plywood and red bean futures were only moderately active and quoted to the next two contracts; all others were only modestly active or completely inactive. Tables 3.28 through 3.47 contain relevant details on BCE's agricultural, chemical and base metal futures.

Futures Contract	Number of identical contracts on domestic exchanges
Corn	7
Soybean	7
Soybean Meal	6
Red Bean	9
Green Bean	5
Rice	5
Sugar	3
Wheat	5
Copper	9
Aluminium	8

Table 3.27 Summary of Identical Contracts on Domestic Exchanges

Contract	Corn Futures
Type	Domestic
Exchange	Beijing Commodity Exchange
Months	January, March, May, July, September, November
Contract Size	10 tons
Tick Value	RMB10/contract
Daily Limit	+/– RMB400/contract against previous day's settlement price
Deliverable Grade	Physical settlement of PRC national standard Grade 2 corn via warehouse receipts*
Last Trading Day	7th business day prior to the last business day of the contract month
Delivery Day	5th business day after the last trading day
Real-time price data	Reuters: <0#BCN:>; Telerate: 56200

* Alternate grades (Grade 1, 3) deliverable into the contract at a premium or discount to the base futures price

Table 3.28 Contract Specifications for BCE Corn Futures

Contract	Red Bean Futures
Type	Domestic
Exchange	Beijing Commodity Exchange
Months	January, March, May, July, September, November
Contract Size	10 tons
Tick Value	RMB20
Daily Limit	+/– RMB1200/contract against previous day's settlement price
Deliverable Grade	Physical settlement of PRC national standard red beans
Last Trading Day	20th business day prior to the last business day of the contract month
Delivery Day	5th business day after the last trading day
Real-time price data	Reuters: <0#BRB:>; Telerate: 56202

Table 3.29 Contract Specifications for BCE Red Bean Futures

Contract	Soybean Futures
Type	Domestic
Exchange	Beijing Commodity Exchange
Months	January, March, May, July, September, November
Contract Size	10 tons
Tick Value	RMB10/contract
Daily Limit	+/– RMB100/contract against previous day's settlement price
Deliverable Grade	Physical settlement of PRC national standard Grade 3 soybeans via warehouse receipts*
Last Trading Day	7th business day prior to the last business day of the contract month
Delivery Day	5th business day after the last trading day
Real-time price data	Reuters: <0#BSB:>; Telerate: 56200

* Alternate grades (Grades 1, 2, 4) deliverable into the contract at a premium or discount to the base futures price

Table 3.30 Contract Specifications for BCE Soybean Futures

Contract	Soybean Meal Futures
Type	Domestic
Exchange	Beijing Commodity Exchange
Months	Every month within next 12 months
Contract Size	10 tons
Tick Value	RMB10/contract
Daily Limit	+/– RMB300/contract against previous day's settlement price
Deliverable Grade	Physical settlement of PRC national standard Grade 2 feedstock soybean meal via warehouse receipts
Last Trading Day	7th business day prior to the last business day of the contract month
Delivery Day	5th business day after the last trading day
Real-time price data	None available

Table 3.31 Contract Specifications for BCE Soybean Meal Futures

Contract	Vegetable Oil Futures
Type	Domestic
Exchange	Beijing Commodity Exchange
Months	April, June, September, October, December
Contract Size	5 tons
Tick Value	RMB5/contract
Daily Limit	+/– RMB100/contract against previous day's settlement price
Deliverable Grade	Physical settlement of PRC national standard Grade 2 vegetable oil via warehouse receipts*
Last Trading Day	7th business day prior to the last business day of the contract month
Delivery Day	5th business day after the last trading day
Real-time price data	Telerate: 56201

*Alternate grades of raw vegetable oil deliverable into the contract at a premium or discount to the base futures price

Table 3.32 Contract Specifications for BCE Vegetable Oil Futures

Contract	Domestic Wheat Futures
Type	Domestic
Exchange	Beijing Commodity Exchange
Months	January, March, May, July, September, November
Contract Size	10 tons
Tick Value	RMB20/contract
Daily Limit	+/– RMB50/contract against previous day's settlement price
Deliverable Grade	Physical settlement of PRC national standard Grade 3 hard/soft North China wheat via warehouse receipts
Last Trading Day	12th day of the contract month
Delivery Day	5th business day after the last trading day
Real-time price data	None available

Table 3.33 Contract Specifications for BCE Domestic Wheat Futures

Contract	Domestic Rice Futures
Type	Domestic
Exchange	Beijing Commodity Exchange
Months	January, March, May, July, September, November
Contract Size	10 tons
Tick Value	RMB10/contract
Daily Limit	+/– RMB60/contract against previous day's settlement price
Deliverable Grade	Physical settlement of PRC national standard hard rice via warehouse receipts*
Last Trading Day	12th day of the contract month
Delivery Day	5th business day after the last trading day
Real-time price data	None available

* Alternate grades of special grade hard rice deliverable into the contract at a premium or discount to the base futures price

Table 3.34 Contract Specifications for BCE Domestic Rice Futures

Contract	Green Bean Futures
Type	Domestic
Exchange	Beijing Commodity Exchange
Months	January, March, May, July, September, November
Contract Size	10 tons
Tick Value	RMB20/contract
Daily Limit	+/– RMB120/contract against previous day's settlement price
Deliverable Grade	Physical settlement of PRC national standard Grade 2 green beans via warehouse receipts
Last Trading Day	12th day of the contract month
Delivery Day	5th business day after the last trading day
Real-time price data	Reuters: <0#BGN:>; Telerate: 56202

Table 3.35 Contract Specifications for BCE Green Bean Futures

Contract	Peanut Kernel Futures
Type	Domestic
Exchange	Beijing Commodity Exchange
Months	January, March, May, July, September, November
Contract Size	10 tons
Tick Value	RMB20/contract
Daily Limit	+/– RMB120/contract against previous day's settlement price
Deliverable Grade	Physical settlement of PRC national standard Grade 3 peanut kernels via warehouse receipts
Last Trading Day	12th day of the contract month
Delivery Day	5th business day after the last trading day
Real-time price data	None available

Table 3.36 Contract Specifications for BCE Peanut Kernel Futures

Contract	White Sugar Futures
Type	Domestic
Exchange	Beijing Commodity Exchange
Months	January, March, May, July, September, November
Contract Size	10 tons
Tick Value	RMB10/contract
Daily Limit	+/– RMB120/contract against previous day's settlement price
Deliverable Grade	Physical settlement of PRC national standard Grade 1 white sugar via warehouse receipts*
Last Trading Day	13th day of the contract month
Delivery Day	5th business day after the last trading day
Real-time price data	Telerate: 56201

* Alternate grades of white sugar deliverable into the contract at a premium or discount to the base futures price

Table 3.37 Contract Specifications for BCE White Sugar Future

Contract	Plywood Futures
Type	Domestic
Exchange	Beijing Commodity Exchange
Months	February, April, June, September, October, December
Contract Size	400 pieces
Tick Value	RMB8/contract
Daily Limit	+/– RMB600/contract against previous day's settlement price
Deliverable Grade	Physical settlement of PRC national standard plywood lumber via warehouse receipts
Last Trading Day	15th day of the contract month
Delivery Day	5th business day after the last trading day
Real-time price data	Reuters: <0#BPW:>

Table 3.38 Contract Specifications for BCE Plywood Futures

Contract	RSS3 Rubber Futures
Type	Domestic/Offshore
Exchange	Beijing Commodity Exchange
Months	January, March, September, December
Contract Size	10 tons
Tick Value	RMB40/contract
Daily Limit	+/– RMB400/contract against previous day's settlement price
Deliverable Grade	Physical settlement of imported RSS3 rubber (ribbed smoked sheet #3) via warehouse receipts
Last Trading Day	15th day of the contract month
Delivery Day	5th business day after the last trading day
Real-time price data	None available

Table 3.39 Contract Specifications for BCE RSS3 Rubber Futures

Contract	Sodium Carbonate Futures
Type	Domestic
Exchange	Beijing Commodity Exchange
Months	Every month up to 12 months forward
Contract Size	10 tons
Tick Value	RMB20/contract
Daily Limit	+/– RMB60/contract against previous day's settlement price
Deliverable Grade	Physical settlement of PRC national standard sodium carbonate with 99% purity via warehouse receipts
Last Trading Day	15th day of the contract month
Delivery Day	5th business day after the last trading day
Real-time price data	Reuters: <0#BSC:>

Table 3.40 Contract Specifications for BCE Sodium Carbonate Futures

Contract	Polypropylene Futures
Type	Domestic
Exchange	Beijing Commodity Exchange
Months	Every month up to 12 months forward
Contract Size	10 tons
Tick Value	RMB50/contract
Daily Limit	+/– RMB150/contract against previous day's settlement price
Deliverable Grade	Physical settlement of PRC national standard polypropylene via warehouse receipts
Last Trading Day	15th day of the contract month
Delivery Day	5th business day after the last trading day
Real-time price data	Reuters: <0#BPQ:>

Table 3.41 Contract Specifications for BCE Polypropylene Futures

Contract	Polyvinyl chloride (PVC) Futures
Type	Domestic
Exchange	Beijing Commodity Exchange
Months	Every month up to 12 months forward
Contract Size	10 tons
Tick Value	RMB50/contract
Daily Limit	+/– RMB150/contract against previous day's settlement price
Deliverable Grade	Physical settlement of PRC national standard Grade 2 polyvinyl chloride via warehouse receipts
Last Trading Day	15th day of the contract month
Delivery Day	5th business day after the last trading day
Real-time price data	None available

Table 3.42 Contract Specifications for BCE Polyvinyl chloride (PVC) Futures

BCE lists two copper and two aluminium contracts, along with wire rod contracts. The copper and aluminium futures compete directly with those offered on China's specialized metals exchanges, SME and SMUFE.

Contract	Copper #1 Futures
Type	Domestic
Exchange	Beijing Commodity Exchange
Months	Every month up to 12 months forward
Contract Size	25 tons
Tick Value	RMB250/contract
Daily Limit	+/– 5% against previous day's settlement price
Deliverable Grade	Physical settlement of PRC national standard copper #1 via warehouse receipts
Last Trading Day	17th day of the contract month
Delivery Day	5th business day after the last trading day
Real-time price data	Reuters: <0#BCU:>

Table 3.43 Contract Specifications for BCE Copper #1 Futures

Contract	Copper BJ Futures
Type	Domestic
Exchange	Beijing Commodity Exchange
Months	Every month up to 12 months forward
Contract Size	25 tons
Tick Value	RMB250/contract
Daily Limit	+/– 5% against previous day's settlement price
Deliverable Grade	Physical settlement of PRC national standard copper #BJ via warehouse receipts
Last Trading Day	17th day of the contract month
Delivery Day	5th business day after the last trading day
Real-time price data	None available

Table 3.44 Contract Specifications for BCE Copper BJ Futures

Contract	Graded Aluminium Futures
Type	Domestic
Exchange	Beijing Commodity Exchange
Months	Every month up to 12 months forward
Contract Size	25 tons
Tick Value	RMB250/contract
Daily Limit	+/– 5% against previous day's settlement price
Deliverable Grade	Physical settlement of PRC national standard graded aluminium via warehouse receipts
Last Trading Day	17th day of the contract month
Delivery Day	5th business day after the last trading day
Real-time price data	Reuters: <0#BAL:>

Table 3.45 Contract Specifications for BCE Graded Aluminium Futures

Contract	Aluminium BJ Futures
Type	Domestic
Exchange	Beijing Commodity Exchange
Months	Every month up to 12 months forward
Contract Size	25 tons
Tick Value	RMB250/contract
Daily Limit	+/– 5% against previous day's settlement price
Deliverable Grade	Physical settlement of PRC national standard aluminium #BJ via warehouse receipts
Last Trading Day	17th day of the contract month
Delivery Day	5th business day after the last trading day
Real-time price data	None available

Table 3.46 Contract Specifications for BCE Aluminium BJ Futures

Contract	Wire Rod Futures
Type	Domestic
Exchange	Beijing Commodity Exchange
Months	Every month up to 12 months forward
Contract Size	50 tons
Tick Value	RMB500/contract
Daily Limit	+/– 5% against previous day's settlement price
Deliverable Grade	Physical settlement of PRC national standard 6.5 wire rods via warehouse receipts
Last Trading Day	17th day of the contract month
Delivery Day	5th business day after the last trading day
Real-time price data	None available

Table 3.47 Contract Specifications for BCE Wire Rod Futures

Although hybrid exchanges have proven popular in China, a handful of those which have been relicensed by the CSRC have chosen to remain specialized exchanges. CUCE is one such exchange, concentrating its product line in the agricultural sector. The Exchange's contracts presently include futures on corn, soybeans, soybean meal, red beans, green beans, and white wheat. CUCE also features two agricultural freight index futures based on the cost of transporting 50 tons of corn to Dalian and Shanghai; the contracts are the first freight derivatives to be offered in China (and Asia Pacific). Tables 3.48 through 3.55 contain details on the CUCE futures.

Contract	Corn Futures
Type	Domestic
Exchange	Changchun United Commodity Exchange
Months	Every month to 12 months forward
Contract Size	10 tons
Tick Value	RMB 2/ton
Daily Limit	+/– RMB400 against previous day's settlement price
Deliverable Grade	Physical settlement of PRC national standard yellow corn
Last Trading Day	10th day of the contract month
Delivery Day	Last day of the contract month
Real-time price data	Reuters: <0#ACN:>

Table 3.48 Contract Specifications for CUCE Corn Futures

Contract	Soybean Futures
Type	Domestic
Exchange	Changchun United Commodity Exchange
Months	January, March, May, July, September, November
Contract Size	10 tons
Tick Value	RMB2/ton
Daily Limit	+/– RMB800 against previous day's settlement price
Deliverable Grade	Physical settlement of PRC national standard soybeans
Last Trading Day	10th day of the contract month
Delivery Day	Last day of the contract month
Real-time price data	Reuters: <0#ASB:>

Table 3.49 Contract Specifications for CUCE Soybean Futures

Contract	Soybean Meal Futures
Type	Domestic
Exchange	Changchun United Commodity Exchange
Months	January, March, May, July, September, November
Contract Size	10 tons
Tick Value	RMB2/ton
Daily Limit	+/– RMB 600 against previous day's settlement price
Deliverable Grade	Physical settlement of PRC national standard soybean meal
Last Trading Day	10th day of the contract month
Delivery Day	Last day of the contract month
Real-time price data	Reuters: <0#ASM:>

Table 3.50 Contract Specifications for CUCE Soybean Meal Futures

Contract	Red Bean Futures
Type	Domestic
Exchange	Changchun United Commodity Exchange
Months	January, March, May, July, September, December
Contract Size	10 tons
Tick Value	RMB2/ton
Daily Limit	+/– RMB1,200 against previous day's settlement price
Deliverable Grade	Physical settlement of PRC national standard red beans
Last Trading Day	10th day of the contract month
Delivery Day	Last day of the contract month
Real-time price data	Reuters: <0#ARB:>

Table 3.51 Contract Specifications for CUCE Red Bean Futures

Contract	Green Bean Futures
Type	Domestic
Exchange	Changchun United Commodity Exchange
Months	January, March, May, July, September, November
Contract Size	10 tons
Tick Value	RMB2/ton
Daily Limit	+/– RMB 1,200 against previous day's settlement price
Deliverable Grade	Physical settlement of PRC national standard green beans
Last Trading Day	10th day of the contract month
Delivery Day	Last day of the contract month
Real-time price data	Reuters: <0#AGN:>

Table 3.52 Contract Specifications for CUCE Green Bean Futures

Contract	White Wheat Futures
Type	Domestic
Exchange	Changchun United Commodity Exchange
Months	January, March, May, July, September, November
Contract Size	10 tons
Tick Value	RMB2/ton
Daily Limit	+/– RMB400 against previous day's settlement price
Deliverable Grade	Physical settlement of PRC national standard white wheat
Last Trading Day	10th day of the contract month
Delivery Day	Last day of the contract month
Real-time price data	Reuters: <0#AWT:>

Table 3.53 Contract Specifications for CUCE White Wheat Futures

Contract	Dalian Freight Futures
Type	Domestic
Exchange	Changchun United Commodity Exchange
Months	January, March, May, July, September, November
Contract Size	50 tons of corn moving cost
Tick Value	RMB20
Daily Limit	+/– RMB400 against previous day's settlement price
Deliverable Grade	Cash settlement
Last Trading Day	10th day of the trading month
Delivery Day	Last day of the trading month
Real-time price data	Reuters: <0#AFD:>

Table 3.54 Contract Specifications for CUCE Dalian Freight Futures

Contract	Shanghai Freight Futures
Type	Domestic
Exchange	Changchun United Commodity Exchange
Months	January, March, May, July, September, November
Contract Size	50 tons of corn moving cost
Tick Value	RMB20
Daily Limit	+/– RMB600 against previous day's settlement price
Deliverable Grade	Cash settlement
Last Trading Day	10th day of the trading month
Delivery Day	Last day of the trading month
Real-time price data	Reuters: <0#AFS:>

Table 3.55 Contract Specifications for CUCE Shanghai Freight Futures

CCFEH began as an exchange focused on three agricultural contracts, including sugar forwards, plywood futures and rubber futures; it added RBD palm olein futures, barley futures, robusta coffee futures, cocoa futures and red bean futures (along with the bond futures described earlier) to its listing in late 1994. Unlike other hybrid exchanges CCFEH has avoided listing base metals, chemicals or petroleum products. It should be noted that several of CCFEH's contracts accept offshore deliverables (e.g. palm olein, rubber, plywood). As of June 1995, the Exchange boasted reasonably strong activity in several of its contracts: palm olein futures were actively traded to the next three contract months and featured open interest of 44,000 contracts; rubber futures were traded to the next six contract months and featured open interest of 45,100 contracts; sugar forwards were also traded to the next six contract months and registered open interest of 23,500 contracts; barley futures were active to two contract months and featured open interest of 5,000 contracts; cocoa futures were also active to two contract months and registered open interest of 830 contracts; and coffee futures were quoted to two contract months and recorded open interest of 7,700 contracts. Tables 3.56 through 3.63 contain details on CCFEH's commodity futures contracts.

Contract	**Sugar Forwards**
Type	Domestic
Exchange	China Commodity Futures Exchange of Hainan
Months	January, March, May, July, September, November
Contract Size	5 tons
Tick Value	RMB5/contract
Daily Limit	+/– RMB500/contract against previous day's settlement price
Deliverable Grade	Cash settlement, or physical settlement of PRC national standard Grade 1 sugar at Zhanjiang, Shanghai, Nantong or Suixi
Last Trading Day	On, or before, the 4th business day counting back from last business day of the month
Delivery Day	Day after the last trading day
Real-time price data	Reuters: <0#HWS:>

Table 3.56 Contract Specifications for CCFEH Sugar Forwards

Contract	RBD Palm Olein Futures
Type	Domestic/Offshore
Exchange	China Commodity Futures Exchange of Hainan
Months	February, April, June, August, October, December
Contract Size	5 tons
Tick Value	RMB5/contract
Daily Limit	+/– RMB200/contract against previous day's settlement price
Deliverable Grade	Cash settlement, or physical settlement of palm olein defined by Palm Oil Refiner Association of Malaysia, delivered at Shanghai, Beihai, Shenzhen, Tianjing, or Zhanjiang
Last Trading Day	On, or before, the 4th business day counting back from last business day of the month
Delivery Day	Day after the last trading day
Real-time price data	Reuters: <0#HPL:>

Table 3.57 Contract Specifications for CCFEH RBD Palm Olein Futures

Contract	Barley Futures
Type	Domestic
Exchange	China Commodity Futures Exchange of Hainan
Months	January, March, May, July, September, November
Contract Size	10 tons
Tick Value	RMB10/contract
Daily Limit	+/– RMB500/contract against previous day's settlement price
Deliverable Grade	Physical settlement of national standard barley
Last Trading Day	On, or before, the 10th business day counting back from last business day of the month
Delivery Day	Day after the last trading day
Real-time price data	Reuters: <0#HBL:>

Table 3.58 Contract Specifications for CCFEH Barley Futures

Contract	Robusta Coffee Futures
Type	Domestic
Exchange	China Commodity Futures Exchange of Hainan
Months	March, May, July, September, December
Contract Size	1 ton
Tick Value	RMB10/contract
Daily Limit	+/– RMB1000/contract against previous day's settlement price
Deliverable Grade	Physical settlement of national standard robusta coffee
Last Trading Day	On, or before, the 10th business day counting back from last business day of the month
Delivery Day	Day after the last trading day
Real-time price data	Reuters: <0#HCF:>

Table 3.59 Contract Specifications for CCFEH Robusta Coffee Futures

Contract	Cocoa Futures
Type	Domestic
Exchange	China Commodity Futures Exchange of Hainan
Months	March, May, July, September, December
Contract Size	1 ton
Tick Value	RMB10/contract
Daily Limit	+/– RMB500/contract against previous day's settlement price
Deliverable Grade	Physical settlement of national standard cocoa beans
Last Trading Day	On, or before, the 10th business day counting back from last business day of the month
Delivery Day	Day after the last trading day
Real-time price data	Reuters: <0#HCC:>

Table 3.60 Contract Specifications for CCFEH Cocoa Futures

Contract	Rubber Futures
Type	Domestic/Offshore
Exchange	China Commodity Futures Exchange of Hainan
Months	January, March, May, June, July, August, September, November, December
Contract Size	2 tons
Tick Value	RMB2/contract
Daily Limit	+/– RMB250/contract against previous day's settlement price
Deliverable Grade	Cash settlement, or physical settlement of PRC national standard SCR rubber (standard China rubber) or RSS1 rubber (ribbed smoked sheet #1), or International Rubber Quality and Packing standard RSS3 rubber (ribbed smoked sheet #3), delivered at Haikou or Zhanjiang
Last Trading Day	On, or before, the 4th business day counting back from last business day of the month
Delivery Day	Day after the last trading day
Real-time price data	Reuters: <0#HRU:>

Table 3.61 Contract Specifications for CCFEH Rubber Futures

Contract	Plywood Futures
Type	Domestic/Offshore
Exchange	China Commodity Futures Exchange of Hainan
Months	January, March, May, July, September, November
Contract Size	300 pieces
Tick Value	RMB3/contract
Daily Limit	+/– RMB200/contract against previous day's settlement price
Deliverable Grade	Cash settlement, or physical settlement of JPIC standard BBCC grade Indonesian plywood delivered at Zhangjiagang, Zhanjiang, or Shanghai
Last Trading Day	On, or before, the 4th business day counting back from last business day of the month
Delivery Day	Day after the last trading day
Real-time price data	None available

Table 3.62 Contract Specifications for CCFEH Plywood Futures

Contract	Red Bean Futures
Type	Domestic
Exchange	China Commodity Futures Exchange of Hainan
Months	January, March, May, September, November
Contract Size	10 tons
Tick Value	RMB20/contract
Daily Limit	+/– RMB300/contract against previous day's settlement price
Deliverable Grade	Cash settlement, or physical settlement of PRC national standard Grade 2 red beans delivered at Tianjing
Last Trading Day	On, or before, the 10th business day counting back from last business day of the month
Delivery Day	Day after the last trading day
Real-time price data	None available

Table 3.63 Contract Specifications for CCFEH Red Bean Futures

CZCE lists and trades futures contracts on wheat, corn, soybeans, green beans, hard rice, peanut kernel, soybean meal, red beans, and cotton yarn; these agricultural products form the mainstay of the Exchange. In 1995 CZCE expanded outside its traditional domain to list and trade contracts on aluminium and Treasury bonds; CZCE's product offering is now almost identical to that of BCE and GUFE. As of June 1995, only three of CZCE's contracts were especially active; the remainder were virtually inactive or dormant. Specifically, wheat futures were quoted to four contract months and featured open interest of 7,000 contracts; corn futures were traded to five contract months and registered open interest of 300 contracts; and green bean futures were quoted to six contract months and featured open interest of nearly 137,000 contracts. Tables 3.64 through 3.73 contain relevant details on all CZCE commodity futures contracts.

Contract	Wheat Futures
Type	Domestic
Exchange	China Zhengzhou Commodity Exchange
Months	January, March, May, July, September, November
Contract Size	10 tons
Tick Value	RMB20/contract
Daily Limit	+/– RMB30 against previous day's settlement price
Deliverable Grade	Physical settlement of PRC national standard wheat (North China Grade 3 hard wheat or soft wheat) via warehouse receipts*
Last Trading Day	7th business day prior to the last business day of the contract month
Delivery Day	Prior to the end of the contract month
Real-time price data	Reuters: <0#CWT:>

* Alternate grades of domestic wheat are deliverable into the contracts at premium or discount prices: North China Grade 1 hard/soft white wheat at a 6% premium, North China Grade 2 hard/soft white wheat at a 3% premium, North China Grade 2 blended hard/soft dotted wheat at a 3% discount, North China Grade 3 blended hard/soft dotted wheat at a 6% discount.

Table 3.64 Contract Specifications for CZCE Wheat Futures

Contract	Corn Futures
Type	Domestic
Exchange	China Zhengzhou Commodity Exchange
Months	January, March, May, July, September, November
Contract Size	10 tons
Tick Value	RMB20/contract
Daily Limit	+/– RMB20 against previous day's settlement price
Deliverable Grade	Physical settlement of PRC national standard Grade 2 yellow corn (from regions other than Northeast China) via warehouse receipts*
Last Trading Day	7th business day prior to the last business day of the contract month
Delivery Day	Prior to the end of the contract month
Real-time price data	Reuters: <0#CCN:>

* Alternate grades of domestic corn are deliverable into the contract at premium or discount prices: Grade 1 yellow corn at a 4% premium, Grade 2 yellow corn at a 4% discount.

Table 3.65 Contract Specifications for CZCE Corn Futures

Contract	Soybean Futures
Type	Domestic
Exchange	China Zhengzhou Commodity Exchange
Months	January, March, May, July, September, November
Contract Size	10 tons
Tick Value	RMB 20/contract
Daily Limit	+/– RMB40 against previous day's settlement price
Deliverable Grade	Physical settlement of PRC national standard Grade 3 yellow soybeans via warehouse receipts*
Last Trading Day	7th business day prior to the last business day of the contract month
Delivery Day	Prior to the end of the contract month
Real-time price data	Reuters: <0#CSB:>

* Alternate grades of domestic soybeans are deliverable into the contract at premium or discount prices: Grade 1 yellow soybeans at a 6% premium, Grade 2 yellow soybeans at a 3% premium, Grade 4 yellow soybeans at a 3% discount.

Table 3.66 Contract Specifications for CZCE Soybean Futures

Contract	Soybean Meal Futures
Type	Domestic
Exchange	China Zhengzhou Commodity Exchange
Months	January, March, May, July, September, November
Contract Size	10 tons
Tick Value	RMB20/contract
Daily Limit	+/– RMB80 against previous day's settlement price
Deliverable Grade	Physical settlement of PRC national standard Grade 2 feedstock soybean meal, via warehouse receipts*
Last Trading Day	7th business day prior to the last business day of the contract month
Delivery Day	Prior to the end of the contract month
Real-time price data	Reuters: <0#CSL:>

* Alternate grades of soybean meal are deliverable into the contract at premium or discount prices: Grade 1 feedstock soybean meal at a 3% premium, Grade 3 feedstock soybean meal at a 3% discount.

Table 3.67 Contract Specifications for CZCE Soybean Meal Futures

Contract	Green Bean Futures
Type	Domestic
Exchange	China Zhengzhou Commodity Exchange
Months	January, March, May, July, September, November
Contract Size	10 tons
Tick Value	RMB20/contract
Daily Limit	+/– RMB80 against previous day's settlement price
Deliverable Grade	Physical settlement of PRC national standard Grade 2 mixed green beans, via warehouse receipts*
Last Trading Day	7th business day prior to the last business day of the contract month
Delivery Day	Prior to the end of the contract month
Real-time price data	Reuters: <0#CGL:>

* Alternate grades of domestic green beans are deliverable into the contract at premium or discount prices: Grade 1 mixed green beans at a 3% premium, Grade 2 mixed green beans at a 3% discount.

Table 3.68 Contract Specifications for CZCE Green Bean Futures

Contract	Hard Rice Futures
Type	Domestic
Exchange	China Zhengzhou Commodity Exchange
Months	January, March, May, October, December
Contract Size	10 tons
Tick Value	RMB20/contract
Daily Limit	+/– RMB60 against previous day's settlement price
Deliverable Grade	Physical settlement of PRC national standard Grade 2 hard rice via warehouse receipts*
Last Trading Day	7th business day prior to the last business day of the contract month
Delivery Day	Prior to the end of the contract month
Real-time price data	Reuters: <0#CRD:>

* Alternate grades of hard rice are deliverable into the contract at premium or discount prices: special grade hard rice at a 9% premium, standard grade hard rice at a 4% premium.

Table 3.69 Contract Specifications for CZCE Hard Rice Futures

Contract	Peanut Kernel Futures
Type	Domestic
Exchange	China Zhengzhou Commodity Exchange
Months	January, March, May, June, November
Contract Size	10 tons
Tick Value	RMB20/contract
Daily Limit	+/– RMB80 against previous day's settlement price
Deliverable Grade	Physical settlement of PRC national standard Grade 3 peanut kernel, via warehouse receipts*
Last Trading Day	7th business day prior to the last business day of the contract month
Delivery Day	Prior to the end of the contract month
Real-time price data	Reuters: <0#CPK:>

* Alternate grades of peanut kernel are deliverable into the contract at premium or discount prices: Grade 1 peanut kernel at a 6% premium, Grade 2 peanut kernel at a 3% premium.

Table 3.70 Contract Specifications for CZCE Peanut Kernel Futures

Contract	Red Bean Futures
Type	Domestic
Exchange	China Zhengzhou Commodity Exchange
Months	January, March, May, September, November
Contract Size	10 tons
Tick Value	RMB20/contract
Daily Limit	+/– RMB60 against previous day's settlement price
Deliverable Grade	Physical settlement of PRC national standard Grade 2 red beans, via warehouse receipts*
Last Trading Day	7th business day prior to the last business day of the contract month
Delivery Day	Prior to the end of the contract month
Real-time price data	Reuters: <0#CRB:>

* Alternate grades of red beans are deliverable into the contract at premium or discount prices: Grade 1 red beans at a 4% premium, Grade 3 red beans at a 4% discount.

Table 3.71 Contract Specifications for CZCE Red Bean Futures

Contract	Cotton Yarn Futures
Type	Domestic
Exchange	China Zhengzhou Commodity Exchange
Months	March, June, August, October, December
Contract Size	10 tons
Tick Value	RMB20/contract
Daily Limit	+/– RMB600 against previous day's settlement price
Deliverable Grade	Physical settlement of PRC national standard cotton yarn
Last Trading Day	7th business day prior to the last business day of the contract month
Delivery Day	Prior to the end of the contract month
Real-time price data	Reuters: <0#CCY:>

Table 3.72 Contract Specifications for CZCE Cotton Yarn Futures

Contract	Aluminium Futures
Type	Domestic
Exchange	China Zhengzhou Commodity Exchange
Months	March, June, August, October, December
Contract Size	10 tons
Tick Value	RMB20/contract
Daily Limit	+/– RMB500 against previous day's settlement price
Deliverable Grade	Physical settlement of PRC national standard aluminium
Last Trading Day	7th business day prior to the last business day of the contract month
Delivery Day	Prior to the end of the contract month
Real-time price data	Reuters: <0#CAL:>

Table 3.73 Contract Specifications for CZCE Aluminium Futures

As mentioned above, DCE is focused strictly on agricultural futures. It presently lists and trades contracts on corn, green beans, red beans, rice, soybeans, soybean meal, soybean oil and wheat; its listing is very similar to that of SCOE and TUFE. Virtually all of DCE's futures contracts are inactive or only modestly active at the present time, with the exception of corn and soybeans. Corn futures are traded to the next six contract months and featured open interest of just over 255,000 contracts as of mid-1995; soybean futures were considerably less active, trading in the near month only and featuring open interest of just 400 contracts. Tables 3.74 through 3.81 contain relevant contract specifications on DCE's futures.

Contract	**Corn Futures**
Type	Domestic
Exchange	Dalian Commodity Exchange
Months	January, March, May, July, September, November
Contract Size	10 tons
Tick Value	RMB20/contract
Daily Limit	+/– 5% against previous day's settlement price
Deliverable Grade	Physical settlement of PRC national standard yellow corn
Last Trading Day	10th business day of the contract month
Delivery Day	Day after the last trading day
Real-time price data	Reuters: <0#DCN:>

Table 3.74 Contract Specifications for DCE Corn Futures

Contract	**Green Bean Futures**
Type	Domestic
Exchange	Dalian Commodity Exchange
Months	January, March, May, July, September, November
Contract Size	10 tons
Tick Value	RMB20/contract
Daily Limit	+/– 5% against previous day's settlement price
Deliverable Grade	Physical settlement of PRC national standard green beans
Last Trading Day	10th business day of the contract month
Delivery Day	Day after the last trading day
Real-time price data	Reuters: <0#DGR:>

Table 3.75 Contract Specifications for DCE Green Bean Futures

Contract	Red Bean Futures
Type	Domestic
Exchange	Dalian Commodity Exchange
Months	January, March, May, July, September, November
Contract Size	10 tons
Tick Value	RMB20/contract
Daily Limit	+/– 5% against previous day's settlement price
Deliverable Grade	Physical settlement of PRC national standard red beans
Last Trading Day	10th business day of the contract month
Delivery Day	Day after the last trading day
Real-time price data	Reuters: <0#DRB:>

Table 3.76 Contract Specifications for DCE Red Bean Futures

Contract	Rice Futures
Type	Domestic
Exchange	Dalian Commodity Exchange
Months	January, March, May, July, September, November
Contract Size	10 tons
Tick Value	RMB20/contract
Daily Limit	+/– 5% against previous day's settlement price
Deliverable Grade	Physical settlement of PRC national standard hard rice
Last Trading Day	10th business day of the contract month
Delivery Day	Day after the last trading day
Real-time price data	Reuters: <0#DRI:>

Table 3.77 Contract Specifications for DCE Rice Futures

Contract	Soybean Futures
Type	Domestic
Exchange	Dalian Commodity Exchange
Months	January, March, May, July, September, November
Contract Size	10 tons
Tick Value	RMB20/contract
Daily Limit	+/– 5% against previous day's settlement price
Deliverable Grade	Physical settlement of PRC national standard soybeans
Last Trading Day	10th business day of the contract month
Delivery Day	Day after the last trading day
Real-time price data	Reuters: <0#DSY:>

Table 3.78 Contract Specifications for DCE Soybean Futures

Contract	Soybean Meal Futures
Type	Domestic
Exchange	Dalian Commodity Exchange
Months	January, March, May, July, September, November
Contract Size	10 tons
Tick Value	RMB20/contract
Daily Limit	+/– 5% against previous day's settlement price
Deliverable Grade	Physical settlement of PRC national standard soybean meal
Last Trading Day	10th business day of the contract month
Delivery Day	Day after the last trading day
Real-time price data	Reuters: <0#DSM:>

Table 3.79 Contract Specifications for DCE Soybean Meal Futures

Contract	Soybean Oil Futures
Type	Domestic
Exchange	Dalian Commodity Exchange
Months	January, March, May, July, September, November
Contract Size	10 tons
Tick Value	RMB20/contract
Daily Limit	+/– 5% against previous day's settlement price
Deliverable Grade	Physical settlement of PRC national standard soybean oil
Last Trading Day	10th business day of the contract month
Delivery Day	Day after the last trading day
Real-time price data	Reuters: <0#DSO:>

Table 3.80 Contract Specifications for DCE Soybean Oil Futures

Contract	Wheat Futures
Type	Domestic
Exchange	Dalian Commodity Exchange
Months	January, March, May, July, September, November
Contract Size	10 tons
Tick Value	RMB20/contract
Daily Limit	+/– 5% against previous day's settlement price
Deliverable Grade	Physical settlement of PRC national standard wheat
Last Trading Day	10th business day of the contract month
Delivery Day	Day after the last trading day
Real-time price data	Reuters: <0#DWT:>

Table 3.81 Contract Specifications for DCE Wheat Futures

As indicated earlier, GUFE is another example of a hybrid exchange which lists and trades futures on softs, energy and base metals (in addition to interest rates, as discussed above); its listing is very similar to that of BCE and CZCE. In softs, the Exchange currently lists sugar forwards, along with soybean, soybean meal, corn and rice futures; in energy products it lists gasoil and 90- and 70-octane gasoline futures; and, in metals, it lists aluminium, national copper and Guangzhou copper futures (note that GUFE previously listed diesel and heating oil futures but abandoned them in 1995). Tables 3.82 through 3.92 contain relevant details on the GUFE contracts.

Contract	**Sugar Forwards**
Type	Domestic
Exchange	Guangdong United Futures Exchange
Months	Every month to 12 months forward
Contract Size	50 tons
Tick Value	RMB50
Daily Limit	+/– 3% against previous day's settlement price
Deliverable Grade	Physical settlement of PRC national standard white sugar
Last Trading Day	20th day of the contract month
Delivery Day	1st business day after the last trading day to the last business day of the delivery month
Real-time price data	Reuters: <0#USF:>

Table 3.82 Contract Specifications for GUFE Sugar Forwards

Contract	**Soybean Futures**
Type	Domestic
Exchange	Guangdong United Futures Exchange
Months	January, March, May, July, September, November
Contract Size	10 tons
Tick Value	RMB10
Daily Limit	+/– 5% against previous day's settlement price
Deliverable Grade	Physical settlement of PRC national standard soybeans
Last Trading Day	15th day of the contract month
Delivery Day	Up to five business days after the 20th day of the contract month
Real-time price data	None available

Table 3.83 Contract Specifications for GUFE Soybean Futures

Contract	Soybean Meal Futures
Type	Domestic
Exchange	Guangdong United Futures Exchange
Months	January, March, May, July, September, November
Contract Size	10 tons
Tick Value	RMB10
Daily Limit	+/– 5% against previous day's settlement price
Deliverable Grade	Physical settlement of PRC national standard soybean meal
Last Trading Day	15th day of the contract month
Delivery Day	Up to five business days after the 20th day of the contract month
Real-time price data	Reuters: <0#USM:>

Table 3.84 Contract Specifications for GUFE Soybean Meal Futures

Contract	Corn Futures
Type	Domestic
Exchange	Guangdong United Futures Exchange
Months	January, March, May, July, September, November
Contract Size	10 tons
Tick Value	RMB10
Daily Limit	+/– 5% against previous day's settlement price
Deliverable Grade	Physical settlement of PRC national standard yellow corn
Last Trading Day	15th day of the contract month
Delivery Day	Up to five business days after the 20th day of the contract month
Real-time price data	None available

Table 3.85 Contract Specifications for GUFE Corn Futures

Contract	Long Grain Rice Futures
Type	Domestic
Exchange	Guangdong United Futures Exchange
Months	January, March, May, July, September, November
Contract Size	10 tons
Tick Value	RMB10
Daily Limit	+/– 5% against previous day's settlement price
Deliverable Grade	Physical settlement of PRC national standard polished, long grain, non-glutinous rice
Last Trading Day	15th day of the contract month
Delivery Day	Up to five business days after the 20th day of the contract month
Real-time price data	Reuters: <0#URC:>

Table 3.86 Contract Specifications for GUFE Long Grain Rice Futures

Contract	Gasoline (90 octane) Futures
Type	Domestic
Exchange	Guangdong United Futures Exchange
Months	Every month to 12 months forward
Contract Size	100 tons
Tick Value	RMB1
Daily Limit	+/– 3% against previous day's settlement price
Deliverable Grade	Physical settlement of PRC national standard grade gasoline, 90 octane
Last Trading Day	15th day of the contract month
Delivery Day	3rd business day after the last trading day until the 10th business day after the last trading day
Real-time price data	Reuters: <0#UAO:>

Table 3.87 Contract Specifications for GUFE Gasoline (90 octane) Futures

Contract	**Gasoline (70 octane) Futures**
Type	Domestic
Exchange	Guangdong United Futures Exchange
Months	Every month to 12 months forward
Contract Size	100 tons
Tick Value	RMB1
Daily Limit	+/– 3% against previous day's settlement price
Deliverable Grade	Physical settlement of PRC national standard grade gasoline, 70 octane
Last Trading Day	15th day of the contract month
Delivery Day	3rd business day after the last trading day until the 10th business day after the last trading day
Real-time price data	None available

Table 3.88 Contract Specifications for GUFE Gasoline (70-octane) Futures

Contract	**Gasoil Futures**
Type	Domestic
Exchange	Guangdong United Futures Exchange
Months	Every month to 12 months forward
Contract Size	100 tons
Tick Value	RMB1
Daily Limit	+/– 3% against previous day's settlement price
Deliverable Grade	Physical settlement of PRC national standard grade #0 gasoil
Last Trading Day	15th day of the contract month
Delivery Day	3rd business day after the last trading day until the 10th business day after the last trading day
Real-time price data	Reuters: <0#UGO:>

Table 3.89 Contract Specifications for GUFE Gasoil Futures

Contract	Aluminium Futures
Type	Domestic
Exchange	Guangdong United Futures Exchange
Months	Every month to 12 months forward
Contract Size	25 tons
Tick Value	RMB250
Daily Limit	+/– 3% against previous day's settlement price
Deliverable Grade	Physical settlement of PRC national standard grade aluminium, 99.7% pure
Last Trading Day	10th day of the contract month
Delivery Day	21st day of the contract month until the 26th day of contract month
Real-time price data	Reuters: <0#UAL:>

Table 3.90 Contract Specifications for GUFE Aluminium Futures

Contract	Copper Futures
Type	Domestic
Exchange	Guangdong United Futures Exchange
Months	Every month to 12 months forward
Contract Size	25 tons
Tick Value	RMB250
Daily Limit	+/– 3% against previous day's settlement price
Deliverable Grade	Physical settlement of PRC national standard grade aluminium, 99.95% pure
Last Trading Day	10th day of the contract month
Delivery Day	21st day of the contract month until the 26th day of the contract month
Real-time price data	Reuters: <0#UCU:>

Table 3.91 Contract Specifications for GUFE Copper Futures

Contract	Guangzhou Copper Futures
Type	Domestic
Exchange	Guangdong United Futures Exchange
Months	Every month to 12 months forward
Contract Size	25 tons
Tick Value	RMB250
Daily Limit	+/– 3% against previous day's settlement price
Deliverable Grade	Physical settlement of PRC national standard grade aluminium, 99.95% pure, Guangzhou origin
Last Trading Day	10th day of the contract month
Delivery Day	21st day of the contract month until the 26th day of the contract month
Real-time price data	Reuters: <0#UCF:>

Table 3.92 Contract Specifications for GUFE Guangzhou Copper Futures

NNME's activity is still based on standardized forward contracts rather than futures contracts (though a conversion to the latter is under discussion). The Exchange currently offers aluminium forwards, Shanghai copper forwards and Guangzhou copper forwards. The aluminium contract is its most active derivative, with quotes to the next three contract months and open interest of 10,100 contracts as of mid-1995. The NNME contracts compete with those offered via SME, BCE, SMUFE and GUFE (note that GUFE offers a Guangzhou copper contract as well). Tables 3.93 through 3.95 contain relevant contract specifications on NNME's derivatives.

Contract	Aluminium Forwards
Type	Domestic
Exchange	Nanfang Non-ferrous Metals Exchange
Months	Every month to 12 months forward
Contract Size	25 tons
Tick Value	RMB250
Daily Limit	+/– 3% against previous day's settlement price
Deliverable Grade	Physical settlement of PRC national standard grade aluminium, 99.95% pure
Last Trading Day	22nd day of the contract month
Delivery Day	Last business day of the contract month
Real-time price data	Reuters: <0#NAL:>

Table 3.93 Contract Specifications for NNME Aluminium Forwards

Contract	Shanghai Copper Forwards
Type	Domestic
Exchange	Nanfang Non-ferrous Metals Exchange
Months	Every month to 12 months forward
Contract Size	25 tons
Tick Value	RMB250
Daily Limit	+/– 3% against previous day's settlement price
Deliverable Grade	Physical settlement of standard grade copper, Shanghai origin
Last Trading Day	22nd day of the contract month
Delivery Day	Last business day of the contract month
Real-time price data	Reuters: <0#NCU:>

Table 3.94 Contract Specifications for NNME Shanghai Copper Forwards

Contract	Guangzhou Copper Forwards
Type	Domestic
Exchange	Nanfang Non-ferrous Metals Exchange
Months	Every month to 12 months forward
Contract Size	25 tons
Tick Value	RMB250
Daily Limit	+/– 3% against previous day's settlement price
Deliverable Grade	Physical settlement of standard grade copper, Guangzhou origin
Last Trading Day	22nd day of the contract month
Delivery Day	Last business day of the contract month
Real-time price data	Reuters: <0#NCF:>

Table 3.95 Contract Specifications for NNME Guangzhou Copper Forwards

NANPEX currently lists futures on gasoil and gasoline, though it is in the process of reviewing additional energy-related derivatives. It is also considering conversion to a hybrid exchange (tentatively to be known as Nanjing Commodity

Exchange), offering non-energy contracts; timing of such a conversion remains uncertain. Note that NANPEX's contracts compete with those offered on BCE and GUFE. Tables 3.96 and 3.97 contain relevant contract details on the NANPEX energy futures.

Contract	**Gasoil Futures**
Type	Domestic
Exchange	Nanjing Petroleum Exchange
Months	Spot month plus 12 consecutive months
Contract Size	100 tons
Tick Value	RMB 2
Daily Limit	N/A
Deliverable Grade	Physical settlement of PRC national standard grade #0 gasoil, delivered at Nanjing Port or Nantong Port
Last Trading Day	Last business day of the month prior to the contract month
Delivery Day	Last business day of the contract month
Real-time price data	None available

Table 3.96 Contract Specifications for NANPEX Gasoil Futures

Contract	**Gasoline Futures**
Type	Domestic
Exchange	Nanjing Petroleum Exchange
Months	Spot month plus 12 consecutive months
Contract Size	100 tons
Tick Value	RMB 2
Daily Limit	N/A
Deliverable Grade	Physical settlement of PRC national standard gasoline, delivered at Nanjing Port
Last Trading Day	Last business day of the month prior to the contract month
Delivery Day	Last business day of the contract month
Real-time price data	None available

Table 3.97 Contract Specifications for NANPEX Gasoline Futures

SCOE trades corn, green bean, red bean, rice, soybean and wheat futures; its product listing is virtually identical to that of DCE and TUFE. SCOE's most active contracts at the present time are on soybeans and corn. The soybean future is generally quoted to the next four contract months and featured open interest of 120,000 contracts at mid-1995; the corn future is quoted to the next two contract months and registered open interest of 7,200 contracts at mid-1995. Tables 3.98 through 3.103 contain relevant details on the Exchange's agricultural contracts.

Contract	**Corn Futures**
Type	Domestic
Exchange	Shanghai Cereals and Oils Exchange
Months	March, May, July, September, December
Contract Size	5 tons
Tick Value	RMB5
Daily Limit	+/– RMB300 against previous day's settlement price
Deliverable Grade	Physical settlement of PRC national standard yellow corn
Last Trading Day	3rd Monday of the contract month
Delivery Day	Day after the last trading day
Real-time price data	Reuters: <0#SCN:>

Table 3.98 Contract Specifications for SCOE Corn Futures

Contract	**Green Bean Futures**
Type	Domestic
Exchange	Shanghai Cereals and Oils Exchange
Months	January, April, June, July, September, November
Contract Size	5 tons
Tick Value	RMB5
Daily Limit	+/– RMB600 against previous day's settlement price
Deliverable Grade	Physical settlement of PRC national standard green beans
Last Trading Day	3rd Monday of the contract month
Delivery Day	Day after the last trading day
Real-time price data	Reuters: <0#SGB:>

Table 3.99 Contract Specifications for SCOE Green Bean Futures

Contract	Red Bean Futures
Type	Domestic
Exchange	Shanghai Cereals and Oils Exchange
Months	January, March, May, August, November
Contract Size	5 tons
Tick Value	RMB5
Daily Limit	+/– RMB600 against previous day's settlement price
Deliverable Grade	Physical settlement of PRC national standard red beans
Last Trading Day	3rd Monday of the contract month
Delivery Day	Day after the last trading day
Real-time price data	Reuters: <0#SRB:>

Table 3.100 Contract Specifications for SCOE Red Bean Futures

Contract	Long Grain Rice Futures
Type	Domestic
Exchange	Shanghai Cereals and Oils Exchange
Months	January, March, April, May, September, October, December
Contract Size	5 tons
Tick Value	RMB5
Daily Limit	+/– RMB300 against previous day's settlement price
Deliverable Grade	Physical settlement of PRC national standard long grain rice
Last Trading Day	3rd Monday of the contract month
Delivery Day	Day after the last trading day
Real-time price data	Reuters: <0#SRC:>

Table 3.101 Contract Specifications for SCOE Long Grain Rice Futures

Contract	**Soybean Futures**
Type	Domestic
Exchange	Shanghai Cereals and Oils Exchange
Months	January, March, May, July, September, November
Contract Size	5 tons
Tick Value	RMB5
Daily Limit	+/– RMB300 against previous day's settlement price
Deliverable Grade	Physical settlement of PRC national standard soybeans
Last Trading Day	3rd Monday of the contract month
Delivery Day	Day after the the last trading day
Real-time price data	Reuters: <0#SSB:>

Table 3.102 Contract Specifications for SCOE Soybean Futures

Contract	**White Wheat Futures**
Type	Domestic
Exchange	Shanghai Cereals and Oils Exchange
Months	January, March, May, July, September, November
Contract Size	5 tons
Tick Value	RMB5
Daily Limit	+/– RMB300 against previous day's settlement price
Deliverable Grade	Physical settlement of PRC national standard white wheat
Last Trading Day	3rd Monday of the contract month
Delivery Day	Day after the last trading day
Real-time price data	Reuters: <0#SWW:>

Table 3.103 Contract Specifications for SCOE White Wheat Futures

SCE, which was created following the merger of four specialized exchanges in Shanghai, presently offers futures contracts on plywood, rubber and polyvinyl chloride (PVC) (note that SCE's plywood and rubber contracts accept deliverables from offshore). SCE expects to introduce additional contracts in the near future. Tables 3.104 through 3.106 highlight the relevant contract specifications for each SCE future.

Contract	**Plywood Futures**
Type	Domestic/Offshore
Exchange	Shanghai Commodity Exchange
Months	January, March, May, July, September, November
Contract Size	200 sheets
Tick Value	RMB20
Daily Limit	+/– 3% against previous day's settlement price
Deliverable Grade	Physical settlement of standard size, 3 ply, plywood from Indonesia, delivered to Exchange determined warehouses
Last Trading Day	15th day of the contract month
Delivery Day	25th through 27th of the contract month
Real-time price data	Reuters: <0#SPW:>

Table 3.104 Contract Specifications for SCE Plywood Futures

Contract	**Rubber Futures**
Type	Domestic/Offshore
Exchange	Shanghai Commodity Exchange
Months	Every month to 12 months forward
Contract Size	1 ton
Tick Value	RMB10
Daily Limit	+/– 3% against previous day's settlement price
Deliverable Grade	Physical settlement of domestic first class SCR5 (Standard China Rubber #5) or imported RSS3 (ribbed smoked sheet #3), delivered to Exchange approved warehouses
Last Trading Day	15th day of the contract month
Delivery Day	25th through 27th of the contract month
Real-time price data	Reuters: <0#SNR:>

Table 3.105 Contract Specifications for SCE Rubber Futures

Contract	Polyvinyl Chloride (PVC) Futures
Type	Domestic
Exchange	Shanghai Commodity Exchange
Months	Every month to 12 months forward
Contract Size	1 ton
Tick Value	RMB10
Daily Limit	+/– 3% against previous day's settlement price
Deliverable Grade	Physical settlement of domestic first class ethylene polymerization SG5 polyvinyl chloride, delivered to Exchange approved warehouses
Last Trading Day	15th day of the contract month
Delivery Day	25th through 27th of the contract month
Real-time price data	Reuters: <0#SPC:>

Table 3.106 Contract Specifications for SCE Polyvinyl Chloride (PVC) Futures

Although exchanges such as BCE, CZCE, NNME and GUFE list a series of base metals futures (e.g. copper, aluminium), SME and SMUFE (discussed later in this section) remain China's primary metals trading exchanges. The forerunner of SMUFE, the Shenzhen Metal Exchange (ShME) and SME were both established to trade non-ferrous metals on a spot, forward and futures basis, and both have posted significant increases in volume over the past few years. Major reasons for the success of the metals-focused exchanges include the non-perishable nature of the commodities, the relative lack of price intervention by the government, and the affordable transportation costs (particularly in relation to the underlying value of the commodities being traded). China's role as a net importer of certain metals has also contributed to more significant activity by hedgers.

SME's dominant contract is its copper future, though it also features active trading in aluminium futures and growing trading in zinc, nickel, lead and tin futures; the latter four contracts were converted from forwards to futures in 1994. The copper contract is active to five consecutive months while the aluminium contract is generally active to four consecutive months, though both are offered to a total of 12 consecutive months. It should be noted that 80% of the brands deliverable into the copper contract are LME registered brands; physical delivery of metals occurs on 10% to 20% of all contracts traded. Tables 3.107 through 3.112 contain details on all SME futures.

Contract	Copper Futures
Type	Domestic/Offshore
Exchange	Shanghai Metals Exchange
Months	Every month to 12 months forward
Contract Size	25 tons
Tick Value	RMB250
Daily Limit	+/– 2% against previous day's settlement price
Deliverable Grade	Physical settlement of PRC national standard electrolyzed copper #1* (blocks or cut plates) delivered to Exchange approved warehouses
Last Trading Day	15th day of the contract month, or following day if a holiday
Delivery Day	25th day of the contract month, or following day if a holiday
Real-time price data	Reuters: <0#SCF:>

* Specific brands of copper #1 deliverable into the contract include: Shangye, Kuanggong, Tiefeng, Daxiang, Baiyin, Guiye, Tongguan, Jingjing, Tianheng, Yuhang, Shanbao, and Dajiang. The SME also permits delivery of LME approved copper, provided that the owner of the copper submits commodity import certificates.

Table 3.107 Contract Specifications for SME Copper Futures

Contract	Aluminium Futures
Type	Domestic/Offshore
Exchange	Shanghai Metals Exchange
Months	Every month to 12 months forward
Contract Size	25 tons
Tick Value	RMB250
Daily Limit	+/– 2% against previous day's settlement price
Deliverable Grade	Physical settlement of PRC national standard aluminium*, 99.7% pure, in ingots of 15-25 kg, delivered to Exchange approved warehouses
Last Trading Day	15th day of the contract month, following day if a holiday
Delivery Day	25th day of the contract month, following day if a holiday
Real-time price data	Reuters: <0#SAF:>

* Specific brands of high grade aluminium deliverable into the SME contract include: LLL, Xueshan, Haihu, Bailu, Yinjian, Baolu, Lanlu, Shanlu and Qinglu. The SME also permits delivery of LME approved aluminium, provided that the owner of the aluminium submits commodity import certificates.

Table 3.108 Contract Specifications for SME Aluminium Futures

Contract	Lead Futures
Type	Domestic
Exchange	Shanghai Metals Exchange
Months	Every month to 12 months forward
Contract Size	25 tons
Tick Value	RMB250
Daily Limit	+/– 2% against previous day's settlement price
Deliverable Grade	Physical settlement of PRC national standard lead, delivered to Exchange approved warehouses
Last Trading Day	15th day of the contract month, following day if a holiday
Delivery Day	25th day of the contract month, following day if a holiday
Real-time price data	Reuters: <0#SPF:>

Table 3.109 Contract Specifications for SME Lead Futures

Contract	Nickel Futures
Type	Domestic
Exchange	Shanghai Metals Exchange
Months	Every month to 12 months forward
Contract Size	3 tons
Tick Value	RMB30
Daily Limit	+/– 2% against previous day's settlement price
Deliverable Grade	Physical settlement of PRC national standard nickel, delivered to Exchange approved warehouses
Last Trading Day	15th day of the contract month, following day if a holiday
Delivery Day	25th day of the contract month, following day if a holiday
Real-time price data	Reuters: <0#SNF:>

Table 3.110 Contract Specifications for SME Nickel Futures

Contract	Tin Futures
Type	Domestic
Exchange	Shanghai Metals Exchange
Months	Every month to 12 months forward
Contract Size	2 tons
Tick Value	RMB20
Daily Limit	+/– 2% against previous day's settlement price
Deliverable Grade	Physical settlement of PRC national standard tin, delivered to Exchange approved warehouses
Last Trading Day	15th day of the contract month, following day if a holiday
Delivery Day	25th day of the contract month, following day if a holiday
Real-time price data	Reuters: <0#SSF:>

Table 3.111 Contract Specifications for SME Tin Futures

Contract	Zinc Futures
Type	Domestic
Exchange	Shanghai Metals Exchange
Months	Every month to 12 months forward
Contract Size	25 tons
Tick Value	RMB250
Daily Limit	+/– 2% against previous day's settlement price
Deliverable Grade	Physical settlement of PRC national standard zinc, delivered to Exchange approved warehouses
Last Trading Day	15th day of the contract month, following day if a holiday
Delivery Day	25th day of the contract month, following day if a holiday
Real-time price data	Reuters: <0#SZF:>

Table 3.112 Contract Specifications for SME Zinc Futures

SyCE, another of China's hybrid exchanges, lists and trades futures on interest rates (discussed above), as well as base metals (aluminium, copper, wire rod (structured as a forward)), and agriculturals (plywood, various classes of wood, sorghum, barley and peanut kernel). Tables 3.113 through 3.120 contain relevant contract details on SyCE's futures.

Contract	**Peanut Kernel Futures**
Type	Domestic
Exchange	Shenyang Commodity Exchange
Months	January, March, May, July, September, November
Contract Size	5 tons
Tick Value	RMB10
Daily Limit	+/– RMB80 against previous day's settlement price
Deliverable Grade	Physical settlement of PRC national standard peanut kernel
Last Trading Day	15th business day counting back from the last business day of the contract month
Delivery Day	Day after the last trading day
Real-time price data	Reuters: <0#YPK:>

Table 3.113 Contract Specifications for SyCE Peanut Kernel Futures

Contract	**Sorghum Futures**
Type	Domestic
Exchange	Shenyang Commodity Exchange
Months	January, March, May, July, September, November
Contract Size	10 tons
Tick Value	RMB10
Daily Limit	+/– RMB50 against previous day's settlement price
Deliverable Grade	Physical settlement of PRC national standard sorghum
Last Trading Day	15th business day counting back from the last business day of the contract month
Delivery Day	Day after the last trading day
Real-time price data	Reuters: <0#YSH:>

Table 3.114 Contract Specifications for SyCE Sorghum Futures

Contract	Barley Futures
Type	Domestic
Exchange	Shenyang Commodity Exchange
Months	March, April, May, September, November, December
Contract Size	10 tons
Tick Value	RMB10
Daily Limit	+/– RMB80 against previous day's settlement price
Deliverable Grade	Physical settlement of PRC national standard barley
Last Trading Day	Last business day of the month before the contract month
Delivery Day	Day after the last trading day
Real-time price data	Reuters: <0#YBL:>

Table 3.115 Contract Specifications for SyCE Barley Futures

Contract	Wood Futures
Type	Domestic/Offshore
Exchange	Shenyang Commodity Exchange
Months	February, April, June, August, October, December for Mandshurica and Bungeana wood, March, April, June, August, October, December for Gmelinii wood
Contract Size	50 square meters
Tick Value	RMB1
Daily Limit	+/– RMB80, RMB40, RMB70 against previous day's settlement price for Mandshurica, Gmelinii and Bungeana, respectively
Deliverable Grade	Physical settlement of Mandshurica, Bungeana or Gmelinii wood
Last Trading Day	On, or after, the 18th of the contract month
Delivery Day	Day after the last trading day
Real-time price data	Reuters: <0#YWD:>, <0#YWE:>, <0#YWF:>

Table 3.116 Contract Specifications for SyCE Wood Futures

Contract	Plywood Futures
Type	Domestic
Exchange	Shenyang Commodity Exchange
Months	Every month to 12 months forward
Contract Size	200 units
Tick Value	RMB0.1
Daily Limit	+/– RMB2.5 against previous day's settlement price
Deliverable Grade	Physical settlement of PRC national standard plywood
Last Trading Day	On, or after, the 18th of the contract month
Delivery Day	Day after the last trading day
Real-time price data	Reuters: <0#YPW:>

Table 3.117 Contract Specifications for SyCE Plywood Futures

Contract	Copper Futures
Type	Domestic
Exchange	Shenyang Commodity Exchange
Months	Every month to 12 months forward
Contract Size	5 tons
Tick Value	RMB10
Daily Limit	+/– RMB600 against previous day's settlement price
Deliverable Grade	Physical settlement of PRC national standard copper
Last Trading Day	On, or after, the 18th of the contract month
Delivery Day	Day after the last trading day
Real-time price data	Reuters: <0#YCU:>

Table 3.118 Contract Specifications for SyCE Copper Futures

Contract	Aluminium Futures
Type	Domestic
Exchange	Shenyang Commodity Exchange
Months	Every month to 12 months forward
Contract Size	5 tons
Tick Value	RMB10
Daily Limit	+/– RMB300 against previous day's settlement price
Deliverable Grade	Physical settlement of PRC national standard aluminium
Last Trading Day	On, or after, the 18th of the contract month
Delivery Day	Day after the last trading day
Real-time price data	Reuters: <0#YAL:>

Table 3.119 Contract Specifications for SyCE Aluminium Futures

Contract	Wire Rod Forwards
Type	Domestic
Exchange	Shenyang Commodity Exchange
Months	Every month between March and December
Contract Size	10 tons
Tick Value	RMB5
Daily Limit	+/– RMB120 against previous day's settlement price
Deliverable Grade	Physical settlement of PRC national standard wire rods
Last Trading Day	On, or after, the 18th of the contract month
Delivery Day	Day after the last trading day
Real-time price data	Reuters: <0#YWR:>

Table 3.120 Contract Specifications for SyCE Wire Rod Forwards

As indicated earlier in the chapter, SMUFE is now focused primarily on base metals contracts (though it retains a presence in bond futures as well). The Exchange currently lists and trades futures contracts on aluminium, copper, nickel, tin and zinc, as well as standard forward contracts on antimony, lead and magnesium; SMUFE competes most directly with the SME and, to a lesser degree, with BCE and GUFE. The Exchange's copper future is its most active contract, routinely quoted and traded to the next seven contract months; aluminium contracts are also very active, trading in the next three contracts months at any time. Total trading across all futures amounted to RMB160 bln (US$19.2 bln) in 1994; by first quarter 1995 turnover amounted to RMB41.5 bln (US$5 bln), three times more than the first quarter of 1994 (AWSJ, 1995). Since its founding (i.e. when it existed as ShME), the Exchange's mix of business has gravitated from primarily spot with physical delivery to forward/futures (82% of volume) with virtually no physical delivery (less than 1%), as is more traditional for a conventional futures exchange. Tables 3.121 through 3.128 contain relevant contract specifications on SMUFE's futures.

Contract	**Aluminium Futures**
Type	Domestic
Exchange	Shenzhen Metal and United Futures Exchange
Months	Every month to 12 months forward
Contract Size	25 tons
Tick Value	RMB250
Daily Limit	+/– 3% against previous day's settlement price
Deliverable Grade	Physical settlement of PRC national standard aluminium at Guangzhou or Shanghai
Last Trading Day	On, or after, the 20th of the contract month
Delivery Day	Day after the last trading day
Real-time price data	Reuters: <0#ZAL:>

Table 3.121 Contract Specifications for SMUFE Aluminium Futures

Contract	**Copper Futures**
Type	Domestic
Exchange	Shenzhen Metal and United Futures Exchange
Months	Every month to 12 months forward
Contract Size	25 tons
Tick Value	RMB250
Daily Limit	+/– 3% against previous day's settlement price
Deliverable Grade	Physical settlement of PRC national standard copper at Guangzhou or Shanghai
Last Trading Day	On, or after, the 20th of the contract month
Delivery Day	Day after the last trading day
Real-time price data	Reuters: <0#ZCU:>

Table 3.122 Contract Specifications for SMUFE Copper Futures

Contract	Nickel Futures
Type	Domestic
Exchange	Shenzhen Metal and United Futures Exchange
Months	Every month to 12 months forward
Contract Size	2 tons
Tick Value	RMB20
Daily Limit	+/– 3% against previous day's settlement price
Deliverable Grade	Physical settlement of PRC national standard nickel at Guangzhou or Shanghai
Last Trading Day	On, or after, the 20th of the contract month
Delivery Day	Day after the last trading day
Real-time price data	Reuters: <0#ZNI:>

Table 3.123 Contract Specifications for SMUFE Nickel Futures

Contract	Tin Futures
Type	Domestic
Exchange	Shenzhen Metal and United Futures Exchange
Months	Every month to 12 months forward
Contract Size	2 tons
Tick Value	RMB20
Daily Limit	+/– 3% against previous day's settlement price
Deliverable Grade	Physical settlement of PRC national standard tin at Guangzhou or Shanghai
Last Trading Day	On, or after, the 20th of the contract month
Delivery Day	Day after the last trading day
Real-time price data	Reuters: <0#ZSN:>

Table 3.124 Contract Specifications for SMUFE Tin Futures

Contract	Zinc Futures
Type	Domestic
Exchange	Shenzhen Metal and United Futures Exchange
Months	Every month to 12 months forward
Contract Size	25 tons
Tick Value	RMB250
Daily Limit	+/– 3% against previous day's settlement price
Deliverable Grade	Physical settlement of PRC national standard zinc at Guangzhou or Shanghai
Last Trading Day	On, or after, the 20th of the contract month
Delivery Day	Day after the last trading day
Real-time price data	Reuters: <0#ZZN:>

Table 3.125 Contract Specifications for SMUFE Zinc Futures

Contract	Antimony Forwards
Type	Domestic
Exchange	Shenzhen Metal and United Futures Exchange
Months	Every month to 12 months forward
Contract Size	25 tons
Tick Value	RMB250
Daily Limit	+/– 3% against previous day's settlement price
Deliverable Grade	Physical settlement of PRC national standard antimony at Guangzhou or Shanghai
Last Trading Day	On, or after, the 20th of the contract month
Delivery Day	Day after the last trading day
Real-time price data	Reuters: <0#ZSB:>

Table 3.126 Contract Specifications for SMUFE Antimony Forwards

Contract	Lead Forwards
Type	Domestic
Exchange	Shenzhen Metal and United Futures Exchange
Months	Every month to 12 months forward
Contract Size	25 tons
Tick Value	RMB250
Daily Limit	+/– 3% against previous day's settlement price
Deliverable Grade	Physical settlement of PRC national standard lead at Guangzhou or Shanghai
Last Trading Day	On, or after, the 20th of the contract month
Delivery Day	Day after the last trading day
Real-time price data	Reuters: <0#ZPB:>

Table 3.127 Contract Specifications for SMUFE Lead Forwards

Contract	Magnesium Forwards
Type	Domestic
Exchange	Shenzhen Metal and United Futures Exchange
Months	Every month to 12 months forward
Contract Size	25 tons
Tick Value	RMB250
Daily Limit	+/– 3% against previous day's settlement price
Deliverable Grade	Physical settlement of PRC national standard magnesium at Guangzhou or Shanghai
Last Trading Day	On, or after, the 20th of the contract month
Delivery Day	Day after the last trading day
Real-time price data	Reuters: <0#ZMG:>

Table 3.128 Contract Specifications for SMUFE Magnesium Forwards

SuCE remains small by Chinese standards in terms of product line, offering contracts on only three different commodities, including plywood, red beans and rod coils. SuCE's plywood contract is regularly quoted to the next three contract months and featured open interest of 819,000 contracts as of mid-1995; its red bean contract is quoted to two contract months and registered open interest of 38,000 contracts at mid-1995, while rod coil futures are also quoted to two contract months and recorded open interest of 19,300 contracts as of mid-1995. Additional contracts are expected to be listed on SuCE in the near-term. Tables 3.129 through 3.131 provide details on SuCE's futures contracts.

Contract	**Red Bean Futures**
Type	Domestic
Exchange	Suzhou Commodity Exchange
Months	Every month to 6 months forward
Contract Size	2 tons
Tick Value	RMB10
Daily Limit	+/– 3% against previous day's settlement price
Deliverable Grade	Physical settlement of PRC national standard red beans
Last Trading Day	On, or before, the 20th of the contract month
Delivery Day	Day after the last trading day
Real-time price data	Reuters: <0#ORB:>

Table 3.129 Contract Specifications for SuCE Red Bean Futures

Contract	**Plywood Futures**
Type	Domestic
Exchange	Suzhou Commodity Exchange
Months	Every month to 6 months forward
Contract Size	200 sheets
Tick Value	RMB20
Daily Limit	+/– 3% against previous day's settlement price
Deliverable Grade	Physical settlement of PRC national standard plywood
Last Trading Day	On, or before, the 25th of the contract month
Delivery Day	Day after the last trading day
Real-time price data	Reuters <0#OPW:>

Table 3.130 Contract Specifications for SuCE Plywood Futures

Contract	Rod Coil Futures
Type	Domestic
Exchange	Suzhou Commodity Exchange
Months	Every month to 6 months forward
Contract Size	10 tons
Tick Value	RMB10
Daily Limit	+/– 3% against previous day's settlement price
Deliverable Grade	Physical settlement of PRC national standard rod coils
Last Trading Day	On, or before, the 15th of the contract month
Delivery Day	Day after the last trading day
Real-time price data	Reuters: <0#OHP:>

Table 3.131 Contract Specifications for SuCE Rod Coil Futures

TUFE's futures contracts are based strictly on agricultural products; unlike several of the other exchanges discussed in this section, TUFE has elected not to expand into a hybrid exchange. The Exchange currently offers futures contracts on corn, green beans, red beans, Tianjin red beans, soybeans and soybean meal; its contracts compete most directly with those offered by DCE and SCOE. Tables 3.132 through 3.137 contain relevant contract details on all TUFE futures.

Contract	Corn Futures
Type	Domestic
Exchange	Tianjin United Futures Exchange
Months	January, March, May, July, September
Contract Size	10 tons
Tick Value	RMB10
Daily Limit	+/– RMB300 against previous day's settlement price
Deliverable Grade	Physical settlement of PRC national standard yellow corn
Last Trading Day	6th business day of the contract month counting back from the last business day of the month
Delivery Day	Last business day of the contract month
Real-time price data	Reuters: <0#TCN:>

Table 3.132 Contract Specifications for TUFE Corn Futures

Contract	Green Bean Futures
Type	Domestic
Exchange	Tianjin United Futures Exchange
Months	January, March, May, July, September, November
Contract Size	10 tons
Tick Value	RMB10
Daily Limit	+/– RMB1,200 against previous day's settlement price
Deliverable Grade	Physical settlement of PRC national standard green beans
Last Trading Day	6th business day of the contract month counting back from the last business day of the month
Delivery Day	Last business day of the contract month
Real-time price data	Reuters: <0#TGB:>

Table 3.133 Contract Specifications for TUFE Green Bean Futures

Contract	Red Bean Futures
Type	Domestic
Exchange	Tianjin United Futures Exchange
Months	January, March, May, July, September, November
Contract Size	5 tons
Tick Value	RMB5
Daily Limit	+/– RMB900 against previous day's settlement price
Deliverable Grade	Physical settlement of PRC national standard red beans
Last Trading Day	6th business day of the contract month counting back from the last business day of the month
Delivery Day	Last business day of the contract month
Real-time price data	Reuters: <0#TRB:>

Table 3.134 Contract Specifications for TUFE Red Bean Futures

Contract	Tianjin Red Bean Futures
Type	Domestic
Exchange	Tianjin United Futures Exchange
Months	January, March, May, July, September, December
Contract Size	6 tons
Tick Value	RMB6
Daily Limit	+/– RMB1,200 against previous day's settlement price
Deliverable Grade	Physical settlement of red beans of Tianjin province origin
Last Trading Day	6th business day of the contract month counting back from the last business day of the month
Delivery Day	Last business day of the contract month
Real-time price data	Reuters: <0#TRN:>

Table 3.135: Contract Specifications for TUFE Tianjin Red Bean Futures

Contract	Soybean Futures
Type	Domestic
Exchange	Tianjin United Futures Exchange
Months	January, March, May, July, September, November
Contract Size	5 tons
Tick Value	RMB10
Daily Limit	+/– RMB500 against previous day's settlement price
Deliverable Grade	Physical settlement of PRC national standard soybeans
Last Trading Day	6th business day of the contract month counting back from the last business day of the month
Delivery Day	Last business day of the contract month
Real-time price data	Reuters: <0#TSB:>

Table 3.136 Contract Specifications for TUFE Soybean Futures

Contract	Soybean Meal Futures
Type	Domestic
Exchange	Tianjin United Futures Exchange
Months	January, March, May, July, September, November
Contract Size	10 tons
Tick Value	RMB10
Daily Limit	+/– RMB800 against previous day's settlement price
Deliverable Grade	Physical settlement of PRC national standard soybean meal
Last Trading Day	6th business day of the contract month counting back from the last business day of the month
Delivery Day	Last business day of the contract month
Real-time price data	Reuters: <0#TSM:>

Table 3.137 Contract Specifications for TUFE Soybean Meal Futures

LISTED/OVER-THE-COUNTER WARRANTS, CONVERTIBLES AND HYBRIDS

Equity

Equity Warrants

The SHSE, one of China's two stock exchanges, lists and trades a small number of domestic issuer equity warrants. Chinese equity warrants are divided into two broad categories, including A1 warrants and A2 warrants; exercise of A1 and A2 warrants results in the flotation of new equity by the underlying issuer. A1 warrants are offered as public securities and can be traded by a broad range of local investors, while A2 warrants are securities which are transferred from state (or legal person) shareholders to other shareholders. Until 1994, warrants were only issued on A shares (local shares); in June 1994, however, the Exchange permitted the listing and trading of equity warrants on B shares (foreign shares). In order to list B share warrants the Exchange must approve a separate application from the issuer; all B share warrants are traded in 2,000 share lots under the B share trading system. Representative Chinese warrant issuers include Dalian Refrigeration Equipment, Foshan Lighting, Fujian Fufa, Hefei Meran, Jilin Light, Mindong Electric Machine, Ocean Fishing Development, Shenyan Resources, Wuhan Phoenix, Zhongyi Electrical Appliance, Zhuzhai Lizhu Pharmaceutical, Luigong Engineering, Shenbao, Shenyang Resources and Sichuan Salt. Despite the availability of equity warrants, overall liquidity is extremely thin.

Basket/Index Warrants

The domestic market features no basket or index warrants based on local shares or indexes. The offshore market has not issued such warrants either, primarily because executing transactions in the local market to cover exposures resulting from such warrants is difficult and time consuming. China-related basket warrants have been limited to those written on 'H' shares, which are the SEHK-listed shares of Chinese companies (see chapter 4 for additional details).

Convertibles

The local market features a single issue of renminbi-denominated convertible bonds, floated by Baoan and listed on the SHSE; no other renminbi convertibles have been sold to date and prospects for future issuance are uncertain. Given their relative lack of importance in the market, we shall not consider domestic convertibles further.

Despite the lack of active domestic convertible issuance by local companies, certain Chinese companies have accessed the offshore Euroconvertible market in recent years. Issuance of Chinese Euroconvertibles most often occurs in US dollars, with bonds listed on overseas stock exchanges (e.g. Luxembourg) and traded in bearer form on an OTC basis. To date, bonds have carried long maturities (ten years), intermediate coupons (3% to 5%) and intermediate conversion premiums (10% to 15%). If offshore bonds result in conversion, investors receive a fixed amount of local B shares which are traded through the SSE or SHSE. Appendix III contains details on all Chinese convertible bonds.

Index-linked Notes

Onshore or offshore index-linked notes providing enhanced coupons or principal based on appreciation (or depreciation) of local indexes (such as the Shanghai or Shenzhen A or B share indexes), have not been structured to date.

Fixed Income

Fixed Income Warrants

Although the local fixed income market has been growing in size and depth and has been attracting the attention of local investors (e.g. those interested in buying inflation-linked Treasury bonds), fixed income warrants based on local bonds or bond indexes have not been issued to date.

Currency

Currency Warrants

The local and offshore markets do not feature renminbi currency warrants; all domestic currency derivatives activity is expected to be concentrated in the new forward renminbi market which will commence trading in 1996 (as discussed below).

Commodity

Commodity Warrants

Although the Chinese market is very active in commodity trading it has concentrated its resources and efforts in creating commodity forward and futures contracts and has not, to date, listed or traded commodity warrants.

OVER-THE-COUNTER FORWARDS, SWAPS AND OPTIONS

Equity

Equity Forwards/Swaps

OTC equity forwards and swaps are not currently transacted in the domestic or offshore markets, primarily as a result of low investor demand and difficulties in hedging exposures through the local market.

Equity Options

OTC options referencing local Chinese shares are not presently transacted in the domestic or offshore markets, for the same reasons cited above.

Basket/Index Forwards/Swaps

Basket and index forwards and swaps are not presently transacted in the domestic or offshore markets, for the reasons indicated above.

Index Options

OTC index options referencing local Chinese indexes in Shanghai or Shenzhen are not currently transacted either domestically or offshore, for the reasons cited above.

Fixed Income

Fixed Income Forwards/Swaps

A market for domestic fixed income forwards and swaps does not currently exist. OTC fixed income derivatives are not available in the local market primarily because (a) a regime of market-determined domestic interest rates is not yet in existence, (b) actual need for fixing local borrowing costs through local forwards and swaps is negligible; and (c) no meaningful pricing or hedging tools exist for structuring or managing renminbi IRSs or forwards. In the offshore market, certain swaps are structured where fixed renminbi is exchanged for floating renminbi based on the rates implied by offshore FX forwards; such transactions, however, are exceptionally rare. Until the points detailed above are resolved and broader deregulation of the financial market occurs, it is unlikely that the market for renminbi forwards and IRSs will expand.

Fixed Income Options

There is presently no market for renminbi caps, floors, swaptions or bond options, for the same reasons cited in the section immediately above. In most derivative markets introduction of fixed income options tends to lag introduction of vanilla forwards and swaps; as such, it is likely to be some time before renminbi fixed income options are featured in the local market.

Currency

Currency Forwards/Swaps

Although the renminbi is a tightly controlled currency, the Shanghai-based Foreign Exchange Centre (FEC) began 'paper trading' RMB/US$ forwards on a trial basis in mid-1995, with the intent of introducing official forward trading in 1996. Renminbi forwards will be available in maturities of 30, 60, 90 and 180 days. Trading will occur on a daily basis through the FEC in Shanghai and prices will be based on the previous day's spot closing of RMB/US$. The 30-day forward will be permitted to fluctuate by as much as 500 basis points around the previous day's spot, the 60-day contract up to 800 basis points, the 90-day contract up to 1,200 basis points and the 180-day contract up to 1,800 basis points. Foreign banks are currently permitted to buy spot renminbi with foreign currencies (US dollars, yen and Hong Kong dollars) but cannot buy foreign currencies with renminbi; likewise, foreign banks will only be allowed to buy forward renminbi with US dollars, but will not be able to buy forward US dollars with renminbi. Foreign-funded Chinese enterprises will be permitted to take either side of the forward transaction. It should be noted that firms wanting to trade FX forwards will be required to demonstrate they have existing FX positions at trade date and can do so by producing FX contracts or certificates. Although domestic forwards are still in the preliminary stages of development, the offshore market already features a small amount of non-deliverable forwards (NDFs, or dollar-settled exchange agreements). NDFs are forwards tied to the value of RMB/US$ which result in net dollar settlement of the market value of the contract at maturity rather than exchange of physical currencies; use of NDFs permits offshore institutions to gain access to the movement in renminbi without having to deal with restrictions regarding currency conversion.

There is currently no domestic onshore market for CCSs. Institutions in the offshore market, however, arrange very intermittent CCSs of renminbi against US dollars. Such transactions are generally short-term in maturity and do not typically result in the exchange of principal (given substantial currency restrictions and sovereign risk considerations); as with NDFs, non-deliverable CCSs result in the net exchange of US dollars (or some other foreign currency) at the conclusion of the transaction rather than physical exchange of principal or coupon flows.

Currency Options

There is currently no market for domestic onshore renminbi currency options. OTC currency options of renminbi against the US dollar (and occasionally the Hong Kong dollar or yen) are structured on an *ad hoc* basis in the offshore market. Such transactions generally carry short-term maturities (one to six months) and most often result in foreign currency cash settlement of the net market value of the option rather than exercise into physical delivery of renminbi and foreign currency.

Commodity

Commodity Forwards/Swaps

The market for OTC commodity forwards and swaps is not yet established within China. Although there is an active market for listed forwards and futures based on local commodities (and certain offshore commodities), the same interest has not yet transferred to the OTC market.

Commodity Options

As with commodity forwards and swaps above, the market for local OTC commodity options is not yet in existence.

LOCAL REGULATORY/LEGAL TREATMENT OF DERIVATIVES

The primary regulators of China's financial markets, institutions and instruments include the China Securities Regulatory Commission (CSRC), the People's Bank of China (PBC) and the Securities Commission of the State Council (SCSC). The CSRC is responsible for implementation, control and supervision of all activities related to the issuance and trading of securities, including futures. The PBC is primarily responsible for approving applications for the establishment of securities institutions and for regulating their business activities once established. The SCSC, created as recently as 1994, is charged with overseeing the administration of the national securities market at a macro level; the department, working in cooperation with the CSRC, has as one of its main priorities the guiding, planning, co-ordinating and supervising of futures exchanges at the national level. Other government bodies involved in regulatory matters (though often in a more indirect fashion) include the Ministry of Finance, the Assets Administration Bureau, the Shanghai Stock Exchange and the Shenzhen Stock Exchange (as well as the municipal governments which control the exchanges).

One of the most significant challenges facing China in the development and expansion of its financial markets is regulatory reform, particularly as applied to its derivatives market. Reform of the local futures market, and of regulations governing the futures market, has been a priority for the CSRC since 1993. The CSRC and the China Securities Supervisory Administrative Committee are responsible for supervising futures trading within the country and the two bodies are presently considering a number of changes in order to bring futures trading to a more advanced stage of development. Key priorities for the regulators include: reducing the number of regional exchanges/commodity trading centres in order to avoid fragmenting the market (which might reduce the probabilities of creating national markets and contracts with sustainable liquidity); fostering more price independence and less government intervention in the cash markets so that forward and future prices are not distorted; developing a sound and secure clearinghouse system for listed contracts, in order that all participants are adequately protected; encouraging the abandonment of unsuccessful contracts in order to focus attention on those which have an opportunity of succeeding; and establishing more effective financing, transportation and warehousing mechanisms to encourage more hedgers and arbitrageurs to participate in the market. If these tasks can be completed it is likely that the Chinese futures market will emerge as a successful derivatives forum.

The first major regulatory effort towards reform took place in April 1993 when the State Administration for Industry and Commerce (SAIC) adopted the 'Futures Brokerage Firms Registration and Management Regulation'. The aim of the regulation was to provide tighter control of futures brokers. To that end, regulations now require futures brokers to be registered with the SAIC, to have at least RMB10 mln (US$1.2 mln) in capital, to place 25% of capital on deposit in a guarantee fund, to have in place a marketing/sales staff of at least 20 people, and to ensure availability and use of appropriate accounting and control mechanisms.

A second major regulatory step was taken in May 1994 when the China State Council issued Directive 69; the aim of the Directive was to begin consolidating and controlling the country's burgeoning futures industry. The Directive was issued as it became apparent that speculative futures trading was causing price inflation in raw materials such as coal, petroleum, sugar and steel bars; futures trading on such commodities was banned on a temporary basis, and was followed by subsequent bans on rice and rapeseed in September 1994. The Directive was also aimed at controlling the activity of unauthorized brokers, particularly those operating in Guangdong and Fujian. The specific elements of the Directive included: a moratorium on the establishment of new exchanges; relicensing of all existing exchanges, which would only be done if an exchange could prove that 90% of its business was from forwards/futures, physical settlement of commodities was less than 5% of turnover, average daily turnover in the first four months of 1994 exceeded RMB95 mln (US$11.5MM), at least 50 members belonged to the exchange, at least ten exchange officials had futures experience, and the exchange was located in a major city and was housed in adequate facilities (note: the relicensing process was performed by the State Industrial and Commercial Executive Management Bureau, and monitored by the CSRC); suspension on the licensing of new futures brokers; re-registration of existing brokers by the CSRC and the SAIC (note that in mid-1994, a total of 300 futures brokers were suspended and forced to re-register (CSB, 7/94)); ban on foreign-owned/joint venture brokers; restrictions on sending customer orders overseas (through omnibus accounts); and ban on speculative futures transactions by state-owned enterprises (enterprises posting profits were still permitted to use overseas exchanges for hedging purposes). On the latter point, the CSRC (in co-operation with the State Economic and Trading Commission and the Ministry of Internal Trade (MIT)) drew up separate orders requiring all state enterprises to receive approval before engaging in any type of futures trading. The MIT initially reviewed individual applications by state enterprises to determine hedging needs and suitability of such hedging, and now requires submission of quarterly reports detailing both profits/losses and futures positions. All state enterprises using futures trading for hedging purposes are subject to periodic audits. As a result of Directive 69, dozens of exchanges were closed down and there are now only 15 recognized exchanges (in various stages of the re-licensing process, as discussed at the beginning of the chapter).

As mentioned earlier, the Chinese Treasury bond futures speculation of early 1995 prompted a further tightening of regulations. The CSRC, in its document entitled 'Provisional Regulations on Management in Treasury Bond Futures Trading', outlined a series of steps designed to prevent further abuse of the cash and futures markets, including: raising minimum margins on bond futures to 10% (e.g. RMB 2,000 (US$238) per contract) in ordinary months and 20% in spot months (and up to 85% three days prior to delivery); establishing maximum daily price movement of RMB 0.5 per contract (from a previous high of RMB 2.5) – the price limit was raised to RMB 2 in late March after trading stabilized; banning overdrafts on Treasury futures; requiring physical delivery of Treasury bonds through transfers of bonds or, in the case of paperless securities, via bank accounts – no cash delivery permissible; permitting bond futures dealing only on approved trading floors; requiring adherence to both intra-day and end-of-day position limits; lowering the ceiling on open interest in the bond contract; setting position limits for both retail investors (ranging from 10,000 to 30,000 contracts) and brokers (up to 30% of outstanding contracts); and re-registering via CSRC and MOF all exchanges and brokers for specific dealing in Treasury bond futures. These are rather broad reforms, designed to prevent a re-occurrence of the February 1995 events. While there was initial concern the reforms would be perceived as overly restrictive, draining activity from the market, such appears not to have happened. Immediately after the reforms were put in place, daily turnover in bond futures subsided to RMB7 bln to RMB10 bln (US$830 mln to US$1.2 bln); however, after just four weeks daily volumes increased to the RMB 70 bln to 80 bln range (US$8.3 bln to US$9.5 bln) (Foo, 1995). Speculative activity in bond futures resumed in April/May 1995, at which time all bond futures trading was temporarily suspended. The suspension led to a flow of funds into local equities as well as other futures contracts (e.g. green bean futures, plywood futures, and so on which experienced soaring prices and volumes on the basis of speculative buying). Timing of the reinstatement of bond futures is uncertain but is expected in the near term.

In the midst of various regulatory attempts to control and restructure the futures markets, the CSRC put forth a further regulatory change in June 1995, calling for all approved exchanges to convert from profit organizations into non-profit membership organizations by December 1995. By restructuring the exchanges into non-profit entities the CSRC has indicated that it hopes to re-order the priorities of exchanges (e.g. the safety of participants as opposed to the profits of exchanges).

As a final note, the Hong Kong Securities and Futures Commission (SFC) and the CSRC signed a joint agreement in July 1995 calling for mutual co-operation on the regulatory front between 1995 and 1997. The SFC hopes to provide the CSRC with information on its own experience in creating and regulating what is now a very active and successful futures exchange.

LOCAL ACCOUNTING PRACTICES FOR DERIVATIVES

Given that the Chinese domestic derivative market is still very underdeveloped (and focused almost exclusively on listed futures), and given that the accounting framework in China is still in the very early stages of development (and attempting to conform to fundamental international accounting procedures such as dual entry (debit/credit) accounting, and so on), it is not surprising to note that there are no specific local accounting practices for domestic derivatives. Until the accounting practice is more firmly integrated in the local financial system and domestic derivative activity is more widespread, introduction of specific derivative accounting rules is unlikely to occur.

PROSPECTS FOR THE LOCAL DERIVATIVE MARKET

Summarized below are the near-term (one to three year) and medium-term (three to five year) prospects for Chinese domestic derivatives.

Near-term:

- Greater turnover in key commodity futures as exchange and contract consolidation continue and regulatory reforms promote greater balance between speculators and hedgers.
- Abandonment of listed commodity futures which generate no turnover or open interest.
- Re-introduction of listed bond futures trading on select exchanges; expanded liquidity in such derivatives as the fixed income market continues deregulating and exchanges attract a more balanced mix of hedgers and speculators.

- Gradual growth of spot and forward renminbi trading as currency forwards are launched.
- Creation of new listed financial derivatives (e.g. index, currency) as the market gains additional experience in futures trading, regulators promote further financial deregulation, and financial markets stabilize and become less dependent on speculative flows.
- Development of new onshore OTC financial derivatives (e.g. IRSs, CCSs, fixed income and currency options) as commercial and financial deregulation progresses, domestic benchmarks are established and market volatility increases.

Medium-term:

- Increased volume and liquidity in listed commodity futures trading as the domestic market completes regulatory reform.
- Expanded liquidity in bond futures as financial deregulation frees interest-rate movements and as exchanges, hedgers and speculators gain experience in trading such instruments.
- Growth in liquidity of OTC interest rate and currency derivatives as the financial marketplace becomes more sophisticated, financial deregulation leads to market-driven rates/prices (with greater volatility), and foreign institutions are permitted to participate in the domestic market (perhaps selectively).
- Increased co-operation with exchanges in Hong Kong regarding mutual product offering/trading as sovereign changeover is concluded.

Note: unlike other chapters in this text where we summarize contract volumes for each listed future/option contract we elect not to do so in this chapter, primarily because: (a) most contracts were developed in 1994; and (b) most have undergone changes in contract specifications such that volume comparison may be misleading.

	Overall Liquidity	**Liquid/ Maximum Maturity**	**Interbank dealing size**	**Average bid-offer spread**
Equity/Index Swaps	non-existent	n/a	n/a	n/a
Equity/Index Options	non-existent	n/a	n/a	n/a
Interest Rate Swaps	non-existent	n/a	n/a	n/a
Interest Rate Options	non-existent	n/a	n/a	n/a
Currency Swaps	non-existent	n/a	n/a	n/a
Currency Options	non-existent	n/a	n/a	n/a

Table 3.138 Summary of Domestic OTC Derivatives

4: Hong Kong

FINANCIAL MARKET OVERVIEW

Hong Kong's domestic financial markets are among the most dynamic and advanced of the Asia Pacific region. The local financial system features a vibrant equity market with substantial primary and secondary activity from both domestic and offshore participants. The local currency market is also very active and features unrestricted trading of spot and forward Hong Kong dollars. The fixed income market, while less developed than the equity and currency markets, is growing on both a primary and secondary basis; although the Hong Kong bond market has historically been corporate in nature (featuring regular private sector issuance of fixed and floating rate bonds and certificates of deposit (CDs)), government borrowing has become more apparent in recent years through rejuvenated bill and bond programmes. As a result of its vibrant cash markets, Hong Kong's derivative market has developed into an important component of the domestic financial system: listed and OTC derivatives are common, innovation is considerable, and liquidity is on the rise.

The Hong Kong equity market dates back to 1871 when the original Hong Kong Stock Exchange (HKSE) was established. The HKSE existed as the territory's sole equity trading forum for nearly a hundred years until several regional exchanges were created, including the Far East Exchange (1969), the Kam Ngan Stock Exchange (1971), and the Kowloon Stock Exchange (1972). In 1986, after nearly 20 years of independent trading, all three exchanges were absorbed by the HKSE and the combined entity was renamed the Stock Exchange of Hong Kong (SEHK). The SEHK is Hong Kong's sole equity trading centre at the present time.

Trading in the local equity market is very extensive. Domestic investors have a long history of investing in both larger capitalization blue chip companies and smaller capitalization local companies and the combination provides the market with excellent liquidity. Foreign investors, who have unrestricted access to local shares, have also been active and were a major reason for the local market's strong performance in 1993. Though the market receded from its peak during 1994, primary and secondary activity remained buoyant; total market capitalization of US$269.5 bln at the end of 1994 ranks the Hong Kong market as the third largest of Asia Pacific's 13 markets (after Japan and Australia). Figure 4.1 traces the historical movement of the bellwether Hang Seng Index, while Table 4.1 contains key data regarding the Hong Kong stock market.

Figure 4.1 Historical Movement of the Hang Seng Index

Year*	Market Capitalization (US$ bln)	Trading Value (US$ bln)	Listed Companies (#)
1994	269.5	147.1	529
1993	385.2	131.6	450
1992	172.1	78.6	386
1991	122.0	38.6	333
1990	83.4	34.6	284

* to December of each year; Source: IFC, 1995

	1/92–6/95 Annualized Return*	1/92–6/95 Total Return*
Hang Seng Index	25.26%	111.78%

* dividends reinvested in index

Table 4.1 Domestic Equity Market Indicators

Hong Kong's fixed income market features growing issuance and trading of sovereign and private sector instruments. The Hong Kong sovereign market is based on Exchange Fund Bills (EFBs) and Exchange Fund Notes (EFNs) which were originally introduced in 1990–91 as replacements to the government's original, and rarely used, medium-term bond programme. Early EFB issues were available with maturities of three, six and 12 months, while EFNs were available with maturities of two and three years; five-year notes were added in 1994 and seven year notes were added in late 1995. Primary and secondary activity has increased steadily since 1990 and further growth appears likely. Total sovereign outstandings amounted to HK$44.3 bln (US$5.73 bln) at the end of 1994 (and included HK$36.8 bln (US$4.75 bln) of EFBs, HK$6 bln (US$775 mln) of EFNs and HK$1.5 bln (US$200 mln) of medium-term government bonds). Figure 4.2 illustrates the historical movement of the Hong Kong sovereign yield curve, while Figure 4.3 traces the movement of the benchmark two year EFN yield. The private sector fixed income market features active issuance of short-term CDs (either fixed rate or floating rate (pegged to Hong Kong Interbank Offer Rate (HIBOR)), as well as medium-term fixed rate CDs, and fixed and floating rate corporate bonds (with maturities ranging from one to ten years). Banks, corporations and supranational organizations are all active participants in the local market and overall volumes have been growing on both a primary and secondary basis for several years. Although there are still sovereign risk considerations associated with Hong Kong's handover to China, overall issuance appears not to have been slowed by the prospect of sovereign transfer; indeed, larger and more frequent debt issues have been apparent in recent years and bond maturities routinely exceed the July 1997 changeover date (though paper maturing after 1997 still commands a risk premium). Total private sector outstandings amounted to HK$148 bln (US$19.15 bln) at the end of 1994 (and included HK$ 87.8 bln (US$11.35 bln) of short-term CDs and HK$60.2 bln (US$7.8 bln) of medium-term CDs and bonds).

The primary interest rates in the Hong Kong market include HIBOR (the borrowing cost for prime banks in the interbank market), EFB and EFN yields (the short- and medium-term borrowing costs of the government (through the Exchange Fund)), Hong Kong dollar CD rates (the borrowing cost for local and foreign banks in the domestic CD market), and Hong Kong dollar swap rates (the rate for transacting domestic interest rate swaps in the interbank market). Table 4.2 summarizes the payment frequency, compounding frequency and day count convention for each of the key Hong Kong rates.

The Hong Kong dollar (HK$) is a freely convertible currency pegged to the value of the US dollar. The peg to the dollar has been in place since October 1983; prior to 1972, the Hong Kong dollar had been linked to sterling. Hong Kong features an unrestricted and active market for spot trading of the local currency, with average daily volume of HK$23 bln (US$3 bln) to HK$27 bln (US$3.5 bln). Average interbank dealing size is HK$77 mln (US$10 mln), though transactions of up to HK$380 mln and HK$770 mln (US$50 mln and US$100 mln) are reasonably

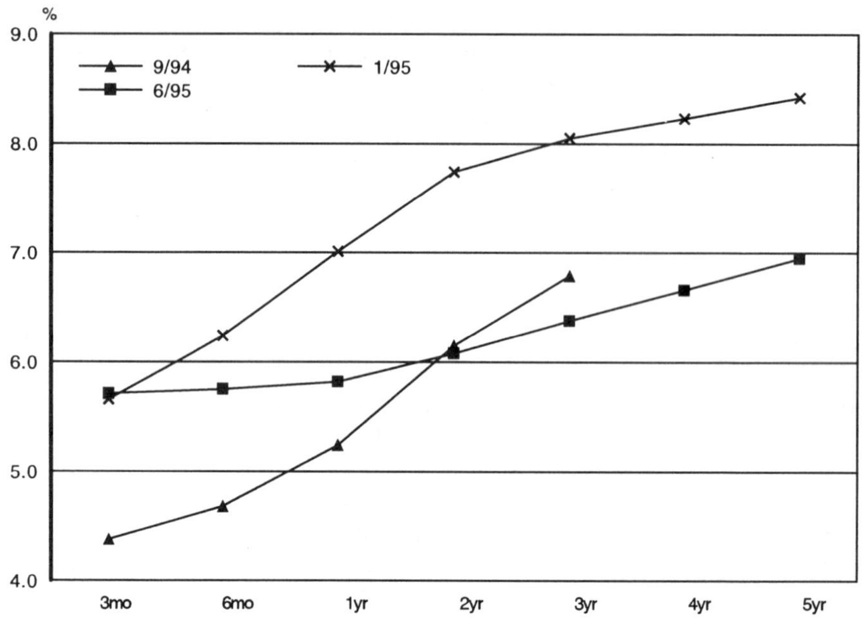

Figure 4.2 Historical Movement of Hong Kong Government Yield Curve

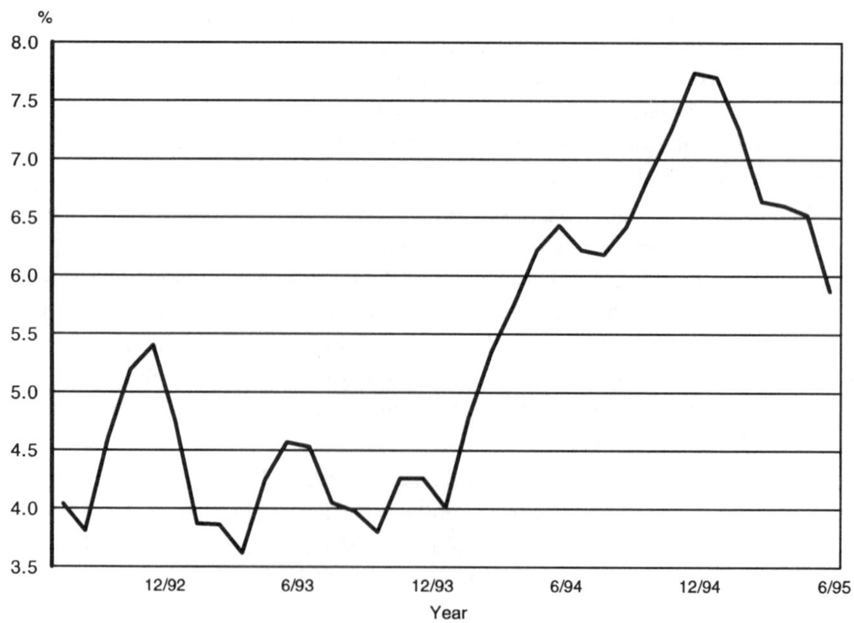

Figure 4.3 Historical Movement of Two-year Exchange Fund Note Yields

Rate	Payment Frequency	Compounding Frequency	Day Count Convention
HIBOR	–	–	Actual/360
EFB	–	–	Actual/365
EFN	semi-annual	semi-annual	Actual/365
HK$ CD	quarterly	quarterly	Actual/365
Swaps	quarterly	quarterly	Actual/365

Table 4.2 Domestic Interest Rate Summary

common and can be executed without moving the market; bid-offer spreads are approximately HK$0.001/US$ under normal market conditions. Unlike other Southeast Asian currency centres, the absence of restrictions means that virtually all trading in Hong Kong dollars takes place onshore, rather than offshore or some combination of the two. In addition to liquid spot trading, the domestic market also features active dealing in Hong Kong dollar OTC forwards and options (discussed later in the chapter); it also features trading in listed currency futures and options, but such derivatives are related to offshore currencies, not the Hong Kong dollar. Figure 4.4 illustrates the historical movement of spot HK$/US$.

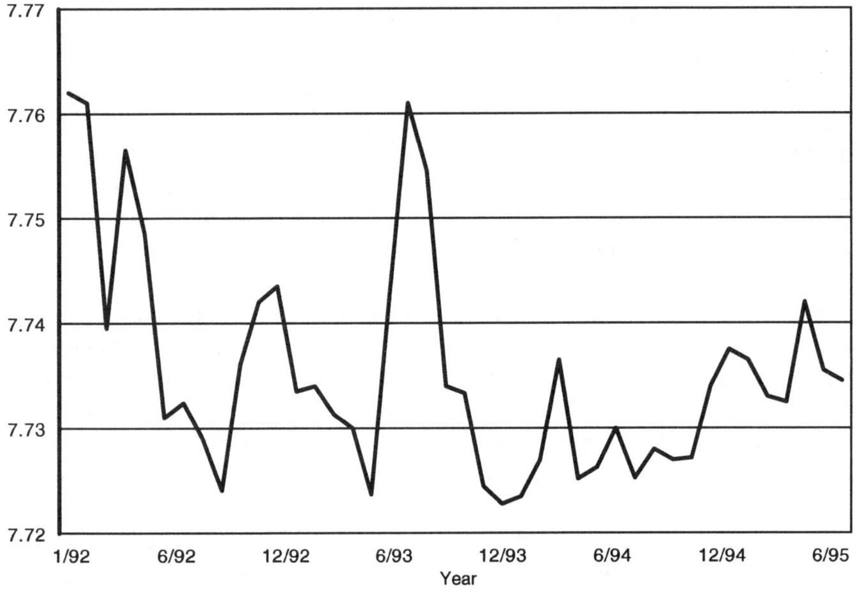

Figure 4.4 Historical movement of Spot HK$/US$

DERIVATIVE MARKETS AND PRODUCTS

LISTED DERIVATIVE EXCHANGES

Hong Kong features two exchanges with trade listed derivatives, the Hong Kong Futures Exchange (HKFE) and the Stock Exchange of Hong Kong (SEHK).

Although Hong Kong has been an active commodity trading centre for many years (beginning with the first formal commodity trading forum, the Chinese Gold and Silver Exchange Society, in 1910), it was not until 1975 that the Commodity Trading Ordinance (CTO) was enacted and the first official trading regulatory body, Office of the Commissioner for Securities, was created. In 1977, two years after the CTO was passed, a group of private investors formed the Hong Kong Commodity Exchange (HKCE), the colony's first futures exchange. The HKCE was granted an original five-year license and, from 1977 until 1982, specialized in trading futures on sugar, cotton, gold and soybeans; only the gold contract remains listed on the HKCE's successor, the Hong Kong Futures Exchange (HKFE), today. In 1982, at the expiry of the five year trading license, regulators requested a re-organization of the HKCE as they were uncomfortable with the ownership structure of the Exchange (e.g. the International Commodity Clearinghouse, which cleared all HKCE's futures trades, was the effective owner of the Exchange). Re-organization of the original exchange took place at the same time interest in financial futures was developing. In 1984 the Exchange, with various local financial institutions, sponsored the creation of the Hang Seng Index (HSI) stock index futures contract. The contract, guaranteed by the Futures Guarantee Corporation (FGC), was launched in 1986 on the HKCE's newly established successor, the HKFE.

The initial success of the HSI futures contract was overshadowed by events surrounding the October 1987 stock market crash. The sharp selloff in global equity markets forced the SEHK to close for several days, leaving certain futures participants with open positions on the HKFE with large losses. At the time of the closure open interest in HSI futures was 36,000 contracts long, 94% with clients; the long positions were all speculative in nature, with a single party (and associates) holding more than 50% of the positions. Short futures positions were concentrated with five brokers (who held 90% of the short outstandings); half of the positions were related to index arbitrage portfolios. From the time of the crash, the subsequent closure of the market, and the re-opening several days later, the value of the HSI fell nearly 69%. The contract guarantor, FGC, was unable to cover losses on all contracts as it had a modest HK$22 mln (US$2.8 mln) guarantee fund and a government/ bank-sponsored bailout was arranged. A total of HK$2 bln (US$258 mln) was raised (50% from the Hong Kong Government, the balance from members and other financial institutions) and HK$1.8 bln (US$237 mln) was utilized to cover contract losses; the loan was eventually repaid through the levy of special fees on HSI contracts and other transactions. A number of regulatory reforms were enacted in the wake of the 1987 problems (which we discuss later in this chapter) aimed at providing additional security for the HKFE and designed to avoid a repeat of 1987's events.

Despite the problems encountered in 1987, the HKFE has emerged as an important global exchange (ranking as the 27th most active exchange in the world in 1994 (FI, 1995)), primarily on the strength of its HSI futures contract and, more recently, its HSI options contract. During the early 1990s the Exchange also pioneered a number of other products (which have met with varying degrees of success, as discussed below), including HIBOR futures (1990), Hang Seng sub-index futures (1991), the aforementioned HSI options (1993), share futures (1995) and currency futures (1995); it has also created a link with the Philadelphia Stock Exchange (PHLX) to trade PHLX's currency options contracts during Asian hours, beginning in 1996. The HKFE trades by open-outcry on its physical trading floor (except for currency futures, which are traded electronically), with trades matched by competitive auction; trades are cleared and settled through a separate wholly-owned, subsidiary, known as the HKFE Clearing Corporation. Membership in the HKFE takes one of four forms: floor traders (who are permitted to trade for their own accounts (and where legal status must be as an individual or corporation owned by an individual)), floor brokers (who are permitted to trade for their own accounts and to act as agents for other members), futures commission merchants (who are permitted to trade for their own accounts and client accounts, and who may act as agents for other members) and merchant traders (who are permitted to trade for their own accounts (and where legal status must be as a corporation)).

The second derivative exchange of Hong Kong is the SEHK, briefly described in the section above. Although the main function of the SEHK is to trade domestic equities, which it does on an electronic order-matching basis through its AMS system, it has also expanded over the past few years to trade in various domestic derivatives. The SEHK presently lists and trades issuer equity warrants, third-party equity warrants, currency warrants, gold warrants, fixed income warrants and, more recently, individual equity options. Equity warrants remain the most active, and well-established, of the Exchange's derivatives; indeed, Hong Kong features one of the world's largest and most liquid listed equity warrant markets. All of SEHK's derivatives are traded through the AMS system and clearing and settlement is effected through a separate subsidiary, the Hong Kong Securities Clearing Company (HKSCC). Membership in the Exchange, for the purposes of trading listed options, takes one of three forms: self-clearing participants (who are permitted to deal and clear for their own accounts, but not client accounts), full clearing participants (who are permitted to deal and clear for their own accounts and client accounts), and managing clearing participants (who are permitted to deal and clear for their own accounts and client accounts, as well as the accounts of other trading members and their clients). Institutions wanting to qualify for one of the above memberships must also be members of the SEHK. Table 4.3 highlights Hong Kong's listed exchanges and derivatives.

Exchange	Primary Derivatives
Hong Kong Futures Exchange (HKFE)	Index futures, options; share futures; deposit futures; gold futures; currency futures, options# (proposed)
Stock Exchange of Hong Kong (SEHK)	Equity options; issuer equity warrants; third-party equity warrants; currency warrants; fixed income warrants; gold warrants

via PHLX link

Table 4.3 Listed Derivative Exchanges

LISTED FUTURES /OPTIONS

Equity

Equity Futures/Options

Although Hong Kong's index derivatives, HKFE HSI futures and options, have been the primary focus of the listed market for several years, we commence our discussion with the colony's newest equity derivatives, HKFE's equity futures and SEHK's equity options.

In 1994 the HKFE announced plans to begin trading cash-settled equity futures on two blue-chip stocks, Hongkong Shanghai Banking Corporation (HSBC) and Hong Kong Telecom (HKT). The SEHK reacted with vocal opposition, arguing primarily that they had not been consulted prior to the HKFE announcement. There was also some concern on the part of the SEHK that share futures would compete directly with SEHK's options on individual equities, slated for introduction a full six months after the commencement of share futures trading. Despite the SEHK's opposition, the Securities and Futures Commission (SFC) approved the listing of equity futures on companies with a large market capitalization (in excess of HK$10 bln (US$1.3 bln)) and a substantial public float. Trading in the two futures commenced at the end of March 1995 (following a government amendment to commodities trading laws to allow the buying and selling of share futures); a third contract, on Cheung Kong was added in late 1995.

The introduction of domestic share futures provides participants with the means of obtaining leveraged exposure to individual equities or of hedging out, on a micro basis, very specific equity exposure. It also enables participants to go short of the market in leveraged form through a listed instrument. At the time share futures were introduced institutions were unable (and remain unable) to borrow warrants and sell them short, and stock options were not yet in existence. As such, selling share futures was the only simple means of obtaining a short derivative position in the listed market. Note that although a share future permits purchasers to command a leveraged position in the underlying equity, it does entitle buyers to dividends or voting rights.

It is interesting to note that initial and variation margins for individual share futures were originally set at twice the level of those required for HSI futures, under the assumption that individual share exposure represents no diversification and, as such, risk of greater market movement. After a modest start (e.g. turnover of 200–300 contracts per day for the first month of trading) activity soon declined, primarily because of the high margin requirements; margins were reduced by 40% to 50% in late 1995 in order to build interest and liquidity, but trading volumes remain light. Over the medium term share futures will be forced to compete with the SEHK's listed equity options, which may prove challenging. It should be noted that the HKFE is currently reviewing plans to trade additional share futures on several other domestic blue-chip companies (Swire Pacific and CITIC Pacific are the next candidates). Table 4.4 contains contract specifications for equity futures.

Contract	**Equity Futures**
Type	Domestic
Exchange	Hong Kong Futures Exchange
Months	Spot month, next month plus next two quarterly months on March, June, September, December cycle
Contract Size	HK$10,000 * share price (HKT) HK$2,000 * share price (HSBC) HK$5,000 * share price (CK)
Tick Value	HK$100 (HKT), HK$20 (HSBC), HK$50 (CK)
Daily Limit	No limit
Deliverable Instrument	Cash settlement
Last Trading Day	Business day immediately preceding the last business day of the contract month
Delivery Day	First business day after the last trading day
Real-time price data	Bloomberg: HKA <Cmdty>, HBA <Cmdty>, HHA<Cmdty>; Reuters: <0#HKB:>, <0#HKT:>, <0#HCK:>; Telerate: 9532-34

Table 4.4 Contract Specifications for HKFE Equity Futures

The SEHK introduced domestic equity options in the third quarter of 1995, following years of discussion and planning. With the introduction of local options Hong Kong becomes the seventh stock market, out of the world's top eight markets, to feature such derivatives (Japan remains the only market among the top eight which does not list options). SEHK's listed equity options are American exercise derivatives which result in physical delivery of shares; determination of strike intervals is based on the price of the underlying share: strikes are set at HK$0.10 intervals when the stock price is below HK$2, HK$0.20 intervals between HK$2 and

HK$5, HK$0.50 intervals between HK$5 and HK$10, HK$1 intervals between HK$10 and HK$20, HK$2 intervals between HK$20 and HK$50, HK$5 intervals between HK$50 and HK$100, HK$10 intervals between HK$100 and HK$200, and HK$20 intervals over HK$200. All options are traded on the SEHK and are cleared through the HKSCC clearing subsidiary. Options are presently available on five stocks, including HSBC, HKT, Cheung Kong, Swire Pacific A, and CITIC Pacific; other options will be added over time, and will be selected based on the following criteria: (a) reference stocks must meet all guidelines applicable to warrant issuance (which we discuss below); (b) trading volume in the underlying stock must have maintained a daily average of at least 500,000 shares for the past 12 months; (c) the share price of the reference stock must have been over HK$10 for the past 12 months; and (d) the stock must be eligible for short-selling (note that the authorities introduced a short-selling 'pilot' programme in order to accommodate the new options). Table 4.5 contains contract details on listed equity options. Table 4.6 summarizes the stocks on which share futures and equity options are available (as at third quarter 1995).

Contract	Equity Options
Type	Domestic
Exchange	Stock Exchange of Hong Kong
Months	Next three calendar months plus next two quarterly months on March, June, September, December cycle
Contract Size	One board lot of the underlying shares
Tick Value	HK$0.01
Daily Limit	No limit
Deliverable Instrument	Physical settlement of shares
Last Trading Day	Business day immediately preceding the last business day of the contract month
Exercise Day	American exercise – any business day up to, and including, the last trading day
Real-time price data	Reuters: <0#0001*.HK>, <0#0005*.HK>, <0#0008*.HK>, <0#0019*.HK>, <0#0267*.HK>; Telerate: 35466-97

Table 4.5 Contract Specifications for SEHK Equity Options

Stock	Share Futures	Equity Options
Cheung Kong	Yes	Yes
CITIC Pacific		Yes
HK Telecom	Yes	Yes
HSBC	Yes	Yes
Swire Pacific A		Yes

Table 4.6 Availability of HKFE Share Futures and SEHK Equity Options

Index Futures/Options/Futures Options

The HSI index futures contract, HKFE's most popular and active listed derivative, was introduced in 1986; following the brief disruption in 1987 (cited above) the contract has emerged as the centrepiece of the Exchange, attracting a broad range of foreign and domestic participants. The HSI is a market value-weighted index of 33 stocks representing approximately 75% of the capitalization of the domestic stock market. In late 1994 the index was realigned after the Jardine group of companies (Jardine Matheson, Jardine Strategic, Dairy Farms International, Hong Kong Land) delisted in favour of Singapore; several new companies were added to replace the departing companies. The HSI is compiled by HSI Services, a wholly-owned subsidiary of Hang Seng Bank (itself majority-owned by HSBC), and is considered the bellwether index for both cash and derivatives trading. The HSI future is a cash-settled contract valued at HK$50 times the index, and is routinely quoted to six contract months.

Growth in HSI futures has been impressive. Trading volume increased from 2.4 mln contracts in 1993 to a record 4.19 mln contracts in 1994 (surpassing the previous record of 3.7 mln contracts set in 1987). Year-end open interest increased from 26,888 contracts in 1993 to 38,008 contracts in 1994 (HKFE, 1995). Activity in the futures market generally outweighs activity in the cash market. In 1994, for instance, the total value of futures turnover was 308% of the turnover in the cash market; the influence of the contract is so significant that futures trading often establishes the direction of the underlying cash market. Specifications on HSI futures are included in Table 4.7; Figure 4.5 illustrates the historical price movement of the HSI contract.

Contract	**Hang Seng Index Futures**
Type	Domestic
Exchange	Hong Kong Futures Exchange
Months	Next two calendar months plus quarter months on March, June, September, December cycle
Contract Size	HK$50 * Hang Seng Index
Tick Value	1 index point
Daily Limit	+/–500 index points against previous day's settlement price (not applicable to spot month or next spot month on delivery day)
Deliverable Instrument	Cash settlement based on the average of the index at 5 minute intervals during the last trading day
Last Trading Day	2nd to last business day of the contract month
Delivery Day	1st business day after last trading day
Real-time price data	Bloomberg: HIA <Cmdty>; Reuters: <0#HSI:>; Telerate: 2470, 2473

Table 4.7 Contract Specifications for HKFE Hang Seng Index Futures

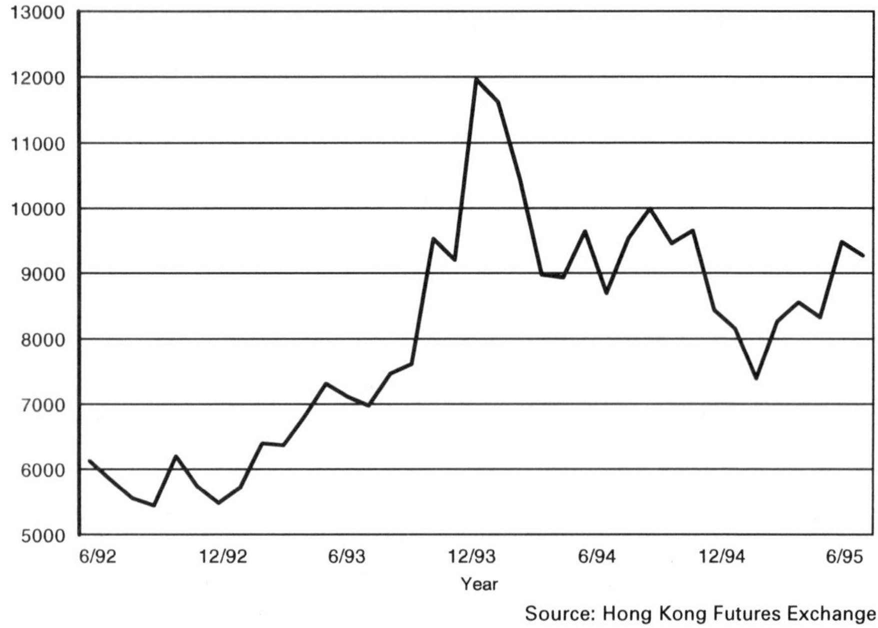

Figure 4.5 Historical Movement of HKFE Hang Seng Index Futures

HSI sub-index futures contracts were designed to give hedgers and speculators protection against (or exposure to) specific sectors of the Hong Kong equity market; sub-index futures on four sectors, including commerce and industry, finance, utilities and properties, were introduced in 1991. As with the HSI contract, each sub-index contract is cash-settled; contract value is determined by multiplying the sub-index by HK\$50. Success of sub-index futures has been minimal, even in the property sub-index (which was expected to very popular, given the heavy concentration of property stocks in the HSI), as most hedgers/speculators have turned to the very liquid HSI contract to obtain cover or exposure. Although the contracts attracted some attention when they were originally introduced they failed to gain widespread acceptance and remain inactive today; no turnover or open interest were recorded in 1993 or 1994 in the sub-index contracts. The Exchange is presently reviewing the contracts to determine whether they should be restructured in order to attract more trading volume. Details on sub-index futures are contained in Table 4.8. Figures 4.6 through 4.9 illustrate the historical futures price movement of all four sub-indexes.

HKFE's cash-settled, European exercise HSI options were launched in March 1993 and have proven extremely popular with both investors and dealers. The additional leverage gained through options has made the instruments appealing to an investor base interested in both equity exposure and leveraged investment, while the liquidity and tight pricing has made the contracts useful for commercial and invest-

Contract	**HSI Sub-index Futures (Commerce & Industry, Finance, Utilities, Property)**
Type	Domestic
Exchange	Hong Kong Futures Exchange
Months	Next two months plus two quarter months on March, June, September, December cycle
Contract Size	HK$50 * HSI sub-index
Tick Value	1 index point
Daily Limit	+/–300 index points against previous day's settlement price (except property sub-index, which is +/–450 points). No limit on spot month contracts
Deliverable Instrument	Cash settlement based on closing level of index on the last trading day
Last Trading Day	2nd to last business day of the contract month
Delivery Day	1st business day after the last trading day
Real-time price data	Bloomberg: HCA <Cmdty>, HFA <Cmdty>, HTA <Cmdty>, HCA <Cmdty>; Reuters: <0#HSC:>, <0#HSF:>, <0#HUT:>, <0#HSP:>; Telerate: 6216, 6217, 6219, 6220

Table 4.8 Contract Specifications for HKFE HSI Sub-index Futures

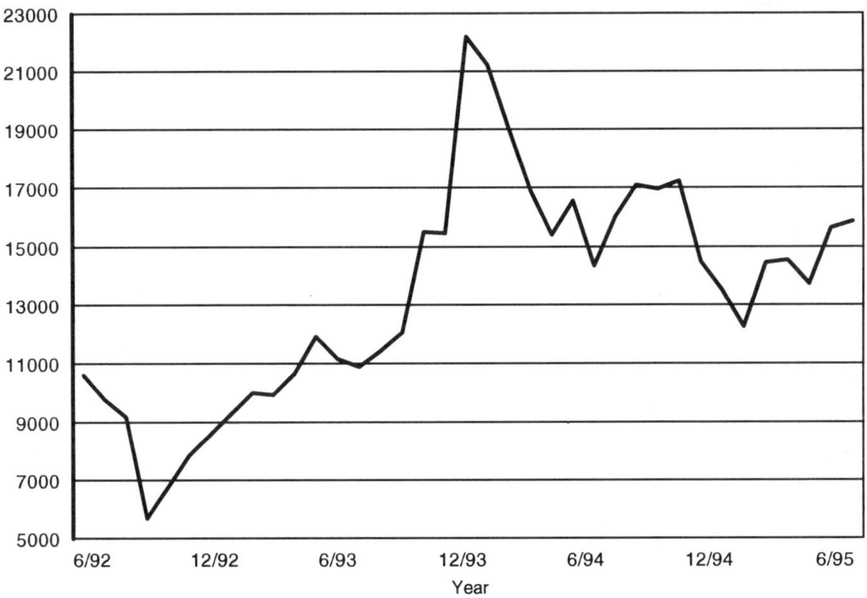

Source: Hong Kong Futures Exchange

Figure 4.6 Historical Movement of HKFE HSI Property Sub-index Futures

Figure 4.7 Historical Movement of HKFE HSI Utilities Sub-index Futures

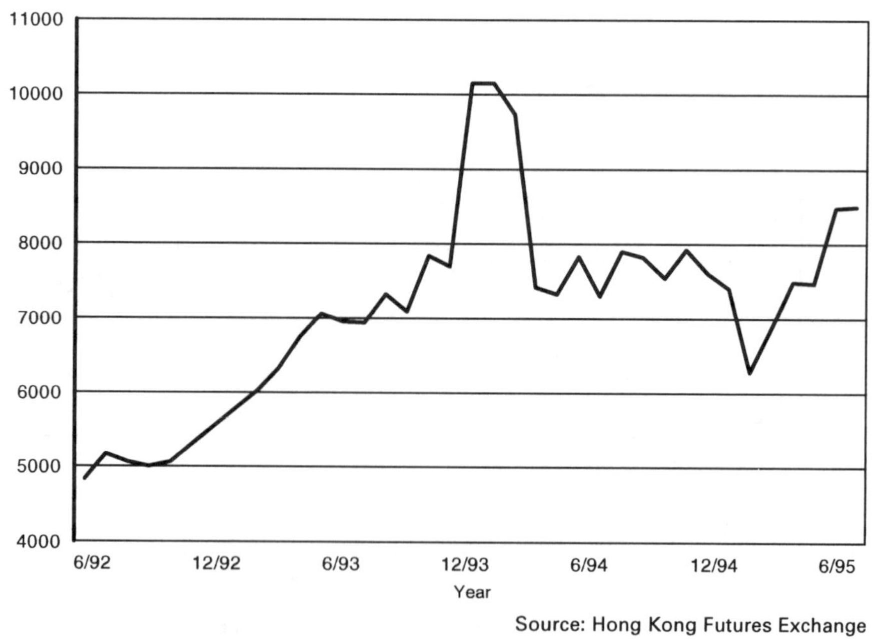

Figure 4.8 Historical Movement of HKFE HSI Finance Sub-index Futures

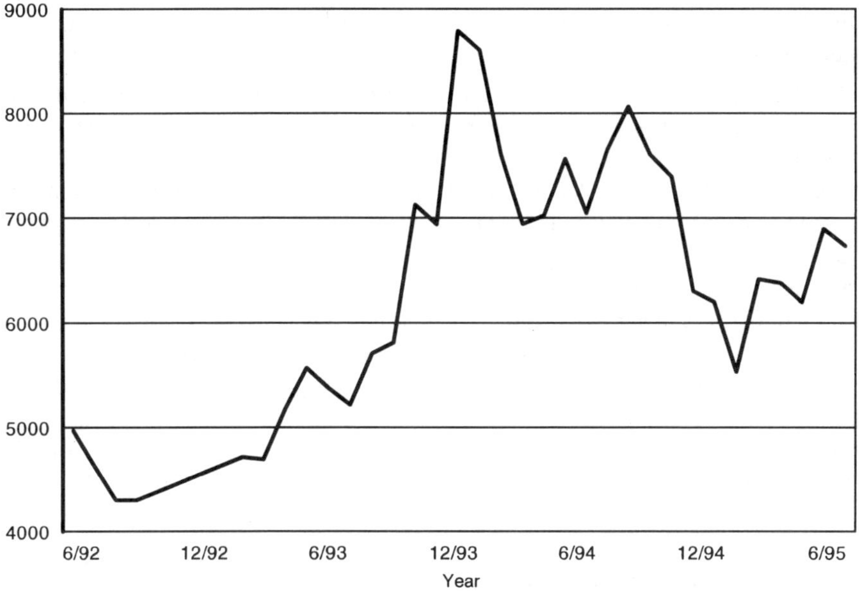

Source: Hong Kong Futures Exchange

Figure 4.9 Historical Movement of HKFE HSI Commerce & Industry Sub-index Futures

Contract	**Hang Seng Index Options**
Type	Domestic
Exchange	Hong Kong Futures Exchange
Months	Next two calendar months plus next two quarter months on March, June, September, December cycle
Contract Size	HK$50 * Hang Seng Index
Tick Value	1 index point
Daily Limit	No limit
Deliverable Instrument	Cash settlement based on average value of the index at five-minute intervals during the last trading day.
Last Trading Day	Business day preceding exercise day
Exercise Day	European exercise – on 2nd to last business day of the contract month only.
Real-time price data	Bloomberg: HSI <Index> OMON; Reuters: <0#HSI*.HF:>; Telerate: 44140-47

Table 4.9 Contract Specifications for HKFE Hang Seng Index Options

ment banks who utilize them to manage market risks generated through OTC equity derivative portfolios.

Registered traders who make markets in HSI puts and calls on all listed series (e.g. different strikes for all current contract months) can trade at favourable rates; this arrangement has fostered greater liquidity and a stronger sense of two-way prices. In addition, in 1994 the HKFE introduced a two-tier maximum bid-offer spread system for quotes on HSI options which permits registered dealers to extract larger spreads for larger customer trades (to compensate for the increased risk inherent in dealing in larger volumes). Option strikes are set at 100 point intervals when the HSI is under 8,000 and 200 point intervals when the index is over 8,000; new strikes are added so there are three option strikes above/below the closing index level at all times. Trading volume has increased dramatically since the introduction of the option contract: total turnover rose from just under 300,000 contracts in 1993 to just over 606,000 contracts in 1994; year-end open interest amounted to 17,702 contracts in 1993 and 15,979 contracts in 1994 (HKFE, 1995). Table 4.9 highlights contract specifications for HSI options.

In addition to the Hang Seng-related derivatives described above, the HKFE announced that it will begin trading Hang Seng China Enterprise (HSCE) Index futures in 1996; the China Enterprise Index is comprised of 13 Chinese companies listed on the SEHK. No contract details have yet been released.

Fixed Income

Deposit Futures/Options/Futures Options

The HKFE introduced three month Hong Kong Interbank Offer Rate (HIBOR) futures, referencing the local benchmark deposit rate, in February 1990. Despite being the only listed fixed income derivative based on local interest rates the contract remains virtually inactive today. HIBOR futures began on a strong note, recording impressive first month turnover of 17,750 contracts; one year later monthly volume had plunged to 175 contracts and, by 1993, the contract was completely inactive. Local and foreign institutions have opted to use other derivatives to hedge or speculate on short-term interest rates. In particular, institutions prefer to utilize the Hong Kong dollar FRA market or the short-dated interest rate swap/FX swap market to obtain cover or exposure; both markets (discussed later in this chapter) feature greater liquidity than HIBOR futures have ever displayed. In addition to Hong Kong dollar-based OTC agreements, certain institutions utilize US$ LIBOR (Eurodollar) contracts listed on IMM, TIFFE, LIFFE or SIMEX to achieve similar results. The direct peg between the US dollar and the Hong Kong dollar implies a link between US and Hong Kong interest rates. The strong positive correlation means that it is possible to utilize Eurodollar futures against short-term HIBOR exposures to remove directional interest rate risk (though a significant amount of basis risk would still exist (Figures 4.35 to 4.38 in the section on currency basis swaps trace the historical movement and spread of HIBOR and US$ LIBOR)).

Given the lacklustre performance of the HIBOR contract its prospects appear uncertain; Exchange officials are presently reviewing the feasibility of restructuring the derivative. Table 4.10 contains contract details on HIBOR futures.

Contract	**Three-Month Hong Kong Interbank Offer Rate (HIBOR) Futures**
Type	Domestic
Exchange	Hong Kong Futures Exchange
Months	March, June, September, December
Contract Size	HK$1 mln
Tick Value	HK$25
Daily Limit	+/– 125 basis points against previous day's settlement. Once reached, a +/–250 basis point limits is applied for next three days. No limit on last five trading days of delivery month
Deliverable Instrument	Cash settlement
Last Trading Day	Two business days prior to 3rd Thursday of month
Delivery Day	Same as last trading day
Real-time price data	Bloomberg: HRA <Cmdty>; Reuters: <0#HIR:>; Telerate: 6218

Table 4.10 Contract Specifications for HKFE Three Month HIBOR Futures

Interest Rate Futures/Options/Futures Options

The Hong Kong derivative market features no domestic bond futures at the present time, although the HKFE has announced that it is in active discussions with both the Hong Kong Monetary Authority (HKMA) and the SFC regarding the introduction of a futures contract on the local Exchange Fund Note (EFN). Primary issuance of two-, three-, five, and seven-year EFNs has been on the rise and it appears that further supply of bonds will be forthcoming in the future, suggesting such a contract could be both useful and viable. There are still many factors which would have to be established prior to the development of an EFN future, including: investor need for such contracts (certain other hedging alternatives already exist, as discussed immediately below); impact of restrictive EFN short-selling rules on futures (short-selling is presently limited to market-makers); consistency of bond supply in the near and intermediate term; and so on. No definitive timetable for the introduction of EFN futures has been established.

In the absence of domestic bond futures participants utilize other instruments to manage domestic interest rate exposures. As mentioned above, the foreign exchange link between the Hong Kong dollar and the US dollar implies a direct link between Hong Kong and US interest rates. For institutions needing to hedge medium- or long-term Hong Kong dollar interest rate exposure, alternatives are available through the US Treasury bond market (which features liquid securities with maturities of one to 30 years), and the US Treasury bond futures market (which features contracts on two, five, ten and 20 year bonds). Although some level of basis risk results in covering Hong Kong dollar interest rate exposure with US Treasury bonds or futures, the strong positive correlation permits directional interest rate exposures to be reduced or eliminated. Participants may also use US dollar swaps for the same purposes and would once again replace directional interest rate risk with more manageable basis risk. Use of Hong Kong dollar swaps is a further alternative available to hedgers, though bid-offer spreads are significantly wider than those found on US dollar swaps, suggesting a more expensive, though more accurate, hedging exercise.

Currency

Currency Futures/Options/Futures Options

During 1995 Hong Kong made substantial progress toward becoming a broader-based foreign exchange trading centre. Although Hong Kong has always featured a vibrant FX trading market it was not until early 1995 that the HKFE announced it would list its own currency futures beginning in the fourth quarter of 1995. The HKFE also announced the formation of a link with the Philadelphia Stock Exchange (PHLX), which will permit trading of PHLX currency options during Asian hours, starting in 1996; we discuss this development in the section below.

In late 1995 the HKFE launched currency futures on JPY/US$ and DM/US$; it plans to introduce additional contracts on CHF/US$ and US$/C$ in the second phase of the program (note that HKFE considered, but rejected, US$/A$, US$/GBP and ECU/US$ contracts; the Exchange has also indicated it has no plans to list Hong Kong dollar or Chinese renminbi futures). Unlike traditional currency contracts the HKFE contract is structured as a one-day rolling currency future and behaves in a manner similar to a spot FX position (note that SIMEX's deferred currency contracts are structured in the same fashion); the contract is an agreement to buy or sell currency at a predetermined rate on the spot date and is automatically rolled into the next spot date unless it is specifically closed out (e.g. it is equivalent to establishing a spot position from value date to the next business day and rolling the position through a spot/next currency swap). For each day that the position is held open, a swap point cash adjustment is debited or credited to the account, in an amount equal to one day's interest cost based on the interest rate differential between the two currencies. Swap points are determined by taking quotes from six banks, dropping the highest and lowest, and averaging the balance. It should be noted that all contracts are denominated in US dollars and settled on a cash basis, rather than in physical; unlike other HKFE futures/options, the currency contracts trade through the ATS electronic trading system, rather than through open outcry on the floor of the Exchange. In introducing its rolling spot contract the HKFE becomes the fourth exchange in Asia to list and trade currency futures (the others being SIMEX, TIFFE and MIFE; NZFOE abandoned its contract in 1994 while the SFE delisted its futures in the early 1990s). Tables 4.11 to 4.14 contain specifications on the current and proposed currency contracts.

Contract	**JPY/US$ One-Day Rolling Currency Futures**
Type	Offshore
Exchange	Hong Kong Futures Exchange
Months	Two near months
Contract Size	US$50,000
Tick Value	JPY500
Daily Limit	No limit
Deliverable Instrument	Cash settlement in US dollars
Last Trading Day	2nd business day after open positions are closed
Delivery Day	Same as the last trading day
Real-time price data	Bloomberg: HYA<Cmdty>; Reuters:<0#HFX:>; Telerate: 6221

Table 4.11 Contract Specification for HKFE JPY/US$ One-day Rolling Currency Futures

Contract	**DM/US$ One-Day Rolling Currency Futures**
Type	Offshore
Exchange	Hong Kong Futures Exchange
Months	Two near months
Contract Size	US$50,000
Tick Value	DM5
Daily Limit	No limit
Deliverable Instrument	Cash settlement in US dollars
Last Trading Day	2nd business day after open positions are closed
Delivery Day	Same as last trading day
Real-time price data	Bloomberg: HMA<Cmdty>; Reuters:<0#HFX:>; Telerate: 6221

Table 4.12 Contract Specification for HKFE DM/US$ One-day Rolling Currency Futures

Contract	CHF/US$ One-Day Rolling Currency Futures
Type	Offshore
Exchange	Hong Kong Futures Exchange
Months	Two near months
Contract Size	US$50,000
Tick Value	CHF5
Daily Limit	No limit
Deliverable Instrument	Cash settlement in US dollars
Last Trading Day	2nd business day after the open positions are closed
Delivery Day	Same as the last trading day
Real-time price data	To be determined

Table 4.13 Contract Specification for HKFE CHF/US$ One-day Rolling Currency Futures

Contract	US$/C$ One-Day Rolling Currency Futures
Type	Offshore
Exchange	Hong Kong Futures Exchange
Months	Two near months
Contract Size	US$50,000
Tick Value	C$5
Daily Limit	No limit
Deliverable Instrument	Cash settlement in US dollars
Last Trading Day	2nd business day after the open positions are closed
Delivery Day	Same as the last trading day
Real-time price data	To be determined

Table 4.14 Contract Specification for HKFE US$/C$ One-day Rolling Currency Futures

In March 1995 the HKFE and PHLX reached an agreement to trade PHLX currency options via the HKFE, commencing in 1996. The HKFE was selected by PHLX over numerous other Asian exchanges (most notably SIMEX) to trade PHLX's very popular contracts and will form part of a continuous 20-hour trading day in currency options. Option trades executed in Hong Kong through the HKFE will flow through PHLX's Options Clearing Corporation (OCC), which clears and guarantees trades; surveillance of trading activity will be done through the US Securities and Exchange Commission (SEC) which regulates PHLX's US business. Profits generated from trades out of the HKFE are to be split between the two exchanges. Although trading in PHLX options has not commenced as of this writing, Tables 4.15 through 4.22 contain specifications on the conventional PHLX currency options which will be traded via HKFE.

Contract	**A$/US$ Currency Options**
Type	Offshore
Exchange	Hong Kong Futures Exchange/Philadelphia Stock Exchange
Months	March, June, September, December plus two near months, on one, three, six, nine and 12 month expiration cycles
Contract Size	A$50,000, at US$0.01 strike intervals
Tick Value	US$5
Daily Limit	No limit
Deliverable Instrument	Physical settlement of currencies; foreign currency purchasers deliver US dollars to OCC account in US, foreign currency sellers deliver foreign currency to OCC account in country of currency
Last Trading Day	Friday before the 3rd Wednesday of the month
Exercise Day	American exercise – any business day up to, and including, the last trading day. Also available as European exercise – on the last trading day only.
Real-time price data	Bloomberg: ADY <Cmdty> OMON, ADE <Cmdty> OMON; Reuters: <0#XAD*.X>, <0#CAD*.X>; Telerate: 15020-29, 16075-84

Table 4.15 Contract Specifications for HKFE/PHLX A$/US$ Currency Options

Contract	GBP/US$ Currency Options
Type	Offshore
Exchange	Hong Kong Futures Exchange/Philadelphia Stock Exchange
Months	March, June, September, December plus two near months, on one, three, six, nine and 12 month expiration cycles
Contract Size	GBP31,250 at US$0.025 strike intervals
Tick Value	US$3.125
Daily Limit	No limit
Deliverable Instrument	Physical settlement of currencies; foreign currency purchasers deliver US dollars to OCC account in US, foreign currency sellers deliver foreign currency to OCC account in country of currency
Last Trading Day	Friday before the 3rd Wednesday of the month
Exercise Day	American exercise – any business day up to, and including, the last trading day. Also available as European exercise – on the last trading day only.
Real-time price data	Bloomberg: BPY <Cmdty> OMON, BPE <Cmdty> OMON; Reuters: <0#XBP*.X>, <0#CBP*.X>; Telerate: 15030-39, 16015-24, 16085-87

Table 4.16 Contract Specifications for HKFE/PHLX GBP/US$ Currency Options

Contract	C$/US$ Currency Options
Type	Offshore
Exchange	Hong Kong Futures Exchange/Philadelphia Stock Exchange
Months	March, June, September, December plus two near months, on one, three, six, nine and 12 month expiration cycles
Contract Size	C$50,000; strikes set at US$0.005 intervals
Tick Value	US$5
Daily Limit	No limit
Deliverable Instrument	Physical settlement of currencies; foreign currency purchasers deliver US dollars to OCC account in US, foreign currency sellers deliver foreign currency to OCC account in country of currency
Last Trading Day	Friday before the 3rd Wednesday of the month
Exercise Day	American exercise – any business day up to, and including, the last trading day. Also available as European exercise – on the last trading day only.
Real-time price data	Bloomberg: CDY <Cmdty> OMON, CDE <Cmdty> OMON; Reuters: <0#XCD*.X>, <0#CCD*.X>; Telerate: 15090-99, 16055-64

Table 4.17 Contract Specifications for HKFE/PHLX C$/US$ Currency Options

Contract	US$/DM Currency Options
Type	Offshore
Exchange	Hong Kong Futures Exchange/Philadelphia Stock Exchange
Months	March, June, September, December plus two near months, on one, three, six, nine and 12 month expiration cycles
Contract Size	DM62,000; strikes set at US$0.01 intervals (and US$0.005 in three near months only)
Tick Value	US$6.25
Daily Limit	No limit
Deliverable Instrument	Physical settlement of currencies; foreign currency purchasers deliver US dollars to OCC account in US, foreign currency sellers deliver foreign currency to OCC account in country of currency
Last Trading Day	Friday before the 3rd Wednesday of the month
Exercise Day	American exercise – any business day up to, and including, the last trading day. Also available as European exercise – on the last trading day only.
Real-time price data	Bloomberg: DMY <Cmdty> OMON, DME <Cmdty> OMON; Reuters: <0#XDM*.X>, <0#CDM*.X>; Telerate: 15060-69, 16025-34, 16088-90

Table 4.18 Contract Specifications for HKFE/PHLX US$/DM Currency Options

Contract	ECU/US$ Currency Options
Type	Offshore
Exchange	Hong Kong Futures Exchange/Philadelphia Stock Exchange
Months	March, June, September, December plus two near months, on one, three, six, nine and 12 month expiration cycles
Contract Size	ECU62,000; strikes set at US$0.02 intervals
Tick Value	US$6.25
Daily Limit	No limit
Deliverable Instrument	Physical settlement of currencies; foreign currency purchasers deliver US dollars to OCC account in US, foreign currency sellers deliver foreign currency to OCC account in country of currency
Last Trading Day	Friday before the 3rd Wednesday of the month
Exercise Day	American exercise – any business day up to, and including, the last trading day.
Real-time price data	Bloomberg: ECY <Cmdty> OMON; Reuters: <0#ECU*.X>; Telerate: 15080-89

Table 4.19 Contract Specifications for HKFE/PHLX ECU/US$ Currency Options

Contract	US$/FRF Currency Options
Type	Offshore
Exchange	Hong Kong Futures Exchange/Philadelphia Stock Exchange
Months	March, June, September, December plus two near months, on one, three, six, nine and 12 month expiration cycles
Contract Size	FRF250,000; strikes set at US$0.0025 intervals
Tick Value	US$5
Daily Limit	No limit
Deliverable Instrument	Physical settlement of currencies; foreign currency purchasers deliver US dollars to OCC account in US, foreign currency sellers deliver foreign currency to OCC account in country of currency
Last Trading Day	Friday before the 3rd Wednesday of the month
Exercise Day	American exercise – any business day up to, and including, the last trading day. Also available as European exercise – on the last trading day only.
Real-time price data	Bloomberg: FRY <Cmdty> OMON, FRE <Cmdty> OMON; Reuters:<0#XFF*.X>, <0#FFW*.X>, <0#CFF*.X>; Telerate: 15070-79, 16065-74

Table 4.20 Contract Specifications for HKFE/PHLX US$/FRF Currency Options

Contract	US$/CHF Currency Options
Type	Offshore
Exchange	Hong Kong Futures Exchange/Philadelphia Stock Exchange
Months	March, June, September, December plus two near months, on one, three, six, nine and 12 month expiration cycles
Contract Size	CHF62,500; strikes set at US$0.01 intervals (US$0.005 strikes available in three near months)
Tick Value	US$6.25
Daily Limit	No limit
Deliverable Instrument	Physical settlement of currencies; foreign currency purchasers deliver US dollars to OCC account in US, foreign currency sellers deliver foreign currency to OCC account in country of currency
Last Trading Day	Friday before the 3rd Wednesday of the month
Exercise Day	American exercise – any business day up to, and including, the last trading day. Also available as European exercise – on the last trading day only.

Contract	US$/CHF Currency Options
Real-time price data	Bloomberg: SFY <Cmdty> OMON, SFE <Cmdty> OMON; Reuters: <0#XSF*.X>, <0#CSF*.X>; Telerate: 15050-59, 16045-54, 16094-96

Table 4.21 Contract Specifications for HKFE/PHLX US$/CHF Currency Options

Contract	US$/JPY Currency Options
Type	Offshore
Exchange	Hong Kong Futures Exchange/Philadelphia Stock Exchange
Months	March, June, September, December plus two near months, on one, three, six, nine and 12 month expiration cycles
Contract Size	JPY6,250,000; strikes set at US$0.0001 intervals (US$0.00005 strikes available in three near months)
Tick Value	US$6.25
Daily Limit	No limit
Deliverable Instrument	Physical settlement of currencies; foreign currency purchasers deliver US dollars to OCC account in US, foreign currency sellers deliver foreign currency to OCC account in country of currency
Last Trading Day	Friday before the 3rd Wednesday of the month
Exercise Day	American exercise – any business day up to, and including, the last trading day. Also available as European exercise – on the last trading day only.
Real-time price data	Bloomberg: JYY <Cmdty> OMON, JYE <Cmdty> OMON; Reuters: <0#XJY*.X>, <0#CJY*.X>; Telerate: 15040-49, 16035-44, 16091-93

Table 4.22 Contract Specifications for HKFE/PHLX US$/JPY Currency Options

In addition to the conventional options detailed above, PHLX also trades long-term options, month-end options and crossrate options (as well as a special dollar-denominated delivery option on Deutschmarks). Long-term options are available on seven currencies (Australian dollars, British pounds, Canadian dollars, Deutschmarks, French francs, Swiss francs and Japanese yen); the European exercise options carry maturities of 36 months and are offered on the June and December cycle. The Exchange's month-end options have a final maturity of approximately 30 days and, as the name suggests, expire at the end of each month. Month-end options are American exercise derivatives resulting in physical delivery of currencies; contracts are offered on the March, June, September, December cycle, along with two near months. PHLX also trades options on two key crossrates,

DM/JPY and GBP/JPY; the options are available as European exercise derivatives in conventional, long-term and month-end form. The options described above will be accessible to Asia Pacific participants through the HKFE/PHLX link once it is operational.

Commodity

Commodity Futures/Options/Futures Options

Over the course of the past decade the HKFE (and HKCE) has listed and traded commodity futures on gold, soybeans, sugar and copra. Only the gold contract remains listed today, though trading volume is non-existent; cotton futures were delisted in 1981, soybean futures in March 1992, and sugar futures in October 1992.

Although gold futures have existed in the Hong Kong market since the HKCE (HKFE's successor) introduced a contract in 1980, there has never been much interest or activity in the derivative; much greater activity and liquidity exists in domestic spot physical gold, which is traded through the Chinese Gold and Silver Market. HKFE gold futures registered no turnover or open interest in either 1993 or 1994; despite the inactivity the Exchange has elected to continue listing the contract. Table 4.23 contains specifications on the gold contract while Figure 4.10 traces the historical price of the future.

Contract	**Gold Futures**
Type	Domestic/Offshore
Exchange	Hong Kong Futures Exchange
Months	Even months, spot plus following two months
Contract Size	100 troy ozs. of fine gold
Tick Value	US$0.10/oz.
Daily Limit	+/– US$40 against previous day's settlement price. No limit imposed on spot month.
Deliverable Grade	Physical settlement of refined gold .955 pure, in bars of 50 oz., 100 oz., or 1 kg.
Last Trading Day	Last business day of the contract month
Delivery Day	Same as the last trading day
Real-time price data	Bloomberg: HLA <Cmdty>; Reuters: <0#HAU:>; Telerate: 6211

Table 4.23 Contract Specifications for HKFE Gold Futures

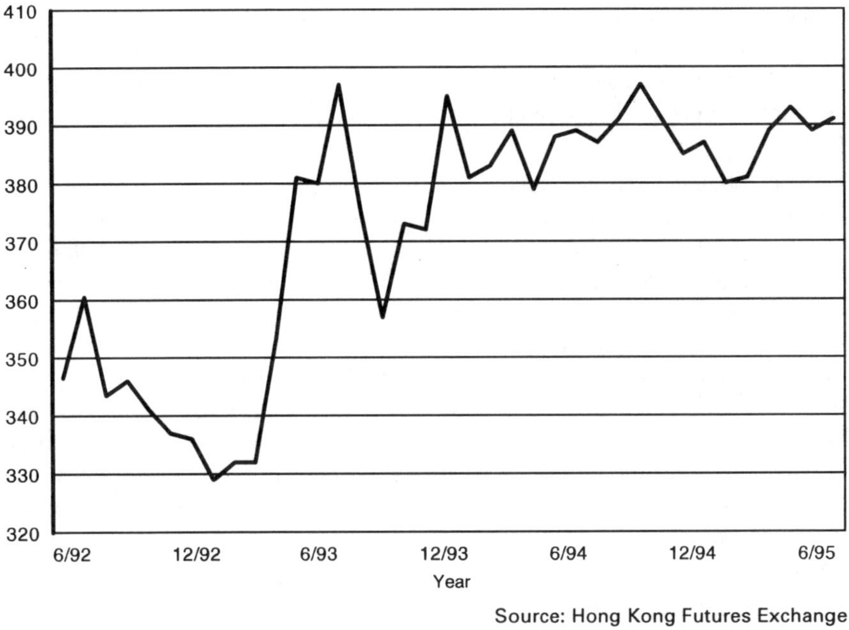

Figure 4.10 Historical Movement of HKFE Gold Futures

It should be noted that the Chinese Gold and Silver Market, established in the early 1900s, continues to operate to this day, trading precious metals based on Chinese measurements. The market is a purely local forum which trades and settles either on a cash basis, or by rolling open positions forward one day at a time (as a type of undated futures contract).

LISTED/OVER-THE-COUNTER WARRANTS, CONVERTIBLES AND HYBRIDS

Equity

Equity Warrants

Hong Kong features the most vibrant equity warrant market in Asia Pacific, with substantial activity in both the listed and OTC sectors.

Listed Hong Kong equity warrants are divided into two broad categories: covered warrants and non-collateralized warrants. Covered warrants are issued by companies on their own shares and result in the issuance of new equity upon exercise. Such warrants are American style derivatives with maturities of one to five years, which are listed on, and traded through, the SEHK. Trading of covered warrants has been exceptionally popular with domestic retail and institutional investors, and many issues feature very deep liquidity. Literally hundreds of listed covered warrants have been floated by companies over the past few years; as of mid-1995 the SEHK listed in excess of 250 domestic covered warrants (Appendix II contains details on all covered (and non-collateralized) warrants traded as of June 1995).

Non-collateralized warrants are issued by third parties on a domestic company's shares, with the obligations provided for in a form other than a charge on existing securities; unlike covered warrants, exercise of non-collateralized warrants results in re-allocation of existing shares rather then flotation of new corporate equity. Local and foreign investment banks have been particularly active issuers of non-collateralized equity warrants since late 1989 (note that non-collateralized warrants are issued in the listed and OTC markets alike; we discuss the latter immediately below). The first listed non-collateralized warrants were launched in September and October 1989 by Salomon Brothers, which sold call warrants on two of the territory's most familiar derivative references, HSBC and HKT; the issues were listed on the SEHK in December 1989. Dozens of non-collateralized warrants have been listed on the Exchange since the inaugural issues of 1989 and further growth in the market appears virtually certain.

In order to control issuance of non-collateralized warrants in a more effective fashion the SEHK released rules limiting warrant references to stocks of companies with a market capitalization in excess of HK$10 bln (US$1.3 bln) and a public float in excess of HK$5 bln (US$650 mln). In addition, the maturity of the warrant must be less than two years, the size must be at least HK$50 mln, and the ratio of warrants to shares must be set at either 1:1 or 10:1. Exercise can result in either physical delivery of existing shares or a cash payment. If warrants are constructed as cash settlement derivatives the valuation must be the higher of the average of the closing price of the underlying security for the past 30 business days and the closing price on the business day before the exercise day, so that there can be no price manipulation before issue date or at expiry date.

Along with standard non-collateralized warrants, the SFC permitted introduction of listed call spread warrants in 1994. Call spread warrants, issued by third parties on another company's underlying shares, are European-style derivatives which cap the potential returns an investor can earn in exchange for lower upfront premium. Call spread warrants are precisely equal to call spread structures constructed in any listed or OTC market; that is, the investor purchases a closer-to-the-money call and sells a farther-out-of-the-money call (e.g. one with a higher strike than the one purchased). The higher strike short call caps returns earned on the long call once both options are in-the-money, creating a ceiling on the amount of earnings an investor can earn. In return, the premium for buying the warrant is lower than that of a conventional warrant, while the gearing is generally higher. The listed call spread warrant package was introduced as a simple and cheap way of gaining the payoff profile of a call spread without having to enter into separate transactions. Peregrine and Union Bank of Switzerland were among the first to issue listed call spread warrants on the SEHK. An early spread warrant was a HK$500 mln (US$65 mln), ten for one call spread on HKT, allowing investors a maximum gain of 2.24 times the issue price.

In addition to domestic listed warrants, numerous US and European investment banks have been at the forefront of offering OTC covered third-party warrants on domestic stocks; such warrants are either unlisted or listed on overseas exchanges and are traded on an OTC basis. OTC covered warrants are distinct from the listed covered warrants discussed above, which are issued by a company on its own shares; covered warrants in the OTC market are issued by third parties on another company's shares (just as the listed non-collateralized warrants described above), and are backed by shares from the market (or other securities or derivatives) enabling the issuer to deliver shares upon exercise. As with listed non-collateralized warrants, covered OTC warrants carry final maturities of one to two years. Dozens of OTC covered warrants have been issued by major financial institutions on many of Hong Kong's blue-chip equities over the past few years (e.g HSBC, HKT, Cheung Kong, Hutchison Whampoa, Hang Seng Bank, and so on).

It should be noted that the recent introduction of listed equity options on the SEHK may provide the domestic warrant market with a certain amount of competition. This is particularly true for warrants on the largest blue-chips in the market (i.e. HSBC, HKT, Cheung Kong, and so on) which are referenced by both warrants and options. Despite the possibility of competition, however, the local warrant market is very well established and extremely popular with both retail and institutional investors, and is likely to survive the challenge.

Basket/Index Warrants

In addition to listed and OTC single stock warrants discussed above, listed and OTC warrants are also written on the broad Hong Kong market and on baskets of domestic stocks. Index and basket warrants permit investors to gain leveraged exposure to the entire market or specific segments of the market, rather than just single stocks. Although the local market permits listing of such structures, most activity occurs in the OTC market; as of June 1995, there were only two index warrants listed on the SEHK, including an HSI call warrant floated by Barclays de Zoete Wedd and a similar warrant underwritten by Morgan Stanley.

While the listed index warrant market is relatively inactive, institutions in the OTC market float index and basket warrants on a frequent basis (particularly when the HSI, or sectors of the HSI, are entering an upturn). Offshore OTC index/basket warrants are listed on overseas exchanges (or remain unlisted) and are traded primarily on an OTC basis; warrants may be American or European exercise, and generally mature in one to three years. OTC index warrants on the HSI have been underwritten by many financial institutions over the past few years, including Swiss Bank Corporation, Robert Fleming, Lehman Brothers, Paribas and others; certain issues have been denominated in Hong Kong dollars, while others have been denominated in US dollars or European currencies. Warrants have also been written on indexes other than the HSI, such as Citibank's Deutschmark index call and put warrants on the Citibank Hong Kong Index (1994) and Salomon Brothers' US dollar index call warrants on the Hong Kong 30 Index (1994). The European Options Exchange in Amsterdam lists, on an ongoing basis, index put and call warrants on the Citibank Hong Kong Index.

Basket warrants are written on groups of domestic bank stocks, property company stocks, utility stocks, and so on; the potential combinations are numerous. Representative issues in this category include Swiss Bank Corporation's US dollar basket call and put warrants on a weighted group of 14 domestic blue-chip stocks (1995) and Bankers Trust's US dollar basket call warrants on a diversified group of domestic stocks (1994). Another popular basket warrant executed on a periodic basis is the H share basket warrant (also known as the 'red chip', or China, basket); H shares are the Hong Kong listed shares of Chinese companies and flotation of H share basket warrants provides investors with a leveraged equity investment in major Chinese stocks. Swiss Bank Corporation, Robert Fleming and Bankers Trust are among the institutions which floated H share basket warrants during 1994 and 1995.

Convertibles

The Hong Kong market does not feature issuance of local convertibles at the present time. The lack of a local convertible market has led numerous Hong Kong issuers to access the offshore convertible market over the past few years and local companies are now frequent issuers of both Eurodollar and domestic Swiss franc convertibles. Eurodollar convertibles, such as those floated by Amoy Properties, Wharf Capital, Sino Land, Sun Hung Kai and Applied International, are most often issued in bearer form, with maturities extending from five to 15 years (though certain issues, such as one by Amoy Properties, have been floated as perpetuals); Eurodollar convertibles are generally listed on overseas exchanges and traded OTC. Activity by Hong Kong companies in the domestic Swiss franc market has also been considerable. Swiss franc convertibles are floated on either a public or private placement basis, with public deals listed and traded on Swiss stock exchanges and private deals unlisted and traded on an OTC basis. Hong Kong convertibles in the Swiss market carry much shorter maturities than those in the Eurodollar market (e.g primarily under five years), and are issued with investor puts (allowing the investor to put the securities to the issuer at any time) and provisional calls (allowing the issuer to call the bond once the market price exceeds a certain level); Swiss franc convertibles are generally non-callable for the first half of a bond's life. Conversion of Eurodollar and Swiss franc bonds is into the shares of the domestic issuer at a Hong Kong dollar conversion price. Offshore convertible issuance by Hong Kong companies has risen from under US$100 mln in 1990 to nearly US$4 bln in 1993 and US$1.45 bln in 1994. Appendix III contains details on convertible bonds issued by domestic companies.

Index-linked Notes

Index-linked note issuance is very active in both the domestic and offshore markets. The HSI is a frequent reference for index-linked securities (e.g. CDs and notes with embedded long or short call or put options); such notes are floated on both a listed and OTC basis by domestic and foreign banks. Given the HSI's strong performance over the past few years, most index-linked notes have been constructed in the form of 'bull market' securities, paying investors a percentage of the appreciation in the index in the form of either an enhanced coupon or an increase in the note's principal redemption value. Those which are listed on the SEHK can be actively traded, while those issued on an OTC basis are most often structured as private placements and held until maturity. Index-linked structures are floated as both CDs and notes, with maturities ranging from one to five years; most securities are denominated in Hong Kong dollars, through certain issues intended for offshore investors are denominated in foreign currencies (with returns converted at a fixed Hong Kong dollar exchange rate). A representative example of the index-linked note structure can be found in the two tranche note planned by Peregrine Securities in 1995. The two year, HK$500 mln (US$65 mln) note was to be available in two forms: the first tranche paying 100% of principal at maturity plus 65% of the appreciation in the HSI over the period, and the second tranche paying at least 90% of principal at maturity (e.g. the investor could suffer up to a 10% loss in principal if the HSI declined) but providing 100% of appreciation in the index. Only tranche one was successfully launched; tranche two remained undersubscribed and was cancelled.

More complex index-linked notes with embedded exotic options (e.g. barriers, Asians, lookbacks, and others) are created on occasion, generally as private placements. One example is a barrier step-up CD paying a 0% coupon and at least par at redemption. The CD permits the investor to earn 100% of the appreciation in the HSI; if the HSI rises by more than 30%, however, the investor receives no appreciation (e.g. the barrier is triggered and the option is extinguished), but earns a stepped-up coupon of 10%. The risk/return combinations of index-linked structures are virtually limitless when utilizing embedded exotic options.

In addition to index-linked notes, single stock-linked notes (and CDs) are also available. Such instruments, which provide enhanced coupons based on the appreciation in a domestic stock (e.g. the investor purchases a call option embedded in a note), are typically purchased by retail investors. Notes with embedded short puts have also proven popular with the retail sector. Such structures provide enhanced coupons (generated from the sale of the put option) but expose investors to lower principal redemption, or the possibility of having to accept shares, as the price of the reference equity falls; WI Carr has issued several tranches of such notes, with each tranche tied to a group of three stocks (but with payoff determined by selecting the performance of only one of the stocks).

Fixed Income

Fixed Income Warrants

Despite the presence of an active domestic listed warrant market very few domestic fixed income warrants have been issued to date. This is true primarily because investor demand for fixed income warrants in Hong Kong is thin and the domestic fixed income market is still growing in depth and breadth; though issuance of sovereign-related Hong Kong dollar fixed income instruments has been on the rise since the early 1990s, total outstandings are still relatively modest. Few investors have been eager to speculate, through the warrant market, on the direction of bill and bond prices, since there are more established and efficient means of accomplishing the same task (e.g. OTC swaps, forwards, options). The few bond warrants floated to date have been structured as one to two year cash-settled derivatives, and have been listed on, and traded through, the SEHK. A representative issue in this category is Union Bank of Switzerland's call warrants on Exchange Fund Notes (1994).

Currency

Currency Warrants

The Hong Kong market features both listed and OTC currency warrants based on major foreign currencies (though not the Hong Kong dollar). Domestic currency warrants debuted on the SEHK in 1991, with inaugural 12 month call US$/DM warrants floated by both Citibank and Morgan; these were followed by several other issues over the next few years, including 12 month put and call warrants on A$/US$ by Morgan in 1993. Listed currency warrants are underwritten by international banks and are listed and traded on the SEHK; most issues carry maturities ranging from 12 to 18 months and pay profits in Hong Kong dollars at a pre-determined fixed rate. As of June 1995 the SEHK listed and traded five distinct issues, including two underwritten by Nomura (DM put/US$ call and JPY put/US$ call) and three by Morgan (JPY call/US$ put, JPY put/US$ call and DM put/US$ call).

The Hong Kong market features occasional issuance of OTC currency warrants, such as those floated by Swiss Bank in 1994 on US$/JPY and US$/DM. OTC currency warrants are often launched at very short notice by large domestic and international banks operating in Hong Kong and, as such, are often unlisted; trading takes place domestically on an OTC basis, not through the SEHK. The need to issue the warrants in the span of just several days, or even hours, makes it inappropriate for full exchange listing which can take several days or weeks to complete. It should be noted that issues of OTC HK$/US$ OTC currency warrants have been non-existent, primarily because of low investor demand. Although domestic investors frequently speculate on the direction of currency movements, such speculation is based primarily on G10 currencies and not the Hong Kong dollar.

Commodity

Commodity Warrants

In contrast to the listed equity and currency warrant markets, the domestic commodity warrant market is extremely small, and limited at the present time to warrants on gold. Despite the local market's propensity for investing in gold, most investment occurs on a physical basis rather than through derivatives (witness the absence of activity in HKFE's gold futures). Widespread activity in gold warrants is unlikely in the future as the commodity warrant market faces extreme competition for investment funds from more accepted and established instruments (e.g equity warrants, currency warrants, currency options, physical gold, and so on). Despite the relative lack of activity, certain deals have been structured in the recent past, including Swiss Bank Corporation's American gold put and call warrants; ten warrants command one troy ounce of gold and settlement is in cash rather than physical (1994).

OVER-THE-COUNTER FORWARDS, SWAPS AND OPTIONS

Equity

Equity Forwards/Swaps

The market for OTC equity derivative forwards and swaps is reasonably active in Hong Kong. Equity forwards, which involve the sale or purchase of domestic equities for settlement on a forward basis, typically carry maturities of six months to three years; settlement may be either in cash or physical. Equity swaps, which exchange deferred floating rate premium (e.g. HIBOR or US$ LIBOR) for appreciation (or depreciation) in the value of single stocks, also carry maturities extending to three years. Secondary liquidity in both derivatives is negligible given the customized nature of the transactions. Although single stock forwards and swaps are quite active, they are not as popular as equity options and index options/swaps, discussed below.

Equity Options

OTC equity options based on individual Hong Kong stocks are executed with frequency by domestic and foreign financial institutions. The absence of domestic listed equity options until the third quarter of 1995 (as well as the very narrow base of stocks on which listed options are available), has caused the OTC equity option market to flourish. OTC equity options have the advantage of conforming to the precise requirements of clients and can be customized with respect to underlying equity, strike, maturity and so on; despite the flexibility of the OTC market, many options are structured as six- to 12-month American or European derivatives exercisable into cash or physical settlement. Unlike the listed equity option market, which permits secondary trading of positions, the OTC equity option market is quite illiquid; virtually all option transactions result in expiry, exercise or close-out with the arranging bank.

Basket/Index Forwards/Swaps

The onshore/offshore market for short-to intermediate-maturity (e.g. one- to three-year) basket and index forwards/swaps is very active in Hong Kong. Index forwards and swaps referencing the HSI are very popular in the local market; typical transactions exchange a floating rate (e.g HIBOR or US$ LIBOR) for appreciation (or depreciation) in the HSI. These structures are equivalent to investors purchasing index calls (or puts), and paying deferred premium in the form of the floating rate flow. In addition to conventional index call and put swaps (and long or short index forwards) the market also features packages of long call swaps and short put swaps (enabling investors to receive appreciation but obligating them to pay depreciation) and long call spread swaps (enabling investors to receive a pre-defined maximum upside through the purchase of a near-the-money call swap and the sale of a farther out-of-the money call swap); both structures have the advantage of eliminating, or reducing, the floating rate premium payment. In addition to index forwards/swaps, basket forwards and swaps are also executed by combining groups of stocks into target baskets (e.g. property baskets, bank baskets, hotel baskets, 'H' share baskets, and so on). Exotic basket/index swaps (e.g. swaps with embedded barrier options, Asian options, and so on) are also available, though far less common. As with other OTC structures, basket/index forwards and swaps are illiquid on a secondary basis.

Basket/Index Options

Although listed HSI index options are readily available and very liquid, the onshore and offshore market for OTC index options has proven popular and active as well. Investors and intermediaries have been attracted by the flexibility offered by such structures (e.g. the ability to set strikes, maturities, notionals and so on). Despite complete flexibility in creating customized basket/index options, most transactions in the local market are American or European cash-settled derivatives with maturities of up to one year. In addition to standard OTC basket/index puts and calls there is a gradually expanding market for exotic options, including index barriers, Asians, digitals, outperformances and quantos.

Fixed Income

Fixed Income Forwards/Swaps

Hong Kong features an active and liquid interest rate forward and swap market which has been in existence for more than a decade. Growth in the market has been impressive in recent years and Hong Kong now features the third largest domestic IRS market in Asia Pacific (after Japan and Australia). According to statistics released by the International Swap Dealers Association (ISDA), total Hong Kong dollar notional outstandings increased from HK$73.2 bln (US$9.46 bln) in 1993 to HK$165.6 bln (US$21.4 bln) in 1994, giving it the highest growth rate of any market in the Pacific region (Choudhury, 1995). Growth has come primarily from increased fixed and floating rate funding in the domestic market, with institutions swapping proceeds to achieve lower overall funding costs.

The Hong Kong dollar FRA market, which references either HIBOR or the interest rates implied in FX forwards, is liquid primarily to 12 months, particularly in benchmark FRAs of 1 x 4, 2 x 5 and 3 x 6. Though the short-end is most liquid, dealers also quote long-term FRAs to three and five years. Typical interbank dealing size is HK$50 mln to HK$100 mln (approximately US$6.5 mln to US$13 mln) and bid-offer spreads are ten basis points under normal market conditions.

The Hong Kong dollar IRS market was established in the mid-1980s as funding via Hong Kong dollar loans and debt issues began increasing in size and scope. As is natural in the creation of any swap market, credit segmentation made it possible for institutions with different funding capabilities to raise funds and engage in swaps to obtain relative or comparative advantages. During the 1980s the structure of fund raising and swapping was based on local corporations issuing floating rate (HIBOR) liabilities and swapping into fixed Hong Kong dollars; banks issuing HIBOR CDs and swapping into either US$ LIBOR or fixed Hong Kong dollars; banks raising fixed, medium-term, Hong Kong dollar funds through the CD market and swapping back into US$ LIBOR or HIBOR; and local corporations with foreign exchange receipts swapping back into fixed Hong Kong dollars. There was also an active basis swap market driven by syndicated loans, where Hong Kong prime rate flows were swapped back into HIBOR. The swap market of the 1990s is not markedly different than ten years ago, although the basis segment (prime/HIBOR) is now virtually non-existent. Corporations still tend to be the primary fixed rate payers, while banks and other institutional investors are fixed rate receivers and HIBOR payers. Foreign banks with excess liquidity from the local marketplace often enter into HIBOR/LIBOR cross currency basis swaps (as discussed in the next section).

The local IRS market is most liquid in short-end maturities although ready quotes are available in both intermediate and long maturities. The short-term market is most active to three years, where bid-offer spreads are approximately five basis points. The availability of hedging instruments (including FX swaps/forwards and FRAs) and the relative lack of sovereign risk has made the short-term market quite liquid. In the intermediate sector (three to five years), spreads widen out to ten basis points. This segment of the market is very sensitive to the level of medium-term CD issuance occurring in the financial system and liquidity can disappear if there is a lack of bank funding activity. The intermediate sector is also faced with a more difficult hedging task and with political/sovereign risk considerations; both items command a risk premium. Liquidity in long-term swaps is reasonably thin and is driven primarily by long-term Hong Kong dollar issues by supranationals such as the World Bank, Nordic Investment Bank, European Bank for Reconstruction and

Development and others. The relative infrequency of seven to ten year issues, coupled with significant hedging challenges and the aforementioned sovereign risk considerations, places bid offer spreads on long-term year swaps in excess of 15 basis points.

Given the infancy of the local sovereign debt market, domestic IRSs are quoted on an absolute basis rather than as a spread to EFNs. The quoting convention is fixed Hong Kong dollars (quarterly, on an Actual/365 day basis) against three month HIBOR. Typical corporate dealing size ranges from HK$50 mln to HK$100 mln (approximately US$6.5 mln to US$13 mln), while standard interbank dealing size ranges from HK$300 mln to HK$400 mln (approximately US$38 mln to US$52 mln); recent estimates place average daily IRS turnover at HK$300 mln to HK$400 mln (approximately US$38 mln to US$52 mln). Table 4.24 provides indicative bid-offer spreads for Hong Kong dollar fixed/floating swaps under normal market conditions while Figure 4.11 depicts the historical movement of the Hong Kong dollar swap curve. Although Hong Kong dollar swaps are priced on an absolute basis we present for informational purposes, in Figures 4.12 to 4.17, the historical rates and spreads of Hong Kong dollar IRSs and EFNs in key maturities.

Maturity	Bid-Offer Spread
2 years	5 bps
3 years	5 bps
4 years	10 bps
5 years	10 bps
7 years	10 bps
10 years	15–20 bps

Table 4.24 HK dollar IRS Bid-Offer Spreads

Hedging in the Hong Kong dollar swap market, as mentioned above, tends to be simpler in the short maturities. In the one- to three-year sector dealers have at their disposal a number of hedge instruments, including FRAs, forward FX/FX swaps and HIBOR futures. Most dealers use FRAs and forward FX to manage positions as HIBOR futures have traditionally demonstrated little liquidity, even in the front month contract. It should also be pointed out that, although the government features sovereign issuance through its EFB/EFN programmes, restrictions regarding short selling of bills and notes (which is prohibited for all institutions except recognized market-makers) make government securities unattractive hedges.

In the intermediate and long sectors of the swap curve, many institutional participants elect to hedge their books with US Treasury bonds or Treasury bond futures. Given the currency link between the Hong Kong dollar and US dollar it is possible to construct an effective US Treasury hedge against a Hong Kong dollar swap position. As US interest rates rise and the US dollar strengthens, Hong Kong dollar interest rates tend to rise to keep the peg in place; the strong positive corre-

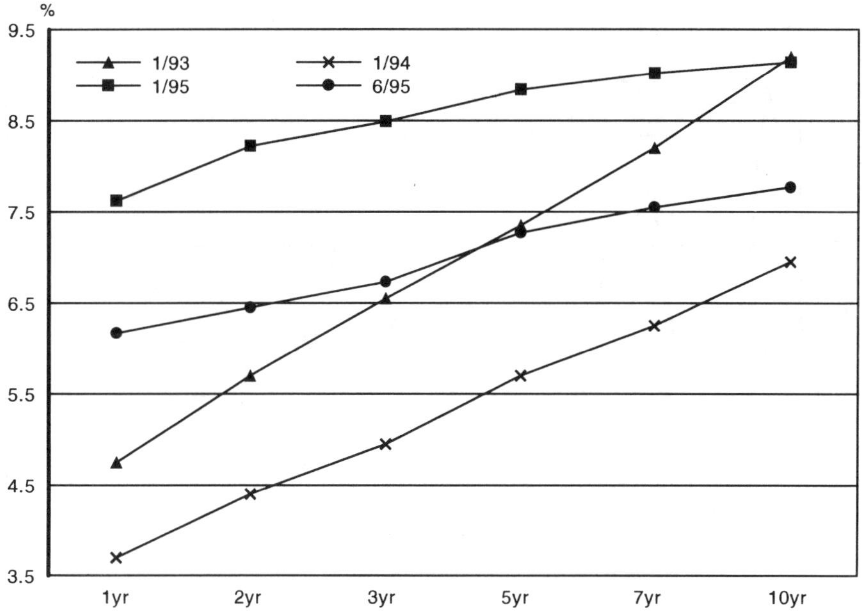

Figure 4.11 Historical Movement of the Hong Kong Dollar IRS Curve

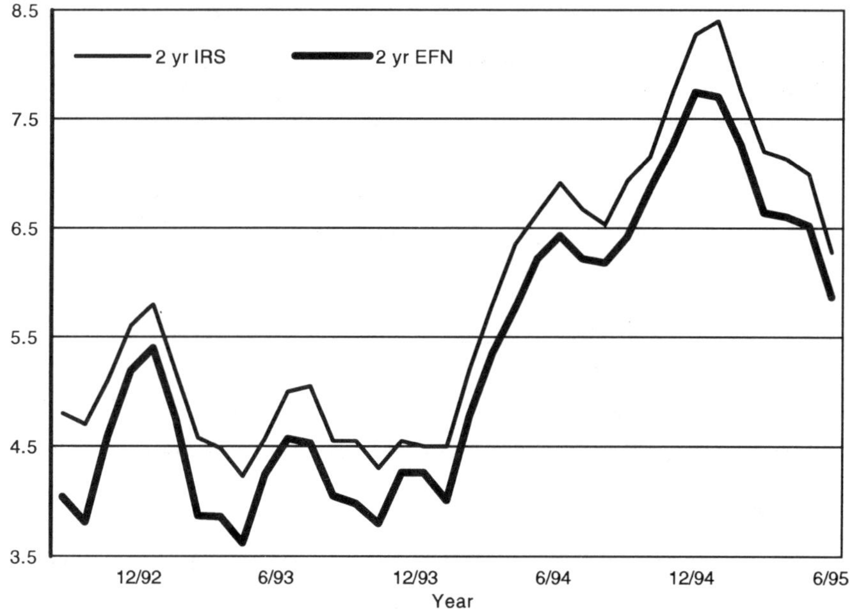

Figure 4.12 Historical Movement of Two-year HK$ IRS and Two-year EFN

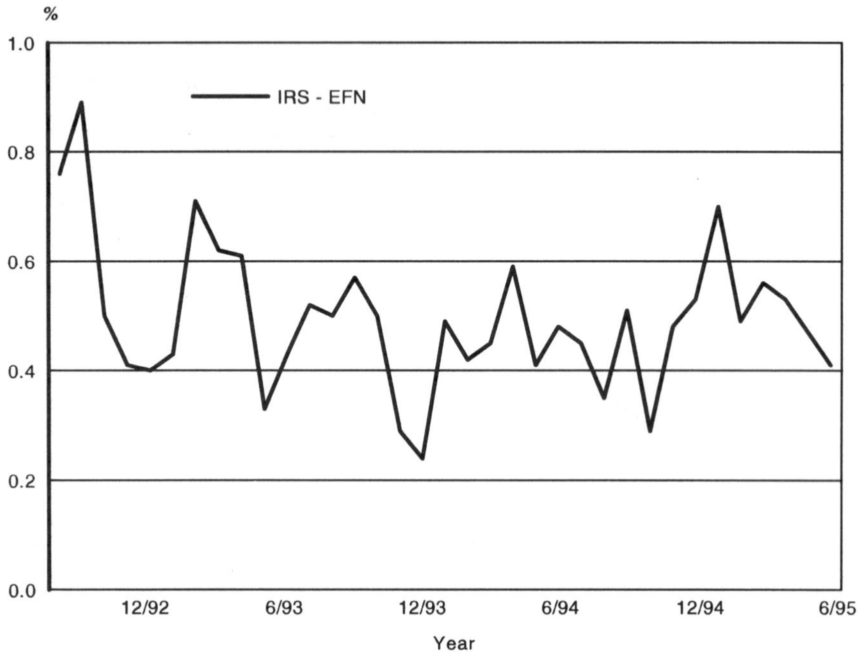

Figure 4.13 Spread of Two-year HK$ IRS and EFN

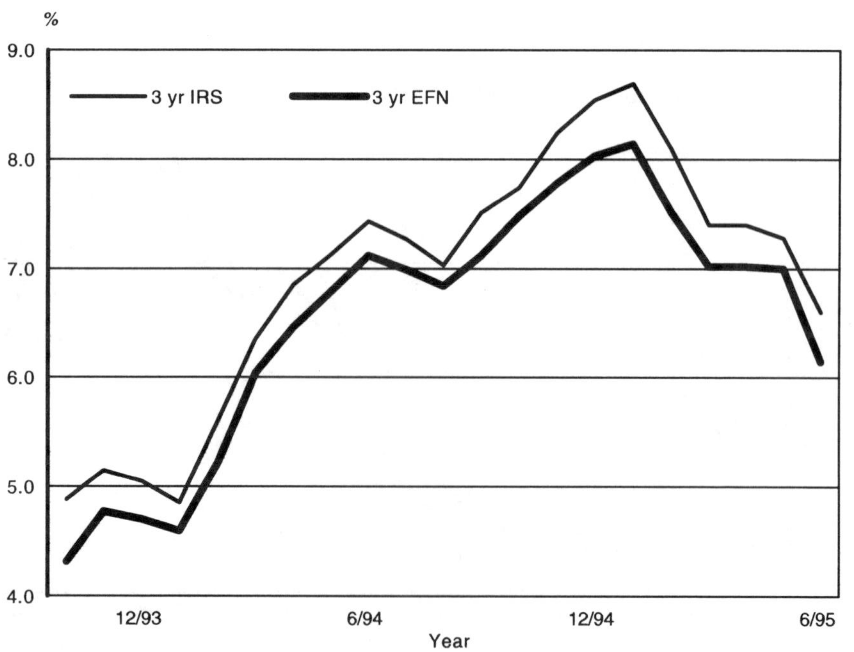

Figure 4.14 Historical Movement of Three-year HK$ IRS and Three-year EFN

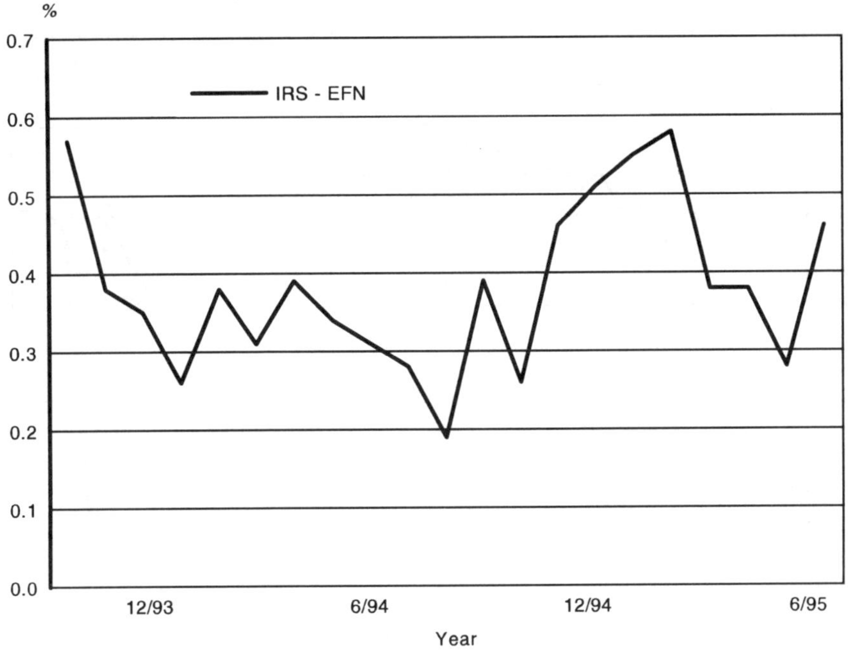

Figure 4.15 Spread of Three-year HK$ IRS and EFN

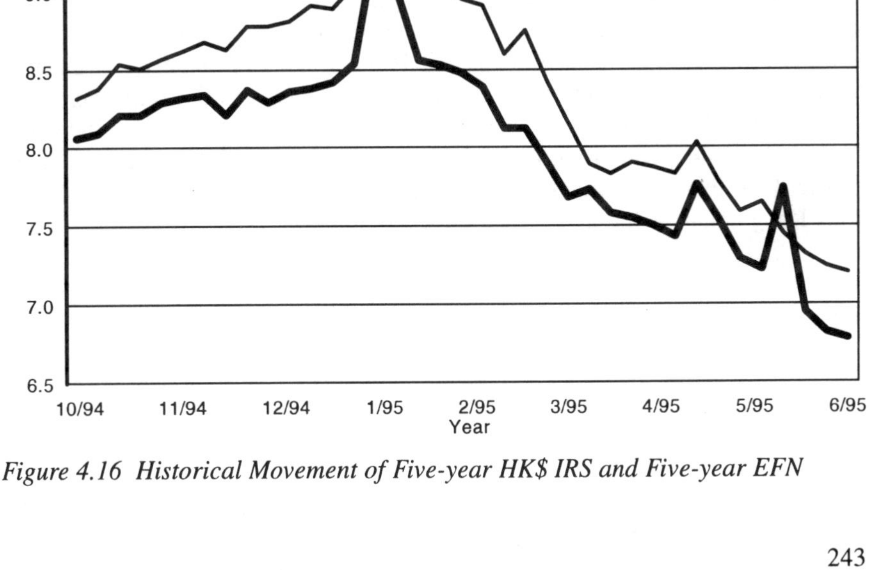

Figure 4.16 Historical Movement of Five-year HK$ IRS and Five-year EFN

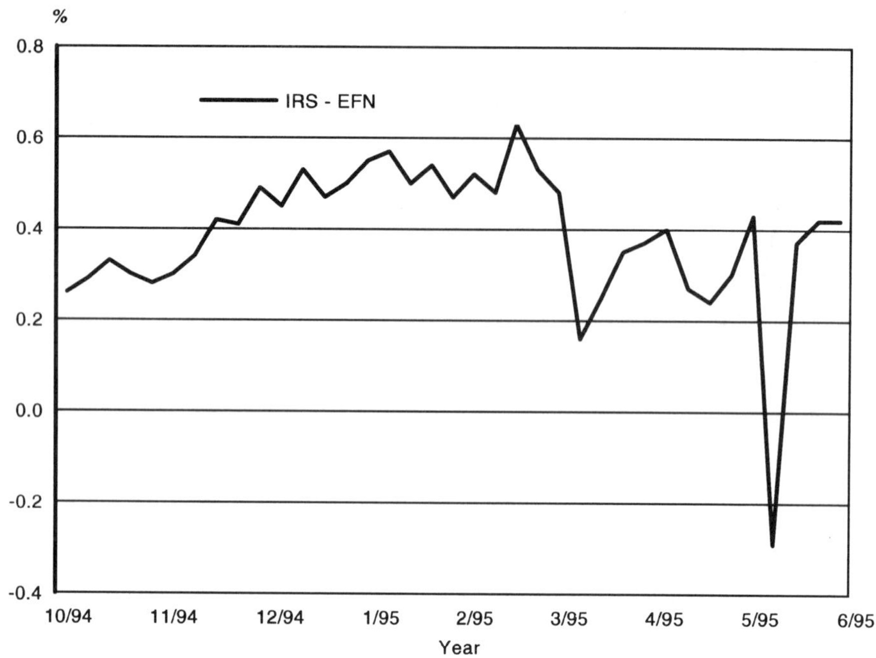

Figure 4.17 Spread of Five-year HK$ IRS and EFN

lation permits dealers to utilize Treasury hedges with some confidence. In doing so they exchange directional interest rate risk for basis risk which is not an insignificant risk to bear, but one which is generally preferable to outright interest rate risk. The spread between US Treasury bonds and Hong Kong dollar swaps fluctuates in relation to myriad political and economic events, causing the efficacy of the hedge to vary. The historical spread between the two instruments in the five year sector has averaged 90 basis points in recent years, but has been as wide as 160 basis points and as narrow as 40 basis points. In addition to Treasury-related instruments, dealers may also use US dollar interest rate swaps, which are quoted as a spread to US Treasuries. Many of the same basis or spread risks which exist in hedging Hong Kong dollar swaps with Treasuries remain when using US dollar swaps. Figures 4.18 to 4.33 display the historical movement of rates and spreads of benchmark Hong Kong dollar swaps, Treasuries, and US dollar swaps.

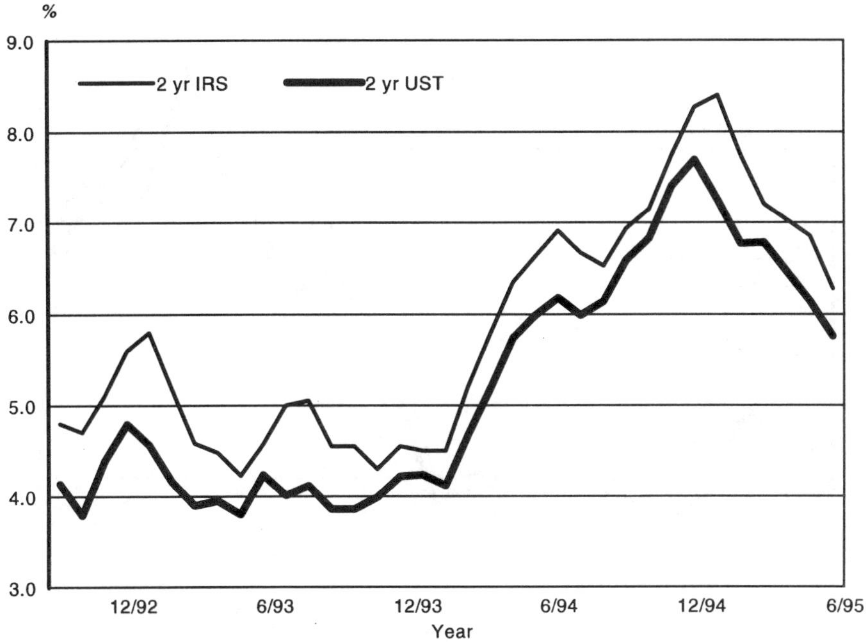

Figure 4.18 Historical Movement of Two-year HK$ IRS and Two-year US Treasury

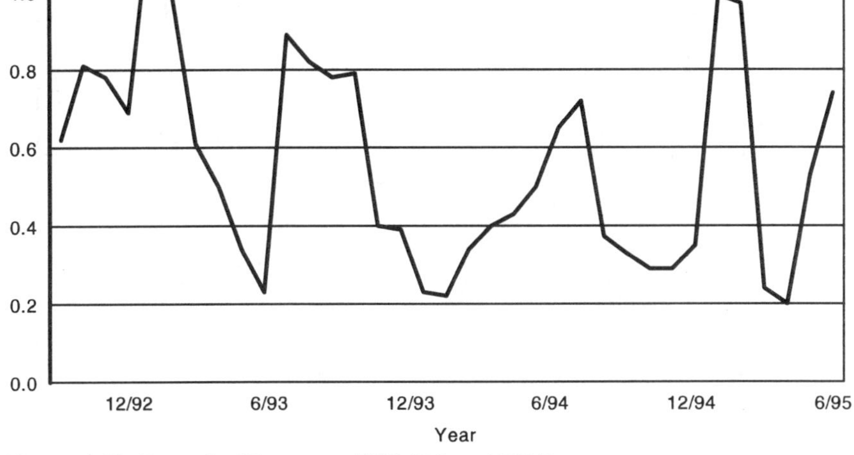

Figure 4.19 Spread of Two-year HK$ IRS and US Treasury

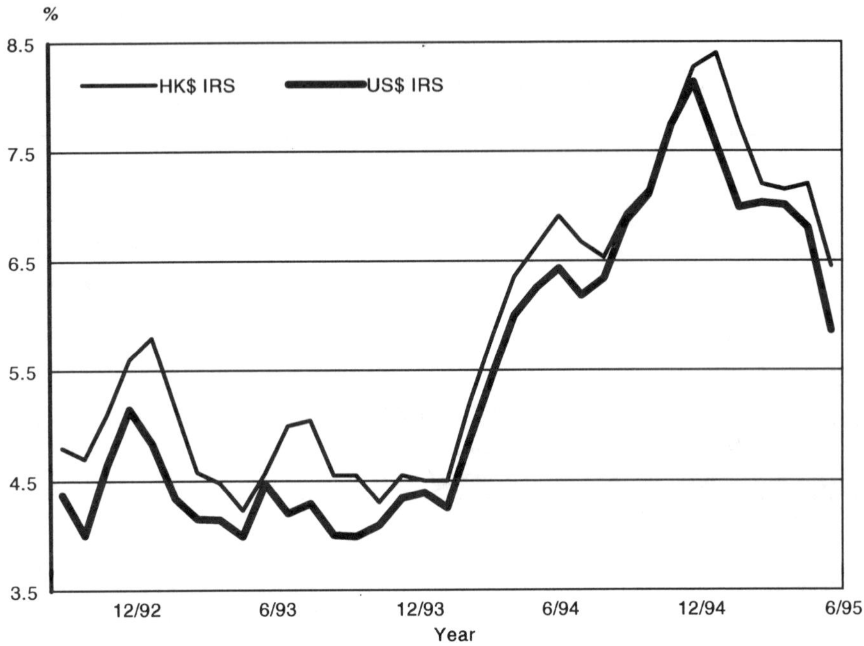

Figure 4.20 Historical Movement of Two-year HK$ IRS and Two-year US$ IRS

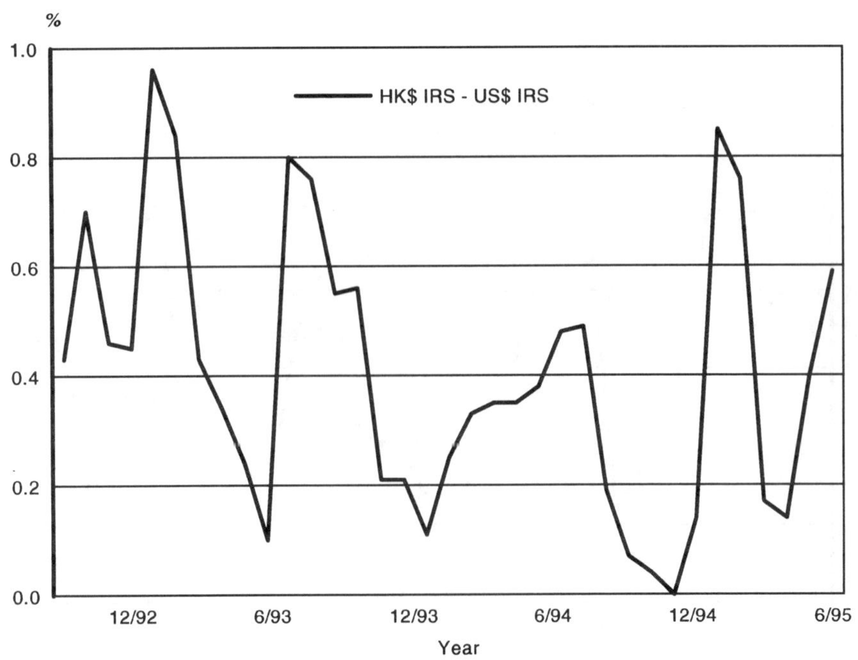

Figure 4.21 Spread of Two-year HK$ IRS and US$ IRS

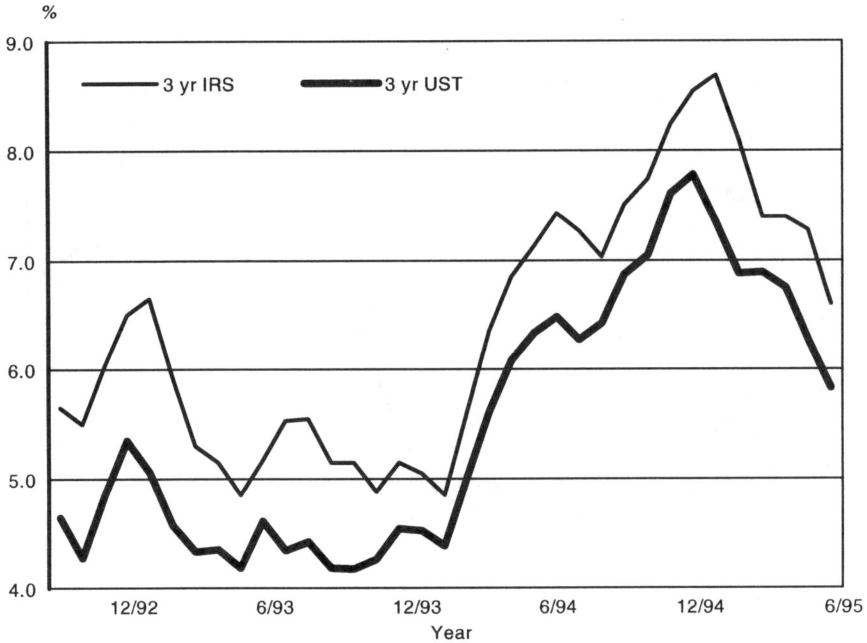

Figure 4.22 Historical Movement of Three-year HK$ IRS and Three-year US Treasury

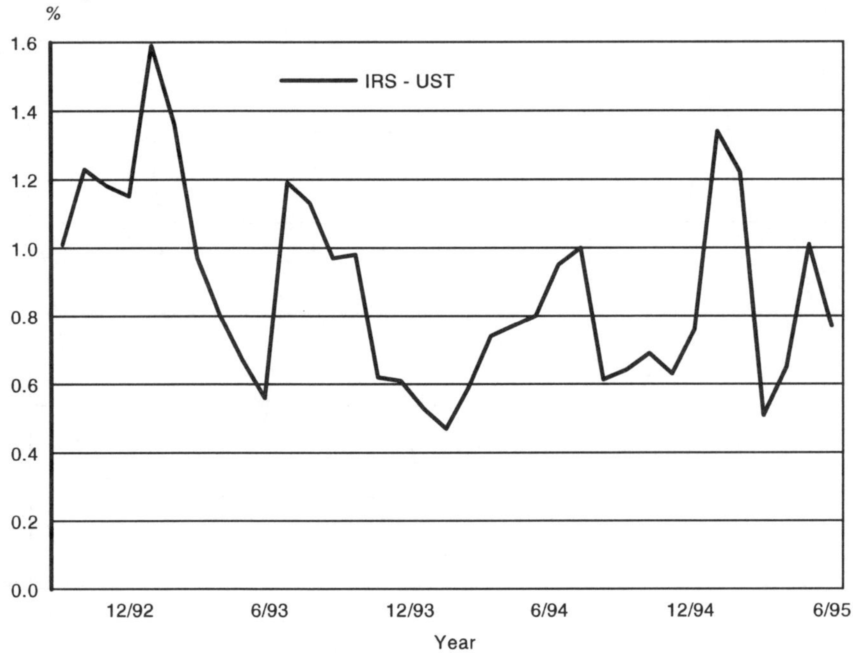

Figure 4.23 Spread of Three-year HK$ IRS and US Treasury

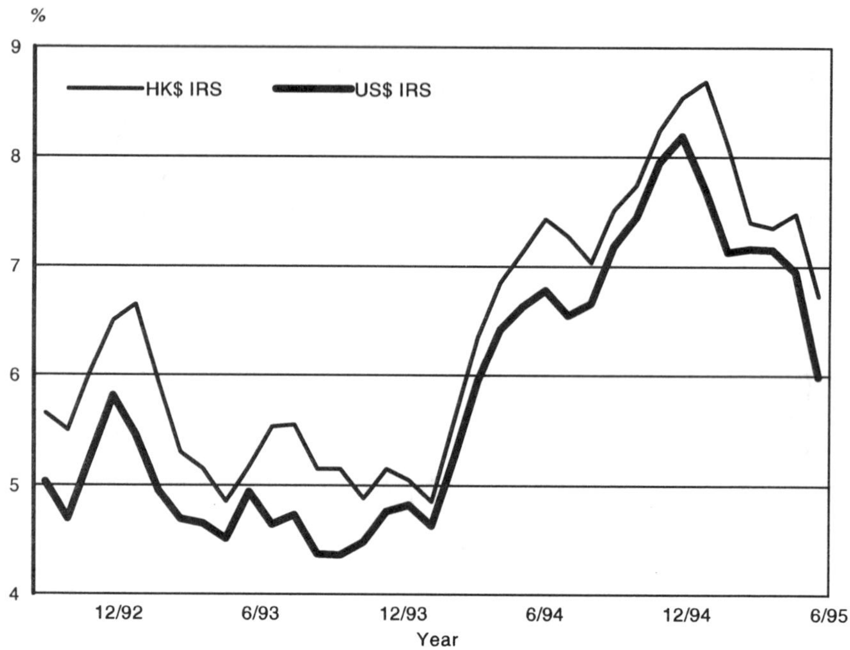

Figure 4.24 Historical Movement of Three-year HK$ IRS and Three-year US$ IRS

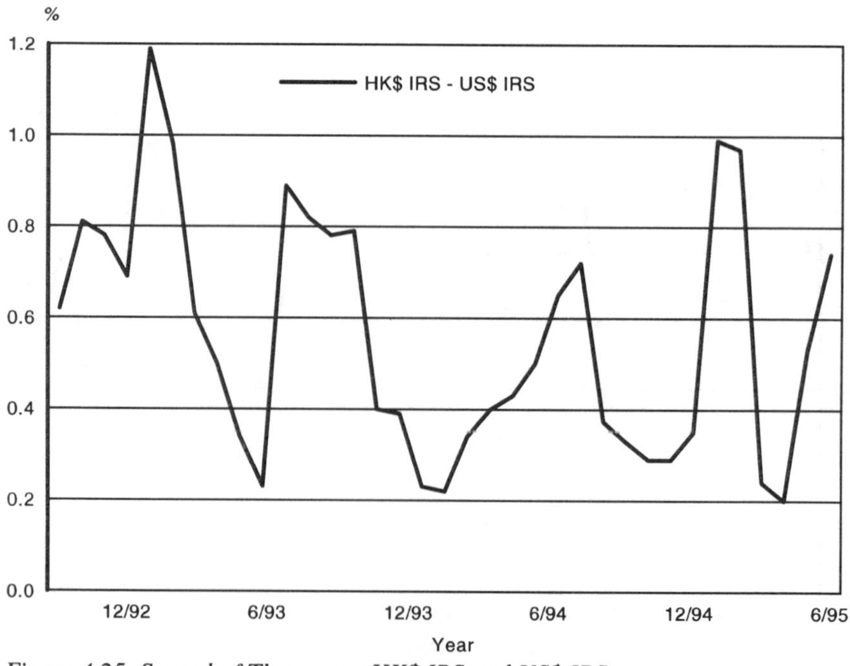

Figure 4.25 Spread of Three-year HK$ IRS and US$ IRS

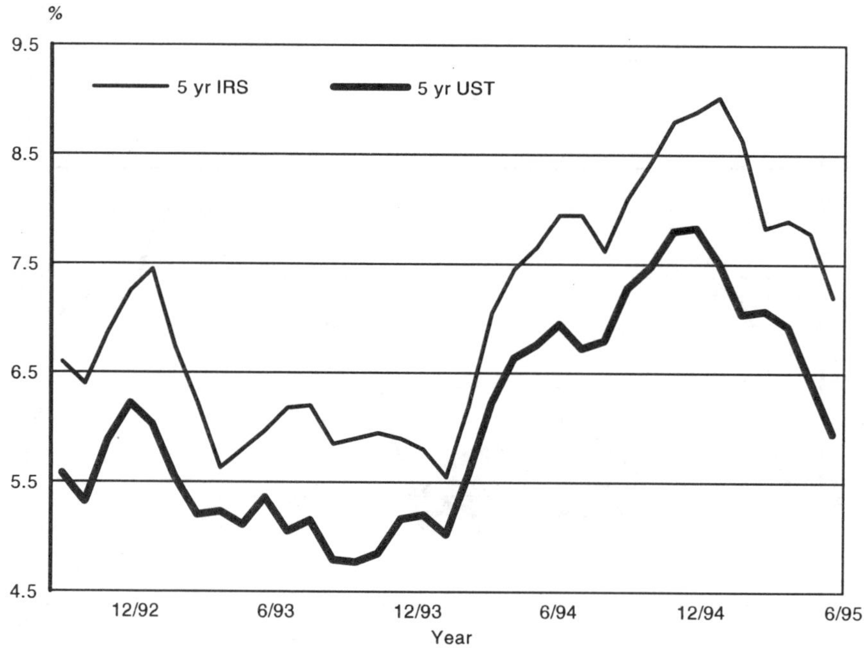

Figure 4.26 Historical Movement of Five-year HK$ IRS and Five-year US Treasury

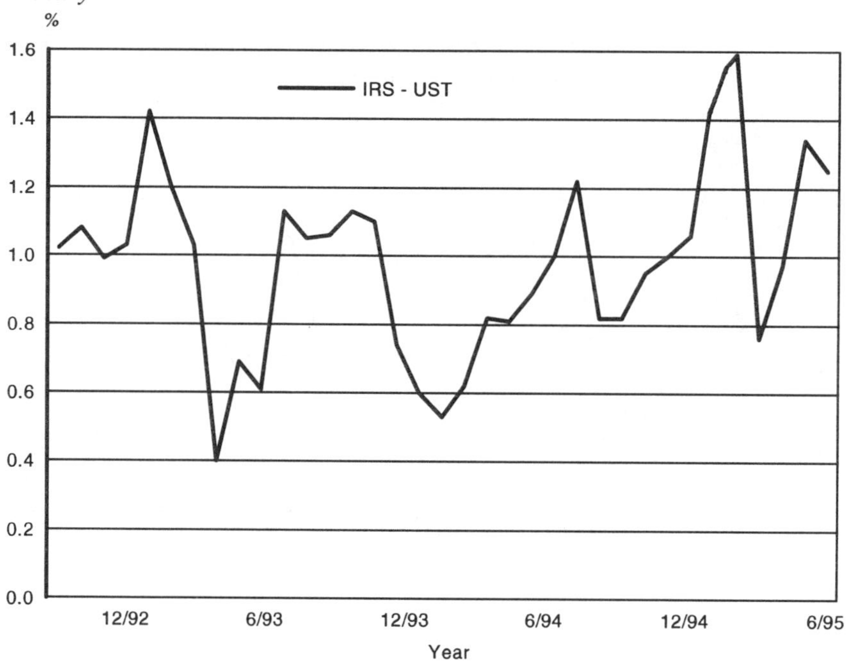

Figure 4.27 Spread of Five-year HK$ IRS and US Treasury

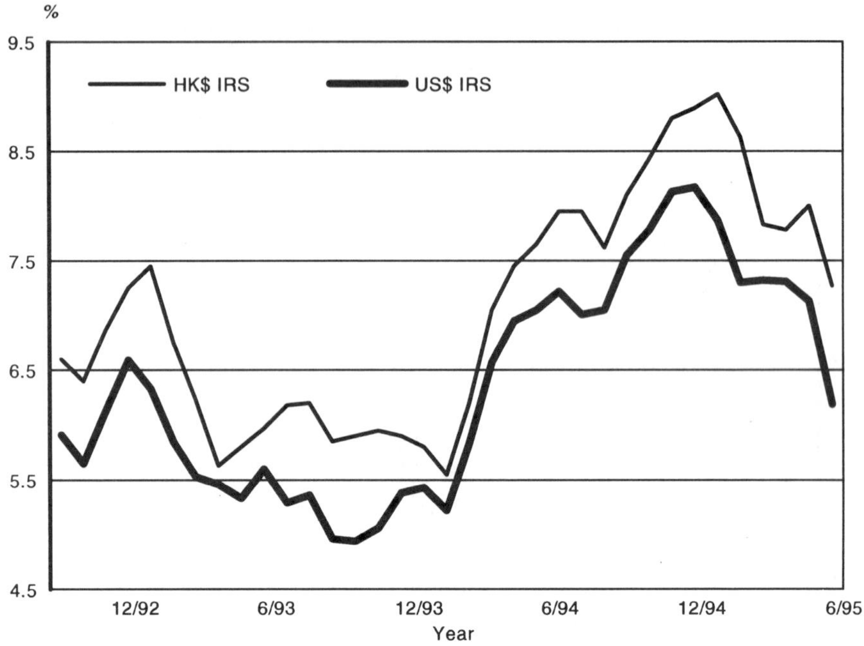

Figure 4.28 Historical Movement of Five-year HK$ IRS and Five-year US$ IRS

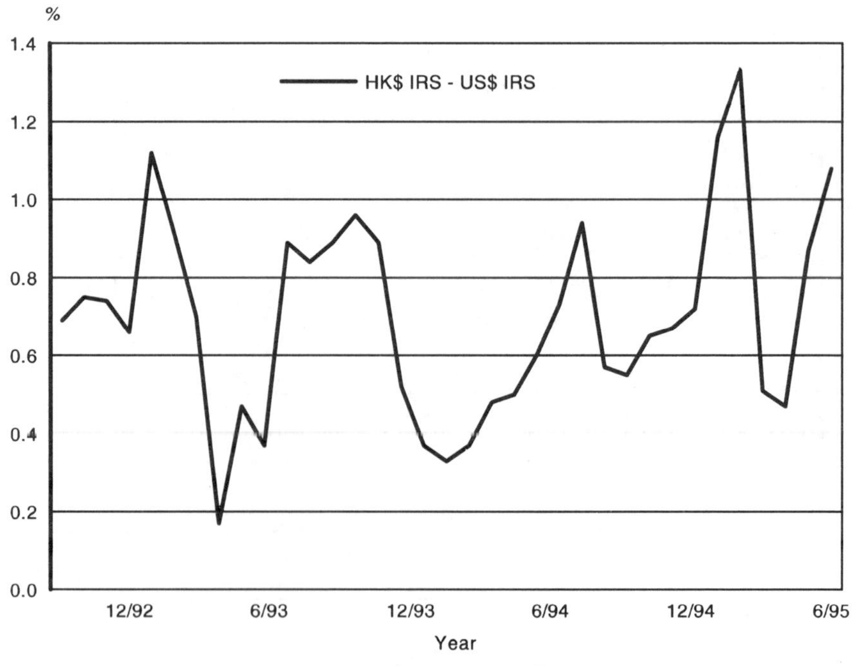

Figure 4.29 Spread of Five-year HK$ IRS and US$ IRS

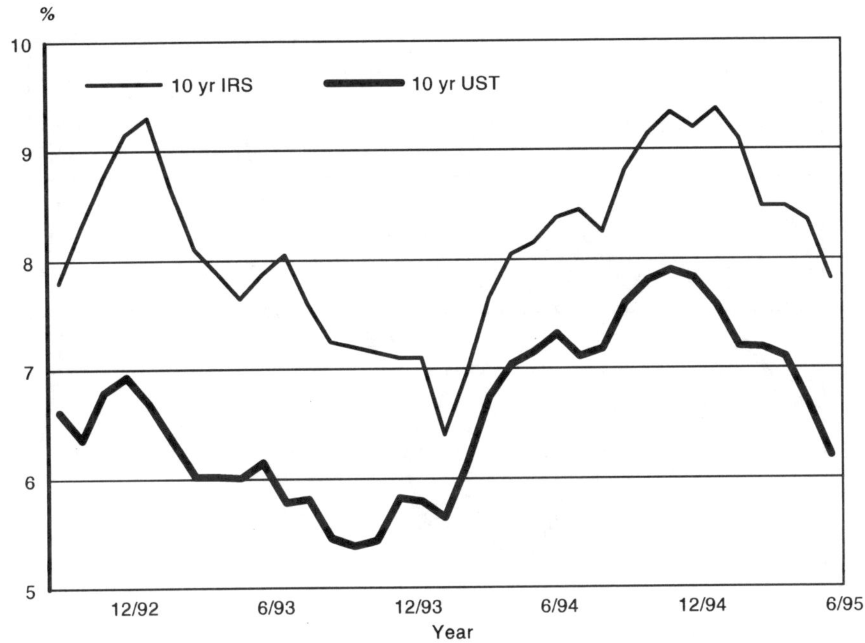

Figure 4.30 Historical Movement of Ten-year HK$ IRS and Ten-year US Treasury

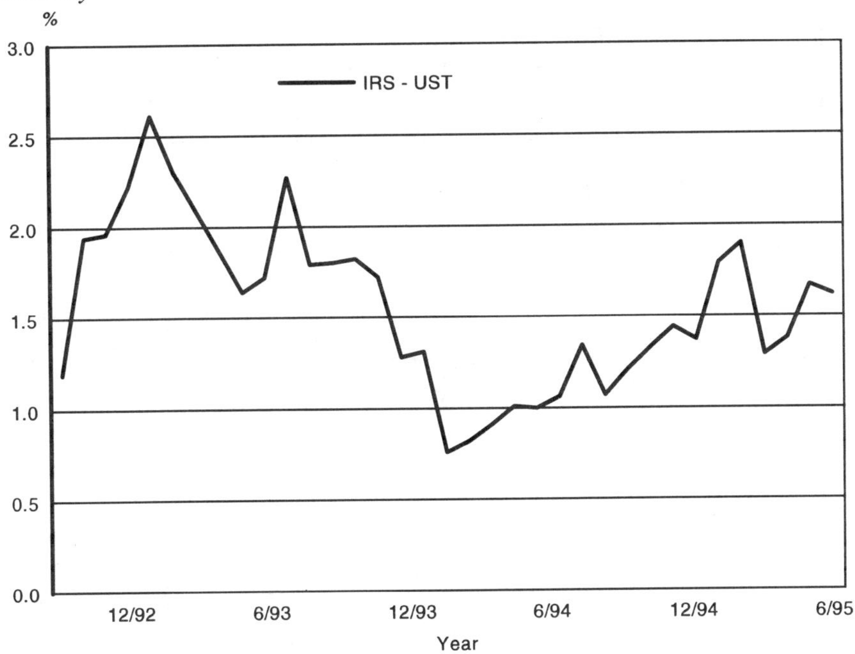

Figure 4.31 Spread of Ten-year HK$ IRS and US Treasury

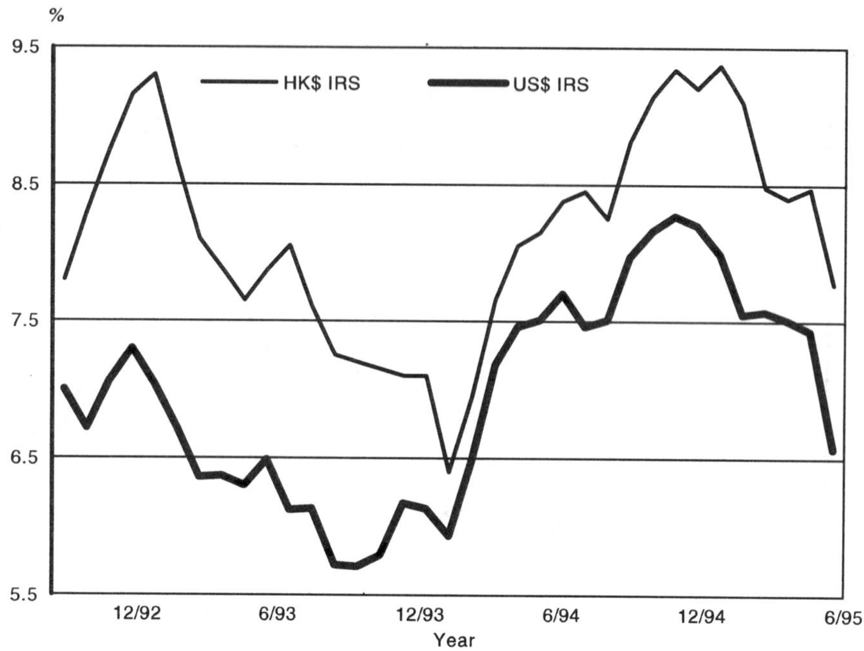

Figure 4.32 Historical Movement of Ten-year HK$ IRS and Ten-year US$ IRS

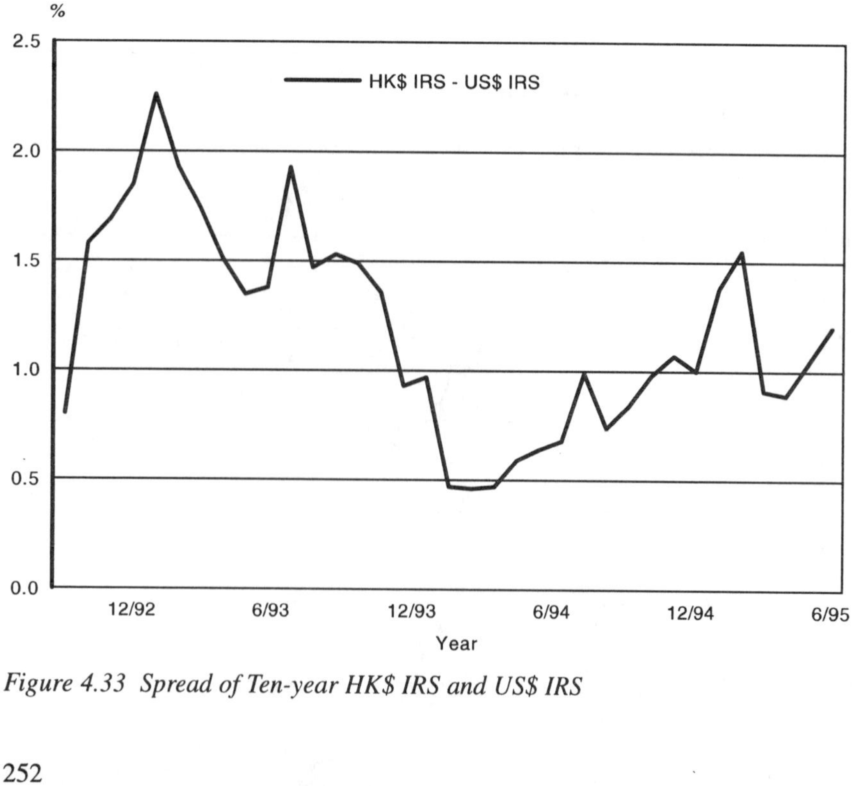

Figure 4.33 Spread of Ten-year HK$ IRS and US$ IRS

Fixed Income Options

Hong Kong features a growing market for caps, floors and swaptions; the market for bond options, however, remains dormant at the present time. Caps and floors generally reference three-month HIBOR though certain options are still structured to reference the interest rates implicit in FX forwards. Maturities for both extend to five years (with most activity occurring in the two- to three-year sector) and typical dealing size is HK$100 mln to HK$200 mln (approximately US$13 mln to US$26 mln); recent estimates indicate that approximately three to five caps/floors are executed per month. The bid-offer spread on intermediate maturity caps/floors is three to four volatility points (approximately half a volatility point over similar US dollar caps/floors), though this varies with strike level, demand and market conditions.

The swaption market features several combinations of American and European payer and receiver structures, but the most common are one- and two-year options into three-year swaps, and one- and two-year options into five-year swaps. Typical swaption dealing size in the interbank market is HK$100 mln (US$13 mln), and approximately HK$300 mln to HK$500 mln (US$38 mln to US$65 mln) of swaptions are executed on a monthly basis. It should be noted that there is presently no formal OTC market for bond options on EFNs, though certain *ad hoc* transactions take place on occasion. Additional activity in all fixed income options is likely to occur as the underlying cash markets expand and the forward/swap markets deepen.

Currency

Currency Forwards/Swaps

Hong Kong features active FX forward and CCS markets, both of which have been in existence since the mid-1980s. The FX forward market in Hong Kong dollars is very liquid to six months, though ready prices are available to 12 months; prices on long-term FX forwards to three and five years can also be obtained but dealing is driven by specific structured transactions (e.g. long-term asset or liability hedging). Typical forward dealing size in the interbank market is HK$150 mln (US$20 mln) (dealing size for corporate customers tends to be approximately half as large). Figure 4.34 traces the historical movement of three and 12 month HK$/US$ forwards.

The CCS market in Hong Kong is less active than the IRS market but still features acceptable liquidity. According to ISDA statistics, total outstanding notional Hong Kong dollar CCSs increased from HK$15.5 bln (US$2 bln) in 1993 to HK$19.2 bln (US$2.48 bln) in 1994; this ranks it as the third largest CCS market in Asia Pacific (after both Japan and Australia) (Choudhury, 1995).

CCSs are utilized by offshore counterparties funding through the domestic fixed and floating rate market (e.g. bonds or medium-term CDs, FRNs or FRCDs), who swap proceeds back into floating US dollars. Likewise, domestic corporations accessing the international capital markets (e.g. in the form of Yankee bonds,

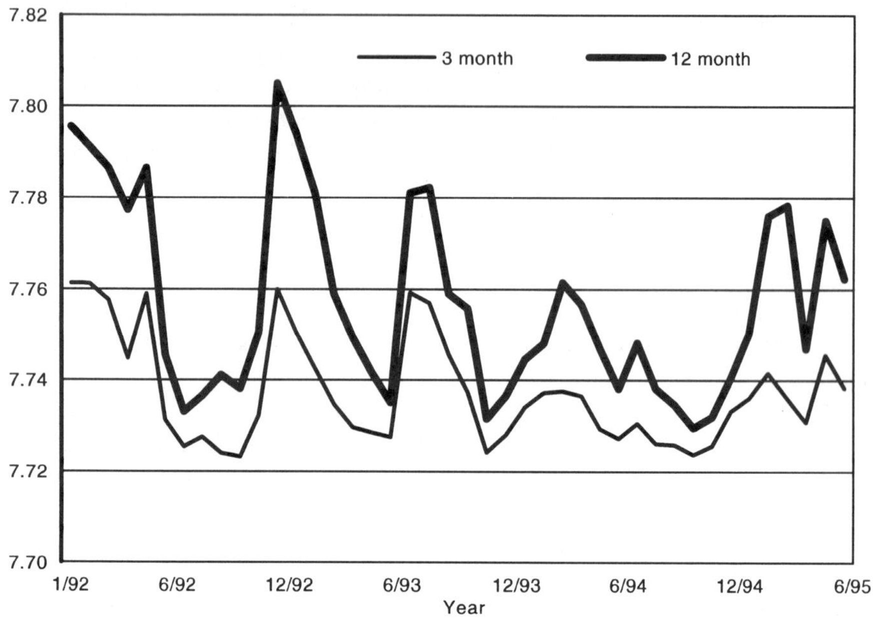

Source: Datastream

Figure 4.34 Historical Movement of Three- and 12-month HK$/US$ Forwards

EuroFRNs, and so on) utilize CCSs to bring funds back into fixed or floating Hong Kong dollars. The market is also used by domestic companies swapping foreign currency receipts into Hong Kong dollars and by offshore companies operating in Hong Kong swapping earnings into a home currency.

The primary structures of the domestic CCS market include cross currency basis swaps and fixed/floating currency swaps. Currency basis swaps are quoted as HIBOR against US$ LIBOR flat (on either a three- or six-month reset basis), out to five years; bid-offer spreads average ten basis points under normal market conditions and standard interbank dealing size is HK$100 mln (US$13 mln). Figures 4.35 through 4.38 chart the historical movement of HIBOR/US$ LIBOR rates and spreads. Fixed/floating currency swaps are quoted as fixed Hong Kong dollars (on an Actual/365 day basis) against six month US$ LIBOR flat, out to five years (though long-term transactions to seven and ten years are available); bid-offer spreads range from ten to 15 basis points under normal market conditions and standard interbank dealing size is HK$100 mln (US$13 mln). The CCS market is supported by an active FX market, as mentioned above, where forwards of three and five years are sufficiently liquid to provide pricing and hedging tools.

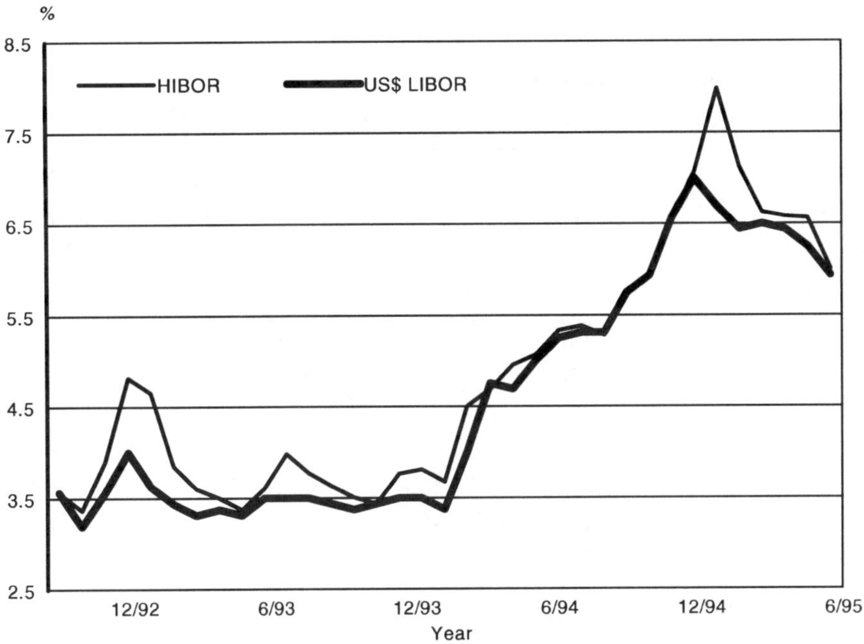

Figure 4.35 Historical Movement of Three-month HIBOR/US$ LIBOR rates

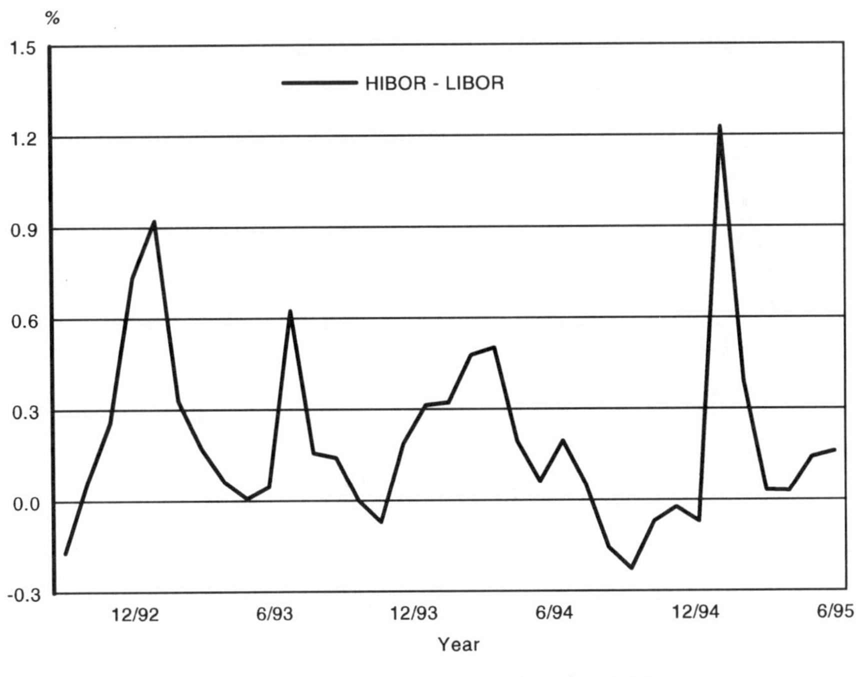

Figure 4.36 Spread of Three-month HIBOR and US$ LIBOR

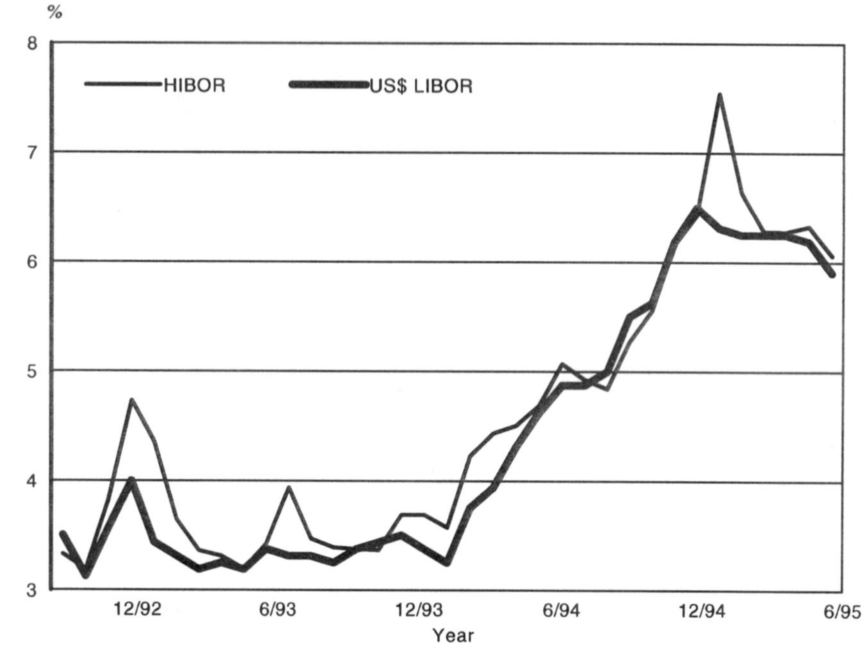

Figure 4.37 Historical Movement of Six-month HIBOR/US$ LIBOR rates

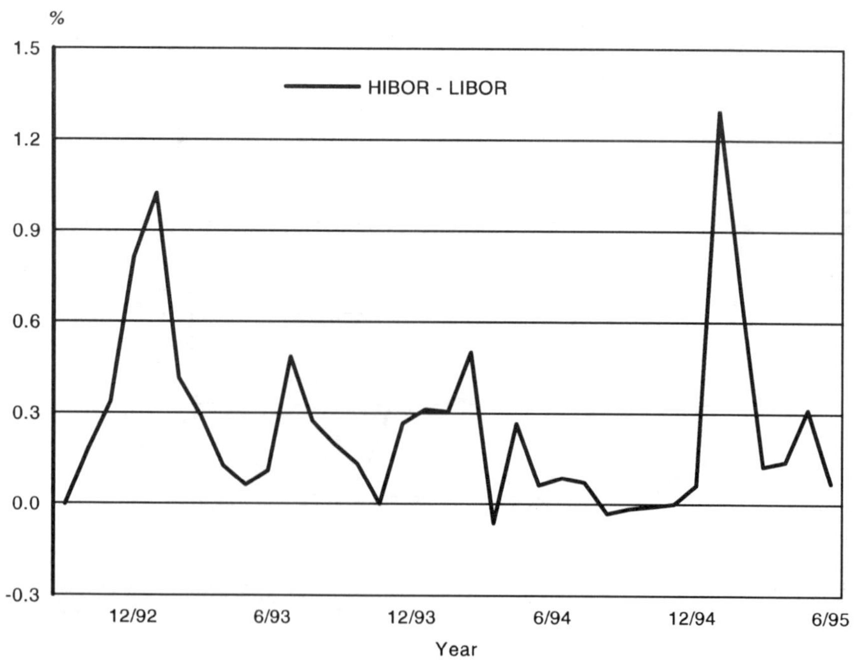

Figure 4.38 Spread of Six-month HIBOR and US$ LIBOR

A specialized segment of the Hong Kong currency market which is accessed by both retail and small institutional customers is the leveraged foreign exchange trading (LEFT) market. LEFT is effectively a margined FX product (based primarily on spot FX, but also including forward FX) which enables participants to assume speculative foreign exchange positions by placing a small deposit with the foreign exchange bank providing the service. Historically margin deposits have ranged from 0% to 20%; the higher the margin, the lower the gearing (e.g. a 20% margin implies a gearing of five times, while a 10% margin implies a gearing of ten times. If a customer places a 10% deposit of HK$1 mln, it may enter into spot/forward OTC currency transactions of up to HK$10 mln). In order to ensure the product is more effectively controlled (particularly at the retail level), the SFC recently imposed a 5% minimum margin requirement; it now also licenses all foreign exchange entities offering the product and encourages the use of stop-loss orders to prevent complete erosion of capital (although stop loss orders do not always permit the closing down of a position, particularly in times of market volatility and illiquidity).

Currency Options

The market for OTC Hong Kong dollar currency options is reasonably well established. The lack of currency restrictions together with underlying liquidity in spot and forward Hong Kong dollar trading have combined to create an active domestic options market. OTC FX options are available on HK$/US$, as well as other major crossrates, in one-, three-, six- and 12-month maturities (though deals to five years are executed on occasion); standard interbank dealing size is HK$50 mln (US$6.5 mln). Options may be structured with either American or European exercise and can result in cash settlement or physical delivery. Pricing of options is in volatility terms, with an average bid-offer spread of one to two volatility points for six-month European at-the-money forward options, depending on market conditions. Participants in the market include interbank institutions, corporations and sophisticated retail clients. Note that in addition to vanilla options, a certain amount of exotic option trading occurs (based on barriers, Asians, lookbacks, digitals and so on); overall exotic activity, however, is still quite limited.

Commodity

Commodity Forwards/Swaps

The market for OTC commodity forwards and swaps is not well established in Hong Kong. Most commodity-related trading is based on speculation in gold, primarily on a physical spot basis rather than through derivatives. As indicated above, listed commodity derivatives (e.g. cotton, soybeans, sugar) have failed to generate interest in the local market; it is not surprising to note, then, that commodity forwards and swaps have remained dormant.

Commodity Options

As with commodity forwards and swaps, the market for commodity options referencing domestic indicators is insignificant. While certain investors buy and sell OTC gold options, overall activity is very thin.

LOCAL REGULATORY/LEGAL TREATMENT OF DERIVATIVES

Hong Kong has maintained rigorous regulation of derivative products over the past few years; oversight and control was made more stringent following the four day closure of the SEHK in October 1987, the resultant losses on HSI futures and the collapse of the FGC. The primary regulators in the Hong Kong market are the Securities and Futures Commission (SFC) and the Hong Kong Monetary Authority (HKMA). The territory's two primary exchanges, Stock Exchange of Hong Kong (SEHK) and Hong Kong Futures Exchange (HKFE) are self-regulated entities.

Futures trading is regulated by the SFC which was given its powers under the 1975 Commodity Trading Ordinance (CTO). The SFC's regulatory powers include: (a) approval of all changes to the HKFE's constitution and approval of new contracts or changes to existing contracts (which must fall into one of three categories, including deliverable contracts, non-deliverable contracts or futures options on non-deliverable contracts); (b) licensing and registration of futures participants (including dealers, commodity trading advisers, dealers representatives, commodities trading advisers representatives and brokers); and, (c) enforcement of trading practices (items (b) and (c) fall under the rules of the CTO). Following the collapse of the FGC in 1987, additional reforms were enacted to protect and regulate market participants. Post-1987 reforms included creation of the Hong Kong Clearing Corporation (HKCC) to guarantee and clear all trades, development of a liquidity reserve fund managed by the HKCC, establishment of a new clearing system, expulsion of non-member shareholders, improvements in reporting of open positions and establishment of position limits based on capital size (by individual member).

In contrast to the long-established regulation of listed derivatives (dating back to 1975, with subsequent amendments), the regulation of OTC derivatives in the Hong Kong marketplace underwent fundamental changes as recently as December 1993. Prior to that time, the government's Gambling Ordinance made OTC options, OTC index options, caps, floors, commodity swaps, index-linked warrants and index/stock futures (except HSI futures) legally unenforceable. In December 1993 the government passed the Gambling (Amendment) Ordinance and deemed the following transactions to be exempt from the Gambling Ordinance (and therefore not legally unenforceable): (a) any contract listed on the SEHK or other major exchange; (b) any contract entered into by a registered dealer under the CTO or Securities Ordinance; and (c) any contract entered into by invitation, where restrictions set out in the Protection of Investors Ordinance are deemed inapplicable. Restrictions would be considered inapplicable if the contract is: (a) governed by an offering document approved by the SFC; (b) transacted outside Hong Kong; or (c) executed within Hong Kong with a sophisticated, professional investor. It should be noted that amendments to the CTO were enacted to permit the creation of equity futures, as discussed above.

In order for listed equity options trading to begin on the SEHK an amendment was required to Section 76(1)(a) of the Securities Ordinance (Cap 333), which had previously prohibited the public trading of options on securities; the amendment was accomplished through changes in regulations rather than changes in primary legislation. In addition, in order to promote development of an options market short selling of equities must be permitted; accordingly, the introduction of options was accompanied by a short selling 'pilot' programme. Amendments to the Stamp Duty Ordinance and the Inland Revenue Ordinance were enacted once the programme was launched.

Three other regulatory guidelines involving derivatives were put forth in 1994 and 1995. First, in late 1994 the Hong Kong Government expanded the powers of the Exchange Fund to include participation in derivatives. The changes are contained in Exchange Fund (Amendment) Bill 1994, and are designed to allow the Financial Secretary to enter into derivative arrangements, following consultation with the Exchange Fund Advisory Committee, to the extent transactions are for hedging purposes (i.e. primarily hedging of fixed rate liabilities arising from the issuance of Exchange Fund securities). Second, in 1995, the Office of the Commissioner of Insurance released guidelines regarding the prudent use of derivatives for domestic insurance companies; the guidelines provide details on the acceptable types of derivatives insurance companies may employ and outlines the proper level of derivative controls required to ensure risks remain well reported and managed. Third, the local treatment of bilateral netting in Hong Kong was clarified in early 1995. The Company and Financial Law Committee of the Law Society of Hong Kong put forth a statement indicating that the right of set-off will apply in Hong Kong when a company in liquidation has mutual dealings (including debits or credits) with other parties; in such instances only the net balance of all obligations (whether a payment or receipt) will be relevant. The provision is contained in Section 35 of the Bankruptcy Ordinance. The HKMA has revised its capital treatment of off-balance sheet exposures based on the concept of bilateral netting. Specifically, as long as a written bilateral netting agreement is in existence between two parties set-off will apply and the HKMA will deem the relevant exposure to be the net exposure of all derivative transactions (including fixed income, currency and equity derivatives).

As use of OTC derivatives has increased in the Hong Kong marketplace during the course of the past decade, the HKMA has been eager to have participants conform to international standards of derivatives risk management. This became particularly true following the release of the Group of 30 derivatives study (and in the face of various derivatives-related losses in 1993 to 1995). The HKMA is in the process of adopting full guidelines regarding derivatives risk management. Each institution involved in the derivatives business will be required to create written risk management policies approved by a bank's directors, understand its risks in advance of transacting, establish and maintain an independent risk management function, adopt prudent risk standards, mark-to-market all derivatives positions on a daily basis, prepare and distribute timely and accurate risk reports and engage in periodic audits of the risk management process. As part of its oversight function, the HKMA will also carry out onsite inspections from time to time. The hope of the regulators is that adherence to the process detailed above will eliminate derivatives-related problems in the local market.

LOCAL ACCOUNTING PRACTICES FOR DERIVATIVES

Despite the fact that Hong Kong features one of the most developed accounting frameworks in Asia Pacific, its treatment of derivatives is still vague; local accounting regulations do not currently require mandatory use of specific standards for derivatives. Hong Kong institutions engaged in derivatives thus tend to draw on accounting guidelines put forth by the International Accounting Standards (IAS) or the British Bankers' Association (BBA); both provide UK-based institutions with guidelines on the treatment of derivatives, and are often utilized by Hong Kong institutions.

Both IAS and BBA guidelines incorporate usage of accrual accounting and market value accounting; use of each depends on whether the derivative exists for trading or hedging purposes (this is consistent with international accounting treatment of derivatives in certain other countries such as the UK, the US and Australia). Most local institutions active in interest rate or currency derivatives used for trading purposes use market value accounting, which revalues the derivative at each reporting period and includes unrealized gains/losses in the current income statement. Gains or losses are not accounted for since they are already embedded in the valuation of the derivative. When flows are paid or received, they are recorded as realized profits or losses and the market value of the derivative automatically adjusts as payments and receipts are no longer included as future cash flows in the valuation of the derivative. If derivatives are used as hedges the accrual accounting method is employed, which simply accrues flows up to the next settlement period, at which point they are recognized. Under the accrual method the current market value of the derivative is not reflected in the accounts.

PROSPECTS FOR THE LOCAL DERIVATIVE MARKET

Summarized below are the near-term (one- to three-year) and medium-term (three- to five-year) prospects for domestic derivatives in Hong Kong.

Near-term:

- Expanded trading volume in index futures and options as domestic and foreign interest in local equities remains buoyant; abandonment or restructuring of HKFE's sub-index futures.
- Potential abandonment or restructuring of HKFE's HIBOR futures and gold futures due to inactivity.
- Growth in listed covered and non-collateralized equity warrants as investors continue to participate in the market and local companies continue expanding capital bases.
- Gradual expansion in domestic IRSs and interest rate derivatives as the change of sovereignty stabilizes risk premia, the domestic sovereign bond market continues to grow and domestic financing opportunities continue to increase.
- Initial growth in listed currency derivatives (i.e. HKFE rolling spot futures and HKFE/PHLX currency options); sustainable liquidity to be determined, but prospects are strong given domestic bias toward currency hedging/speculating.
- Adoption of formal accounting guidelines for derivatives.

Medium-term:

- Growth in IRS, forward and fixed income option trading as the domestic fixed income market deepens, the yield curve lengthens and pricing stabilizes.
- Expansion in CCSs and currency derivatives as offshore funding opportunities continue to increase and hedging of import/export receipts remains buoyant.
- Continued expansion of listed equity warrants as equity financing increases.
- Cooperation with Chinese authorities on developing standardized derivatives for use in both Hong Kong and China.

Exchange	Contract	1993 Volume (contracts)	1994 Volume (contracts)
HKFE	Share futures	n/l*	n/l*
	Hang Seng Index futures	2,400,000	4,190,000
	Hang Seng Index options	300,000	606,000
	Hang Seng Property Sub-index futures	0	0
	Hang Seng Commerce & Industry Sub-index futures	0	0
	Hang Seng Finance Sub-index futures	0	0
	Hang Seng Utilities Sub-index futures	0	0
	HIBOR futures	0	0
	Gold futures	0	0
SEHK	Equity options	n/l*	n/l*

* n/l: contract not yet listed

Table 4.25 Summary of 1993/1994 Listed Futures and Options Turnover

	Overall Liquidity	Liquid/ Maximum Maturity	Interbank dealing size	Average bid-offer spread
Equity/Index Swaps	good	1–3 yrs/5 yrs	n/a	n/a
Equity/Index Options	good	1–12 months/3 yrs	n/a	n/a
Interest Rate Swaps	good	2–3 yrs/10 yrs	HK$300 – HK$400 mln	5–15 bps
Interest Rate Options	fair	1–3 yrs/5 yrs	HK$100 – HK$200 mln	3–4 pts
Currency Swaps	good	2–3 yrs/10 yrs	HK$100 mln	10–15 bps
Currency Options	good	1–12 months/5 yrs	HK$50 mln	1–2 pts

Table 4.26 Summary of Domestic OTC Derivatives

5: India

FINANCIAL MARKET OVERVIEW

India's financial markets are sizeable on a primary basis but generally illiquid on a secondary basis. Secondary trading in key equity, fixed income and currency instruments has been dampened by regionalized domestic markets, restrictive regulations limiting foreign participation in local debt and equity instruments, and strict controls concerning the purchase and sale of foreign exchange. As a result of these barriers the domestic derivative market has been very slow to develop.

The Indian equity market dates back to 1875 when the Bombay Stock Exchange (BSE) was established. The BSE was renamed the Native Share and Stock Brokers' Association in 1887, but reverted to its former name and structure after India gained independence. Although the BSE remains India's primary equity exchange the country also features numerous regional stock exchanges (e.g. the exchanges of Jaipur, Bhubaneswar, Ahmedabad, Cochin, Delhi, Madhya Pradesh, Magadh, Pune, Bangalore, Gauhati, Calcutta, Hyderabad, Kanara, Ludhiana, Madras, Uttar Pradesh and Coimbatore); the country also features two new exchanges, the Over-the-Counter Exchange of India (OTCEI) and the National Stock Exchange (NSE). One of the key challenges presently facing the country is the unification of regional markets and trading; the substantial number of listed companies and the fragmentation of exchanges has created significant secondary liquidity problems. In addition, the market is plagued by operational and trade processing problems which complicate settlement; establishment of the NSE as a central trading forum is designed to alleviate several of these concerns over time. The Indian market featured total market capitalization of US$127.5 bln at the end of 1994 (based on the BSE, which comprises 90% of local market capitalization) ranking it as the ninth largest of Asia Pacific's 13 markets. Figure 5.1 illustrates the historical movement of the key Bombay Sensitive Index while Table 5.1 contains information on the general equity market.

Note that foreign investor access to domestic equities is very strictly controlled. In order for offshore investors to participate in the local market they must first be approved as foreign institutional investors (FIIs) through the Securities and Exchange Board of India (SEBI). Once approved as FIIs (for an initial period of five years), offshore investors may participate in the local market, but must still adhere to two ceilings: shareholdings of all FIIs cannot account for more than 24% of a domestic company's share capital and shareholdings of any single FII cannot account for more than 5% of a domestic company's share capital.

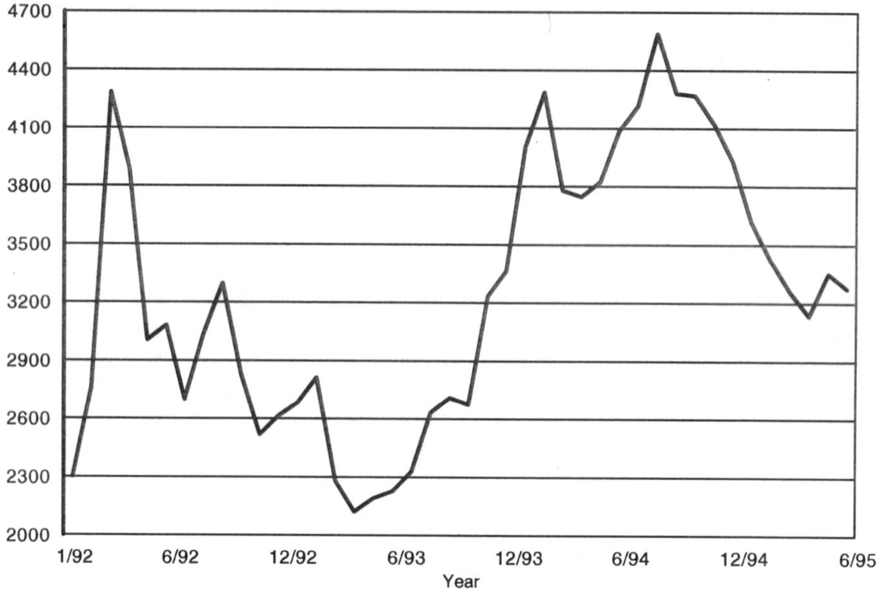

Figure 5.1 Historical Movement of the Bombay Sensitive Index

Year*	**Market Capitalization (US$ bln)**	**Trading Value (US$ bln)**	**Listed Companies (#)**
1994	127.5	27.3	4,413
1993	97.9	21.9	3,263
1992	65.1	20.6	2,781
1991	47.7	24.3	2,556
1990	38.6	21.9	2,435

* to December of each year; Source: IFC, 1995.

Note: data based on BSE figures only, which accounts for 90% of the country's market capitalization and trading value

	1/92–6/95 Annualized Return	**1/92–6/95 Total Return**
Bombay Sensex	11.93%	45.55%

Table 5.1 Domestic Equity Market Indicators

The Indian fixed income market is substantial on a primary basis but often illiquid on a secondary basis. The sovereign segment of the market features issuance of short-term Government of India Treasury bills (to one year) and Government of India bonds (from two to ten years, though longer-term issues have been floated in the past). The sovereign market also includes issuance of state government bonds (floated by various states in their own names), state government guaranteed bonds (floated by state financial corporations and authorities with the backing of each state government) and state bank certificates of deposit (CDs, floated by major banking institutions, most of which are owned by the central or state governments). Government-controlled enterprises (also known in the local market as public sector undertakings, or PSUs) issue public sector bonds (PSBs), in either taxable or tax-free form, with maturities of seven to ten years; PSBs do not carry the explicit backing of the central government. Total outstanding short-and long-term sovereign issues amounted to IRP 2.3 tln (US$72.6 bln) in 1994. The private sector bond market is still modest in size but increasing very rapidly. Instruments issued by private sector corporations (and the newer private sector banks), include commercial paper, commercial bills and CDs in the short end of the curve (to one year), and fixed rate non-convertible debentures, convertible debentures, party convertible debentures and zero coupon debentures in the intermediate and long end of the curve (from two to ten years); secondary trading in many of these securities is now effected through the NSE. Total private sector outstandings reached IRP330 bln (US$10.4 bln) at the end of 1994 (World Bank, 1995).

The key interest rates in the local market include the Government of India treasury bill rate (the short-term borrowing cost of the government), Government of India bond yields (the medium- and long-term borrowing costs of the government), and the interbank call rate (the short-term borrowing cost for banks in the local call market). Table 5.2 contains details on the key domestic interest rates.

Rate	**Payment Frequency**	**Compounding Frequency**	**Day Count Convention**
Gov't bills	–	–	Actual/360
I/B call	–	–	Actual/360
Gov't bonds	semi-annual	semi-annual	Actual/360

Table 5.2 Key Domestic Interest Rates

The Indian rupee (IRP) is not yet a fully convertible currency, though efforts are underway to achieve full convertibility within the next few years. The value of the rupee is managed by the Reserve Bank of India (RBI) which observes activity in the interbank market on a daily basis and sets appropriate buying and selling rates; all FX quotes must remain within the daily range set by the RBI. Average turnover in the interbank market is estimated at IRP9.5 bln to IRP 15.8 bln (US$300 mln to US$500 mln) per day (Rattanaik, 1994, ERG, 1995); standard interbank dealing size is IRP10 mln (US$300,000) and bid-offer spreads are approximately IRP0.02/US$ under normal market conditions. It should be noted that under current regulations Indian banks are only permitted to sell rupees to offshore institutions, and cannot buy rupees from such institutions (on either a spot or forward basis). In order for foreign investors to participate in the local currency market they must first be approved as FIIs, with the intent of using local currency to purchase domestic securities for investment. Once approved as FIIs, institutions also receive dispensation from the RBI to open local bank accounts for the conversion of foreign currencies into rupee; FII's are permitted to convert rupees back into foreign currencies and repatriate funds at any time. Figure 5.2 below traces the historical movement of the rupee.

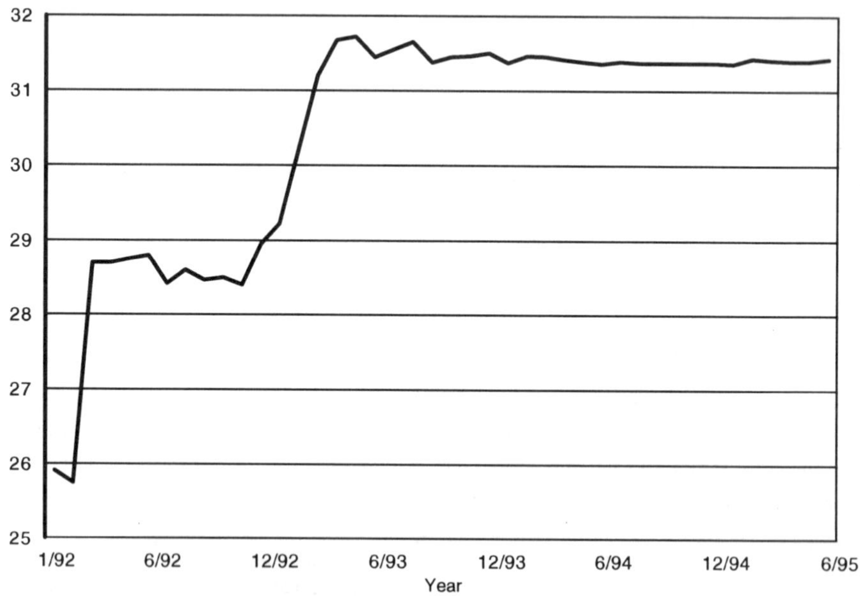

Figure 5.2 Historical Movement of Spot IRP/US$

DERIVATIVE MARKETS AND PRODUCTS

LISTED DERIVATIVE EXCHANGES

India's listed derivative market is presently limited to trading of issuer equity warrants and convertible bonds (also known locally as convertible debentures); listing and trading of both types of derivatives is concentrated on six of the country's largest stock exchanges.

The Bombay Stock Exchange (BSE), established in 1875 and restructured into its present form in 1956, is the country's primary forum for equity trading; in addition to equities the Exchange also trades convertible debentures and partly convertible debentures. Trading of all equities and derivatives recently shift from open-outcry on the floor of the Exchange to electronic screen-based trading through the automated BOLT system. Clearing and settlement of trades is effected through a separate clearinghouse.

The Cochin Stock Exchange (CSE), a regional equity exchange established in 1878, lists convertible debentures. The Exchange trades all securities via open-outcry auction, and clears and settles all transactions itself.

The Delhi Stock Exchange (DSE), created in 1913 and restructured into its present form in 1956, is a reasonably active trading forum for equities, convertible debentures and equity warrants. All trading occurs on an open outcry auction basis, and clearing and settling is effected by the Exchange itself.

The National Stock Exchange (NSE), which began operations in 1994, lists and trades equities, convertible debentures and warrants. All trading on the NSE occurs via computerized trading systems and trades are cleared and settled in automated fashion by the Exchange itself.

The Over-the-Counter Exchange of India (OTCEI), founded in 1990, is a diverse exchange active in equities, debentures and convertible debentures. Convertible (and partly convertible) debentures are traded via the Exchange's screen-based system, and trades are cleared and settled through an independent settlement bank.

The Stock Exchange of Ahmedabad (SEA), originally established in 1894, is one of the country's largest regional stock exchanges. In addition to trading equities the SEA also lists and trades convertible debentures. Trading occurs via open outcry on the floor of the Exchange, and clearing and settling of trades is accomplished through a separate clearinghouse.

Note that unlike virtually every other country discussed in this text, India has no firm plans to proceed with the establishment of a domestic futures exchange to trade financial derivatives. Although there have been discussions and vague references regarding the creation of an exchange at some future time, no details or

Exchange	**Primary Derivatives**
Bombay Stock Exchange (BSE)	Convertible debentures
Cochin Stock Exchange (CSE)	Convertible debentures
Delhi Stock Exchange (DSE)	Convertible debentures; issuer equity warrants
National Stock Exchange (NSE)	Convertible debentures
Over-the-Counter Exchange of India (OTCEI)	Convertible debentures
Stock Exchange of Ahmedabad (SEA)	Convertible debentures

Table 5.3 Listed Derivative Exchanges

timetable have been released. It should be noted that a small number of specialized commodity trading associations (which trade standardized "futures contracts") are presently in existence in India. Such associations are informal in nature, however, and are not generally considered legitimate derivative exchanges; we shall not consider them in this chapter. Table 5.3 summarizes the key domestic exchanges which trade in derivative securities.

LISTED FUTURES AND OPTIONS

Equity

Equity Futures/Options

The domestic Indian market features no equity futures or options at the present time. Although the Indian government approved trading in equity options in January 1995 by lifting a 38 year ban on such products (through amendments to the Securities and Exchange Board of India Act of 1992 and the Securities Contracts (Regulation) Act of 1956), it is unlikely that equity options will be introduced to the marketplace in a meaningful fashion in the foreseeable future. Underlying turnover in cash equities is still low (and made lower by the ban on forward trading, as discussed below) and the stock exchanges of India are still fragmented and unable to produce critical mass in trading; since option markets depend on broad and liquid cash equity markets to achieve success, it is unlikely India will launch a comprehensive options programme until trading is unified and liquidity improves.

Index Futures/Options/Futures Options

Although the Indian market does not feature index futures, it took an important, though very preliminary, step in 1994 when it created a new, broad-based market-capitalization index known as the BSE 200. The index, comprised of 200 equities, was established to give a broader, and more representative, view of the Indian equity market, under the belief that the widely quoted Bombay Sensitive Index is too heavily weighted toward large blue-chip stocks (e.g. the 30 largest Indian stocks). To the extent stock index futures are introduced in the Indian market in the medium term, the BSE 200 index is likely to be the reference for such contracts.

Fixed Income

Deposit Futures/Options/Futures Options

The domestic market does not presently list deposit futures or options and there are no plans to introduce such derivatives in the near term.

Interest Rate Futures/Options/Futures Options

The domestic market does not presently list interest rate futures or options and has no plans to introduce such contracts in the near term. Although India's bond market is significant in size (e.g. US$83 bln) and creation of bond futures could be both useful and viable, there have been no co-ordinated efforts regarding the development of such contracts.

Currency

Currency Futures/Options/Futures Options

The Indian market does not presently list currency futures or options and has no near term plans to do so; until currency convertibility becomes a reality and foreign access to rupees becomes unrestricted, such futures would in any event meet with limited demand or success.

Commodity

Commodity Futures/Options/Futures Options

India has a very small commodity futures market which is centred exclusively on specialized Indian agricultural products (e.g. pepper, turmeric, jaggery (sugar), jute). A small number of minor regional exchanges and associations (e.g. the Indian Pepper and Spice Trade Association at Kochi and the Bombay Oil and Oilseeds Exchange at Bombay) list and trade certain contracts, though overall turnover is still negligible. Given the relatively small size and specialized nature of these exchanges/associations, we shall not consider them further in this text.

LISTED/OVER-THE-COUNTER WARRANTS, CONVERTIBLES AND HYBRIDS

Equity

Equity Warrants

India features a large domestic equity warrant market. Domestic equity warrants, which are generally attached to rupee bond issues (known in the local market as non-convertible debentures (NCDs)), are issued by companies on their own equity; exercise results in the flotation of new equity by the underlying company. These derivatives, which carry maturities ranging from one to five years, are typically listed on one of India's stock exchanges; the derivatives are detached from NCDs and traded separately, either on an exchange or OTC. Representative warrant issuers in the local market include Kesoram Industries, Sabeor Organics Gujarat, Indian Rayon, DCM Shriram Industries and Bombay Dyeing and Manufacturing, among many others.

In addition to flotation of domestic warrants, OTC equity warrants attached to

Indian global depository receipts (GDRs) have been floated on a periodic basis for several years. Representative issuers in this category include Bombay Dyeing and Manufacturing, CESC Limited, Hindustan Development Corporation, Hindalco Industries, Tata Engineering and ITC Limited. Most issues are US dollar-denominated instruments with maturities of two to four years which are listed on, and traded through, offshore exchanges; conversion is into underlying rupee-denominated shares of the Indian issuer. It should be noted that flotation of offshore equity warrants has been sufficiently widespread over the past few years that in August 1994 SEBI banned warrant issues ahead of initial public offerings of stock; in October 1994 it also banned issuance of warrants attached to new GDR issues. Whether future issues of GDRs with attached warrants will be permitted remains to be seen; thus far the ban has not extended to offshore bonds-with-warrants, so future warrant issues may be floated through such structures. Appendix II contains details on Indian equity warrants.

It should be noted that, unlike equities in other Asia Pacific markets, equities in the Indian market have not been references for issues of OTC covered warrants. While foreign financial institutions operating offshore routinely float covered warrants on single stocks in Malaysia, Hong Kong and Singapore, among others, they have not done the same in the Indian market, primarily because foreign investor access to shares is restrictive and liquidity in the local market is poor. As FII restrictions are loosened, OTC Indian single stock warrants may become more prevalent.

Basket/Index Warrants

Although the domestic market does not feature listed or OTC basket/index warrants, institutions in the offshore market float periodic issues of such derivatives. Basket and index warrants, which reference groups of domestic stocks or the broader Indian market, are generally unlisted, or listed on an overseas exchange, and traded on an OTC basis; maturities range from one to three years. One representative issue in this category is Bankers Trust's two tranche, US dollar index call warrants on the Bombay Index (1994). Given the poor secondary liquidity of the Indian market and the restrictions placed on foreign investor access to local shares, overall offshore warrant activity is still negligible (particularly in comparison with other Asia Pacific markets). As the market liberalizes and investor access to local shares is made simpler, additional warrant issues are expected.

Convertibles

Indian companies have been very active issuers of convertible securities in both the domestic and offshore markets. The onshore market features significant issuance of domestic convertible bonds, known locally as fully convertible debentures (FCDs) (note that although domestic FCDs are now convertible on a voluntary basis, bonds were previously convertible on a compulsory basis). The onshore market also features a second class of convertibles known as partly convertible debentures

(PCDs); such securities include a debt component (known as a khokha) which is repaid in tranches, along with an embedded equity option which can be exchanged for a pre-specified number of shares should conversion occur. The khokha is often traded as a separate discount security by financial institutions. The local Indian market also features issuance of zero-coupon convertible debentures (ZCCDs); the Government of India launched the market's inaugural ZCCD with an IRP28.5 bln (US$900 mln) issue in 1993. Domestic Indian convertibles generally carry maturities of five to ten years and pay semi-annual coupons which are often 100-200 basis points lower than those found on conventional fixed rate debentures. Issues may be listed on one of the country's regional exchanges or the NSE, and may be traded on an exchange or OTC. Overall liquidity in domestic convertibles is very thin, however, as most investors purchase securities with a view towards holding until maturity or conversion. The market is currently characterized by a large number of small issues from a broad range of corporations.

In addition to domestic convertible bond issues, Indian companies are active issuers of Euro-convertibles in the offshore market; unlike other Asia Pacific companies, Indian issuers have only utilized the Eurodollar market and have not accessed the domestic Swiss market. Blue-chip Indian companies began floating convertibles in the Eurodollar market in 1993; total issuance reached an impressive US$555 mln in 1993 though this figure declined to US$330 mln in 1994 after the Ministry of Finance imposed a series of regulations intended to control the amount of offshore issuance (e.g. individual companies are now only permitted to issue one offshore convertible per year, while industrial groups can only issue two bonds; in addition, bonds can only be floated to raise funds for the financing of domestic capital investment, early repayment of foreign debts or the importation of capital goods). Blue-chip Indian companies such as Reliance Industries, Jindal Strips, SCICI, Essar Gujarat, Sterlite Industries and Gujarat Ambjua, among others, have all accessed the Eurodollar convertible market with five- to ten-year issues. Bonds are typically issued in bearer form, and are listed on offshore exchanges and traded OTC; all securities are convertible into the shares of the Indian issuer at a rupee conversion price. Indian domestic and offshore convertible issues are highlighted in Appendix III.

Index-linked Notes

Institutions in the domestic and offshore markets have not yet floated index-linked notes tied to the overall value of the Indian stock market.

Fixed Income

Fixed Income Warrants

Institutions operating in the domestic and offshore markets have not floated listed or OTC fixed income warrants related to Indian government bonds, primarily because investor demand for such instruments is non-existent.

Currency

Currency Warrants

Institutions in the domestic and offshore markets have not issued rupee listed or OTC currency warrants, primarily as a result of the country's strict currency controls.

Commodity

Commodity Warrants

Institutions operating in the domestic and offshore markets have not floated listed or OTC commodity warrants referencing Indian commodity prices/rates.

OVER-THE-COUNTER FORWARDS, SWAPS AND OPTIONS

Equity

Equity Forwards/Swaps

India has featured an OTC equity forward market for several decades which has been instrumental in adding liquidity to the underlying share market. The 'badla' system, as it is known, is described at greater length below. Before embarking on a description of badlas it should be noted that trading in the forward market was suspended in March 1994 based on SEBI's belief that forwards were significant in promoting widespread speculation in the stock market. Forward trading was ultimately reinstated in the third quarter of 1995 after a review of the previous system and the drafting of new procedures. While forward trading was in suspension overall volume in the Indian cash equity markets dropped to 20% to 30% of previous levels; badlas were thus essential in adding liquidity to the underlying cash market. Whether liquidity recovers with the re-introduction of badlas remains to be seen, as the new forward trading rules are very restrictive.

The badla system in its original form (i.e. before regulatory reform) was effectively a forward trading mechanism for equities. Under a typical badla transaction, an investor could buy shares on margin (15%) and, at the end of two weeks, close out the position and pay or receive any losses or gains generated during the two-week period, without marking-to-market the initial margin, and without delivering the remaining 85% of the cash or taking delivery of the shares. For investors who wanted to preserve the position beyond two weeks, the only amount due would be an interest charge on the balance being financed (at rates of 24%–36% p.a.); once again, there would be no delivery of either the cash balance or shares. Although regulations stipulated that trades could only be rolled for 90 days, in practice positions were often rolled for periods of up to several years. If either buyer or seller was unwilling to continue the rollover, the lending of cash or shares would be provided by a badla financier. Forward transactions were limited to shares on four of

India's 22 exchanges, including the Bombay, Delhi, Calcutta and Ahmedabad exchanges.

The original badla system was believed to have fuelled widespread speculation in the market, which was of particular concern to the regulatory authorities; between June and December 1993 the Indian market rose sharply, largely on the basis of speculative forward trading. The original system was also susceptible to abuse, with many brokers routinely extending trades beyond maximum settlement date. As a result of these problems SEBI announced in December 1993 that it would suspend badlas on main board or group A stocks (also known as specified shares) beginning in March 1994; by January 1995 SEBI had added a similar ban to second board or Group B stocks (also known as non-specified shares). As mentioned above, the ban on forwards caused turnover to plummet and reduced liquidity dramatically. Following complaints from the Indian broker community, a government committee was established to study how badlas could be employed in the Indian market without causing excessive speculation and abuse. Following a review of the process (which was accompanied by intense lobbying from brokers who were financially impacted by the ban), the committee recommended to SEBI that badlas be reinstated with a stricter system of margins and forced termination of transactions on due date. The new system, implemented in the third quarter of 1995, met with unenthusiastic response from the brokerage community, which declared the rules to be overly restrictive. Under the new badla system the following rules apply: (a) trades will be financed to a maximum of 90 days and the cutoff date will be strictly enforced; (b) the 90-day period will consist of six 15-day sub-periods, where amounts due gradually increase (e.g. at the end of the first period a 20% deposit will be due, at the end of the second period an additional 10% will be due, and so on, until the end of the fifth period when a total of 50% will be due; at that stage trades will have to be net settled in cash, or enter the final period with delivery of shares and cash at the conclusion); (c) deals executed on a forward basis cannot account for more than 25% of a single broker's daily trading; (d) badla trades can only be executed by well-capitalized brokers who meet certain capital adequacy norms; (e) brokers will be required to differentiate between proprietary and client trades; (f) normal trades and badla trades cannot be commingled on the books of brokers; and (g) badlas will only be permitted on stocks traded through screen-based systems (such as those of the NSE or BSE). Given the very strict regulations, it is uncertain whether forwards will continue to be employed and/or whether underlying liquidity in the market will improve; as of this writing industry groups are lobbying for a relaxation of the new rules.

Equity Options

Despite the government's removal of the ban on equity options in early 1995 the market for domestic OTC equity options is non-existent at the present time. Foreign institutions operating in the offshore market buy and sell options on Indian equities on a periodic basis, though overall activity is negligible (particularly in comparison with other Asia Pacific markets). Activity is limited by poor liquidity of the cash market and restrictive foreign access to local shares; the inability to buy and sell local shares in a simple fashion makes it difficult for foreign institutions to manage risk in an efficient manner. As liquidity in the underlying cash market increases and foreign investor restrictions are loosened, it is possible that these types of derivatives will become more prevalent (both onshore and offshore).

Basket/Index Forwards/Swaps

The market for domestic OTC index forwards/swaps is non-existent at the present time. Institutions operating in the offshore market occasionally structure short-term index or basket derivatives, but overall activity remains insignificant (particularly in relation to other emerging Asian equity markets, where foreign banks have been particularly active). Volume is negligible as a result of low investor demand, poor domestic market liquidity, restricted access to local shares and absence of listed index derivatives. As with equity options, the market for basket/index forwards and swaps may become more active as liquidity improves and foreign investor restrictions are loosened.

Basket/Index Options

The market for domestic OTC index options does not exist at the present time. As with basket/index forwards/swaps, the market for offshore OTC basket and index options is very small. Though certain foreign banks buy and sell very short-term options (primarily on baskets of domestic blue-chip stocks), overall activity is negligible for many of the same reasons cited above. Future growth will depend on market liberalization and investor demand.

Fixed Income

Fixed Income Forwards/Swaps

India does not currently feature a true market for interest rate forwards/swaps based on local rates. Although certain onshore and offshore domestic swap transactions are structured on a sporadic basis, the Indian market is still negatively impacted by: (a) lack of a benchmark floating rate through which to value the floating rate segments of IRSs; (b) lack of a robust government bond yield curve by which to provide the market with additional swap pricing information; and (c) lack of liquid government bonds to hedge swap portfolios. In addition, the authorities have discouraged development or expansion of interest rate derivatives, and foreign institutions (with derivatives expertise) cannot freely access the domestic fixed income market. The rupee forward/swap market is likely to remain inactive until these hurdles are overcome. Onshore swaps exchanging fixed rupees for treasury bill rates are structured on a very irregular basis; most transactions are very short-term in nature and designed for specific hedging purposes. Offshore swaps exchanging fixed rupees for the interest rates implicit in FX forwards are equally rare. Given the very low volume of both onshore and offshore rupee swaps, there is no standard interbank dealing size, quoting convention or bid-offer spread.

Fixed Income Options

The domestic Indian market features no OTC fixed income options at the present time. Local bond options, swaptions, caps and floors have not been developed, primarily because there is no established floating rate benchmark and there is virtually no activity in rupee forwards or swaps. Until the challenges cited in the section above are overcome, a meaningful domestic fixed income option market is unlikely to develop.

Currency

Currency Forwards/Swaps

Although India's FX market remains severely restricted, certain steps have been taken toward deregulating the forward market. During early 1995 the RBI granted permission for non-resident equity investors to access forward foreign exchange via local banks; this makes it possible for investors to hedge out currency risk on a forward basis up to a maximum of six months (rollovers for longer terms can be granted by the authorities). In addition, local banks are now permitted to engage in short dated IRP/US$ forwards to manage their foreign currency balances. Despite these reforms the onshore forward market remains very inactive.

It should be noted that the offshore market features a very modest amount of non-deliverable forwards (NDFs, or dollar-settled exchange agreements); NDFs are transactions referencing forward IRP/US$ which result in net US dollar settlement of the market value of the contract at maturity rather than physical delivery of rupees and US dollars. NDFs are active to a maximum of six months.

There is no true market for CCSs exchanging rupees for US dollars (or other reserve currencies). Although specific onshore transactions may be arranged between institutions to provide appropriate currency hedging cover, such deals are very limited and generally short-dated in nature (e.g. six to 12 months). The market is likely to remain thin until currency and foreign investment regulations are liberalized.

Currency Options

As a further step towards reform of the local financial markets the RBI announced liberalization of currency options trading in early 1994. In its announcement the RBI granted institutions permission to enter into FX options based solely on foreign currencies against other foreign currencies (i.e. not against the rupee). At the present time foreign currency options may only be transacted against genuine currency exposures (e.g. they must be hedge transactions) and may only be resold in the market once; transactions can be executed in minimum size of US$250,000 (versus the US$1 mln parcels common in the international OTC FX options market). Corporations may buy such options, but cannot at present sell them. Development of rupee currency options is likely to occur over time as rupee liquidity increases and currency convertibility is implemented; the regulatory authorities are presently studying the matter.

While the onshore market currently prohibits use of the rupee in option transactions, the offshore market has developed a small turnover in short-term (e.g. six to 12 month) non-deliverable rupee options, which function just as the NDFs described above; the market, however, remains extremely limited.

Commodity

Commodity Forwards/Swaps

India's fledgling commodity forward market was born out of physical trading of agricultural commodities on a spot basis. Though forwards were banned in the early 1960s, dispensation was granted in the late 1980s and early 1990s for forward trading on select agricultural commodities. At the present time, participants may trade forwards on raw sugar (also known in the local market as jaggery), edible oils (e.g. palm oil, palm kernel oil, palm olein), rice, potatoes, castor seed, hessian, turmeric and pepper; there is also a more restricted market for forward trading in cotton and raw jute. As with commodity futures mentioned earlier in the chapter, all forward trading occurs through informal associations or small specialized regional exchanges where terms are generally negotiated between buyer and seller. Use of standardized forward contracts is not widespread.

Commodity Options

India does not currently feature an OTC commodity option market.

LOCAL REGULATORY/LEGAL TREATMENT OF DERIVATIVES

The primary regulators of the Indian financial system, institutions and instruments include the Reserve Bank of India (RBI) and the Securities Exchange Board of India (SEBI). The RBI is responsible, on a macro level, for conducting monetary policy for the country; within a regulatory context, it is responsible for general oversight of the financial system. SEBI, which was established in 1988 and which became a statutory body in 1992 under the SEBI Act of the same year, regulates all matters related to the stock market and the securities market. It is also responsible for supervising brokers, agents, bankers, underwriters and dealers. Given the absence of listed futures/options and OTC derivatives in the local market (with the exception of badla forward trading, as discussed above), there have been no specific derivatives regulations or guidelines enacted by SEBI or the RBI. Matters related to the study of local derivatives (e.g. currency options, interest rate swaps) fall under the jurisdiction of SEBI.

LOCAL ACCOUNTING PRACTICES FOR DERIVATIVES

Given India's relative inexperience with derivatives and the very underdeveloped nature of its derivative market, the financial and regulatory authorities have not, to date, issued specific rules regarding the treatment of derivatives. There is at present no uniform accounting policy utilized by local institutions with derivative exposures on their books. Full development of accounting policies for such instruments is likely to take several years to implement.

PROSPECTS FOR THE LOCAL DERIVATIVE MARKET

Summarized below are the near-term (one- to three-year) and medium-term (three- to five-year) prospects for Indian domestic derivatives.

Near-term:

- Introduction of vanilla rupee currency derivatives as currency deregulation continues.
- Introduction of onshore, and gradual expansion of offshore, equity derivatives as FII restrictions are loosened, local currency becomes more accessible, and foreign derivative technologies are imported.
- Very gradual expansion of IRS activity as the domestic debt market continues to grow and a floating rate benchmark is established.
- Conversion of certain agricultural forward contracts into formal futures contracts.
- Further expansion of domestic warrants and convertibles as the Indian equity market grows and the need for domestic financing increases; deeper liquidity in both instruments as exchanges are consolidated and trading is focused on fewer locations.
- Limited growth in forward equity trading given the restrictive nature of the new badla system.

Medium-term:

- Creation of a listed futures exchange to trade key financial futures (e.g. stock index futures, bond futures).
- Development of listed equity options.
- Continued expansion of IRSs and CCSs as financing opportunities continue to increase and derivatives become accepted by a broader base of institutions.

	Overall Liquidity	Liquid/ Maximum Maturity	Interbank dealing size	Average bid-offer spread
Equity/Index Swaps	non-existent	n/a	n/a	n/a
Equity/Index Options	poor	1-6 mos/12 mos	n/a	n/a
Interest Rate Swaps	poor	12 mos/2 yrs	none	none
Interest Rate Options	non-existent	n/a	n/a	n/a
Currency Swaps	poor	6-12 mos	none	varies
Currency Options	non-existent	n/a	n/a	n/a

Table 5.4 Summary of Domestic OTC Derivatives

6: Indonesia

FINANCIAL MARKET OVERVIEW

Indonesia's underlying financial markets are still in the process of development; the markets for domestic equity, debt, currency and commodities are still modest in comparison with those of other Asia Pacific nations, both in terms of absolute size and overall liquidity. The developing nature of the cash markets is reflected in the domestic derivative market, which is in the early stages of development. Although derivative product range and liquidity are still limited there are various initiatives underway designed to expand the use of derivatives in the local market over the coming years (as discussed below).

The domestic Indonesian equity market is comprised of three separate exchanges including the Jakarta Stock Exchange (JSE) (the country's main bourse), the Surabaya Stock Exchange (SSE) (a significant regional exchange) and the Indonesian Parallel Stock Market (an OTC trading forum for stocks (and bonds) of smaller companies); the regulatory authorities are presently considering a merger of all three. JSE, the country's primary exchange, has been in existence since the early 1900s when it listed shares of Dutch-owned companies with interests in Indonesia. After several decades of only moderate activity the JSE was closed in 1940 and remained inoperative until approximately 1977, when it was re-opened through presidential decree; the JSE was privatized in 1992 and exists today as a self-regulating, member-owned exchange.

Following several years of relative inactivity in the late 1980s and early 1990s, the Indonesian equity market experienced substantial gains in 1993 as domestic and foreign investors began participating heavily in local shares; investment flows more than doubled trading volume (to 3.8 mln shares per annum) and nearly tripled market capitalization (to US$32.9 bln). Although foreign and domestic investment receded in 1994, market capitalization remained buoyant as a result of privatizations, secondary placements and initial public offerings (including Indosat's US$1 bln initial public offering); total capitalization reached US$47.2 bln at the end of 1994, ranking the Indonesian market as the eleventh largest of Asia Pacific's 13 stock markets. Figure 6.1 below illustrates the historical movement of the benchmark Jakarta Composite Index (JCI). Table 6.1 contains key indicators on the domestic equity market.

Note that foreign investor access to the domestic market is largely unrestricted, up to 49% of a local company's outstanding shares. Once the 49% ceiling is reached separate foreign shares are listed on the JSE; given significant investment activity by offshore investors in the domestic market foreign shares generally trade at a substantial premium to local shares.

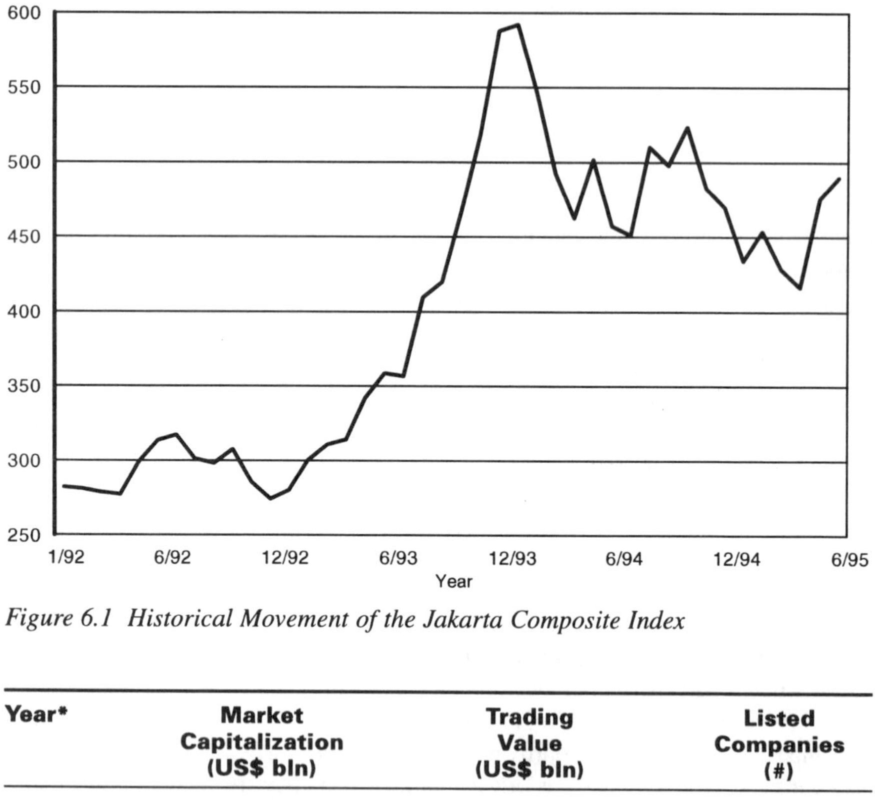

Figure 6.1 Historical Movement of the Jakarta Composite Index

Year*	Market Capitalization (US$ bln)	Trading Value (US$ bln)	Listed Companies (#)
1994	47.2	11.8	216
1993	32.9	9.2	174
1992	12.0	3.9	155
1991	6.8	2.9	141
1990	8.0	4.0	125

* to December of each year; Source: IFC, 1995

	1/92–6/95 Annualized Return	1/92–6/95 Total Return
Jakarta Composite Index	16.93%	68.39%

Table 6.1 Domestic Equity Market Indicators

The Indonesian fixed income market is among the smallest of those in Asia Pacific, with virtually all primary and secondary activity concentrated in short-term sovereign securities. The local market is dominated by issuance of short-term central bank bills (Sertifikat Bank Indonesia, or SBIs), which carry maturities of 90, 180 and 360 days; total SBI outstandings amounted to nearly IDR29 tln (US$13 bln) at the end of 1994 (far outweighing outstanding private sector certificates of deposit (CDs) and commercial paper (CP)). The government itself is not an issuer of medium- or long-term debt obligations as it is prohibited through its constitution from raising debt to finance budgetary shortfalls. As such, the country has no true sovereign fixed income benchmarks, which has been an impediment to growth in the private sector/state enterprise bond market (and the domestic swap market) (e.g. there are no pricing references for private sector bonds or swaps, there are no government bonds which can be used to hedge swap positions, and so on). Accordingly, private sector bond and state enterprise bond issuance is still extremely modest; outstanding state enterprise and corporate bonds (many with state bank guarantees) amounted to only IDR4.9 tln (US$2.2 bln) at the end of 1994. Virtually all corporate and state enterprise bonds are issued with final maturities under five years, though certain seven year deals have been floated in the recent past. It should be noted that Indonesian fixed income instruments are generally structured with coupons which pay a fixed rate for an initial period of one to three years, followed by a floating rate (set as a fixed spread over the average of state bank time deposits (SBTDs)) for the balance of the bond's life.

Although debt issuance in the Indonesian market is still modest in comparison with other Asia Pacific nations, a number of interest rates are beginning to emerge as important domestic financial market indicators. The key Indonesian interest rates include Jakarta Interbank Offered Rate (JIBOR) (the borrowing cost for financial institutions in the interbank market), SBI yields (the short-term borrowing cost of the central bank), SBTD yields (the borrowing cost for state banks in the deposit market) and rupiah interest rate swap rates (the rate for transacting interest rate swaps in the interbank swap market). Table 6.2 below highlights the payment frequency, compounding frequency and day count conventions of key Indonesian domestic interest rates.

Rate	Payment Frequency	Compounding Frequency	Day Count Convention
JIBOR	–	–	Actual/360
SBI	–	–	Actual/360
SBTD	semi-annual	semi-annual	Actual/360
Swaps	semi-annual	semi-annual	Actual/360

Table 6.2 Domestic Interest Rate Summary

Indonesia's currency, the rupiah (IDR), is a fully convertible, floating currency depreciated on a daily basis against the US dollar based on the inflation differential between the two countries; past annual depreciation of the currency has been in the range of 3% to 6%. The country's general policy of devaluing on a consistent basis has allowed it to maintain competitive export prices, which has helped stabilize the country's trade account over the past decade (note that Indonesia has not experienced a major devaluation of its currency since 1986, when the rupiah devalued by 27%). The value of the rupiah is set twice per day, at 8 a.m. and 3 p.m., and is traded at a maximum spread of 44 rupiah (the band was widened from 30 rupiah in mid-1995). Indonesia's onshore FX market is among the most active in Southeast Asia, featuring average daily turnover of approximately IDR1.3 tln (US$600 mln) (Paisley and Woodcock, 1995). While this is below the onshore daily turnover of Singapore dollars in Singapore (US$1.2 bln), it is well above the onshore turnover of Thai baht within Thailand (US$300 mln) and Malaysian ringgit within Malaysia (US$250 mln). Offshore activity in spot rupiah is significant as well, with average daily turnover of IDR5.6 tln to IDR 6.7 tln (US$2.5 bln to US$3 bln). Standard interbank dealing size in spot rupiah is IDR11 bln to IDR22 bln (US$5 mln to US$10 mln) and bid-offer spreads range from IDR0.50/US$ to IDR1/US$ under normal market conditions; spreads can widen to IDR2/US$ to IDR3/US$ during volatile times. Figure 6.2 traces the historical movement of spot IDR/US$.

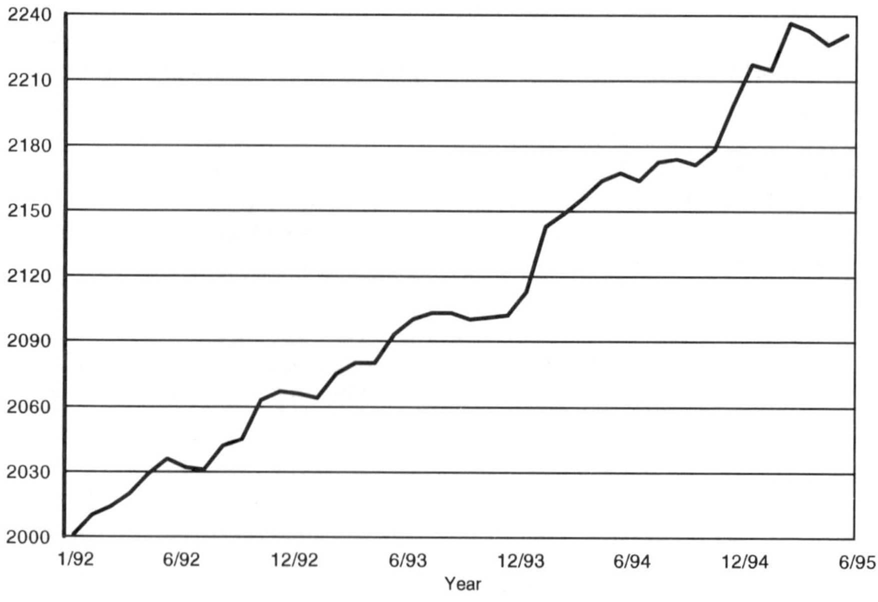

Figure 6.2 Historical Movement of Spot IDR/US$

DERIVATIVE MARKETS AND PRODUCTS

LISTED DERIVATIVE EXCHANGES

Indonesia features two exchanges which list and trade financial and commodity derivatives, the Jakarta Stock Exchange (JSE) and the Indonesian Commodity Exchange Board (ICEB).

JSE, the country's primary equity trading centre, also lists and trades domestic convertible bonds and is in the process of considering introduction of listed issuer equity warrants. Though the listed convertible market in Indonesia is still in its infancy, there is substantial room for growth as companies and investors appear eager to issue and trade such instruments. The same is true of equity warrants, which were nearly introduced in late 1994 and again in mid-1995; regulatory authorities appear close to permitting listing of such derivatives but have not yet announced specific timing. Trading of convertibles occurs on a continuous basis on the floor of the Exchange and all trades are settled and cleared through PT KDEI, the Indonesian clearing and depository house.

Indonesia's second exchange, known as the Indonesian Commodity Exchange Board (ICEB), or Bursa Komoditi Indonesia, was founded in 1985 as a forum for listing and trading commodities on a spot and forward basis. In January 1986 ICEB began trading standardized forwards on a series of rubber and coffee grades, with all delivery settled in physical. Trading on ICEB occurs through open outcry and clearing and settlement of trades is effected through a separate subsidiary known as the Indonesian Commodities Clearing House. It should be noted that ICEB is in the process of reviewing conversion of its standardized forward contracts into futures contracts; precise timing of a conversion is uncertain. Note that, unlike other Southeast Asian countries (e.g. Thailand, Taiwan, Korea), Indonesia has announced no formal plans regarding the introduction of domestic financial futures. Table 6.3 highlights the country's listed exchanges and derivatives.

Exchange	Primary Derivatives
Indonesian Commodity Exchange Board (ICEB)	Rubber forwards; coffee forwards
Jakarta Stock Exchange (JSE)	Convertible bonds; issuer equity warrants (proposed)

Table 6.3 Listed Derivative Exchanges

LISTED FUTURES AND OPTIONS

Equity

Equity Futures/Options

The Indonesian market features no listed equity futures or options at the present time. Although the equity market is expanding on both a primary and secondary basis, there have been no proposals put forth regarding the introduction of listed equity derivatives. The lack of listed equity options has created activity in the offshore OTC equity option market, as discussed later in the chapter.

Index Futures/Options/Futures Options

The Indonesian market features no index futures or options at the present time and no proposals have been put forward regarding the creation of such derivatives. As with listed equity options, the lack of listed index futures and options has led to the development of OTC index forwards, swaps and options in the offshore market (as discussed below).

Fixed Income

Deposit Futures/Options/Futures Options

Indonesia does not list or trade deposit futures at the present time. Although JIBOR is gradually emerging as a key short-term benchmark it is not firmly established as the primary short-term rate of the local financial system; there has been no interest to date in designing contracts related to JIBOR.

Interest Rate Futures/Options/Futures Options

The domestic market does not currently feature interest rate futures or options. The prospects for introducing such derivatives in the near-term are non-existent, primarily because Indonesia lacks a government bond programme. The absence of government bond benchmarks and supply makes it difficult, if not impossible, to create a meaningful interest rate futures programme. In the absence of a listed bond futures programme institutions requiring protection against domestic interest rate movements must utilize the developing rupiah forward/swap market (discussed later in the chapter).

Currency

Currency Futures/Options/Futures Options

Indonesia does not feature listed currency futures or options at the present time, and there do not appear to be plans to create such contracts in the foreseeable future.

The absence of listed currency derivatives has led to increasing activity in the OTC currency forward, swap and options market (discussed later in the chapter).

Commodity

Commodity Futures/Options/Futures Options

Although listed financial futures have not yet been introduced in Indonesia, domestic commodity derivatives have been in existence for the past decade. As indicated earlier in the chapter, ICEB was created in 1985 as a forum for listing and trading select commodities on a spot and forward basis. Indonesia already features substantial physical trading of commodities such as rubber and coffee (it is one of the world's top three producers of both commodities); forward trading of the same commodities was deemed a necessity in order to provide producers and consumers with the ability to protect against price movements. The ICEB currently lists standard physical delivery forward contracts on coffee and rubber, and is contemplating introduction of forwards on cocoa and palm oil. ICEB rubber forwards are based on RSS1 and RSS3 (ribbed smoked sheet #1 and #3) as well as local SIR 3L, 10 and 20 (Standard Indonesian Rubber #3L, #10 and #20). While other Asian exchanges trade the RSS contract (e.g. SICOM, KRE, TOCOM as well as various Chinese exchanges), ICEB is the only exchange to trade the SIR contract. ICEB coffee forwards are based on robusta beans (just as those offered via SICOM, MIFE and various Chinese exchanges). ICEB trades three forwards designed for local delivery (RSS1/RSS3, SIR, and robusta denominated in rupiah, for local delivery points) and three forwards designed for offshore delivery (RSS1/RSS3, SIR, and robusta denominated in US dollars, delivery free on board (f.o.b., e.g. cargo, insurance and freight costs not included in the quoted price)).

Total turnover in the offshore RSS/SIR rubber forwards amounted to 532,000 tons in 1993 (almost exclusively in the form of RSS1), with forward periods ranging from one to five months; turnover was almost unchanged in 1994. 1993 and 1994 tonnage equates to approximately 31,000 RSS contracts in each year. Turnover in domestic RSS/SIR rubber forwards amounted to 1.54 mln tons in 1993 and 2.94 mln tons in 1994; forward periods ranged from one to three months. In 1993 the composition of domestic rubber delivered under forwards included RSS1 (31%), RSS3 (48%), SIR 20 (3%), SIR 3L (8%) and others (10%); this equates to approximately 80,800 RSS contracts and 10,600 SIR contracts. In 1994 the composition of domestic rubber delivered under forwards included RSS1 (12%), RSS3 (55%), SIR 20 (21%), SIR 3L (8%) and others (4%); this equates to approximately 116,000 RSS contracts and 53,250 SIR contracts (ICEB, 1995). Tables 6.4 through 6.9 contain details on the ICEB rubber and coffee contracts.

As indicated earlier, ICEB is presently exploring the possibility of converting its forwards into futures (and converting the Exchange itself from a physical trading forum into a conventional futures exchange) but has not provided details on timing of proposed conversion.

Contract	SIR Rubber Forwards (Local)
Type	Domestic
Exchange	Indonesian Commodity Exchange Board
Months	Spot month plus next five months
Contract Size	16 tons
Tick Value	IDR5/kg.
Daily Limit	No limit
Deliverable Grade	Physical settlement of SIR rubber (Standard Indonesia Rubber), grades 3L, 20 and 10, local delivery
Last Trading Day	10th day of the current delivery month
Delivery Day	1st day of the delivery month
Real-time price data	None available

Table 6.4 Contract Specifications for ICEB SIR Rubber Forwards (Local)

Contract	RSS Rubber Forwards (Local)
Type	Domestic
Exchange	Indonesian Commodity Exchange Board
Months	Spot month plus next five months
Contract Size	17 tons
Tick Value	IDR5/kg.
Daily Limit	No limit
Deliverable Grade	Physical settlement of RSS rubber (ribbed smoked sheet), grades 1 and 3, local delivery
Last Tradin Day	10th day of the current delivery month
Delivery Day	1st day of the delivery month
Real-time price data	None available

Table 6.5 Contract Specifications for ICEB RSS Rubber Forwards (Local)

Contract	SIR Rubber Forwards (Offshore)
Type	Offshore/Domestic
Exchange	Indonesian Commodity Exchange Board
Months	Spot month plus next five months
Contract Size	16 tons
Tick Value	US$0.125/kg.
Daily Limit	No limit
Deliverable Grade	Physical settlement of SIR rubber (Standard Indonesian Rubber), grades 3L, 20 and 10, free on board
Last Trading Day	10th day of the current delivery month
Delivery Day	1st day of the delivery month
Real-time price data	None available

Table 6.6 Contract Specifications for ICEB SIR Rubber Forwards (Offshore)

Contract	RSS Rubber Forwards (Offshore)
Type	Offshore/Domestic
Exchange	Indonesian Commodity Exchange Board
Months	Spot month plus next five months
Contract Size	17 tons
Tick Value	US$0.125/kg.
Daily Limit	No limit
Deliverable Grade	Physical settlement of RSS rubber (ribbed smoked sheet), grades 1 and 3, free on board
Last Trading Day	10th day of the current delivery month
Delivery Day	1st day of the delivery month
Real-time price data	None available

Table 6.7 Contract Specifications for ICEB RSS Rubber Forwards (Offshore)

Contract	Robusta Coffee Forwards (Local)
Type	Domestic
Exchange	Indonesian Commodity Exchange Board
Months	Spot month plus next five months
Contract Size	5 tons
Tick Value	IDR5/kg.
Daily Limit	No limit
Deliverable Grade	Physical settlement of Robusta coffee beans, grades 4 and 5, local delivery
Last Trading Day	10th day of the current delivery month
Delivery Day	1st day of the delivery month
Real-time price data	None available

Table 6.8 Contract Specifications for ICEB Robusta Coffee Forwards (Local)

Contract	Robusta Coffee Forwards (Offshore)
Type	Offshore/Domestic
Exchange	Indonesian Commodity Exchange Board
Months	Spot month plus next five months
Contract Size	5 tons
Tick Value	US$0.125/kg.
Daily Limit	No limit
Deliverable Grade	Physical settlement of Robusta coffee beans, grades 4 and 5, free on board
Last Trading Day	10th day of the current delivery month
Delivery Day	1st day of the delivery month
Real-time price data	None available

Table 6.9 Contract Specifications for ICEB Robusta Coffee Forwards (Offshore)

LISTED/OVER-THE-COUNTER WARRANTS, CONVERTIBLES AND HYBRIDS

Equity

Equity Warrants

Indonesian equity warrants are presently only available in covered form through the offshore OTC market. There are efforts underway, however, to introduce listed issuer equity warrants to the domestic market in the near term.

In response to widespread demand by corporate issuers and domestic investors, BAPEPAM, the Indonesian capital markets authority, announced in 1994 that it would release rules regarding the listing of issuer equity warrants on the JSE. In late 1994 Moderland Realty announced plans to float an inaugural five-year mandatory convertible bond issue with attached warrants; the warrants were to be detachable and traded through the JSE. The proposed transaction was ultimately rejected by BAPEPAM which was concerned that the derivatives would be too complex for domestic investors to understand; the timing of the decision coincided with the announcement that several Indonesian firms had posted losses in global derivatives, perhaps causing the authorities to take an overly cautious stance regarding the listing of new domestic derivatives. A subsequent attempt at launching warrants was made in mid-1995 by Bank Bali, which proposed a rights issue with attached warrants; as with the original Modernland deal, the Bank Bali warrants were to be detachable from the rights and traded separately through the JSE. BAPEPAM eventually rejected the Bali warrant (for the same reasons) and the transaction proceeded as a pure rights offering. Although it seems likely that listed warrants will eventually be floated in the domestic market, precise timing is uncertain.

Although the domestic market has not yet listed issuer equity warrants, numerous financial institutions operating in the offshore market float periodic covered OTC warrants based on individual Indonesian equities. Unlike issuer equity warrants which result in the flotation of new corporate equity upon exercise, covered warrants result in the re-allocation of a company's shares from the seller to the buyer of the warrant. Indonesian OTC covered warrants generally carry maturities of one to two years, are listed on offshore exchanges (or may remain unlisted) and are traded on an OTC basis; the derivatives may be structured with American or European exercise and are typically denominated in foreign currencies (and not rupiah). Note that unlike other Southeast Asian markets (e.g. Malaysia, Thailand, Singapore), offshore single stock warrants referencing Indonesian stocks are still comparatively rare.

Basket/Index Warrants

Given that domestic listed equity warrant market is not yet operational it follows that the domestic basket/index warrant market is dormant. International institutions, however, float occasional offshore OTC warrants linked to Indonesian equity indexes and baskets. Basket/index warrants generally carry maturities of one to three years and are most often denominated in US dollars or European currencies; the derivatives are typically unlisted or listed on offshore exchanges, and traded OTC. Representative issues in this category include Swiss Bank Corporation's Deutschmark basket call warrants on a group of 14 blue-chip Indonesian companies (1994), Bankers Trust's two tranche US dollar index call warrants on the Indonesian Index (1994) and Credit Lyonnais' US dollar basket call warrants on a diversified group of eight Indonesian blue-chip companies (1994); several other transactions have been executed since 1994.

Convertibles

Indonesian convertible bonds are issued in the domestic and offshore markets, though total outstandings in each market remain relatively modest.

The domestic market features issuance of rupiah convertible bonds which are both listed on, and traded through, the JSE. Despite an increase in activity in 1994, overall primary and secondary turnover remains negligible; total outstanding rupiah convertibles amounted to IDR236 bln (US$106 mln) at the end of 1994 (JSE, 1994), a fraction of what Indonesian companies have issued in the offshore convertible market. Virtually all securities in the local market carry maturities under five years (though there have been certain issues extending as far as ten years); bonds are issued with conversion premia of 20% to 30% and coupons approximately 100–300 basis points lower than comparable fixed rate securities. Secondary trading of local convertibles is dormant; most issues trade irregularly through the JSE or through brokers. Representative issuers in the local convertible market include Sari Husada (which has issued a zero coupon convertible), Charoen Pokphand Indonesia, Astra, Bank Niaga, Tigaraksa Satria, Indocement and Matahari Putra Prima.

While issuance by Indonesian corporates in the domestic rupiah convertible bond market has been very modest to date, issuance in the offshore market has been somewhat more active. Various Indonesian companies have accessed both the domestic Swiss franc convertible market and the offshore Eurodollar convertible market since 1991 (though most have opted for the latter). A total of US$360 mln of Indonesian offshore convertibles was floated in 1991; following a quiet year in 1992, issuance increased to over US$500 mln in 1993 and US$540 mln in 1994. Indonesian Eurodollar convertibles are listed on offshore exchanges and are traded in bearer form in the OTC market. Maturities of most issues range from five to ten years and conversion is into the underlying shares of the Indonesian company based on a rupiah conversion price. The Swiss franc market, which can be accessed on a public or private placement basis, features bonds with maturities of less than five years). Public deals are listed on, and traded through, the Swiss stock exchanges, while private deals are unlisted and traded on an OTC basis. Swiss franc convertibles are most often issued with investor puts (enabling the investor to put the bond to the issuer) as well as provisional calls (enabling the issuer to call the bond, following a non-call period, once a certain market price has been reached). Appendix III contains details on Indonesian convertible bonds.

Index-linked Notes

Index-linked notes referencing key domestic equity indexes such as the JCI are structured with relative infrequency, primarily because investor demand for such securities is limited and management of risk positions by underwriters is relatively inefficient (given the absence of index futures/options). Basket-linked notes are somewhat more common, primarily because they are simpler to structure and can be customized to include the best performing blue-chip stocks in the market. Basket notes are typically structured to provide investors with upside appreciation in the value of a group of Indonesian stocks (i.e. embedded long calls); such securities are generally short- to medium-term in nature (e.g. one to five years) and are most often denominated in foreign currencies. Most notes are arranged offshore on a private placement basis and are not actively traded. Note that in addition to bonds with embedded long calls, the market also features a very small amount of securities with embedded long puts or short puts, resulting in greater gains or liabilities, respectively, as the market declines.

Fixed Income

Fixed Income Warrants

Indonesia does not list fixed income warrants, primarily because investor demand for such derivatives is negligible; in addition, the local market is still in the process of development and no firm interest rate benchmarks have yet emerged.

Currency

Currency Warrants

Institutions in the domestic and offshore markets have not yet floated currency warrant issues referencing the Indonesian rupiah.

Commodity

Commodity Warrants

Despite featuring a rather active agricultural commodity sector, the Indonesian market does not currently list or trade domestic commodity warrants.

OVER-THE-COUNTER FORWARDS, SWAPS AND OPTIONS

Equity

Equity Forwards/Swaps

The Indonesian domestic market features no OTC equity forwards or swaps. Though activity in the offshore market is extremely limited as well, foreign banks occasionally structure individual OTC equity forwards with maturities ranging from several months to three years; equity swaps (e.g. exchange of a floating rate flow for appreciation or depreciation in a single Indonesian stock) are rare. Somewhat more common are equity options and index swaps/options, discussed below.

Equity Options

While the domestic market features no listed equity options, financial institutions operating in the offshore market offer puts and calls on individual domestic stocks. Although OTC equity options are available in virtually any form, vanilla transactions (i.e. three to 12 month, American or European exercise puts/calls on larger capitalization blue-chip stocks) appear to be most popular; OTC options generally involve cash settlement upon exercise, though delivery or acceptance of shares is also possible. Given the customized nature of these instruments, liquidity is non-existent; virtually all transactions result in expiry, exercise into settlement with the seller, or close-out with the seller; resales to third parties are extremely unusual. Note that there is presently no market for exotic options on Indonesian equities.

Basket/Index Forwards/Swaps

The local market features no OTC basket or index forwards/swaps at the present time. Foreign financial institutions, however, execute a modest amount of index/basket swaps in the offshore market, typically providing investors with appreciation in an Indonesian index (e.g. JCI) or a basket of domestic blue-chip stocks, in exchange for premium in the form of a floating rate flow; basket forwards and swaps tend to be more prevalent (in what is still a small market), primarily because risks are simpler to manage from the dealer's viewpoint. As with any OTC structure, basket and index forwards/swaps can be customized with regard to notional, maturity, target basket or index, and so on. Standard transactions carry short- to medium-term maturities (e.g. one to three years) and are denominated in either foreign currencies or rupiah.

Basket/Index Options

Indonesia features no domestic OTC index options. Institutions operating in the offshore market, however, are modestly active in buying and selling puts and calls on the broad Indonesian market (typically the JCI) or on smaller baskets of Indonesian blue-chip stocks; as with other index derivatives, risk management of positions can be inefficient and expensive given the lack of listed index derivatives. Basket/index options are customized for individual investors with regard to target basket/index, maturity, strike, and notional, and are not traded on a secondary basis. Typical transactions are centred on American or European options with maturities of six months to two years, exercisable into cash settlement. There is currently no formal OTC market for exotic options on Indonesian baskets or indexes, though certain institutions execute such transactions on an *ad hoc* basis.

Fixed Income

Fixed Income Forwards/Swaps

The Indonesian interest rate forward/swap market is gradually developing in size and liquidity but is faced with a series of hurdles which will have to be overcome before the market becomes liquid and efficient. Specifically, the Indonesian fixed income derivative market is impacted by: (a) lack of a widely accepted, and robust, floating-rate benchmark to value floating-rate segments of IRSs; (b) lack of a government yield curve to provide the market with additional swap pricing references; and (c) lack of government bond supply to hedge interest rate risks generated by swaps.

The rupiah forward market, which quotes to JIBOR (for onshore transactions) or the interest rates implied by FX forwards (for offshore transactions) is still very thinly traded and is only active to 12 months; given the infancy of this segment of the market, no standard interbank dealing size has yet developed and bid-offer spreads are wide and volatile.

The rupiah IRS market, like the Thai baht, Malaysian ringgit and Singapore dollar IRS markets, is challenged by the lack of an accepted, and accessible, onshore floating rate benchmark. While SBIs are very actively traded, the yields implied by such instruments are not widely utilized as benchmark domestic floating rates. JIBOR, the interbank rate, is increasingly used as a domestic short-term benchmark but has not yet been adopted by all swap market participants, primarily because it is not efficient to replicate the JIBOR flow and management of cash rolls is difficult; in addition, foreign institutions often have problems accessing the onshore market and, as such, cannot rely on onshore JIBOR rates to drive business flows. While onshore swaps of fixed rupiah (semi-annual, on an Actual/360-day basis) against six-month JIBOR are executed on occasion, the market is still very thinly traded.

In order to circumvent these difficulties, an increasing number of institutions utilize the Singapore-based rupiah swap offer rate (SOR). The SOR, also used in other Southeast Asian swap markets (e.g. Thailand, Malaysia, Singapore), is the rate obtained from borrowing US dollars and converting into rupiah of the same maturity through forward FX. The SOR uses the offer side of the FX swap to swap out of US dollars and into rupiah. Use of the rupiah SOR adds a dimension of uniformity to the market, provides offshore participants with greater access to rupiah IRSs and permits dealers to manage their cash rolls more effectively. SOR is calculated on a daily basis through the average of spot and forward point quotes from leading domestic and international banks based in Singapore; quotes of one, three, six and 12 months are carried on Telerate page 44178. Quoting convention for offshore swaps is fixed rupiah (semi-annual, on an Actual/360-day basis) against rupiah SOR.

IRSs (against either JIBOR or rupiah SOR) are active primarily in the two- and three-year sector, though quotes are available to five years. Deal flow is dominated by onshore participants; the market executes only two to three swaps per week but deals tend to be very large in size (e.g. IDR22 bln to IDR110 bln, or US$10 mln to US$50 mln). Bid-offer spreads on standard transactions are approximately 20–30 basis points throughout the curve, though the relative illiquidity of the market and the volatility of domestic rates makes spreads wide and variable. Figure 6.3 below highlights a representative rupiah IRS curve (fixed rupiah against rupiah SOR) from mid-1995.

In addition to the absence of an accepted domestic floating rate benchmark, participants in the rupiah swap market must also contend with a lack of comprehensive hedging instruments. As indicated above, Indonesia does not presently feature deposit or bond futures and its sovereign sector debt programme is non-existent (except for short-term bills). Participants are therefore restricted to money market instruments (deposits, forward FX contracts) to manage interest rate positions; this suggests deals in the market are likely to remain concentrated in short tenors until long-term cash markets develop further. Although two-way flow is increasing it is not yet sufficient to permit dealers to warehouse risk in anticipation of finding offsetting swaps.

Fixed Income Options

As with the IRS market, the rupiah fixed income options market is still in the initial stages of development. OTC bond options are not presently available, primarily because there are no established bond benchmarks; prospects for the development

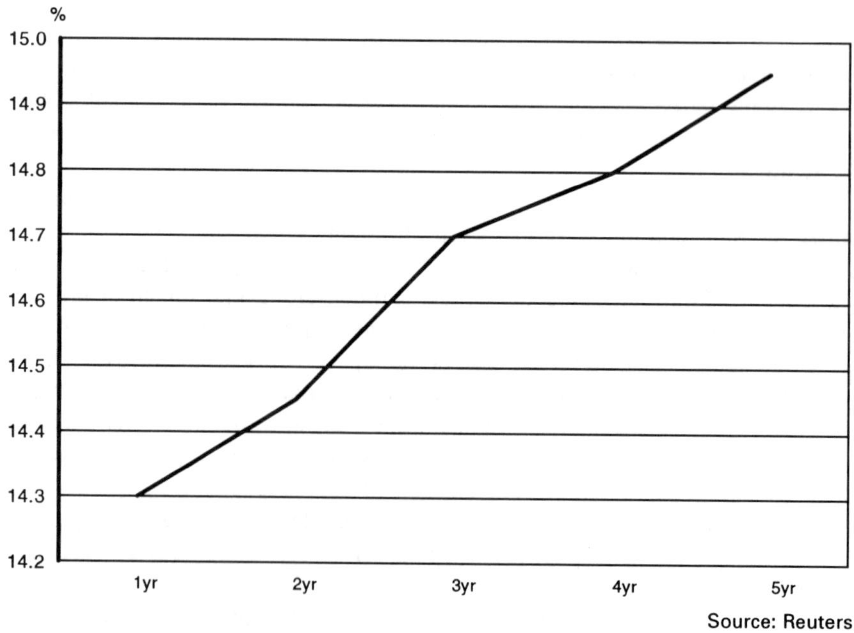

Figure 6.3 Representative Rupiah IRS Curve

of such derivatives are poor. Caps and floors, in contrast, are available in the market, though overall activity is still very limited. As with rupiah IRSs, caps and floors are concentrated primarily in short-term maturities up to one year, though two- and three-year transactions are executed on occasion; transactions in the offshore market most often reference rates implied in FX forwards while those in the onshore market reference JIBOR. Despite the availability of caps and floors, no standard interbank dealing size exists and bid-offer spreads (quoted in volatility terms) are still volatile. Rupiah swaptions are not widely utilized by participants, as the cost of buying such structures is very expensive. Broader development of caps, floors and swaptions is likely to occur as the underlying forward/swap market expands in size and liquidity, and as a robust and uniform floating rate benchmark is developed.

Currency

Currency Forwards/Swaps

The rupiah forward FX market is reasonably well developed, and features average daily turnover of approximately IDR1.8 tln (US$800 mln). There is now acceptable liquidity in FX forwards to six months and quotes are provided by both local and foreign banks out to 12 months. Interbank dealing size in forwards is IDR4.5 bln to IDR11.5 bln (US$2 mln to US$5 mln) and spreads range from IDR1/US$ for one month forwards to IDR5/US$ for six month forwards under normal market conditions. Long-term FX forwards are also available out to three and, occasionally, five years. It should be noted that Bank Indonesia (BI), the country's central bank, maintained an FX swap facility for a number of years in order to provide domestic institutions with the ability to hedge US dollar borrowings against movements in the rupiah; since the local FX market was not sufficiently deep in the late 1980s and early 1990s to provide the necessary FX swap facilities, BI provided the service. Total FX swaps transacted through BI reached a peak of IDR30 tln (US$13 bln) in 1991, but declined to IDR2.2 tln (US$1 bln) in 1994 as commercial banks operating in the local market became more active in forward FX trading. BI disbanded the swap facility in 1995 and all FX swaps are now carried out on a commercial basis through domestic and international financial institutions.

Currency swaps of rupiah against the US dollar are increasingly common among institutions desiring to hedge assets, liabilities or currency receipts, or by those wishing to take a medium-term view on the currency market; there is, in fact, more activity in the rupiah CCS market than in the IRS market, though both are still in the early stages of development. The quoting convention for rupiah CCSs is fixed rupiah (semi-annual, on an Actual/360-day basis) against six-month US$ LIBOR flat. Typical dealing size in rupiah CCSs is IDR22 bln (US$10 mln) and recent estimates suggest that one or two deals are transacted on a daily basis. Virtually all activity occurs in two- and three-year maturities, though quotes to five years are available. Given the lack of market liquidity and the currency volatility which has been in evidence since late 1994, it is not surprising to see CCS spreads ranging from 20 to 30 basis points in most segments of the curve. By way of comparison, the liquid JPY/US$ swap market features reasonably constant spreads of 7–8 basis points throughout the curve. Figure 6.4 illustrates the historical movement of the IDR/US$ CCS curve, while Figure 6.5 traces the movement of two- and three-year CCS rates. Table 6.10 illustrates indicative bid offer spreads of IDR/US$ swaps out to five years.

Maturity	Bid-Offer Spread
1 year	25–30 bps
2 years	15–20 bps
3 years	15–20 bps
4 years	20–25 bps
5 years	20–30 bps

Table 6.10 IDR/US$ CCS Bid-Offer Spreads

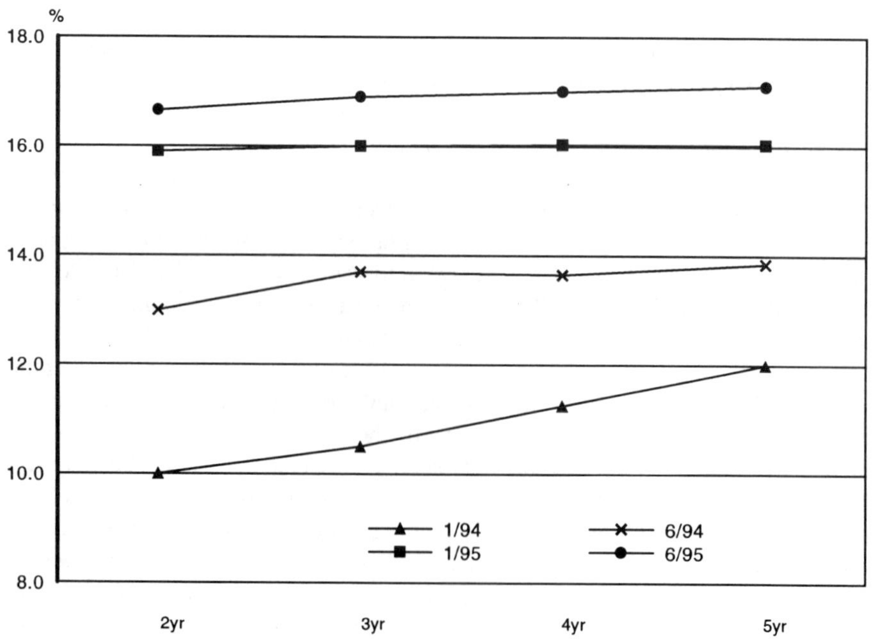

Figure 6.4 Historical Movement of IDR/US$ CCS Curve

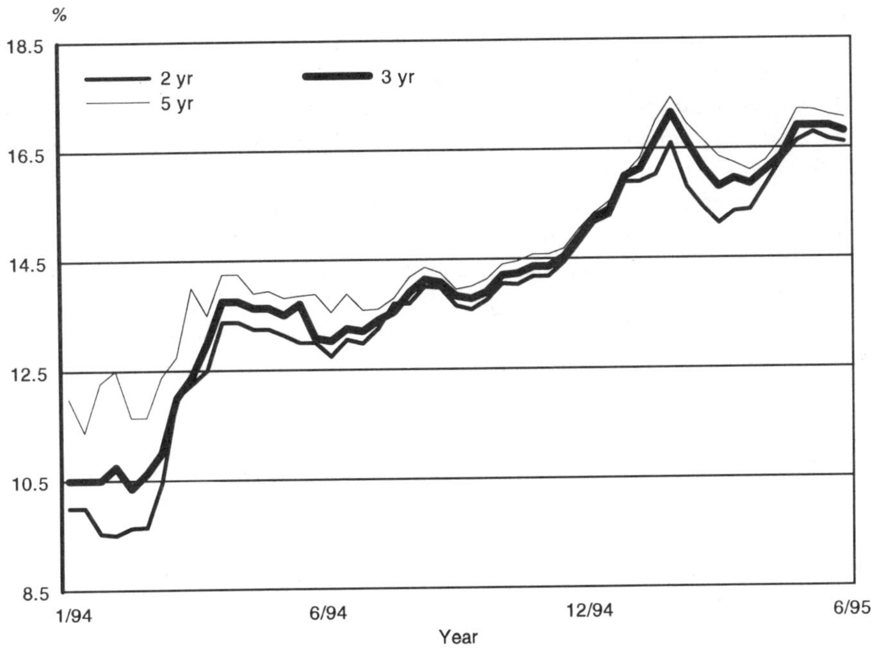

Figure 6.5 Historical Movement of Two-, Three- and Five-year IDR/US$ CCS Rates

Currency Options

The OTC rupiah FX options market is developing in size and liquidity and is now estimated to be the one of the most active in Southeast Asia. Maturities of rupiah options tend to be concentrated in the short end, primarily to 12 months, though longer-term options are quoted with increasing frequency. Pricing of options is in volatility terms, with one-month options offered at approximately 2.5–3.0 points, six-month options at 5.5–6.0 points and 12-month options at 7 points (all under normal market conditions); typical bid-offer spreads range from 1 point in short maturity deals to 1.5 points in 12-month deals. Standard interbank dealing size for IDR/US$ options is IDR22 bln (US$10 mln) and estimates suggest three to four transactions are executed on a typical day, for total weekly volume of IDR335 bln to IDR445 bln (US$150 mln to US$200 mln). Though virtually all options are struck against the IDR/US$ FX rate, IDR/JPY options are written on occasion as well. The market for exotic options is still very limited, though certain institutions arrange rupiah barrier options on occasion.

Commodity

Commodity Forwards/Swaps

Although Indonesia is a major commodity producer (e.g. oil, rubber, coffee, rice) and features a reasonably active listed market for physical spot and forward trading (i.e. through ICEB), it does not presently feature a local OTC commodity forward or swap market. The various grades of Indonesian crude oil (e.g. Minas, Cinta, Duri, Attaka, Lalang, Widuri, Belida, and so on) trade almost exclusively on a spot basis; OTC oil/forwards swaps designed to hedge Indonesian production or delivery are based primarily on the Asian regional benchmark, Tapis, rather than on specific Indonesian crudes, and are often executed through the Singapore energy market (see chapter 11 for additional details). Domestic institutions seeking to enter into OTC commodity forwards and swaps to gain hedging protection base transactions on regional or international energy benchmarks and often operate through the Singaporean energy derivative market.

Commodity Options

As with local OTC commodity forwards/swaps, the market for local OTC commodity options is non-existent at the present time. Domestic institutions requiring hedging (particularly of energy products) occasionally utilize OTC options through the offshore market.

LOCAL REGULATORY/LEGAL TREATMENT OF DERIVATIVES

The primary regulators of the Indonesian financial markets are the Ministry of Finance and BAPEPAM, the capital markets regulatory authority. BAPEPAM is the primary supervisor of Indonesia's capital markets and is responsible for guiding and regulating all aspects of the securities industry; BAPEPAM is accountable to the Ministry of Finance on all regulatory matters. All exchanges in Indonesia, including the three stock exchanges and ICEB, are organized as self-regulated entities. The exchanges, which are private sector institutions, regulate their own members but do so under broad guidance provided by BAPEPAM.

Given the relative infancy of Indonesia's local derivative market, it is not surprising to note that specific laws and regulations regarding derivative transactions have not been passed. To date the main regulatory communiques from the MOF and BAPEPAM on derivatives have been in the form of warnings on the use of OTC forwards, swaps and options and an urging that use of such instruments be considered for hedging purposes only. The cautions were sounded following a series of losses by Indonesian companies (as discussed in chapter 1), including those by Sinar Mas group companies, Dharmala group companies and Indorayon. Until derivatives become a more significant component of the local financial system, it is unlikely that specific regulatory treatment of derivatives will be put forth.

LOCAL ACCOUNTING PRACTICES FOR DERIVATIVES

Given the developing nature of Indonesia's local derivative market firm accounting rules for the treatment of such instruments have not yet been created. Despite the absence of established rules, most financial institutions operating in the local market tend to utilize generally accepted principles established by the Indonesian Accountants Association and the Indonesian Banking Accounting Principles (SKAPI) to prepare financial statements; such principles contain certain references regarding the accounting treatment of select derivatives. In instances where a currency forward or swap is held for funding or hedging purposes, the difference between the market value and the contracted value of the derivative is recorded as either a premium (gain) or discount (loss) and amortized over the life of the contract; such amortization is recorded as a gain or loss in the interest account in the income statement. Where a currency forward or swap is held primarily as a trading or speculating position, the net market value is taken to the income statement in the current period; unrealized profits on outstanding contracts as of reporting date are not recognized, while unrealized losses are recognized. In the absence of guidelines regarding the reporting of interest rate derivatives, various local institutions tend to apply the same approach used for currency forwards/swaps.

PROSPECTS FOR THE LOCAL DERIVATIVE MARKET

Summarized below are the near-term (one to three year) and medium-term (three to five year) prospects for Indonesia's domestic derivatives.

Near-term:

- Gradual expansion of rupiah IRSs as domestic financing needs continue to build; market still concentrated in shorter maturities given the absence of a medium-/long-term government bond market.
- Continued growth in rupiah CCSs as domestic financing needs expand and trading in the local currency becomes more liquid.
- Issuance of domestic equity warrants and convertibles as both issuers and investors are drawn to the instruments.
- Only modest expansion in OTC equity derivative structures as the market remains limited by both illiquidity and lack of listed index futures.

Medium-term:

- Conversion of ICEB into a futures exchange, and conversion of current rubber and coffee forwards into futures contracts. Introduction of new contracts (e.g. cocoa, palm oil).
- Introduction of select listed financial derivatives (perhaps index futures and deposit futures) as the underlying cash markets mature and the need for such derivatives becomes apparent.
- Increased liquidity in rupiah IRSs and CCSs, together with lengthening of maturities, as two-way flow improves and extends out the curve.

	Overall Liquidity	**Liquid/ Maximum Maturity**	**Interbank dealing size**	**Average bid-offer spread**
Equity/Index Swaps	poor	1 yr/3 yrs	n/a	n/a
Equity/Index Options	poor	1–12 mos/12 mos	n/a	n/a
Interest Rate Swaps	fair	2–3 yrs/5 yrs	US$10–50 mln	20–30 bps
Interest Rate Options	poor	1 yr/3 yrs	none	varies
Currency Swaps	fair	2–3 yrs/5 yrs	US$10 mln	20–30 bps
Currency Options	fair	1–12 mos/12 mos	US$10 mln	1–1.5 pts

Table 6.11 Summary of Domestic OTC Derivatives

7: Japan

FINANCIAL MARKET OVERVIEW

Japan's financial markets are among the largest, most developed and most liquid in the world. By most measures the Japanese domestic equity and fixed income markets are the second largest in the world, behind those of the US; the currency and commodity markets are sizeable on a primary and secondary basis as well. The very large and liquid nature of the cash markets has resulted in the development of broad and sophisticated local derivative capabilities. Though regulatory barriers continue to impede the introduction of certain derivatives (as discussed later in the chapter), most vanilla and exotic derivatives found in other advanced trading nations are well represented, and utilized, in the Japanese market.

The history of Japanese equity trading dates back to the late 1800s when the original Tokyo and Osaka stock exchanges were formed. Creation of smaller regional exchanges followed over ensuing decades and in the mid-1940s all exchanges were combined into a single national trading organization; by the late 1940s, however, the central organization was dissolved and the regional exchanges became independent non-profit membership organizations. Japan presently features equity trading on eight separate exchanges, namely those of Tokyo, Osaka, Nagoya, Kyoto, Hiroshima, Fukuoka, Niigata and Sapporo. Tokyo accounts for approximately 80% of market volume and capitalization, followed by Osaka (15%), and the remaining regional exchanges (approximately 1% each). A new OTC equity market, designed to raise capital for small domestic companies, was established in 1995.

Japan's equity market is the second largest in the world (and the largest in Asia Pacific) as measured by market capitalization; for a brief period in 1989 and 1990, when the domestic market was at its peak, capitalization exceeded that of the US market. After a strong performance in the 1980s (culminating in a market peak in late 1989), the domestic market of the 1990s has been plagued by low trading volume and poor returns; both are due primarily to the country's economic recession, caused in large part by tight monetary policy employed to burst the speculative 'bubble economy' of the 1980s. Despite its difficulties, the local equity market remains a vital component of the domestic (and global) financial markets; total domestic market capitalization amounted to nearly US$3.7 tln in 1994, up from US$3 tln in 1993 (following several significant privatizations (e.g. Japan Tobacco,

Japan Railways East)). Figures 7.1 and 7.2 highlight the movement of the benchmark Nikkei 225 and Topix stock indexes while Table 7.1 provides data on the domestic equity market.

Note that foreign access to local shares is generally unrestricted, though if foreign ownership of a domestic company's outstanding shares exceeds 10%, prior approval must be obtained from the Ministry of Finance.

Year*	Market Capitalization (US$ bln)	Trading Value (US$ bln)	Listed Companies (#)
1994	3,719.9	1,121.4	2,205
1993	2,999.7	954.3	2,155
1992	2,399.0	635.2	2,118
1991	3,130.8	995.9	2,107
1990	2,917.7	1,602.4	2,071

* to December of each year; Source: IFC, 1995

	1/92–6/95 Annualized Return*	1/92–6/95 Total Return*
Nikkei 225	–9.92%	–29.40%
Topix	–7.40%	–22.61%

* dividends reinvested in index

Table 7.1 Domestic Equity Market Indicators

Japan's fixed income market is the second largest in the world on both a primary and secondary basis. The range of instruments in the Japanese bond market is broad and includes Japanese Government Bonds (JGBs), local government bonds, public corporation bonds, corporate bonds and foreign bonds. The general category of JGBs consists of revenue bonds (including construction bonds, special authority bonds and refinancing bonds), treasury accommodation bonds (including Treasury bills and foreign exchange fund bills), and deferment bonds (including government compensation bonds and fiscal investment bonds). JGBs, the centrepiece of the fixed income market, have been actively floated since 1975 (though periodic issues appeared between 1965 and 1975). JGBs are presently issued as short-term bonds (with maturities under four years), medium-term bonds (four to six years), long-term bonds (seven to ten years), superlong bonds (20 years), and zero-coupon bonds. The size of the primary JGB/bill market increased from JPY185 tln (US$2.05 tln) at the end of 1993 to JPY201 tln (US$2.23 tln) at the end of 1994 (BOJ, 1995). Figure 7.3 illustrates the historical movement of thc JGB

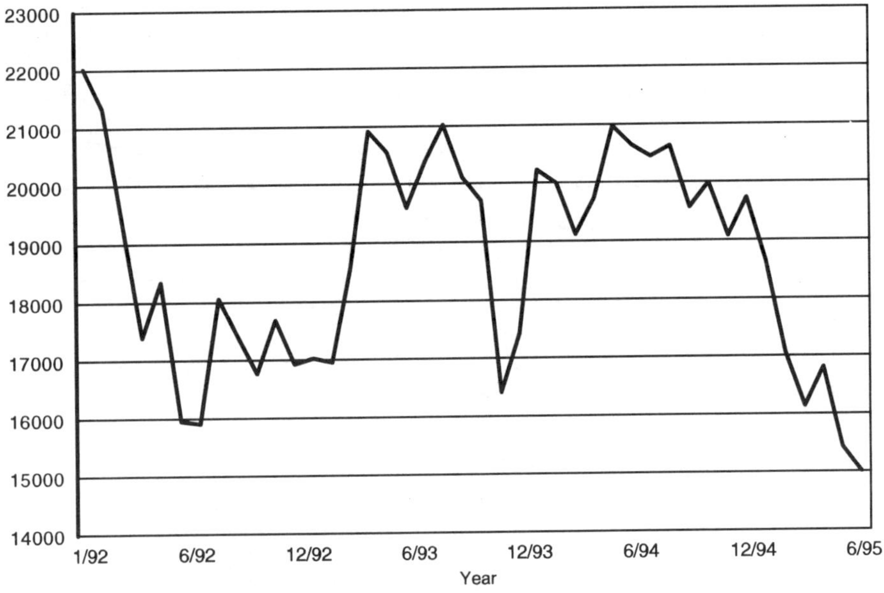

Figure 7.1 Historical Movement of the Nikkei 225 Index

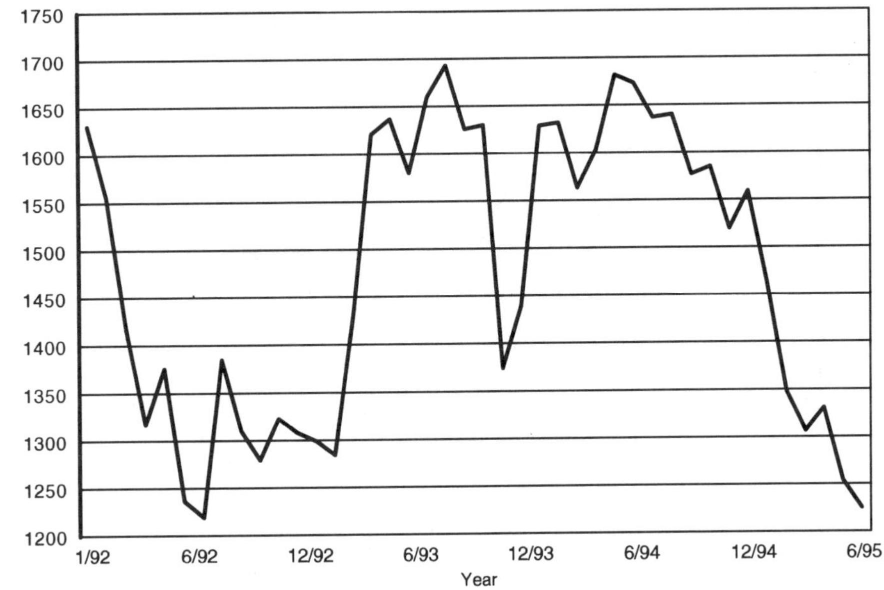

Figure 7.2 Historical Movement of the Topix Index

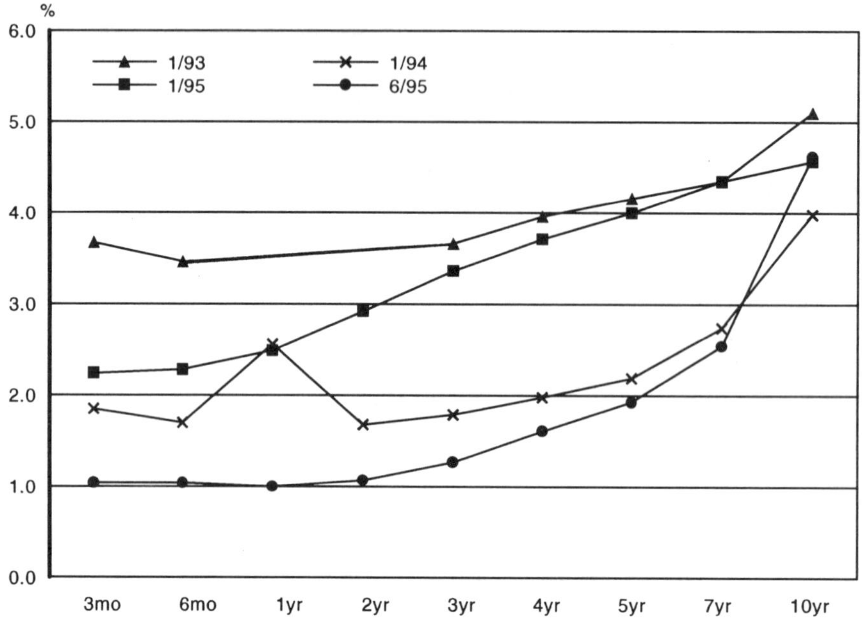

Figure 7.3 Historical Movement of Japanese Government Yield Curves

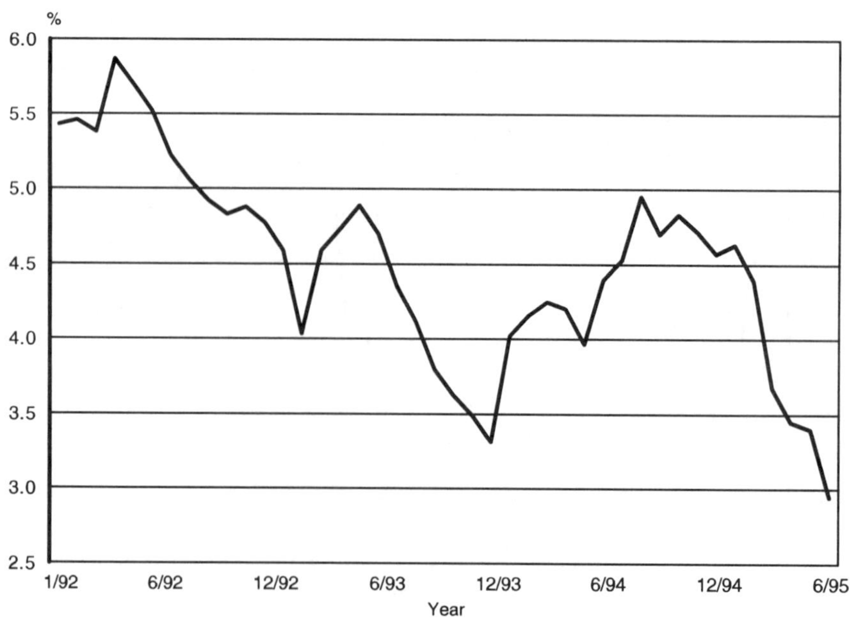

Figure 7.4 Historical Movement of Ten-year Japanese Government Bond Yields

yield curve while Figure 7.4 traces the movement of the benchmark ten-year JGB yield.

Local government bonds include the obligations of prefectural and municipal governments, while public corporation bonds include securities issued by government agencies; the latter obligations tend to be explicitly guaranteed by the central government. Corporate bonds include bank debentures, industrial/electric power bonds, straight (fixed rate) bonds, convertible bonds and bonds-with-warrants; corporate securities may be issued on a secured or unsecured basis with maturities ranging from one to ten-years (though longer-term fixed rate convertible bonds are floated on a periodic basis). The general category of foreign bonds includes samurai bonds (yen-denominated bonds issued by foreign entities in the domestic market), shogun bonds (foreign currency bonds issued by foreign entities in the domestic market), shibosai bonds (private placement bonds), daimyo bonds (bonds issued by supranationals in the domestic market), and dual currency bonds and reverse dual currency bonds (bonds which pay coupons and principal redemptions in different currencies). Total outstanding local government, public corporation, corporate and foreign bonds amounted to JPY142 tln (US$1.65 tln) in 1994 (note that Euroyen bonds are not included in the total as they are considered offshore securities). Secondary trading in the OTC market (the primary trading forum for most bonds) during 1993 and 1994 is highlighted in Table 7.2 below.

US$ bln	JGBs	Bank Debentures	Corp Bonds	Public Corp/ Agency Bonds	Muni/Prov Bonds
1994	39,307	567	118	279	66
1993	38,144	785	155	361	86

Source: Bank of Japan Quarterly Bulletins, 1995

Table 7.2 Secondary Turnover in Japanese Fixed Income Securities

The key interest rates in the Japanese onshore and offshore markets include Japanese yen LIBOR (the borrowing cost for prime Japanese banks in the offshore market), long-term prime rate (LTPR) (the long-term domestic borrowing cost for large corporations), JGB yields (the intermediate- and long-term borrowing costs of the government itself), Euroyen bond rates (the borrowing cost for domestic and offshore issuers in the offshore market), samurai bond rates (the borrowing cost for domestic and offshore issuers in the domestic market), and yen swap rates (the rate for transacting yen interest rate swaps in the interbank market). We shall discuss the interaction of these rates in our section on fixed income forwards and swaps later in the chapter. Table 7.3 below summarizes the payment frequency, compounding frequency and day count conventions for each of the key Japanese rates.

Rate	Payment Frequency	Compounding Frequency	Day Count Convention
Yen LIBOR	–	–	Actual/360
LTPR	semi-annual	annual	Actual/365
JGB	semi-annual	annual	363/365
Euroyen	annual	annual	30/360
Samurai	semi-annual	annual	Actual/365
Swaps	semi-annual	semi-annual	Actual/365

Table 7.3 Domestic Interest Rate Summary

The Japanese yen (JPY) is a freely convertible currency and the JPY/US$ rate is one of the most actively traded currency pairs in the global financial markets; there are no restrictions imposed on trading of the yen and the value of the currency is determined entirely by market forces. Within the Tokyo market average daily turnover in spot JPY/US$ was JPY520 bln (US$5.82 bln) in 1994, down from JPY540 bln (US$6.02 bln) in 1993; in addition to JPY/US$ there are several actively traded crossrates (e.g. DM/JPY, GBP/JPY) which add to total daily trading volume. Typical dealing size in the interbank market is JPY5 bln (US$55 mln) and bid-offer spreads are a very thin JPY0.05/US$, reflecting the liquid nature of

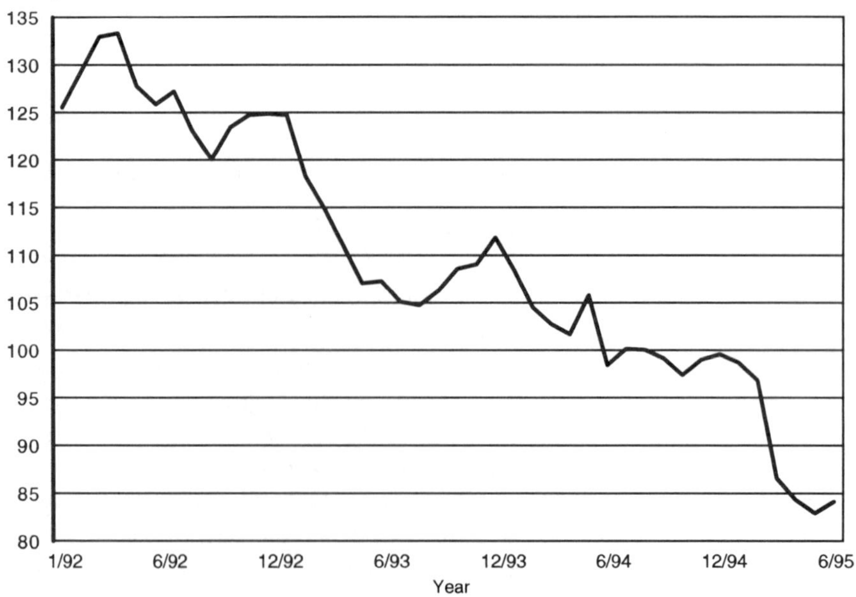

Figure 7.5 Historical Movement of JPY/US$ Spot Rate

JPY/US$ trading. The appreciation of the yen against the US dollar has been well reported in the financial press; Figure 7.5 illustrates the movement of spot JPY/US$ since 1992.

DERIVATIVE MARKETS AND PRODUCTS

LISTED DERIVATIVE EXCHANGE

Formal trading of commodity futures dates back to the mid-17th century when Tokugawa-era rice merchants in Osaka engaged in trading of rice, often against future delivery of the grain. In 1730 Japan introduced the Osaka Dojima, or Osaka rice trading board, where merchants traded 'rice tickets' against future deliveries of rice. In 1893 the country developed its first commodity trading regulations and established the Rice Exchange. This forum served as the primary commodity futures exchange of the country until 1950, when new futures regulations were introduced; following the establishment of the new regulations a series of regional agricultural commodity exchanges were created. Many of the exchanges created in the 1950s are still in existence today, though a series of exchange mergers has reduced the overall number somewhat. Financial authorities and government ministries are urging a continuation of the merger process in order to reduce market fragmentation and ensure achievement of deeper liquidity in certain futures contracts; several mergers of exchanges described below are pending completion. The country's 'modern era' exchanges include the following:

Hokkaido Grain Exchange (HGE) was established in 1893 as the Otaru Rice, Herring and Fertilizer Exchange. It re-opened in 1951 as the Agricultural and Fishery Products Exchange and relocated to Sapporo in 1961, when it was renamed the HGE; futures trading in soybeans, white beans, red beans and potato starch followed shortly thereafter. The HGE merged with the Tokyo Grain Exchange (TGE) in mid-1995; details are presently being finalized on which contracts will be traded on the merged exchange and which will be abandoned (though we present full details on all 'pre-merger' contracts later in the chapter, for the benefit of comparison).

Kanmon Commodity Exchange (KCE) was originally established as the Kanmon Grain Exchange (KGE) in 1805 and was restructured in 1953 to trade soybeans, red beans and potato starch. The Exchange was renamed the KCE in 1954 and corn and sugar contracts were added to the product listing shortly afterwards. The Exchange is constituted as a non-profit membership organization; trading on the KCE occurs via open-outcry auction, known as itayose.

Kansai Agricultural Commodities Exchange (KANEX) was created in 1993 through the merger of three historic exchanges, including the Osaka Grain Exchange, the Kobe Grain Exchange and the Osaka Sugar Exchange. KANEX lists and trades futures on red beans, soybeans, and sugar, as well as options on sugar;

KANEX was the 26th most active exchange in the world in 1994, primarily on the strength of its red bean and soybean contracts (FI, 1995). The Exchange is constituted as a non-profit membership organization (with members categorized as grain traders or sugar traders). Trading on the KANEX follows the auction principle and leads to the establishment of a single price at the end of each session, but is completed through an electronic trading system rather than open-outcry. Note that KANEX has agreed in principle to merge with the Kobe Raw Silk Exchange (KRSE).

Kobe Raw Silk Exchange (KRSE) was established in 1928 to trade raw silk futures. It did so until 1943, when it was closed for a brief period; after its re-opening the Exchange was restructured as a non-profit membership organization, a status it holds at the present time. KRSE continues to trade only in raw silk futures, via open-outcry auction. As indicated above, KRSE has agreed to merge with KANEX.

Kobe Rubber Exchange (KRE) was founded in 1952 as the country's first rubber trading centre; the Exchange was originally organized as a non-profit membership organization and retains the same structure today. KRE lists rubber futures and a new rubber index future; trading of all contracts occurs via open-outcry, where the auction process leads to the establishment of a single price at the end of each session. KRE was the 37th most active exchange in the world in 1994 (FI, 1995).

Maebashi Dried Cocoon Exchange (MDCE), originally created in 1952 as a non-profit membership organization, trades only in dried cocoons, the raw material used in the production of silk; trading of dried cocoon futures occurs via the open-outcry auction method. It should be noted that following a failed merger attempt with the Yokohama Raw Silk Exchange, MDCE has publicly declared its desire to find another merger candidate.

Nagoya Grain and Sugar Exchange (NGSE) was originally created as the Nagoya Rice Exchange in 1877 to trade rice futures. The Exchange was eventually converted into a non-profit membership organization and renamed NGSE; new contracts (e.g. sugar, red beans) were added to its product line shortly thereafter. Trading on the NGSE occurs via open-outcry auction. Note that in late 1995 the NGSE, Nagoya Textile Exchange and Toyohashi Dried Cocoon Exchange agreed to merge; details are being finalized as of this writing.

Nagoya Textile Exchange (NTE) was founded in 1951 as a non-profit membership organization to trade in cotton, woollen yarn and staple fibre yarn futures; the NTE's original product line has remained unchanged over the past four decades. Futures trading on the NTE occurs via the open outcry auction method on the floor of the Exchange. NTE was the 44th most active exchange in the world in 1994 (FI, 1995). As indicated immediately above, NTE is in final discussions with NGSE and Toyohashi Dried Cocoon Exchange on a planned merger.

Osaka Textile Exchange (OTE) was created in 1984 through the merger of the Osaka Chemical Textile Exchange and the Osaka Sampin Exchange and is constituted as a non-profit membership organization. Like the NTE above, the Exchange trades in cotton yarn, woollen yarn and staple fibre yarn futures, and establishes prices through competitive auction. As a result of strong turnover in cotton futures, OTE was the 34th most active exchange in the world in 1994 (FI, 1995).

Tokyo Commodity Exchange (TOCOM) was created in 1984 through the merger of three established exchanges, namely Tokyo Rubber Exchange (1952), Tokyo Gold Exchange (1982) and Tokyo Textile Commodities Exchange (1951). TOCOM now lists and trades precious metal futures, rubber futures and cotton and wool futures; it is the largest trading centre in the world for platinum, palladium and rubber futures. TOCOM was the 13th largest exchange in the world in 1994, with total turnover of 30.4 mln contracts (FI, 1995). Rubber, wool and cotton futures are traded via itayose open-outcry auction, while precious metals futures are traded via an electronic screen-based system.

Tokyo Grain Exchange (TGE), established in 1952 as a non-profit membership organization to trade red bean, soybean and potato starch futures, merged with the Tokyo Sugar Exchange in October 1993. Following the merger the Exchange added raw and refined sugar futures, as well as options on soybeans and raw sugar, to its listing; trading in all futures and options occurs via computerized systems. Based on very strong activity in red bean and soybean futures, TGE was the 22nd most active exchange in the world in 1994 (FI, 1995). As indicated above, TGE merged with HGE in 1995 and is in the process of incorporating certain of HGE's contracts into its listing.

Toyohashi Dried Cocoon Exchange (TDCE), founded in 1937 and restructured in 1951 as a non-profit membership organization, trades exclusively in dried cocoon futures; all trading is executed via the open-outcry auction method. As indicated above, TDCE has agreed in principle to merge with NGSE and NTE.

Yokohama Raw Silk Exchange (YRSE), established in 1894 to trade futures on raw silk, tea, textiles, fish and sugar, merged with the Yokohama Stock and Rice Exchange in 1910 and was restructured as a non-profit membership organization in 1951. The Exchange currently lists a single futures contract, on raw silk, and trades via the open-outcry auction method. YRSE was the 47th most active exchange in the world in 1994 based on turnover (FI, 1995).

It should be noted that membership in Japanese commodity exchanges is divided into two broad categories, including futures commission merchants (FCMs) (also referred to as commodity commission merchants) and general members (also referred to as associate members). FCMs are permitted to trade for their own accounts as well as client accounts, though they must be relicensed on an annual basis by the Ministry for International Trade and Industry (MITI); general members are only permitted to trade for their own accounts and must execute through FCMs.

While commodity-focused spot and futures trading has always been important in Japan given the country's agricultural history, it was the creation of financial futures which propelled the Japanese markets into the mainstream of listed derivatives. The leading exchanges for Japanese financial futures trading are the Tokyo Stock Exchange (TSE), Osaka Stock Exchange (OSE), Nagoya Stock Exchange (NSE) and Tokyo International Financial Futures Exchange (TIFFE). Japanese financial futures trading commenced in October 1985 when the TSE introduced a futures contract on the benchmark ten-year JGB. In September 1988 the TSE created the first widely accepted domestic stock index future, based on the Topix index, and was followed shortly thereafter by the OSE, which introduced the Nikkei 225 index contract (note that the OSE had introduced an earlier physical settlement stock index contract, the Stock Futures 50, in mid-1987, which failed to draw interest – it was abandoned in 1988 in favour of the Nikkei 225 contract, which has become enormously successful). NSE joined the domestic derivative market by introducing an index option contract in 1989 and TIFFE commenced trading of Euroyen deposit futures in the same year.

The TSE was originally established in 1878 as the Tokyo Stock Exchange Company, with responsibility for trading domestic equities. The original exchange merged with other Japanese exchanges in 1943 but was restructured in 1948 as an independent non-profit organization to trade equities and bonds; trading in issuer equity warrants, convertible bonds, futures and options followed over ensuing decades. The Exchange's futures/options programme is currently centred on two JGB contracts, the Topix stock index contract and a US Treasury bond contract; the TSE was the 17th most active exchange in the world in 1994, with total turnover of 17.4 mln contracts (FI, 1995). Although trading in liquid equities occurs on the floor of the Exchange, all derivative instruments, including convertibles, warrants, futures and options, are traded via electronic screen-based trading systems (e.g. CORES-F for futures and CORES-O for options), which match orders by price and time through a central order book. Settlement and clearing of all transactions on the TSE are handled by the Japan Securities Clearing Corporation (JSCC), a subsidiary of the TSE.

The history and evolution of the OSE is very similar to that of the TSE: the OSE was founded in 1878 as a profit-making corporation and, in 1943, became part of a merged national exchange. In 1948 the Exchange was restructured as an independent, non-profit membership organization and began trading in equities and bonds. Further trading in futures, options, issuer equity warrants and convertibles followed during the next 40 years; the Exchange's futures/options programme presently includes contracts on the Nikkei 225 and Nikkei 300 stock indexes. OSE was the 18th most active exchange in the world in 1994, with total turnover of 14.9 mln contracts (FI, 1995). As with the TSE, all OSE warrants, futures, options and convertibles are traded through an electronic screen-based trading system which matches orders by price and time through a central order book; only liquid equities are traded directly on the floor of the Exchange. Transactions executed on the OSE are cleared and settled through the Osaka branch of the Japan Securities Depository Centre (JASDEC).

The NSE was created in 1886 as a corporate entity to trade equities, and was restructured as a non-profit organization in mid-1949 to trade both equities and bonds. The NSE entered the derivative market in the mid-1980s when it introduced trading of convertible bonds and issuer equity warrants; it followed in 1989 with its index option contract. Trading of all securities (equities, bonds, convertibles, options, warrants) occurs via the Exchange's computerized trading system which matches orders through a central order book based on price and time.

TIFFE was established in 1989 by the Federation of Bankers Association to list and trade a series of money market derivatives; the Exchange began operations in June 1989 with a three month Euroyen deposit futures contract and followed with a JPY/US$ futures contract, a three-month Eurodollar futures contract, a three-month Euroyen futures options contract and a 12-month Euroyen futures contract. TIFFE was the tenth most active exchange in the world in 1994, with total turnover of 38 mln contracts (FI, 1995). Trading occurs through the FACTS electronic trading system which matches orders on the basis of price and time through a central order book. TIFFE features 100 clearing members (including city, trust and long-term credit banks, insurance companies, domestic and foreign securities firms and foreign bank branches) who settle and clear all trades.

Membership in Japan's financial futures exchanges generally takes one of three forms: regular members (who are permitted to execute trades for their own accounts or for client accounts), special participants (who are permitted to execute trades for their own accounts, in approved products only), and saitori members (who are permitted to execute transactions for two regular members, two special participants or one of each; saitori members cannot execute for either their own accounts or client accounts). Under the Securities and Exchange Law, members must be financial institutions legally permitted to engage in broking and dealing in the underlying cash markets.

It should be noted that in addition to the TSE, OSE and NSE, other regional stock exchanges (e.g. Fukuoka Stock Exchange, Hiroshima Stock Exchange) feature a modest amount of trading in convertible bonds and issuer equity warrants. Table 7.4 summarizes Japan's listed exchanges and derivatives.

Exchange	**Primary Derivatives**
Fukuoka Stock Exchange (FSE)	Convertible bonds; issuer equity warrants
Hiroshima Stock Exchange (HSE)	Convertible bonds; issuer equity warrants
Hokkaido Grain Exchange (HGE)	Soybean futures; red bean futures; white bean futures; potato starch futures
Kanmon Commodity Exchange (KCE)	Soybean futures; corn futures; red bean futures; sugar futures
Kansai Agricultural Exchange (KANEX)	Sugar futures, options; soybean futures; red bean futures
Kobe Raw Silk Exchange (KRSE)	Silk futures
Kobe Rubber Exchange (KRE)	Rubber futures; rubber index futures
Maebashi Dried Cocoon Exchange (MDCE)	Dried cocoon futures

Exchange	Primary Derivatives
Nagoya Grain and Sugar Exchange (NGSE)	Red bean futures; potato starch futures; sugar futures
Nagoya Stock Exchange (NSE)	Index options; convertible bonds; issuer equity warrants
Nagoya Textile Exchange (NTE)	Cotton yarn futures; wool yarn futures; staple fibre yarn futures
Osaka Stock Exchange (OSE)	Index futures, options; convertible bonds; issuer equity warrants
Osaka Textile Exchange (OTE)	Cotton yarn futures; staple fibre yarn futures; wool yarn futures
Toyohashi Dried Cocoon Exchange (TDCE)	Dried Cocoon futures
Tokyo Commodity Exchange (TOCOM)	Gold futures; silver futures; platinum futures; palladium futures; rubber futures; cotton yarn futures; wool yarn futures
Tokyo Grain Exchange (TGE)	Soybean futures, options; corn futures; red bean futures; sugar futures, options
Tokyo International Financial Futures Exchange (TIFFE)	Deposit futures, options; currency futures
Tokyo Stock Exchange (TSE)	Index futures, options; bond futures, options; convertible bonds; issuer equity warrants
Yokohama Raw Silk Exchange (YRSE)	Raw silk futures

Table 7.4 Listed Derivative Exchanges

LISTED FUTURES AND OPTIONS

Equity

Equity Futures/Options

The Japanese market features no listed equity futures or equity options at the present time. While the absence of domestic equity futures is not surprising, as such derivatives are still relatively unique in the global financial markets, it is interesting to note that of the eight largest stock markets in the world, Japan is the only one which does not list and trade individual equity options (Hong Kong held the same status until it introduced its options in the third quarter of 1995). Listing of domestic equity options in the future remains uncertain although the TSE has reportedly been in discussions with the regulatory authorities regarding the introduction of such derivatives, on a trial basis, during 1996. The TSE's proposed plan is to list options on five large blue-chip companies and to add new options over a period of time; no further details have been released and the regulatory authorities have made no statements regarding the proposal.

Index Futures/Options/Futures Options

As mentioned above, Japan's three largest equity exchanges list and trade stock index futures. The TSE features trading of the Topix contract while the OSE features trading of the popular Nikkei 225 contract and the newer Nikkei 300 contract (it should be noted that OSE was not the first exchange to list a future on the Nikkei 225; both SIMEX and CME introduced Nikkei 225 contracts up to two years before the OSE introduced its own contract). The Nikkei 225 is an arithmetic average price-based index, while the Topix and the Nikkei 300 are market capitalization-weighted indexes. The Nikkei 225 index is calculated by dividing the sum of current prices by the number of companies on base date. The Topix and Nikkei 300 are calculated by dividing the current market value of stocks by the base market value, and multiplying by 100. The creation of the market capitalization Nikkei 300 index came from a desire to change the bias present in the Nikkei 225. Under the current index bias a given percentage change in the price of an equity whose price is greater than the average has a greater effect on the index than an equity whose price is lower than the average (even if the company has a larger market capitalization); the value of the Nikkei 225 index can thus be influenced by a relatively small amount of trading in a high priced stock.

The TSE's cash-settled Topix futures contract was introduced in 1988 and quickly attracted significant domestic and foreign attention; average daily turnover amounted to nearly 15,000 contracts during the first year of trading. After its initial success, however, activity shifted towards the OSE's Nikkei 225 contract and by June 1989 average daily trading volume in the Nikkei 225 outweighed trading in the Topix. Annual Topix trading volume declined from a peak of 3.7 mln contracts in 1989 to a low of 1.35 mln contracts in 1992; it rebounded, however, to 2.16 mln contracts in 1993 and 2.62 mln contracts in 1994; year-end open interest increased from 3,300 contracts in 1993 to 4,209 contracts in 1994 (TSE, 1994, BOJ, 1995).

The cash-settled Nikkei 225 contract was launched in 1988, just months after the introduction of the Topix future. The Nikkei 225 future quickly became popular and in late 1989 and early 1990, when the Tokyo equity market was at its peak, it was the most actively traded index future in the world (averaging daily turnover of 75,000 contracts and boasting open interest of 300,000 contracts). Activity in the contract was heavily weighted towards proprietary trading by domestic and foreign securities firms; one estimate suggests that 70% to 80% of all contract turnover during this time was related to institutional proprietary trading by securities companies, much based on index arbitrage of cash equity baskets against index futures (Park and Schoenfeld, 1993). Index arbitrage activity was thought to be sufficiently destabilizing, particularly with regard to volatility at settlement, that procedures were altered so that settlement of futures would be based on the next day's opening price (so-called special quotation). The regulatory authorities were also concerned that rapid, and sizeable, trading in index futures would destabilize the domestic financial markets; the concern eventually led to an increase in index futures margins and the imposition of daily price limits and 'circuit breakers'. With the gradual decline of the Tokyo equity market during the early 1990s turnover in Nikkei 225 futures declined dramatically; trading volume decreased from 8.48 mln contracts in 1993 to 5.55 mln contracts in 1994, though year-end open interest increased from 69,876 contracts in 1993 to 105,458 contracts in 1994 (OSE, 1994).

The OSE's Nikkei 300 contract, which began trading in 1994, achieved total turnover of 4.18 mln contracts during its first year. While this appears to be a respectable figure it is important to note that the difference in index composition and pricing means that average daily market value total turnover in 1994 was only JPY56.6 bln (US$625 mln), versus JPY503 bln (US$5.6 bln) for the Nikkei 225 contract.

As mentioned earlier in the chapter, several global exchanges feature competing Japanese stock index futures contracts. SIMEX trades Nikkei 225 and Nikkei 300 futures while the CME trades Nikkei 225 futures. Both exchanges feature significant volume and continually challenge the OSE (and, more indirectly, the TSE) for market share. Tables 7.5 though 7.7 contain contract specifications for the three domestic index futures contracts, while Figures 7.6 to 7.8 highlight the historical movement of index futures prices.

Contract	**Nikkei 225 Stock Index Futures**
Type	Domestic
Exchange	Osaka Stock Exchange
Months	March, June, September, December to five contract months
Contract Size	JPY1,000 * Nikkei 225 Index
Tick Value	JPY10 * Nikkei 225 Index
Daily Limit	Approximately +/– 3% against previous day's settlement price (e.g. +/– 900 points if the index is between 20,000 – 30,000; 1,200 points if the index is between 30,000 – 40,000)
Deliverable Instrument	Cash settlement based on special quotation of index (total opening price of each issue on business day following last trading day)
Last Trading Day	Business day preceding the 2nd Friday of the contract month
Delivery Day	4th business day following the last trading day of the contract month
Real-time price data	Bloomberg: NKA <Cmdty>; Reuters: <0#JNI:>; Telerate: 9192

Table 7.5 Contract Specifications for OSE Nikkei 225 Index Futures

Contract	Nikkei 300 Stock Index Futures
Type	Domestic
Exchange	Osaka Stock Exchange
Months	March, June, September, December plus two consecutive near months
Contract Size	JPY10,000 * Nikkei 300 Index
Tick Value	0.1 index point
Daily Limit	+/– 5% against previous day's settlement price
Deliverable Instrument	Cash settlement
Last Trading Day	Business day before the 2nd Friday of each contract month (previous business day if a holiday)
Delivery Day	4th business day following the last trading day
Real-time price data	Bloomberg: NEA <Cmdty>; Reuters: <0#JNW:>; Telerate: 9193

Table 7.6 Contract Specifications for OSE Nikkei 300 Index Futures

Contract	Topix Index Futures
Type	Domestic
Exchange	Tokyo Stock Exchange
Months	March, June, September, December to five contract months
Contract Size	JPY10,000 * Topix Index
Tick Value	1 index point
Daily Limit	Approximately +/– 3% against previous day's settlement price (e.g. +/– 60 points if the index is below 2,000, +/– 90 points if the index is between 2,000–3,000)
Deliverable Instrument	Cash settlement
Last Trading Day	Business day prior to the 2nd Friday of the contract month (or preceding Thursday if Friday is a holiday)
Delivery Day	3rd business day following the 2nd Friday of each contract month (or Thursday if Friday is a holiday)
Real-time price data	Bloomberg: TPA <Cmdty>; Reuters: <0#JTI:>; Telerate: 9186

Table 7.7 Contract Specifications for TSE Topix Index Futures

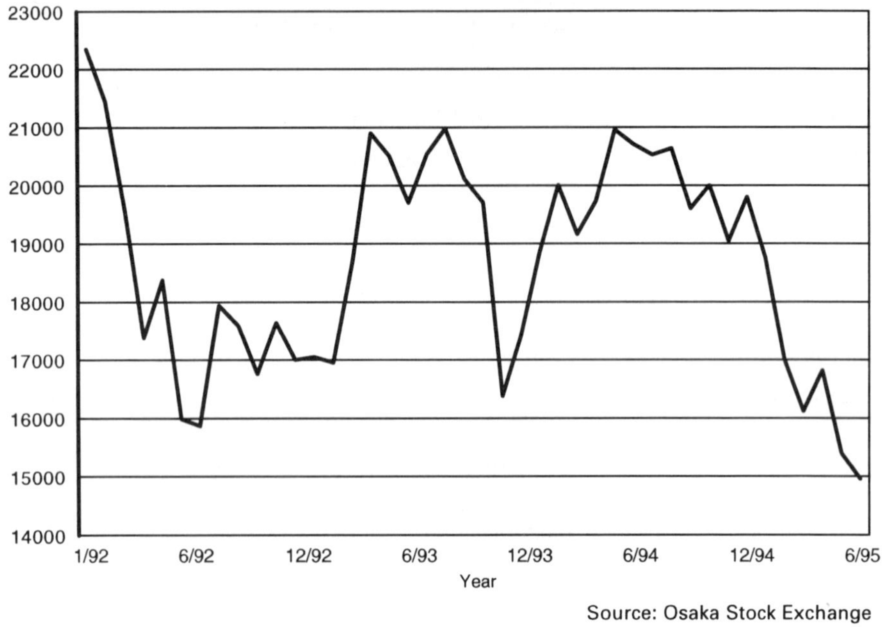

Figure 7.6 Historical Movement of OSE Nikkei 225 Index Futures

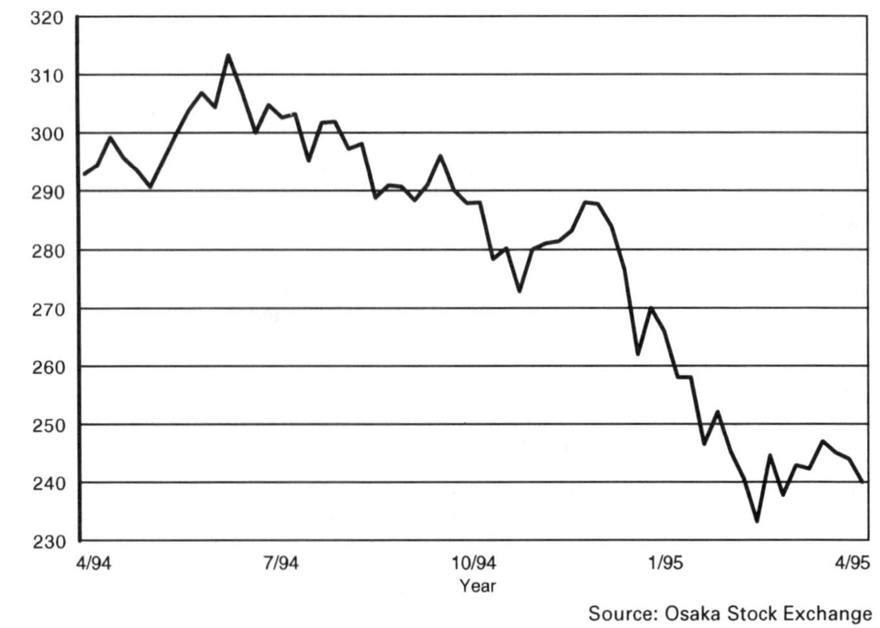

Figure 7.7 Historical Movement of OSE Nikkei 300 Index Futures

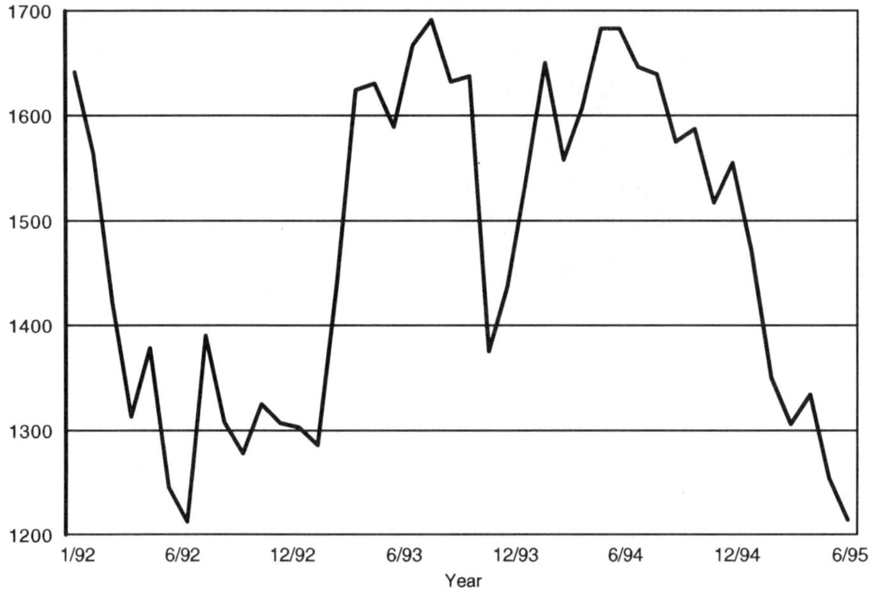

Figure 7.8 Historical Movement of TSE Topix Index Futures

The domestic market currently features four distinct index options contracts, including Nikkei 225 index options, Nikkei 300 index options, Topix index options and Nagoya 25 index options.

Trading in listed index options began in mid-1989 when the OSE launched its Nikkei 225 contract. The contract is structured as a modified American option (e.g. exercisable on any Thursday up to, and including, expiration) which is settled on a cash basis; strikes are set at 500 point intervals and four contract months are quoted at all times. Trading volume in Nikkei 225 options amounted to 6.08 mln contracts in 1993 and 4.27 mln contracts in 1994; year-end open interest increased from 80,466 contracts in 1993 to 97,026 contracts in 1994 (OSE, 1995).

Just six months after the introduction of the Nikkei 225 options, the TSE introduced Topix index options and the NSE introduced Nagoya 25 index options. The TSE Topix option is structured as an American exercise, cash-settled derivative with strikes set at 50 point intervals; four contract months are quoted at any given time. Although initial turnover in Topix options was promising the contract failed to sustain investor interest, mainly because the Nikkei had developed as the market's primary index. Annual trading volume in Topix options fell from a peak of 4.8 mln contracts in 1989 to a mere 37,831 contracts in 1993 and 20,078 contracts in 1994; year-end open interest fell from 8,037 contracts in 1993 to 3,396 contracts in 1994 (TSE, 1994, NSE, 1995). The Nagoya option, based on an index of the 25 largest companies quoted on the TSE, OSE and NSE, is structured as a

European exercise, cash-settlement option with strikes set at 25 point intervals; four contract months are quoted at any time. Turnover in Nagoya options has been only modestly active: trading amounted to 160,104 contracts in 1993 and 80,682 contacts in 1994; year-end open interest remained negligible at 70 contracts in 1993 and 310 contracts in 1994 (NSE, 1995).

The OSE introduced Nikkei 300 index options in 1994. The contract is designed as a European, cash-settled option with strikes set at 25 point intervals for quarter months and five point intervals for near months; six contracts are quoted at all times. Overall volume in Nikkei 300 options has been very modest, particularly in comparison with Nikkei 225 options. Total trading volume amounted to 269,067 contracts in 1994 (versus 4.27 mln for its counterpart); on a market value basis this equates to an average of JPY190 mln (US$2 mln) per day (versus JPY4.8 bln (US$550 mln) per day for its counterpart) (OSE, 1995).

Note that SIMEX features futures options contracts on the Nikkei 225 and Nikkei 300 which compete directly with the OSE's contracts; in the US, the CME lists Nikkei 225 futures options, while the CBOE lists Nikkei 300 options. Tables 7.8 though 7.11 contain relevant details on the four Japanese index option contracts. Figures 7.9 and 7.10 illustrate the historical movement of implied volatility for Nikkei 225 and Topix at-the-money puts and calls.

Contract	**Nikkei 225 Stock Index Options**
Type	Domestic
Exchange	Osaka Stock Exchange
Months	Four near months
Contract Size	JPY1,000 * Nikkei 225 Index
Tick Value	JPY5,000 per contract when within JPY1,000 of index; JPY10,000 per contract when more than JPY1,000 over index
Daily Limit	Approximately +/– 3% against previous day's settlement price (e.g. +/– 900 points if between 20,000 and 30,000)
Deliverable Instrument	Cash settlement
Last Trading Day	Business day preceding the 2nd Friday of each month
Exercise Day	Modified American exercise – once per week up to, and including the second Friday of contract month
Real-time price data	Bloomberg: NKY <Index> OMON; Reuters: <0#JNI*.OS:>; Telerate: 9120–27

Table 7.8 Contract Specifications for OSE Nikkei 225 Index Options

Contract	Nikkei 300 Stock Index Options
Type	Domestic
Exchange	Osaka Stock Exchange
Months	March, June, September, December plus two consecutive near months
Contract Size	JPY10,000 * Nikkei 300 Index
Tick Value	0.1 point
Daily Limit	+/– 5% against previous day's settlement price
Deliverable Instrument	Cash settlement
Last Trading Day	Day before 2nd Friday of each expiration month
Exercise Day	European exercise – on last trading day only
Real-time price data	Bloomberg: NEY <Index> OMON; Reuters: <0#JNW*.OS:>; Telerate: 56946–57

Table 7.9 Contract Specifications for OSE Nikkei 300 Index Options

Contract	Topix Index Options
Type	Domestic
Exchange	Tokyo Stock Exchange
Months	Monthly, up to next four months
Contract Size	JPY10,000 * Topix Index
Tick value	0.5 points
Daily Limit	+/– 3% against previous day's settlement price
Deliverable Instrument	Cash settlement
Last Trading Day	Business day prior to the 2nd Friday of the contract month
Exercise Day	American exercise – any business day up to, and including, the business day prior to the second Friday of the month, except for March, June, September, December contracts, which expire on the second Friday
Real-time price data	Bloomberg: TPX <Index> OMON; Reuters: <0#JTI*.T:>; Telerate: 9187–90, 9128–31

Table 7.10 Contract Specifications for TSE Topix Index Options

Contract	Nagoya 25 Index Options
Type	Domestic
Exchange	Nagoya Stock Exchange
Months	Four near term months
Contract Size	JPY10,000 * Nagoya 25 Index
Tick value	0.5 points if index is below 1,000; 1 point if index is over 1,000
Daily Limit	Approximately +/– 3% against previous day's settlement price
Deliverable Instrument	Cash settlement
Last Trading Day	Same day as exercise day
Exercise Day	European exercise – on the business day prior to the 2nd Friday of the contract month only
Real-time price data	Bloomberg: NSY <Index> OMON; Reuters: <0#JNG*.NG:>; Telerate: 28970–77

Table 7.11 Contract Specifications for NSE Nagoya 25 Index Options

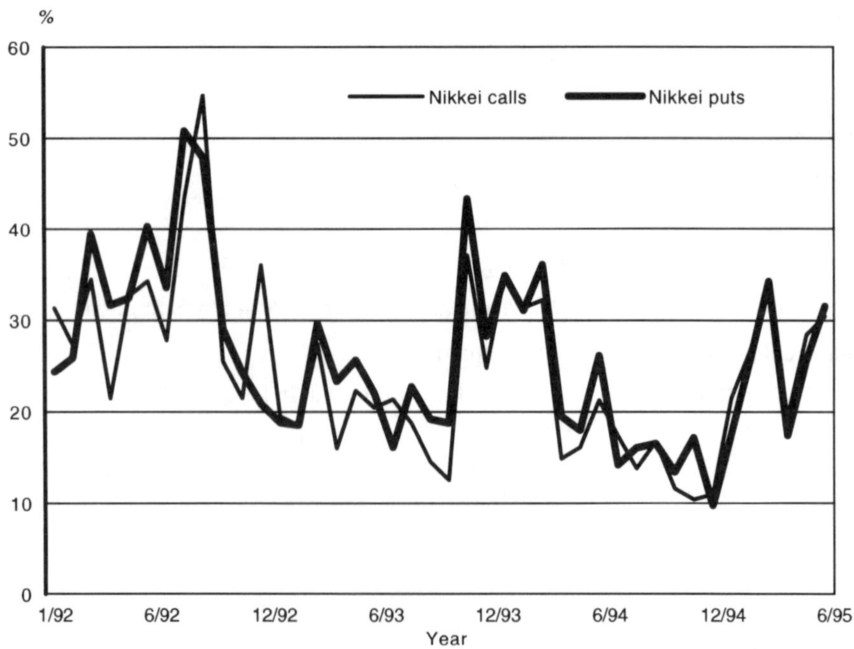

Figure 7.9 Historical Movement of Nikkei 225 At-the-Money Option Implied Volatilities

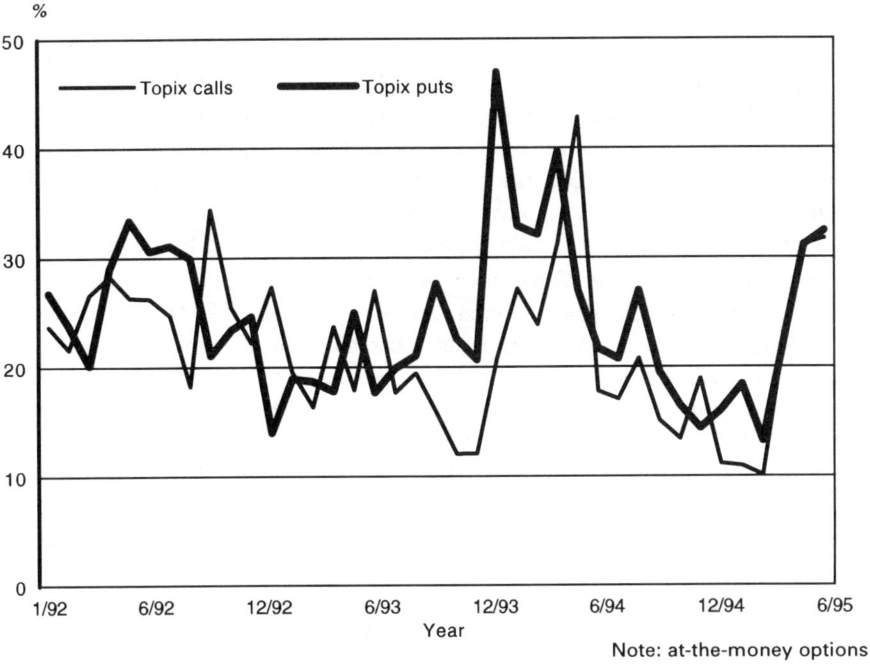

Figure 7.10 Historical Movement of Topix At-the-Money Option Implied Volatilities

Fixed Income

Deposit Futures/Options/Futures Options

In June 1989 Japan's newest listed derivative exchange, TIFFE, introduced futures contracts on three-month Euroyen and three-month Eurodollars. The Euroyen contract, referencing three-month yen LIBOR, quickly became the most active derivative on TIFFE and has, over the course of the past six years, risen to become the most actively traded futures contract in Japan. It has also become one of the world's most active contracts, ranking fifth in turnover among all global listed derivatives in 1994. Total trading volume increased from 23.4 mln contracts in 1993 to 37.4 mln contracts in 1994; year-end open interest rose from 1 mln contracts in 1993 to 1.127 mln contracts in 1994 (TIFFE, 1995). The Euroyen contract, which is used by a broad range of hedgers and speculators, is typically active to 24 months at any point, with good to excellent liquidity out to 18 months.

In 1995 TIFFE and LIFFE signed a letter of agreement calling for the creation of a fungible LIFFE Euroyen contract which would give participants the ability to trade short-term Japanese interest rates on a 16-hour basis every business day. The contract is expected to be offsettable for LIFFE members, but not TIFFE members (e.g. LIFFE members can establish, transfer or close out positions on either exchange, while TIFFE members cannot); the 'one-sided' offset is designed to provide LIFFE members with access to TIFFE's liquidity while at the same time preserving TIFFE's liquidity (e.g. not permitting TIFFE-originated business to flow to LIFFE). The LIFFE contract will be launched in the second quarter of 1996. It should be noted that SIMEX lists a competing Euroyen futures contract which features reasonable liquidity; although the SIMEX contract is actively used, turnover and open interest have always been far greater in the TIFFE contract.

In sharp contrast to the Euroyen contract the performance of the TIFFE three-month Eurodollar future, which references three-month US$ LIBOR, has been disappointing. Though trading began on an acceptable note volume soon dwindled, and the contract registered no turnover or open interest in either 1993 or 1994. The contract's lacklustre performance is attributable primarily to competition from SIMEX's own Eurodollar futures; the SIMEX contract is the primary choice for regional hedgers and speculators and features a very liquid strip to 24 months. Despite the dormant status of TIFFE Eurodollar futures, the Exchange has indicated that it is not planning to abandon the contract. Tables 7.12 and 7.13 contain relevant details on the TIFFE three-month deposit futures contracts.

Contract	**Three-month Euroyen Futures**
Type	Domestic
Exchange	Tokyo International Financial Futures Exchange
Months	March, June, September, December on two year cycle
Contract Size	JPY100 mln
Tick Value	0.01 point
Daily Limit	No limit
Deliverable Instrument	Cash settlement
Last Trading Day	2nd business day prior to the 3rd Wednesday of the contract month
Delivery Day	Business day after the last trading day
Real-time price data	Bloomberg: YEA <Cmdty>; Reuters: <0#JEY:>; Telerate: 9945, 9768–69

Table 7.12 Contract Specifications for TIFFE Three-month Euroyen Futures

Contract	**Three-month Eurodollar Futures**
Type	Offshore
Exchange	Tokyo International Financial Futures Exchange
Months	March, June, September, December
Contract Size	US$1 mln
Tick Value	0.01 point

Contract	Three-month Eurodollar Futures
Daily Limit	No limit
Deliverable Instrument	Cash settlement
Last Trading Day	2nd business day prior to the 3rd Wednesday of the contract month
Delivery Day	Business day following the last trading day
Real-time price data	Bloomberg: JDA <Cmdty>; Reuters: <0#JED:>; Telerate: 9780

Table 7.13 Contract Specifications for TIFFE Three-month Eurodollar Futures

In July 1992, following several years of success with its three-month Euroyen contract, TIFFE introduced a 12-month Euroyen contract referencing 12-month yen LIBOR. Though trading volume has increased modestly over the past few years, it remains negligible as most participants continue to utilize the very liquid three-month derivative. Total turnover increased from 4,434 contracts in 1993 to 25,100 contracts in 1994; year-end open interest amounted to less than 100 contracts in 1993 and 1994 (TIFFE, 1995). Table 7.14 contains details on 12-month Euroyen LIBOR futures, while Figures 7.11 and 7.12 trace the historical price movement of three- and 12-month Euroyen futures.

Contract	12-month Euroyen Futures
Type	Domestic
Exchange	Tokyo International Financial Futures Exchange
Months	March, June, September, December to 15 months
Contract Size	JPY100 mln
Tick Value	0.01 point
Daily Limit	No limit
Deliverable Instrument	Cash settlement
Last Trading Day	2nd business day prior to the 3rd Wednesday of the contract month
Delivery Day	Business day following the last trading day
Real-time price data	Bloomberg: YOA <Cmdty>; Reuters: <0#JFY:>; Telerate: 9946, 9778

Table 7.14 Contract Specifications for TIFFE 12-month Euroyen Futures

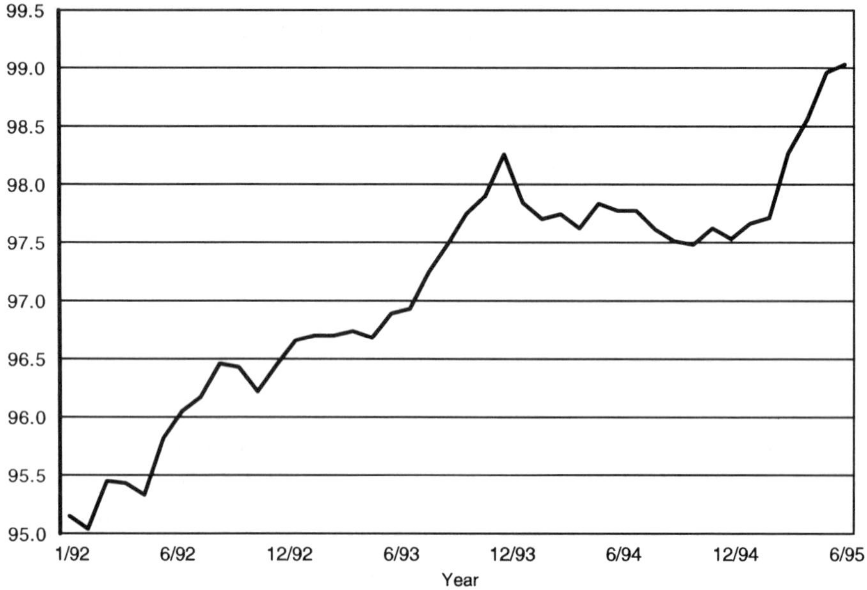

Source: Tokyo International Financial Futures Exchange

Figure 7.11 Historical Movement of TIFFE Three-month Euroyen Futures

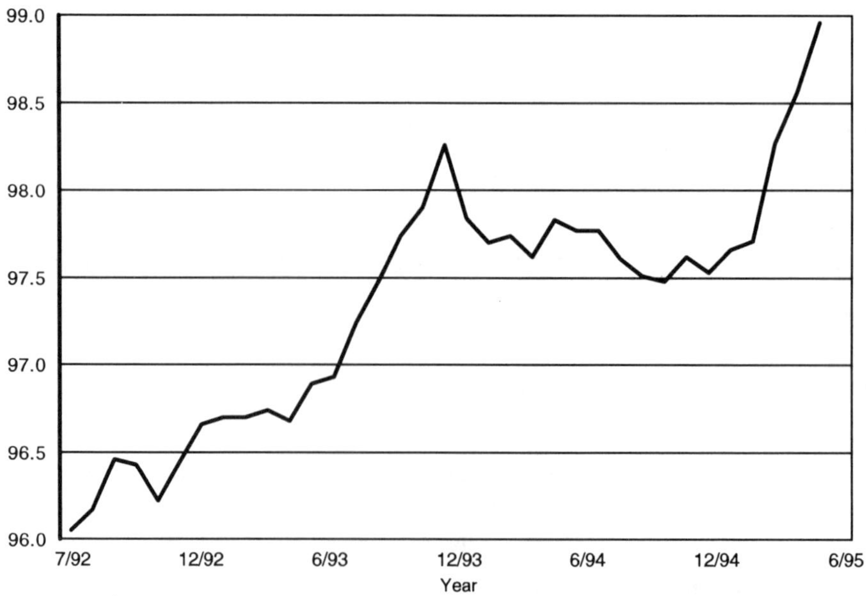

Source: Tokyo International Financial Futures Exchange

Figure 7.12 Historical Movement of TIFFE 12-month Euroyen Futures

TIFFE complemented its Euroyen product line with the introduction of three-month Euroyen futures options in July 1991. The option is structured as an American exercise, physical delivery contract with strikes set at 0.25% intervals. Trading volume in the contract amounted to 686,500 contracts in 1993 and 520,237 contracts in 1994; year-end open interest increased from 81,600 contracts in 1993 to 86,650 contracts in 1994 (TIFFE, 1995). As with Euroyen futures, TIFFE faces modest competition from SIMEX, which lists and trades its own three-month Euroyen futures options contract (the SIMEX contract was actually introduced before the TIFFE contract); despite the presence of a competing contract, however, trading volume on TIFFE has always exceeded that of SIMEX. Table 7.15 contains relevant details on the option contract.

Contract	**Options on Three-month Euroyen Futures**
Type	Domestic
Exchange	Tokyo International Financial Futures Exchange
Months	March, June, September, December to nine months
Contract Size	One Euroyen future
Tick Value	0.01 point
Daily Limit	No limit
Deliverable Instrument	Physical settlement into underlying futures contract
Last Trading Day	2nd business day prior to the 3rd Wednesday of the contract month
Exercise Day	American exercise – any business day up to, and including, the last trading day
Real-time price data	Bloomberg: YEA <Index> OMON; Reuters: <0#JEDmy+>; Telerate: 9949–54, 35304–09, 56940–42

Table 7.15 Contract Specifications for TIFFE Options on Three-month Euroyen Futures

Interest Rate Futures/Options/Futures Options

The TSE lists and trades interest rate futures contracts on the ten-year benchmark JGB and the 20-year superlong JGB. The ten-year contract was launched in 1985 and has, over the past decade, become an extremely liquid derivative; it was the 20th most active futures contract in the world in 1994 with turnover of more than 13 mln contracts (FI, 1995). The 20-year future, in contrast, has been virtually inactive since its launch in 1988.

The ten-year JGB future has been successful primarily because it is a useful hedging/speculating instrument for those active in the world's second largest fixed income market. As indicated earlier in the chapter, there is substantial OTC JGB trading in both Tokyo and London, primarily in the benchmark ten-year sector (which accounts for 80% of all JGB trading (Park and Schoenfeld, 1993)); liquid trading in the benchmark has prompted substantial use of ten-year futures by both hedgers and speculators. Further use of the contract has developed through growth in yen IRSs; market-makers often utilize JGB futures to hedge swap books on a temporary basis until offsetting swaps can be executed. The success of the ten-year future, therefore, is related to the substantial trading which occurs in underlying cash and OTC derivative instruments. During 1989 (the peak year for JGB futures trading) 18.9 mln contracts were traded; given the large notional amount of the contract (JPY100 mln), the market value turnover of the future was the highest of any contract in the world. Though volume declined to 11.8 mln contracts by 1992, it experienced a resurgence to 15.1 mln contracts in 1993 and 13 mln contracts in 1994; year-end open interest increased from 151,542 contracts in 1993 to 162,146 contracts in 1994 (TSE, 1995).

As indicated above, the 20-year futures contract has remained virtually dormant since its creation. After trading a record 28,734 contracts in 1989, volume dropped to 3,106 contracts in 1993 and 3,194 contracts in 1994; year-end open interest amounted to a mere 142 contracts in 1993 and 194 contracts in 1994 (TSE, 1994). The primary reason for the low futures turnover is attributable to poor liquidity in the underlying 20-year superlong cash bond, which often suffers from prolonged periods of inactivity. Despite its poor showing the TSE has elected not to delist the contract.

It should be noted that SIMEX introduced trading in ten-year JGB futures in 1994; though the SIMEX contract is still relatively new it has already achieved significant volume and open interest, and is challenging the TSE for a portion of the Japanese interest rate futures market. LIFFE also lists and trades a ten-year JGB contract. The LIFFE contract is very actively traded and provides JGB traders in Asia with an extended trading day; though settlement of the LIFFE future is to the TSE closing price the contract is settled in cash, not physical, and, as such, is not perfectly fungible with the TSE contract. There is presently discussion on converting the LIFFE JGB into a deliverable contract so that the TSE and LIFFE futures become completely fungible. Tables 7.16 and 7.17 contain contract details for ten- and 20-year JGB futures, while Figures 7.13 and 7.14 trace the historical movement of ten- and 20-year JGB futures prices.

Following the establishment and success of ten-year JGB futures the TSE developed options on JGB futures. The creation of the listed option (which debuted in May 1990) was also a response to competition from the domestic OTC bond option market, which commenced trading in April 1989 after receiving approval from the Japanese Ministry of Finance (we discuss the OTC bond option market later in this chapter). JGB futures options are structured as American exercise, physical delivery derivatives with seven strikes set at one point intervals around the current futures price. The first year of trading in TSE bond options was the most significant, with turnover reaching nearly 2.3 mln contracts. Trading volumes have declined since then, but remain substantial nonetheless: total turnover amounted to 1.5 mln contracts in 1993 and 1.69 mln contracts in 1994, with year-end open interest of 59,883 contracts in 1993 and 63,764 contracts in 1994 (TSE, 1995). As indicated above, SIMEX introduced JGB futures in 1993 and it followed with JGB futures options in 1994; total SIMEX turnover remains small, however, in comparison with TSE turnover. Table 7.18 highlights contract details on JGB futures options.

Contract	Ten-year Japanese Government Bond Futures
Type	Domestic
Exchange	Tokyo Stock Exchange
Months	March, June, September, December to five quarterly months
Contract Size	JPY100 mln face value of Ten-year, 6% coupon Japanese Government Bonds
Tick Value	JPY10,000 per contract
Daily Limit	+/– 2 points against previous day's settlement price
Deliverable Instrument	Physical settlement of listed Japanese Government Bond with final maturity of 7 to 11 years
Last Trading Day	9th business day prior to the delivery day
Delivery Day	20th day of the contract month
Real-time price data	Bloomberg: JBA <Cmdty>; Reuters: <0#JGB:>; Telerate: 9137

Table 7.16 Contract Specifications for TSE Ten-Year Japanese Government Bond Futures

Contract	20-year Japanese Government Bond Futures
Type	Domestic
Exchange	Tokyo Stock Exchange
Months	March, June, September, December to five quarterly months
Contract Size	JPY100 mln face value of 20-year, 6% coupon, Japanese Government Bonds
Tick Value	JPY10,000 per contract
Daily Limit	+/– 3 points against previous day's settlement price
Deliverable Instrument	Physical settlement of listed Japanese Government Bond with final maturity of 15 to 21 years
Last Trading Day	9th business day prior to the delivery day
Delivery Day	20th day of the contract month
Real-time price data	Bloomberg: JLA <Cmdty>; Reuters: <0#JTB:>; Telerate: 9137

Table 7.17 Contract Specifications for TSE 20-year Japanese Government Bond Futures

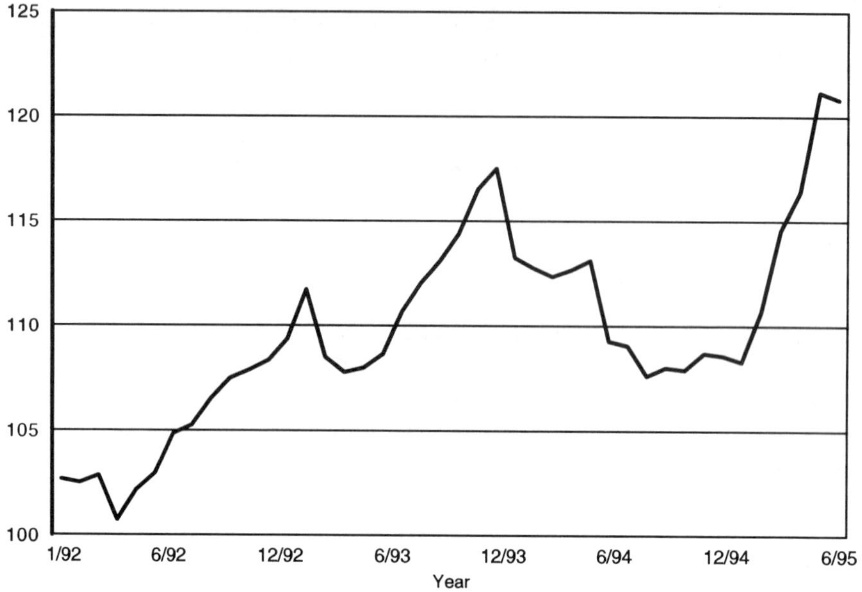

Source: Tokyo Stock Exchange

Figure 7.13 Historical Movement of TSE Ten-year JGB Futures

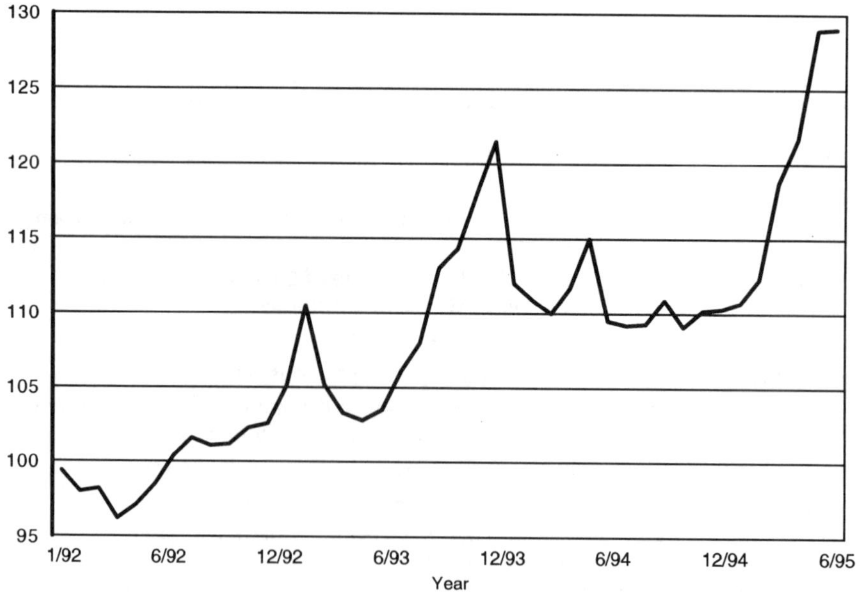

Source: Tokyo Stock Exchange

Figure 7.14 Historical Movement of TSE 20-year JGB Futures

Contract	Options on Ten-year Japanese Government Bond Futures
Type	Domestic
Exchange	Tokyo Stock Exchange
Months	Closest two months from March, June, September, December cycle
Contract Size	1 JGB future
Tick Value	JPY10,000 per contract
Daily Limit	+/– 2 points against previous day's settlement price
Deliverable Instrument	Physical settlement into underlying futures contract
Last Trading Day	Exercise day
Exercise Day	American exercise – any business day up to, and including, the last business day of the month prior to the delivery month of the relevant future.
Real-time price data	Bloomberg: JBA <Cmdty> OMON; Reuters: <0#JGBmy+> ; Telerate: 27750–55

Table 7.18 Contract Specifications for TSE Options on Japanese Government Bond Futures

In addition to futures/options on domestic Japanese interest rates, the TSE also features a physical settlement contract on the US 20-year Treasury bond. The US bond future was introduced in December 1989 as a means of providing Japanese participants with a US bond derivative in the Asian time zone. During the late 1980s and early 1990s, when Japanese institutions were substantial investors in US bonds, local access to a hedge instrument based on such securities was particularly important. During the peak year of 1990 total turnover in TSE Treasury bond futures amounted to a respectable 518,400 contracts. With the decline of Japanese investment in US Treasury securities in recent years, however, turnover in the TSE's contract has declined as well: total volume amounted to 112,600 contracts in 1993 and 115,750 contracts in 1994, with year-end open interest of 2,200 contracts in 1993 and 2,120 contracts in 1994 (TSE, 1995). Table 7.19 contains relevant contract details on the 20-year Treasury future while Figure 7.15 illustrates the historical price movement of the contract.

With regard to new products, there is widespread expectation that a five-year JGB future will be introduced on the TSE during the first quarter of 1996 (though no specific details on contract specifications have been released). Benefits of having such a contract would be twofold: it would provide participants, particularly hedgers, with a listed derivative much closer in duration to medium-term Euroyen bonds, which are typically issued with maturities of three to five years; such would make for more accurate hedging of positions. In addition, liquidity in intermediate maturity JGB's deliverable into the contract (e.g. bonds with four- to six-year maturities) would almost certainly increase. As indicated above, liquidity in the JGB

Contract	20-year US Treasury Bond Futures
Type	Offshore
Exchange	Tokyo Stock Exchange
Months	March, June, September, December to five contract months
Contract Size	US$100,000 face value of US Treasury bonds, 8% coupon, 20 year maturity
Tick Value	1/32 of a point
Daily Limit	+/– 3 points against previous Chicago Board of Trade (CBOT) settlement price
Deliverable Instrument	Physical settlement of US Treasury bonds with maturity of 15+ years, or callable after 15 years
Last Trading Day	Last trading date at CBOT (7th day prior to the CBOT's last business day of the month)
Delivery Day	Last business day of the contract month
Real-time price data	Bloomberg: JTA <Cmdty>; Reuters: <0#JUS:>; Telerate: 9132

Table 7.19 Contract Specifications for TSE 20-year US Treasury Bond Futures

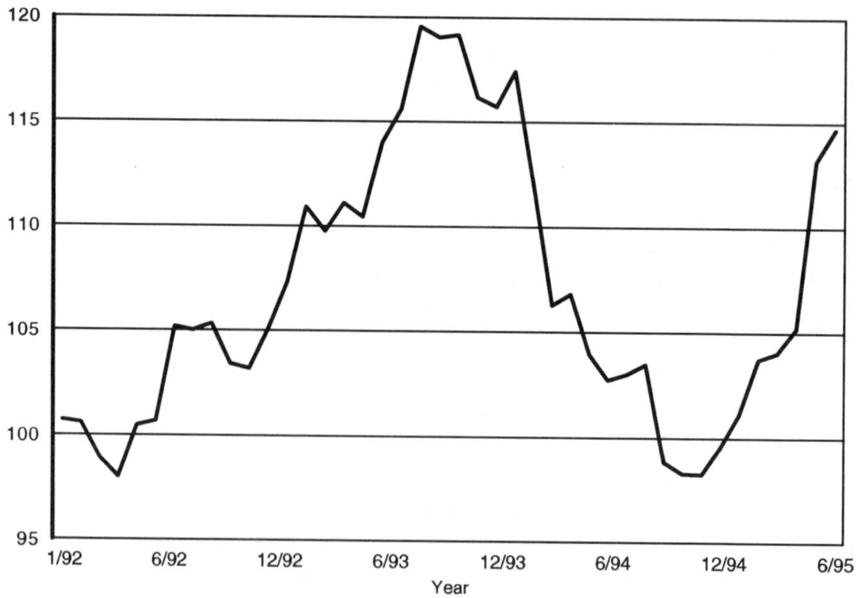

Source: Tokyo Stock Exchange

Figure 7.15 Historical Movement of TSE 20-year US Treasury Bond Futures

market is driven by trading activity in the ten-year benchmark. During 1994, average daily trading in the benchmark was approximately JPY160 bln (US$1.8 bln), while trading in the four- to six-year sector was only JPY20 bln (US$220 mln) (Morse, 1995). A five-year future could shift more trading into the four to six year range and help strengthen the JGB yield curve. Issues related to bond deliverability, pricing of reference bonds, and so on, would have to be resolved prior to introduction of such futures.

Currency

Currency Futures/Options/Futures Options

As indicated above, TIFFE is the sole exchange within the Japanese market permitted to list and trade currency derivatives. In 1989 the Exchange introduced its first currency contract, based on the US$/JPY exchange rate; the contract met with very limited demand and was altered in February 1991 to make the terms more appealing to a broader base of participants (e.g the quote was changed to the more acceptable financial industry practice of JPY/US$). Interest has remained lacklustre, however, primarily because the Japanese OTC spot, forward and FX swap markets are extremely well developed and very liquid; most professional participants prefer to use the OTC market for hedging or establishing JPY/US$ exposures (note that in addition to the OTC market, TIFFE also faces competition from MIFE, SIMEX and HKFE, which all feature listed JPY/US$ contracts). Turnover in the currency future dropped from 48,241 contracts in 1993 to 13,770 contracts in 1994; year-end open interest declined from 1,600 in 1993 to 1,240 contracts in 1994 (TIFFE, 1995). Table 7.20 contains details on the TIFFE currency contract while Figure 7.16 illustrates the historical movement of the futures price.

Commodity

Commodity Futures/Options/Futures Options

Japan features the broadest, and most diverse, range of commodity futures in Asia Pacific (though China's commodity listings are comprehensive as well, they are still subject to trading restrictions and are not accessible by foreign institutions); 13 different exchanges list 46 futures/options contracts on agricultural commodities and precious metals. As the reader will note in this section there is currently a reasonable amount of contract duplication between exchanges, suggesting some exchanges and contracts have (or will have) difficulty achieving sufficient volume to provide hedgers and speculators with the required level of liquidity; this may result in further consolidation of exchanges and/or reconstruction or delisting of contracts. As indicated earlier in the chapter, the authorities are encouraging mergers between exchanges so that duplication can be reduced and volume can be concentrated in one or two contracts per product category. Table 7.21 summarizes the number of identical (or very nearly identical) contracts by category, when more than two contracts exist for a single category.

Contract	JPY/US$ Currency Futures
Type	Domestic
Exchange	Tokyo International Financial Futures Exchange
Months	March, June, September, December
Contract Size	US$50,000
Tick Value	¥2,500 per contract
Daily Limit	No limit
Deliverable Instrument	Physical delivery of yen in Tokyo, US dollars in New York
Last Trading Day	2nd business day prior to the 3rd Wednesday of the contract month
Delivery Day	3rd Wednesday of the contract month
Real-time price data	Bloomberg: YNA <Cmdty>; Reuters: <0#JYJ:>; Telerate: 9947

Table 7.20 Contract Specifications for TIFFE JPY/US$ Currency Futures

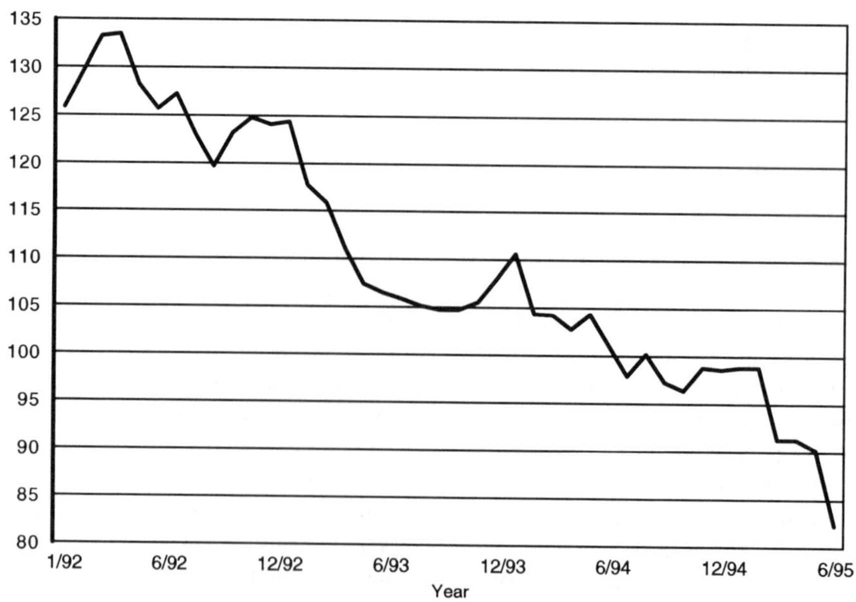

Source: Tokyo International Financial Futures Exchange

Figure 7.16 Historical Movement of TIFFE JPY/US$ Currency Futures

Futures/options contract	Number of identical contracts on domestic exchanges
Red (Azuki) Beans	5
Soybeans	6
Refined Sugar	4
Raw Sugar	4
Cotton Yarn	5
Woollen Yarn	3

Table 7.21 Summary of Identical Contracts on Domestic Exchanges

HGE currently trades futures on imported and domestic soybeans, red beans, white beans, and potato starch. During 1993 and 1994 the Exchange's white bean, potato starch and domestic soybean contracts were inactive. The red bean and imported soybean contracts were moderately active: turnover in red bean futures increased from 182,611 contracts in 1993 to 241,555 contracts in 1994, with year-end open interest of 5,084 contracts in 1993 and 3,507 contracts in 1994; turnover in imported soybean futures declined from 106,152 contracts in 1993 to 89,916 contracts in 1994, with year-end open-interest of 3,191 contracts in 1993 and 929 contracts in 1994 (HGE, 1995). Although the Exchange is in the process of merging with the TGE, we present below, in Tables 7.22 through 7.26, relevant contract details on HGE futures as they existed just prior to the merger. Current plans call for combining the HGE imported soybean contract and the TGE US soybean contract, and consolidating the HGE and TGE red bean futures; futures trading in domestic soybeans, white beans and potato starch is expected to be abandoned.

Contract	Imported Soybean Futures
Type	Domestic/Offshore
Exchange	Hokkaido Grain Exchange
Months	Next six alternate, even months
Contract Size	250 bags (15,000 kg)
Tick Value	JPY10/bag
Daily Limit	+/– 7% against previous day's settlement price
Deliverable Grade	Physical settlement of imported soybeans through delivery of warehouse certificates
Last Trading Day	Two business days before delivery day
Delivery Day	Business day prior to the last business day of the contract month
Real-time price data	None available

Table 7.22 Contract Specifications for HGE Imported Soybean Futures

Contract	Domestic Soybean Futures
Type	Domestic
Exchange	Hokkaido Grain Exchange
Months	Three consecutive months, starting with current month
Contract Size	40 bags (2,400 kg)
Tick Value	JPY10/bag
Daily Limit	+/– 7% against previous day's settlement price
Deliverable Grade	Physical settlement of domestic soybeans through delivery of warehouse certificates
Last Trading Day	20th day of every month, day before if a holiday (for December contracts 8th of the month)
Delivery Day	Business day prior to the last business day of the contract month
Real-time price data	None available

Table 7.23 Contract Specifications for HGE Domestic Soybean Futures

Contract	Red Bean Futures
Type	Domestic
Exchange	Hokkaido Grain Exchange
Months	Six consecutive months, starting with current month
Contract Size	80 bags (2,400 kg)
Tick Value	JPY10/bag
Daily Limit	+/– 7% against previous day's settlement price
Deliverable Grade	Physical settlement of red beans through delivery of warehouse certificates
Last Trading Day	20th day of every month, day before if a holiday (for December contracts 8th of the month)
Delivery Day	Business day prior to the last business day of the contract month
Real-time price data	None available

Table 7.24 Contract Specifications for HGE Red Bean Futures

Contract	White Bean Futures
Type	Domestic
Exchange	Hokkaido Grain Exchange
Months	Six consecutive months, starting with current month
Contract Size	40 bags (2,400 kg)
Tick Value	JPY10/bag
Daily Limit	+/– 7% against previous day's settlement price
Deliverable Grade	Physical settlement of white beans through delivery of warehouse certificates
Last Trading Day	20th day of every month, day before if a holiday (for December contracts 8th of the month)
Delivery Day	Business day prior to the last business day of the contract month
Real time price data	None available

Table 7.25 Contract Specifications for HGE White Bean Futures

Contract	Potato Starch Futures
Type	Domestic
Exchange	Hokkaido Grain Exchange
Months	Three consecutive months, starting with current month
Contract Size	100 bags (2,500 kg)
Tick Value	JPY1/bag
Daily Limit	+/– 7% against previous day's settlement price
Deliverable Grade	Physical settlement of potato starch through delivery of warehouse certificates
Last Trading Day	20th day of every month, day before if a holiday (for December contracts 8th of the month)
Delivery Day	Business day prior to the last business day of the contract month
Real-time price data	None available

Table 7.26 Contract Specifications for HGE Potato Starch Futures

The KCE trades futures contracts on red beans, US soybeans, yellow corn and refined sugar; its primary domestic competitors include KANEX, NGSE and TGE (which all list similar contracts). Total turnover in KCE's red bean future declined from 579,751 contracts in 1993 to 492,294 contracts in 1994; open interest at the end of each year amounted to just over 13,400 contracts. Turnover in the Exchange's soybean contract dropped from 486,850 contracts in 1993 to 213,271 contracts in 1994; year-end open interest amounted to 24,906 contracts in 1993 and 11,342 contracts in 1994 (despite the apparent decline in volume and open interest it should be noted that the soybean contract size increased from 15,000 to 30,000 kilograms in August 1993 and, as such, the turnover figures are not directly comparable). Corn futures continue to be KCE's most active derivative, recording turnover of 1 mln contacts in 1993 and 1.7 mln contracts in 1994; year-end open interest increased from 57,396 contracts in 1993 to 79,958 contracts in 1994. In contrast to the very active corn future, the KCE refined sugar future is all but dormant. Total turnover has been just slightly more than 1,400 contracts per year for each of the past few years; no open interest was recorded at the end of 1993 or 1994 (KCE, 1995). (Note: KCE has also traded raw sugar and potato starch contracts in the past, but such are not active at the present time). Tables 7.27 through 7.30 contain relevant contract details on the KCE's futures.

Contract	**Red Bean Futures**
Type	Domestic/Offshore
Exchange	Kanmon Commodity Exchange
Months	Six consecutive months
Contract Size	80 bags (2,400 kg)
Tick Value	JPY10/bag
Daily Limit	+/– 10% against previous day's settlement price
Deliverable Grade	Physical settlement of No.2 polished red beans from Hokkaido (premiums or discounts applied to substitute beans from PRC, Taiwan or other areas of Japan), delivered to warehouses at Shimonoseki, Kitakyushu and Fukuoka
Last Trading Day	3rd business day prior to the final business day of the contract month
Delivery Day	1st business day prior to the final business day of the contract month
Real-time price data	None available

Table 7.27 Contract Specifications for KCE Red Bean Futures

Contract	US Soybean Futures
Type	Domestic/Offshore
Exchange	Kanmon Commodity Exchange
Months	January, March, May, plus every other month to 12 months forward
Contract Size	30,000 kg
Tick Value	JPY10/1,000 kg
Daily Limit	+/– 10% against previous day's settlement price
Deliverable Grade	Physical settlement of non-screened yellow soybeans from Indiana, Ohio or Michigan, delivered to warehouses in Shimonoseki, Kitakyushu and Fukuoka
Last Trading Day	3rd business day prior to the final business day of the contract month
Delivery Day	1st business day prior to the final business day of the contract month
Real-time price data	None available

Table 7.28 Contract Specifications for KCE US Soybean Futures

Contract	Yellow Corn Futures
Type	Domestic/Offshore
Exchange	Kanmon Commodity Exchange
Months	February, April, June, plus every other month to 12 months forward
Contract Size	100,000 kg
Tick Value	JPY10/1,000 kg
Daily Limit	+/– 10% against previous day's settlement price
Deliverable Grade	Physical settlement of US No. 3 yellow corn to piers of Hakata, Kagoshima, Shibushi or Mizushima
Last Trading Day	15th day of the month preceding delivery month, or preceding business day if a holiday
Delivery Day	1st business day to final business day of delivery month
Real-time price data	None available

Table 7.29 Contract Specifications for KCE Yellow Corn Futures

Contract	Refined Sugar Futures
Type	Domestic
Exchange	Kanmon Commodity Exchange
Months	Six consecutive months
Contract Size	9,000 kg
Tick Value	JPY0.10/kg
Daily Limit	+/– JPY10 against previous day's settlement price
Deliverable Grade	Physical settlement of NO brand white soft refined sugar to designated warehouses at Shimonoseki, Kitakyushu and Fukuoka
Last Trading Day	Second session of the business day preceding the last business day before delivery day
Delivery Day	Day preceding the last business day of the delivery month
Real-time price data	None available

Table 7.30 Contract Specifications for KCE Refined Sugar Futures

KANEX presently trades futures on red beans, soybeans, raw sugar and refined sugar, as well as options on raw sugar futures. KANEX's primary domestic competitors include KCE, NGSE and TGE. KANEX, along with TGE, is one of only two Japanese commodity exchanges to list commodity options; the KANEX option on raw sugar futures is an American exercise, physical delivery derivative with strikes set at 1,000 point intervals.

KANEX's red bean contract continues to be its most actively traded derivative, posting annual turnover of 2.91 mln contracts in 1993 and 2.93 mln contracts in 1994; year-end open interest rose from 74,606 contracts in 1993 to 81,600 contracts in 1994. Trading in soybean futures is also significant but has declined somewhat over the past few years; total turnover dropped from 1.58 mln contracts in 1993 to 1.29 mln contracts in 1994, with year-end open interest falling from 98,832 contracts in 1993 to 49,835 contracts in 1994. Turnover in raw sugar futures declined rather dramatically, from 1 mln contracts in 1993 to 664,600 contracts in 1994; year-end open interest dropped from 57,087 contracts in 1993 to 42,116 contracts in 1994. The Exchange's sole option contract, based on raw sugar futures, has gradually increased in popularity. Total option turnover amounted to 26,793 contracts in 1993 and 63,789 contracts in 1994; despite the increase in volume, year-end open interest declined from 2,739 contracts in 1993 to 1,568 contracts in 1994 (KANEX, 1995). Tables 7.31 through 7.35 contain contract specifications on each of the KANEX derivatives. (Note: in an effort to provide assistance to China's rapidly expanding futures industry, KANEX entered into co-operation agreements with two of China's leading commodity futures exchanges, China Zhengzhou Commodities Exchange and Shanghai Cereals and Oils Exchange (both discussed in chapter 3), where KANEX will provide both exchanges with technical advice and consultancy regarding futures products and markets).

Contract	**Red Bean Futures**
Type	Domestic
Exchange	Kansai Agricultural Commodity Exchange
Months	Six consecutive months
Contract Size	80 bags (2,400 kg)
Tick Value	JPY10/bag
Daily Limit	+/– JPY350 to JPY450 against previous day's settlement price
Deliverable Grade	Physical settlement of No.2 grade red beans produced in Hokkaido, by delivery of warehouse certificates
Last Trading Day	Two business days before delivery day
Delivery Day	Penultimate business day of the contract month
Real-time price data	Telerate: 35374

Table 7.31 Contract Specifications for KANEX Red Bean Futures

Contract	**Imported Soybean Futures**
Type	Domestic/Offshore
Exchange	Kansai Agricultural Commodity Exchange
Months	Six even months to 12 months forward
Contract Size	30 tons
Tick Value	JPY10/ton
Daily Limit	+/– JPY1,200 to JPY1,800 against previous day's settlement price
Deliverable Grade	Physical settlement of non-screened yellow soybeans from Indiana, Ohio or Michigan, by delivery of warehouse certificates
Last Trading Day	Two business days before delivery day
Delivery Day	Penultimate business day of the contract month
Real-time price data	Telerate: 35375

Table 7.32 Contract Specifications for KANEX Imported Soybean Futures

Contract	Raw Sugar Futures
Type	Domestic/Offshore
Exchange	Kansai Agricultural Commodity Exchange
Months	January, March, May, July, September, November; nine odd months to 20 months forward
Contract Size	20 tons (50 tons from March 1996 on)
Tick Value	JPY0.1/kg (JPY10/ton from March 1996 on)
Daily Limit	+/– JPY1 to JPY1.6 against previous day's settlement price (JPY1,000 to JPY1,600 from March 1996 on)
Deliverable Grade	Physical settlement of raw centrifugal cane sugar (96 degree polarization), CIF Japan
Last Trading Day	Two days before the end of the delivery month
Delivery Day	15th day of each even-numbered month
Real-time price data	Telerate: 22621

Table 7.33 Contract Specifications for KANEX Raw Sugar Futures

Contract	Refined Sugar Futures
Type	Domestic
Exchange	Kansai Agricultural Commodity Exchange
Months	Six consecutive months
Contract Size	9 tons
Tick Value	JPY0.1/kg
Daily Limit	+/– JPY2.50 against previous day's settlement price
Deliverable Grade	Cash settlement
Last Trading Day	Three business days before the last business day of the delivery month
Delivery Day	Day before the last business day of the contract month (24th in December)
Real-time price data	Telerate: 22622

Table 7.34 Contract Specifications for KANEX Refined Sugar Futures

Table 7.35 Contract Specifications for KANEX Options on Raw Sugar Futures

Contract	**Options on Raw Sugar Futures**
Type	Domestic
Exchange	Kansai Agricultural Commodity Exchange
Months	Last three delivery months of raw sugar futures
Contract Size	1 Raw Sugar future
Tick Value	JPY10/kg
Daily Limit	+/– JPY1,000 to JPY1,600 against previous day's settlement price
Deliverable Grade	Physical settlement into underlying futures contract
Last Trading Day	Last business day of the month six months after the 1st trading day
Expiry Day	American exercise – any business day up to, and including, last trading day
Real-time price data	Telerate: 42089–94

KRSE trades exclusively in raw silk futures. Overall turnover in the future increased from 687,723 contracts in 1993 to 695,172 contracts in 1994; year-end open interest rose from 21,123 contracts in 1993 to 27,610 contracts in 1994 (KRSE, 1995). Note that the KRSE faces direct competition from YRSE, which trades an identical contract. Table 7.36 contains relevant details on the KRSE's silk contract.

Contract	**Raw Silk Futures**
Type	Domestic
Exchange	Kobe Raw Silk Exchange
Months	Six consecutive months
Contract Size	150 kg (5 bales)
Tick Value	JPY1/kg
Daily Limit	+/– JPY200 against previous day's settlement price (no limits on current month after the 15th)
Deliverable Grade	Physical settlement of raw silk bales through delivery of warehouse certificates
Last Trading Day	Three business days before delivery day
Delivery Day	Penultimate business day of the contract month
Real-time price data	None available

Table 7.36 Contract Specifications for KRSE Raw Silk Futures

Given Japan's substantial industrial production base it is not surprising that the country is one of the world's largest rubber importers and one of the world's most active rubber traders. Two Japanese exchanges, TOCOM (which we discuss later in this section) and KRE (which we discuss immediately following), list and trade various rubber futures.

KRE is one of several Asian forums which trade rubber futures (others include TOCOM, which trades RSS3 futures, SICOM, which trades RSS1, RSS3, TSR20 (technically specified rubber grade 20) futures and RCS rubber index futures (an index of TOCOM RSS3 and KRE RSS3), KLCE, which trades RSS1 and SMR (standard Malaysian rubber) futures, ICEB which trades RSS1, RSS3, and SIR (standard Indonesian rubber) forwards, and several Chinese exchanges, which trade RSS1 and RSS3 futures.

KRE RSS3 futures volume has remained rather buoyant for the past few years: total turnover amounted to 2.9 mln contracts in 1993 and 2.93 mln contracts in 1994; year-end open interest increased from 118,000 contracts in 1993 to 124,290 contracts in 1994 (KRE, 1995). Although the KRE has traded the RSS3 contract for several decades, it launched its rubber index futures contract as recently as March 1995. The composite index is comprised primarily of futures prices quoted on other exchanges, although New York and London trading association quotes are based on the physical market. The precise components of the index include SICOM RSS1 (where RSS1, though declining in terms of production and market share, is still considered the global rubber benchmark), TOCOM, KRE and SICOM RSS3 (the most active rubber product in the Japanese market), SICOM, New York and London TSR20 (noting that TSR production/consumption has steadily outweighed that of RSS over the past few years) and Malaysian SMR (as a proxy for high grade TSR latex rubber). Contract specifications for KRE's RSS3 and Composite Index futures are detailed in Tables 7.37 and 7.38.

The MDCE trades a single futures contract on dried cocoons, the raw material used in silk production. Trading volume in dried cocoon futures declined from 1.78 mln contracts in 1993 to 475,978 contracts in 1994, with year-end open interest falling from 20,493 contracts in 1993 to 13,275 contracts in 1994 (MDCE, 1995). Note that MDCE faces domestic competition from TDCE and offshore competition from MIFE. Table 7.39 contains relevant information on the MDCE contract.

The NGSE currently lists and trades futures on red and white beans, sweet potato starch and refined sugar; its primary domestic competitors include KCE, KANEX and TGE. Red bean futures continue to be the Exchange's main derivative, posting turnover of 1.21 mln contracts in 1993 and 919,371 contracts in 1994; year-end open interest amounted to 31,300 contracts in 1993 and 28,000 contracts in 1994. Soybean trading has been moderately active: turnover reached 287,612 contracts in 1993 but declined to 177,513 contracts in 1994; year-end open interest increased from 13,249 contracts in 1993 to 18,688 contracts in 1994 (NGSE, 1995). Unlike red beans and soybeans, NGSE's refined sugar and sweet potato starch contracts have been all but dormant for the past few years. Sweet potato starch futures

Contract	RSS3 Rubber Futures
Type	Domestic/Offshore
Exchange	Kobe Rubber Exchange
Months	Spot month plus next five months
Contract Size	5,000 kg
Tick Value	JPY0.1/kg
Daily Limit	+/– JPY4 to JPY7, against previous day's settlement price
Deliverable Grade	Physical settlement of RSS3 rubber (ribbed smoked sheet #3) to designated warehouses in Kobe and Osaka
Last Trading Day	6th business day before the end of the contract month
Delivery Day	Last business day of the contract month
Real-time price data	Reuters: <0#JKR:>; Telerate: 22626

Table 7.37 Contract Specifications for KRE RSS3 Futures

Contract	Rubber Composite Index Futures
Type	Domestic/Offshore
Exchange	Kobe Rubber Exchange
Months	March, June, September and December (nearest three months)
Contract Size	JPY20,000 * Rubber Index
Tick Value	0.01 index points
Daily Limit	+/– 2 index points against previous day's settlement price
Deliverable Grade	Cash settlement
Last Trading Day	10th day of each contract month, following day if a holiday
Delivery Day	Same as last trading day
Real-time price data	Telerate: 22628

Table 7.38 Contract Specifications for KRE Rubber Composite Index Futures

have traded less than 50 contracts per year since 1992, while sugar futures volume has been only marginally better, at 2,874 contracts in 1993 and 1,789 contracts in 1994; year-end open interest in both futures has been under 100 contracts for several years. (It should be noted that even with the merger with NTE and TDCE, NGSE is likely to retain its current contract listing.) Tables 7.40 to 7.43 contain relevant details on NGSE's contracts.

Contract	Dried Cocoon Futures
Type	Domestic
Exchange	Maebashi Dried Cocoon Exchange
Months	Six consecutive months
Contract Size	300 kg
Tick Value	JPY1/kg
Daily Limit	+/- JPY110 against previous day's settlement price
Deliverable Grade	Physical settlement of dried cocoons at designated warehouses
Last Trading Day	Seven days prior to the delivery day
Delivery Day	Three days prior to the end of the contract month
Real-time price data	Telerate: 17110

Table 7.39 Contract Specifications for MDCE Dried Cocoon Futures

Contract	Red Bean Futures
Type	Domestic
Exchange	Nagoya Grain and Sugar Exchange
Months	Six consecutive months
Contract Size	80 bags (2,400 kg)
Tick Value	JPY10/bag
Daily Limit	+/- 7% against previous day's settlement price
Deliverable Grade	Physical settlement of red beans at designated warehouses
Last Trading Day	Two business days before the delivery day
Delivery Day	Penultimate business day of the contract month
Real-time price data	None available

Table 7.40 Contract Specifications for NGSE Red Bean Futures

Contract	Imported Soybean Futures
Type	Domestic/Offshore
Exchange	Nagoya Grain and Sugar Exchange
Months	Six consecutive months
Contract Size	40 bags (2,400 kg)
Tick Value	JPY10/bag
Daily Limit	+/– 7% against previous day's settlement price
Deliverable Grade	Physical settlement of imported soybeans at designated warehouses
Last Trading Day	Two business days before the delivery day
Delivery Day	Penultimate business day of the contract month
Real-time price data	None available

Table 7.41 Contract Specifications for NGSE Imported Soybean Futures

Contract	Sweet Potato Starch Futures
Type	Domestic
Exchange	Nagoya Grain and Sugar Exchange
Months	Three consecutive months
Contract Size	100 bags (2,500 kg)
Tick Value	JPY10/bag
Daily Limit	+/– 7% against previous day's settlement price
Deliverable Grade	Physical settlement of sweet potato starch at designated warehouses
Last Trading Day	Two business days before the delivery day
Delivery Day	Penultimate business day of the contract month
Real-time price data	None available

Table 7.42 Contract Specifications for NGSE Sweet Potato Starch Futures

Contract	Refined Sugar Futures
Type	Domestic
Exchange	Nagoya Grain and Sugar Exchange
Months	Six consecutive months
Contract Size	9,000 kg
Tick Value	JPY0.1/kg
Daily Limit	+/– JPY3 against previous day's settlement price
Deliverable Grade	Physical settlement of refined sugar at designated warehouses
Last Trading Day	Two business days before the delivery day
Delivery Day	Six days before contract expiry
Real-time price data	None available

Table 7.43 Contract Specifications for NGSE Refined Sugar Futures

The NTE currently lists and trades futures on cotton yarn, woollen yarn and dull staple fibre yarn; NTE's contracts compete directly with those offered by OTE and TOCOM. Total turnover in cotton yarn, the Exchange's most active future, amounted to 822,683 contracts in 1993 and 1.1 mln contracts in 1994; year-end open interest increased from 25,924 in 1993 to 28,860 contracts in 1994. Turnover in wool yarn futures has been negligible in comparison with cotton yarn futures: total volume amounted to only 79,114 contracts in 1993 and 87,240 contracts in 1994, with year-end open interest of approximately 3,200 contracts in each year. Turnover in staple fibre yarn futures has been even more modest: total volume declined from 18,729 contracts in 1993 to 13,114 contracts in 1994, with year-end open interest of less than 500 contracts in each year (NTE, 1995). As with NGSE and TDCE, NTE will retain its product listing post-merger. Tables 7.44 through 7.46 contain relevant details on the NTE contracts.

OTE presently lists futures on three different cotton yarns, woollen yarn and staple fibre yarn; the Exchange's contracts compete specifically with those offered by NTE and TOCOM. OTE's most active contracts are based on 20 and 40 strand cotton yarn. Trading volume in 20S cotton futures increased from 648,345 in 1993 to 2 mln contracts in 1994; year-end open interest rose from 23,635 contracts in 1993 to 107,904 contracts in 1994. Trading in 40S cotton futures experienced similar increases: total volume rose from 574,724 in 1993 to 833,283 contracts in 1994, with year-end open interest increasing from 10,358 contracts in 1993 to 27,109 contracts in 1994. In contrast to cotton yarn futures, woollen yarn futures volume and open interest declined between 1993 and 1994. Total turnover fell from an exchange peak of nearly 470,000 contracts in 1993 to 267,000 contracts in 1994, while year-end open interest dropped from 22,355 contracts in 1993 to 7,239 contracts in 1994 (OTE, 1995). Note that OTE recorded no trading volume or open interest in either 30S cotton futures or staple fibre yarn futures in 1994. Tables 7.47 to 7.51 contain relevant contract specifications for all OTE products.

Contract	Cotton Yarn Futures (40S)
Type	Domestic
Exchange	Nagoya Textile Exchange
Months	Six consecutive months
Contract Size	4,000 lbs.
Tick Value	JPY0.1/lb.
Daily Limit	+/– JPY7 to JPY10 against previous day's settlement price
Deliverable Grade	Physical settlement of 40S cotton yarn at designated warehouses
Last Trading Day	Three business days before the delivery day
Delivery Day	Last day of the contract month (24th in December)
Real-time price data	Reuters: <0#JNC:>

Table 7.44 Contract Specifications for NTE Cotton Yarn Futures

Contract	Woollen Yarn Futures
Type	Domestic
Exchange	Nagoya Textile Exchange
Months	Six consecutive months
Contract Size	500 kg
Tick Value	JPY1/kg
Daily Limit	+/– JPY55 to JPY85 against previous day's settlement price
Deliverable Grade	Physical settlement of woollen yarn at designated warehouses
Last Trading Day	Three business days before the delivery day
Delivery Day	Last day of the contract month (24th in December)
Real-time price data	None available

Table 7.45 Contract Specifications for NTE Woollen Yarn Futures

Contract	Staple Fibre Yarn Futures
Type	Domestic
Exchange	Nagoya Textile Exchange
Months	Six consecutive months
Contract Size	5,000 lbs
Tick Value	JPY0.1/lb
Daily Limit	+/– JPY5 to JPY8 against previous day's settlement price
Deliverable Grade	Physical settlement of dull staple fibre yarn at designated warehouses
Last Trading Day	Three business days before the delivery day
Delivery Day	Last day of the contract month (24th in December)
Real-time price data	None available

Table 7.46 Contract Specifications for NTE Staple Fibre Yarn Futures

Contract	Cotton Yarn Futures (20S)
Type	Domestic
Exchange	Osaka Textile Exchange
Months	Six consecutive months
Contract Size	2,000 lbs.
Tick Value	JPY0.1/lb.
Daily Limit	+/– JPY6 to JPY9 against previous day's settlement price
Deliverable Grade	Physical settlement of 20S cotton yarn at designated warehouses in Osaka Prefecture and Kobe City; presentation of warehouse warrants acceptable
Last Trading Day	Four business days before the delivery day
Delivery Day	Last business day of the contract month, or the day before if a holiday
Real-time price data	Reuters: <0#JON:>; Telerate: 22623

Table 7.47 Contract Specifications for OTE Cotton Yarn (20S) Futures

Contract	Cotton Yarn Futures (30S)
Type	Domestic
Exchange	Osaka Textile Exchange
Months	Six consecutive months
Contract Size	2,000 lbs.
Tick Value	JPY0.1/lb.
Daily Limit	+/– JPY7 to JPY10 against previous day's settlement price
Deliverable Grade	Physical settlement of 30S cotton yarn at designated warehouses in Osaka Prefecture and Kobe City; presentation of warehouse warrants acceptable
Last Trading Day	Four business days before the delivery day
Delivery Day	Last business day of the contract month, or the day before if a holiday
Real-time price data	Telerate: 22623

Table 7.48 Contract Specifications for OTE Cotton Yarn (30S) Futures

Contract	Cotton Yarn Futures (40S)
Type	Domestic
Exchange	Osaka Textile Exchange
Months	Six consecutive months
Contract Size	4,000 lbs.
Tick Value	JPY0.1/lb.
Daily Limit	+/– JPY7 to JPY10 against previous day's settlement price
Deliverable Grade	Physical settlement of 40S cotton yarn at designated warehouses in Osaka Prefecture and Kobe City; presentation of warehouse warrants acceptable
Last Trading Day	Four business days before the delivery day
Delivery Day	Last business day of the contract month, or the day before if a holiday
Real-time price data	Reuters: <0#JOC:>; Telerate: 22623

Table 7.49 Contract Specifications for OTE Cotton Yarn (40S) Futures

Contract	Woollen Yarn Futures
Type	Domestic
Exchange	Osaka Textile Exchange
Months	Six consecutive months
Contract Size	500 kg
Tick Value	JPY1/kg
Daily Limit	+/– JPY55 to JPY85 against previous day's settlement price
Deliverable Grade	Physical settlement of woollen yarn at designated warehouses in Osaka Prefecture and Kobe City; presentation of warehouse warrants acceptable
Last Trading Day	Four business days before the delivery day
Delivery Day	Last business day of the contract month, or the day before if a holiday
Real-time price data	Reuters <0#JOW:>; Telerate: 22625

Table 7.50 Contract Specifications for OTE Woollen Yarn Futures

Contract	Staple Fibre Yarn Futures
Type	Domestic
Exchange	Osaka Textile Exchange
Months	Six consecutive months
Contract Size	5,000 lbs
Tick Value	JPY0.1/lb
Daily Limit	+/– JPY5 to JPY8 against previous day's settlement price
Deliverable Grade	Physical settlement of staple fibre yarn at designated warehouses in Osaka Prefecture and Kobe City; presentation of warehouse warrants acceptable
Last Trading Day	Four business days before the delivery day
Delivery Day	Last business day of the contract month, or the day before if a holiday
Real-time price data	Telerate: 22624

Table 7.51 Contract Specifications for OTE Staple Fibre Yarn Futures

TOCOM, which was created through the merger of three previously existing exchanges, currently lists precious metal and agricultural contracts. The Exchange's most active contracts, ranked by trading volume, are its gold and rubber futures; the two contracts are among the most actively traded commodity futures in the world. Within the metals category, TOCOM lists futures on gold, silver, platinum and palladium. Gold futures were originally introduced in March 1982 (on what was then the Tokyo Gold Exchange); silver and platinum contracts débuted in January 1984 and palladium contracts followed in August 1992 (following the merger). Total trading volume in gold futures amounted to 8.76 mln contracts in 1993 and 12.48 mln contracts in 1994, making it Japan's most active commodity futures contract; year-end open interest amounted to 468,965 contracts in 1993 and 564,386 contracts in 1994. Turnover in silver futures increased from 861,463 contracts in 1993 to 1.04 mln contracts in 1994, with year-end open interest rising from 64,429 in 1993 to 66,835 contracts in 1994. Turnover in platinum futures fell from 4.98 mln contracts in 1993 to 4.55 mln contracts in 1994, with year-end open interest remaining reasonably constant at 261,810 contracts in 1993 and 260,113 contracts in 1994. Trading in palladium futures dropped rather dramatically, from 2.27 mln contracts in 1993 to 774,284 contracts in 1994; year-end open interest declined from 92,606 in 1993 to 65,648 contracts in 1994 (TOCOM, 1995). Tables 7.52 through 7.55 contain relevant contract details on each precious metal future. Figures 7.17 through 7.20 highlight the historical price movement of all TOCOM precious metals futures.

Contract	**Gold Futures**
Type	Domestic/Offshore
Exchange	Tokyo Commodity Exchange
Months	February, April, June, August, October, December plus current or following odd month
Contract Size	1 kg
Tick Value	JPY1/gram
Daily Limit	+/– JPY40 to JPY70 against previous day's settlement, price
Deliverable Grade	Physical settlement of 1 kg bar of gold of 99.99% fineness, with stamp of refiner approved by TOCOM
Last Trading Day	4th business day before the delivery day
Delivery Day	Last business day of the current month (24th in December)
Real-time price data	Reuters: <0#JAU:>; Telerate: 17102

Table 7.52 Contract Specifications for TOCOM Gold Futures

Contract	Silver Futures
Type	Domestic/Offshore
Exchange	Tokyo Commodity Exchange
Months	Even numbered months within 12 month period plus odd numbered month following current even numbered month
Contract Size	30 kg
Tick Value	JPY0.1/10 grams
Daily Limit	+/– JPY6 to JPY15 against previous day's settlement price
Deliverable Grade	Physical settlement of 30 kg bar of silver of 99.99% fineness, with stamp of refiner approved by TOCOM
Last Trading Day	4th business day before the delivery day
Delivery Day	Last business day of the current month (24th in December)
Real-time price data	Reuters: <0#JSV:>; Telerate: 17104

Table 7.53 Contract Specifications for TOCOM Silver Futures

Contract	Platinum Futures
Type	Domestic/Offshore
Exchange	Tokyo Commodity Exchange
Months	Even numbered months within 12 month period plus odd numbered month following current even numbered month
Contract Size	500 gram
Tick Value	JPY1/gram
Daily Limit	+/– JPY60 to JPY120 against previous day's settlement price
Deliverable Grade	Physical settlement of 500 gram bar of platinum of 99.95% fineness, with stamp of refiner approved by TOCOM
Last Trading Day	4th business day before the delivery day
Delivery Day	Last business day of the current month (24th in December)
Real-time price data	Reuters <0#JPL:>; Telerate: 17103

Table 7.54 Contract Specifications for TOCOM Platinum Futures

Contract	Palladium Futures
Type	Domestic/Offshore
Exchange	Tokyo Commodity Exchange
Months	Even numbered months within 12 month period plus odd numbered month following current even numbered month
Contract Size	1.5 kg
Tick Value	JPY1/gram
Daily Limit	+/– JPY25 against previous day's settlement price
Deliverable Grade	Physical settlement of 3 kg bar (or 3 1 kg bars) of palladium of 99.95% fineness, with stamp of refiner approved by TOCOM
Last Trading Day	4th business day before the delivery day
Delivery Day	Last business day of the current month (24th in December)
Real-time price data	Reuters <0#JPA:>; Telerate: 17099

Table 7.55 Contract Specifications for TOCOM Palladium Futures

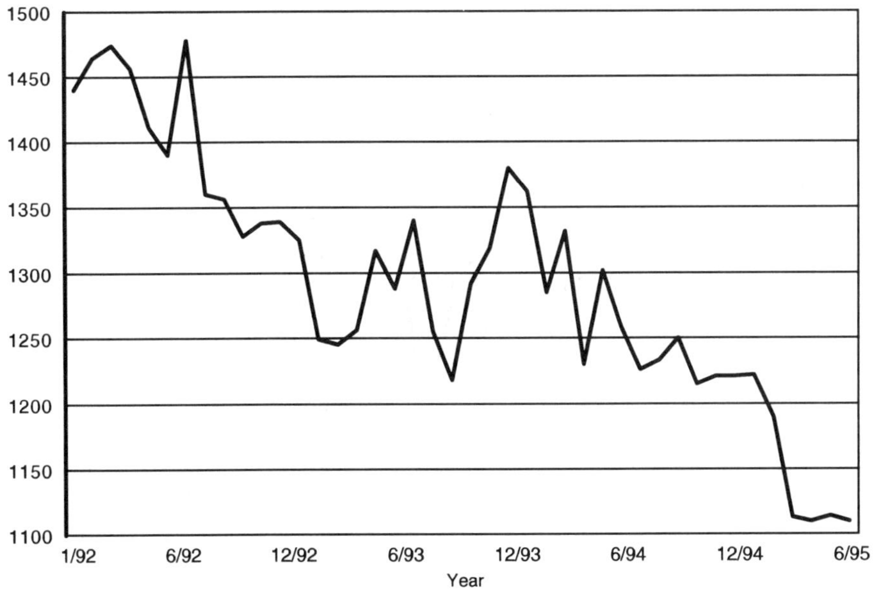

Source: Tokyo Commodity Exchange

Figure 7.17 Historical Movement of TOCOM Gold Futures

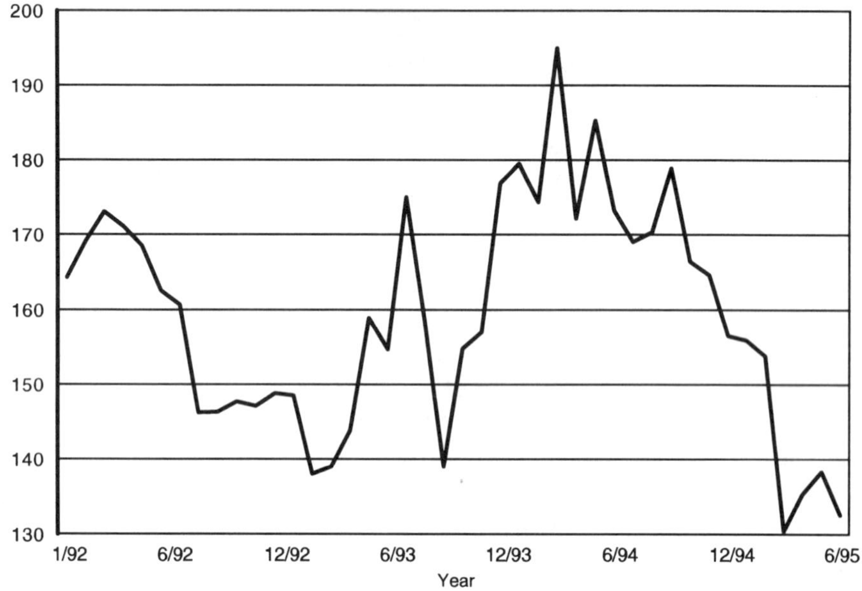

Source: Tokyo Commodity Exchange

Figure 7.18 Historical Movement of TOCOM Silver Futures

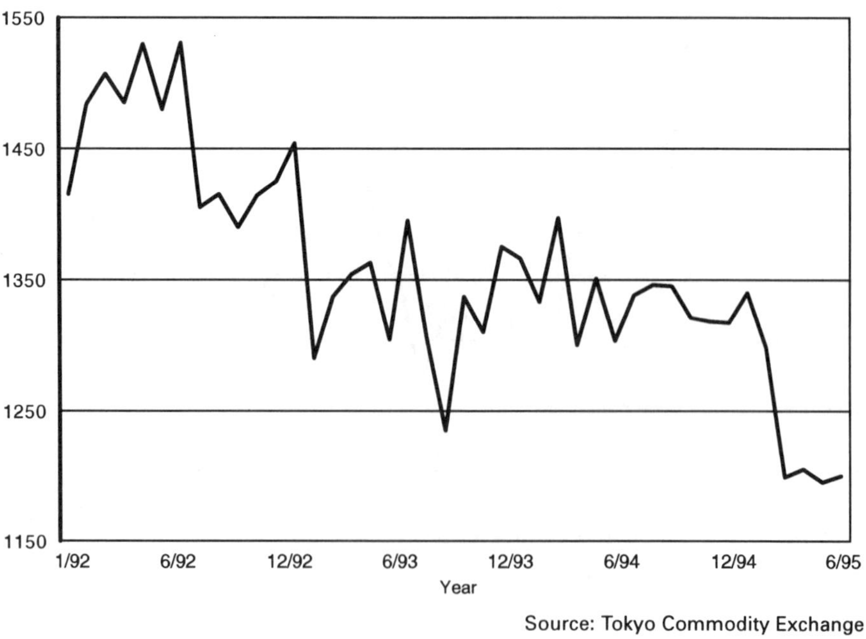

Source: Tokyo Commodity Exchange

Figure 7.19 Historical Movement of TOCOM Platinum Futures

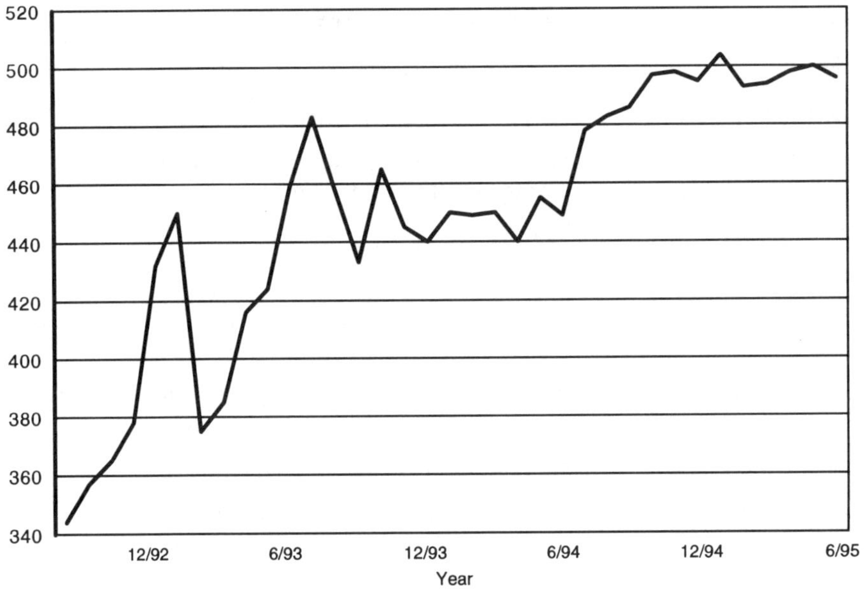

Source: Tokyo Commodity Exchange

Figure 7.20 Historical Movement of TOCOM Palladium Futures

In the agricultural category, TOCOM lists rubber, cotton yarn and woollen yarn futures. The rubber contract competes with the KRE's RSS3 future (along with other rubber contracts offered on Asian exchanges, as discussed above), while the textile contracts compete with those offered by NTE and OTE. TOCOM's rubber contract was originally listed on the Tokyo Rubber Exchange in December 1952; cotton yarn futures and woollen yarn futures were originally introduced on the Tokyo Textile Exchange in 1951 and 1953, respectively.

Trading volume in RSS3 rubber futures soared from 2.97 mln contracts in 1993 to 9.02 mln contracts in 1994, making it the second most active Japanese commodity future (after TOCOM's own gold contract); year-end open interest increased from 214,729 contracts in 1993 to 362,672 contracts in 1994. Trading volume in cotton futures increased from 1.3 mln contracts in 1993 to 2.57 mln contracts in 1994; year-end open interest amounted to 110,107 contracts in 1993 and 108,896 contracts in 1994. Trading in wool futures remained very modest, with total turnover of only 32,800 contracts in 1993 and 36,400 contracts in 1994; year-end open interest was a mere 3,497 contracts in 1993 and 3,691 contracts in 1994 (TOCOM, 1995). Relevant details on the TOCOM contracts are contained in Tables 7.56 to 7.58; historical futures prices for each commodity are illustrated in Figures 7.21 to 7.23.

Contract	RSS3 Rubber Futures
Type	Domestic/Offshore
Exchange	Tokyo Commodity Exchange
Months	Four consecutive months plus even numbered months within next four months
Contract Size	5000 kg
Tick Value	JPY0.1/kg
Daily Limit	+/– JPY4 to JPY7 against previous day's settlement price
Deliverable Grade	Physical settlement of RSS3 rubber (ribbed smoked sheet #3) to warehouses approved by TOCOM
Last Trading Day	5th business day before the delivery day
Delivery Day	Last business day of the current month except December, when it is second to the last business day
Real-time price data	Reuters: <0#JRU:>; Telerate: 17105

Table 7.56 Contract Specifications for TOCOM RSS3 Rubber Futures

Contract	Cotton Yarn Futures
Type	Domestic
Exchange	Tokyo Commodity Exchange
Months	Six consecutive months
Contract Size	1814 kg
Tick Value	JPY0.1/0.45 kg
Daily Limit	+/– JPY7 to JPY10 against previous day's settlement price
Deliverable Grade	Physical settlement of 40 count single grey weaving yarn, Murasakifuji brand
Last Trading Day	4th business day before the delivery day
Delivery Day	Last business day of the current month (in December on the 24th)
Real-time price data	Reuters: <0#JCT:>; Telerate: 17100

Table 7.57 Contract Specifications for TOCOM Cotton Yarn Futures

Contract	Woollen Yarn Futures
Type	Domestic/Offshore
Exchange	Tokyo Commodity Exchange
Months	Six consecutive months
Contract Size	500 kg
Tick Value	JPY1/kg
Daily Limit	+/– JPY50 to JPY70 against previous day's settlement, depending on settlement price
Deliverable Grade	Physical settlement of 48 count double, worsted weaving yarn, AG brand
Last Trading Day	4th business day before the delivery day
Delivery Day	Last business day of the current month or day before if a holiday
Real-time price data	Reuters: <0#JPW:>; Telerate: 17101

Table 7.58 Contract Specifications for TOCOM Woollen Yarn Futures

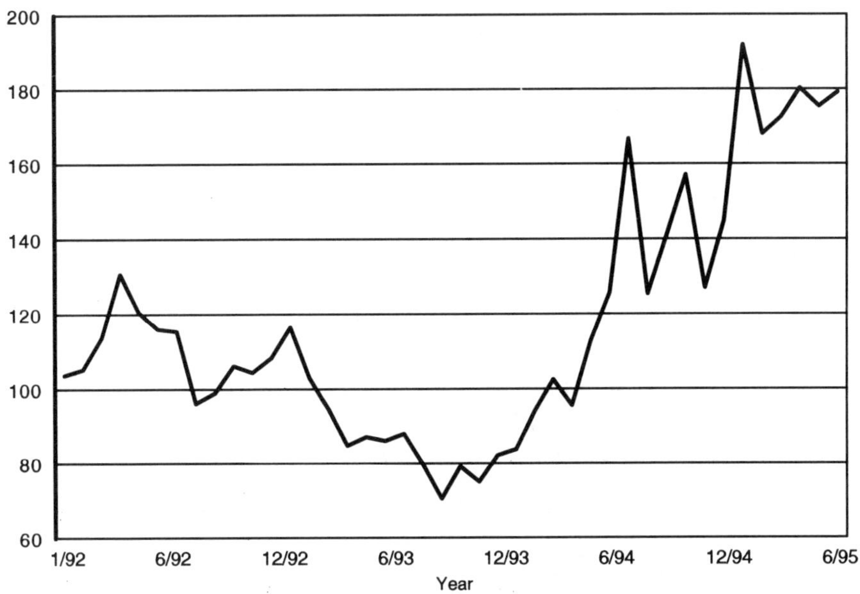

Source: Tokyo Commodity Exchange

Figure 7.21 Historical Movement of TOCOM RSS3 Rubber Futures

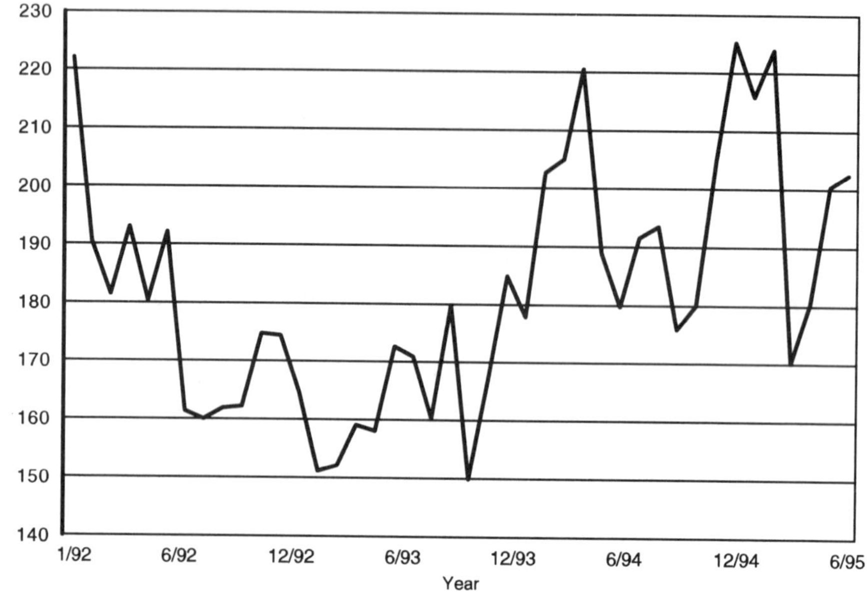

Source: Tokyo Commodity Exchange

Figure 7.22 Historical Movement of TOCOM Cotton Futures

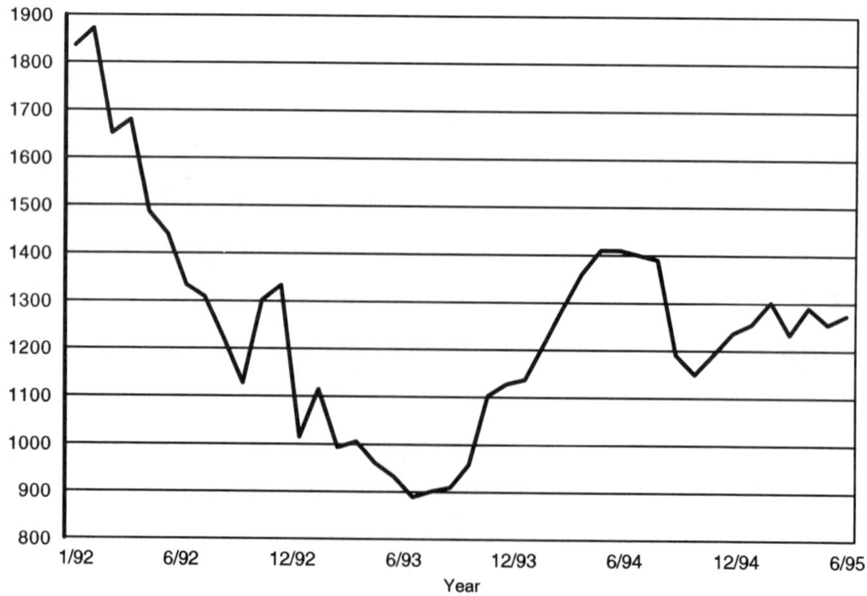

Source: Tokyo Commodity Exchange

Figure 7.23 Historical Movement of TOCOM Wool Futures

In addition to its current range of commodity derivatives, TOCOM is presently considering the introduction of an energy-related futures contract, possibly in 1996. Given Japan's role as a major importer and consumer of energy products, there is logic to shifting hedging of such imports to a domestic exchange, challenging energy contracts on NYMEX, IPE and SIMEX (as well as the Japanese and Singaporean OTC energy derivative markets, discussed below and in chapter 11) in the process. TOCOM is presently studying the feasibility of introducing a sweet crude oil contract, based on either Arabian Light, West Texas Intermediate or Dubai crude. It is also examining the possibility of listing a gasoline contract, though it has reportedly ruled out listing of naphtha and fuel oil contracts.

The TGE is focused strictly on grain futures; it is the second largest grain exchange in the world, with trading volumes exceeded only by those of the CBOT. The Exchange presently trades futures on US soybeans, corn, red beans, raw sugar and refined sugar, as well as options on both US soybean futures and raw sugar futures; the TGE's primary competitors include KCE, NGSE and KANEX. The original futures contracts of the TGE (and the Tokyo Sugar Exchange, which TGE absorbed in 1993) were based on raw sugar, refined sugar and red beans; all three contracts débuted in 1952. Soybean futures followed in 1984 and corn futures were added in April 1992. TGE's red bean contract is its most active derivative; based on recent statistics, it is the third most actively traded agricultural commodity future in the world. Total volume in red bean futures amounted to 6.35 mln contracts in 1993 and 5.12 mln contracts in 1994; year-end open interest declined from 182,096 contracts in 1993 to 129,779 contracts in 1994. Corn futures are TGE's second most active contract, trading 1.26 mln contracts in 1993 and 3 mln contracts in 1994; year-end open interest increased from 86,625 contracts in 1993 to 175,734 contracts in 1994. Turnover in soybean futures amounted to 3.75 mln contracts in 1993 and 2.56 mln contracts in 1994; year-end open interest declined from 241,076 contracts in 1993 to 145,088 contracts in 1994. Trading in raw sugar futures has continued to dominate trading in refined sugar futures: raw sugar futures registered turnover of 2.21 mln contracts in 1993 and 1.22 mln contracts in 1994, with year-end open interest of 178,105 contracts in 1993 and 126,644 contracts in 1994; refined sugar futures traded a mere 2,864 contracts in each of 1993 and 1994, and recorded no open interest at the end of either year (TGE, 1995). Note that the TGE is presently in discussions with the Ministry of Agriculture, Forestry and Fisheries regarding the listing of beef futures in 1996; such futures could be used by importers and producers to protect against movements in the price of beef. TGE is also in discussions with the SFE regarding trading of TGE's futures through the SFE. Tables 7.59 through 7.63 contain details on TGE's futures.

Contract	US Soybean Futures
Type	Domestic/Offshore
Exchange	Tokyo Grain Exchange
Months	February, April, June, August, October, December to 12 months
Contract Size	30,000 kg
Tick Value	JPY10/1,000 kg
Daily Limit	+/– JPY1,200 against previous day's settlement price. No limits from 15th of the contract month onwards
Deliverable Grade	Physical settlement of unscreened yellow soybeans from Indiana, Ohio or Michigan, at designated warehouses in Tokyo, Kanagawa, Chiba or Saitama
Last Trading Day	2nd business day prior to the delivery day
Delivery Day	1st business day prior to the last business day of the delivery month
Real-time price data	Reuters: <0#JAS:>; Telerate: 17108

Table 7.59 Contract Specifications for TGE US Soybean Futures

Contract	Corn Futures
Type	Domestic/Offshore
Exchange	Tokyo Grain Exchange
Months	January, March, May, July, September, November to 12 months
Contract Size	100 tons
Tick Value	JPY10/1,000 kg
Daily Limit	+/– JPY400 against previous day's settlement price. No limits from the first business day preceding the month of delivery
Deliverable Grade	Physical settlement of No.3 grade yellow corn from the US, at piers of Kashima, Chiba, Kawasaki or Yokohama
Last Trading Day	15th day of the month prior to the delivery month
Delivery Day	1st business day to the last business day of the delivery month
Real-time price data	Reuters: <0#JCR:>; Telerate: 17107

Table 7.60 Contract Specifications for TGE Corn Futures

Contract	Red Bean Futures
Type	Domestic
Exchange	Tokyo Grain Exchange
Months	Six consecutive months
Contract Size	80 bags (2,400 kg)
Tick Value	JPY10/bag
Daily Limit	+/– JPY350 against previous day's settlement price. No limits from the 15th day of the delivery month onwards
Deliverable Grade	Physical settlement of No.2 grade red beans from Hokkaido, at designated warehouses of Tokyo, Kanagawa, Chiba, or Saitama
Last Trading Day	2nd business day prior to the delivery day
Delivery Day	1st business day prior to the last business day of the delivery month
Real-time price data	Reuters: <0#JRB:>; Telerate: 17106

Table 7.61 Contract Specifications for TGE Red Bean Futures

Contract	Raw Sugar Futures
Type	Domestic/Offshore
Exchange	Tokyo Grain Exchange
Months	January, March and every other month within 20 months
Contract Size	20,000 kg (50,000 kg from May 1996 on)
Tick Value	JPY0.1/kg (JPY10/1,000 kg from May 1996 on)
Daily Limit	+/– JPY1.5 against previous day's settlement price (JPY1,000 from May 1996 on). No limits from the first business day two months prior to the delivery month
Deliverable Grade	Physical settlement of centrifugally separated raw cane sugar syrup of 96 degree polarization, CIF Japan, to piers of Tokyo, Chiba, Funabashi, Yokohama, Shimizu, Kinuura, Nagoya, Izumisano, Sakai, Osaka, Kobe, Unot, Shimonoseki, Moji, Hakata or Hosojima
Last Trading Day	2nd session of the last trading day two months prior to the delivery month
Delivery Day	15th of every even month to the end of the subsequent month
Real-time price data	Reuters: <0#JSG:>; Telerate: 22629

Table 7.62 Contract Specifications for TGE Raw Sugar Futures

Contract	Refined Sugar Futures
Type	Domestic
Exchange	Tokyo Grain Exchange
Months	Six consecutive months
Contract Size	9,000 kg
Tick Value	JPY0.1/kg
Daily Limit	+/– JPY2.5 against the previous day's settlement. No limits from the first business day two months prior to the delivery month
Deliverable Grade	Physical settlement of TI brand white soft sugar refined within 3 months by Toyo Seito, to designated warehouses in Tokyo
Last Trading Day	2nd session two business days before the delivery day
Delivery Day	Day preceding delivery day
Real-time price data	Reuters: <0#JWS:>

Table 7.63 Contract Specifications for TGE Refined Sugar Futures

TGE presently lists options on both US soybean futures and raw sugar futures, based on the underlying futures contracts described above; soybean futures options were originally introduced in June 1991 while raw sugar futures options were launched in May 1992. Soybean futures options and sugar futures options are structured as American exercise, physical delivery derivatives with strikes set at 1,000 point intervals. Trading volume in soybean options increased from 60,000 contracts in 1993 to 96,000 contracts in 1994; year-end open interest increased from 3,303 contracts in 1993 to 9,592 contracts in 1994. Trading volume in raw sugar options doubled from 38,000 contracts in 1993 to 67,500 contracts in 1994; year-end open interest increased from 1,413 contracts in 1993 to 6,970 contracts in 1994 (TGE, 1995). Note that the TGE is considering listing options on its corn futures in the third quarter of 1996. Tables 7.64 and 7.65 contain relevant details on the two TGE option contracts.

The TDCE lists a single futures contract, on dried cocoons; the Exchange's contract faces onshore competition from MDCE and offshore competition from MIFE. After several years of strong growth overall volume declined in 1993 and 1994: total turnover dropped from 1.07 mln contracts in 1993 to 488,558 contracts in 1994; year-end open interest declined from 15,710 contracts in 1993 to 14,589 contracts in 1994 (TDCE, 1995). Note that TDCE is expected to retain its contract following the merger with NGSE and NTE. Table 7.66 contains relevant contract details on the TDCE's dried cocoon future.

Contract	Options on US Soybean Futures
Type	Domestic/Offshore
Exchange	Tokyo Grain Exchange
Months	February, April, June, August, October, December to 12 months
Contract Size	1 Soybean Future
Tick Value	JPY10/1,000 kg
Daily Limit	+/– JPY1,200 against previous day's settlement price. No limits from the 15th of the contract month onwards
Deliverable Grade	Physical settlement into underlying futures contract
Last Trading Day	15th day of the month preceding the delivery month of the underlying futures
Exercise Day	American exercise – any business day up to, and including, the last trading day
Real-time price data	Telerate: 35274–85

Table 7.64 Contract Specifications for TGE Options on US Soybean Futures

Contract	Options on Raw Sugar Futures
Type	Domestic/Offshore
Exchange	Tokyo Grain Exchange
Months	January, March, May, July, September, November to 15 months
Contract Size	1 Raw Sugar Future
Tick Value	JPY0.05/1 kg
Daily Limit	+/– JPY1.5 against previous day's settlement price. No limits from the first business day two months prior to the delivery month
Deliverable Grade	Physical settlement into underlying futures contract
Last Trading Day	Last business day three months prior to the delivery month of the underlying futures contract
Exercise Day	American exercise – any business day up to, and including, the last trading day
Real-time price data	Telerate: 42077–88

Table 7.65 Contract Specifications for TGE Options on Raw Sugar Futures

Contract	Dried Cocoon Futures
Type	Domestic
Exchange	Toyohashi Dried Cocoon Exchange
Months	Six consecutive months
Contract Size	300 kg
Tick Value	JPY1/kg
Daily Limit	+/– JPY110 to JPY140 against previous day's settlement price
Deliverable Grade	Physical settlement of dried cocoons at designated warehouses
Last Trading Day	Seven business days prior to the delivery day
Delivery Day	Two days before the last business day of the month; if a holiday, the day before
Real-time price data	None available

Table 7.66 Contract Specifications for TDCE Dried Cocoon Futures

The YRSE, like its primary competitor, KRSE, lists a single futures contract on raw silk. Total turnover amounted to 1.51 mln contracts in 1993 and 1 mln contracts in 1994; despite the drop in turnover, year-end open interest increased from 33,305 contracts in 1993 to 36,684 contracts in 1994 (YRSE, 1995). Table 7.67 contains relevant contract details on raw silk futures.

Contract	Raw Silk Futures
Type	Domestic
Exchange	Yokohama Raw Silk Exchange
Months	Six consecutive months
Contract Size	300 kg
Tick Value	JPY1/kg
Daily Limit	+/– 5% against previous day's settlement price
Deliverable Grade	Physical settlement of raw silk at designated warehouses
Last Trading Day	Three business days prior to the delivery day
Delivery Day	Previous business day to the last business day of the contract month
Real-time price data	Reuters: <0#JSK:>; Telerate: 17109

Table 7.67 Contract Specifications for YRSE Raw Silk Futures

LISTED/OVER-THE-COUNTER WARRANTS, CONVERTIBLES AND HYBRIDS

Equity

Equity Warrants

Japanese equity warrants are available in three distinct forms, including domestic listed yen warrants, offshore listed foreign currency warrants, and offshore OTC covered warrants.

The main segment of the onshore and offshore Japanese equity warrant market consists of conventional warrants issued by companies on their own stock which result in the flotation of new corporate equity upon exercise. Japanese equity warrants are somewhat unique in having developed as both domestic, yen-denominated derivatives and offshore, foreign currency-denominated derivatives. Although trading in Japanese equity warrants technically began in September 1967 with a US dollar issue, the instruments did not become truly popular until the 1980s. The first yen-denominated warrant was issued in 1981 by Daiei as part of a bond-with-warrant package, and was followed by two more later in the same year, from Meiji Milk and Sankyo Electric. All three bond-with-warrant issues were listed on the TSE but the warrants were not detachable and could not be traded separately. In 1982, Mitsubishi Chemical became the first company to attach a warrant to an offshore Euroyen issue (where, again, the warrant could not be removed from the bond).

In the mid-1980s certain regulatory changes were enacted which made warrants more flexible and popular. In January 1986 regulatory authorities approved the detachment of warrants from bonds, permitting the two to be traded as separate instruments. In addition, Japanese investors were permitted to purchase non-yen warrants of Japanese companies, opening up a broader investor base for the product. These two fundamental changes led to much greater domestic and offshore warrant issuance, a phenomenon which would last for the next five years. The flotation of Eurobonds-with-warrants became extremely popular during the 1980s, when literally hundreds of Japanese corporations accessed the market; one estimate indicates that by 1992 more than 1,000 warrants had been issued by TSE 1st section, 2nd section and OTC companies, in both yen and foreign currencies (including Swiss francs, US dollars, Deutschmarks, sterling, and French francs, though all were ultimately exercisable into a fixed amount of yen shares, implying a fixed yen FX rate embedded in each derivative) (Connolly and Philip, 1992).

The peak year for Japanese warrants was 1989, when primary warrant issuance outweighed primary equity issuance; most domestic companies were able to achieve exceptionally low funding costs through the flotation of bonds-with-warrants, particularly when deals were packaged with interest rate or currency swaps (as discussed later in this chapter). Although the warrant market experienced several years of success in the late 1980s and early 1990s, the broad range of instruments and currencies, the general oversupply of product, and the small issue size characteristic of typical deals (e.g. US$50 mln equivalent in the relevant currency) contributed to fragmentation and illiquidity in the overall market; these problems became particularly pronounced in 1994 when several major market-makers ceased quoting two way prices as a result of losses. In addition to problems encountered by dealers and market-makers, issuers also experienced substantial difficulties: many warrants issued in the late 1980s, with five-year maturities, expired worthless as the Japanese equity market receded from its 1989 peak, meaning hundreds of companies were forced to arrange alternate forms of financing (e.g. bank loans, private placements) to repay maturing bonds, often at a much higher cost.

Figure 7.24 below highlights the movement of the James Capel Warrant Index, which tracks the weighted average movement of actively traded warrants of all currencies in the Japanese market. The dramatic rise of the index in the mid- to late-1980s and the subsequent decline in the 1990s (as a result of the collapse of the Nikkei, the general contraction of the warrant market, and the disappearance of market-makers) are apparent in the illustration.

Warrants in the Japanese market are issued primarily as American exercise, bearer derivatives with maturities of one to five years (though long-term, seven- to ten-year, issues are floated on occasion). The derivatives are typically issued at a premium, where the premium is defined as the differential between the cost of

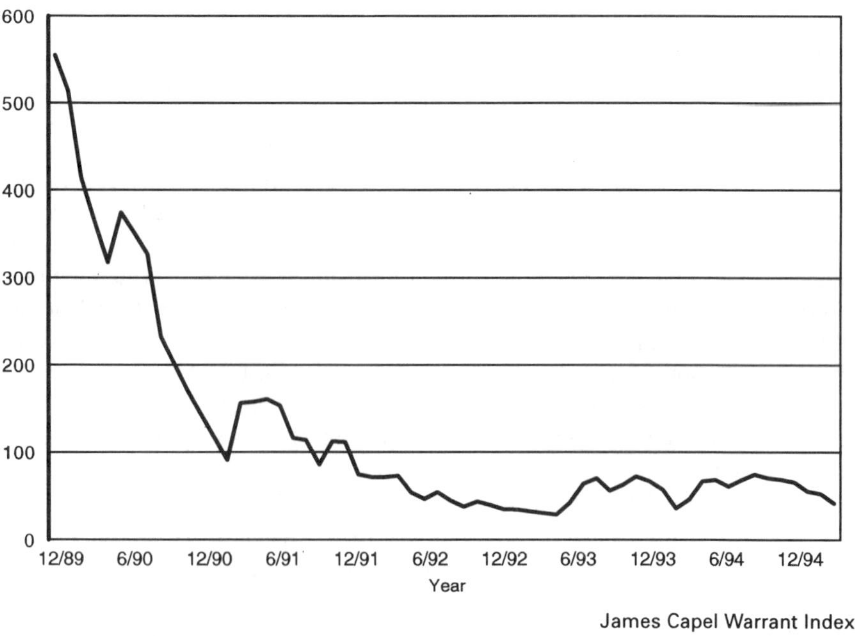

Figure 7.24 Historical Movement of Japanese Domestic Warrants 1989–1995

buying the warrant and exercising immediately at the current stock price. The holder of a warrant receives no dividends but if exercise occurs the ensuing allocation of new shares results in full shareholder benefits, including dividends. Domestic warrants are listed on the TSE, but are traded primarily in the OTC market; the Japan Bond Trading Company, a brokers' broker, provides quotes in the OTC market for certain issues, though many remain unquoted and the general market, as indicated above, is very illiquid. Offshore issues are most often denominated in US dollars, Deutschmarks or Swiss francs and are sold via public offering and listed in Luxembourg, Germany or Switzerland; Swiss franc issues may also be sold on a private placement basis. It should be noted that in 1995 the Japanese MOF announced that unlisted companies would be permitted to issue domestic bonds-with-detachable warrants from January 1996 onwards; issuance in the market had previously been restricted to listed companies. Appendix II contains a detailed listing of all Japanese warrants in existence as at June 1995, including those denominated in yen and traded through the TSE or brokers' broker and those denominated in foreign currencies and listed/traded on overseas exchanges.

Although listed equity warrants issued by companies on their own stock feature prominently in the domestic market, third party covered equity warrants are not available as domestic listed instruments (as they are in other countries, such as Hong Kong, Australia, Malaysia, Singapore, Thailand and so on); the lack of domestic covered warrants has led to the development of an offshore market over the past decade. The Japanese offshore OTC covered equity warrant market began in 1985 when Citicorp issued a covered warrant on Mitsubishi Corporation shares; the issue was followed shortly thereafter by warrants on Casio Corporation and Kobe Steel, and dozens of others have been underwritten since that time. Unlike the listed warrants discussed immediately above, OTC equity warrants are effectively long dated call options which are 'covered' by shares of the underlying target company (or by other warrants, convertibles or options); exercise of the warrant results in re-allocation of existing equity from the seller to the buyer of the warrant, as opposed to the issuance of new shares. Covered warrants are typically denominated in foreign currencies and carry maturities of one to three years; the derivatives are either unlisted or listed on overseas exchanges and traded OTC.

Basket/Index Warrants

Current regulations do not permit the issuance of basket or index warrants in the onshore market. Financial institutions operating offshore, however, routinely sell warrants on baskets of Japanese stocks or on broad Japanese indexes. Merrill Lynch issued the first basket warrant on Japanese non-life insurance companies, in the 1980s and dozens of others have followed since then (including warrants on media baskets, bank baskets, automobile baskets, construction baskets, oil company baskets and so on). Japanese index warrants have also proven popular. During the ascendancy of the Japanese stock market during the late 1980s a number of firms sold OTC call warrants on Japanese indexes. After the trend of the market reversed and it became clear that a protracted market decline was underway, US financial institutions introduced customized index put warrants; the American Stock Exchange (AMX) became a primary location for the listing of Japanese index call and put warrants. Japanese basket and index warrants issued in the offshore market generally carry maturities of one to three years; issues are denominated in various foreign currencies and may be structured with either American or European exercise. Warrants may be listed on overseas exchanges (or can remain unlisted) and are traded on an OTC basis.

It should be noted that in 1994 the Ministry of Finance (MOF) approved the issuance of offshore warrants on the Nikkei 300 with the proviso that such instruments be denominated in currencies other than yen and not be sold to Japanese investors. Following the MOF's ruling, numerous financial institutions (including Bankers Trust, Barclays de Zoete Wedd, Merrill Lynch, SG Warburg and Nomura) came forth with Nikkei 300 issues denominated in US dollars, Deutschmarks and Swiss francs. In March 1995 the Japan Securities Dealers Association (JSDA) announced the removal of restrictions on all offshore index warrant issuance; offshore warrants on the Nikkei 225 and Topix indexes can now be issued in any currency but must not be sold to Japanese investors. Dozens of issues have been floated since the deregulation measures were announced; most are listed on offshore exchanges (e.g. Luxembourg, Switzerland) and are traded OTC. Along with vanilla index put and call warrants on the Nikkei 225 and Nikkei 300, certain institutions such as Nomura and Swiss Bank Corporation have floated index warrants with embedded exotic options. Representative issues in this category include Nikkei 300 'up and out' warrants (where the warrants are extinguished once an upper barrier is triggered), Nikkei 300 'down and in' warrants (where warrants are activated once a lower barrier is triggered), and Nikkei 300 lookback warrants (where the warrants pay the maximum level attained over a pre-specified period, regardless of the terminal value of the index).

Convertibles

The origin of Japanese domestic convertible bonds dates back to 1938 when revisions to the Common Law made it possible for companies to issue such derivative securities; the first issue followed in 1949 but the market remained dormant until the early 1960s when Shin Mitsubishi and Tokyo Shibura floated long-term convertibles with maturities of 15 and 16 years, respectively. The TSE began listing domestic convertibles in 1970, but overall issuance remain subdued. Despite a slow start, primary volumes increased throughout the 1970s after amendments to the Japanese Commercial Code made it possible for domestic corporations to float convertibles with a simple board resolution, rather than full shareholder approval. In addition, previous maximum and minimum issuance limits (i.e. JPY30 bln (US$330 mln) and JPY2.5 bln (US$27 mln), respectively) were relaxed (i.e. the upper limit was abolished and the lower limit dropped to JPY2 bln (US$22 mln)). The two regulatory changes attracted a broader range of issuers and by the late-1970s convertibles were a significant source of financing for small and large Japanese corporations; with the dramatic rise in equity prices in Japan during the 1980s convertibles became even more popular. Convertibles (along with bonds-with-warrants, discussed above) dominated domestic financing during the 1980s, reaching record primary issuance in late 1989 and early 1990 when the Japanese equity market was at a peak. Domestic convertible issuance subsided in the early 1990s, following the drop in domestic equity prices (and a decline in corporate financing needs as a result of the economic slowdown), but began strengthening again in 1993 and 1994. Domestic convertible issuance amounted to JPY6.6 tln (US$73 bln) in 1988, JPY6.8 tln (US$75.5 bln) in 1990 and a low of JPY600 bln (US$6.7 bln) in 1992; by 1993 and 1994 annual issuance was up near JPY1,275 bln (US$14 bln) once again (Redmayne, 1994).

During the 1980s most convertible issues were purchased by domestic investors as equity investments; coupons on virtually all bonds were minimal, ranging from 1% to 3%. Most yen convertibles were (and are) purchased by investors who view the securities primarily as equity investment vehicles (albeit with downside protection in the form of the underlying bond); the preferred issues are those with low prices, low premiums and negligible yield pickup. Bonds with low premiums mean that investors are not as susceptible to premium contraction against investment value. Virtually all convertibles issued in the Japanese market are floated as conventional convertibles, meaning they are issued and redeemed at par. Far less common are premium redemption convertibles, which are redeemed at a premium at maturity, and zero coupon convertibles, which are issued at a discount and redeemed at par at maturity.

Domestic convertibles are available with three different forms of security: secured convertibles (which are backed by specific collateral pledged in support of the bonds), unsecured convertibles with reserved assets (which are backed by general, though not specific, collateral), and unsecured convertibles without reserved assets (which are not collateralized in any form). Prior to 1973 all bonds were secured; in 1973 the reserved asset variation was introduced and in 1979 unsecured convertibles entered the market. Virtually all convertibles issued in the domestic market have maturities ranging from four to 15 years; while ten-year issues were the norm for many years, four-year issues (introduced in 1988), seven-year issues (introduced in 1987), and 15-year issues are now very popular. According to TSE statistics, the maturity profile of listed convertibles is skewed toward the intermediate sector, with more than 80% of bonds falling in the six- to 11-year category (and approximately 15% in the under-six-year category and less than 5% in the over 11-year category).

Very few domestic convertible bonds have put features, though most have call features; instances of issuers calling yen convertibles are extremely rare (though calls of Japanese issues in the Euroconvertible market are somewhat more common). In practice, most bonds are either repurchased in the market or are partially repaid after a call lockout period (where the balance (up to 90% of the bond) is repaid at maturity unless otherwise converted). For weaker-rated issuers use of sinking funds to provide for repayment at maturity is mandatory. Actual conversion periods for yen convertibles begin 30 days after issuance and are effective until maturity. Bonds are typically issued at a premium over conversion value; conversion prices are generally set at 5% over an average equity price, where the average price covers from one to four weeks. Though coupons are generally minimal, interest is payable on a semi-annual or annual basis, based on an Actual/365-day count. Bonds are listed and traded on one of the country's stock exchanges (generally the TSE, but occasionally one of the regional exchanges) as bearer securities, though investors may choose to register their securities if desired (note: issues of private placement convertibles are exceptionally rare, and must be approved by the MOF). As indicated above, minimum bond issue size is JPY2 bln (US$27 mln) and trading size is generally JPY1 mln (US$11,000); price quotes on an exchange exclude accrued interest. Figure 7.25 displays the historical price movement of the Tokyo Convertible Bond Index, an index of liquid yen convertibles.

It should be noted that in addition to issuance in the domestic yen convertible market, Japanese corporations have been active issuers in the offshore Euroconvertible market. Japanese companies have historically been very active in both the Eurodollar and domestic Swiss Franc convertible markets; such issues are typically sold with conversion premiums and coupons similar to those in the domestic market. Maturities in the Eurodollar market are comparable to those in the

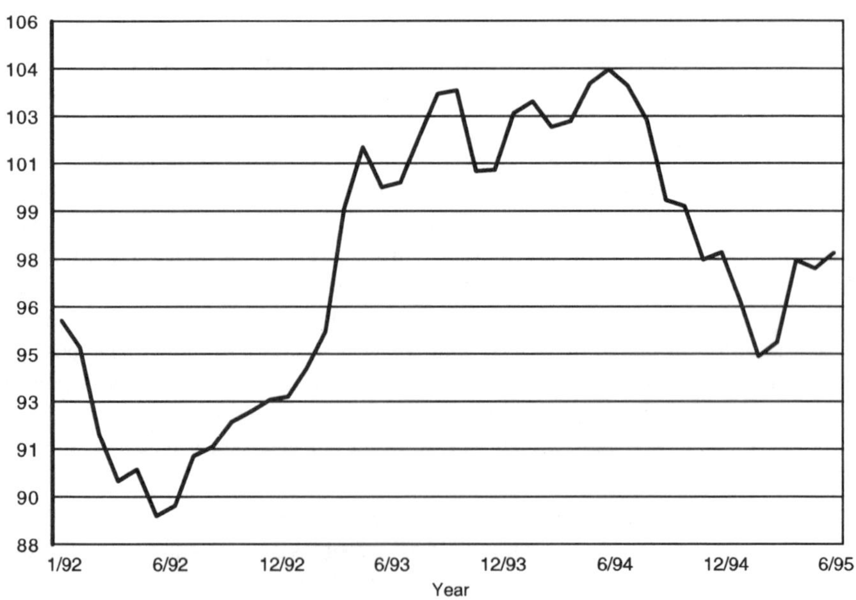

Figure 7.25 Historical Movement of the Tokyo Convertible Bond Index

domestic market (e.g. five to ten years) while maturities in the Swiss market tend to be much shorter (e.g. under five years). In addition to the Eurodollar and Swiss franc convertible markets, Japanese corporations began issuing offshore convertibles in the Euroyen market with some frequency in 1992 through 1994 as a means of refinancing maturing bond-with-warrant deals. Offshore Japanese convertibles (denominated in any currency and issued in any market) may be floated as public deals (listed and traded through overseas exchanges, such as the Luxembourg Stock Exchange or the Swiss exchanges) or private placement deals (unlisted and traded on an OTC basis). Appendix III contains details on all domestic and offshore convertible bonds.

Index-linked Notes

Japanese index-linked notes have proven extremely popular with issuers and investors in the domestic and offshore markets over the past decade. The Japanese MOF first authorized the issuance of 'high risk/return' Euroyen bonds in June 1985; these securities were effectively index-linked bonds (e.g. bonds with embedded long calls or puts), which paid enhanced coupons and/or principal based on the appreciation or depreciation of an index, generally the Nikkei 225 or Topix. Index-linked notes became particularly popular in the mid- to late-1980s as the domestic stock market was climbing to new highs; investors eager to capture returns based on the appreciation of the Nikkei and Topix indexes often found index-linked notes a convenient mechanism for gaining such exposure. Many notes were issued in the Euroyen market, either as bonds or from Euro Medium-Term Note programmes, generally with maturities of one to five years. One of the earliest securities was the two tranche 'bull and bear' note issued in 1986 by Swedish Export Credit. The four-year note, with an 8% coupon, was split into two tranches of JPY10 bln (US$110 mln) notional each. In each case principal redemption was based on the difference between the level of the Nikkei at inception and maturity; redemption had a floor of 0% (e.g. the investor could lose all principal due) and a ceiling of 170%. Index-linked notes proved so popular that just six months after the initial MOF approval, 32 separate issues had been launched (Fabozzi, 1990). As the level of the Japanese equity market has subsided in the mid-1990s equity-linked structures have become less common. Notes currently available are based primarily on linking coupon payouts, rather than full principal payouts, to appreciation or depreciation in equity indexes; such structures provide investors with less potential return but also far less risk.

In addition to 'vanilla' index-linked notes, certain structures are also created using embedded exotic options; such securities provide very unique payoff and risk profiles. Examples of these derivative securities include bonds with barrier options (e.g. bonds which activate or extinguish coupon payments based on the level of the index); bonds with lookback options (e.g. bonds which provide the investor with the maximum index appreciation or depreciation attained during the life of the note, regardless of the index level at expiry); bonds with Asian options (e.g. bonds which provide the investor with an average index appreciation or depreciation achieved over a pre-specified time), and so on. Dozens of other combinations can be structured through the use of embedded exotic options.

It should be noted that index-linked notes are not listed on domestic Japanese exchanges and are not generally traded on a secondary basis; since these structures are custom-made to meet the specific requirements of investors, they are often held until maturity or are redeemed by the issuing or structuring bank. Securities which are not sold on a private placement basis may be listed on overseas exchanges.

Fixed Income

Fixed Income Warrants

Issuance and trading of onshore listed fixed income warrants is not presently permissible under Japanese law. Although the Japanese authorities recently permitted the issuance of offshore warrants based on fixed income references such as JGBs, such instruments cannot be sold onshore to domestic investors and exist strictly as offshore, OTC instruments. Numerous international institutions have issued call warrants on benchmark JGBs over the past few years and new issues appear in the market on occasion (particularly when volatility is increasing or the market is trending). JGB warrants, which may be American or European exercise derivatives, typically have one- to two-year final maturities and are either unlisted or listed on overseas exchanges; all warrants trade on an OTC basis. Representative issues in this category include Bankers Trust's call warrants on JGB#157 (1993) (calls on the same benchmark were also sold by Merrill Lynch, Nomura, and JP Morgan in 1993 and 1994), Société Générale's call warrants on JGB#174 (1995) and SBC Warburg's put warrants on JGB#174 (1995). Despite the presence of certain issues overall activity remains modest, primarily because investors have at their disposal more liquid bond futures and bond futures/options (as discussed above), as well as OTC bond options (as discussed below), to achieve similar risk/return profiles.

Interest rate-linked notes

In addition to the equity-linked index bonds mentioned above, the offshore market also features various interest rate-linked notes. The most common are JGB-linked bonds and yen LIBOR range floaters. JGB-linked bonds, issued in the offshore Euroyen market, are structured as straight bonds with embedded JGB call options; to the extent the price of a reference JGB rises in excess of the strike, investors receive enhanced coupons or enhanced principal. Range floaters (and other variations such as corridor notes, range binary notes, range digital notes, daily accrual notes, and so on) are issued in the Euroyen market and typically reference yen LIBOR. Under a basic range floater structure a bond is embedded with a strip of short digital options (or a short strangle or a corridor) pegged to yen LIBOR. For every day yen LIBOR trades within the range dictated by the strikes of the digitals the investor receives one day's interest; if yen LIBOR trades outside the range, one day's interest is sacrificed. Under a range binary structure an investor sells a digital strangle or corridor which pays a lower (or zero) coupon for an entire period if the index trades outside the range. In return for selling digital options (through range floaters or range binaries, and so on), the investor stands the chance of receiving an enhanced yield. Notes such as these are often placed privately, though certain issues are listed on overseas exchanges and traded OTC on a limited basis.

Currency

Currency Warrants

Like covered equity and fixed income warrants, listed currency warrants are not presently permitted under Japanese law (though the regulatory authorities are presently reviewing the listing and trading of domestic currency warrants as part of broader financial deregulation measures; we discuss this matter in the regulatory section at the end of the chapter). Despite the current ban on domestic listed warrants, offshore OTC currency warrants referencing the yen are executed with great frequency (i.e. one to five issues in a given week). Such issues, which are underwritten by foreign financial institutions, are either unlisted or listed on overseas exchanges and traded primarily on an OTC basis; the warrants may be structured with American or European exercise, and carry maturities ranging from one to five years. Note that in addition to JPY/US$ warrants, institutions also actively underwrite DM/JPY, CHF/JPY and GBP/JPY warrants. In addition, there is a smaller market for exotic currency warrants, which combine standard currency warrants and embedded exotic options such as barriers, Asians and digitals. One representative issue is Chase Manhattan's JPY/US$ binary range warrant (1995) which provides a full payout if JPY/US$ trades within a range defined by an upper and lower band, and provides no payout if the exchange rate trades outside the band (in a fashion similar to the yen LIBOR range floater structures mentioned above). A second representative issue is the yen outperformance warrant, which provides the investor with a payout based on the better performing of JPY/US$ and JPY/DM.

Currency-linked bonds

Currency-linked bonds are available in the offshore Euroyen market in the form of short- to intermediate-term securities with embedded currency options. Various foreign exchange-linked structures have been introduced in the past, including dual currency bonds and reverse dual currency bonds (discussed at greater length in the section on currency swaps below), duet bonds, and 'heaven and hell' bonds; these securities are generally a combination of a fixed income instrument and one or more vanilla currency options. An example of the 'heaven and hell' structure is the 1985 bond issued by IBM Credit Corporation, which linked redemption of principal to the level of JPY/US$ rates at maturity. To the extent the dollar strengthened against yen, investors received an additional capital gain ('heaven'); if yen outperformed US dollars, investors received a lower principal redemption ('hell'). In addition to bonds with embedded vanilla currency options, the market also features bonds with embedded exotic currency options; the structures detailed in the sections above are equally applicable to currency-linked bonds (e.g. range floater structures which link coupon payments to the level of JPY/US$ rather than yen LIBOR, and so on).

Commodity

Commodity Warrants

The domestic and offshore markets do not presently feature commodity warrants which reference Japanese commodity prices or indexes.

Commodity-linked bonds

Issues of commodity-linked bonds are floated in the Euroyen market periodically. Gold and crude oil have tended to be the two main commodity indexes used in the construction of derivative notes; commodity-linked notes are thus combinations of straight bonds and either gold calls or crude oil calls, and provide investors with either enhanced coupons or enhanced principal redemption should the option move (or end) in-the-money. Though commodity-linked notes are an easy means for investors to gain exposure to the commodity markets, overall issuance has been relatively scarce, particularly in comparison with equity-linked bonds. Issues executed to date have been structured as private placements or offshore listed deals with maturities ranging from one to five years.

OVER-THE-COUNTER FORWARDS, SWAPS AND OPTIONS

Equity

Equity Forwards/Swaps

OTC equity forwards and swaps referencing individual Japanese equities are available in the offshore market; since the domestic onshore market for equity derivatives is very strictly regulated at the present time all activity takes place offshore, between non-resident institutions. Although one- to five-year equity forwards based on blue-chip stocks occur with some frequency, equity swaps (i.e. structures which exchange a floating rate flow for appreciation or depreciation in a single equity) are relatively rare (far more active are the offshore OTC equity option, index swap and index option markets, described below).

Equity Options

The buying and selling of OTC equity options (of any structure) in the Japanese onshore market is prohibited under Section 201 of the Securities and Exchange

Law. Though deregulation measures have called for a re-examination of the restriction, there is no timetable as to when it might be reviewed.

The lack of onshore OTC (and listed) Japanese equity options has resulted in the creation of a very active offshore market for OTC puts and calls on 1st section, 2nd section and OTC Japanese stocks. Japanese OTC equity options can be structured as American or European derivatives exercisable into physical or cash settlement; maturities may extend from several months to several years. In addition to vanilla equity options, there is a smaller market for exotic equity options (including digital options, outperformance options, Asian options and barrier options). Note that there is no secondary trading in vanilla or exotic equity options, as the custom-made nature of the derivatives makes them illiquid; transactions either end in exercise, expire worthless or are closed out with the arranging institution.

Basket/Index Forwards/Swaps

Offshore OTC forwards and swaps targeting baskets of Japanese equities or broad Japanese indexes are executed with frequency; they have become especially popular with Japanese institutions wishing to hedge their equity portfolios on a customized basis (though such hedging must occur through an offshore subsidiary, as onshore activity is not yet permissible). Japanese basket/index forwards and swaps are available on traditional indexes such as the Nikkei 225 and the Topix, new indexes such as the Nikkei 300, and sub-indexes, index sectors and baskets of individual stocks. Swaps and forwards generally carry intermediate maturities of one to five years.

The original Japanese index forward and swap market originated in the late 1980s and was based primarily on institutions exchanging a LIBOR flow for appreciation in the value of the Nikkei 225 index over a single period or an extended period; this is effectively equal to an institution buying a long-dated index call and paying the premium over the life of the transaction in the form of the LIBOR flow. As the Nikkei reached its peak index put swaps became more prevalent, with institutions exchanging LIBOR flows for depreciation in the index (e.g. purchasing index put swaps). OTC index put and call swaps were also employed as hedges by institutions issuing index-linked bonds (discussed above).

In addition to long-dated calls and puts embedded in swaps, combinations of swap structures are also available. For instance, investors may purchase an index call swap and sell an index put swap; depending on the relative strike levels, there is also generally a LIBOR flow paid or received. This combination has the advantage of reducing (and occasionally eliminating), the investor's periodic premium payments but obligates it to make a payment if the index depreciates. Index corridor swaps are also prevalent in the market (e.g. purchase of a call and sale of a higher strike call, embedded in a swap); these index swaps also act to lower premium paid on the transaction (via the floating rate flow) but cap potential returns. Index swaps with embedded barrier options, Asian options, digital options, and so on, are also available and are structured to provide more specific or unique risk/return profiles.

Basket/Index Options

Although the onshore market prohibits activity in OTC basket and index options, offshore equity derivative firms are very active in buying and selling options on both baskets of stocks and broader domestic indexes. Although the onshore market features very liquid listed index options (as discussed above), the offshore OTC market has proven successful as it offers derivatives with customized risk/return parameters. Vanilla European and American index/basket options are readily available in a range of maturities from one-month to five-years; most transactions are structured to settle in cash, though physical delivery (primarily for basket options) is also possible. As with other OTC structures there is very little liquidity given the customized nature of the product; options are generally closed out with the arranging bank, expire worthless if out-of-the-money or exercised into cash or physical settlement if in-the-money (resales to third parties are non-existent). In addition to vanilla puts and calls on baskets, sectors or indexes, the offshore market has also introduced a variety of exotics on the same references. Barrier options, digital options, quanto options, outperformance options, and others are structured with frequency. Such options provide investors with specific risk or payoff profiles, often at a lower cost than conventional options (though occasionally with higher risks or lower potential returns).

Fixed Income

Fixed Income Forwards/Swaps

Japan features a well developed yen IRS market and a developing yen FRA market. The yen interest rate swap market, which has been in existence since the early 1980s, has developed into one of the most liquid segments of the global swap market. Based on International Swap Dealers Association (ISDA) figures for the end of 1994, the yen IRS market continues to rank as the second largest component of the global market, second only to US dollar IRSs. At December 1994 notional Japanese yen IRSs amounted to JPY180 tln (US$1.98 tln) notional, equal to 22.6% of global outstandings (note that US dollar IRSs held a 36.6% share) (Choudhury, 1995). Growth in the Japanese IRS market has occurred as a result of: (a) increasing deregulation of the market (leading to introduction of new structures (e.g. yen FRAs, exotic swaps, credit derivatives)); (b) growing sophistication of end-users in asset/liability management (leading to increased use of swaps to manage portfolios and balance sheets); (c) increasing participation by local financial institutions as dealers (leading to more active quoting of swaps in all segments of the curve); (d) expanding Euroyen issuance (leading to credit arbitrage-related swaps); and (e) declining yen interest rates (leading to swaps as a means of locking-in lower funding costs).

The very short end of the interest rate swap market, based on yen FRAs, is new to Japan. Although domestic and foreign institutions in Japan have been permitted to deal in non-yen FRAs for several years (and foreign banks have actively dealt in

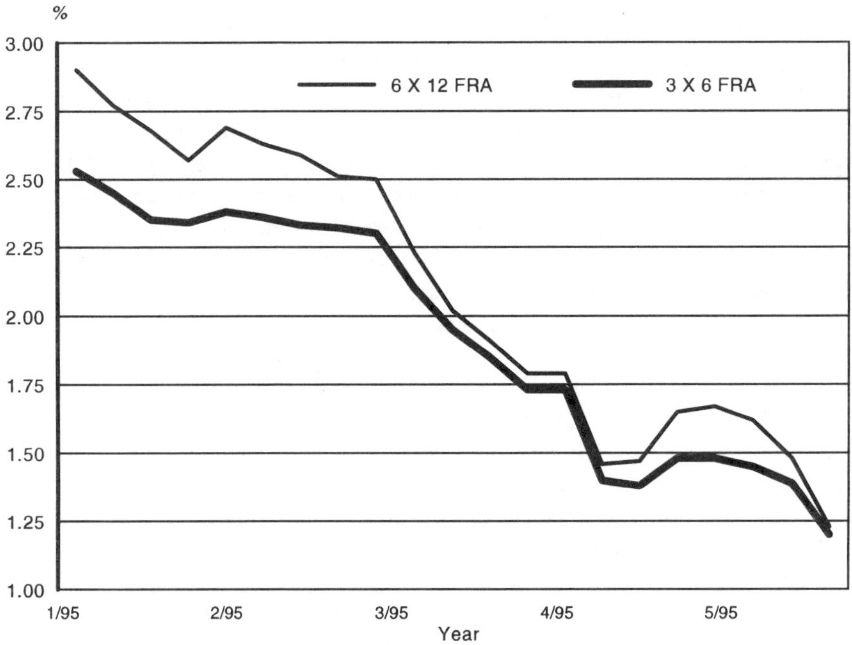

Figure 7.26 Historical Movement of 3 x 6 and 6 x 12 yen FRAs

yen FRAs in the offshore market for several years), domestic yen FRAs were not permissible under Japanese law until 1994. Deregulation measures introduced at that time opened the domestic market for yen FRAs to both local and foreign institutions. Actual trading of FRAs began in October 1994, with first month turnover reaching JPY5.4 tln (US$60 bln); turnover since that time has averaged JPY3 tln to JPY4 tln (US$33 bln to US$44 bln) per month (by way of comparison foreign currency FRA trading in Japan averaged US$9 bln to US$10 bln per month over the same time period). The introduction of yen FRAs has been especially important for swap dealers, who now have at their disposal another short-term interest rate tool through which to manage interest rate risk exposures. FRAs are very liquid to 12 months and are offered in various standard combinations of one-, three-, six-, nine-, and 12-months; long-term quotes to three and five years are available but turnover is much thinner. Bid-offer spreads on deals to 12 months average approximately 3–4 basis points under normal market conditions, which is consistent with spreads found on yen IRSs; standard interbank dealing size is JPY5 bln (US$55 mln). Figure 7.26 traces the movement of 3 x 6 and 6 x 12 yen FRAs since their introduction in the local market.

In contrast to the yen FRA market, the yen IRS market has been in existence since the early 1980s. Unlike other major global swap markets, the driving force behind the development and growth of the Japanese IRS market has been related to structural and regulatory barriers rather than strict credit arbitrage (though credit arbitrage certainly contributes to activity in the market).

The presence of funding restrictions placed on domestic financial institutions has resulted in the use of swaps to circumvent such restrictions; by employing swaps financial institutions have been able to access a broader range of funding sources at relative cost savings. For instance, Japanese city banks and trust banks have historically dominated access to short-term yen funding (up to two years) but have not been permitted to access medium- and long-term fixed yen funding; they have thus held a comparative advantage in short-term, floating rate funds. Long-term credit banks (Industrial Bank of Japan, Long-Term Credit Bank and Nippon Credit Bank), certain special co-operative banks (Norinchukin and Shokochukin) and the Bank of Tokyo, in contrast, have been the only institutions permitted to raise funds in the medium- and long-term domestic market, primarily through the issuance of five-year, fixed coupon, bank debentures; these banks hold a comparative advantage in medium- and long-term fixed rate funding. Long-term credit banks have also been the country's primary long-term lenders and, in the IRS market, the only natural fixed yen receivers. As a result of these restrictions long-term credit banks, city banks and trust banks have been able to employ fixed/floating IRSs to develop and expand the overall domestic swap market. Pure credit arbitrage opportunities have also fuelled growth in the market, with lower-rated domestic corporates typically retaining a comparative advantage in fixed rate funding and swapping into yen LIBOR, and higher-rated corporates most often paying fixed yen in exchange for yen LIBOR, particularly in the intermediate sector of the curve.

In addition to standard fixed/floating IRSs, the Japanese market now also features exotic structures such as index amortizing rate swaps, range floater swaps, leveraged swaps, yield curve swaps, differential swaps, arrears swaps, callable/puttable swaps, zero-coupon swaps, forward start swaps, and others. Demand by end-users for customized payoff or risk profiles has been on the rise and exotic swaps have found a ready client base. The liquidity of the IRS market, the availability of yen swaptions, caps and floors (described below) and a liquid Euroyen strip has made it possible for dealers to create, price and hedge such transactions. The market for credit-related derivatives has also been expanding as domestic participants become more interested in trading the credit spreads of both domestic and international issuers, and as credit derivatives gain greater acceptance in the global market. Strategies in the credit derivative market often call for repackaging assets (generally illiquid, high-yielding samurais, for instance) with attached swaps. The swaps can be simple structures which convert coupons from fixed into floating yen for the life of the asset, or can be more complex structures which allow intermediaries to call back the package once a strike has been reached, or put bonds to an investor once a strike has been reached; certain other derivatives require intermediaries to pay investors a stepped-up coupon if the asset/swap package is not called back on a particular remarketing date. There are numerous other structures employed in the credit derivative market which are beginning to gain more focus from institutions in the Japanese market.

Unlike other major swap markets (e.g. US, Australia), yen IRSs are not priced as a spread to domestic government bonds. As mentioned earlier in the chapter, the JGB market is a benchmark market with excellent liquidity in ten year JGBs (particularly in the current benchmark bond) but thin liquidity in other segments of the curve. As such, the yen IRS curve cannot derive sufficient pricing information from JGBs to price on a spread basis, and is therefore created on an absolute basis through a blend of rates. Given the importance of long-term credit banks in fixed yen funding and lending (and the swap opportunities generated through such liability and asset transactions), the relationship between the five-year bank debenture and the long-term prime rate (LTPR) influences yen swap rates to a significant degree. The rate paid on prime bank debentures is used by the Bank of Japan (BOJ) as a base for the monthly setting of LTPR (which is done by the BOJ in consultation with the MOF and the long-term credit banks); LTPR is effectively a semi-floating rate used as a reference for yen corporate lending to prime customers. The yen swap curve is thus influenced by Euroyen deposits in the short-end of the curve, bank debenture rates and Euroyen bond rates in the middle of the curve, and fixed domestic lending rates (determined, in great part, by LTPR) and benchmark JGBs in the long-end of the curve. The actual direct or indirect influence of domestic rates on yen swap rates may be traced as follows: the government dictated official discount rate (ODR) is used as a benchmark for time deposits, which influences one-year bank debentures offered by banks; the one-year bank debenture rate has a bearing on the five-year bank debenture offered by the long-term credit banks. The five-year debenture influences both LTPR and JGBs. Benchmark JGBs, in turn, influence the level of AA corporate paper. The confluence of LTPR, corporate paper, debentures and JGBs determines the market level of domestic yen swap rates.

Quoting convention for IRSs is fixed yen (semi-annual, on an Actual/365-day basis), against yen LIBOR flat. Standard dealing size in the interbank market is JPY5 bln (US$55 mln) and liquidity is readily available to ten years; unlike other Asia Pacific swap markets, ten-year transactions are very commonplace and obtaining competitive quotes is generally not difficult. In addition to active interbank dealing of fixed yen against yen LIBOR, there is also a liquid market for basis swaps of LTPR against yen LIBOR (where the quoting convention is LTPR flat against three- or six-month yen LIBOR plus a spread) and short-term prime rate (STPR) against yen LIBOR (quoted in the same fashion). Liquidity in the yen swap market has improved dramatically over the past few years, to the point where bid-offer spreads on vanilla fixed/floating swaps have fallen from 10 basis points to 2 to 5 basis points in most segments of the curve (bid-offer spread on LTPR basis swaps are 30 basis points in most segments of the curve); since 1993 bid-offer spreads on vanilla swaps have fallen by 4 basis points, as competition among domestic and foreign banks and securities firms has increased. Under typical IRSs corporate end-users can expect to receive bids from at least five banks; this suggests, of course, that margins are very thin, with dealer profits generated primarily on the basis of volume, not spread. Figure 7.27 illustrates the historical movement of the yen IRS curve. Table 7.68 highlights typical bid-offer spreads on yen fixed/floating and LTPR basis swaps under normal market conditions.

Figures 7.28 through 7.40 illustrate the historical rate and spread movement of benchmark maturity yen IRSs against LTPR, bank debentures, AAA/AA-rated Euroyen bonds and JGBs.

Maturity	JPY Fixed/LIBOR Bid-Offer Spread	LTPR/JPY LIBOR Bid-Offer Spread
2 years	2–3 bps	30 bps
3 years	2–3 bps	30 bps
4 years	4–5 bps	30 bps
5 years	3–4 bps	30 bps
7 years	4–5 bps	30 bps
10 years	4–5 bps	30–40 bps

Table 7.68 JPY Fixed/JPY LIBOR and LTPR/JPY LIBOR Bid-Offer Spreads

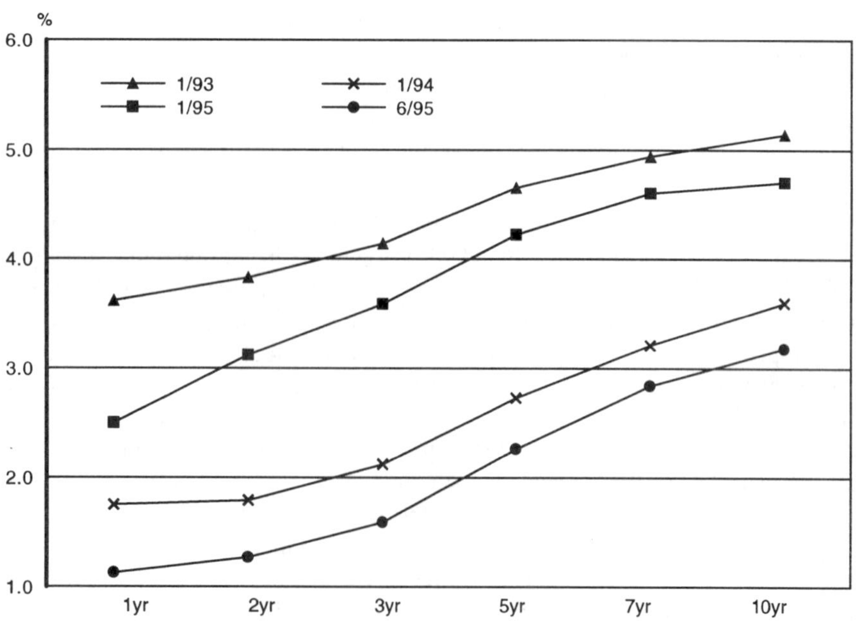

Figure 7.27 Historical Movement of the Yen IRS Swap Curve

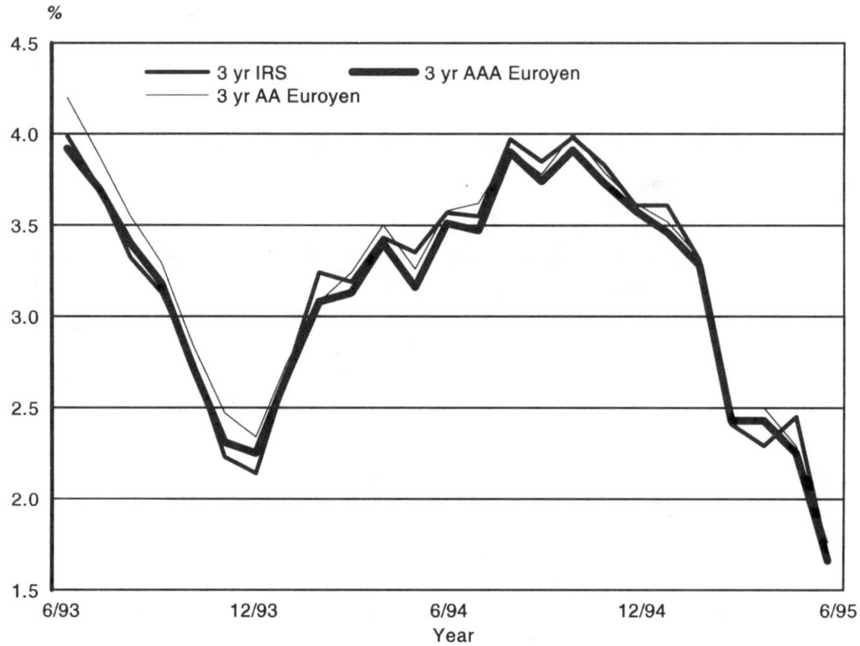

Figure 7.28 Historical Movement of Three-year Yen IRS and Three-year AAA/AA Euroyen Bonds

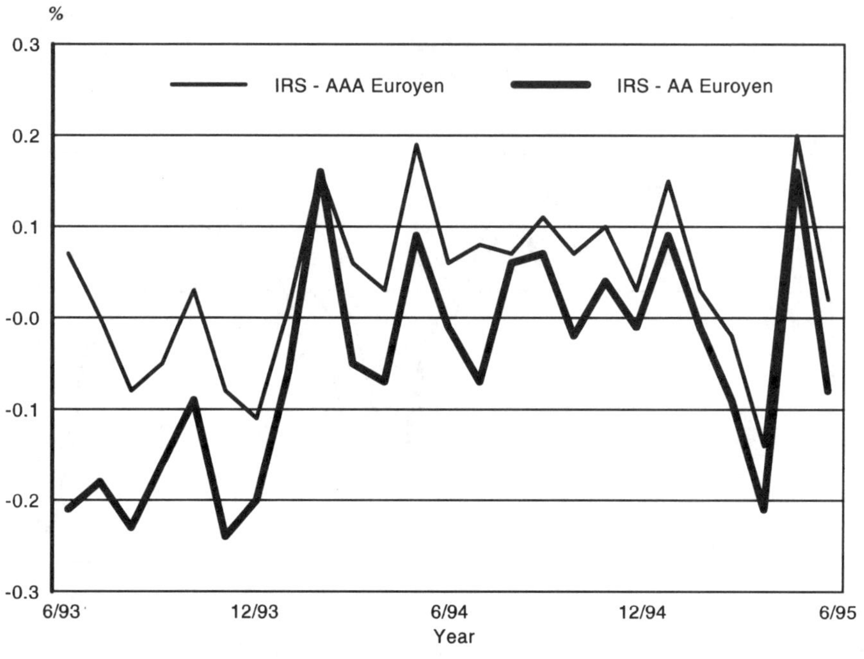

Figure 7.29 Spread of Three-year Yen IRS and AAA/AA Euroyen Bonds

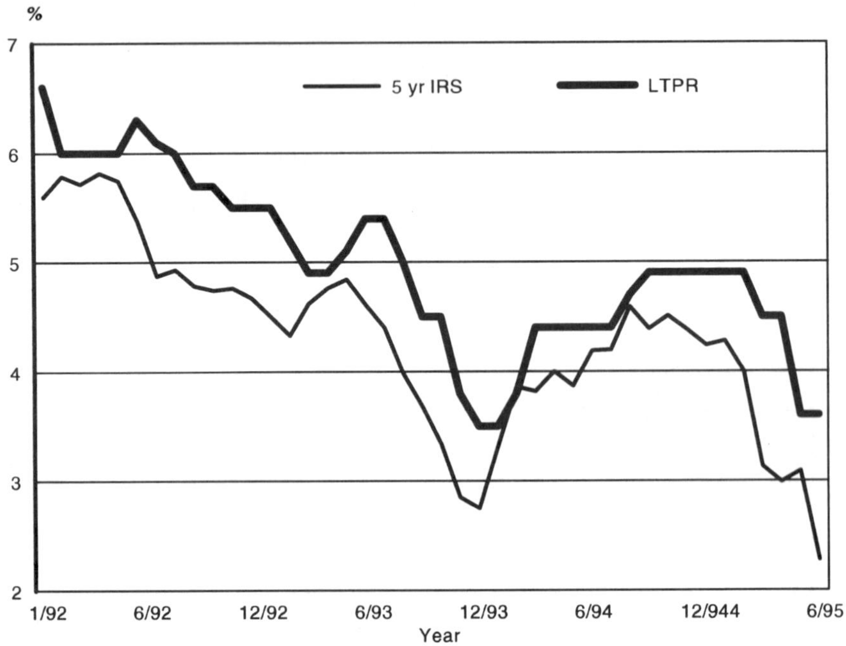

Figure 7.30 Historical Movement of Five-year Yen IRS and Five-year LTPR

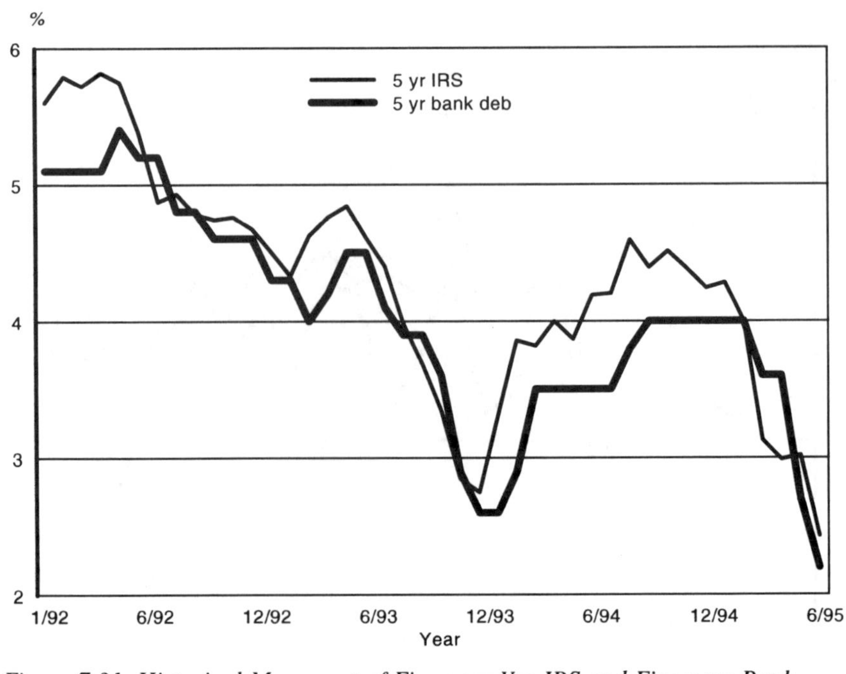

Figure 7.31 Historical Movement of Five-year Yen IRS and Five-year Bank Debentures

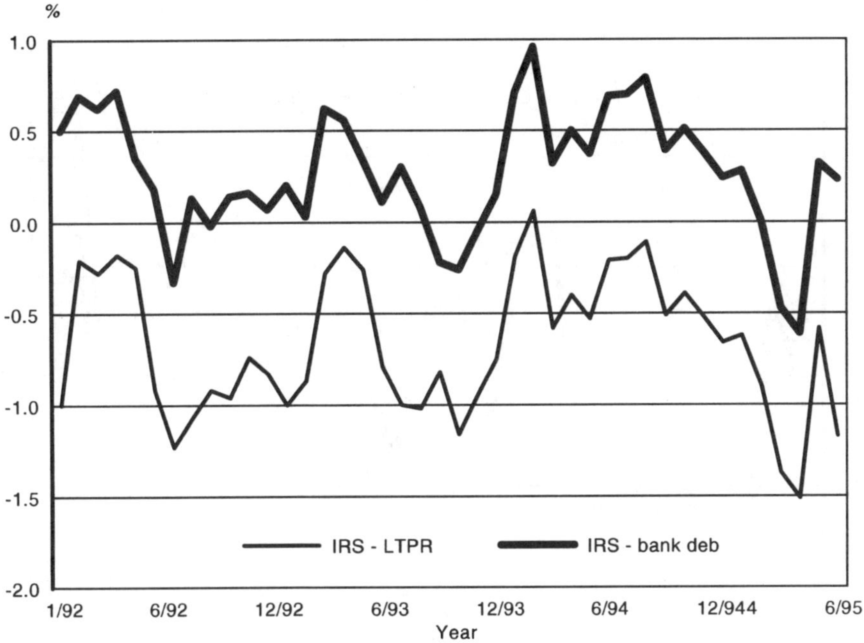

Figure 7.32 Spread of Five-year Yen IRS, LTPR and Bank Debentures

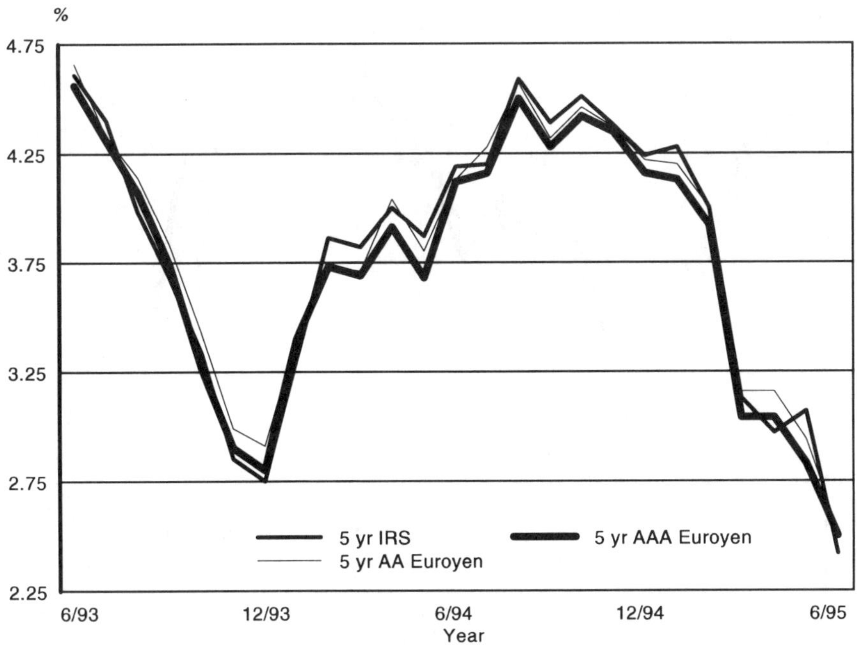

Figure 7.33 Historical Movement of Five-year Yen IRS and Five-year AAA/AA Euroyen Bonds

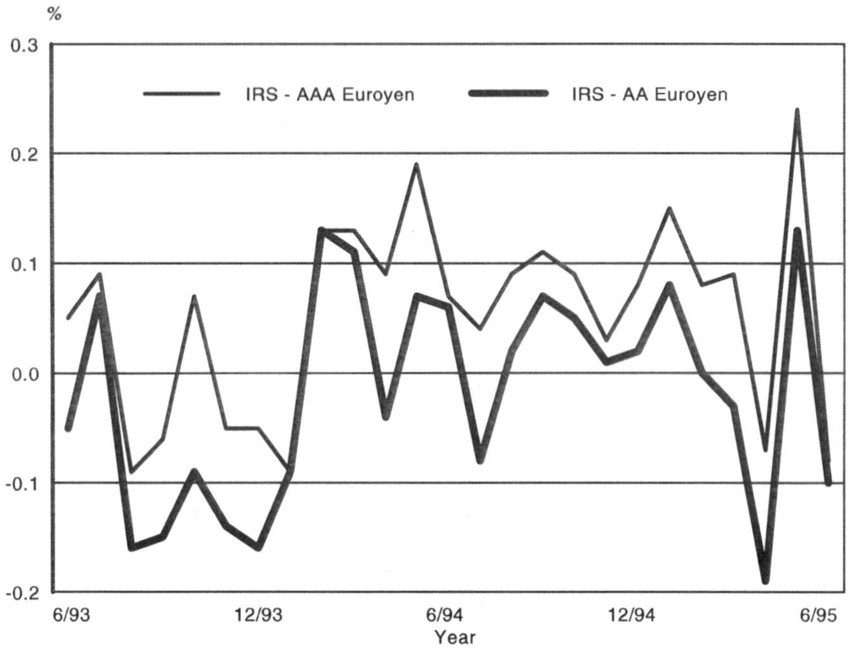

Figure 7.34 Spread of Five-year Yen IRS and AAA/AA Euroyen Bonds

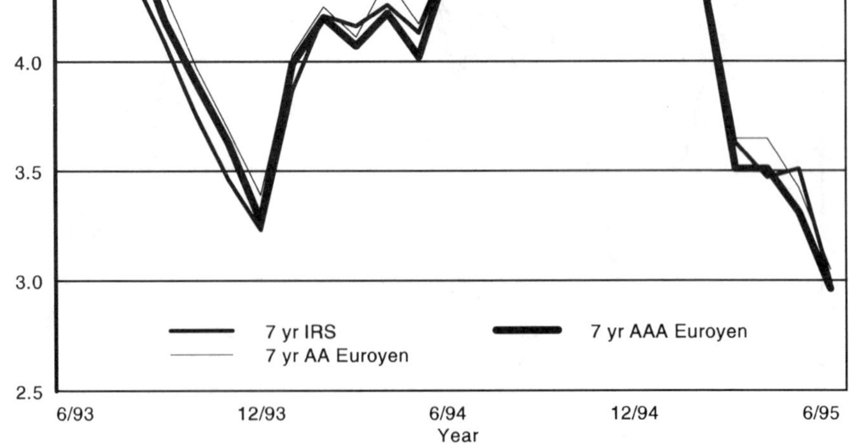

Figure 7.35 Historical Movement of Seven-year Yen IRS and Seven-year AAA/AA Euroyen Bonds

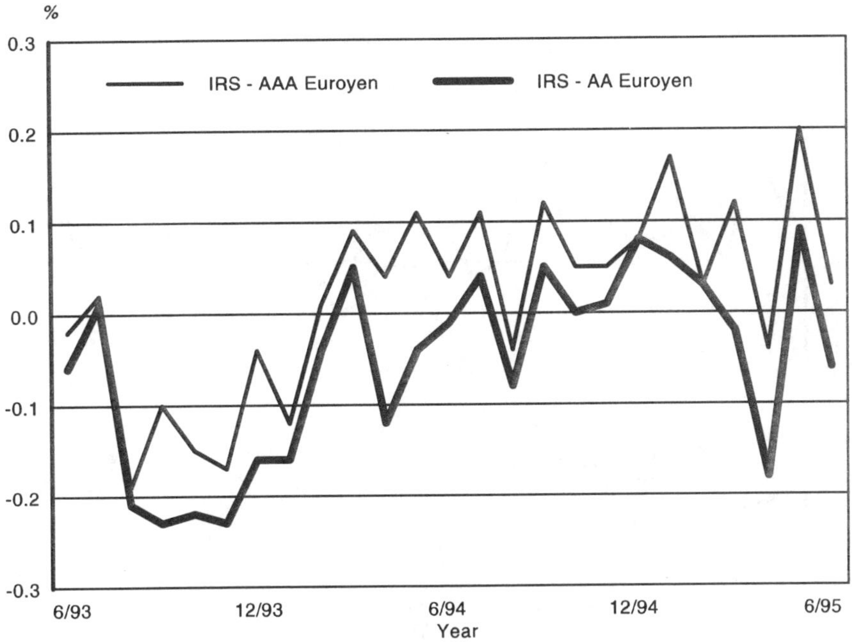

Figure 7.36 Spread of Seven-year Yen IRS and AAA/AA Euroyen Bonds

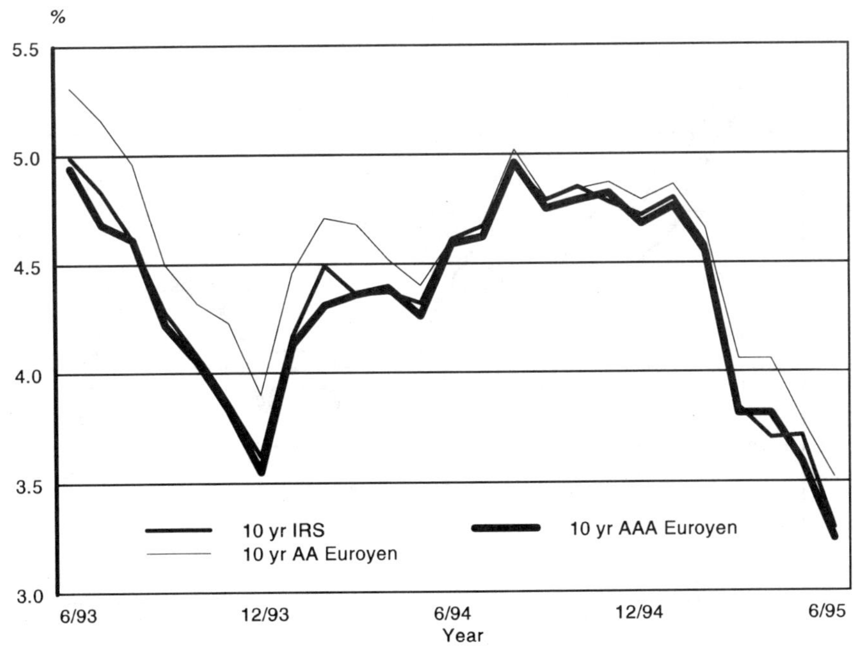

Figure 7.37 Historical Movement of Ten-year Yen IRS and Ten-year AAA/AA Euroyen Bonds

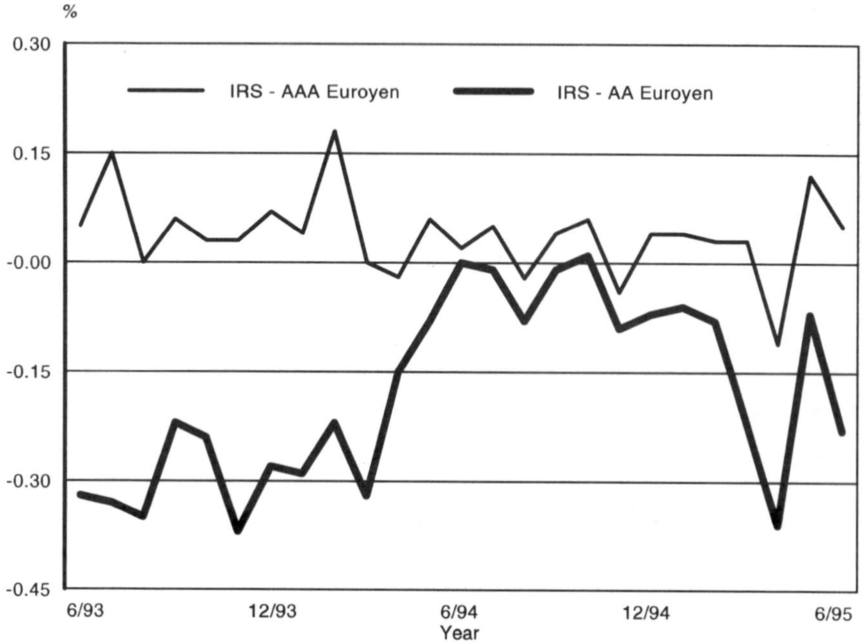

Figure 7.38 Spread of Ten-year Yen IRS and AAA/AA Euroyen Bonds

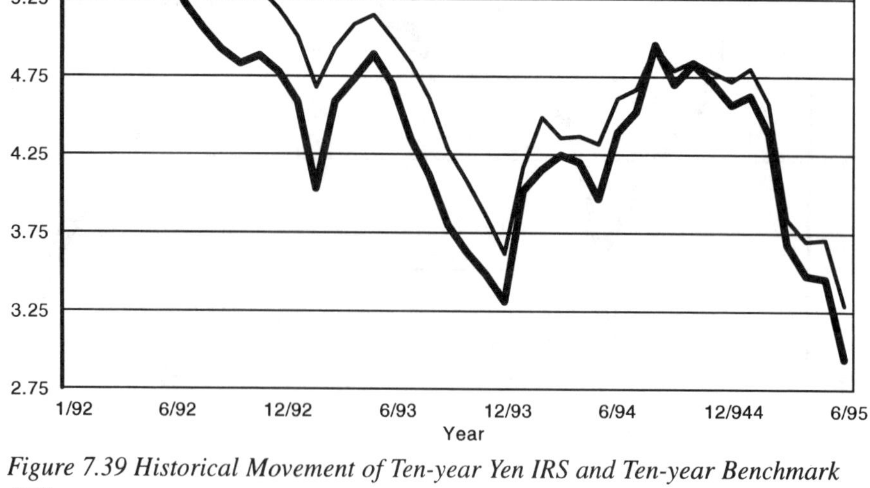

Figure 7.39 Historical Movement of Ten-year Yen IRS and Ten-year Benchmark JGB

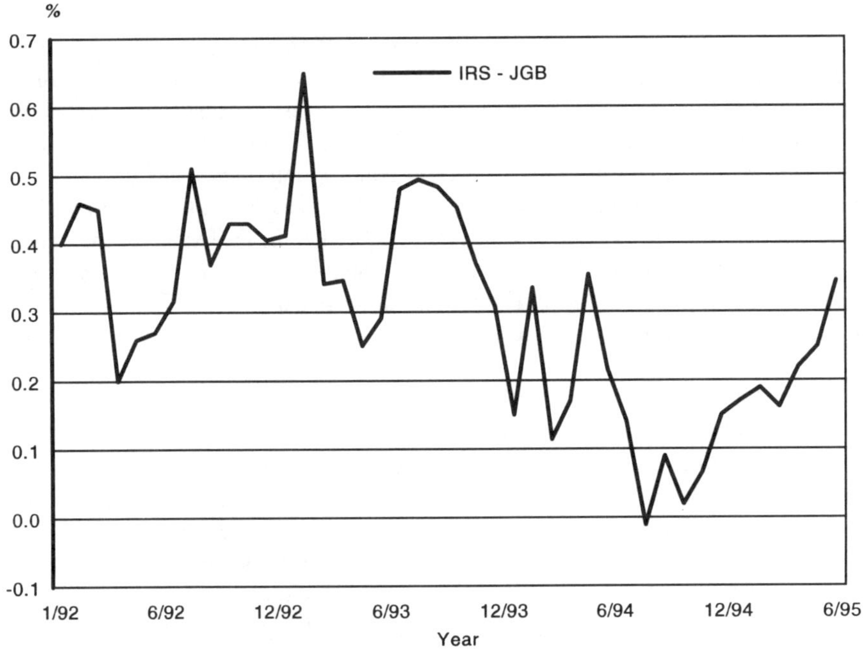

Figure 7.40 Spread of Ten-year Yen IRS and Benchmark JGB

The primary hedge instruments for short-term yen swaps include Euroyen futures/options (described earlier in the chapter) and yen FRAs. Euroyen contracts on TIFFE and SIMEX feature liquid strips out to 24 months, enabling participants to hedge short-term exposures efficiently and inexpensively. As mentioned above, the domestic short-term market now also features yen FRAs which are already sufficiently liquid to be effective hedging tools. Medium- and long-term swaps are most often hedged with JGBs or JGB futures, on a duration-weighted basis. A JGB-related hedge acts primarily to remove directional interest rate risk; a swap book would still retain significant elements of spread risk and/or basis risk when utilizing such hedges. Given the liquidity of the yen market plus the presence of very strong two-way flow, swap dealers can generally replace temporary futures or cash hedges with yen IRSs in a very short time frame (removing basis or spread risks in the process).

Fixed Income Options

The Japanese market features very liquid OTC bond option, cap, floor and swaption markets. Formal trading of domestic OTC fixed income options began in April 1989, following a MOF ruling permitting the establishment of an OTC market for bond options on JGBs, local government bonds, straight (fixed) bonds and offshore bonds; the OTC bond option market actually began trading before the TSE created its listed bond futures options contract in 1990. Though the listed option described earlier in the chapter has proven very successful and attracts strong trading interest, the OTC market continues to enjoy widespread participation and reasonably deep liquidity, particularly for OTC options on benchmark JGBs. Note that in addition to being structurally flexible, OTC options are generally less expensive to execute than listed bond options, primarily because listed derivatives must adhere to a fixed commission schedule set by the TSE. The OTC bond option market has developed to the point where certain market conventions are followed by participants: standard interbank dealing size is set at JPY100 mln (US$1.1 mln) face value of the underlying and is increased in JPY100 mln increments; option maturities extend from three months to a maximum of 12 months (note that offshore OTC options may extend beyond 12 months); exercise may be either American or European; and, option trades are closed out by either entering into offsetting transactions or by exercising into physical delivery (resales to third parties are not permitted).

In addition to bond options, the Japanese fixed income option market also features caps, floors and swaptions; all three instruments are actively traded and very liquid. While the market for investor sales of caps, floors and swaptions has always been popular as a means of generating premium income, investors have been more active in recent years in purchasing caps and floors as a means of locking in funding costs or protecting portfolios. Many such options, however, are still purchased in combinations of spreads or collars so that the effective cost is equal, or close, to zero; since many investors are reluctant to pay premium, zero-cost transactions are the preferred alternative, despite the fact that such structures leave residual risk exposure or cap potential returns.

Yen caps and floors, which reference yen LIBOR, are actively quoted by brokers and dealers up to ten years, though true liquidity is found in the short- and medium-term maturities; standard interbank dealing size is JPY5 bln (US$55 mln). Caps and floors maturing in one year are quoted against three-month yen LIBOR while those maturing in excess of one year are quoted against six-month yen LIBOR. Caps/floors are priced in volatility terms, with near-term options carrying higher volatilities than medium-term options; Table 7.69 provides indicative bid-offer spreads for yen caps and floors under normal market conditions.

Maturity	Cap Bid-Offer Spread	Floor Bid-Offer Spread
1 year*	5–6 pts	5–6 pts
2 year	3–4 pts	3–4 pts
3 years	2–4 pts	2–4 pts
4 years	2–4 pts	2–4 pts
5 years	1–3 pts	1–3 pts
7 years	1–3 pts	1–3 pts
10 years	1–3 pts	1–3 pts

* Three-month resets; all others six-month resets

Table 7.69 Yen Cap/Floor Bid-Offer Spreads

Yen swaptions are actively quoted by both brokers and dealers, and are traded in standard interbank size of JPY5 bln (US$55 mln). The domestic market features a range of European and American payer and receiver swaptions, with option maturities ranging from one month to ten years, exercisable into underlying swaps with maturities ranging from one to ten years. As with caps/floors, swaptions are quoted in volatility terms, with short-term options exercisable into short-term swaps carrying higher volatilities than long-term deals.

Exotic fixed income derivatives such as compound options, barrier caps/floors, spread options and others have become increasingly popular in the domestic market. Such options generally reference yen LIBOR and are available in a range of short- and intermediate-maturities (though most activity occurs in the three- to 12-month sector). Spread options, which are generally based on the spread between two points on the swap curve or JGB yield curve, or between swaps and JGBs, are often embedded in swaps in order to adhere to regulatory restrictions (which prohibit the outright sale or purchase of spread options or other exotic structures in the onshore market); spreads in the offshore market between non-resident counterparties are typically bought and sold on an outright basis.

Currency

Currency Forwards/Swaps

Japan features substantial activity in yen currency forwards, long-term FX swaps and CCSs. Currency forwards and FX swaps (effectively long-term FX forwards) are most liquid to 12 months but are quoted out to ten years; standard interbank dealing size is JPY5 bln (US$55 mln). Average daily turnover in JPY/US$ forwards and FX swaps (though not CCSs) was JPY740 bln (US$8.25 bln) in 1994, down from JPY930 bln (US$10.3 bln) in 1993 (BOJ, 1995). Figure 7.41 illustrates the historical movement of three- and 12-month JPY/US$ forwards.

Unlike certain other national swap markets, the creation of the domestic currency swap market preceded the development and acceptance of the domestic interest rate swap market by several years; indeed, transaction volume and average transaction size remained larger in the yen CCS market until 1989. Growth and volume in the local market has historically been driven by four fundamental factors: availability of yen liquidity, credit arbitrage opportunities, foreign currency restrictions and, more recently, commercial risk hedging opportunities. Statistics provided by ISDA reflect continued expansion in yen CCSs: total notional yen CCSs outstanding increased from JPY14.3 tln (US$158.8 bln) in 1993 (17.6% market share) to JPY15.3 tln (US$169.9 bln) in 1994 (18.6% market share) (Choudhury, 1995).

The origin of the Japanese yen CCS market dates back to the late 1970s and early 1980s when a series of basic swap transactions were executed between French and Japanese companies; French companies raised yen funds via public or private placement bonds, and swapped back to dollars or French francs. During the early 1980s the market was also driven by foreign currency ‘impact loans’ granted to Japanese borrowers. As a result of tight liquidity in the local market Japanese bor-

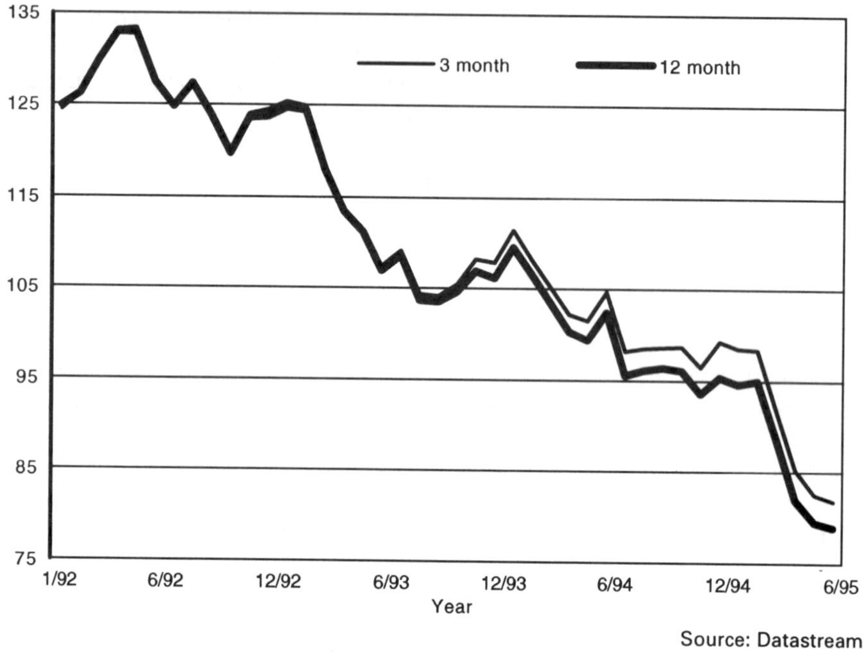

Figure 7.41 Historical Movement of Three- and 12-month JPY/US$ Forwards

rowers sourced foreign currency funds from foreign banks (the only institutions permitted to lend in foreign currencies at the time), swapping loan proceeds back into yen. The market also saw major Japanese institutions accessing the Eurodollar bond market and swapping proceeds back into yen; institutions such as Japan Development Bank and Japan Airlines were early issuers of US dollar bonds, which they would convert back into fixed yen for use in local operations.

The next phase of the CCS market occurred in the mid- to late-1980s when the tight liquidity situation reversed itself and Japan enjoyed excess liquidity. During this time Japan became a major capital exporter to the rest of the world. Foreign borrowers found many opportunities to fund themselves through yen loans granted by Japanese banks and would swap proceeds back into US dollars; direct yen loans to corporations and sovereign entities was a main line of business for many Japanese banks during this time. In the mid-1980s the Ministry of Finance also deregulated bond issuance guidelines, particularly those related to Euroyen bonds. Though the Euroyen market had been in existence since 1977 (when the European Investment Bank launched the first issue), the MOF had limited the market to six individual issues per year and had forbidden domestic companies from accessing the market. In 1984 it abolished all such restrictions as well as those previously imposed on issuance of convertible Euroyen bonds and bonds-with-warrants; it followed with further liberalization of dual currency bonds, zero-coupon bonds, deep discount bonds and floating rate notes in April 1985. A range of high rated offshore corporates, supranational organizations and sovereign institutions soon issued offshore Euroyen bonds, swapping proceeds back into fixed or floating US dollars; domestic corporations followed with their own issues shortly thereafter. In 1986 further deregulation occurred, with a broader range of borrowers permitted to access the market, issuance of subordinated structures approved, and the seasoning period for resales of offshore paper into Japan reduced from 180 to 90 days; these changes brought more borrowers to the market and generated additional JPY/US$ swap opportunities. Under a typical transaction, a borrower would raise fixed yen through the Euroyen market while a bank would raise Eurodollars on a LIBOR basis in its market; the borrower would then pay US$ LIBOR in exchange for fixed yen from the bank. Estimates indicate that 90% of all Euroyen financings during this time were swapped (Viner, 1987). During the 1980s trust banks, long-term credit banks, foreign banks and foreign securities firms were active in offering long-dated FX facilities for converting Eurobond flows.

While the liability segment of the market drove many CCS opportunities, the asset segment also contributed to overall activity. Japanese investors, who were becoming significant purchasers of US dollar (and other foreign currency) securities, often acquired such instruments and swapped coupons back into yen. Japanese investor purchases of US dollar EuroFRNs, Eurobonds and shogun bonds were widespread, with investors receiving fixed yen and paying US$ LIBOR or fixed US dollars. Given investor appetite for yield during these years, a number of innovative swap-driven structures were created. Among the most popular was the dual currency bond/swap package, where borrowers would issue in yen and offer enhanced yen coupons 100 to 200 basis points over straight yen bonds; principal repayment, rather than being in yen, was in a foreign currency (generally US dollars or Australian dollars), at a pre-specified rate different than that of the issue. Issuers hedged their open currency risk on yen coupons through the swap market, converting yen to fixed dollars, and fixed dollars into US$ LIBOR; they carried no exposure on the principal redemption as that was already denominated in the relevant home currency. The reverse dual currency bond structure exposed the investor to potential currency risk; the investor would thus enter into swaps to lock in an enhanced yield. Under a typical transaction, a company would issue and redeem in yen, but would peg coupons to a high yielding currency such as Australian dollars. In such instances the issuer would engage in a series of swaps which amounted to the issuer paying a LIBOR-based flow to a bank in exchange for fixed Australian dollars, which it would pass on to the investor. The swap bank would engage in both a CCS exchanging the LIBOR flow for a fixed yen flow, and a coupon swap exchanging the fixed yen for the fixed Australian dollars, which would be passed on to the investor through the borrower.

During the period of excess liquidity Japanese banks would often issue US dollar bonds offshore and enter into CCSs to onlend proceeds to Japanese borrowers in yen terms. The bond-with-warrant market (discussed earlier in the chapter), also generated swap activity during the late 1980s and very early 1990s. Under the warrant structure, a Japanese company would issue a foreign currency warrant bond (e.g. US dollars) and detach the equity warrant. The Japanese borrower would enter into a series of CCSs, converting fixed US dollar flows into fixed yen flows. A swap bank would pay the borrower the fixed dollar coupon in exchange for deep sub-LIBOR flows, which it would offset in the dollar IRS market. The borrower would then enter the CCS market and exchange the sub-LIBOR flow for a very low yen fixed rate, equal to perhaps 50% of the coupon on the original warrant bond; thus, final borrowing costs were exceptionally low. The size of the bond-with-warrant market grew at a substantial pace in the late 1980s, primarily on the basis of the very cheap funding Japanese issuers were able to obtain. The asset side of this transaction, where a Japanese investor converted foreign currency warrant bond flows into yen, also helped fuel growth in the CCS market.

As the Euroyen market grew throughout the late 1980s and early 1990s, so too did currency swap activity. During 1993 and 1994, when yen rates were particularly low and Euroyen new issue arbitrage was possible, issuance of Euroyen bonds soared; substantial issuance by both foreign and offshore Japanese issuers created additional activity in the yen CCS market. Toward the end of 1994 and early 1995, however, the tremendous strength of the yen against the dollar and a tightening of swap spreads forced a slowdown in issuance and swap volume. While the strength of the yen was a factor in slowing Euroyen issuance and reducing new issue swap flow, it had the offsetting effect of prompting more commercial currency hedging. Use of yen CCSs to hedge commercial exposures from further appreciation in the currency became more prevalent as the yen breached important technical levels on numerous occasions in late 1994 and early 1995.

It should be noted that in 1994 the MOF altered regulations permitting domestic securities firms to execute CCSs on foreign currency bonds underwritten by their offshore subsidiaries; until that time securities firms had been barred from participating in the CCS market. It now also permits securities firms to enter into CCSs with Japanese investors if they are executed simultaneously with investor purchases of foreign securities. The MOF is also preparing to allow securities firms to engage in CCSs based on samurai bond, foreign currency warrant and foreign currency convertible underwritings.

Like IRSs, CCSs in the Japanese market are priced on an absolute basis. Quoting convention in the market is fixed yen (semi-annual, on an Actual/365-day basis) against six month US$ LIBOR flat. The FX rate used at the time of quotation is the prevailing spot rate. The market is very liquid to ten years and transactions to 15 and 20 years are executed on occasion; standard interbank dealing size is JPY5 bln (US$55 mln). Figures 7.42 and 7.43 below trace the movement of the JPY/US$ CCS curve, as well as the movement of benchmark two-, five- and ten-year rates. It should be noted that increased liquidity in the market has lowered five-year CCS spreads from 12–15 basis points to 7–8 basis points over the past five years; by way of reference, CCSs executed in the early 1980s carried bid-offer spreads in excess of 100 basis points. Table 7.70 illustrates indicative CCS yen/US$ bid-offer spreads under normal market conditions. In addition to standard fixed JPY/US$ LIBOR CCSs there is also an active market for cross currency basis swaps of yen LIBOR against US$ LIBOR. The basis market is readily quoted and active to ten years; as with standard CCSs, interbank dealing size in basis swaps is JPY5 bln (US$55 mln). Figures 7.44 and 7.45 below trace the movement and the spread of six-month JPY and US$ LIBOR.

Maturity	Bid-Offer Spread
2 years	7–8 bps
3 years	7–8 bps
4 years	7–8 bps
5 years	7–8 bps
7 years	7–8 bps
10 years	7–8 bps

Table 7.70 Yen/US$ CCS Bid-Offer Spreads

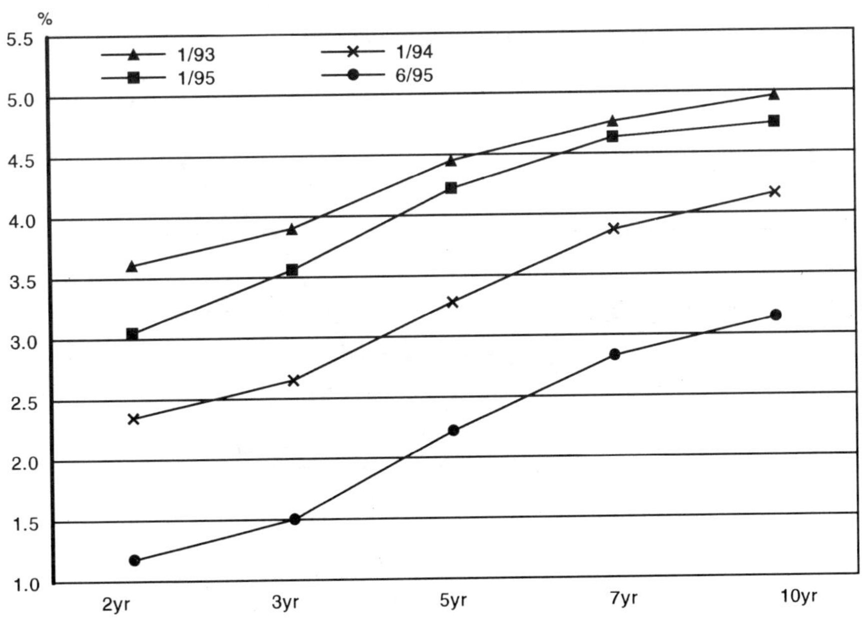

Figure 7.42 Historical Movement of JPY/US$ CCS Curves

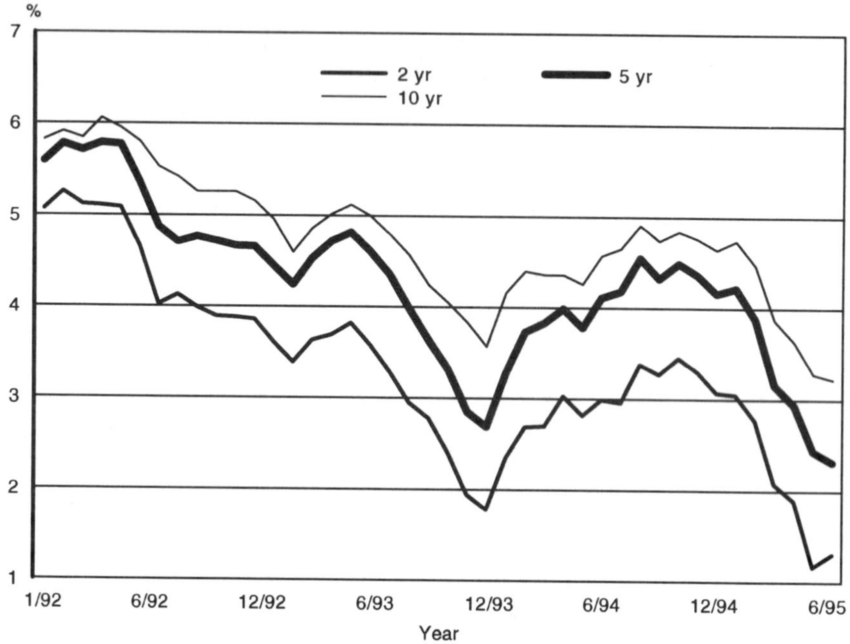

Figure 7.43 Historical Movement of Benchmark JPY/US$ CCS Rates

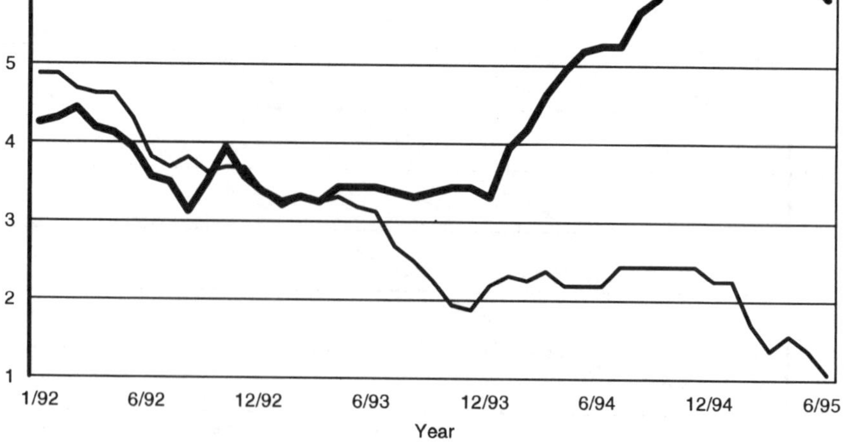

Figure 7.44 Historical Movement of Six-month JPY LIBOR and Six-month US$ LIBOR

Figure 7.45 Spread of Six-month JPY and US$ LIBOR

Currency Options

The Japanese FX options market was founded in early 1984 when the Bank of Tokyo introduced OTC options on JPY/US$. Despite the early introduction of currency options, the market remained relatively stagnant for a number of years as Japanese participants were not attracted to the idea of paying upfront premium for derivatives (the same general sentiment exists among many Japanese institutions today). By 1988 volume had increased somewhat, primarily through the introduction of zero cost structures (e.g. purchase and sale of options with offsetting premiums); users of JPY/US$ currency options were particularly attracted to zero cost options as no premium outflow was required. In 1988 the market expanded as FX brokers and dealers, primarily foreign banks, began quoting two-way markets; they were soon joined by major Japanese banks. Today's market is based primarily on vanilla American and European options with maturities of one to 12 months; standard interbank dealing size ranges from JPY3 bln (US$33 mln) to JPY5 bln (US$55 mln) and most deals flow through brokers (and only rarely from bank to bank). Quotes are generally given in volatility terms (and only occasionally in price, or premium terms) and trades are often executed on a delta neutral basis, through a combination of an option and associated spot FX, which leaves the institution with no directional exposure to JPY/US$ at the time of trade. The historical movement of one- and 12-month JPY/US$ option volatility quotes is illustrated in Figure 7.46.

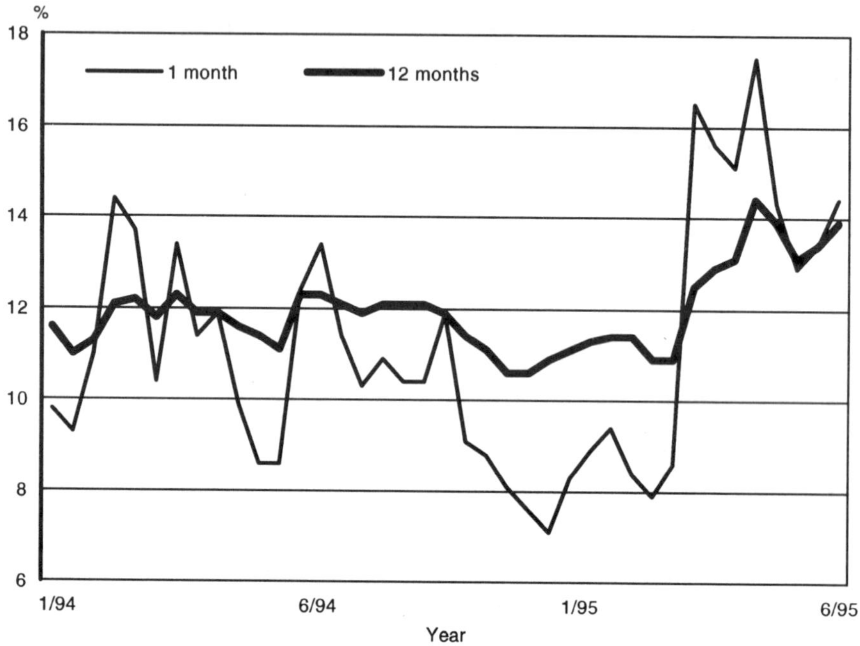

Figure 7.46 Historical Movement of One- and 12-month JPY/US$ FX Option Volatilities

In addition to standard FX options the Japanese (and offshore) market has also experienced increasing activity in exotic JPY/US$ FX options, particularly barrier options. Japanese corporates, desiring to hedge portions of their currency exposure but not wanting to pay the full amount of premium due, have found knock-in and knock-out options to be particularly attractive. With such barriers the core of the exposure institutions need to hedge is most often covered for the life of the transaction, but the premium paid for such cover is lower than under a comparable vanilla option; as with all barrier structures there is always a possibility that the barrier will be triggered and the currency hedge will disappear. Other variations of barriers are also executed, including the purchase of barriers which provide hedging cover over a broad range of FX rates, packaged with the sale of out-of-the-money barriers in order to reduce premium payments even further. As the yen appreciated against the US dollar in late 1994 and early 1995, many investors with simple or compound barrier structures found themselves without currency cover (or with greater option liabilities, or both) as the yen surged to previously 'unimaginable' levels. In addition to barrier options, other exotic FX options are also available on JPY/US$, including Asian options, digital options, lookback options, compound options and so on. The deep liquidity of the underlying FX market, together with investor demand for specific payout or risk profiles, has prompted reasonably active use of exotic currency structures.

Commodity

Commodity Forwards/Swaps

Japan is a significant trading centre for OTC energy products, on both a spot and forward/swap basis. Although it is not as active as Singapore (see chapter 11 for details), Japan's role as a significant importer of energy products (from outright crudes to refined products such as gasoil, naphtha and fuel oil) makes it an important centre for trading of such products. Japan's primary commodity trading is based on forwards and swaps on naphtha, jet kerosene, gasoil, fuel oil and crude. Most OTC energy forwards and swaps are very short-dated, extending primarily from one to two months (though certain longer-dated structures can be negotiated); the Asia Pacific physical energy market trades primarily in the near month and the second near month (as compared with the European market, which trades to four months forward, and the US market, which trades to 12 months forward). Forwards/swaps may be either 'paper' transactions, which result in net cash settlement rather than physical delivery, or physical transactions which result in the exchange of cash for physical product; paper forwards and swaps are often used to hedge physical deliveries.

As in Singapore, short-dated energy forwards and swaps traded in the Japanese market follow conventions used in the cash energy markets. For gasoil transactions, quotes are in US dollars/barrel for 0.5% (maximum) sulphur gasoil (0 degrees centigrade pour point); for naphtha, quotes are in US dollars/barrel for petrochemcial light or full range grade naphtha (minimum 65% paraffins) (note that naphtha deliverable under a forward into Japan is presently limited to product originating from the Middle East, Asia (excluding Southeast Asia) and Australia; a proposal is presently under consideration by Japanese traders to consider including naphtha from the US and Southeast Asia); for fuel oil, quotes are in US dollars/ton for 3.5% sulphur (maximum) fuel oil (380 centistoke viscosity); for gasoline, quotes are in US dollars/barrel for 97 octane gas (0.15 grams of lead/litre); and, for jet kerosene, quotes are in US dollars/barrel for DERD 2494 jet kerosene. Quotes for forwards in Japan are generally done on a c & f basis (meaning cargo and freight costs are included in the quoted price) as opposed to the f.o.b. (free on board) basis customary in Singapore (meaning cargo, insurance and freight costs are not included in the quoted priced).

As mentioned, in addition to pure physical delivery forwards (for instance purchase of two-month forward Tapis (Malaysian benchmark grade) at a given price, open spec) forwards and swaps are often executed on a paper basis, without exchange of the underlying commodity. Under a typical paper transaction one party pays a fixed price while the other pays a floating price (generally based on the average of a floating index over a pre-specified period of time) on a certain quantity of fuel. At the conclusion of the trade the net differential between the fixed price and the average floating price is settled in cash. Paper transactions are often executed in order to hedge physical deliveries or an open spec position taken on a particular cargo of energy products. Further details on paper forwards/swaps (including the trading of paper forward spreads) are included in chapter 11.

Commodity Options

Japanese firms have been reasonably active users of OTC commodity options, particularly as a means of hedging production or imports; most commodity options executed are related to international energy products, such as crude, jet fuel or naphtha. In comparison with the commodity forward and swap market, however, OTC commodity options activity remains modest.

LOCAL REGULATORY/LEGAL TREATMENT OF DERIVATIVES

Regulation of derivatives within Japan is divided into four separate segments. Commodity futures and options are regulated by the Commodity Exchange Act (CEA), with oversight provided by the relevant ministries (e.g. Ministry of Agriculture, Fisheries and Food for softs, Ministry of International Trade and Industry for metals, and so on). Securities futures and options (e.g. index futures/options, JGB futures/options) are governed by the revised Securities and Exchange Law (SEL) and the rules of the Japan Securities Dealers' Association (JSDA), a self-regulating body acting under the auspices of the SEL. Financial futures and options are governed by the Financial Futures Transaction Law of 1988 (FFTL), which established the legal framework for the listing and trading of financial contracts not explicitly recognized by the SEL (e.g. deposit and currency futures/options). OTC transactions are governed by the rules established by the National Federation of Bankers Association.

Contracts listed on the OSE, TSE and NSE (including Nikkei 225 and Nikkei 300 futures and options, Topix futures and options, JGB futures and options, US Treasury bond futures and Nagoya 25 options) fall under the regulations of the SEL. Interestingly, OTC options written on any of the above also fall under the jurisdiction of the SEL. The SEL was amended in 1988 to permit stock exchanges to launch derivatives as long as the derivatives were based on securities recognized by the SEL (e.g. stock indexes, government bonds). Under the SEL regulations, all orders for derivatives must be routed through an exchange member though the use of a 'special participant' order. OTC options on the same derivatives must be routed through securities companies or other authorized dealers, who then become principals, not brokers. No trades in this category can be executed on the basis of exchange quotes unless they are actually traded on an exchange; the sole exception is for OTC options. In addition to the regulations set forth by the SEL, the JSDA has established specific rules regarding the financial sophistication of customers and securities companies participating in such derivative transactions. Customers must demonstrate a sufficient capability for dealing in futures and options and must maintain certain mandated levels of assets on deposit with securities firms (note that sophisticated institutional investors such as banks and listed companies may be exempt from this requirement). Deposit and currency contracts offered via TIFFE, which are regulated under the FFTL, include Euroyen futures and options, Eurodollar futures, and JPY/US$ futures. Trading in these contracts must be conducted via TIFFE, through a financial futures trading company which is a MOF-licensed general or clearing member. Customer deposits, such as those required by the JSDA, are also required by TIFFE. Non-resident customers must adhere to the same deposit requirements.

Japanese swap law is reasonably well defined though certain areas, such as netting of exposures, are in the process of being evaluated; there is, as of this writing, no legal precedent related to netting or set-off of exposures under default or bankruptcy. Japanese law does not require the use of signed documentation, though parties to the transaction must be licensed. A binding agreement can be executed on an oral basis, and the exchange of confirms is not technically required. Consideration is not required to create a legally binding contract, only a declaration of reciprocal intention. Although documentation is not a legal requirement, in practice most participants in the market adhere to some documentary standard, primarily the International Swap Dealers' Association (ISDA) agreement. Relevant ISDA clauses are typically translated in summary form in Japanese where necessary. Master swap agreements (e.g. an ISDA master document, where attached confirms form part of the overall agreement) are increasingly used in Japan, though set-off and netting under such agreements have not yet been tested under Japanese law. Authorization to conduct swaps by non-financial institutions is generally interpreted rather broadly under articles of incorporation, as few corporations involved in swaps have articles which specifically delineate swaps as permissible financial contracts in which to deal. The only exception to such interpretation would occur in instances when articles specifically refute the use of swap transactions.

Although financial deregulation is occurring within Japan, there is still a significant amount of regulatory change required before the markets will be regarded as completely free and open. During the course of the past two years, however, a number of significant changes have occurred in the local derivative market. For instance, banks can now trade in domestic yen FRAs; mutual funds and insurance companies are permitted to use swaps for hedging purposes; warrants can be written and listed on the new Nikkei 300 index as well as other equity indexes; and, perhaps most significantly, the division between banks and securities companies has begun to fade (primarily as a result of the Financial Services Reform Act of 1993), and the two groups are actively competing on each other's territories, adding competition and innovation to the industry.

As the Japanese financial market deregulates, the range of permissible derivatives activity has been a central point of focus. In 1994 the US and Japan agreed on a range of measures designed to provide offshore participants with greater financial access to the local markets. Though the proposed changes, as contained in the key document 'Measures of the Government of Japan and the Government of the United States Regarding Financial Services', encompass a broad range of financial services, we highlight in this section several key statements made with regard to derivatives. We first discuss changes which have already been enacted, and we then summarize proposed changes to be enacted at some future date.

Changes which have been enacted, and where activities are now permissible under Japanese law, include the following: need for administrative notices to be issued when floating offshore warrants linked to either JGBs or indexes has been abolished, making the warrant issuance process more flexible; use of yen-yen interest rate agreements (e.g. FRAs), as well as forward exchange agreements is now permissible; local financial institution trading of stock index futures and options on offshore exchanges is permitted; non-designated financial institution investment in offshore derivatives is now permitted; and, the range of cross currency swaps which can be executed directly by Japanese securities firms in respect of their overseas subsidiaries' underwriting business has been expanded.

Several items are presently under review as a result of the agreement. For instance, an examination of expanded activity in exchange-traded derivatives on equities, and on OTC equity derivatives, is being undertaken; product study of currency derivatives not presently contained under Article 2 of the SEL is being prepared, with a specific view towards permitting onshore currency warrant transactions (note: allowing such currency derivatives will require expansion of powers under the existing Foreign Exchange and Foreign Trade Control Law); permission for corporate investors to deal in derivatives on offshore exchanges is being investigated (though such investors would still have to adhere to an ex-post reporting mechanism); exemption for securities companies, insurance companies and investment and trust companies to deal in own account trading of spot currency options is being considered; and, comprehensive approvals regarding netting of exposures is being reviewed.

LOCAL ACCOUNTING PRACTICES FOR DERIVATIVES

Accounting for derivatives in the Japanese marketplace is based primarily on accrual accounting. Under the accrual method of accounting, gains or losses on interest or currency derivatives (whether for hedge or speculative purposes) are accrued to the next settlement period, at which point they are recognized through the income statement. Under this process, the current market value of derivatives is not considered. Use of market value accounting, where positions are marked-to-market (e.g. the contracted value is compared with the market value, and a differential reflecting an unrealized gain or loss is obtained) is not permitted, since Japanese accounting principles do not permit unrealized gains to be shown as profits in the income statement. It should be noted that certain Japanese institutions are required to provide statements conforming to US Generally Accepted

Accounting Principles for listing purposes (e.g. Mitsubishi Bank, which is listed on the NY Stock Exchange). Under such circumstances, institutions convert derivatives used for trading positions to current market values (with gains/losses shown in the trading account and with unrealized gains/options (including option premium) shown in the other asset/liability account); derivatives used for hedging purposes follow accrual methods, as is typical for Japanese financial institutions in the domestic market. It should be noted that Japanese authorities are presently reviewing a change to market value accounting.

PROSPECTS FOR THE LOCAL DERIVATIVE MARKET

Summarized below are near-term (one- to three-year) and medium-term (three- to five-year) prospects for domestic Japanese derivatives.

Near-term:

- Additional growth in yen IRSs and CCSs as domestic and offshore companies continue to raise funds in the samurai and Euroyen markets.
- Expansion of yen currency derivatives as institutions attempt to protect against, or take advantage of, volatility of the yen; initial expansion into listed currency warrants once onshore deregulation occurs.
- Continued growth in key listed fixed income futures (e.g. Euroyen, JGBs) as domestic rates remain volatile and financing and swapping opportunities increase.
- Little expansion in onshore equity-related derivatives as the domestic equity markets remain subdued and regulatory authorities embark on an extensive review of current onshore listed and OTC regulations.
- Growth in domestic credit-related derivatives as institutions become more interested and adept at trading, via derivatives, the credit spreads of domestic issuers in the domestic market, domestic issuers in the offshore market, and offshore issuers in the domestic market.
- Modest expansion in exotic derivatives as domestic institutions become more comfortable with the risks and opportunities inherent in such derivatives.
- Abandonment or restructuring of listed financial/commodity derivatives which generate no trading volume or open interest.

Medium-term:

- Expansion in onshore equity derivatives (e.g. listed/OTC equity options, basket/index warrants, equity forwards/swaps) as the regulatory authorities loosen restrictions presently imposed on such businesses.
- Greater liquidity in key agricultural commodity futures as exchange mergers continue and consolidation of contracts occurs.
- Continued deepening of the fixed income and currency derivative markets (forwards, swaps and options).

Exchange	Contract	1993 Volume (contracts)	1994 Volume (contracts)
HGE	Red bean futures	182,611	241,555
	US Soybean futures	106,152	89,916
	White bean futures	0	0
	Potato starch futures	0	0
	Domestic soybean futures	0	0
KCE	Red bean futures	579,751	492,294
	Soybean futures	486,850#	213,271#
	Corn futures	1,000,000	1,700,000
	Refined sugar futures	1,400	1,400
KANEX	Red bean futures	2,910,000	2,930,000
	Soybean futures	1,580,000	1,290,000
	Raw sugar futures	1,000,000	664,600
	Raw sugar futures options	26,793	63,789
KRSE	Raw silk futures	687,723	695,172
KRE	RSS3 rubber futures	2,900,000	2,932,000
	Rubber Index futures	n/l*	n/l*
MDCE	Dried cocoon futures	1,780,000	475,978
NGSE	Red bean futures	1,210,000	919,371
	Soybean futures	287,612	177,513
	Refined sugar futures	0	0
	Potato starch futures	0	0
NSE	Nagoya Index options	160,104	80,682
NTE	Cotton futures	822,683	1,100,000
	Wool yarn futures	79,114	87,240
	Staple fibre yarn futures	18,729	13,114
OSE	Nikkei 225 Index futures	8,480,000	5,550,000
	Nikkei 300 Index futures	n/l*	4,180,000
	Nikkei 225 Index futures options	6,080,000	4,270,000
	Nikkei 300 Index futures options	n/l*	269,067
OTE	Cotton (20) futures	648,345	2,000,000
	Cotton (30) futures	0	0
	Cotton (40) futures	574,729	833,283
	Wool yarn futures	470,000	267,000
	Staple fibre yarn futures	0	0
TDCE	Dried cocoon futures	1,070,000	486,558

Exchange	Contract	1993 Volume (contracts)	1994 Volume (contracts)
TOCOM	Gold futures	8,760,000	12,480,000
	Silver futures	861,463	1,040,000
	Platinum futures	4,980,000	4,550,000
	Palladium futures	2,270,000	774,284
	RSS3 rubber futures	2,970,000	9,020,000
	Cotton futures	1,300,000	2,570,000
	Wool yarn futures	32,800	36,400
TGE	Red bean futures	6,350,000	5,120,000
	Corn futures	1,260,000	3,000,000
	Soybean futures	3,750,000	2,560,000
	Raw sugar futures	2,210,000	1,220,000
	Refined sugar futures	2,864	2,864
	Soybean futures options	60,000	96,000
	Raw sugar futures options	38,000	67,500
TIFFE	Three-month Euroyen futures	23,400,000	37,400,000
	12-month Euroyen futures	4,434	25,100
	Three-month Eurodollar futures	0	0
	Three-month Euroyen futures options	686,500	520,237
	JPY/US$ currency futures	48,241	13,770
TSE	Topix Index futures	2,156,9600	2,623,067
	·Topix Index futures options	37,831	20,078
	Ten-Year JGB futures	15,165,265	13,002,892
	20-Year JGB futures	3,106	3,194
	Ten-Year JGB futures options	1,506,386	1,691,834
	20-Year US Treasury futures	112,600	115,750
YRSE	Raw silk futures	1,510,000	1,000,000

* n/l: contract not yet listed; # contract specification altered to half size in August 1993

Table 7.71 Summary of 1993/1994 Listed Futures and Options Turnover

	Overall Liquidity	Liquid/ Maximum Maturity	Interbank dealing size	Average bid-offer spread
Equity/Index Swaps	good	1–3 yrs/5 yrs	n/a	n/a
Equity/Index Options	good	1–3 yrs/5 yrs	n/a	n/a
Interest Rate Swaps	excellent	1–10 yrs/10 yrs+	US$ 55 mln	2–5 bps
Interest Rate Options	good	1–5 yrs/10 yrs	US$ 55 mln	1–6 pts
Currency Swaps	excellent	1–10 yrs/10 yrs+	US$ 55 mln	7–8 bps
Currency Options	excellent	3–12 mos/5 yrs	US$ 55 mln	1–2 pts

Table 7.72 Summary of Domestic OTC Derivatives

8: Malaysia

FINANCIAL MARKET OVERVIEW

Malaysia's financial markets are growing in size, liquidity and sophistication. The country's equity market has drawn the attention of domestic and offshore investors in recent years and growth and returns have been significant. The fixed income market is among the most advanced of those in Southeast Asia and features a diverse array of government and private sector securities; primary issuance and secondary trading continue to increase and the market has become an important and legitimate source of financing for both the government and local companies. Although Malaysia's currency market has been subject to temporary restrictions in the past the local currency is freely convertible and actively traded (primarily offshore). In addition to financial instruments, Malaysia's role as a key regional commodity producer (e.g. crude palm oil, rubber, tin, cocoa, coffee) has resulted in the development of liquid physical cash markets for such products. The rapidly developing cash markets have resulted in the creation of a reasonably broad, and growing, range of domestic derivatives.

Malaysian equity trading dates back to 1960, when the Malaysian Stock Exchange (MSE), with trading centres in both Kuala Lumpur and Singapore, was established; the two trading centres were merged in 1964 and the MSE was renamed the Stock Exchange of Malaysia and Singapore (SEMS). In 1973, several years after Singapore gained independence, SEMS was disbanded and the Malaysian authorities created the Kuala Lumpur Stock Exchange (KLSE), which exists as the primary equity exchange of the country today (the smaller Bumiputra Stock Exchange was founded in 1969, but remains rather inactive in comparison with the KLSE). Despite the break-up of SEMS in the early 1970s the KLSE and the Stock Exchange of Singapore (SES) continued to list each other's stocks; in 1989 the KLSE and SES elected to delist each other's 'guest' stocks, and each exchange now features only local shares (note that certain Malaysian shares are still traded via the SES's CLOB international OTC dealing system).

After many years of slow growth and only moderate returns, the Malaysian equity market attracted substantial domestic and foreign investment between 1992 and 1994. During 1993, when the Malaysian market reached its peak, annual trading volume rose to a record 100 mln shares (from previous average annual turnover of only 15 to 20 mln shares); liquidity at that time was considerable and spread among large and small capitalization stocks. Taking advantage of the market's considerable strength in 1993 and early 1994 the government privatized several state enterprises (e.g. Malaysian Airlines, Malaysian Industrial Shipping, STM, Tenaga), which added significantly to both market liquidity and capitalization. Since the decline of the market from its peak annual trading volume has subsided to 20–30 mln shares per year, with liquidity in smaller stocks declining dramatically. Despite several large IPOs and privatizations, overall market capitalization has declined slightly as well; total capitalization amounted to US$199.3 bln in 1994, ranking it as the fifth largest of Asia Pacific's 13 markets. Figure 8.1 below illustrates the trend of the benchmark Kuala Lumpur Composite Index (KLCI) stock index. Table 8.1 contains information on domestic equity market indicators.

Note that foreign investors generally have unrestricted access to domestic shares. The only exception to this occurs when an investor seeks to acquire more than 15% of a domestic company or more than 30% of a domestic company's voting shares; in such instances the investor must obtain prior approval from the Foreign Investment Committee (in certain instances a company may specify the maximum level of permissible foreign ownership through its articles of incorporation; in such cases foreign investment cannot exceed the pre-specified level).

Malaysia features one of the most diverse and advanced fixed income markets in Southeast Asia. In the short-end of the curve sovereign benchmarks are found in both central bank bills (known as Bank Negara Bills) and government treasury bills; there is also active issuance of fixed and floating rate certificates of deposit (CDs)

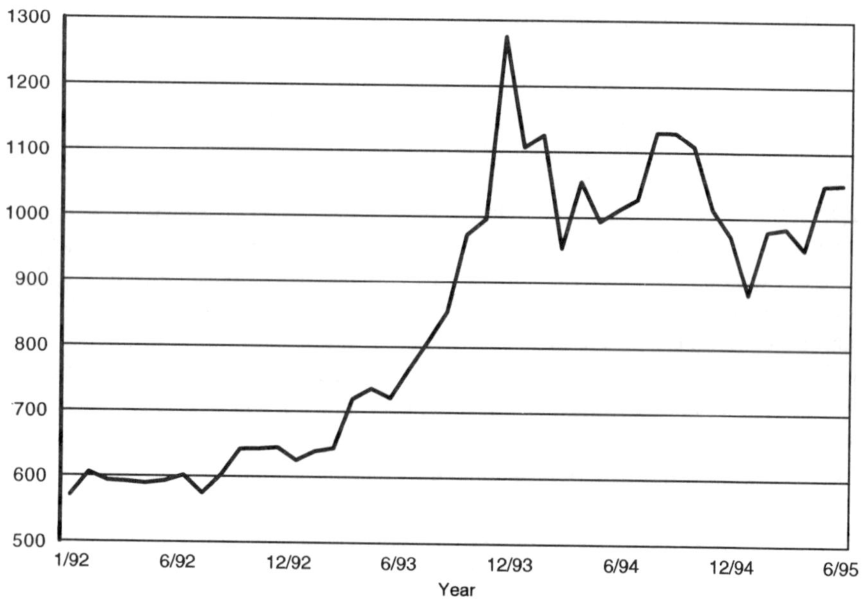

Figure 8.1 Historical Movement of the Kuala Lumpur Composite Index

Year*	Market Capitalization (US$ bln)	Trading Value (US$ bln)	Listed Companies (#)
1994	199.3	126.5	478
1993	220.3	153.7	410
1992	94.0	21.7	369
1991	58.6	10.7	321
1990	48.6	10.9	282

* to December of each year; Source: IFC, 1995

	1/92–6/95 Annualized Return*	1/92–6/95 Total Return*
Kuala Lumpur Composite Index	20.71%	87.22%

* dividends reinvested in index

Table 8.1 Domestic Equity Market Indicators

by private-sector financial institutions and less active, though growing, issuance of commercial paper by corporations. Total short-term fixed income outstandings amounted to MYR21.75 bln (US$8.7 bln) at the end of 1994. The intermediate- and long-end of the curve (from two to 20 years) is dominated by Malaysian Government Securities (MGS), which represent the primary obligations of the Malaysian government. Figure 8.2 below traces the historical movement of benchmark two- and five-year MGS yields. The intermediate sector of the curve is also supplemented by issues of mortgage-backed bonds and notes known as Cagamas securities; these instruments are available as both fixed and floating rate securities (the latter pegged to the Kuala Lumpur Interbank Offer Rate, KLIBOR). Total outstanding MGS and Cagamas reached MYR74.25 bln (US$29.7 bln) at the end of 1994. Corporate issuance through the Private Debt Securities (PDS) market is modest but increasing. Corporate bonds are issued as fixed rate obligations with maturities extending from one to ten years. The corporate market also features convertible bonds and bonds with transferable subscription rights (TSRs), the Malaysian equivalent of warrants. Total private sector outstandings amounted to MYR9.75 bln (US$3.9 bln) at the end of 1994 (Paisley, 1995).

Key interest rates in the Malaysian market include KLIBOR (the borrowing cost for financial institutions in the interbank market), treasury bill yields (the short-term borrowing cost of the government), MGS yields (the medium- and long-term borrowing cost of the government), and ringgit interest rate swaps (the rate for transacting swaps in the domestic interbank swap market). Table 8.2 contains payment frequency, compounding frequency and day count conventions for each rate.

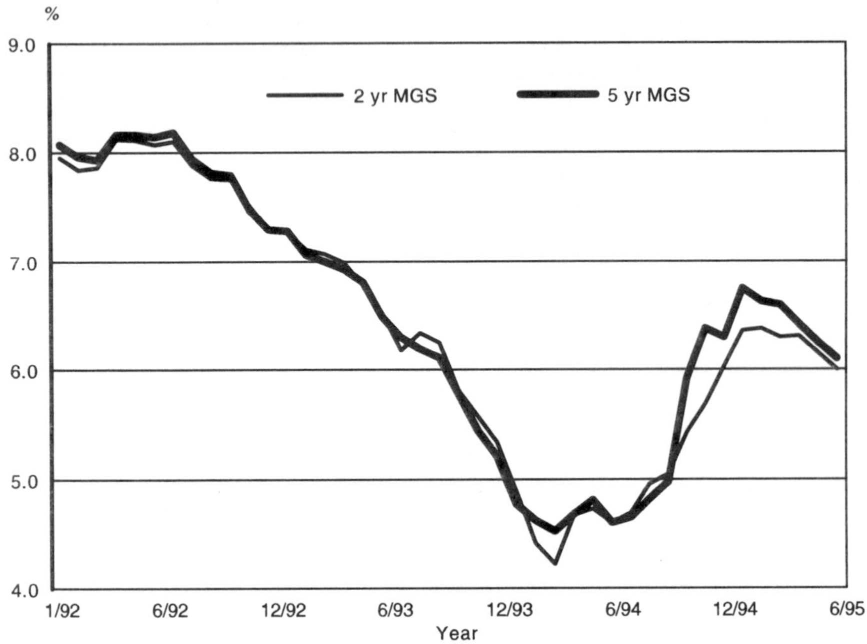

Figure 8.2: Historical Movement of Benchmark Malaysian Government Securities Yields

Rate	Payment Frequency	Compounding Frequency	Day Count Convention
KLIBOR	–	–	Actual/365
Bills	–	–	Actual/365
MGS	semi-annual	semi-annual	Actual/Actual
Swaps	semi-annual	semi-annual	Actual/365

Table 8.2 Domestic Interest Rate Summary

The Malaysian ringgit (MYR) is a freely convertible currency managed on a floating basis against a trade-weighted basket; through the precise composition of the basket is not disclosed by the authorities it is generally thought to include the US dollar, Japanese yen and Singapore dollar. Bank Negara Malaysia (BNM), the central bank, participates actively in the currency market to bid up, or sell down, the value of the ringgit. Although there are technically no major restrictions regarding the trading and convertibility of the ringgit, temporary restrictions in the past regarding onshore/offshore FX swaps have dampened overall activity in the onshore market. Average daily spot trading in ringgit within Malaysia is estimated at MYR625 mln to MYR750 mln (US$250 mln to US$300 mln), where trades of MYR12.5 mln (US$5 mln) can move market prices; the offshore market, in

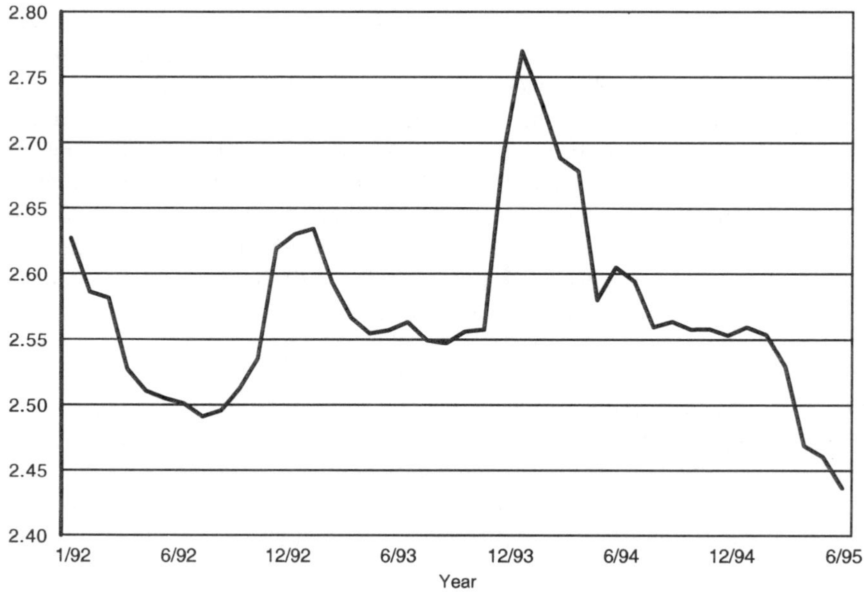

Figure 8.3 Historical Movement of Spot MYR/US$

contrast, is extremely liquid, with approximately MYR8.75 bln (US$3.5 bln) traded on a spot basis during an average trading day (Paisley and Woodcock, 1995). Standard dealing size in the offshore interbank spot market is MYR12.5 mln (US$5 mln) and bid-offer spreads are approximately MYR0.001/US$ under normal market conditions. Figure 8.3 illustrates the historical movement of spot MYR/US$ since 1992.

DERIVATIVE MARKETS AND PRODUCTS

LISTED DERIVATIVE EXCHANGES

Malaysia has been among the most active of all nations in Asia Pacific in establishing forums for trading listed derivatives; it currently features four exchanges which trade (or will trade) listed derivatives, including Kuala Lumpur Commodity Exchange (KLCE), Kuala Lumpur Options and Financial Futures Exchange (KLOFFE), Malaysia Monetary Exchange (MME) and Kuala Lumpur Stock Exchange (KLSE).

Malaysia has been engaged in trading of spot commodities such as rubber, tin, cocoa and palm oil, four of its major exports, for several decades. As it became apparent that development of a commodity-based futures market was required to provide protection against commodity price movements, the Malaysian government, through the Ministry of Primary Industry, began studying the framework for developing such a derivatives forum. In 1980, after four years of design, the Kuala Lumpur Commodity Exchange (KLCE) was established, along with its wholly-owned clearing subsidiary, the Kuala Lumpur Commodity Clearing House (KLCCH). Trading in crude palm oil (CPO) futures began in late 1980 and the contract became the focal point of the KLCE for the next few years. Though trading of futures on the KLCE was regulated by the Commodity Trading Act of 1980 (discussed in the regulatory section at the end of the chapter), difficulties with member brokers meeting margin calls in late 1984 after the KLCCH raised CPO margins led to a review of trade procedures and, shortly thereafter, the establishment of new regulations via the Commodity Trading Act of 1985. As part of the process a new clearinghouse, the Malaysia Futures Clearing Corporation (MFCC), was created; MFCC has sought to avoid a repeat of the 1984 difficulties through the imposition of much stricter membership requirements. Following its regulatory reforms, KLCE expanded the CPO contract to include additional trading months, and introduced new futures contracts on rubber, tin, cocoa, palm olein and crude palm kernel oil. Not all of these contracts were successful, as we shall discuss later in the chapter, and some were eventually redesigned or phased out. Trading of KLCE futures occurs via continuous open-outcry on the floor of the Exchange. Membership on the KLCE takes one of four forms: clearing members (who are permitted to trade for their own accounts and for client accounts), corporate members (who are permitted to trade for their own accounts and for client accounts, but must be guaranteed by a clearing member), trade affiliate members (who can trade for their own accounts or for accounts of overseas clients, but cannot trade with other affiliate members and must deal only through clearing members) and local members (who are permitted to trade only on their own accounts).

In addition to being an early developer and promoter of Asian commodity futures, Malaysia has also made substantial progress in preparing for local financial futures trading by creating KLOFFE and MME.

KLOFFE was created in 1991 by a consortium of private companies (i.e. Renong (33.3% ownership), Rashid Hussain (22.2%), Zalik Securities (22.2%) and New Straits Times Press (22.2%)) to trade domestic equity derivatives. After several years of planning the Exchange began trading stock index futures in 1995, and will follow with listed index options and equity options in mid- to late-1996 (details on all contracts have already been released and are discussed later in the chapter). KLOFFE has been established as an electronic, screen-based exchange, with trades executed through the KATS trading system; trades are cleared through the Malaysian Derivative Clearing House (MDCH), a joint clearinghouse which will be used by both KLOFFE and MME (though not KLCE, which clears through MFCC, as indicated above). Membership on KLOFFE takes one of three forms: trading members (who are permitted to trade for their own accounts and client accounts), local members (who are permitted to trade for their own accounts only) and trading permit holders (who are permitted to trade for their own accounts only, during set time periods). KLOFFE is also establishing a separate category of market-makers to provide two-way quotes for index and equity options (in exchange for lower fees); designated market-makers are often necessary in order to ensure a minimum level of liquidity for options.

In 1992 the KLCE created a wholly-owned subsidiary, the MME (originally known as the Kuala Lumpur Futures Market), to trade money market and interest rate futures (under the jurisdiction of the Ministry of Finance). The Exchange is slated to introduce Kuala Lumpur Interbank Offer Rate (KLIBOR) deposit futures by early 1996 and will begin trading interest rate futures, based on the MGS discussed above, in mid-1996 (currency derivatives will follow at a later date). Malaysia will thus join Japan, Hong Kong, Philippines, Australia and New Zealand in trading futures on its own domestic rates. MME will trade through open-outcry on the floor of the Exchange and all orders will be routed through KL Trades Allocation and Confirmation System (KLTACS); transactions are to be cleared through the MDCH mentioned above. Though membership structure is in the final stages of preparation, it appears that MME will divide membership into two broad categories, including corporate members and individual members. Individual members will only be permitted to trade for their own accounts. Corporate members will be sub-divided into brokers (permitted to trade and clear for their own accounts and client accounts) and non-brokers (permitted to trade for their own accounts only); non-brokers will include locally incorporated members (who may be clearing or non-clearing members), and associate foreign members (who may also be clearing or non-clearing members).

Exchange	**Primary Derivatives**
Kuala Lumpur Commodity Exchange (KLCE)	Crude palm oil futures; crude palm kernel oil futures; cocoa futures; rubber futures; tin futures
Kuala Lumpur Options and Financial Futures Exchange (KLOFFE)	Equity options (proposed); Index futures, options (latter proposed)
Kuala Lumpur Stock Exchange (KLSE)	Equity warrants; transferable subscription rights (TSRs); convertible unsecured loan stocks (CULS); redeemable convertible unsecured notes (RCUN)
Malaysia Monetary Exchange (MME)	Deposit futures (proposed); interest rate futures (proposed)

Table 8.3 Listed Derivative Exchanges

The KLSE, described above, is the country's main forum for equity trading (which occurs on an automated basis through the SCORE system). In addition to equities, the Exchange is active in the local derivative market through the listing and trading of both convertible bonds and warrants. The KLSE features trading of convertible unsecured loan stocks (CULS) and redeemable convertible unsecured notes (RCUN), along with two distinct types of warrants, issuer warrants (also known in the local market as transferable subscription rights, or TSRs) and covered warrants. Convertible securities and TSRs have been actively traded in the local market for several years; covered warrants, in contrast, were introduced as recently as May 1995. Table 8.3 highlights Malaysia's listed derivative exchanges and products.

LISTED FUTURES AND OPTIONS

Equity

Equity Futures/Options

Although the Malaysian market does not yet feature listed equity options, one of KLOFFE's near-term priorities is to introduce such derivatives; although no definitive timetable has been established, preliminary indications point to listing and trading of equity options in mid- to late-1996. The Exchange has already released contract specifications on the proposed options, though they have not yet announced the stocks on which options will be available. Malaysian stock options will be structured as American exercise, physical settlement derivatives, with each contract commanding 1,000 shares of underlying stock. Strike intervals will be established according to the price of the underlying shares; shares priced below MYR4.98 will have strike intervals of MYR0.25, shares priced between MYR5 and MYR9.95 will have strike intervals of MYR0.50 and shares priced over MYR10 will have strike intervals of MYR1. As indicated above, a group of market-makers will be introduced in order to ensure availability of continuous two-way prices and liquidity. It should be noted that the authorities are presently reviewing liberalization of onshore short-selling rules (such short-selling is not currently permissible); option markets depend on short-selling to be successful. Table 8.4 contains preliminary contract specifications for KLOFFE equity options. It should be noted that the Exchange presently has no plans to introduce equity futures.

Index Futures/Options/Futures Options

Following several years of planning and design KLOFFE introduced its first listed derivative contract, KLCI futures, in December 1995. As indicated above, creation of the index future forms the first stage of KLOFFE's derivative programme, which will grow to include equity options and index options. The KLCI future, which is designed as a cash-settled contract valued at MYR100 times the index, becomes the

Contract	Equity Options
Type	Domestic
Exchange	Kuala Lumpur Options and Financial Futures Exchange
Months	Spot month, next month and the next two quarterly months on March, June, September, December cycle
Contract Size	1,000 shares
Tick Value	MYR0.01
Daily Limit	No limit
Deliverable Instrument	Physical settlement
Last Trading Day	Last business day of the contract month
Exercise Day	American exercise – any business day up to, and including, the last trading day
Real-time price data	To be determined

Table 8.4 Contract Specifications for KLOFFE Equity Options (Proposed)

ninth listed index future in the Asia Pacific region. The underlying KLCI, created in 1977, is a market capitalization-weighted index of Malaysia's top 100 stocks. Introduction of the KLCI future is expected to generate additional activity in equity-related derivatives (e.g. index warrants, OTC index options, index swaps) by making the risks of such positions simpler to manage. It is also expected to appeal to a broad base of investors and fund managers seeking to take a view on the broad Malaysian market in a simple and efficient form. Details on KLCI futures are highlighted in Table 8.5.

In addition to KLCI futures, KLOFFE intends to introduce KLCI options to the Malaysian market during mid- to late-1996. Preliminary details point to the listing and trading of European, cash-settled index options with strikes set at 20 point intervals. The contracts will be offered on two near months as well as two quarter months and settlement will be determined through a simple average of the KLCI at one minute intervals during the last 30 minutes of trading on settlement day. As with equity options, a group of market-makers will be in place to quote two-way prices for index options. Table 8.6 contains contract specifications for KLOFFE's proposed KLCI options.

Contract	Kuala Lumpur Composite Index Futures
Type	Domestic
Exchange	Kuala Lumpur Options and Financial Futures Exchange
Months	Spot month, next month and the next two quarterly months on March, June, September, December cycle
Contract Size	MYR100 * KLCI
Tick Value	0.1 index point
Daily Limit	To be determined by KLOFFE on a periodic basis. No price limits on the last trading day of the contract month.
Deliverable Instrument	Cash settlement based on closing level of the index on the last trading day.
Last Trading Day	Last business day of the contract month
Delivery Day	Business day following the last trading day
Real-time price data	Bloomberg: IKA <Cmdty> Reuters:<0#KL17; Telerate: 39889

Table 8.5 Contract Specifications for KLOFFE Kuala Lumpur Composite Index Futures

Contract	Kuala Lumpur Composite Index Options
Type	Domestic
Exchange	Kuala Lumpur Options and Financial Futures Exchange
Months	Spot month, next month and the next two quarterly months on March, June, September, December cycle
Contract Size	MYR100 * KLCI
Tick Value	0.1 index point
Daily Limit	No limit
Deliverable Instrument	Cash settlement based on average price during the last 30 minutes of trading on the last trading day.
Last Trading Day	Last business day of the contract month
Exercise Day	European exercise – on the last trading day only
Real-time price data	Bloomberg: IKA <Cmdty> OMON

Table 8.6 Contract Specifications for KLOFFE Kuala Lumpur Composite Index Options (Proposed)

Fixed Income

Deposit Futures/Options/Futures Options

As indicated above, the MME was established to develop the market for local deposit and interest rate derivatives. The MME's first contract will be a cash-settled deposit future referencing 90-day KLIBOR, which is gradually emerging as Malaysia's benchmark short-term floating rate. KLIBOR futures are expected to be used by those seeking to take an outright view on short-term Malaysian rates or by those seeking to hedge short-term interest rate exposures generated from interest rate swaps or floating rate securities. The contract will be offered on a quarterly cycle up to three years in advance (though liquidity is likely to be concentrated only in the near month contracts). Table 8.7 contains details on the proposed KLIBOR future, which is expected to begin trading in early 1996.

Contract	**90-day Kuala Lumpur Interbank Offer Rate (KLIBOR) Futures**
Type	Domestic
Exchange	Malaysia Monetary Exchange
Months	March, June, September, December
Contract Size	MYR1 mln
Tick Value	0.01%
Daily Limit	N/A
Deliverable Instrument	Cash settlement through arithmetic mean of quotes from 20 banks (less five highest and five lowest) on last trading day
Last Trading Day	3rd Wednesday of the contract month, or 1st business day following the 3rd Wednesday if the latter is a holiday
Delivery Day	Same as the last trading day
Real-time price data	Reuters:<0#KLB:7

Table 8.7 Contract Specifications for MME 90-day KLIBOR Futures (Proposed)

MME has announced no plans regarding the introduction of KLIBOR options or futures options.

Interest Rate Futures/Options/Futures Options

MME's first medium-term interest rate futures contract will be based on five-year Malaysian Government Securities (MGS), the country's benchmark sovereign bond. The contract is designed as a cash-settled derivative based on an 8% coupon, five-year MGS. Use of the MGS contract will permit speculators to take a directional view on medium-term Malaysian interest rates; it will also permit hedgers to manage interest rate risk arising from government bond portfolios, corporate bond portfolios and interest rate swap portfolios. It is interesting to note that the Exchange has opted not to make the contract deliverable, primarily because supply of intermediate sector MGS is still limited; whether the MGS future will become deliverable in the medium term has yet to be determined. Table 8.8 below contains preliminary details on the proposed MGS future, which is expected to trade in mid-1996.

Contract	**Five-year Malaysian Government Securities Futures**
Type	Domestic
Exchange	Malaysia Monetary Exchange
Months	March, June, September, December
Contract Size	MYR200,000 face value of 8% coupon, five-year MGS
Tick Value	0.01%
Daily Limit	N/A
Deliverable Instrument	Cash settlement through arithmetic mean of randomly selected quotes from 12 of 23 primary dealers (less two highest and two lowest) on last trading day
Last Trading Day	3rd Wednesday of the contract month, or 1st business day following the 3rd Wednesday if the latter is a holiday
Delivery Day	Same as the last trading day
Real-time price data	To be determined

Table 8.8 Contract Specifications for MME Five-year Malaysian Government Securities Futures (Proposed)

MME has announced no plans regarding the introduction of MGS options or MGS futures options.

Currency

Currency Futures/Options/Futures Options

Malaysia features no listed currency futures or options at the present time. Although MME's mandate permits it to list and trade currency derivatives it has made no announcement regarding the introduction of such derivatives.

Commodity

Commodity Futures/Options/Futures Options

Malaysian commodity futures trading commenced in 1980 with the introduction of crude palm oil (CPO) futures on the KLCE. Following the initial success of the contract trading was expanded in 1982 to include the spot month plus the next five months. After strong trading in 1982 and 1983 volume receded in 1984 as a sharp sell-off in CPO kept many players on the sidelines; the inability by certain member brokers to meet higher margin requirements resulted in the closure of the KLCE for one week and the eventual introduction of new regulatory measures (discussed at greater length in the regulatory section below). Strong trading resumed following the reorganization of the KLCE and the passage of the Commodity Trading Act of 1985. To continue building momentum in the contract the KLCE made the CPO contract more flexible in the late 1980s and early 1990s by granting favourable margins for spreaders and accepting delivery of offshore CPO into the contract. Total turnover in CPO futures amounted to 358,177 contracts in 1993 and 569,482 contracts in 1994; average annual growth in turnover has been an impressive 87% since 1986 (RT, 4/95). Year-end open interest amounted to 9,584 contracts in 1993 and 8,110 contracts in 1994 (KLCE, 1995). According to Exchange officials, 70% of trades in 1994 were by speculators or traders on their own accounts; nearly 20% of turnover was from direct foreign trading. Table 8.9 highlights contract specifications for the KLCE's key CPO contract.

Contract	Crude Palm Oil Futures
Type	Domestic/Offshore
Exchange	Kuala Lumpur Commodity Exchange
Months	Spot month plus next five months, plus alternate months thereafter to 12 months
Contract Size	25 tons crude palm oil
Tick Value	MYR1.00/ton
Daily Limit	1st day MYR50/ton; 2nd day MYR75/ton; 3rd day MYR100/ton; 4th day no limit; 5th day MYR50/ton, and so on
Deliverable Grade	Physical settlement of crude palm oil at Port Kelang, or Butterworth. Oil of all origins tenderable.
Last Trading Day	15th of the contract month, or preceding business day
Delivery Day	1st business day to 20th business day of the contract month
Real-time price data	Bloomberg: KOA; Reuters: <0#KPO:>; Telerate: 19872, 25904-10

Table 8.9 Contract Specifications for KLCE Crude Palm Oil Futures

Success of CPO futures spurred the development of other oil-related futures on the KLCE, including palm kernel oil futures in 1988 and RBD palm olein futures in early 1990. Lack of activity in palm kernel oil futures caused the contract to be delisted in 1992, and to be reconstructed, renamed and relisted as crude palm kernel oil futures in October 1992; the future underwent a further change in August 1993 when the contract size was increased from 15 to 25 metric tons. Despite these changes, activity in the redesigned contract has remained negligible, with only 5,442 contracts traded in 1993 and 208 contracts traded in 1994; year-end open interest amounted to 74 contracts in 1993 and zero in 1994 (KLCE, 1995). Table 8.10 below contains contract details on crude palm kernel oil futures. In addition to lacklustre performance of the crude palm kernel oil contract, the RBD palm olein contract became inactive shortly after its introduction and was delisted in 1993.

While the focal point of the KLCE during the 1980s was primarily on edible oils, it also made advances in the development and listing of rubber, tin and cocoa futures. The Exchange's first rubber contract, on RSS1 (ribbed smoked sheet #1), was launched in late 1983. Three years later, it launched its second rubber contract, on SMR20 (Standard Malaysian Rubber #20). Though RSS1 and SMR20 were ini-

Contract	Crude Palm Kernel Oil Futures
Type	Domestic/Offshore
Exchange	Kuala Lumpur Commodity Exchange
Months	Spot month plus next five months, plus alternate months thereafter to 12 months
Contract Size	25 tons crude palm kernel oil
Tick Value	MYR1.00/ton
Daily Limit	+/– MYR70/ton against previous day's settlement price except current month. Limits expanded for non-current month contracts when at limit: 1st day MYR70/ton; 2nd day MYR100/ton; 3rd day MYR130/ton; 4th day no limit; 5th day MYR70/ton, and so on
Deliverable Grade	Physical settlement of crude palm kernel oil (free fatty acids) delivered into port tank installations at Butterworth, Port Klang or Pasir Gudang. Kernel oil of all origins tenderable.
Last Trading Day	15th of the contract month, or preceding business day
Delivery Day	1st business day to 20th business day of the contract month
Real-time price data	Reuters: <0#KPK:>; Telerate: 25904-11

Table 8.10 Contract Specifications for KLCE Crude Palm Kernel Oil Futures

tially quite successful, volume soon dwindled as global rubber prices stabilized in the early 1990s and the need for hedging disappeared. In recent years Malaysian contracts have received significant competition from RSS1, RSS3, TSR20 (Technically Specified Rubber #20) and SIR (Standard Indonesian Rubber) contracts listed on the KRE, TOCOM, SICOM and ICEB; KLCE recorded no turnover or open interest in RSS1 or SMR20 futures in 1993 or 1994. Despite the lack of activity, the Exchange has announced no plans regarding restructuring or delisting of either rubber contract. Tables 8.11 and 8.12 highlight details on the KLCE's rubber contracts.

The KLCE's tin and cocoa futures, which are both physical settlement contracts accepting offshore deliverables, were introduced in 1988. The tin contract has historically achieved only modest trading volume; the future traded 14,231 contracts in 1993 but registered no turnover or open interest in 1994. Activity in the cocoa contract has been negligible as well, with total turnover of just 156 contracts in 1993 and with no turnover or open interest in 1994 (KLCE, 1995). As with rubber futures, the Exchange has announced no plans regarding delisting or restructuring of either contract. Tables 8.13 and 8.14 highlight contract details on tin futures and cocoa futures.

Contract	**RSS1 Rubber Futures**
Type	Domestic/Offshore
Exchange	Kuala Lumpur Commodity Exchange
Months	Three consecutive months plus two quarter months
Contract Size	10 tons
Tick Value	MYR0.025/kg
Daily Limit	+/– MYR0.10/kg against previous day's settlement price except current month. If trading is at limit, there is a 15 minute halt, followed by resumption of trading within a new MYR0.10/kg band
Deliverable Grade	Physical settlement of RSS1 rubber (ribbed smoked sheet #1) specified by International Rubber Quality and Packaging standards, at Penang or Port Kelang
Last Trading Day	15th day of the contract month, or next business day if 15th is not a business day
Delivery Day	Last business day of the month preceding the contract month to 2nd business day of the contract month
Real-time price data	Telerate: 19878-81

Table 8.11 Contract Specifications for KLCE RSS1 Rubber Futures

Contract	SMR20 Rubber Futures
Type	Domestic
Exchange	Kuala Lumpur Commodity Exchange
Months	Three consecutive months plus two quarter months
Contract Size	20 tons for single contract months, 60 tons for quarter months
Tick Value	MYR0.025/kg
Daily Limit	+/– MYR0.10/kg against previous day's settlement price except current month. If trading is at limit, there is a 15 minute halt, followed by resumption of trading within a new MYR0.10/kg band
Deliverable Grade	Cash settlement or physical settlement of SMR20 rubber (Standard Malaysian Rubber #20) specified by Rubber Research Institute of Malaysia's latest technical specifications, at Penang, Port Kelang or Singapore
Last Trading Day	15th day of the contract month, or next business day if the 15th is not a business day
Delivery Day	Last business day of the month preceding the contract month to 2nd business day of the contract month
Real-time price data	Reuters: <0#KRU:>; Telerate: 19878-81

Table 8.12 Contract Specifications for KLCE SMR20 Rubber Futures

Contract	Tin Futures
Type	Domestic/Offshore
Exchange	Kuala Lumpur Commodity Exchange
Months	Spot month and next three months, plus alternate months to 12 months forward
Contract Size	Five tons
Tick Value	US$25/contract
Daily Limit	+/– US$250/ton against previous day's settlement price except current month. If trading occurs at limit for three consecutive days, limits will be removed on the 4th day
Deliverable Grade	Physical settlement of KLCE-approved refined tin (brand names Banka, DKS, Mentok, MSC, Thaisarco, Koba, Bera do Brasil, Monsa), 99.85% pure, at Exchange approved warehouses in Penang, Singapore or Rotterdam
Last Trading Day	Business day immediately preceding the last two business days of the contract month
Delivery Day	First business day to last business day of the contract month
Real-time price data	Reuters: <0#TIN:>; Telerate: 25904-11

Table 8.13 Contract Specifications for KLCE Tin Futures

Contract	Cocoa Futures
Type	Domestic/Offshore
Exchange	Kuala Lumpur Commodity Exchange
Months	January, March, May, July, September, November, December
Contract Size	Ten tons
Tick Value	US$10/contract
Daily Limit	+/– US$80/ton against previous day's settlement price except for current month. Limits expanded for non-current month contracts when at limit: 1st day US$80/ton; 2nd day US$100/ton; 3rd day US$120/ton; 4th day no limit; 5th day US$80/ton, and so on
Deliverable Grade	Physical settlement of Group A (Malaysia, Papua New Guinea) cocoa at par or Group B (Indonesia, Thailand, Philippines), cocoa at US$45/ton discount with a bean count of 140 per 100 grams. Delivery at KLCE approved warehouses at Tawau, Pasir Gudang, Johore Baru, Port Kelang
Last Trading Day	20th day of the contract month, or preceding day if a holiday
Delivery Day	1st business day to last business day of the contract month
Real-time price data	Reuters: <0#KCO:>; Telerate: 19882

Table 8.14 Contract Specifications for KLCE Cocoa Futures

It should be noted that the KLCE is in the process of designing CPO futures options, though a specific launch date has not yet been determined. Under exchange proposals, puts and calls on CPO futures will trade in 25 ton lots (e.g one underlying CPO future), with strike prices set at intervals of MYR25/ton. The minimum price fluctuation will be MYR0.50/ton, and the maximum daily price limit will be MYR50/ton. Proposed contract months include the first six months of the calendar year; the last trading day will be five business days before the first tender day of the CPO futures contract. The KLCE has no other commodity options or futures options under consideration at present.

LISTED/OVER-THE-COUNTER WARRANTS, CONVERTIBLES AND HYBRIDS

Equity

Equity Warrants

The listed equity warrant market in Malaysia is divided into three categories, including listed transferable subscription rights (TSRs), listed covered equity warrants and OTC covered equity warrants. TSRs and offshore covered warrants have been in existence for several years, while listed covered equity warrants are relatively new, having been approved by regulators in December 1994 and introduced to the market in May 1995.

TSRs are long-term warrants, with maturities ranging from one to five years, issued by corporations on their own equity; exercise of a TSR results in the issuance of new equity by the corporation. TSRs, which are denominated in ringgit and structured as American exercise instruments, are most often attached to local bond issues, and are then be stripped and traded separately through the KLSE; liquidity in many TSRs, particularly those of blue-chip companies, is good. As of June 1995 there were 64 TSRs listed on, and traded through, the KLSE; Appendix II contains details on all warrants in existence as of mid-1995.

Listed covered equity warrants are new to the Malaysian market. Covered warrants are issued by third-party financial institutions on the stock of Malaysian corporations; if exercise of the warrant occurs shares are re-allocated from the seller to the buyer of the warrant, but no new equity is issued by the corporation. Covered equity warrants are American exercise derivatives denominated in ringgit and issued with final maturities of one to two years; all issues are listed on, and traded through, the KLSE. Regulators amended regulations in December 1994 to permit issuance of third-party equity warrants, and the first transaction was executed by Merrill Lynch and CIMB in May 1995, on Malaysian Banking shares. A second transaction followed by Fleming and Arab-Malaysia Bank in August 1995, on Renong shares; futures issues are expected.

Offshore covered Malaysian equity warrants have been floated by foreign financial institutions for a number of years. Like the listed covered warrants described immediately above, offshore covered warrants result in the re-allocation of shares from the seller to the buyer of the warrant upon exercise. Offshore warrants, which are denominated in foreign currencies, are either unlisted or listed on overseas exchanges, and traded OTC; issues may be structured with European or American exercise and carry maturities ranging from one to three years. Offshore warrants have been floated by foreign financial institutions on numerous Malaysian blue-chip stocks, including Magnum, Genting, Sime Darby, Malaysian Banking, Berjaya and others.

Basket/Index Warrants

Although the local market does not feature listed basket or index warrants, offshore OTC warrants based on baskets of Malaysian stocks and key Malaysian equity indexes are floated with frequency by foreign financial institutions. Such transactions are either unlisted or listed on offshore exchanges and are traded on an OTC basis. Most warrants carry short or intermediate maturities of one to three years and are denominated in foreign currencies. Representative index warrants include Paribas' US dollar quanto index call warrants on the KLCI (1993), Credit Suisse's Swiss franc index call warrants on the KLCI (1993), Barings' US dollar index call warrants and capped call warrants on the KL Index (1994), Nomura's US dollar index call warrants on the NRI-AP Malaysian Index (1993), Lehman Brothers' US dollar index call warrants on the KLSE Index (1995), Citibank's US dollar index call warrants on the Citibank Malaysian Index (1995), and Union Bank of Switzerland's US dollar index put and call warrants on the KL 50 Index (1995). Representative basket warrants include JP Morgan's US dollar basket call warrants on a group of ten Malaysian stocks (1994), Société Générale's US dollar Malaysian basket call warrants (1993), Swiss Bank Corporation's US dollar Malaysian basket call warrants (1994), and Merrill Lynch's US dollar Sarawak basket call warrants (1995).

Convertibles

The Malaysian market features modest issuance of domestic convertible bonds, known locally as convertible unsecured loan stocks (CULS) or redeemable convertible unsecured notes (RCUN). CULS are standard unsecured convertible bonds which pay a fixed coupon and can be converted into the issuer's shares at a preset price; RCUNs are identical to CULS except investors retain the option of receiving principal (par value) rather than converting into stock. The first issues of domestic convertible securities date back to 1988, when a total of MYR36 mln (US$14 mln) was floated. Although issuance reached an impressive MYR921 mln (US$370 mln) in 1991, new flotations decreased dramatically between 1992 and 1994, primarily as issuers turned to the more popular conventional bond market. CULS and RCUN issues floated in the local market are generally listed on the KLSE, though they may trade either through the Exchange or in the OTC market. Maturities of local convertibles extend from three to seven years; coupons range from 4% to 8% while initial conversion premiums range from 10% to 14%.

Malaysian companies have been increasingly active issuers of offshore Eurodollar convertibles in recent years. The country's inaugural Eurodollar convertible was floated in 1991 by the Malaysian government (with conversion into shares of the newly privatized STM telecommunications company). The US$190 mln issue was followed by a US$230 mln bond floated by United Engineers in 1994, along with public and private US dollar deals for TRI in the same year. Total outstanding issues floated in 1994 amounted to US$1.33 bln, making Malaysia the fourth most active Euroconvertible issuer for the year (after Japan, Taiwan and

Thailand). Eurodollar convertibles floated by Malaysian companies are generally listed on offshore exchanges and traded on an OTC basis. Issues typically have low coupons (1.5% to 4.5%), intermediate conversion premiums (5% to 8%) and long maturities (ten years). Appendix III contains details on Malaysian domestic and offshore convertible bond issues.

Index-linked Notes

Malaysian index-linked notes have not been floated with frequency in either the domestic or offshore markets. Notes which are issued generally take the form of index-linked CDs or bonds which provide investors with enhanced coupons or enhanced principal redemption based on the upside of a broad Malaysian market indicator, such as the KLCI, or smaller baskets of stocks (and occasionally single stocks). Such securities tend to be unlisted or, in certain cases, listed on offshore exchanges; since many issues are structured as private placements there is little secondary trading. While most notes are structured to provide investors with an embedded long call, certain notes carry long puts (providing enhanced returns based on index depreciation) or short puts (providing investors with enhanced returns when the market rises but paying lower principal if the market declines).

Fixed Income

Fixed Income Warrants

The local and offshore markets feature no listed or OTC fixed income warrants at the present time; this is due primarily to low investor demand for such derivatives.

Currency

Currency Warrants

Malaysia features no listed or OTC currency warrants at the present time. Institutions in the offshore market float occasional warrants pegged to the value of the ringgit, though such issues are still comparatively rare. Offshore ringgit warrants are either listed on overseas exchanges or remain unlisted, and trade strictly on an OTC basis; most issues are short- to intermediate-term in maturity (e.g. six months to two years).

Commodity

The domestic and offshore markets feature no listed or OTC commodity warrants based on Malaysian commodities.

OVER-THE-COUNTER FORWARDS, SWAPS AND OPTIONS

Equity

Equity Forwards/Swaps

The market for Malaysian OTC equity forwards and swaps is limited at the present time. Although offshore counterparties occasionally structure short-to medium-term forwards referencing Malaysian equities, actual equity swaps (e.g. transactions which exchange floating rate premium for appreciation (or depreciation) in the value of a single local equity) are rare. More common are basket and index options, as well as outright index swaps, described immediately following.

Equity Options

While the market for listed equity options is not yet operational (but will commence trading in 1996 via KLOFFE), the market for OTC equity options has become popular with both domestic and offshore institutions. Foreign institutions routinely buy and sell puts and calls on Malaysian stocks (particularly larger capitalization blue-chips), tailoring parameters such as strike, maturity, notional and underlying equity to match the specific requirements of clients. Though any type of option can be structured in the OTC market, the most common transactions are six-month to two-year, American or European options, exercisable into cash settlement. As with all OTC structures, secondary liquidity in OTC equity options is negligible given the customized nature of the transactions; options most often expire unexercised (if out-of-the-money), exercised into cash or equity (if in-the-money), or closed out with the arranging bank. Resales to third parties are exceptionally rare.

Basket/Index Forwards/Swaps

Certain offshore institutions offer OTC index forwards and swaps, where clients exchange a floating rate flow (KLIBOR or perhaps US$ LIBOR) for appreciation (or depreciation) in a local index, such as the KLCI. These index derivatives are equivalent to investors purchasing long-dated calls (or puts) on the KLCI, and paying option premium through the floating rate stream; typical maturities range from six-months to three-years. Basket forwards and swaps pegged to groups of Malaysian stocks (e.g. resort companies, financial institutions, property companies, and so on) are also available.

Recent introduction of KLOFFE index futures is likely to both challenge and benefit the OTC index forward/swap market. From the investors' point of view futures will be able to duplicate, at a cheaper cost and more efficiently, many of the payoff profiles currently available through the OTC market; futures are therefore likely to compete with OTC structures for market share. From the dealers' perspective, introduction of index futures will make management of risk positions simpler, as they will be able to turn to the listed market for hedging, rather than attempting to arrange time-consuming (and often expensive) offsetting swaps/forwards to keep market risks in balance; such should increase dealers' ability to structure transactions.

Basket/Index Options

Since KLOFFE has not yet introduced listed index options (but will do so in 1996) the market for offshore OTC index options has been quite active. Investors, eager to gain or hedge exposure on the KLCI, have been able to do so in an effective fashion through the purchase or sale of OTC index options. Intermediaries wanting to hedge elements of market risk in their overall option portfolios have also been active participants in the market. Most index options written are vanilla in nature (e.g. three- to 12-month European or American derivatives exercisable into cash settlement), though a certain amount of specialized exotic options (e.g. barriers, outperformances, Asians) are also available. Basket options, combining groups of Malaysian stocks into a single basket, have also been popular with investors, particularly since they can be customized to include any group of reference stocks. The introduction of KLCI index futures should strengthen the OTC market by providing dealers with alternate risk management instruments (e.g. for directional risks). Future introduction of listed index options on KLOFFE may present more of a competitive challenge for the OTC market (but will also provide alternate means of hedging volatility and gamma risks).

Fixed Income

Fixed Income Forwards/Swaps

Malaysia's domestic fixed income derivative market is gradually expanding in size. The market is still impacted by the absence of an established floating rate benchmark but it now features a reasonably robust government yield curve (which provides the market with important pricing references) and a sufficiently active domestic money and bond market (which provides swap dealers with hedging instruments).

Malaysian FRAs, which reference either KLIBOR (for onshore transactions) or the interest rates implied by FX forwards (for offshore transactions), are liquid to six months and are offered in various standard combinations of one, three, and six months; FRAs to three years are also executed on occasion but are far less liquid. Typical dealing size in FRAs is MYR12.5 mln to MYR25 mln (US$5 mln to US$10 mln) and the market is dominated by interbank players.

Malaysian interest rate swap activity is developing rather rapidly. The ringgit IRS market benefits from reasonable two-way flows as well as a comprehensive and increasingly liquid fixed income market (which makes hedging of swap positions manageable). The market remains somewhat fragmented, however, as it continues to distinguish between onshore and offshore swaps. Given restrictions which have existed regarding foreign access to the onshore market, international institutions have not always been permitted to buy and sell KLIBOR-based instruments (and to therefore use KLIBOR references to price swaps); in addition, though KLIBOR is emerging as the country's main floating rate benchmark, it has not been universally adopted by all participants. To overcome these difficulties, the Singapore-based ringgit swap offer rate (SOR) has developed as an alternate offshore floating benchmark (note that it is also used in other Southeast Asian swap markets, i.e. Thailand, Indonesia and Singapore). Ringgit SOR is the rate derived from borrowing US dollars and converting into ringgit of identical maturity through forward FX; SOR uses the offer side of the FX swap rate to swap from dollars to ringgit. Use of SOR, which is quoted in maturities of one, three, six and 12 months, makes it simpler for offshore counterparties to price swaps and manage cash rolls. Although restrictions impacting offshore institutions have disappeared for the present, local ringgit interest rate swaps are still quoted in two forms: onshore swaps are quoted as fixed ringgit (semi-annual, on an Actual/365-day basis) against three-month KLIBOR (set on Reuters page KLIA, which represents the daily average of quotes from 20 banks); offshore swaps are quoted as fixed ringgit (semi-annual, on an Actual/365-day basis) against ringgit SOR (set on Telerate page 44178, which represents the daily average of spot and forward point quotes from Singapore-based banks).

Most IRS activity (whether onshore or offshore) is centred in the short end of the curve, where two- and three-year transactions are quite common; swaps in the long end (seven to ten years) are driven solely by structured deals. Average volume in the IRS market is two to three deals per week, with deal size ranging from MYR12.5 mln to MYR75 mln (US$5 mln to US$30 mln). Bid-offer spreads range from 10 basis points in the one- and two-year sector to 30 basis points in five years and 30–40 basis points in seven years; the relative immaturity of the market combined with volatility in domestic rates causes spreads to widen on occasion. Figure 8.4 illustrates a representative ringgit IRS curve from mid-1995 (fixed ringgit against six month ringgit SOR).

Though two-way flow is increasingly evident in ringgit swaps the market is occasionally skewed towards liability transactions. This is less problematic in Malaysia than other Southeast Asian nations because the fixed income market is sufficiently developed to give dealers cost effective hedging alternatives through CDs, bills and MGS; the new KLIBOR and MGS futures contracts to be launched on MME will provide dealers with even more alternatives in the near future. The ability to hedge allows dealers to position swaps without immediately having to lay risk off through back-to-back swaps. Note that as in any hedging exercise, use of cash or futures removes directional interest rate risk but not spread or basis risk.

Fixed Income Options

The local fixed income option market, based on caps/floors, swaptions and bond options, remains rather underdeveloped as the present time. Caps and floors represent the most developed segment of the ringgit fixed income option market.

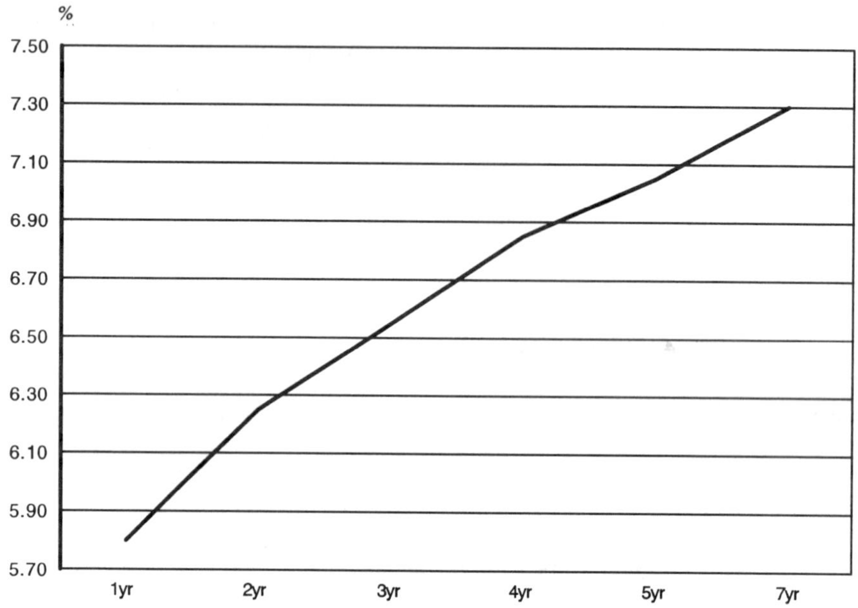

Source: Reuters

Figure 8.4 Representative Ringgit IRS Curve

Domestic caps and floors are quoted to three years and are structured to reference either KLIBOR (for onshore transactions) or the rates implied by FX forwards (for offshore transactions). Despite the presence of such options, the market is often one-sided; the lack of two-way flow means dealers are forced to charge higher prices for the options and assume greater risk on their books. Note that no standard interbank dealing size has yet developed, and bid-offer spreads (quoted in volatility terms) remain rather wide. While ringgit caps and floors are developing, the same is not yet true for ringgit bond options or swaptions. Though issuance of MGS is substantial (i.e. US$27 bln), a market for MGS bond options has not yet developed; it may be some time before investor demand for such derivatives becomes evident. The swaption market is very thinly traded at the present time, primarily because the cost of executing transactions is still very high; that has kept many institutions from participating in this segment of the market. Until more liquidity is evident in vanilla ringgit swaps and forwards it is likely that activity in ringgit interest rate options will remain subdued.

Currency

Currency Forwards/Swaps

The Malaysian currency forward market is growing in size and scope. Like the spot market, the forward market is divided into onshore and offshore segments: the onshore market displays fair liquidity to six months and features average dealing size of MYR10 mln (US$4 mln); the offshore market is liquid to six months (though quotes can be obtained to three years), and features average dealing size of MYR10 mln (US$4 mln) as well. As with spot trading, forward trading is most liquid offshore, though removal of onshore/offshore FX swap restrictions may act to shift volume to the onshore market over time. Figure 8.5 illustrates the historical movement of three- and 12-month MYR/US$ forwards.

Turnover in cross currency swaps is gradually increasing as domestic institutions funding in the international capital markets swap back to ringgit, local companies with foreign exchange receipts bring such flows back into ringgit and international firms with ringgit receipts swap into home currencies; there is also a growing amount of CCS activity related to onshore and offshore investments. Quoting convention for currency swaps is fixed ringgit (semi-annual, on an Actual/365-day basis) against six-month US$ LIBOR flat. Transactions are executed out to

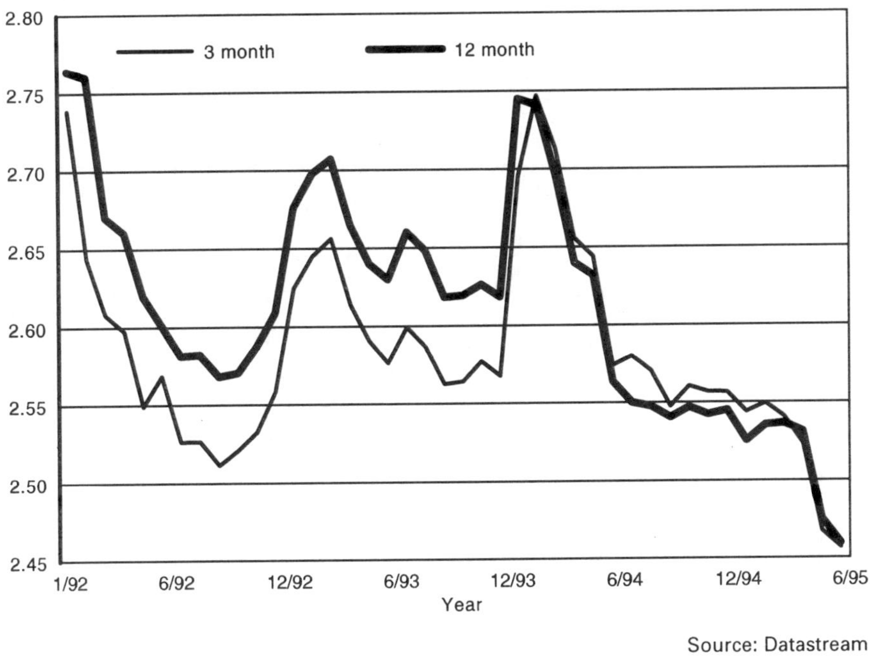

Figure 8.5 Historical Movement of Three- and 12-month MYR/US$ Forwards

approximately five years; there is virtually no activity beyond five years, unless structured against specific assets, liabilities or anticipated currency receipts. Typical deal size is MYR12 mln to MYR25 mln (US$5 mln to US$10 mln), though swaps related to large investment or funding transactions can result in larger dealing size. Given the relative illiquidity of the market and the volatility of the currency, it is not unusual to see ringgit CCS bid-offer spreads in excess of 15–20 basis points; by way of comparison, JPY/US$ CCSs, representing the most liquid CCSs in Asia Pacific, generally display bid-offer spreads of 7–8 basis points throughout the curve. Figures 8.6 and 8.7 illustrate the historical movement of MYR/US$ swap curves and two-, three- and five-year benchmark CCS rates. Table 8.15 contains indicative bid-offer spreads on MYR/US$ CCSs out to five years.

Maturity	Bid-Offer Spread
1 year	15–20 bps
2 years	15–20 bps
3 years	15–20 bps
4 years	20 bps
5 years	20 bps

Table 8.15 MYR/US$ CCS Bid-Offer Spreads

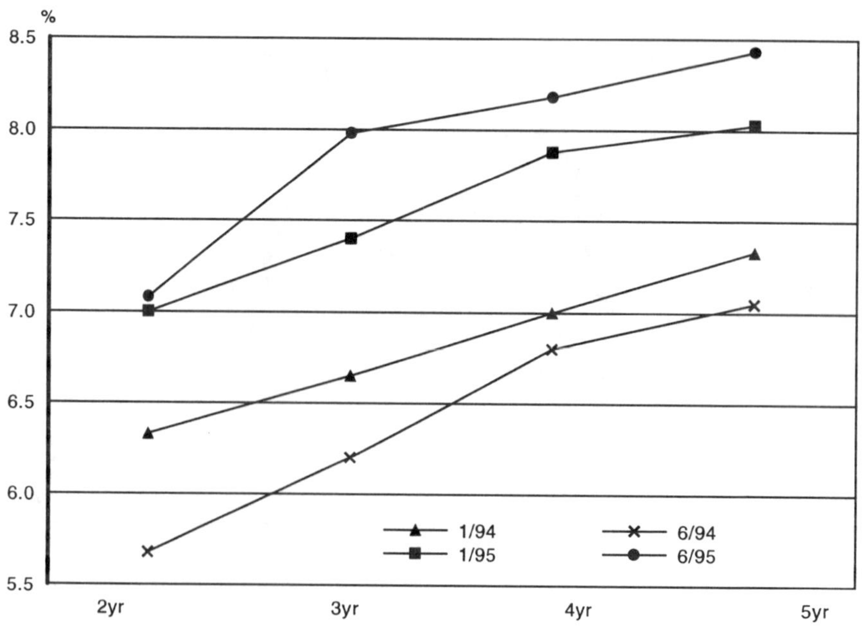

Figure 8.6 Historical Movement of MYR/US$ CCS Curves

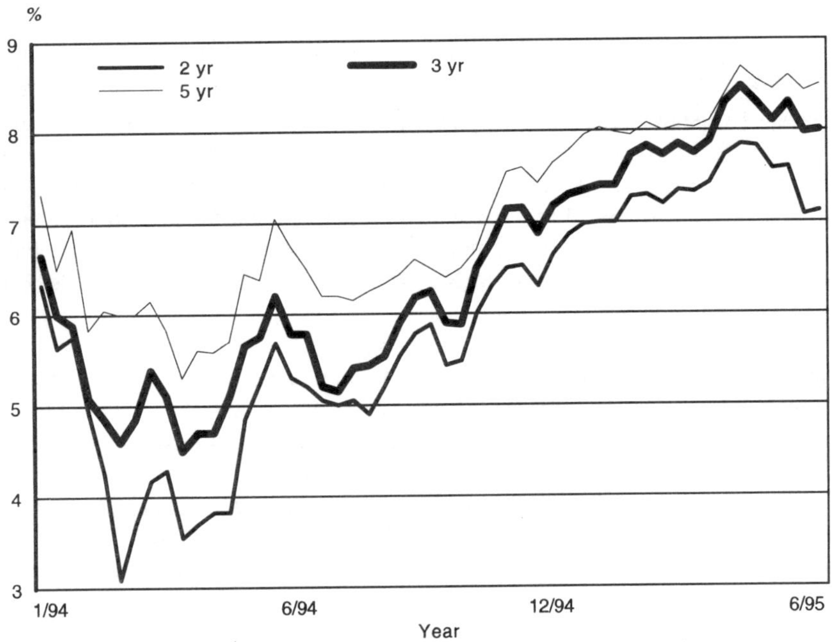

Figure 8.7 Historical Movement of MYR/US$ Two-, Three- and Five-year Swap Rates

Currency Options

The market for ringgit FX options is still modest in size, though it is growing in volume and lengthening in tenor. The most liquid segment of the market is concentrated in three- and six-month deals, through quotes to 12 months are readily available. Transactions are typically structured as vanilla European or American derivatives, struck at-the-money spot or forward; standard dealing size is MYR12 mln to MYR25 mln (US$5 mln to US$10 mln). Volatility quotes range from four points for one-month options to five points for six-month options and six points for 12-month options; bid-offer spreads range from one to two volatility points, depending on maturity and market conditions. Most dealing tends to be concentrated among major domestic and offshore financial institutions; corporate activity is still negligible. Virtually all business occurs in MYR/US$ options, though there is a small amount of activity in MYR/SGD and MYR/JPY options as well. Ringgit exotics (e.g. barriers, Asians, digitals) are evident in the market, but overall activity is still extremely limited.

Commodity

Commodity Forwards/Swaps

Malaysia is a significant producer and exporter of rubber, crude palm oil, crude palm kernel oil, cocoa and tin (as described above) and features a significant amount of OTC forward trading in all commodities. OTC contracts are bought and sold to six months forward and are quoted on both a domestic and offshore basis (f.o.b., free on board); trading results in physical delivery or acceptance of the underlying commodity. The most active trading occurs in SMR, RSS, crude palm oil, RBD palm olein and RBD palm stearin.

In addition to soft commodities, there is also an active offshore forward and swap market for Tapis, Malaysia's primary grade of crude oil, which has emerged as a regional benchmark for energy traders. Tapis is a light, sweet crude oil which is routinely bought and sold on a physical basis to two months forward. In addition, it is often used as a reference in regional OTC commodity swap transactions (e.g. fixed crude oil against floating crude oil, based on the average monthly price of Tapis over a pre-determined period), known as 'paper' swaps. Despite the fact that Tapis originates in Malaysia the domestic market is not a significant trading location for the crude; virtually all spot, forward and swap trading of Tapis (and other energy products) occurs through the Singapore energy market, which is discussed at greater length in chapter 11 (note that a much smaller amount of forward and swap trading in energy products, including Tapis, occurs in the Japanese market).

Commodity Options

OTC commodity options based on Malaysian commodity prices or indicators are not presently available in the domestic market; crude oil options referencing the local/regional Tapis grade are executed strictly through the Singapore market.

LOCAL REGULATORY/LEGAL TREATMENT OF DERIVATIVES

The main regulators of the Malaysian financial system are Bank Negara Malaysia (BNM) (the central bank) and the Securities Commission (SC). BNM is responsible for regulating financial institutions and their activities, while the SC, established in 1993 under the Securities Commission Act, is responsible for regulating the issuance of securities, designing and developing financial futures (though not commodity futures), supervising the activities of all exchanges (KLSE, KLCE, MME, KLOFFE) and clearinghouses (MFCC, MDCH), and ensuring the safety of members dealing in securities and futures. The SC reports directly to the Ministry of Finance (MOF) and advises the MOF on all matters related to securities and futures. It should be noted that under the present regulatory structure matters related to commodity futures contracts themselves fall under the regulatory jurisdiction of the Ministry of Primary Industry and the Commodity Trading Act (CTA) of 1985. The primary legislation regulating listed derivatives is contained in the CTAs of 1980 and 1985, and the Futures Industry Act (FIA) of 1993.

The regulatory treatment of Malaysian derivatives dates back to 1980, when creation of the KLCE was accompanied by regulatory control through the CTA of 1980. The CTA was designed to provide appropriate control over commodity trading within Malaysia, and did so through the Commodity Trading Council (CTC). The CTC was initially responsible for supervising the KLCE, advising the Ministry of Primary Industries on all matters related to the Exchange, contracts and commodity trading, safeguarding the interests of both the Exchange and member brokers, and ensuring that all contracts were properly cleared and guaranteed by the KL Commodity Clearing House. As indicated above, the sharp sell-off in crude palm oil futures in 1984, and the subsequent increase in margins by the clearing-house, left several member brokers unable to meet margin calls; the KLCE itself suspended trading for one week in order to review the nature and source of difficulties. A committee was created to study the fundamental problems of the Exchange and the end result was new regulation set forth in the CTA of 1985. The CTA of 1985 created a new supervisory body, also known as the Commodity Trading Council, which had very broad powers in emergency situations. It also created a new clearinghouse, the MFCC, which imposed much stricter membership requirements; small, financially impaired, brokers (such as those unable to meet calls in 1984), were effectively prevented from joining the Exchange.

In 1993, the FIA was enacted to provide specific support for the regulation of financial futures and options traded on exchanges other than the KLCE. Under the FIA, the SC is empowered to regulate financial futures exchanges and clearing-houses, license brokers and advisers acting through such exchanges, establish a code of conduct for members and impose penalties or disciplinary action for infractions. Regulation of the MME and KLOFFE falls under the terms of the FIA.

In line with the general tone of the CTA, the MME recently announced that in creating the new fixed income futures exchange it would strive to keep membership very low. It is the MME's intent to limit membership to only 15 broker members for the first five years of the Exchange's life; the MME wants to restrain broker membership while the market is still small and will only expand membership once trading volumes reach certain critical levels. It should be noted that the MME does not intend to constrain membership levels of non-broker members, under the assumption that non-brokers will be true corporate hedgers interested in participating in the market on their own account, primarily for hedging purposes.

There are presently no specific regulations governing Malaysian OTC derivatives, simply a series of guidelines the BNM expects domestic and foreign institutions operating in Malaysia to follow. In 1995 BNM released general OTC guidelines, which included the following: BNM must approve all onshore derivatives trades – such derivatives should be used for hedging, not speculating; local banks will only be permitted to market derivatives to customers with underlying commercial interests to hedge (such will make it easy to establish approvals for IRSs and CCSs, but more difficult for equity-linked structures); banks and corporations will be required to put forth evidence that the boards of both institutions are aware of derivative obligations and the liabilities which could be incurred; and, banks and other financial institutions involved in derivatives should be required to meet minimum standards with regard to risk management practices, public disclosure of derivatives risks, and capital adequacy.

LOCAL ACCOUNTING PRACTICES FOR DERIVATIVES

Local accounting treatment of OTC derivatives has not been firmly established to date; the Malaysian regulators, accounting authorities and Inland Revenue Department have not yet created mandatory guidelines for the accounting (or tax) treatment of instruments such as forwards, swaps and options. Nonetheless, a series of voluntary guidelines are generally utilized by major local participants (e.g. banks and merchant banks) to account for derivative exposures. Gains or losses arising from interest rate swaps used as legitimate hedges are recognized over the life of the swap as interest income or interest expense in the income statement. Gains or losses arising from interest rate futures, forwards or options used as legitimate hedges are deferred and amortized over the life of the underlying hedge positions as adjustments to interest income or interest expense in the income statement. If an institution employs interest rate derivatives of any type to speculate, positions are marked-to-market with resulting gains or losses posted as income/losses in the securities dealing account in the current income statement. In the case of currency derivatives, outstanding positions are valued at relevant forward rates on balance sheet date, with gains or losses reported in the year they are recognized.

PROSPECTS FOR THE LOCAL DERIVATIVES MARKET

Summarized below are the near-term (one- to three-year) and medium-term (three- to five-year) prospects for Malaysian domestic derivatives.

Near-term:

- Introduction of financial futures via MME (KLIBOR futures, MGS futures).
- Introduction of financial futures/options via KLOFFE (i.e. index options and equity options).
- Introduction of CPO futures options on KLCE.
- Potential abandonment or restructuring of commodity futures which have exhibited no turnover for several years (e.g. KLCE rubber, tin, cocoa); this is

particularly likely as other regional exchanges increase their own market shares in the same futures (e.g. SICOM and TOCOM in rubber futures).

- Expansion of onshore IRSs as KLIBOR becomes a more established and accessible short-term floating rate benchmark, domestic fund-raising increases and the yield curve strengthens.
- Growth in the covered warrants and TSRs as the equity market continues to expand and local companies continue to raise equity capital.
- Additional activity in ringgit currency derivatives (forwards, CCSs, options) as the currency becomes completely liberalized and hedging and funding opportunities continue to expand.
- Expansion of OTC equity derivatives as the introduction of KLCI futures (and options, at a later date) makes risk management of OTC books simpler and local institutions demand more specific risk/return profiles.
- Further issuance of domestic and offshore convertibles as the equity market expands, domestic companies require additional sources of financing and investors are drawn to the securities.

Medium-term:

- Introduction of a deliverable MGS futures contract as intermediate bond supply builds.
- Creation of meaningful fixed income options activity as ringgit swaps and forwards deepen, the fixed income market expands and pricing becomes more efficient.
- Further maturing of vanilla ringgit IRSs and CCSs (to the point where bid-offer spreads are narrow and stable), as hedging becomes simpler, the yield curve becomes more robust and financing/hedging opportunities remain buoyant.

Exchange	Contract	1993 Volume (contracts)	1994 Volume (contracts)
KLCE	Crude palm oil futures	358,117	569,482
	Crude palm kernel oil futures	5,442#	208#
	RSS1 rubber futures	0	0
	SMR20 rubber futures	0	0
	Tin futures	0	0
	Cocoa futures	156	0
KLOFFE	Equity options	n/l*	n/l*
	Index futures	n/l*	n/l*
	Index options	n/l*	n/l*
MME	90-day KLIBOR futures	n/l*	n/l*
	5-year MGS futures	n/l*	n/l*

* n/l: contract not yet listed; # contract size increased from 15 metric tons to 25 metric tons in August 1993

Table 8.16 Summary of 1993/1994 Listed Futures and Options Turnover

	Overall Liquidity	Liquid/ Maximum Maturity	Interbank dealing size	Average bid-offer spread
Equity/Index Swaps	fair	6–12 mos/3 yrs	n/a	n/a
Equity/Index Options	fair	6–12 mos/3 yrs	n/a	n/a
Interest Rate Swaps	fair	2–3 yrs/10 yrs	US$5–US$30mln	10–30 bps
Interest Rate Options	poor	3–6 mos/12 mos	none	varies
Currency Swaps	fair	2–3 yrs/7 yrs	US$5–US$10mln	15–20 bps
Currency Options	fair	3–6 mos/12 mos	US$5–US$10mln	1–2 pts

Table 8.17 Summary of Domestic OTC Derivatives

9: New Zealand

FINANCIAL MARKET OVERVIEW

New Zealand's financial market is advanced and comprehensive, though small in size and often thin in liquidity. The country features well established equity, fixed income and currency markets, though activity tends to be concentrated primarily in a small group of benchmark securities and instruments (i.e. the top ten domestic equities, three- and ten-year New Zealand Government Bonds, and US$/NZ$ and A$/NZ$ currency rates). The country's domestic derivative market mirrors the cash market: the range of local derivative instruments is broad but liquidity in certain listed/OTC contracts tends to be thin.

The New Zealand stock market traces its origins to the 1870s, when informal equity trading began in Auckland, Thames, Dunedin and Reefton. The Auckland Shareholders' Association was formed in 1872 to provide general rules regarding trading of shares, and in 1897 the Auckland Stock Exchange (ASE) was established as the country's first formal stock exchange. The ASE was re-organized as the Stock Exchange Association of New Zealand (SEANZ) in 1915, and operated as the country's first national exchange for 70 years before being converted into the New Zealand Stock Exchange (NZSE); the NZSE is the country's sole equity exchange at the present time. As with other segments of the local financial market, the domestic equity market is well established but small. It features good liquidity among the dozen leading blue-chip stocks but little liquidity in smaller, or second tier, stocks; with more than 200 companies listed on the NZSE, trading activity in a large proportion of issues remains very thin. Overall 1994 market capitalization of US$27.2 bln is small on an absolute basis, though sizeable on a per capita basis; New Zealand's equity market is the smallest of the 13 Asia Pacific markets discussed in this text. Figure 9.1 below traces the historical movement of the New Zealand Stock Exchange 40 Capital Share Price Index (NZSE 40, formerly known as the Barclays Index); note that the NZSE 40 is being replaced by the NZSE 10 (an index comprised of New Zealand's ten most liquid blue-chip stocks) as the country's primary market index; the change in indexes has already resulted in the creation of new listed and OTC equity derivatives, as discussed below. Table 9.1 provides information on key equity market indicators.

Note that foreign investors have unrestricted access to domestic shares, though foreign investment in excess of 25% of a domestic company's outstanding shares requires approval from the Overseas Investment Commission.

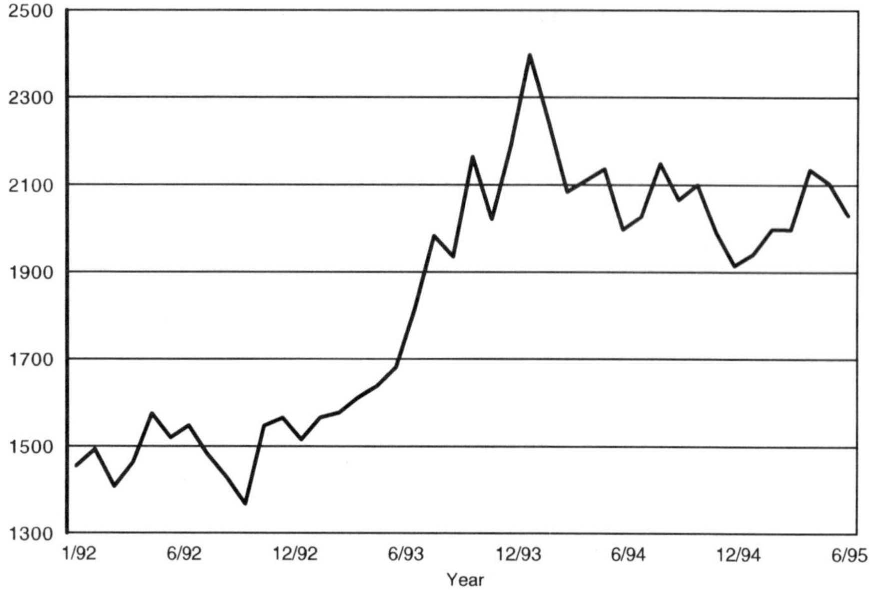

Figure 9.1 Historical Movement of New Zealand Stock Exchange 40 Index

Year*	Market Capitalization (US$ bln)	Trading Value (US$ bln)	Listed Companies (#)
1994	27.2	7.1	207
1993	25.6	6.7	136
1992	15.3	3.2	123
1991	14.3	2.9	139
1990	8.8	1.9	171

* to December of each year; Source: IFC, 1995

	1/92–6/95 Annualized Return*	1/92–6/95 Total Return*
New Zealand Stock Exchange40	16.46%	62.00%

* dividends reinvested in index

Table 9.1 Domestic Equity Market Indicators

The New Zealand fixed income market features modest issuance by both government and private sector borrowers. The sovereign sector consists of New Zealand Government Treasury bills, with maturities extending to one year, and New Zealand Government Bonds (NZGBs) with maturities extending from two- to ten-years (and with benchmarks at three-, five- and ten-years); there have also been issues of sovereign index-linked bonds in the past, but such have declined in overall importance (e.g. no new issues have been floated since 1984) and outstandings are now negligible. There is also a small market for semi-government bonds issued by quasi-government authorities, district/regional councils and public corporations (such as Housing Corporation of New Zealand, Rural Banking and Finance Corporation, the regional councils of Auckland and Wellington, and so on); the semi-government sector is very small, particularly in comparison with the semi-government sector in Australia. At the end of 1994 total outstanding NZGBs amounted to NZ$22.68 bln (US$14.7 bln), while outstanding bills amounted to NZ$6.4 bln (US$4.3 bln); outstanding semi-government notes amounted to less than NZ$3 bln (US$2 bln). Figures 9.2 and 9.3 below trace the historical movement of NZGB yield curves and benchmark three- and ten-year bond yields. The private sector market features issuance of bank transferable certificates of deposit (CDs), promissory notes and bank accepted bills in the short end of the curve (to one year), and fixed rate bonds and convertible bonds in the intermediate sector of the curve (from two- to ten-years). In comparison with the sovereign sector, private sector

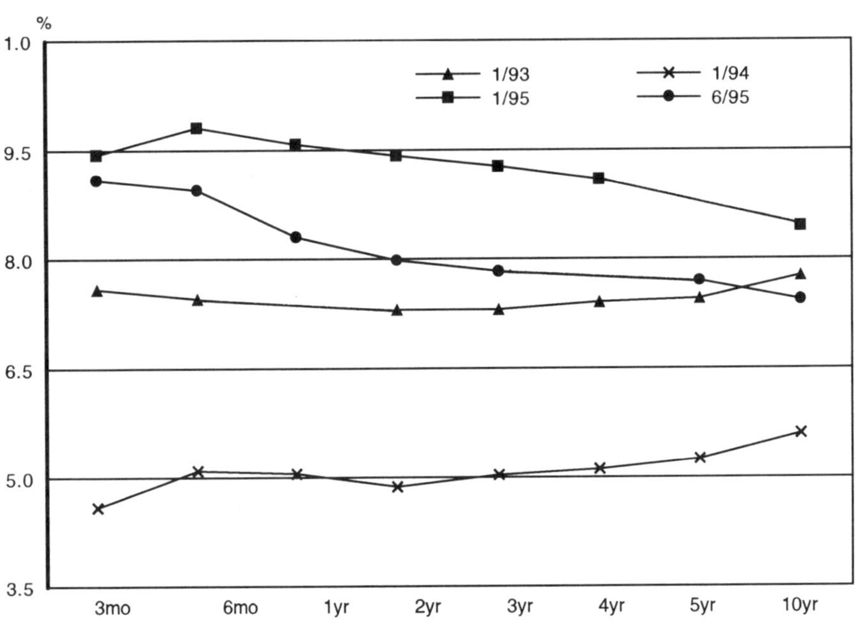

Figure 9.2 Historical Movement of New Zealand Government Yield Curves

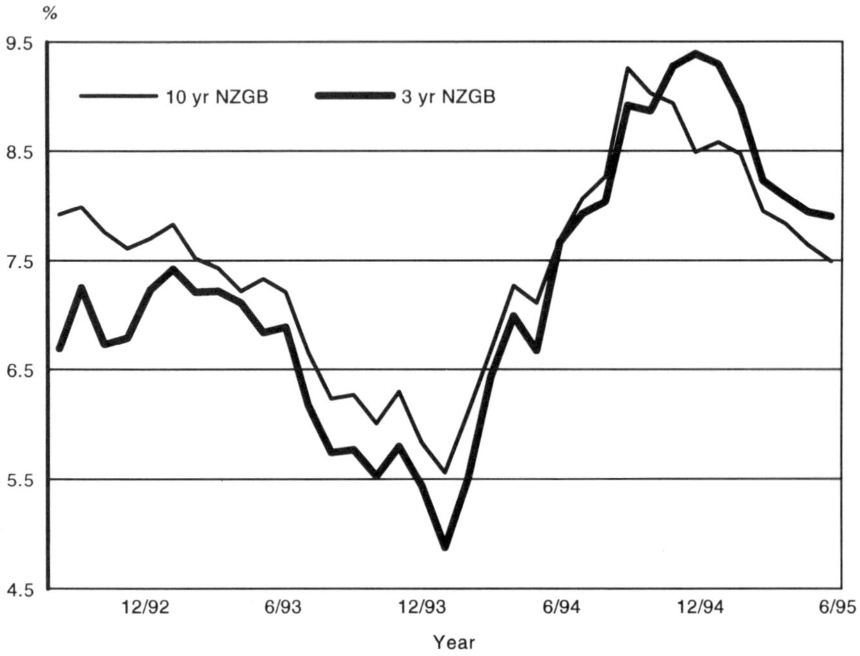

Figure 9.3 Historical Movement of Three- and Ten-year New Zealand Government Bond yields

issuance has remained very modest; total outstandings amounted to just under NZ$4 bln (US$2.6 bln) at the end of 1994.

The key interest rates in the New Zealand financial market include the New Zealand prime commercial bill rate (the short-term borrowing cost for institutions in the bill market), New Zealand dollar LIBOR (the borrowing cost for prime banks in the offshore interbank market), New Zealand Government Bond yields (the intermediate- and long-term borrowing costs of the government), EuroNZ$ bond yields (the borrowing cost for domestic and foreign issuers in the offshore market), and New Zealand dollar swap rates (the rates for transacting domestic interest rate swaps in the interbank market). We shall discuss these interest rate indicators at greater length in our section of fixed income forwards and swaps. Table 9.2 summarizes the payment frequency, compounding frequency and day count convention for each rate.

The New Zealand dollar (NZ$) is a freely convertible currency which can be traded without restriction by domestic and offshore institutions. The value of the local currency is determined by market forces though the Reserve Bank of New Zealand (RBNZ) attempts to manage the currency against a trade-weighted index in order to keep inflation under control; although the weighting of the index fluctuates, it is presently comprised of US dollars (24.3%), Australian dollars (35%), yen (24.9%), sterling (10.1%) and Deutschmarks (5.7%). Average domestic daily spot trading in New Zealand dollars against US dollars and New Zealand dollars against Australian dollars (the two major crossrates of the market), amounted to approximately NZ$7.75 bln (US$5 bln) in 1994 (split almost equally between the two crosses). Standard interbank dealing size is NZ$5 mln (US$3.25 mln) and bid-offer spreads in the interbank market are a narrow NZ$0.0005/US$ under normal market conditions. Figure 9.4 traces the historical movement of spot US$/NZ$.

Rate	Payment Frequency	Compounding Frequency	Day Count Convention
NZ$ Bills	–	–	Actual/365
NZ$ LIBOR	–	–	Actual/360
NZGBs	semi-annual	semi-annual	Actual/360
EuroNZ$	annual	annual	30/360
Swaps	semi-annual	semi-annual	Actual/360

Table 9.2 Domestic Interest Rate Summary

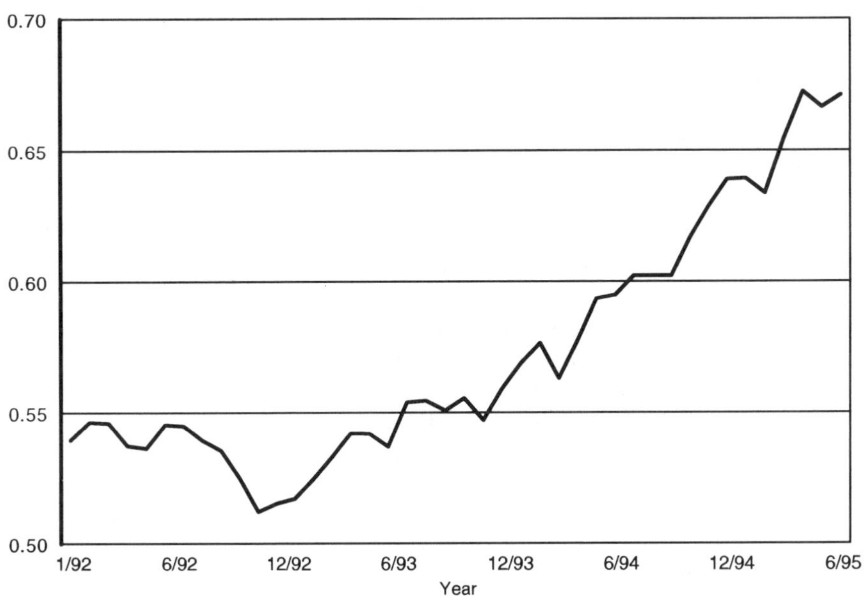

Figure 9.4 Historical Movement of Spot US$/NZ$

DERIVATIVE MARKETS AND PRODUCTS

LISTED DERIVATIVE EXCHANGES

New Zealand features two domestic exchanges which list and trade derivatives, the New Zealand Stock Exchange (NZSE) and the New Zealand Futures and Options Exchange (NZFOE).

The NZSE, discussed above, is primarily responsible for trading domestic equities, which it accomplishes through a national automated screen-based trading system. In addition to equities it also lists and trades domestic convertible bonds and listed issuer equity warrants (known locally as options, though we shall refer to them as warrants in order to avoid confusion with NZFOE's equity options). Although the absolute number of convertibles and warrants in the primary market is still modest (e.g. 26 convertible issues and six equity warrants as of mid-1995), the instruments, and the Exchange, form an important part of New Zealand's listed derivative market.

The origin of New Zealand's most active derivative exchange dates back to 1953 when an informal group of wool traders in London, known collectively as the London Wool Terminal Market Association (LWTMA), commenced trading in wool futures. In 1980 the LWTMA introduced a new contract based on New Zealand cross-bred wool; in 1982, after achieving success with its New Zealand wool contract, the LWTMA established a local branch in New Zealand and changed its name to the London and New Zealand Futures Association (LNZFA). Local brokers who were part of the LNZFA eventually split away from the group and started their own exchange, known as the New Zealand Commodity Market (NZCM), and commenced trading in a new local wool contract. In 1984, after several years of independent trading, the NZCM was re-organized as the New Zealand Futures Exchange (NZFE), an all-electronic forum with automated screen-based trading systems. Trading in new wool futures and financial futures began in 1985 and select financial options contracts were added in 1987. Three years later, in October 1990, the NZFE added equity options to its product line and, given the strong presence of options trading in its business, renamed itself the New Zealand Futures and Options Exchange (NZFOE). The NZFOE, which had existed as an independent organization since its creation in 1984, was nearly acquired by the London Futures Exchange in 1992; after intensive negotiations lasting until late 1992 the Sydney Futures Exchange (SFE) emerged as the final acquirer of the NZFOE. Since the acquisition ties between the two exchanges have grown stronger and a great deal of trading and execution on the NZFOE is carried out by Australian members of the SFE; indeed, SFE members are now permitted to trade NZFOE products directly from the SFE and the entire clearing, settlement and guarantee process for all NZFOE contracts is routed through the Sydney Futures Exchange Clearing House (SFECH). Membership in the NZFOE takes one of three forms: principal traders (who deal primarily on their own accounts but can deal on a give-up basis on behalf of dealers, but cannot accept client orders), public brokers (who deal for their own accounts or client accounts and can hold client funds), and introducing brokers (who can deal for their own accounts or client accounts but cannot hold client funds). Based on 1994 turnover, NZFOE was the 50th most active futures exchange in the world (FI, 1995). Table 9.3 highlights the country's listed exchanges and derivative products.

Listed Exchange	Primary Derivatives
New Zealand Stock Exchange (NZSE)	Issuer equity warrants; convertible bonds
New Zealand Futures and Options Exchange (NZFOE)	Equity options; index futures, options; deposit futures, options; interest rate futures, options; wool futures

Table 9.3 Listed Derivative Exchanges

LISTED FUTURES AND OPTIONS

Equity

Equity Futures/Options

NZFOE introduced domestic equity options in 1990. The Exchange's listed equity options are American exercise contracts which result in physical delivery of shares; strikes on all options are set at NZ$0.10 intervals. While the number of options has remained relatively constant over the past five years (seven options in total, including two added in 1994), trading volume has been on the rise and total annual turnover is becoming significant. Total volume for all listed equity options amounted to 49,987 contracts in 1993 and 146,399 contracts in 1994 (this compares with only 13,135 contracts for all other NZFOE listed options combined (e.g. deposit, bond and index options)); year-end open interest increased from 10,863 contracts in 1993 to 28,282 contracts in 1994 (NZFOE, 1995).

Options are presently available on Brierley Investments (1994 trading volume of 38,254 contracts), Carter Holt Harvey (23,637 contracts), Fletcher Challenge Forestry (1,780 contracts), Fletcher Challenge Ordinary (39,797 contracts), Goodman Fielder (854 contracts), Lion Nathan (17,616 contracts), and Telecom Corporation (24,425 contracts); Fletcher Challenge Forestry and Goodman Fielder are the Exchange's newest options. Table 9.4 contains contract details for listed equity options.

Note that the NZFOE does not list equity futures and has no immediate plans to introduce such derivatives.

Contract	Equity Options
Type	Domestic
Exchange	New Zealand Futures and Options Exchange
Months	Quarterly, on independent cycle
Contract Size	1,000 shares of underlying stock
Tick Value	NZ$0.01
Daily Limit	No limit
Deliverable Instrument	Physical settlement of underlying shares
Last Trading Day	2nd to last business day of the contract month
Exercise Day	American exercise – any business day up to, and including, the last trading day
Real-time pricing data	Reuters: <0#NUS*.NZ>, <0#NZW*.NZ>, <0#BRY*.NZ>, <0#CAH*.NZ>, <0#FLC*.NZ>, <0#FFS*.NZ>, <0#GMF*.NZ>, <0#LNN*.NZ>, <0#TEL*.NZ>; Telerate: 38166-79

Table 9.4 Contract Specifications for NZFOE Equity Options

Index Futures/Options/Futures Options

Although NZFOE has featured index futures and options since 1987 and 1989, respectively, its index derivative programme underwent a major change in mid-1995 as the reference for both contracts shifted from the traditional NZSE 40 index to the new NZSE 10 share index. After several years of disappointing turnover in NZSE 40 futures and options the Exchange determined that use of a smaller, more accurate, index for its derivatives would attract more participants. The NZSE 40 index has historically been plagued by the presence of many illiquid shares, which has made pricing of index derivatives difficult and inaccurate; pricing difficulties, in turn, have kept institutions from participating in the market. By shifting to an index with more underlying liquidity and more accurate pricing, the Exchange hopes to gain more participation in its derivatives. The NZSE 10 index futures and options contracts débuted in August 1995 while the NZSE 40 index contracts were delisted in September 1995. Although the reference index and contract multiplier have changed, the index future is still offered on the same cycle as the old contract (i.e. spot month, two near months and two quarter months); the new option contract remains structured as an American exercise, cash-settled derivative with strikes set at NZ$25 intervals.

Contract	New Zealand Stock Exchange Ten Index Futures
Type	Domestic
Exchange	New Zealand Futures and Options Exchange
Months	Spot month plus two near months, plus quarter months to one year on March, June, September, December cycle
Contract Size	NZ$25 * NZSE 10 Index
Tick Value	1 index point
Daily Limit	No limit
Deliverable Instrument	Cash settlement
Last Trading Day	2nd to last business day of contract month
Delivery Day	Business day following last trading day
Real-time price data	Bloomberg: ZGA <Cmdty>; Reuters: <0#NTP:>; Telerate: 6205

Table 9.5 Contract Specifications for NZFOE New Zealand Stock Exchange Ten Index Futures

Contract	New Zealand Stock Exchange Ten Index Futures Options
Type	Domestic
Exchange	New Zealand Futures and Options Exchange
Months	March, June, September, December
Contract Size	1 NZSE Ten Index Future
Tick Value	1 index point
Daily Limit	No limit
Deliverable Instrument	Physical settlement into underlying futures contract
Last Trading Day	2nd to last business day of the contract month
Exercise Day	American exercise – any business day up to, and including, the last trading day
Real-time price data	Bloomberg: ZGA <Cmdty> OMON; Reuters: <0#NTPmy+>; Telerate: 38165

Table 9.6 Contract Specifications for NZFOE New Zealand Stock Exchange Ten Index Futures Options

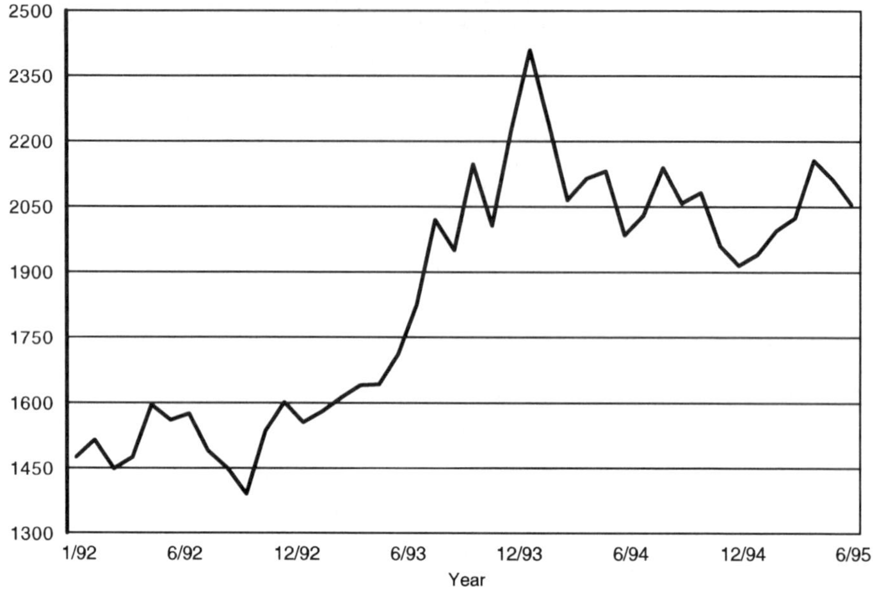

Source: New Zealand Futures and Options Exchange

Figure 9.5 Historical Movement of NZFOE NZSE 40 Index Futures

As indicated above, trading in NZSE 40 index futures has been negligible for several years. Total annual turnover amounted to a mere 3,633 contracts in 1993 and 7,397 contracts in 1994; year-end open interest was less than 500 contracts in each year. Turnover in index options has been even poorer: total trading volume amounted to just 596 contracts in 1993 and 1,985 contracts in 1994, with year-end open interest falling below 500 contracts in each year (NZFOE, 1995). It was on the basis of these poor turnover statistics that the Exchange elected to revamp its index derivatives programme. Figure 9.5 traces the historical price movement of the NZSE 40 index future, while Tables 9.5 and 9.6 contain contract specifications for the new NZSE 10 index futures and options.

Fixed Income

Deposit Futures/Options/Futures Options

NZFOE's most active contract is the 90-day bank accepted bill future, introduced in late 1986 (as a replacement to the Exchange's original prime commercial bill contract, which proved unsuccessful). The 90-day Bank Accepted bill rate (BBR) is widely regarded as New Zealand's benchmark short-term interest rate, with a number of derivatives (including Bill futures, New Zealand dollar FRAs and interest rate swaps) priced against the rate. The physical market, based on 90-day bank accepted bills, arises from the extension of short-term credit to local borrowers. A borrower issues a bill in exchange for funds, with a promise to repay such funds at a future date; banks typically accept the bills at a discount (based on the borrower's creditworthiness) and trade the securities in the secondary market. Note that unlike the Australian bill future, the New Zealand bill future is strictly a cash-settled derivative. It should also be noted that the face value of the New Zealand contract is NZ$500,000; the Australian contract carried a face value of A$500,000 until 1995, when members elected to double the notional to A$1 mln. NZFOE has no plans to double the size of its contract.

As with Australian bill futures, the tick value of the New Zealand bill contract changes with interest rates. In order to determine the tick value at a specific yield the following formula may be used:

$$P = \frac{365 \times 500{,}000}{365 + (I \times 90/100)}$$

where $I = 100 -$ quoted bill futures price.

The value of the contract can then be recalculated for a given change in yield (e.g. one basis point higher or lower); the differential between the two provides the tick value for a particular interest rate level. For example, if the quoted futures price is 95 (indicating a yield of 5%), the contract value is NZ$493,910.69. If the futures price is 94.99 (e.g. the yield is increased by one basis point, to 5.01%), the new contract value is NZ$493,898.66. The tick value is simply the difference between the two contract values, or NZ$12.03. As yields increase, tick values decrease.

As mentioned above, NZFOE's bill contract is its most active future; turnover amounted to 463,141 contracts in 1993 and a record 608,460 contracts in 1994; year-end open interest increased from 14,856 contracts in 1993 to 22,608 contracts in 1994 (NZFOE, 1995). Table 9.7 contains contract specifications on the bank bill future, while Figure 9.6 traces the historical price of the contract.

NZFOE introduced bank bill futures options in mid-1989; the contracts, which are American exercise, physical-settlement derivatives, are struck at 0.25% intervals. Unlike turnover in bank bill futures, activity in bank bill options has been subdued since introduction: total turnover declined from 8,193 contracts in 1993 to 6,870 contracts in 1994, with year-end open interest of 320 contracts in 1993 and 700 contracts in 1994 (NZFOE, 1995). Despite the low turnover and open interest the Exchange has made no announcement regarding potential redesign of the contract. Table 9.8 contains contract details on the bank bill futures option.

Interest Rate Futures/Options/Futures Options

For the first nine years of its operation the NZFOE listed interest rate futures on both five- and ten-year NZGBs. In mid-1993 the Exchange replaced the five-year future with a three-year future as turnover in the five-year contract was declining and physical supply of five-year bonds was becoming irregular; the five-year contract was delisted in December 1993.

Contract	90-day Bank Accepted Bill Futures
Type	Domestic
Exchange	New Zealand Futures and Options Exchange
Months	Spot month plus next two months plus quarter months on March, June, September, December cycle to eighteen months
Contract Size	NZ$500,000 face value of bank accepted bills
Tick Value	0.01% of yield (approximately NZ$12, varies with interest rates)
Daily Limit	No limit
Deliverable Instrument	Cash settlement based on 3 month FRA rate published on last trading day on Reuters page BKBM. If not available, cash settlement based on clearinghouse accepted quotes calculated on last trading day (clearinghouse selects 8 random quotes, discards those with spreads in excess of 0.1%, calculates mid rates, discards 3 highest and lowest and averages remainder)
Last Trading Day	1st Wednesday after the 9th day of the contract month
Delivery Day	Business day following the last trading day
Real-time price data	Bloomberg: ZBA <Comdty>; Reuters: <0#NBB:>; Telerate: 6207

Table 9.7 Contract Specification for NZFOE 90-day Bank Accepted Bill Futures

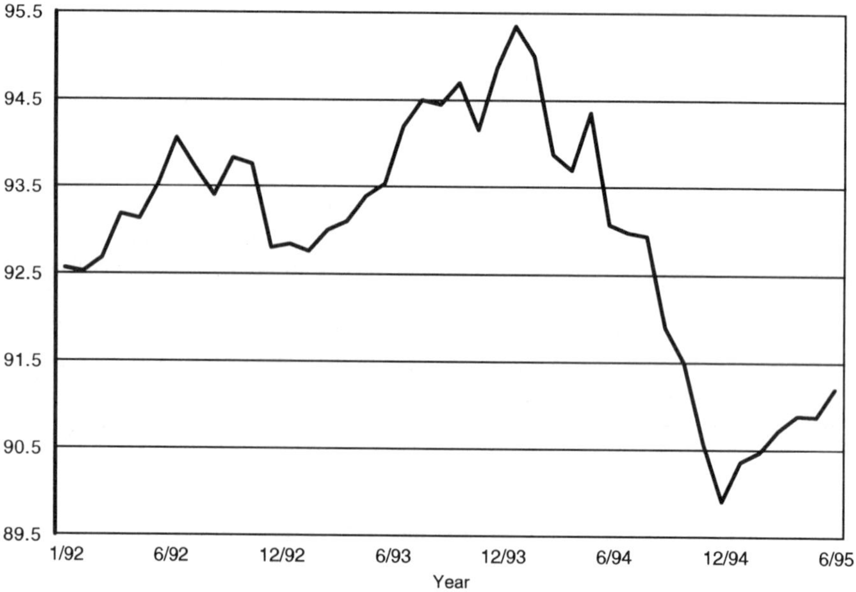

Source: New Zealand Futures and Options Exchange

Figure 9.6 Historical Movement of NZFOE 90-day Bank Accepted Bill Futures

Contract	Options on 90-day Bank Accepted Bill Futures
Type	Domestic
Exchange	New Zealand Futures and Options Exchange
Months	March, June, September, December to six quarter months forward
Contract Size	1 Bank Accepted Bill Future
Tick Value	0.01% of yield (approximately NZ$12, varies with interest rates)
Daily Limit	No limit
Deliverable Instrument	Physical settlement into underlying futures contract
Last Trading Day	Same as futures
Exercise Day	American exercise – any business day up to, and including, the last trading day
Real-time price data	Bloomberg: ZBA <Cmdty> OMON; Reuters: <0#NBBmy+>; Telerate: 38164

Table 9.8 Contract Specifications for NZFOE Options on 90-day Bank Accepted Bill Futures

As with bill futures discussed above, the tick value for interest rate futures varies with the level of rates. To determine the tick value at a given yield the value of the contract must first be determined through the following formula:

$$P = NZ\$1000 \times (6(1 - V^n)/i + 100V^n)$$

where i is a per annum yield/200
V is $1/(1 + \mathrm{i})$
n is 6 for three-year bonds, 20 for ten-year bonds

After calculating the initial value of the contract the yield is increased or decreased by one basis point and a new value is derived; the tick value is simply the differential between the two prices.

Volume in the three-year future has risen steadily since its introduction and it now ranks as the second most active derivative on the NZFOE: turnover increased from 74,128 contracts in 1993 to 101,229 contracts in 1994; year-end open interest declined from 4,390 contracts in 1993 to 1,888 contracts in 1994 (NZFOE, 1995). While activity in the ten-year contract is not as great as the three-year contract, it stands as the Exchange's third most active derivative: total turnover increased from 20,996 contracts in 1993 to 42,541 contracts in 1994; year-end open interest declined from 1,271 contracts in 1993 to 1,018 contracts in 1994 (NZFOE, 1995).

It is interesting to note that unlike bond futures contracts in most major financial markets, the New Zealand contracts are not deliverable; this is related, in part, to lack of strong and continuous supply of deliverable government bonds in the three- and ten-year maturities. No plans have been put forth by the NZFOE regarding deliverability of the contracts in the future. Tables 9.9 and 9.10 contain contract details on the two bond futures while Figures 9.7 and 9.8 trace the historical price movement of the two contracts.

Contract	Three-year New Zealand Government Bond Futures
Type	Domestic
Exchange	New Zealand Futures and Options Exchange
Months	March, June, September, December
Contract Size	NZ$100,000 face value of New Zealand Government Bonds, 8% coupon, three-year maturity
Tick Value	0.01% of yield (approximately NZ$27, varies with interest rates)
Daily Limit	No limit
Deliverable Instrument	Cash settlement based on clearinghouse accepted quotes (clearinghouse obtains quotes from government dealers, discards those with spreads in excess of 15 basis points, selects ten random quotes, drops two highest and two lowest and averages balance)
Last Trading Day	1st Wednesday after the 9th trading day of the contract month
Delivery Day	Business day following the last trading day
Real-time price data	Bloomberg: ZYA <Cmdty>; Reuters: <0#NGV:>; Telerate: 6206

Table 9.9 Contract Specifications for NZFOE Three-year New Zealand Government Bond Futures

Contract	Ten-year New Zealand Government Bond Futures
Type	Domestic
Exchange	New Zealand Futures and Options Exchange
Months	March, June, September, December
Contract Size	NZ$100,000 face value of New Zealand Government Bonds, 8% coupon, ten-year maturity
Tick Value	0.01% of yield (approximately NZ$78, varies with interest rates)
Daily Limit	No limit
Deliverable Instrument	Cash settlement based on clearinghouse accepted quotes (clearinghouse obtain quotes from government dealers, discards those with spreads in excess of 15 basis points, selects ten random quotes, drops two highest and two lowest and averages the balance)
Last Trading Day	1st Wednesday after the 9th day of the contract month
Delivery Day	Business day following the last trading day
Real-time price data	Bloomberg: ZTA <Cmdty>; Reuters: <0#NGB:>; Telerate: 6215

Table 9.10 Contract Specifications for NZFOE Ten-year New Zealand Government Bond Futures

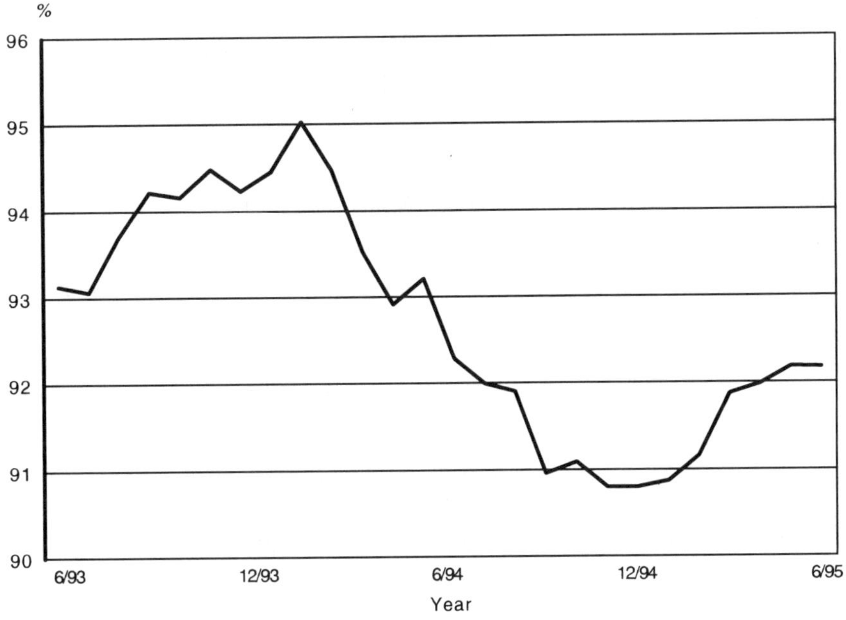

Source: New Zealand Futures and Options Exchange

Figure 9.7 Historical Movement of NZFOE Three-year NZGB Futures

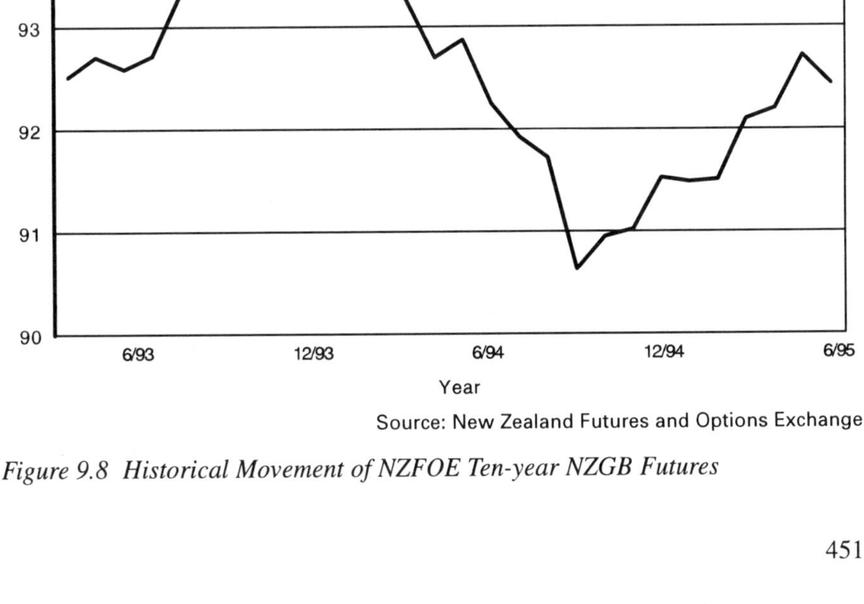

Source: New Zealand Futures and Options Exchange

Figure 9.8 Historical Movement of NZFOE Ten-year NZGB Futures

Contract	Options on Three-year New Zealand Government Bond Futures
Type	Domestic
Exchange	New Zealand Futures and Options Exchange
Months	March, June, September, December
Contract Size	1 Three-year NZ Government Bond future
Tick Value	0.01%, approximately NZ$27 (varies with interest rates)
Daily Limit	No limit
Deliverable Instrument	Physical settlement into underlying futures contract
Last Trading Day	Same as futures
Exercise Day	American exercise – any business day up to, and including, the last trading day
Real-time price data	Bloomberg: ZYA <Cmdty> OMON; Reuters: <0#NGVmy+>; Telerate: 38162

Table 9.11 Contract Specifications for NZFOE Options on Three-year New Zealand Government Bond Futures

Contract	Options on Ten-year New Zealand Government Bond Futures
Type	Domestic
Exchange	New Zealand Futures and Options Exchange
Months	March, June, September, December
Contract Size	1 Ten-year New Zealand Government Bond future
Tick Value	0.01%, approximately NZ$78 (varies with interest rates)
Daily Limit	No limit
Deliverable Instrument	Physical settlement into underlying futures contract
Last Trading Day	Same as futures
Exercise Day	American exercise – any business day up to, and including, the last trading day
Real-time price data	Bloomberg: ZTA <Cmdty> OMON; Reuters: <0#NGBmy+>; Telerate: 38163

Table 9.12 Contract Specifications for NZFOE Options on Ten-year New Zealand Government Bond Futures

NZFOE offers American exercise options on both three- and ten-year NZGB futures; strikes are set at 0.25% intervals and settlement is into the underlying futures contract. Both options have remained relatively inactive in recent years, particularly in comparison with the underlying futures contracts. During 1994, volume shifted from the three-year contract to the ten-year contract: total annual turnover in three year bond futures options fell from 1,000 contracts in 1993 to a mere 80 contracts in 1994, with no year-end open interest in either year; turnover in ten-year bond futures options rose from 120 contracts in 1993 to 4,200 contracts in 1994, with year-end open interest of less than 100 contracts in 1993 and just over 600 contracts in 1994 (NZFOE, 1995). Despite the lack of activity in both contracts the Exchange has made no announcement regarding potential redesign of either derivative. Contract specifications for the two instruments are highlighted in Tables 9.11 and 9.12.

Currency

Currency Futures/Options/Futures Options

Though NZFOE introduced a US$/NZ$ currency futures contract when the Exchange was originally established in 1985 the derivative was immediately plagued by poor turnover, primarily because participants requiring foreign exchange protection or exposure chose to utilize the OTC spot and forward currency market (which has always featured reasonably good liquidity). Turnover in currency futures amounted to a mere nine contracts in 1993 and 21 contracts in 1994, with no year-end open interest in either year (NZFOE,1995). The contract was delisted at the end of 1994 as it became apparent that volume was unlikely to increase. No other listed currency derivatives have been created or are presently contemplated.

Commodity

Commodity Futures/Options/Futures Options

Despite an historic and illustrious past, NZFOE's sole commodity futures contract, on wool, has been completely inactive for the past few years (for many of the same reasons the SFE's original 22 micron wool contract became inactive, e.g. oversupply of wool which is only now being reduced, along with government price supports which were only eliminated in the early 1990s). Although there was no trading volume in the contract during 1993 or 1994 the Exchange has made no announcement regarding redesign or delisting of the contract. Table 9.13 contains details on the wool contract.

Contract	New Zealand Wool Futures
Type	Domestic
Exchange	New Zealand Futures and Options Exchange
Months	February, April, June, August, October, December
Contract Size	2,500 * NZ Wool Board Indicator
Tick Value	NZ$0.01/kg
Daily Limit	No limit
Deliverable Instrument	Cash settlement
Last Trading Day	2nd to last business day of the contract month
Delivery Day	2nd business day following the last trading day
Real-time price data	Bloomberg: ZWA <Cmdty>; Reuters: <0#NZW:>; Telerate: 6209

Table 9.13 Contract Specifications for NZFOE New Zealand Wool Futures

LISTED/OVER-THE-COUNTER WARRANTS, CONVERTIBLES AND HYBRIDS

Equity

Equity Warrants

The New Zealand equity warrant market consists of domestic listed equity warrants (also known locally as options) and offshore OTC covered equity warrants.

Domestic listed equity warrants are floated by local companies on their own shares; exercise of the warrants results in the issuance of new equity by the company. Issuer equity warrants of this type are listed on, and traded through, the NZSE, and carry maturities ranging from one to four years; all warrants are structured as American exercise instruments and are denominated in New Zealand dollars. As of mid-1995, the local market listed and traded six equity warrants; secondary trading in most warrants is thin. Summary details on all domestic warrants are contained in Appendix II.

In addition to the onshore listed warrant market, there is also a modest offshore market for OTC third-party, covered warrants. Such warrants are issued by domestic or international financial institutions on another company's shares, and result in the re-allocation of existing equity, rather than the issuance of new equity, upon exercise. Covered warrants are issued in American or European style, typically carry maturities of one to three years and may be denominated in either New Zealand dollars or foreign currencies. The derivatives are traded strictly on an OTC basis (i.e. not through the NZSE) and are often listed on overseas exchanges (though they may remain unlisted). Warrants have been issued by financial institutions on a number of large capitalization domestic blue-chip stocks.

Basket/Index Warrants

While the domestic market does not currently list or trade basket or index warrants, institutions in the offshore OTC market float periodic issues of index warrants, based primarily on the key NZSE 40 index; basket warrants combining groups of domestic stocks are occasionally floated in the market as well. Offshore basket/index warrants, which carry maturities ranging from one to three years, are either unlisted or listed on overseas exchanges, and trade strictly on an OTC basis. With the declining popularity of the NZSE 40 as a reference for derivatives (as discussed earlier in the chapter), and the introduction of the new NZSE 10 as the primary index for futures and options, it seems likely that future index warrants will target the new index.

Convertibles

New Zealand features a small domestic convertible bond market. Domestic convertibles are listed on, and traded through, the NZSE; overall secondary liquidity remains very modest, as most corporate bond trading is focused on conventional fixed rate securities. Domestic convertibles are issued with a broad range of maturities, extending from three to ten years; coupons are generally set in an intermediate range of 7% to 12% and conversion premiums range from 5% to 10%. While most domestic convertibles are issued in the form of senior securities certain bonds are issued in subordinated form; in addition, there is periodic issuance of mandatory convertibles (where conversion into equity is mandatory at, or before, maturity).

Unlike local companies in other Asia Pacific nations, companies in New Zealand have not accessed the offshore convertible market in recent years, primarily because overall domestic corporate bond issuance is small, domestic convertibles are available in the local market, and domestic blue-chips have historically been able to access the EuroNZ$ market on favourable terms. There is presently only a single New Zealand offshore convertible outstanding in the market (Carter Holt Harvey's Swiss franc domestic bond); all other issues have been called or converted. Appendix III lists all domestic and offshore New Zealand convertible bond issues.

Index-linked Notes

Although index-linked notes are not issued with great frequency in the domestic market, certain institutions float structured notes with principal or coupon payments linked to the appreciation in the NZSE 40 equity index (or smaller baskets of domestic stocks). These notes are one- to five-year debt instruments with embedded call options, and are typically unlisted (e.g. private placements), or listed on offshore exchanges. Index-linked notes of this type are most often sold directly to investors who hold them until maturity; they are not actively traded on a secondary basis. Despite the availability of a small number of index-linked issues, overall activity in the New Zealand market has been negligible in comparison with activity in Japan, Hong Kong and Australia.

Fixed Income

Fixed Income Warrants

The New Zealand market does not presently list or trade domestic fixed income warrants, primarily as a result of the small size of the local fixed income market and the limited investor demand for such derivatives.

Currency

Currency Warrants

The domestic market does not feature listed currency warrants based on New Zealand dollars at the present time. Given the country's lack of success in sustaining interest in a listed US$/NZ$ currency future, it seems unlikely that currency warrants will be introduced in the market. Institutions operating in the offshore market occasionally issue one- to two-year US$/NZ$ currency warrants, listing the securities on offshore exchanges and trading them on an OTC basis; instances of such warrant issuance, however, are infrequent.

Commodity

Commodity Warrants

The local and offshore markets do not presently list or trade commodity warrants referencing local New Zealand commodity indicators.

OVER-THE-COUNTER FORWARDS, SWAPS AND OPTIONS

Equity

Equity Forwards/Swaps

The market for onshore and offshore OTC forwards and swaps based on New Zealand equities is not particularly active at the present time. Although short- to intermediate-term equity forwards (e.g. one- to three-years) referencing domestic blue-chips are structured on a periodic basis by financial institutions, equity swaps exchanging a floating rate flow (e.g. BBR or NZ$ LIBOR) for appreciation or depreciation in a given equity are far less common. The equity option, index swap and index option segments of the OTC market are more active.

Equity Options

While equity forwards and swaps are not particularly popular, OTC options on domestic equities are more common. Although New Zealand already features an active listed equity option market (with 146,399 options traded on seven different stocks in 1994), the OTC market has achieved success by offering flexibility in structuring parameters such as reference equity, strike, maturity, amount and so on. Although virtually any type of option can be created in the OTC market, most institutions structure vanilla European or American options with maturities extending from several months to three years; settlement may be in cash or physical. Unlike listed options, OTC equity options are not traded in the secondary market; they are generally closed out with the arranging bank, exercised if in-the-money, or permitted to expire if out-of-the-money. Note that foreign access to domestic equities is not restricted in any fashion, meaning foreign banks (who often structure such transactions) are able to participate actively in the market.

Basket/Index Forwards/Swaps

Index forwards and swaps referencing the broad domestic market (e.g. NZSE 40) are executed with some frequency in the onshore and offshore markets. Conventional transactions exchange a floating rate (e.g. BBR or NZ$ LIBOR) for appreciation in the NZSE 40; this is identical to an institution purchasing a long-dated index call and paying deferred premium through the floating rate flow. In other structures an institution might exchange a floating rate flow for depreciation in the NZSE 40 (e.g. buying a long-dated index put), or receive appreciation and pay depreciation (e.g. buying a long-dated index call and selling a long-dated index put), and so on. As indicated above, the move to the NZSE 10 index is likely to result in OTC index swap structures shifting toward the new index. In addition to derivatives referencing the broad NZSE 40 market index, forwards and swaps are structured on narrower indexes and baskets (e.g. blue-chip baskets, resource baskets, and so on). Note that there is a very small market for index/basket swaps with embedded exotic options, such as barriers, digitals or Asians; activity, however is very limited.

Basket/Index Options

Although the original NZSE 40 listed options discussed earlier in the chapter have proven illiquid the market for OTC index options targeting the NZSE 40 has been more successful. Domestic and offshore institutions have been attracted by the flexibility offered by OTC index options (e.g. customized strikes, maturities, notionals) and have been reasonably active in the market. Although virtually any option can be created in the OTC market, standard transactions are centred on six- to 12-month, cash-settled, American or European exercise options. Basket options, which band together similar groups of equities, are executed in the local market on occasion as well. In addition to vanilla basket/index options, exotic basket/index options are available, including barriers, lookbacks, Asians, digitals and outperformances. As with other equity derivatives detailed above, a shift to the NZSE 10 as the new reference for OTC index options is expected over time.

Fixed Income

Fixed Income Forwards/Swaps

The New Zealand fixed income market has featured domestic FRAs and IRSs for nearly 15 years. As with other domestic derivative instruments discussed in this chapter, the New Zealand dollar forward and swap market is small in absolute size and is often impacted by illiquidity; nonetheless, FRAs and swaps remain an integral component of the local financial market.

On the short end of the curve FRAs, which reference New Zealand BBR, are offered in various standard one-, three-, six-, nine- and 12-month combinations; quotes are available to five years, though most liquidity exists in transactions maturing in under one year. Bid-offer spreads for FRAs are approximately 10 basis points under normal market conditions, which is consistent with spreads found on domestic IRSs; typical interbank dealing size is NZ$10 mln (US$6.5 mln) to NZ$20 mln (US$13 mln). During 1994, total New Zealand dollar FRAs bought amounted to NZ$10.27 bln (US$6.67 bln), while FRAs sold amounted to NZ$10.55 bln ($6.85 bln) (RBNZ, 1995).

Although the New Zealand interest rate swap market has been in existence since the early 1980s, activity has traditionally been subdued, primarily because the need for swapping fixed/floating New Zealand dollars has been limited (e.g. a small domestic corporate fixed income market with reasonably limited fixed rate funding needs and limited credit arbitrage opportunities). More activity occurs in the offshore market, where swapping fixed New Zealand dollars from Eurobond issues into floating US$ LIBOR is common. Despite the small size of the market there is still a reasonable amount of domestic IRS activity, which has grown more significant with the broader acceptance of BBR as the country's primary floating benchmark; although use of BBR as the floating benchmark for swaps did not originally appeal to all participants, it has now become an accepted rate for most institutions active in the market. IRSs are often generated through domestic fixed New Zealand dollar bonds floated by state agency, bank or corporate issuers; fixed rate proceeds from such bonds are swapped into floating bills. Swaps may also be generated by issuance in the offshore market, where domestic entities (operating through offshore subsidiaries) raise fixed New Zealand dollars and swap into floating bills.

Domestic finance companies and smaller corporations, with comparative advantages in the domestic floating rate market, often swap bank bills into fixed New Zealand dollars. Note that the domestic market is still centred on vanilla swaps; though structures such as forward start, arrears, puttable, callable, zero coupon and amortizing swaps are available, dealing is negligible. Total domestic notional swaps outstanding, as reported by the International Swap Dealers Association (ISDA), declined from NZ$9.55 bln (US$6.21 bln) in 1993 to NZ$8.43 bln (US$5.48 bln) in 1994 (Choudhury, 1995).

Given the relatively small size of the government bond market and the volatility of the spread between government and swap rates, fixed New Zealand dollar swaps are priced on an absolute basis rather than as a spread to NZGBs. Quoting convention for domestic IRSs is fixed New Zealand dollars (semi-annual, on an Actual/360-day basis) against six-month New Zealand dollar BBR (as set on Reuters page BKBM). Typical interbank dealing size is NZ$20 mln (US$13 mln) and bid-offer spreads range from 7 to 10 basis points under normal market conditions (slightly wider in turbulent or illiquid times). The absence of regular issuance of government bonds over five years has been detrimental to the development of medium- and long-term New Zealand dollar swaps and most transactions carry maturities under five years (though quotes can be obtained to ten years). Figure 9.9 traces the historical movement of the New Zealand dollar IRS swap curve; the lack of development in the long-term market is evident by the absence of firm quotes beyond five years. Table 9.14 contains representative bid-offers for New Zealand dollar swaps under normal market conditions.

Maturity	**Bid-Offer Spread**
1 year	7–8 bps
2 years	10–12 bps
3 years	10–12 bps
4 years	10–12 bps
5 years	10–12 bps

Table 9.14 NZ$ IRS Bid-Offer Spreads

It is interesting to note that fixed New Zealand dollar swap rates are occasionally bid below government bond rates, which results in swaps executed at sub-LIBOR levels. While two- to five-year swap rates have historically been in the range of 20 to 40 basis points over NZGBs, such spreads have occasionally been narrower or, as demonstrated below, negative (e.g. swaps trading through government bonds). Figures 9.10 through 9.13 trace rates and spreads of New Zealand dollar IRSs against benchmark government bonds. Figures 9.14 through 9.17 illustrate the historical rates and spreads of New Zealand dollar swaps against AA-rated EuroNZ$ bond issues.

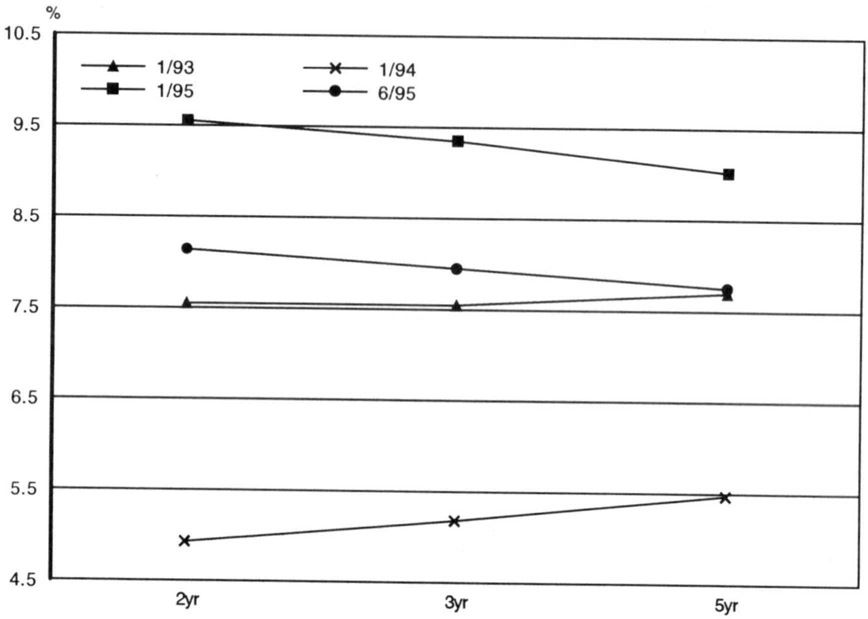

Figure 9.9 Historical Movement of NZ$ IRS Swap Curve

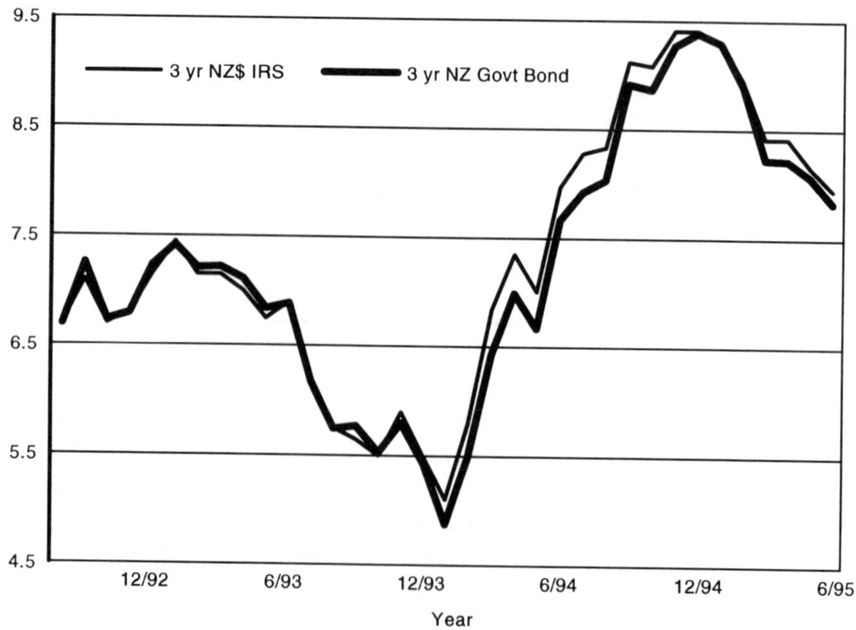

Figure 9.10 Historical Movement of Three-year NZ$ IRS and Three-year NZ Government Bond

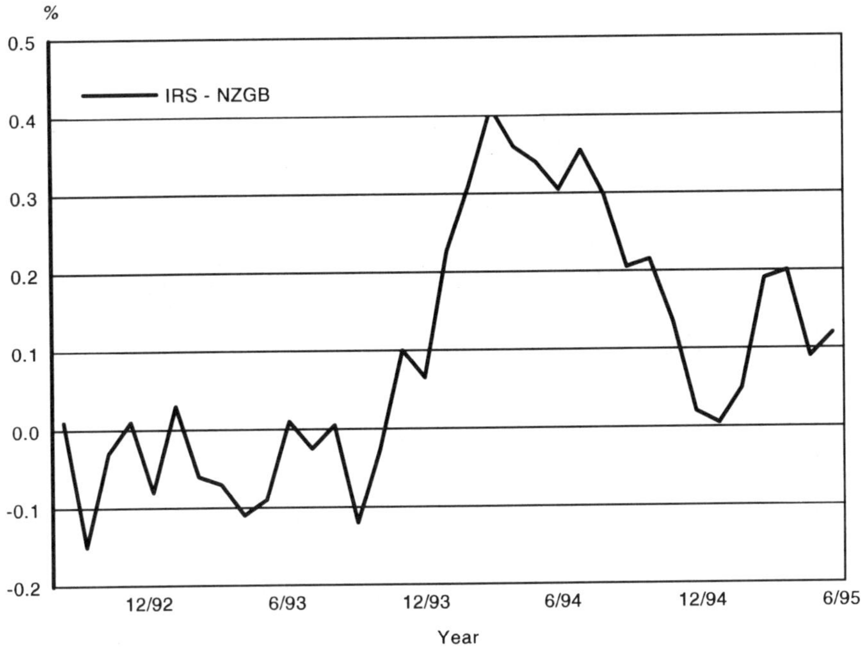

Figure 9.11 Spread of Three-year NZ$ IRS and NZ Government Bond

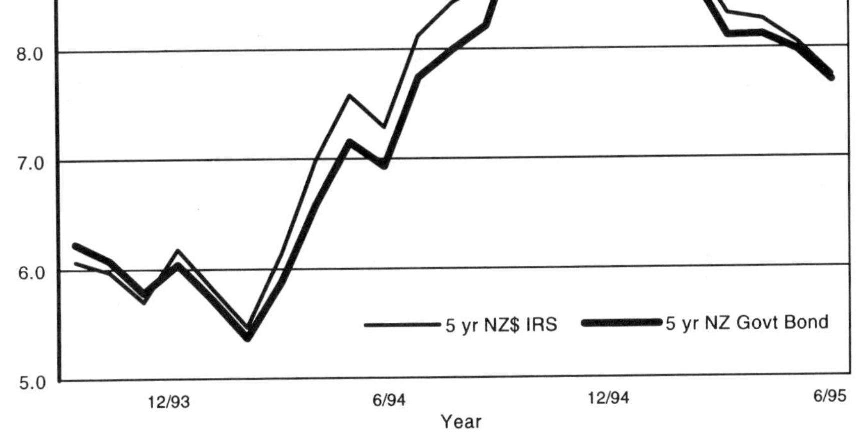

Figure 9.12 Historical Movement of Five-year NZ$ IRS and Five-year NZ Government Bond

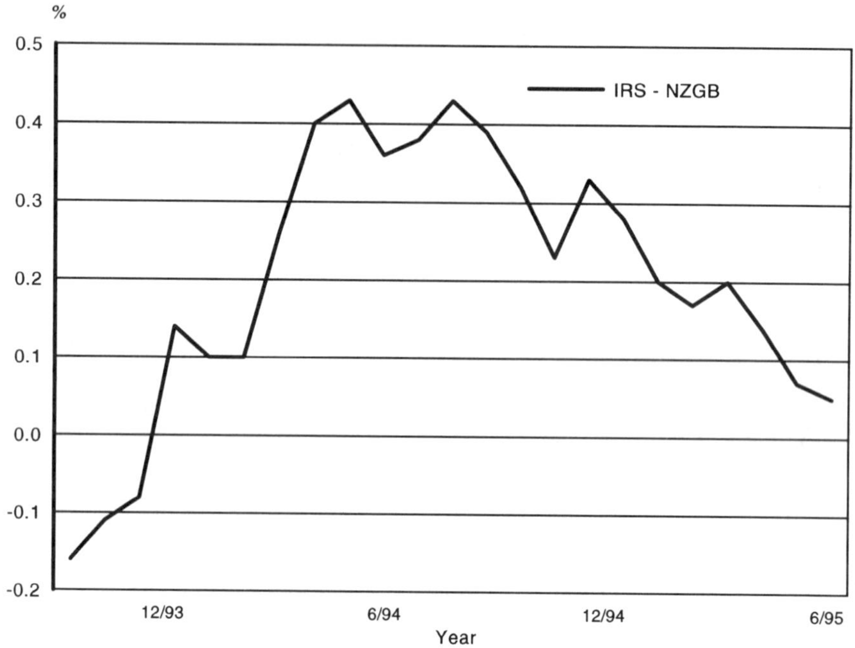

Figure 9.13 Spread of Five-year NZ$ IRS and NZ Government Bond

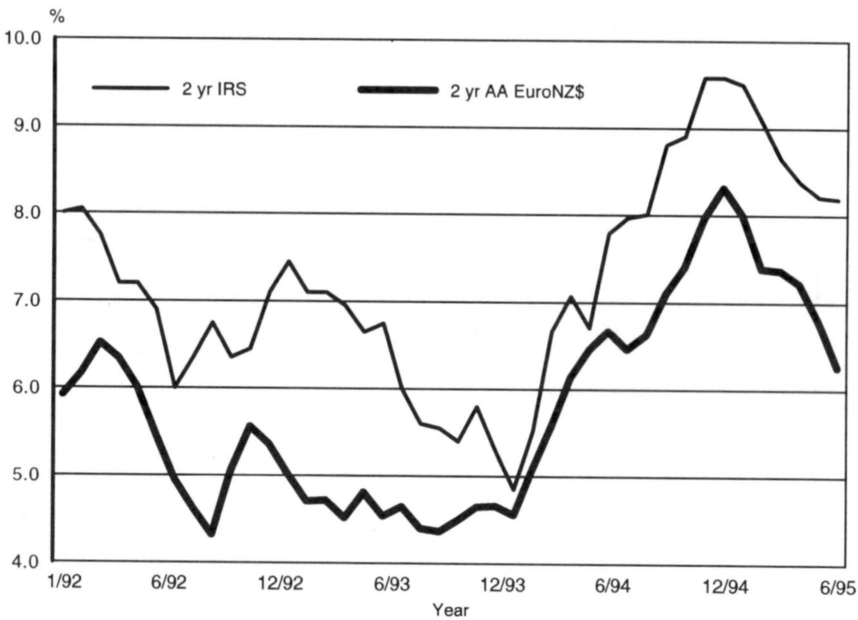

Figure 9.14 Historical Movement of Two-year NZ$ IRS and Two-year AA EuroNZ$ Bond

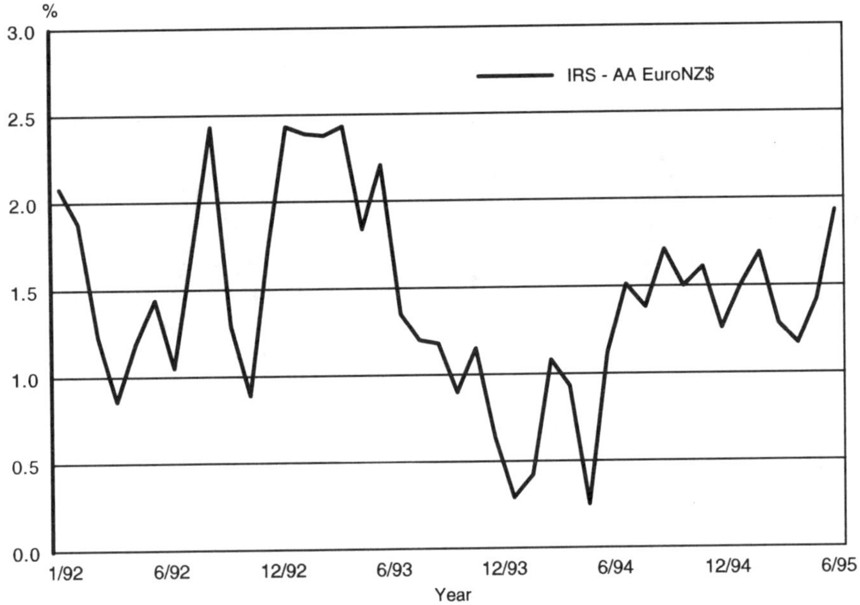

Figure 9.15 Spread of Two-year NZ$ IRS and AA EuroNZ$ Bond

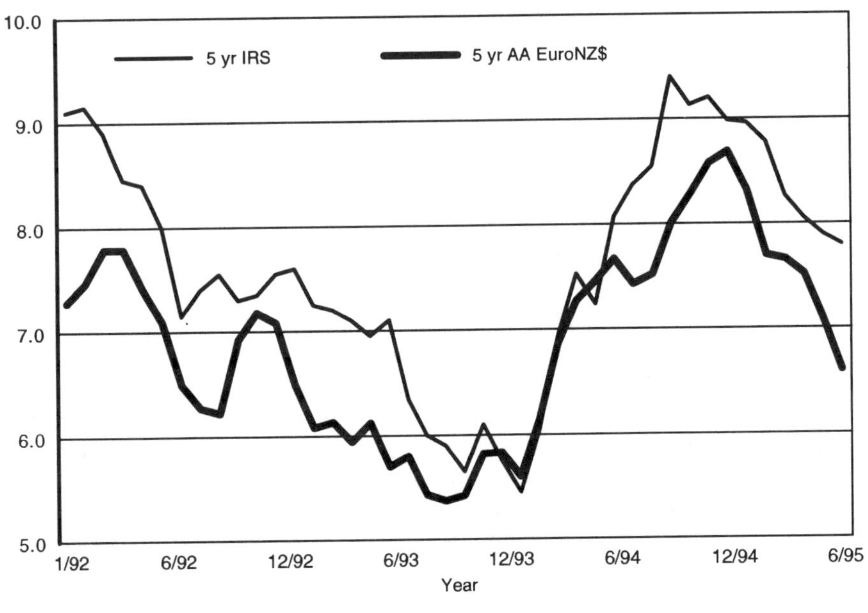

Figure 9.16 Historical Movement of Five-year NZ$ IRS and Five-year AA EuroNZ$ Bond

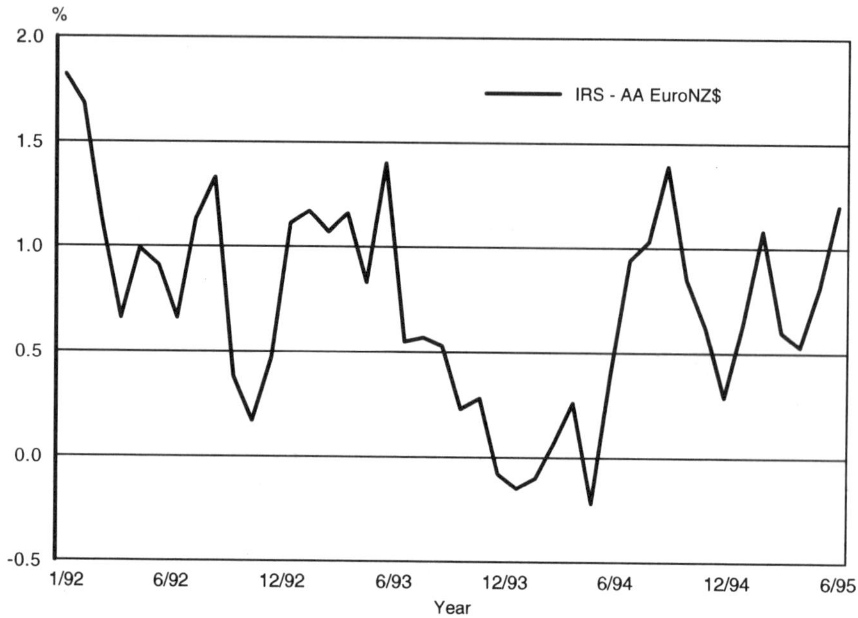

Figure 9.17 Spread of Five-year NZ$ IRS and AA EuroNZ$ Bond

Portfolios of interest rate swaps are generally hedged in the short end with New Zealand dollar FRAs or 90-day bank bill futures; a bill futures strip is available to 12 months and the contracts are the most liquid of NZFOE's futures. Hedging medium-term swaps is generally a manageable task given availability of benchmark NZGBs and three- and ten-year NZGB futures. Reasonable liquidity, particularly in the futures market, makes it possible for swap market-makers to hedge their positions with relative ease and at reasonable cost. Note that there are no restrictions on short-selling NZGBs. Two-way swap flow is generally available such that temporary NZGB or futures hedges can be replaced with offsetting swaps (removing basis or spread risks in the process).

Fixed Income Options

The New Zealand fixed income market features a reasonably broad array of options, including caps, floors, swaptions and bond options. New Zealand dollar caps and floors, which generally reference 90-day BBR, are available to five years, though most activity occurs in the one- to three-year sector; typical interbank dealing size is NZ$20 mln (US$13 mln) and bid-offer spreads, quoted in volatility terms, are approximately one point for short-term transactions. Payer and receiver swaptions are available in a variety of combinations, with two-year options into two-year swaps, two-year options into three-year swaps and two-year options into five-year swaps being the most liquid; as with caps and floors, swaption dealing size is normally NZ$20 mln (US$13 mln) and bid-offer spreads range from one to two points under normal market conditions, depending on maturity. Bond options are bought and sold on various reference instruments, including 90-day bank bills and a series of short-, intermediate- and long-maturity NZGBs. Maturities for bond options generally extend from 30 to 180 days; bid-offer spreads for options on bonds are generally one volatility point, while spreads for options on bills are three volatility points.

Currency

Currency Forwards/Swaps

The domestic market features FX forwards, long-term FX forwards and CCSs with full exchange of principal.

The short-term FX forward market is the most liquid segment of the local currency market and is active primarily to 12 months; the market is dominated by interbank players who deal in standard parcels of NZ$20 mln to NZ$50 mln (US$13 mln to US$32 mln). During 1994, total turnover in New Zealand dollar forwards amounted to NZ$41.2 bln (US$26.8 bln); a further NZ$68 bln (US$44.2 bln) of foreign currency (i.e. non-NZ$) forwards was also executed in the domestic market (RBNZ, 1995). These figures are approximately ten times greater than those evident in the CCS market, discussed below. The long-term FX forward market, featuring maturities to five years, is reasonably small, with only NZ$1.1 bln (US$715 mln) traded in 1994; turnover in long-term forwards involving foreign currencies was only slightly higher, at NZ$2 bln (US$1.3 bln). Figure 9.18 traces the historical movement of three- and 12-month forward US$/NZ$ rates.

While the New Zealand dollar IRS market features reasonably modest turnover, the CCS market has generally been more active (though in 1994 roles were reversed as offshore New Zealand dollar Eurobond issuance, which drives the CCS market, was non-existent). The primary form of CCS in the local market is fixed New Zealand dollars swapped into fixed or floating US dollars; the fixed New Zealand dollars are most often generated through Eurobond issues from supranational, sovereign or offshore corporate borrowers, who utilize a 15% withholding tax to generate significant cost savings. The New Zealand dollar CCS market has thus been driven primarily by issuers generating funding in offshore New Zealand dollars and swapping into US dollars. Sovereigns, corporates and supranationals, issuing EuroNZ$, have been the traditional fixed New Zealand dollar receivers and US$ LIBOR payers. State agencies and large domestic corporations have traditionally been fixed rate New Zealand dollar payers and US$ LIBOR receivers; both groups have had good access to offshore floating rate funding. Since new issue arbitrage generates a significant amount of activity in the local CCS market, currency swap liquidity dries up when the offshore market experiences a decline in issuance, lower yields or tighter swaps spreads. This happened during the late 1980s and early

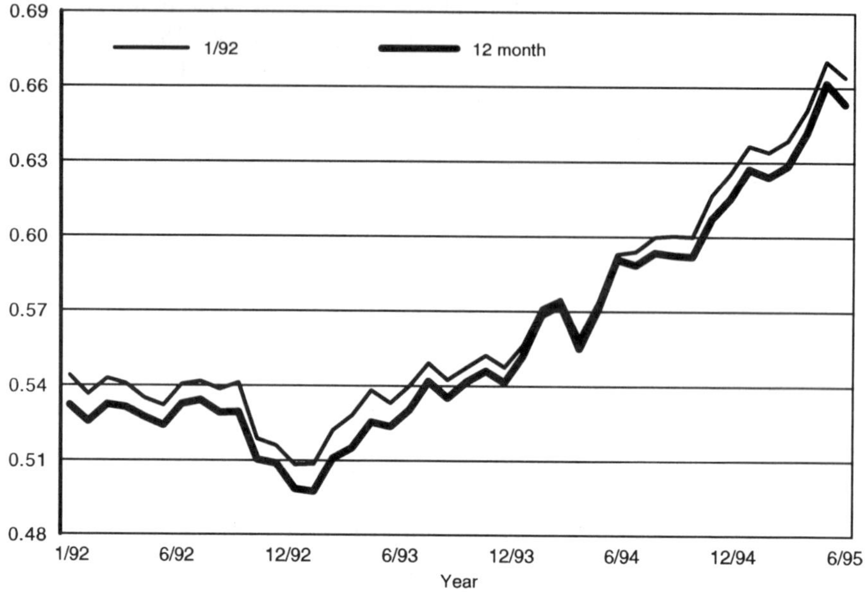

Source: Datastream

Figure 9.18 Historical Movement of Three-and 12-month US$/NZ$ Forwards

1990s when New Zealand was in recession; activity in CCSs was all but non-existent. The local market was also impacted in 1994 as global economies slowed and issuers failed to access the EuroNZ$ market for funding. Total outstanding notional New Zealand dollar CCSs, as reported by ISDA, amounted to NZ$3.74 bln (US$2.43 bln) in 1993 and NZ$3.1 bln (US$2 bln) in 1994 (Choudhury, 1995).

The quoting convention for CCSs is fixed New Zealand dollars (semi-annual, on an Actual/360-day basis) against six month US$ LIBOR flat. Bid-offer spreads range from 10 to 15 basis points across the curve under normal market conditions, but can widen significantly as a result of illiquidity or supply/demand imbalances. Given that turnover in the CCS market is issue-driven, average deal size tends to be significantly larger than in the domestic IRS market; transactions of NZ$100 mln (US$65 mln) and more (to match deal size) are not uncommon. Note that unlike Australia, Hong Kong and Japan, New Zealand does not feature an active currency basis swap market exchanging US$ LIBOR for bank bills; though such transactions are available, they are not as readily quoted as they are in other Asia Pacific markets.

Currency Options

The market for OTC New Zealand dollar currency options has been in existence for many years and, like the market for spot and forward New Zealand dollars, features fair liquidity. Market makers quote European and American exercise options from one- to 12-months (and occasionally longer), in standard interbank dealing size of NZ$50 mln to NZ$100 mln (US$32 mln to US$65 mln); deals for corporate customers are generally executed in NZ$5 mln to NZ$10 mln (US$3.25 mln to US$6.5 mln) parcels. The domestic market prices options in volatility terms, with one month options carrying higher volatilities than 12 month options; bid-offer spreads on options to 12 months are generally one volatility point under normal market conditions. Note that there is a small market for exotic New Zealand dollar currency options; such derivatives, which are centred primarily on barriers, Asians and lookbacks, are created on a deal-specific basis to match the desired risk/payoff requirements of particular clients.

Commodity

Commodity Forwards/Swaps

The market for offshore OTC commodity forwards and swaps is used by certain domestic resource companies, the national airline, electricity authorities, and so on. Such commodity derivatives, however, are based on offshore commodity references rather than local benchmarks. For instance, domestic companies requiring protection from movements in the price of crude oil most often transact OTC forwards or swaps based on Brent crude, West Texas Intermediate crude, or Tapis crude, since New Zealand lacks a benchmark grade of its own; the same is true for commodity forwards and swaps involving gasoil, jet fuel and so on.

Commodity Options

OTC commodity options, like forwards and swaps, are employed by certain domestic companies in the management of commodity exposures. As indicated above, however, such options reference offshore benchmarks and indicators (particularly on energy products), as opposed to domestic ones.

LOCAL REGULATORY/LEGAL TREATMENT OF DERIVATIVES

The primary regulators of New Zealand's financial markets are the Reserve Bank of New Zealand (RBNZ) and the Securities Commission (SC). The RBNZ is charged with general oversight of the operations of banks and securities firms, while the SC is empowered to regulate all aspects of the securities markets, including listed and OTC derivatives, and to authorize the operation of exchanges and dealers. The NZFOE, licensed by the SC, is a self-regulated entity, and oversees the activities of its own members.

Regulatory development and reform involving both listed and OTC derivatives in New Zealand has been implemented during the past decade, though certain issues, related primarily to the legal enforceability of gambling or wagering contracts, remain unresolved.

Although regulatory provisions regarding futures and options trading were enacted in 1988 and are now reasonably well defined, the early period of trading (from NZFE's establishment in 1984 until enactment of laws in 1988) saw relatively few regulatory provisions designed to protect participants. In fact, the only form of regulation from 1984 until 1988 was contained in the NZFE's by-laws and articles of association, which were applicable only to members of the exchange; non-members were not governed by, or included in, the by-laws and there were no other statutory provisions which provided protection. The by-laws of the NZFE (amended to include those applicable to the NZFOE) relate to trading procedures and trading authorities (e.g. public brokers can deal on their own accounts and client accounts, and can hold client funds; introducing brokers can do the same except hold client funds; and principal traders can only deal for their own account).

In 1988 the SC urged the Government to adopt specific regulation related to futures/options and OTC derivatives; such regulations were drafted and adopted in the Securities Amendment Act (SAA) of 1988. While the SAA also deals with securities regulation outside futures and options (e.g. insider trading and so on), Part III of the Act provides specific regulatory support for futures and options contracts, as well as certain types of OTC derivatives. Under Part III of the SAA, the SC is given the power to authorize both dealers and exchanges. Section 41 of the SAA also permits the Commission to establish regulations regarding the business of the exchanges, dealers, disclosure requirements and safekeeping of client funds. Client fund protection was enacted under Section 41 in the form of the Futures Industry (Client Funds) Regulation of 1991. Dealing in futures, futures options and options is governed by Section 38(1), which states that only members of authorized exchanges or those with specific SC approval can deal in futures; at the present time, the NZFOE is the only authorized exchange in New Zealand. The definition of 'dealing' under the Act is applied only to those dealing on behalf of another person or account, not for one's own account.

Futures are defined under Section 37(1) of the SAA as: (a) non-deliverable contracts; (b) futures on indexes; (c) options on equities; (d) interest rate swaps/cross currency swaps; (e) forward foreign exchange transactions and FRAs; and (f) other options. Thus, even select OTC derivative transactions are covered under the SAA. Section 37(2) highlights certain instruments which are excluded from the definition of a futures contract (and, hence, from regulation under the SAA). Specifically, any interest rate or currency swap, forward FX or FRA transaction is excluded when a registered bank or an authorized dealer is a party to the transaction. The rationale for excluding most major derivatives involving banks or authorized financial institutions is that they most likely adhere to regulatory requirements from other regulatory bodies (i.e. the RBNZ).

One of the key questions facing certain regulators in the Asia Pacific region is the legality of gambling, gaming or wagering contracts, and whether derivatives can fairly be considered a form of such contracts. In New Zealand, wagering contracts are deemed unenforceable under Section 28(1)(a) of the Gaming and Lotteries Act of 1977. In order that derivatives not be considered wagering contracts (and thus legally unenforceable), the SAA contains a provision, in Section 40, stating that futures contracts are not to be considered wagering contracts. The remaining 'grey' area relates only to those derivative instruments which are not considered futures contract under Section 37(1); those which are not could be deemed legally unenforceable under the Gaming and Lotteries Act.

LOCAL ACCOUNTING PRACTICES FOR DERIVATIVES

Although New Zealand accounting practices do not require specific accounting treatment of derivative transactions, most major institutions active in the market (e.g. registered banks) tend to follow similar procedures. For New Zealand dollar IRSs, treatment is dependent on whether the swaps exist as legitimate interest rate hedges or as speculative trading positions. Gains or losses (including all yield-related payments) on hedge transactions are accrued over the life of such transactions, except management fees, which are recognized immediately. Gains or losses for swaps which are held for trading purposes are marked to market on a daily basis, with the differential (e.g. the difference between contracted value and market value) posted to the income statement immediately. New Zealand dollar interest rate futures, caps, floors, collars, bond options and FRAs are treated in the same fashion, with gains/losses on trading positions marked daily and posted to the income statement immediately, and with gains/losses on hedge transactions deferred and recognized over the expected remaining life of the hedged transaction. In the case of foreign currency derivatives (e.g. swaps, options, forwards or futures of New Zealand dollars versus foreign currencies, or foreign currencies against other foreign currencies), positions are valued at market rates at balance date; unrealized gains or losses generated from such revaluations are recognized in the income statement at that time.

PROSPECTS FOR THE LOCAL DERIVATIVE MARKET

Summarized below are the near-term (one- to three-year) and medium-term (three- to five-year) prospects for New Zealand's domestic derivatives.

Near-term:

- Expanded liquidity in new NZSE 10 index futures and options.
- Introduction of new OTC equity derivatives based on the NZSE 10 index.
- Introduction of select additional equity options on the NZFOE; modest growth in turnover for existing equity options.

- Continued modest growth in listed bank bill futures and government bond futures; potential restructuring of bill and bond options if trading volume does not recover.
- Potential restructuring or abandonment of wool futures if trading volume does not recover.
- Gradual expansion in IRSs and CCSs, commensurate with offshore financing opportunities and general demand for funds by domestic corporations; very gradual lengthening of the yield curve.

Medium-term:

- Addition of new listed equity options on NZFOE as the market for blue-chip, liquid stocks expands.
- More active use of exotic interest rate and currency derivatives in the local market as demand for specific risk/reward profiles increases and greater comfort is gained in dealing with such structures.
- Continued expansion of the IRS and CCS markets, in a controlled and stable manner.

Exchange	**Contract**	**1993 Volume (contracts)**	**1994 Volume (contracts)**
NZFOE	Equity options	49,987	146,399
	NZSE 40 Index futures	3,633	7,397
	NZSE 10 Index futures	n/l*	n/l*
	NZSE 40 Index futures options	596	1,985
	NZSE 10 Index futures options	n/l*	n/l*
	90-day bill futures	463,141	608,460
	90-day bill futures options	8,193	6,870
	Three-year NZGB futures	74,128	101,299
	Ten-year NZGB futures	20,996	42,541
	Three-year NZGB futures options	1,000	80
	Ten-year NZGB futures options	120	4,200
	US$/NZ$ currency futures#	9	21
	Wool futures	0	0

* n/l: contract not yet listed; # contract now delisted

Table 9.15 Summary of 1993/1994 Listed Futures and Options Turnover

	Overall Liquidity	Liquid/ Maximum Maturity	Interbank dealing size	Average bid-offer spread
Equity/Index Swaps	fair	1 yr/5 yrs	n/a	n/a
Equity/Index Options	fair	1 yr/3 yrs	n/a	n/a
Interest Rate Swaps	good	5 yrs/10 yrs	US$13 mln	7–10 bps
Interest Rate Options	good	1 yr/5 yrs	US$13 mln	1–3 pts
Currency Swaps	good	5 yrs/10 yrs	varies	10–15 bps
Currency Options	good	1 yr/5 yrs	US$33 mln– $65 mln	1 pt

Table 9.16 Summary of Domestic OTC Derivatives

10: Philippines

FINANCIAL MARKET OVERVIEW

The Philippine market features a broad range of financial instruments but overall liquidity in most sectors is thin. The country's currency is not yet freely convertible and spot and forward trading is negligible. The lack of currency convertibility has made foreign access to local debt and equity investments difficult and has kept many institutions from participating. The domestic bond market remains extremely fragmented with true liquidity existing in only certain benchmark instruments; the equity market, though growing on a primary basis, is thinly traded apart from the largest capitalization stocks. The illiquid and restrictive nature of the local markets has slowed development of domestic derivatives considerably; the country's primary success has come in listed commodity futures, where hedging activity in key commodities has created reasonably deep liquidity. Despite the current limitations greater advancements in domestic derivatives are expected as the local financial market deregulates and expands.

The Philippine equity market has historically consisted of two separate exchanges, the Manila Stock Exchange, which was founded in 1927, and the newer Makati Stock Exchange, which was created in 1963. In early 1992 the authorities decided to merge the two exchanges into a nationwide trading forum in order to promote the development of a single, unified market; in late 1992 the Manila and Makati exchanges were combined into the Philippine Stock Exchange (PSE), which is now the country's sole equity trading centre.

With the rebuilding and recovery of the Philippine economy between 1990 and 1993, primary and secondary activity in the domestic equity market expanded substantially. In 1993 foreign and domestic investors, recognizing the potential of the Philippine market, invested actively in local shares, causing the domestic composite exchange to rise by 154%; the increase made the Philippine stock market the top performer among all global equity markets for that year. Between 1992 and 1993 domestic market capitalization more than tripled to US$40 bln; the increase was attributable to higher equity prices, secondary flotations and initial public offerings. Although there was a substantial decline in foreign investment in Asia Pacific during 1994 the Philippine market was not affected, primarily as domestic investment remained buoyant; stock market listings continued to expand and market capitalization increased to just over US$55 bln at the end of 1994, ranking it as the tenth largest of Asia Pacific's 13 markets. Figure 10.1 traces the recent movement of the key Philippine Composite Index, while Table 10.1 provides details on the overall equity market.

Note that foreign investors generally have unrestricted access to domestic shares but are prevented from owning more than 49% of any local company; in very exceptional instances (e.g. companies of 'national importance') no foreign ownership of local shares is permitted. Certain companies issue separate foreign 'B' shares as a means of controlling foreign ownership while other companies simply instruct registrars to reject share transfers which would violate the 49% limit. Foreign investors must also adhere to foreign exchange restrictions (as discussed below) when acquiring domestic shares.

Year*	Market Capitalization (US$ bln)	Trading Value (US$ bln)	Listed Companies (#)
1994	55.5	13.9	189
1993	40.3	6.8	180
1992	13.8	3.1	170
1991	10.2	1.5	161
1990	5.9	1.2	153

* to December of each year; Source: IFC, 1995

	1/92–6/95 Annualized Return*	1/92–6/95 Total Return*
Philippine Composite Index	26.83%	120.73%

* dividends reinvested in index

Table 10.1 Domestic Equity Market Indicators

The Philippine fixed income market is reasonably large on primary basis but remains quite illiquid on a secondary basis as a result of fragmentation. The short-term private sector market (to one year) consists primarily of certificates of deposit (CDs) floated by commercial banks, but also includes a modest amount of commercial paper issued by local corporations. The short-term sovereign sector is comprised of Republic of the Philippines Treasury Bills (RPTBs) and central bank bills (also known as Central Bank Certificates of Indebtedness, or CBCIs). The short- (and intermediate-) sovereign sector also features the benchmark floating rate treasury note (FRTN), a floating rate security linked to yields on 91-day RPTBs. Total outstanding RPTBs, CBCIs, FRTNs and short-term private bank CDs amounted to PHP1.01 tln (US$39.8 bln) in 1994. The intermediate portion of the sovereign curve (three- to five-years) features fixed rate treasury notes (including

Figure 10.1 Historical Movement of the Philippine Composite Index

new five-year notes), while the long end of the curve (five- to ten-years) consists of treasury bonds, a series of national government bonds issued by state authorities, and government enterprise bonds. Total outstanding medium- and long-term sovereign securities reached PHP71.4 bln (US$2.8 bln) at the end of 1994. Medium-term corporate bond issuance (based on fixed rate securities) is still very rare, with less than PHP3.8 bln (US$150 mln) in notes outstanding at the end of 1994 (Paisley, 1995). The overall Philippine fixed income market is in the process of consolidation; after permitting numerous state enterprises and authorities to issue their own debt (often guaranteed by the central government), regulatory authorities are now attempting to cease such issuance and concentrate all borrowing at the government level. This unification may aid in the creation of secondary market liquidity over time.

Key interest rates in the domestic market include RPTB yields (the short-term borrowing cost of the government), interbank call rates (the borrowing cost for financial institutions in the short-term interbank market), and FRTN yields (the medium-term borrowing cost of the government). Table 10.2 contains details on the payment frequency, compounding frequency and day count convention of key local rates.

In contrast to other Asian currencies, trading of the Philippine peso (PHP) is negligible. Spot and forward trading of the peso, which is not yet freely convertible, is controlled very strictly by the Central Bank of the Philippines (CBP), which intervenes with frequency to influence the value of the currency. Foreign investor

Rate	Payment Frequency	Compounding Frequency	Day Count Convention
RPTBs	–	–	Actual/360
I/B call	–	–	Actual/360
FRTNs	semi-annual	semi-annual	Actual/360

Table 10.2 Domestic Interest Rate Summary

participation in onshore peso trading is restricted by a series of regulations. For instance, foreign investors can purchase the peso only up to four days forward and must use proceeds to invest locally; transactions must be documented through a local authorized bank, and documentation must be presented in order to repatriate capital at a future date. Foreign participants cannot sell spot or forward pesos unless they present documentary evidence that the original position was based on an underlying investment in Philippine government securities or equities. With such tight restrictions, average daily spot trading executed through the onshore 36-bank dealing network (the Philippine Dealing System (PDS)) is a negligible PHP765 mln (US$30 mln); bid-offer spreads are very wide at PHP0.10/US$ (with 40% of the spread payable by sellers as a stamp duty). Though turnover is up from the PHP125 mln (US$5 mln) per day recorded two years ago, it is still well short of trading volumes in other emerging Asian nations (where onshore and offshore trading can

Figure 10.2 Historical Movement of Spot PHP/US$

range from US$2 bln to US$4 bln per day). Widespread activity and deeper liquidity are unlikely to occur until the peso is freely convertible and restrictions on offshore investors are eliminated. Figure 10.2 illustrates the historical movement of spot PHP/US$.

DERIVATIVE MARKETS AND PRODUCTS

LISTED DERIVATIVE EXCHANGES

The Philippines features two exchanges which list and trade derivatives, the Philippine Stock Exchange (PSE) and the Manila International Futures Exchange (MIFE).

As indicated above, the PSE is the sole equity trading centre of the Philippines. In addition to its primary equity trading business the Exchange participates in local derivatives (albeit in a very minor way) through listing and trading of issuer equity warrants; the market for such derivatives is currently dormant (i.e. there is only one issue outstanding), though new issues are expected in the near term. Note that although the local market also features a small amount of domestic convertible bonds, such instruments are not listed on the PSE and, as such, are not considered part of the Exchange's derivative product offerings.

MIFE is the primary derivative exchange of the Philippines. The Exchange was established in October 1984, received formal approval from the Philippine Securities and Exchange Commission (SEC) in January 1986, and commenced trading in October 1986. MIFE's original derivatives included sugar and soybean futures; coffee and copra futures were added in 1988, and a dried cocoon (e.g. raw silk) contract followed in 1992. In order to broaden its product focus MIFE created a series of financial futures between 1990 and 1992: its first financial contract was an interest rate future based on 91-day Republic of the Philippines Treasury Bill yields; in 1991 the Exchange followed with a series of foreign currency futures and in 1992 it created a PHP/US$ currency future (note that trading hours for currency contracts span 20 hours, and cover a portion of the US trading day, the entire Asian trading day, and a portion of the London trading day). Based on 1994 trading volume MIFE ranked as the 35th most active futures exchange in the world (FI, 1995).

MIFE's currency futures are traded on the floor of the Exchange through the continuous open-outcry system, while its agricultural futures are traded through the one price group trading system used in the Japanese commodity markets. The one price group system arrives at a single price at the end of each individual session (four per day) by having floor representatives bid or offer based on a co-ordinator's price levels. The RPTB contract trades through the one price group system and the auction-based board trading system. Futures trades executed through MIFE are cleared and guaranteed by the Manila International Futures Clearing House

(MIFCH), an independent clearing organization; management of the Exchange itself is carried out by another independent organization, Moncom Management Services, approved by the SEC. Membership on MIFE takes one of five forms: founding members (who have access to the trading floor and full voting rights, and may deal for their own accounts or client accounts (with express permission from clients)), full members (who have access to the trading floor and full voting rights, may deal for their own accounts or client accounts (with express permission from clients) and must be registered and licensed as commodity futures brokers), trade affiliate members (who have no access to the trading floor and no voting rights, but can deal for their own accounts or client accounts (with express permission from clients), through a full member), associate members (who have no prior affiliation with the Exchange and who may only deal for their own accounts, through a floor member) and individual market members (who have access to the trading floor and can deal for their own accounts only). Table 10.3 highlights the country's listed exchanges and derivatives.

Exchange	Primary Derivatives
Manila International Futures Exchange (MIFE)	Interest rate futures; currency futures; soybean futures; sugar futures; robusta coffee futures; copra futures; dried cocoon futures
Philippine Stock Exchange (PSE)	Issuer equity warrants

Table 10.3 Listed Derivative Exchanges

It should be noted that in addition to MIFE, which presently stands as the only established and approved derivative exchange in the Philippines, a group of private investors has attempted to launch a second exchange, known as the Philippine Options Market Inc. (POMI), to trade equity options. Although establishment of POMI has been mentioned in the past, it has yet to obtain proper licensing or release specific details on potential products.

LISTED FUTURES AND OPTIONS

Equity

Equity Futures/Options

The domestic Philippine market does not presently list or trade equity futures or equity options. Although certain vague proposals have been put forth regarding the creation of an equity option market (e.g. the proposal set forth by POMI), there are no firm plans to introduce equity options in the domestic financial market at the present time.

Index Futures/Options/Futures Options

The Philippine market does not presently list index futures or options, though MIFE has specifically indicated that it will trade an index futures contract in the near term (perhaps during 1996); it is presently studying aspects of both market interest and contract design. Despite MIFE's desire to list an index contract, it should be noted that the PSE has expressed an interest in listing such a derivative as well; given that the PSE's composite index is the primary barometer of the country's stock market (and the most logical reference for an index contract), it is unclear which exchange will ultimately list and trade such derivatives (though expectations favour MIFE).

Fixed Income

Deposit Futures/Options/Futures Options

The Philippine market does not currently list or trade deposit-related contracts. Although the country features a short-term interest rate future, discussed below, it is more appropriately considered an interest rate contract, not a deposit contract. The local market is unlikely to introduce deposit futures until an established deposit benchmark is developed.

Interest Rate Futures/Options/Futures Options

MIFE introduced its short-term interest rate future, based on domestic treasury bill rates, in 1990; the contract references 91-day RPTB yields, the country's primary short-term interest rate benchmark. The future is a cash-settled contract valued at PHP10,000 times the 91-day Treasury bill yield. Although MIFE is unique in that it is one of the few emerging market exchanges in the world to introduce a local interest rate contract, overall activity has been minimal. Total turnover amounted to 5,472 contracts in 1993 and 7,672 contracts in 1994, while year-end open interest plummeted from 5,140 contracts in 1993 to zero in 1994 (MIFE, 1995). Low volume in the futures is attributable to reasonably low liquidity in the underlying cash market, as well as general reluctance among potential participants to employ listed RPTB futures to hedge interest rate risk. Given lacklustre volume its outlook would appear uncertain; the Exchange, however, has made no announcement regarding potential restructuring of the contract. Table 10.4 contains relevant contract specifications, while Figure 10.3 traces the historical price movement of near-month RPTB futures.

The local derivative market does not presently feature medium- or long-term interest rate futures or options. Although the Philippine fixed income market features a number of distinct, and reasonably active, notes and bonds, the need for separate interest rate futures has not yet developed.

Contract	91-day Republic of the Philippines Treasury Bill Futures
Type	Domestic
Exchange	Manila International Futures Exchange
Months	Spot month plus next three months
Contract Size	PHP10,000 * Bill Rate
Tick Value	0.01%
Daily Limit	+/– 0.50% against previous day's settlement yield
Deliverable Instrument	Cash settlement based on weighted average interest rate of 91-day Treasury bills on the 3rd Friday of the contract month
Last Trading Day	Thursday before 3rd Friday of the contract month
Delivery Day	Monday after the last trading day
Real-time price data	Reuters: <MIQH/S>; Telerate: 38696

Table 10.4 Contract Specifications for MIFE 91-day Republic of the Philippines Treasury Bill Futures

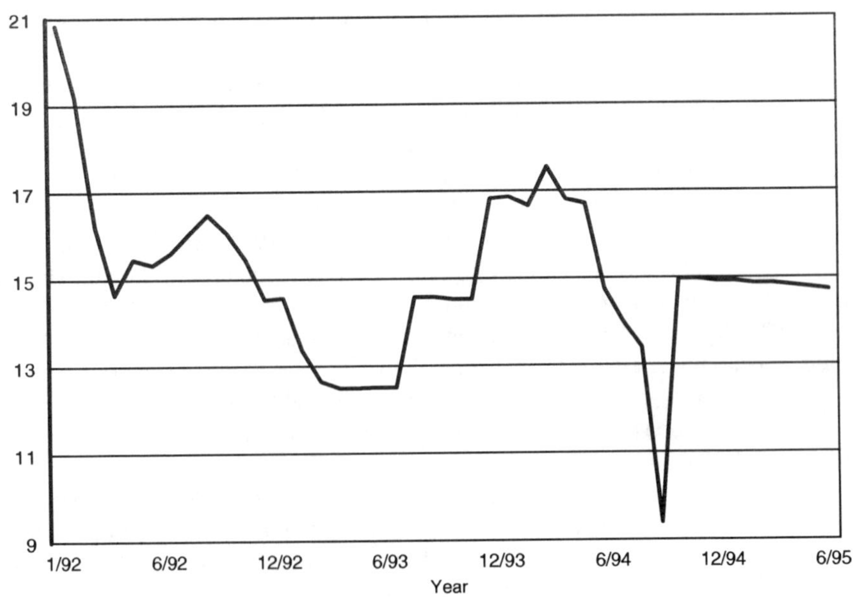

Source: Manila International Futures Exchange

Figure 10.3 Historical Movement of MIFE 91-day Republic of the Philippines Treasury Bill Futures

Currency

Currency Futures/Options/Futures Options

Currency futures were originally introduced on MIFE in 1991, and have become the most active of the Exchange's financial futures contracts. The Exchange presently lists and trades currency futures on PHP/US$, DM/US$, JPY/US$, US$/GBP and CHF/US$. The foreign currency contracts may be settled on a cash or physical basis, while the peso currency contract must be settled on a physical basis; there are four quoted contract months for each pair at any time, through liquidity exists primarily in the front month. Turnover in all foreign contracts has been reasonably strong. Trading in JPY/US$ futures increased from 97,050 contracts in 1993 to 163,542 contracts in 1994; year-end open interest amounted to 3,874 contracts in 1993 and 5,384 contracts in 1994. Turnover in US$/GBP futures amounted to 196,998 contracts in 1993 and 97,004 contracts in 1994; year-end open interest reached 7,026 contracts in 1993 and 4,374 contracts in 1994. Turnover in CHF/US$ futures rose from 58,204 contracts in 1993 to 79,840 contracts in 1994, with year-end open interest of 2,544 contracts in 1993 and 1,212 contracts in 1994. Turnover in DM/US$ futures amounted to 64,972 contracts in 1993 and 43,280 contracts in 1994, with year-end open interest of 2,908 contracts in 1993 and 1,844 contracts in 1994. In contrast to the foreign currency contracts, turnover in the local currency contract has been poor. Trading in PHP/US$ futures reached only 3,634 contracts in 1993 and 2,356 contracts in 1994, and recorded year-end open interest of 1,720 contracts in 1993 and zero in 1994 (MIFE, 1995). The low turnover in the local currency contract is ultimately due to the very low turnover in the OTC peso spot and forward markets, described above.

It is interesting to note that, while currency contracts offered on other Asia Pacific exchanges have failed to generate meaningful turnover (e.g TIFFE, SIMEX), MIFE's currency contracts have posted consistent, and reasonable, trading volumes. MIFE, however, faces strong competition from HKFE which introduced its one-day rolling spot futures in late 1995 (and will commence regional trading of PHLX's currency options in early 1996). Tables 10.5 through 10.9 contain relevant details on each contract. Figure 10.4 highlights the historical price movement of the PHP/US$ currency contract.

Contract	PHP/US$ Currency Futures
Type	Domestic
Exchange	Manila International Futures Exchange
Months	Spot month plus next three months
Contract Size	US$100,000
Tick Value	PHP0.001
Daily Limit	+/– PHP0.30 against previous day's settlement price
Deliverable Instrument	Physical settlement of pesos and US dollars
Last Trading Day	3rd Tuesday of the contract month
Delivery Day	Business day following the last trading day
Real-time price data	Reuters: <MIQF/Q>; Telerate: 39969

Table 10.5 Contract Specifications for MIFE PHP/US$ Currency Futures

Contract	JPY/US$ Currency Futures
Type	Offshore
Exchange	Manila International Futures Exchange
Months	Spot month plus next three months
Contract Size	JPY12.5 mln
Tick Value	JPY0.01
Daily Limit	+/– JPY2 against previous day's settlement price
Deliverable Instrument	Cash or physical settlement based on the average of four hourly spot quotes on the last trading day
Last Trading Day	3rd Tuesday of the contract month
Delivery Day	Business day after the last trading day
Real-time price data	Reuters: <MIQC/N>; Telerate: 39965/6

Table 10.6 Contract Specifications for MIFE JPY/US$ Currency Futures

Contract	DM/US$ Currency Futures
Type	Offshore
Exchange	Manila International Futures Exchange
Months	Spot month plus next three months
Contract Size	DM125,000
Tick Value	DM0.0001
Daily Limit	+/– DM0.02 against previous day's settlement price
Deliverable Instrument	Cash or physical settlement based on the average of four hourly spot quotes on the last trading day
Last Trading Day	3rd Tuesday of the contract month
Delivery Day	Business day after the last trading day
Real-time price data	Reuters: <MIQB>; Telerate: 39965/6

Table 10.7 Contract Specifications for MIFE DM/US$ Currency Futures

Contract	US$/GBP Currency Futures
Type	Offshore
Exchange	Manila International Futures Exchange
Months	Spot month plus next three months
Contract Size	GPB62,500
Tick Value	US$0.0001
Daily Limit	+/– US$0.02 against previous day's settlement price
Deliverable Instrument	Cash or physical settlement based on the average of four hourly spot quotes on the last trading day
Last Trading Day	3rd Tuesday of the contract month
Delivery Day	Business day following the last trading day
Real-time price data	Reuters: <MIQD/Q>; Telerate: 39965/7

Table 10.8 Contract Specifications for MIFE US$/GBP Currency Futures

Contract	CHF/US$ Currency Futures
Type	Offshore
Exchange	Manila International Futures Exchange
Months	Spot month plus next three months
Contract Size	CHF125,000
Tick Value	CHF0.0001
Daily Limit	+/– CHF0.025 against previous day's settlement price
Deliverable Instrument	Cash or physical settlement based on the average of four hourly quotes on the last trading day
Last Trading Day	3rd Tuesday of the contract month
Delivery Day	Business day after the last trading day
Real-time price data	Reuters: <MIQE/P>; Telerate: 39965/7

Table 10.9 Contract Specifications for MIFE CHF/US$ Currency Futures

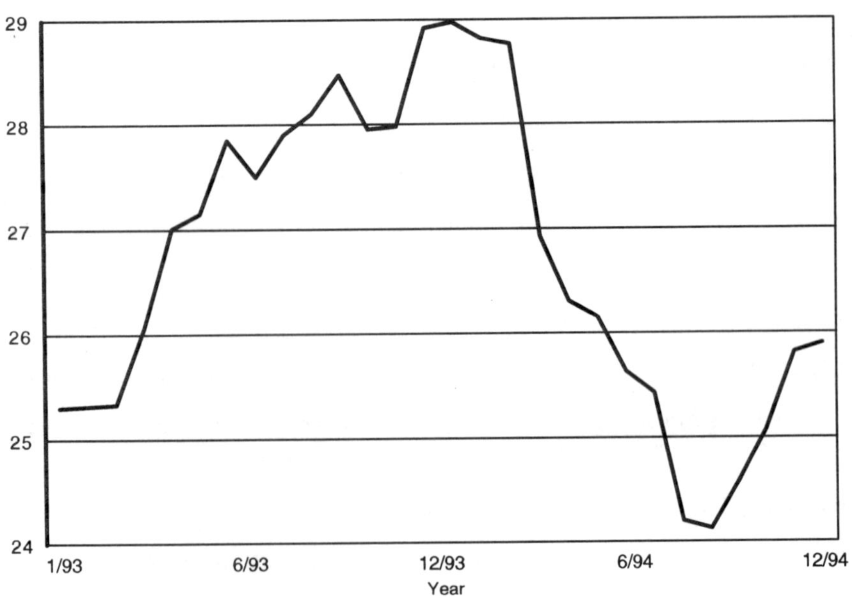

Source: Manila International Futures Exchange

Figure 10.4 Historical Movement of MIFE PHP/US$ Currency Futures

Commodity

Commodity Futures/Options/Futures Options

Although MIFE has achieved modest success with certain financial futures contracts (i.e. its currency derivatives), the Exchange remains primarily a commodity futures trading forum. MIFE's greatest trading volume has come from its agricultural futures on copra, sugar, coffee, soybeans and dried cocoons.

MIFE, which introduced its coffee future in 1988, is one of only five exchanges in the world to trade a coffee contract (the others being SICOM, ICEB (which offers a forward, not a future), London Commodity Exchange (LCE) and the Coffee, Sugar and Cocoa Exchange (CSCE))(note: several Chinese exchanges list coffee futures as well, but such derivatives are not accessible by foreign institutions). The local future, like those on SICOM, LCE and ICEB, is based on the robusta bean (the CSCE is based on the arabica bean); the contract accepts robusta coffee from any one of 17 countries in Asia (Malaysia, Indonesia, India, Philippines), Africa (Angola, Central African Republic, Guinea, Ivory Coast, Nigeria, Zaire, Uganda, Cameroon, Ghana, Tanzania, Togo, Sierra Leone) or the Caribbean (Trinidad). Total turnover in coffee futures increased from 143,788 contracts in 1993 to 516,010 contracts in 1994 (MIFE, 1995); year-end open interest reached 10,030 contracts in 1993 and 20,798 contracts in 1994 (MIFE, 1995). Despite competition from other Asia Pacific exchanges, MIFE's future is the region's most active coffee contract. Table 10.10 contains contract specifications on the MIFE robusta contract, while Figure 10.5 illustrates the historical movement of robusta futures prices.

Contract	**Robusta Coffee Futures**
Type	Domestic/Offshore
Exchange	Manila International Futures Exchange
Months	Nearest six consecutive months
Contract Size	5,000 kgs
Tick Value	PHP0.05/kg
Daily Limit	+/– PHP1.60/kg against previous day's settlement price
Deliverable Grade	Physical settlement of sound robusta (CTMAL standard) beans of Asian, Caribbean or African origin
Last Trading Day	Last trading day of the preceding month
Delivery Day	1st day of the delivery month
Real-time price data	Reuters: <MIQK/V>; Telerate: 38691

Table 10.10 Contract Specifications for MIFE Robusta Coffee Futures

Figure 10.5 Historical Movement of MIFE Robusta Coffee Futures

MIFE's sugar contract, based on raw cane sugar, was originally introduced in 1986; it is one of several raw sugar futures traded in Asia Pacific (along with those on TGE and KANEX; note that several Chinese exchanges offer raw sugar contracts but such are not accessible by offshore institutions). The Exchange's contract accepts deliverable grades from Australia, Indonesia, Thailand, India, Philippines, Fiji, Pakistan, China, Malaysia, Bangladesh and Japan. Total turnover amounted to 315,212 contracts in 1993 and 496,686 contracts in 1994; year-end open interest increased from 21,902 contracts in 1993 to 28,930 contracts in 1994 (MIFE, 1995). Table 10.11 contains relevant specifications on the sugar contract while Figure 10.6 illustrates the historical price movement of the future.

MIFE's soybean contract, which débuted in 1986, was the single most actively traded derivative on the Exchange in 1994. Turnover nearly tripled from 229,640 contracts in 1993 to a record 615,968 contracts in 1994, with year-end open interest rising from 10,208 contracts in 1993 to 22,878 contracts in 1994 (MIFE, 1995). Turnover statistics have been particularly impressive given the large number of competing soybean contracts in Asia Pacific (including six in Japan and seven in China). It should be noted that the MIFE soybean contract accepts tenderables from Dai Ren or Chin Wang Tao in China (i.e. China yellow soybeans) or from Indiana, Ohio or Michigan in the US (i.e. US IOM yellow soybeans). Table 10.12 highlights relevant details on the soybean contract while Figure 10.7 illustrates the historical price movement of the future.

Contract	Sugar Futures
Type	Domestic/Offshore
Exchange	Manila International Futures Exchange
Months	Nearest six consecutive months
Contract Size	112,000 lbs
Tick Value	PHP0.02/lb
Daily Limit	+/– PHP0.10/lb against previous day's settlement price
Deliverable Grade	Physical settlement of raw cane sugar of Asia Pacific origin
Last Trading Day	Last business day of the preceding month
Delivery Day	1st day of the delivery month
Real-time price data	Reuters: <MIQJ/U>; Telerate: 38689

Table 10.11 Contract Specifications for MIFE Sugar Futures

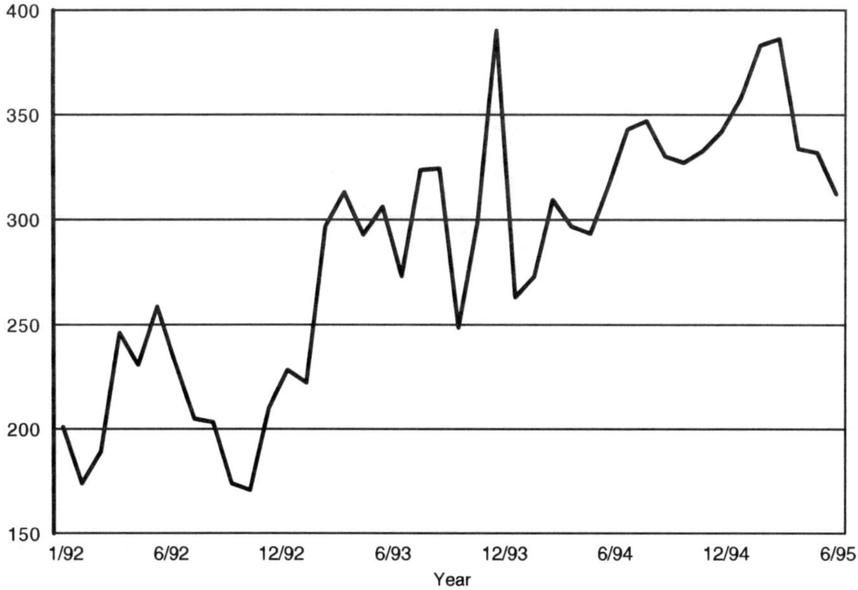

Source: Manila International Futures Exchange

Figure 10.6 Historical Movement of MIFE Sugar Futures

The MIFE copra contract, originally introduced in 1988, is the only copra future traded in Asia Pacific. Like the Exchange's other commodity futures, the copra contract has been extremely active in recent years: total trading volume more than doubled from 203,204 contracts in 1993 to 544,992 contracts in 1994, with year-end open interest increasing from 10,806 contracts in 1993 to 20,660 contracts

Contract	Soybean Futures
Type	Domestic/Offshore
Exchange	Manila International Futures Exchange
Months	Nearest six consecutive months
Contract Size	5,000 bags (60 kgs/bag)
Tick Value	PHP0.50/bag
Daily Limit	+/– PHP20/bag against previous day's settlement price
Deliverable Instrument	Physical settlement of unselected yellow soybeans of Chinese or US origin
Last Trading Day	Last business day of the preceding month
Delivery Day	1st day of the delivery month
Real-time price data	Reuters: <MIQL/W>; Telerate: 38690

Table 10.12 Contract Specifications for MIFE Soybean Futures

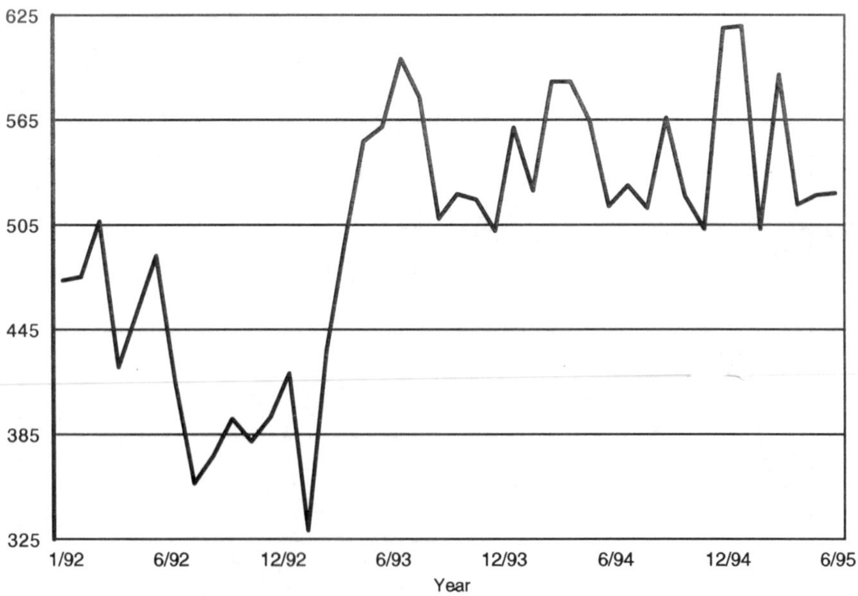

Source: Manila International Futures Exchange

Figure 10.7 Historical Movement of MIFE Soybean Futures

in 1994 (MIFE, 1995). Unlike other MIFE futures, which accept deliverable grades from countries other than the Philippines, the commodity deliverable into the contract must be produced in the Philippines and stored in domestic warehouses. Table 10.13 contains relevant contract details on the copra contract, while Figure 10.8 traces the historical price movement of the future.

Contract	Copra Futures
Type	Domestic
Exchange	Manila International Futures Exchange
Months	Nearest six consecutive months
Contract Size	20,000 kgs
Tick Value	PHP0.01/kg
Daily Limit	+/– PHP0.40/kg against previous day's settlement price
Deliverable Grade	Physical settlement of Philippine copra, FFA 4% moisture content
Last Trading Day	Last business day of the preceding month
Delivery Day	1st day of the delivery month
Real-time price data	Reuters: MIQI/T; Telerate: 38692

Table 10.13 Contract Specifications for MIFE Copra Futures

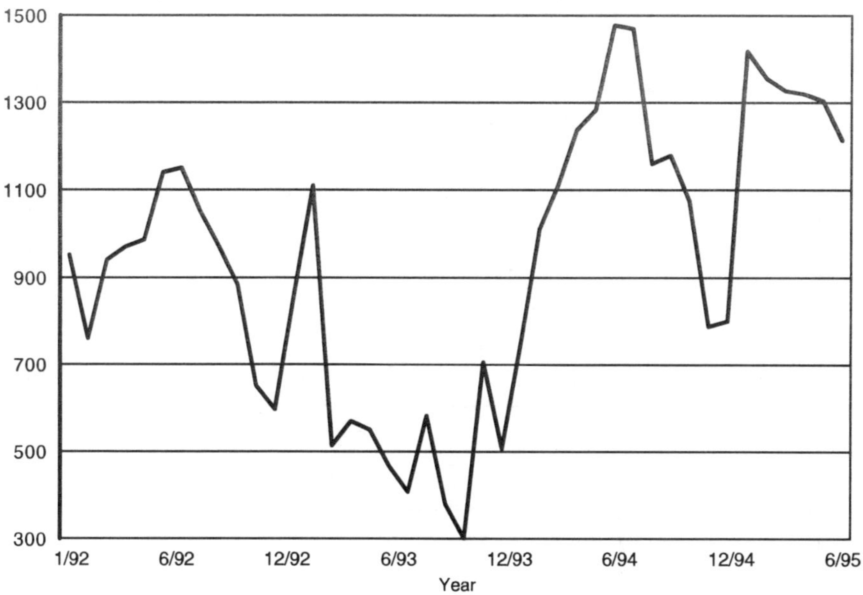

Source: Manila International Futures Exchange

Figure 10.8 Historical Movement of MIFE Copra Futures

MIFE's dried cocoon future, introduced in 1991, is used primarily by producers of silk and those who utilize silk to produce textile; the Exchange's contract is one of three offered in Asia Pacific (along with those of MDCE and TDCE in Japan) and, as such, faces significant regional competition. Despite competition from other exchanges trading in MIFE's future is extremely active; total turnover amounted to 431,476 contracts in 1993 and just over 524,000 contracts in 1994, with year-end open interest rising from 21,294 contracts in 1993 to 25,100 contracts in 1994 (MIFE, 1995). Table 10.14 contains relevant details on the future while Figure 10.9 traces the historical price movement of the contract.

Contract	**Dried Cocoon Futures**
Type	Domestic
Exchange	Manila International Futures Exchange
Months	Nearest six consecutive months
Contract Size	300 kgs
Tick Value	PHP0.50/kg
Daily Limit	+/– PHP25/kg against previous day's settlement price
Deliverable Grade	Physical settlement of dried cocoon, 40% raw silk within three months of sealing
Last Trading Day	Last business day of the preceding month
Delivery Day	1st day of delivery month
Real-time price data	Reuters: <MIQG/R>; Telerate: 38694

Table 10.14 Contract Specifications for MIFE Dried Cocoon Futures

Source: Manila International Futures Exchange

Figure 10.9 Historical Movement of MIFE Dried Cocoon Futures

MIFE is presently considering the introduction of a red bean futures contract (red bean contracts have proven very popular in both China and Japan, where multiple exchanges list and trade such contracts); timing of such a future is uncertain. It should be noted that MIFE does not presently offer options or futures options on commodities.

LISTED/OVER-THE-COUNTER WARRANTS, CONVERTIBLES AND HYBRIDS

Equity

Equity Warrants

The market for domestic listed equity warrants is virtually non-existent at the present time. The PSE lists only a single warrant issue, floated by Easycall Communications in mid-1992 on its own stock; future warrants are expected, though precise timing remains uncertain. Activity in the offshore covered warrant market, targeting individual Philippine stocks, has been dormant as well. While certain foreign financial institutions execute basket and index warrants (discussed immediately below), issues targeting individual stocks are not prevalent.

Basket/Index Warrants

Although the local stock exchange does not currently list or trade equity, basket or index warrants, certain offshore institutions float periodic OTC warrants referencing local Philippine indexes or baskets. Such warrants, which are either unlisted or listed on offshore exchanges and traded OTC, are denominated in foreign currencies and carry maturities ranging from one- to three-years. Representative issues in this category include Salomon Brothers' Deutschmark index call warrants on the Philippine Composite Index (1994), Swiss Bank Corporation's US dollar index call warrants on the Manila Composite Index (1994) and Citibank's US dollar index call warrants on the Citibank Philippines Index (1995). Basket warrants, created on groups of Philippine stocks, are also floated on occasion; such warrants carry the same general characteristics as index warrants.

Convertibles

The Philippine market features a very small amount of domestic convertibles. As of 1994 the total market featured a mere PHP1 bln (US$40 mln) in domestic convertible bonds, issued by three different local firms. The convertibles are not listed on the PSE and trade very infrequently through the OTC market. Future convertible bond flotation remains uncertain at this time, though overall issuance is likely to increase as private sector borrowers become more active users of the domestic capital markets.

Unlike issuers in other Asia Pacific nations (e.g. Hong Kong, Taiwan, Korea, Thailand), those in the Philippines have not been particularly active in the offshore convertible market. The first Philippine convertible issues appeared in the Eurodollar market in late 1993 and early 1994, when JG Summit, Filinvest and Benpres Holdings issued long-term Eurodollar securities; the JG Summit and Filinvest issues were denominated in US dollars and carried ten-year maturities, while the Benpres bond (a perpetual) was denominated in pesos, but traded and settled in US dollars. Total outstanding Philippine issues amounted to US$330 mln in 1994. As is common with most Eurodollar convertibles, those floated by Philippine issuers are listed on overseas exchanges and traded on an OTC bearer basis. Bonds are issued with long maturities (i.e. ten years and over) and are priced with low- to intermediate-coupons (3% to 5.5%) and intermediate conversion premiums (10% to 15%); all are convertible into shares of the issuer (or a subsidiary) at a peso conversion price. Appendix III contains details on Philippine convertible bond issues.

Index-linked Notes

Although several Asia Pacific markets feature active index-linked note issuance (e.g. Japan, Hong Kong, Australia), the Philippine index-linked market has been relatively inactive to date. Foreign financial institutions float only occasional issues referencing the Philippine Composite Index (or, in certain instances, baskets of local blue-chip equities); issues are generally denominated in foreign currencies and carry maturities of one- to three-years. These notes, which typically pay an enhanced coupon and/or enhanced principal redemption if the market rises, provide investors with long-dated calls on the local market. Trading in such securities is extremely limited with many deals arranged strictly on a private placement basis.

Fixed Income

Fixed Income Warrants

The local and offshore markets do not feature fixed income warrants referencing domestic fixed income securities, primarily because investor demand for such derivative securities is negligible and overall secondary activity in domestic fixed income instruments is still modest.

Currency

Currency Warrants

The onshore and offshore markets do not currently feature peso currency warrants, primarily because the currency market is restricted and trading in spot and forward pesos is subdued. As currency deregulation occurs it is likely that offshore institutions and investors will be interested in speculating on the directional movement of the peso through currency warrants.

Commodity

Commodity Warrants

Although the Philippines features active turnover in listed commodity futures, the local market does not list or trade domestic commodity warrants.

OVER-THE-COUNTER FORWARDS, SWAPS AND OPTIONS

Equity

Equity Forwards/Swaps

The market for Philippine OTC equity forwards and swaps is relatively inactive, primarily because the equity market is small and illiquid and foreign investor access to local equities is restricted by currency controls (the same constraints are applicable to all the equity derivatives discussed below). Although certain institutions in the offshore market enter into short- or medium-term (e.g. one- to three-year) equity forwards, overall turnover remains extremely limited. The market for equity swaps (e.g. exchange of deferred premium in the form of a floating rate flow for appreciation or depreciation in the value of a single equity) is non-existent.

Equity Options

The absence of listed equity options in the Philippine market has led to the development of a small market for offshore OTC options. Foreign institutions with equity derivative capabilities periodically buy and sell OTC options on Philippine blue-chip stocks; such transactions are generally short-term in nature (e.g. under one year in maturity) and may be structured with European or American exercise into cash or physical settlement. Note that as with OTC structures in general, there is no secondary market for equity options given the customized nature of each transaction; options either expire worthless if out-of-the-money, are exercised if in-the-money or are closed out with the arranging bank. The overall OTC equity options market is likely to remain small until the underlying equity market expands and investment restrictions ease.

Basket/Index Forwards/Swaps

Certain foreign banks operating in the offshore market deal in basket forwards/swaps (referencing baskets of blue-chip stocks) and index forwards/swaps (based on broad market indicators such as the Philippine Composite Index).

Conventional swaps exchange a floating rate for appreciation or depreciation in the underlying index or basket. These transactions are equivalent to clients buying medium-term (e.g. one- to three-year) calls or puts and paying premium in a deferred fashion. Index/basket put swaps (exchanging premium for depreciation), index/basket collar swaps (buying and selling call swaps or put swaps with different strikes) and other structures are also available. Although these types of derivatives are executed in the offshore market, overall activity is still thin.

Basket/Index Options

The absence of listed index options on MIFE has led certain offshore banks to buy and sell offshore OTC basket/index options for clients or proprietary books. Banks arrange puts and calls based on key Philippine indexes or smaller baskets of local blue-chip stocks; most options are short-term, American or European cash-settlement derivatives denominated in foreign currencies. Although these options are appealing as they permit clients to obtain specific risk protection or exposure, overall activity is still very limited for many of the same reasons outlined above. Note that there is presently no market for exotic index options.

Fixed Income

Fixed Income Forwards/Swaps

The Philippine fixed income derivative market is still in the very early stages of development and features only token trading of peso FRAs and peso swaps. The overall domestic FRA/swap market is impacted by: (a) lack of an established floating rate benchmark through which to value the floating segment of IRSs (although treasury bill rates are becoming a more broadly accepted onshore reference); (b) lack of a robust government yield curve to provide the market with additional swap pricing information; (c) thinly-traded government securities resulting in expensive or difficult hedging of swap positions; and (d) erratic, one-sided flow preventing institutions from matching swaps as a means of reducing risk. Until further advances occur in these areas (which are most likely to be fostered by financial deregulation and easier foreign access to underlying cash instruments), the domestic forward/swap market is likely to remain small and illiquid.

Peso FRAs are technically quoted to three years, though six- and 12-month deals are the norm in what is still a very small market; FRAs generally reference the 91-day treasury bill rate (for onshore deals) or the interest rates implied by FX forwards (for offshore deals). Given the infancy of the FRA market, there is no standard interbank dealing size at the present time and bid-offer spreads on transactions are wide and volatile. Interest rate swaps, which are quoted as either fixed pesos against 91-day treasury bill rates (onshore), or fixed pesos against the interest rates implicit in either three- or six-month FX forwards (offshore), are available to three years. As with FRAs, most liquidity in this thinly-traded segment of the market is concentrated in short-term transactions to one year; there is currently no standard interbank dealing size and bid-offer spreads are very wide.

Fixed Income Options

The market for peso fixed income caps, floors, swaptions and bond options is not presently in existence, for many of the reasons detailed in the section immediately above. Until further advancements are made in the domestic fixed income market (e.g. greater liquidity in bonds, easier foreign access to securities, establishment of an accepted short-term floating benchmark, development of a more robust government curve, expansion of peso FRAs and swaps, and so on), it is unlikely that a meaningful fixed income option market will develop.

Currency

Currency Forwards/Swaps

As a result of the very thin turnover in spot PHP/US$ (primarily a function of currency controls and lack of convertibility), activity in peso currency forwards and swaps is thin as well. Until foreign exchange controls are liberalized and spot trading in pesos increases, turnover in local currency forwards and swaps is likely to remain small.

Although the onshore currency forward market is technically quoted to 12 months, there is very little liquidity beyond six months. Typical interbank dealing size in peso forwards is PHP127.5 mln (US$5 mln), and bid-offer spreads range from 200 to 300 basis points under normal market conditions. It should be noted that in addition to modest onshore activity in peso forwards, there is also a small amount of offshore turnover in non-deliverable forwards (NDFs, also known as dollar-settled exchange agreements). NDFs reference the forward price of PHP/US$ but settlement is effected through a net US dollar payment based on the market value of the forward at maturity, rather than physical exchange of pesos and US dollars.

Currency swaps are occasionally arranged to hedge asset or liability structures on a very specific basis, to a maximum of three years; such deals are still very rare. Although the market is extremely small the two most common varieties of CCSs quoted are fixed pesos against US$ LIBOR flat, and fixed pesos against fixed US dollars (effectively long-term FX forwards). Given the nascent state of the market there is no standard interbank dealing size and bid-offer spreads are very wide and quite volatile. It should be noted that certain offshore currency swaps are structured in the non-deliverable form described above as well.

Currency Options

As with peso currency forwards and swaps, activity in peso currency options is extremely limited, for the same reasons outlined above. Onshore currency options (quoting pesos against US dollars) are based exclusively on hedging of asset or liability transactions; such options are normally vanilla European or American derivatives which mature in under 12 months. Non-deliverable, cash-settled offshore options which reference the peso (but which do not involve physical delivery of pesos and foreign currencies) are executed on occasion but overall activity is thin. Given the small size of the market, there are no established quoting conventions or dealing parameters for peso FX options.

Commodity

Commodity Forwards/Swaps

Although the Philippine listed derivative market is heavily weighted toward commodity futures trading, the market for domestic OTC commodity forward and swap trading on the same references (e.g. soybean, copra, sugar) is non-existent. The only true commodity forward activity which occurs in the country is related to major domestic corporations seeking hedging protection on an OTC basis; such hedges are related to major international commodity references (e.g. oil products, base metals) and are executed offshore.

Commodity Options

As with OTC commodity forwards/swaps, the market for domestic OTC commodity options is non-existent at the present time.

LOCAL REGULATORY/LEGAL TREATMENT OF DERIVATIVES

The two primary regulators of the Philippine financial system include the Central Bank of the Philippines (CBP) and the Securities and Exchange Commission (SEC). The SEC, a quasi-judicial agency, controls all aspects of the local securities market, including matters related to futures trading.

The SEC has direct oversight over the country's futures exchange, MIFE, and of member brokers belonging to MIFE. The SEC has only recognized and licensed a single exchange in the Philippines to date (MIFE), and domestic futures brokers are only permitted to deal on licensed exchanges; as a result, domestic futures brokers are not authorized to trade on overseas or offshore exchanges.

The Philippine listed derivative market is regulated under the Revised Securities Act (RSA) and the Revised Rules and Regulations on Commodity Futures Trading. Under the RSA and the Revised Rules, all futures brokers must be licensed by the SEC. In order to obtain a license (which must be renewed on a continuous basis) brokers must maintain minimum capitalization standards at all times (e.g. minimum capital of PHP3 mln (US$115,000) and minimum unencumbered capital of PHP1 mln (US$40,000)) and must ensure that assets are not less than 20% of liabilities at any time. All brokers are required to report their financial standing and condition to the SEC on a regular basis in the form of daily transaction reports, monthly unaudited financial statements, audited semi-annual statements and other associated documents. Futures brokers are not permitted to trade managed accounts; all buy and sell orders must be obtained in writing from clients (or from third parties through use of a special power of attorney). All brokers must contribute a PHP2 mln (US$80,000) deposit to the MIFE Compensation Fund, which is used to protect clients, and the Exchange, from broker defaults. Given the infancy of the domestic OTC derivative market, there are currently no specific regulations governing OTC forwards, swaps or options.

LOCAL ACCOUNTING PRACTICES FOR DERIVATIVES

Given the Philippines' relatively underdeveloped OTC derivative market, there is no mandatory accounting treatment for derivatives; certain accounting conventions have been adapted by larger domestic financial institutions, but are not followed universally within the country. In the case of unmatured forward foreign exchange contracts and swaps (whether for hedging or speculating purposes), positions are revalued on balance sheet date at prevailing market rates, with unrealized gains or losses taken into the income statement at that time. There is no other specific accounting treatment for local derivatives, though certain large institutional participants use a mark-to-market valuation process for their speculative derivative positions; gains or losses arising from the current market value are reflected in the income statement immediately.

PROSPECTS FOR THE LOCAL DERIVATIVE MARKET

Summarized below are the near-term (one- to three-year) and medium-term (three- to five-year) prospects for Philippine domestic derivatives.

Near-term:

- Introduction of listed index futures and additional commodity futures (e.g. red beans) on MIFE.
- Increased liquidity in peso futures and forwards as currency regulations are eased and the country moves towards full convertibility of the peso; greater activity in CCSs as a result of currency deregulation and as corporate funding needs continue to grow.
- Greater participation in OTC equity derivatives as listed index futures are introduced, the equity market continues expanding, and currency restrictions are

eased (permitting foreign investors easier access to local shares through local currency transactions).

- More widespread use of IRSs as a domestic floating rate benchmark develops and domestic companies increase their funding needs.
- Gradual expansion of warrants and convertibles as the demand for equity-linked financing by domestic companies grows.

Medium-term:

- Further deepening of IRSs and CCSs as financing needs continue to grow, clients become more accustomed to using such derivatives, and hedging becomes simpler for dealers.
- Initial development of fixed income options.
- Continued expansion of commodity trading volume; introduction of select new contracts.

Exchange	Contract	1993 Volume (contracts)	1994 Volume (contracts)
MIFE	Treasury bill futures	5,472	7,672
	JPY/US$ currency futures	97,050	163,542
	US$/GBP currency futures	196,998	97,004
	CHF/US$ currency futures	58,204	79,840
	DM/US$ currency futures	64,972	43,280
	PHP/US$ currency futures	3,634	2,356
	Robusta coffee futures	143,788	516,010
	Sugar futures	315,212	496,686
	Soybean futures	229,640	615,968
	Copra futures	203,204	544,992
	Dried cocoon futures	431,476	524,000

Table 10.15 Summary of 1993/1994 Listed Futures and Options Turnover

	Overall Liquidity	Liquid/ Maximum Maturity	Interbank dealing size	Average bid-offer spread
Equity/Index Swaps	poor	1–3 yrs/3 yrs	n/a	n/a
Equity/Index Options	poor	1–12 mos/12 mos	n/a	n/a
Interest Rate Swaps	poor	1 yr/3 yrs	none	varies
Interest Rate Options	non-existent	n/a	n/a	n/a
Currency Swaps	poor	1 yr/3 yrs	none	varies
Currency Options	poor	1–12 mos/12 mos	none	varies

Table 10.16 Summary of Domestic OTC Derivatives

11: Singapore

FINANCIAL MARKET OVERVIEW

Singapore's domestic financial markets are gradually expanding in size and liquidity. The country's equity market features growing market capitalization and liquidity, while its bond market, though still thinly traded, is expanding on a primary basis. The Singapore dollar (SGD) currency market is quite active, particularly onshore (though it receives substantial scrutiny from the Monetary Authority of Singapore (MAS), the country's primary regulator). In addition to financial instruments, Singapore's geographic location and its role as a centre of commerce and shipping have allowed it to generate significant trading in commodities and energy products. The country's local derivative market is in the developing stages: local derivatives are still limited in availability and liquidity, primarily as turnover in the underlying cash markets is still growing; in addition, the MAS is a strict regulator which does not encourage the development of derivatives based on local indicators. Despite these limitations Singapore has managed to create for itself a successful niche in the global derivative markets by developing a series of listed and OTC derivatives based on important international references.

Equity trading in the local market dates back to 1960, before Singapore existed as an independent nation. In 1960 the Malaysian Stock Exchange (MSE) created equity trading centres in both Kuala Lumpur and Singapore; in 1964 the two centres were merged and the MSE was renamed the Stock Exchange of Malaysia and Singapore (SEMS). When Singapore declared independence in 1965 it agreed to continue operating SEMS in joint co-operation with the Malaysian authorities. In 1973, however, the venture was disbanded and the local authorities created the Stock Exchange of Singapore (SES), which exists today as the country's sole equity exchange (note that SES also operates SESDAQ, an OTC electronic system for trading in smaller capitalization stocks). Despite the existence of separate Malaysian and Singaporean exchanges from 1973 onwards, both centres continued to list each other's shares; these joint listings continued until 1989, when the SES and the Kuala Lumpur Stock Exchange elected to delist the other's shares. The two markets now trade exclusively in their own local shares (though certain Malaysian (and select international) shares are available in Singapore through the SES's CLOB (Central Order Limit Book) Market, an electronic OTC trading system).

The Singaporean equity market experienced a surge in foreign investment between 1992 and 1993 as foreign funds channelled into global emerging stock markets. During this period annual trading volume on the SES rose from nearly 13 mln shares to over 60 mln shares, while overall market capitalization more than doubled to US$133 bln. With the decline of the Singaporean market in 1994 and 1995 trading volume dropped dramatically (e.g. back to 25 mln shares per year), as did liquidity in smaller capitalization stocks. Nevertheless, Singapore's overall market capitalization has remained buoyant as a result of privatizations, initial public offerings and secondary flotations; total capitalization of just under US$134.5 bln ranks it as the seventh largest of Asia Pacific's 13 markets. Figure 11.1 traces the historical movement of the benchmark Straits Times Index (STI) while Table 11.1 highlights key indicators of the local equity market.

Note that foreign investors have complete access to domestic equities and are not restricted from acquiring any amount of shares in local companies; the sole exception is in certain 'national interest' companies, such as banking, defense and aviation, where separate classes of foreign shares are listed on the SES once predetermined foreign ownership levels have been reached (e.g. 20% to 49%, depending on institution/sector).

Year*	Market Capitalization (US$ bln)	Trading Value (US$ bln)	Listed Companies (#)
1994	134.5	81.0	240
1993	132.7	81.6	178
1992	48.8	14.0	163
1991	47.6	18.1	166
1990	34.3	20.2	150

* to December of each year; Source: IFC, 1995

	1/92-6/95 Annualized Return*	1/92-6/95 Total Return*
Straits Times Index	11.92%	45.53%

* dividends reinvested in index

Table 11.1 Domestic Equity Market Indicators

The Singaporean fixed income market is gradually increasing in size, though overall liquidity is still thin. The main segment of the market consists of Singapore Government securities, including short-term bills and medium- and long-term bonds. Bills are available with maturities of 90, 180 and 360 days, while bonds are available with maturities of one- to 20-years (and with benchmarks at two-, five- and seven-years). Although the primary market is expanding, secondary liquidity is

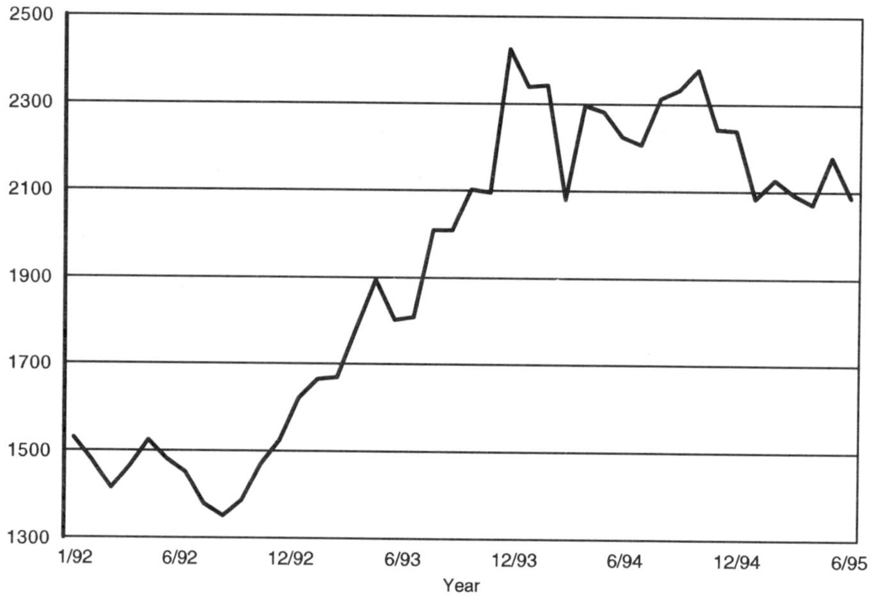

Figure 11.1 Historical Movement of the Straits Times Index

still limited as a result of the Central Provident Fund's (CPF, a major government pension fund) demand for paper; activity by the CPF often squeezes other investors out of the market and dampens secondary trading. Total sovereign securities in the public market amounted to SGD15.8 bln (US$11.2 bln) in 1994 (supplemented by an additional SGD44 bln (US$31.4 bln) of private placement securities held by the CPF). Figure 11.2 traces the historical movement of government bond yield curves while Figure 11.3 illustrates the movement of two- and five-year benchmark government bond yields. Issuance of private sector Singapore dollar bonds is still very limited. Although various blue-chip local companies have accessed the corporate market in the past (through fixed rate bonds, bonds-with-warrants, or convertible bonds, all with maturities ranging from one- to ten-years), most still rely on internal capital generation or bank borrowing to provide necessary financing. Activity in the private sector money market is also limited and focused primarily on domestic bank certificates of deposit; bills of exchange and commercial paper exist but are not actively utilized. Total private sector fixed income outstandings amounted to SGD3.5 bln (US$2.5 bln) at the end of 1994.

The key interest rates in the domestic market include Singapore dollar interbank offer rate (SIBOR) (the borrowing cost for financial institutions in the domestic interbank deposit market), Singapore Government treasury bill rates (the short-term borrowing cost of the government), Singapore Government treasury bond yields (the medium- and long-term borrowing costs of the government) and Singapore dollar swap rates (the rate for transacting domestic interest rate swaps in

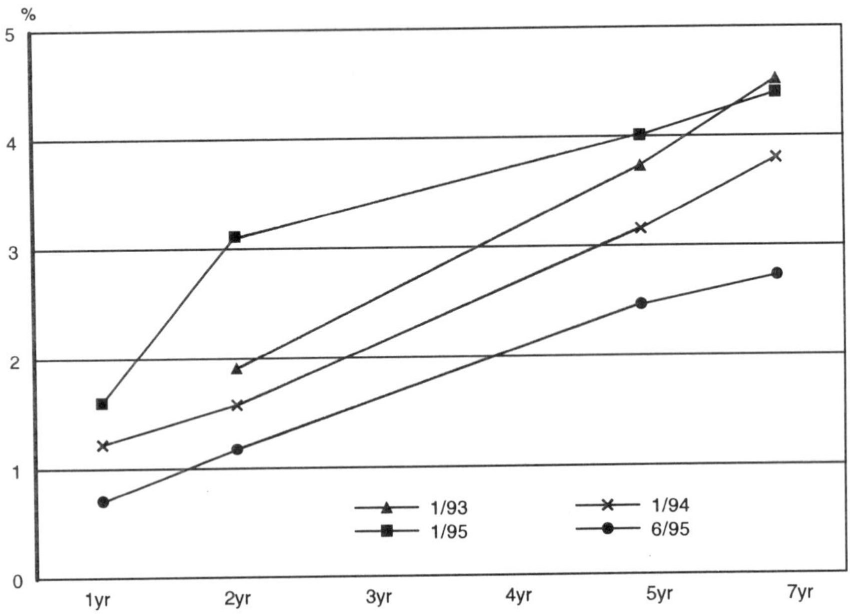

Figure 11.2 Historical Movement of Singapore Government Bond Yield Curves

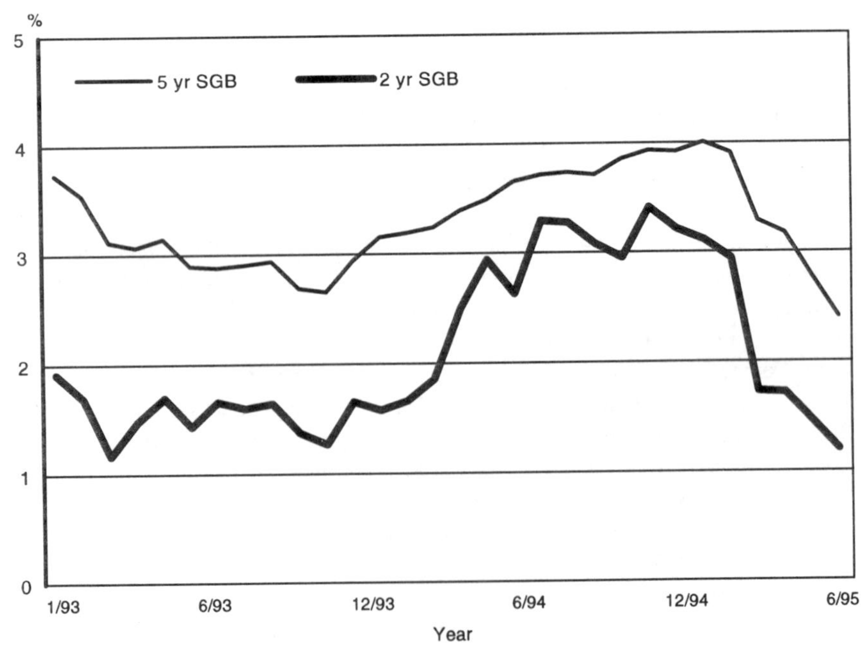

Figure 11.3 Historical Movement of Two- and Five-year Singapore Government Bond Yields

the interbank market). We shall discuss these rates at greater length in our section on fixed income forwards and swaps later in the chapter. Table 11.2 summarizes the payment frequency, compounding frequency and day count conventions for each rate.

Rate	Payment Frequency	Compounding Frequency	Day Count Convention
SGD SIBOR	–	–	Actual/365
Gov't Bills	–	–	Actual/365
Gov't Bonds	semi-annual	semi-annual	Actual/Actual
Swaps	semi-annual	semi-annual	Actual/365

Table 11.2 Key Domestic Interest Rates

The Singapore dollar (SGD) is a freely convertible currency based on a managed float against a trade weighted basket of currencies. Management of the currency is handled with great care in order to ensure low and stable inflation within the country; given a strong desire to manage inflation prudently, the regulatory authorities keep close watch on trading of the Singapore dollar. Spot FX trading of the local currency in the onshore market is highest among all emerging Asian currencies, averaging an estimated SGD1.68 bln (US$1.2 bln) per day; offshore trading is estimated at SGD1.4 bln (US$1 bln) per day (Paisley and Woodcock, 1995).

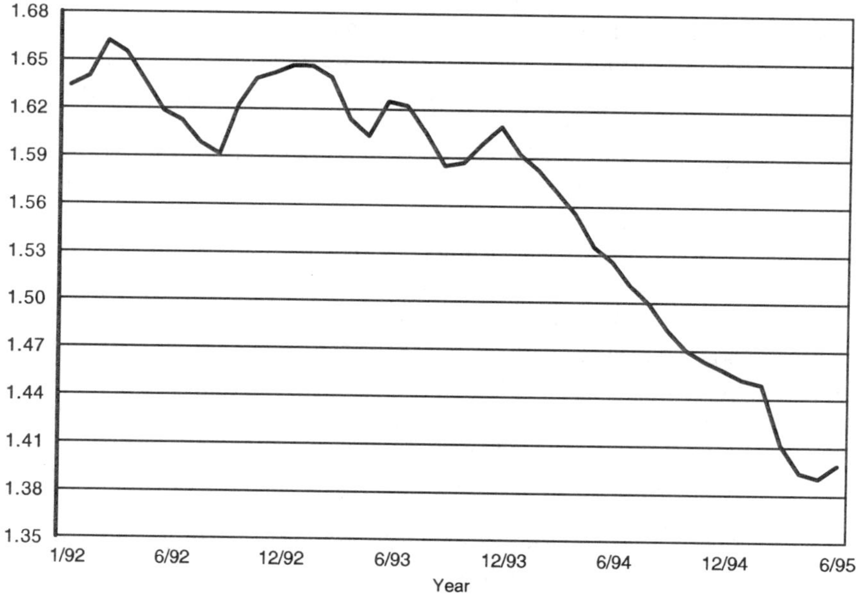

Figure 11.4 Historical Movement of Spot SGD/US$

The skew towards greater dealing in the onshore market is in sharp contrast to other Asian nations, where offshore trading is generally a multiple of onshore trading. The fact that more trading occurs onshore is beneficial for the MAS, which prefers to monitor trading activity in the country's currency for the reasons indicated above. Typical dealing size in the spot interbank market is SGD7 mln to SGD14 mln (US$5 mln to US$10 mln) and bid-offer spreads are SGD0.001/US$ under normal market conditions; dealing in the corporate market, which drives a significant portion of onshore activity, is executed in SGD1.4 mln to SGD2.8 mln (US$1 mln to US$2 mln) parcels. Figure 11.4 illustrates the historical movement of spot SGD/US$.

DERIVATIVE MARKETS AND PRODUCTS

LISTED DERIVATIVE EXCHANGES

Singapore features three separate exchanges which list and trade derivatives: the Stock Exchange of Singapore (SES), Singapore International Monetary Exchange (SIMEX) and Singapore Commodity Exchange (SICOM). Despite the fact that Singapore possesses a reasonably small domestic financial market it has made great efforts to establish itself as an international financial centre. The creation of SIMEX and, to a lesser extent, SICOM and SES, have aided in that process.

The trading of listed derivatives in Singapore dates back to 1977 when the SES introduced options on individual Singaporean equities. Despite a promising beginning, trading soon languished and the options were suspended in 1980; equity options did not reappear in Singapore until 1993, when they were re-introduced by the SES. Along with equity options the SES has traded listed convertibles and issuer/covered equity warrants for several years; activity in warrants has far outweighed activity in both options and convertibles. All SES derivative securities are traded on a fully automated basis through the Exchange's computerized central limit order book (CLOB) system; clearing and settlement occur through the SES's wholly-owned subsidiary, the Options Clearing Company (OCC).

At the time the SES was trading equity options, the Gold Futures Exchange of Singapore was trading gold futures. The original Gold Exchange, founded in 1978, enjoyed several years of success before lack of supervision gave way to trading abuses by certain local participants. The authorities re-organized the Gold Futures Exchange in 1983 as an internationally-focused trading centre and renamed it SIMEX. SIMEX has since made its mark by becoming an active international derivatives forum, listing and trading futures and options based on offshore financial and commodity indexes; SIMEX has also established (or is in the process of finalizing) arrangements with certain offshore exchanges, such as IPE and NYMEX, to trade their contracts during Asian hours, adding to the international stature of the Exchange. It should be noted that none of the SIMEX's contracts currently reference the local equity, interest rate, currency or commodity markets. As a result of its international focus, SIMEX has attracted the interest and attention of offshore hedgers and speculators; approximately 80% of its client base (primarily institutional) resides outside of Singapore. By listing contracts on a number of the world's main financial indexes (e.g. the Nikkei 225 stock index, Euroyen deposits, Japanese Government Bonds (JGBs), Eurodollar deposits, and so on), SIMEX has grown to become the 14th largest futures and options exchange in the world, with annual turnover of 24 mln contracts in 1994 (FI, 1995). In addition to its practice of creating derivatives based on highly liquid international financial instruments, a portion of the Exchange's success is attributable to its policy of charging low commissions, requiring low futures margins, paying interest on margin deposits and imposing no taxes on transactions. Success is also due to the Exchange's decision to calibrate a number of its contracts so that they are completely offsettable with those listed on other exchanges (e.g. the Eurodollar contract is offsettable on the CME, while the Brent oil contract is offsettable on the IPE); the mutual offset system enables clients to establish, transfer or close positions on one of two exchanges at any time and to settle open positions at expiry at the same price on different exchanges. SIMEX trades on an open-outcry basis on the floor of the Exchange (though it is also in the process of establishing an overnight screen dealing system which will permit electronic trading of Euromark, Euroyen, Japanese Government Bond and currency futures from 11.30 to 17.00 GMT; the system is expected to be operational at the end of 1995). Trades are cleared through, and guaranteed by, the SIMEX Clearinghouse, which is backed by the financial resources of its clearing members. Membership on SIMEX is available in one of four forms: corporate clearing members (who have full trading rights on the floor and can execute and clear own account and client trades), corporate non-clearing members (who have full trading rights and can execute own account trades but cannot execute or clear client trades), commercial associate members (who can execute own account trades in energy contracts only) and individual non-clearing members (who can execute own account trades only).

SICOM, which has been somewhat overshadowed by SIMEX is, nonetheless, an important component of the local derivative market. The Exchange, which is viewed primarily as a rubber trading forum, has been in existence in various forms since the 1920s. Trading in rubber and rubber futures began in Singapore in the 1920s, before Singapore existed as an independent nation. Over the course of several decades the trading and clearing of rubber futures was handled by the Singapore Chamber of Commerce Rubber Association, followed by the Rubber Association of Singapore (RAS); the RAS was privatized in 1992 and renamed the RAS Commodity Exchange. In 1994 it changed its name to SICOM as it became clear that commodities other than rubber would be traded on the Exchange over time. The gradual shift away from rubber began in early 1995 when SICOM introduced a robusta coffee contract; plans are currently underway to introduce futures on cocoa, zinc, copper and aluminium. Trading on SICOM is automated and occurs via the NEAT electronic trading system; all futures trades on SICOM are cleared and guaranteed by clearing members. Membership on the Exchange takes one of two forms: clearing members and non-clearing members. Clearing members may be market-makers (who are able to trade for their own accounts or client accounts and are authorized to clear and guarantee trades), brokers (who are able to trade for clients and clear and guarantee trades, and are required to execute via market-makers) or dealers (who are able to trade for their own accounts and are required to execute via market-makers or brokers). Non-clearing members may be brokers (who can trade for client accounts), trade members (who can trade for their own accounts directly with market-makers), associate members (who can trade for their own accounts directly with market-makers but cannot access SICOM systems), and individual members (who can trade for their own accounts through brokers). Table 11.3 summarizes the listed exchanges and derivatives of Singapore.

Exchange	Primary Derivatives
Singapore International Commodity Exchange (SICOM)	Rubber futures; rubber index futures; coffee futures
Singapore International Monetary Exchange (SIMEX)	Deposit futures, options; index futures, options; interest rate futures, options; currency futures; gold futures; fuel oil futures; crude oil futures#,##; gasoline futures##; heating oil futures##; natural gas futures##; propane futures##
Stock Exchange of Singapore (SES)	Equity options; issuer equity warrants; covered equity warrants; convertible bonds

via IPE link; ## via NYMEX link (proposed)

Table 11.3 Listed Derivative Exchanges

LISTED FUTURES AND OPTIONS

Equity

Equity Futures/Options

The domestic market lists and trades equity options through the SES. Equity options, along with convertibles and equity warrants (discussed below), are the only listed derivatives in Singapore based on local financial prices; all other listed contracts are related to offshore prices, rates or indexes.

We indicate above that the SES introduced listed equity options in 1977 but suspended trading in 1980 due to poor turnover. The SES reintroduced options in 1993 on two separate shares, Singapore Airlines (foreign shares) and Keppel

Corporation, and followed shortly thereafter with options on two more shares, City Development and National Steel; in late 1994 it introduced options on three additional shares, United Overseas Bank (foreign shares), Development Bank of Singapore (foreign shares) and Creative Technology. Despite encouraging trading volume of nearly 15,000 contracts in 1993, turnover declined to less than 4,000 contracts in 1994, primarily because investors returned to cheaper and more liquid warrants (which have historically been available on all the stocks covered by options). The absence of option market-makers has also been a detriment to greater activity, as has the restriction on short-selling of equities in the onshore market; both will need to be resolved before activity in options can increase to meaningful levels.

Options on the SES have maturities of either three- or six-months and coincide with a regular contract cycle of March, June, September and December; each option contract, exercisable in American form, commands 1,000 shares of underlying stock. Strike price intervals on options are set in accordance with the underlying share price; shares with prices under SGD1 are set at SGD0.10 intervals, SGD1–SGD3 at SGD0.20 intervals, SGD3–SGD4.20 at SGD0.30 intervals, SGD4.20–SGD5 at SGD0.40 intervals, SGD50–SGD10 at SGD0.50 intervals and SGD10+ at SGD1 intervals. Trading of equity options occurs via the SES's central limit order book; options trades are cleared and guaranteed by the Options Clearing Company. Stock options are governed by the Securities Industry Act (discussed in the regulatory section below) and through By-law XI of the SES, entitled 'Exchange Options Trading via CLOB'. Contract specifications for listed options are detailed in Table 11.4.

Contract	**Equity Options**
Type	Domestic
Exchange	Stock Exchange of Singapore
Months	March, June, September, December
Contract Size	1,000 shares of underlying equity
Tick Value	Varies with price of equity
Daily Limit	No limit
Deliverable Instrument	Cash settlement
Last Trading Day	Business day prior to the option exercise
Exercise Day	American exercise – any business day up to, and including, the last Friday of the contract month
Real-time price data	Reuters: <0#CTDM*.SI>, <0#KPLM*.SI>, <0#NATS:*.SI>, <0#SIAe*.SI>, <0#CREA*.SI>, <0#DBSe*.SI>, <0#UOBe*.SI>; Telerate: 2806, 2811, 2822, 2835, 2841, 2845, 2846, 2867, 2888, 2894, 56930-34

Table 11.4 Contract Specifications for SES Equity Options

Note that equity futures are not currently traded in the local market.

Index Futures/Options/Futures Options

Although Singapore's exchanges do not list domestic stock index futures, SIMEX has been a pioneer in listing overseas stock index contracts. SIMEX currently trades futures on three separate offshore indexes, including the Nikkei 225, the Nikkei 300 and the MSCI Hong Kong Index.

SIMEX introduced Nikkei 225 futures in 1986, two years before the OSE contract was created. The future remains one of SIMEX's most active derivatives, posting total turnover of 5.1 mln contracts in 1993 and 5.8 mln contracts in 1994; year-end open interest increased from 89,786 in 1993 to 98,099 in 1994 (SIMEX, 1995). Participants have been attracted to the SIMEX contract because it offers deep liquidity and low margins; in addition, the SIMEX contract is fungible (though not mutually offsettable) with the CME's contract, providing participants with longer trading days and greater flexibility in managing positions. These advantages have permitted SIMEX to challenge the OSE for a meaningful portion of the total Nikkei futures market.

SIMEX expanded its Japanese derivative listing in early 1995 by introducing Nikkei 300 futures. Although it is still too early to determine whether the Exchange will achieve the same level of success with its Nikkei 300 future, the new contract is expected to challenge the OSE for a meaningful segment of the market. SIMEX's Hong Kong contract, introduced in 1993, is based on the MSCI Hong Kong Index (HKI). The MSCI HKI, tracks, but does not duplicate, the very popular Hang Seng Index underlying HKFE's contract. Although first year turnover in MSCI HKI futures was an impressive 66,000 contracts, volume declined to under 500 contracts in 1994 (SIMEX, 1995); the contract is effectively dormant at the present time, primarily because institutions interested in gaining or managing Hong Kong equity exposure prefer the deep liquidity of HKFE's HSI contract. Tables 11.5 and 11.6 outline the Japanese contracts, while Table 11.7 summarizes the Hong Kong contract. Figure 11.5 displays the historical price movement of near-month SIMEX Nikkei 225 futures.

SIMEX presently features index options on Nikkei 225 and Nikkei 300 futures. The options are structured as American exercise contracts with strikes set at 500 point intervals (for Nikkei 225 options) or five point intervals (for Nikkei 300 options); unlike OSE's cash-settled Nikkei index options, the SIMEX options result in delivery or acceptance of the underlying futures. Activity in Nikkei 225 futures options, as in the futures described above, has been on the rise over the past few years. Total turnover increased from 897,000 contracts in 1993 to 1.49 mln contracts in 1994; year-end open interest increased from 126,649 contracts in 1993 to 203,450 contracts in 1994 (SIMEX, 1995). Trading volume in Nikkei 300 options is still negligible; the contract has only been listed on SIMEX since February 1995 and has not attracted much attention to date. Tables 11.8 and 11.9 contain contract details for the two index futures options.

Contract	**Nikkei 225 Index Futures**
Type	Offshore
Exchange	Singapore International Monetary Exchange
Months	March, June, September, December, plus spot month
Contract Size	JPY500 * Nikkei 225 Index
Tick Value	5 index points
Daily Limit	+/– 5% against previous day's settlement price, after which trading is only permitted within the 5% band for 30 minutes; thereafter the band is expanded to 10%. No price limits on the last trading day.
Deliverable Instrument	Cash settlement
Last Trading Day	3rd Wednesday of the contract month
Delivery Day	Same as the last trading day
Real-time price data	Bloomberg: NIA <Cmdty>; Reuters:<0#SSI:>; Telerate: 6174

Table 11.5 Contract Specifications for SIMEX Nikkei 225 Index Futures

Contract	**Nikkei 300 Index Futures**
Type	Offshore
Exchange	Singapore International Monetary Exchange
Months	March, June, September, December to 5 quarter months
Contract Size	JPY10,000 * Nikkei 300 Index
Tick Value	0.1 index points
Daily Limit	+/– 7.5% against previous day's settlement price, after which trading is only permitted within the 7.5% band for 15 minutes; the band is then expanded to 12.5% for 15 minutes, and is then eliminated. No price limits on the last trading day.
Deliverable Instrument	Cash settlement
Last Trading Day	Last business day before the 2nd Friday of the contract month
Delivery Day	2nd Friday of the contract month
Real-time price data	Bloomberg: SNA <Cmdty>; Reuters: <0#SNW:>; Telerate: 44170

Table 11.6 Contract Specifications for SIMEX Nikkei 300 Index Futures

Contract	MSCI Hong Kong Index Futures
Type	Offshore
Exchange	Singapore International Monetary Exchange
Months	Two serial months and March, June, September, December, up to five quarter months
Contract Size	HK$100 * MSCI HK Index
Tick Value	1 point
Daily Limit	No limit
Deliverable Instrument	Cash settlement based on closing price on the last business day of the contract month
Last Trading Day	2nd to last business day of the contract month
Delivery Day	Last business day of the contract month
Real-time price data	Bloomberg: HSA <Cmdty>; Reuters: <0#SHI:>; Telerate: 22975

Table 11.7 Contract Specifications for SIMEX MSCI Hong Kong Index Futures

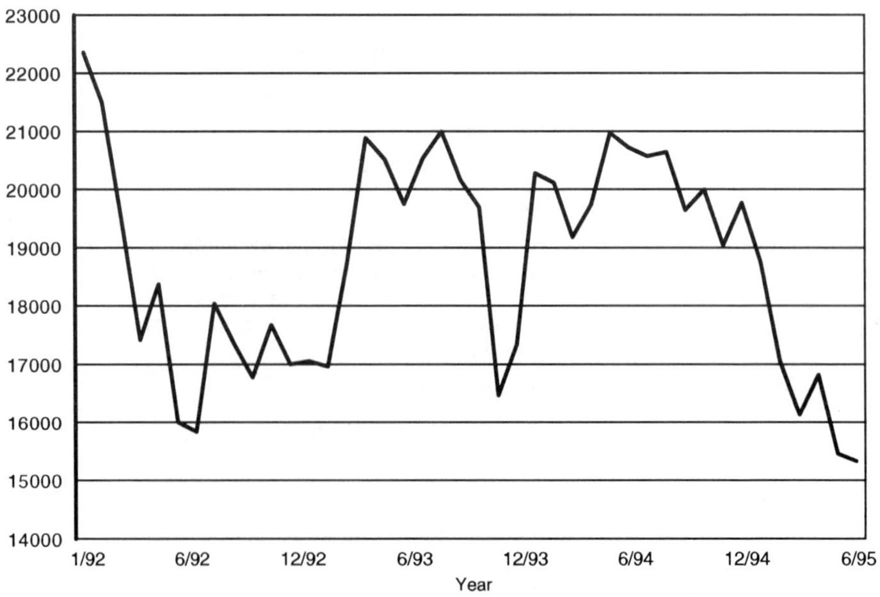

Figure 11.5 Historical Movement of SIMEX Nikkei 225 Index Futures

Contract	Options on Nikkei 225 Index Futures
Type	Offshore
Exchange	Singapore International Monetary Exchange
Months	Two serial months plus March, June, September, December
Contract Size	1 Nikkei 225 Index future
Tick Value	5 index points; 0.2 index points if trade results in liquidation
Daily Limit	Same as SIMEX Nikkei 225 Index futures
Deliverable Instrument	Physical settlement into underlying futures contract
Last Trading Day	Day before 2nd Friday of the contract month
Exercise Day	American exercise – any business day up to, and including, the last trading day
Real-time price data	Bloomberg: NIA <Cmdty> OMON; Reuters: <0#SSImy+>, <SSISUM>; Telerate: 7346-47, 26540-53

Table 11.8 Contract Specifications for SIMEX Options on Nikkei 225 Index Futures

Contract	Options on Nikkei 300 Index Futures
Type	Offshore
Exchange	Singapore International Monetary Exchange
Months	Three near non-quarter months, plus five quarter months on March, June, September, December cycle
Contract Size	1 Nikkei 300 Index future
Tick Value	0.1 index point
Daily Limit	Same as SIMEX Nikkei 300 Index futures
Deliverable Instrument	Physical settlement into underlying futures contract
Last Trading Day	Business day before the 2nd Friday of the contract month
Exercise Day	American exercise – any business day up to, and including, the last trading day
Real-time price data	Bloomberg: SNA <Cmdty> OMON; Reuters: <0#SNWmy+>, <0#SNWs:>; Telerate: 9108-11, 9112-15, 57278-86, 27808-23

Table 11.9 Contract Specifications for SIMEX Options on Nikkei 300 Index Futures

Fixed Income

Deposit Futures/Options/Futures Options

SIMEX lists and trades deposit futures based on three of the world's most active Eurodeposit rates, Eurodollars, Euromarks and Euroyen. The Eurodollar contract offered on SIMEX is the Exchange's most liquid derivative, used throughout the region to gain exposure to, or protect positions from, changes in three-month US$ LIBOR movements; SIMEX Eurodollar futures utilize the SIMEX-CME mutual offset link, meaning positions can be established, traded, transferred or closed out on either exchange. Turnover in Eurodollar futures increased from 5.35 mln contracts in 1993 to a record 8.69 mln contracts in 1994; year-end open interest also rose, from 53,366 contacts in 1993 to 82,585 contracts in 1994 (SIMEX, 1995). It should be noted that Eurodollar futures are also available in Asia Pacific through TIFFE; the SIMEX contract, however, is much more actively traded, offering a liquid strip out to 18-24 months (and quotes to 48 months).

SIMEX Euroyen futures are very actively traded, despite extreme competition from TIFFE's Euroyen contract. Trading volume increased from 3.53 mln contracts in 1993 to 6.82 mln contracts in 1994; year-end open interest rose from 202,657 contracts in 1993 to 336,299 contracts in 1994. SIMEX's Euromark futures are less actively traded than Eurodollars or Euroyen; total volume amounted to 23,127 contracts in 1993 and 231,068 contracts in 1994, with year-end open interest of 575 contracts in 1993 and 1,542 contracts in 1994 (SIMEX, 1995). (Note that SIMEX and LIFFE are in discussions to make their Euromark contracts fungible by 1996, which could provide an extended trading day for participants and boost trading volume in both locations). Tables 11.10, 11.11 and 11.12 provide details on the three SIMEX deposit futures contracts, while Figures 11.6 through 11.8 illustrate the historical price movement of each future.

Contract	Three-month Eurodollar Futures
Type	Offshore
Exchange	Singapore International Monetary Exchange
Months	Two serial months plus March, June, September, December to four years
Contract Size	US$1 mln
Tick Value	0.01%
Daily Limit	No limit
Deliverable Instrument	Cash settlement based on CME clearing house quote determination for 90-day US$ LIBOR
Last Trading Day	2nd London business day preceding the 3rd Wednesday of the contract month
Delivery Day	3rd Wednesday of the contract month
Real-time price data	Bloomberg: DEA <Cmdty>; Reuters: <0#SED:>; Telerate: 6175, 6172, 7296, 7251

Table 11.10 Contract Specifications for SIMEX Three-month Eurodollar Futures

Contract	Three-month Euroyen Futures
Type	Offshore
Exchange	Singapore International Monetary Exchange
Months	March, June, September, December to two years
Contract Size	JPY100 mln
Tick Value	0.01%
Daily Limit	No limit
Deliverable Instrument	Cash settlement based on average of Singapore-based yen LIBOR quotes taken randomly during last 90 minutes of expiry day session
Last Trading Day	2nd business day preceding the 3rd Wednesday of the contract month
Delivery Day	3rd Wednesday of the contract month
Real-time price data	Bloomberg: EYA <Cmdty>; Reuters: <0#SEY:>; Telerate: 6173, 38990

Table 11.11 Contract Specifications for SIMEX Three-month Euroyen Futures

Contract	Three-month Euromark Futures
Type	Offshore
Exchange	Singapore International Monetary Exchange
Months	March, June, September, December to one year
Contract Size	DM1 mln
Tick Value	0.01%
Daily Limit	No limit
Deliverable Instrument	Cash settlement
Last Trading Day	2nd business day preceding the 3rd Wednesday of the contract month
Delivery Day	3rd Wednesday of the contract month
Real-time price data	Bloomberg: MSA <Cmdty>; Reuters: <0#SEM:>; Telerate: 6170

Table 11.12 Contract Specifications for SIMEX Three-month Euromark Futures

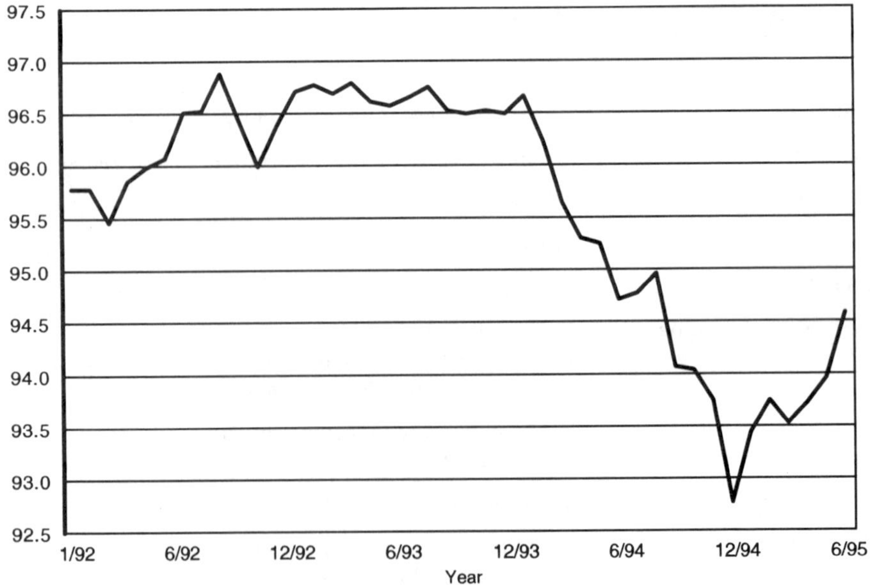

Figure 11.6 Historical Movement of SIMEX Three-month Eurodollar Futures

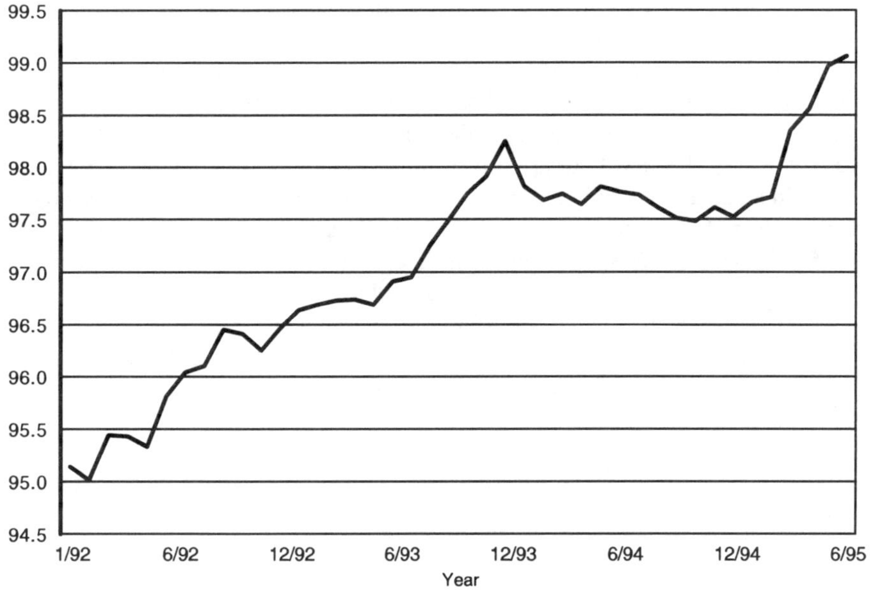

Figure 11.7 Historical Movement of SIMEX Three-month Euroyen Futures

Figure 11.8 Historical Movement of SIMEX Three-month Euromark Futures

In addition to the LIBOR-based futures contracts discussed above, SIMEX also lists deposit futures options on both Eurodollars and Euroyen. The options are structured as American exercise, physical delivery contracts; Eurodollar option strikes are set at 0.25% intervals when the futures price is greater than 91, and 0.50% intervals when less than 91, while Euroyen option strikes are always set at 0.25% intervals. Though trading volume in both contracts is growing, it remains modest in comparison with turnover in the underlying futures contracts. Total volume in Eurodollar futures options was a very modest 6,525 contracts in 1993 and 13,545 contracts in 1994; year-end open interest amounted to 1,436 contracts in 1993 and 1,483 contracts in 1994. Total volume in Euroyen futures options amounted to 57,395 contracts in 1993 and 126,280 contracts in 1994; year-end open interest nearly tripled from 7,027 contracts in 1993 to 19,240 contracts in 1994 (SIMEX, 1995). Tables 11.13 and 11.14 contain details on the two deposit futures options contacts.

Contract	**Options on Three-month Eurodollar Futures**
Type	Offshore
Exchange	Singapore International Monetary Exchange
Months	March, June, September, December to one year
Contract Size	1 Eurodollar future
Tick Value	0.01%; tick can be US$1 equivalent if trade results in liquidation
Daily Limit	No limit
Deliverable Instrument	Physical settlement into underlying futures contract
Last Trading Day	2nd London business day preceding the 3rd Wednesday of the contract month
Exercise Day	American exercise – any business day up to, and including, the last trading day
Real-time price data	Bloomberg: DEA <Cmdty> OMON; Reuters: <0#SEDmy+>, <SEDSUM>; Telerate: 27800-07

Table 11.13 Contract Specifications for SIMEX Options on Three-month Eurodollar Futures

Contract	Options on Three-month Euroyen Futures
Type	Offshore
Exchange	Singapore International Monetary Exchange
Months	March, June, September, December to 1 year
Contract Size	1 Euroyen Future
Tick Value	0.01%; tick value can be JPY100 equivalent if trade results in liquidation
Daily Limit	No limit
Deliverable Instrument	Physical settlement into underlying futures contract
Last Trading Day	2nd business day preceding the 3rd Wednesday of the contract month
Exercise Day	American exercise – any business day up to, and including the last trading day
Real-time price data	Bloomberg: EYA <Cmdty> OMON; Reuters: <0#SEYmy+>, <SEYSUM>; Telerate: 27828-39, 44150-51

Table 11.14 Contract Specifications for SIMEX Options on Three-month Euroyen Futures

Interest Rate Futures/Options/Futures Options

The sole interest rate future traded on SIMEX is the ten-year Japanese Government Bond (JGB) contract; the future is a cash-settled contract quoted to five quarter months at any time. Despite having been introduced as recently as 1993, trading volume and open interest have grown quickly: turnover increased from 29,254 contracts in 1993 to an impressive 443,564 contracts in 1994; year-end open interest rose from 575 contracts in 1993 to 3,060 contracts in 1994 (SIMEX, 1995). The SIMEX JGB is offered as an alternative to the TSE's physical settlement contract as well as LIFFE's cash settlement contract. Table 11.15 contains contract specifications for JGB futures, while Figure 11.9 illustrates the historical movement of SIMEX JGB futures prices.

Contract	Ten-year Japanese Government Bond Futures
Type	Offshore
Exchange	Singapore International Monetary Exchange
Months	March, June, September, December to five quarter months
Contract Size	JPY50 mln face value of ten-year Japanese Government Bonds, 6% coupon
Tick Value	JPY0.01 per JPY100 face value of bonds
Daily Limit	No limit
Deliverable Instrument	Cash settlement based on official opening price (hajimane) on the TSE's last trading day
Last Trading Day	One business day immediately preceding the TSE's last trading day in JGB futures
Delivery Day	Last trading day in TSE JGB futures
Real-time price data	Bloomberg: BJA <Cmdty>; Reuters:<0#SJB:>; Telerate: 7253

Table 11.15 Contract Specifications for SIMEX Ten-year Japanese Government Bond Futures

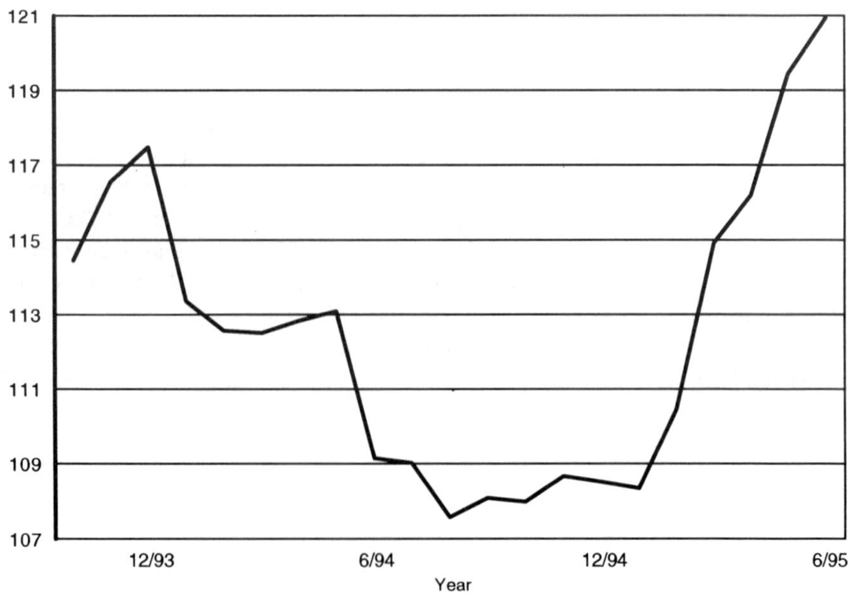

Figure 11.9 Historical Movement of SIMEX Ten-year Japanese Government Bond Futures

In addition to JGB futures, SIMEX also lists and trades JGB futures options; the option is structured as an American exercise, physical delivery contract with strikes set at 0.50% intervals. JGB futures options were introduced in late 1993 and completed their first full year of trading in 1994 with modest turnover: total trading volume amounted to 39,808 contacts while year-end open interest reached 1,994 contracts (SIMEX, 1995). Both figures suggest future interest in the contract should be strong, despite rather formidable competition from the TSE's own JGB futures option contract. Table 11.16 contains information on the contract.

Contract	Options on Ten-year Japanese Government Bond Futures
Type	Offshore
Exchange	Singapore International Monetary Exchange
Months	Two nearest serial months and two nearest quarter months in March, June, September, December cycle
Contract Size	1 ten-year Japanese Government Bond Future
Tick Value	JPY0.01 per JPY100 face value bonds
Daily Limit	No limit
Deliverable Instrument	Physical settlement into underlying futures contract
Last Trading Day	Last TSE business day of the calendar month which precedes expiring contract month
Exercise Day	American exercise – any business day up to, and including, the last trading day
Real-time price data	Bloomberg: BJA <Cmdty> OMON; Reuters: <0#SJBmy+>, <0#SJBs:>; Telerate: 44154-69

Table 11.16 Contract Specifications for SIMEX Options on Ten-year Japanese Government Bond Futures

Currency

Currency Futures/Options/Futures Options

SIMEX currently features two physical settlement foreign exchange futures, the deferred spot US$/JPY contract and the deferred spot US$/DM contract; prior to July 1995 it also listed conventional US$/JPY, US$/DM and GBP/US$ contracts (all offsettable on the CME) but it delisted all three as a result of inactivity. Deferred spot contracts provide participants with the ability to automatically roll a position into the next business day, incurring a one day interest charge equal to the interest rate differential between the two currencies. Although trading volume in conventional currency futures proved lacklustre, overall activity in the deferred contracts has been on the rise. Turnover in US$/JPY deferred spot futures increased from 13,182 contracts in 1993 to 68,605 contracts in 1994; year-end open interest declined slightly, from 716 contracts in 1993 to 337 contract in 1994. Trading volume in US$/DM deferred spot futures increased from 26,298 contracts in 1993 to 131,210 contracts in 1994; year-end open interest dropped from 877 contracts in 1993 to 336 contracts in 1994 (SIMEX, 1995). Note that SIMEX currency futures face direct competition from listed currency products offered via MIFE, TIFFE and HKFE. The SIMEX contracts also face competition from the OTC spot and forward currency markets of Singapore, Hong Kong and Tokyo (which deal in G10 as well as Asian currencies). Tables 11.17 and 11.18 contain contract details on the SIMEX currency futures; Figures 11.10 and 11.11 illustrate the historical prices of the conventional US$/JPY and US$/DM futures contracts just prior to delisting.

Contract	**US$/JPY Deferred Spot Futures**
Type	Offshore
Exchange	Singapore International Monetary Exchange
Months	One contract month in March, June, September, December cycle (except from the fifth to last business day of contract month, when next quarterly month contract is also listed)
Contract Size	US$100,000
Tick Value	JPY0.01/US$
Daily Limit	No limit
Deliverable Instrument	Physical settlement of yen and US dollars
Last Trading Day	2nd business day immediately before the 2nd Wednesday of the contract month
Delivery Day	2nd Singapore bank business day following the last trading day (if not a business day in home countries of the currencies, delivery day is the next business day which is not a holiday in all three locations)
Real-time price data	Bloomberg: UJA <Cmdty>; Reuters: <0#2SFX:> ; Telerate: 7314

Table 11.17 Contract Specifications for SIMEX US$/JPY Deferred Spot Futures

Contract	US$/DM Deferred Spot Futures
Type	Offshore
Exchange	Singapore International Monetary Exchange
Months	One contract month in March, June, September, December cycle (except from the fifth to last business day of contract month, when next quarterly month contract is also listed)
Contract Size	US$100,000
Tick Value	DM0.0001/US$
Daily Limit	No limit
Deliverable Instrument	Physical settlement of Deutschmarks and US dollars
Last Trading Day	2nd business day immediately before the 2nd Wednesday of the contract month
Delivery Day	2nd Singapore bank business day following the last trading day (if not a business day in home countries of the currencies, delivery day is next business day which is not a holiday in all three locations)
Real-time price data	Bloomberg: UDA <Cmdty>; Reuters: <0#2SFX:>; Telerate: 7314

Table 11.18 Contract Specifications for SIMEX US$/DM Deferred Spot Futures

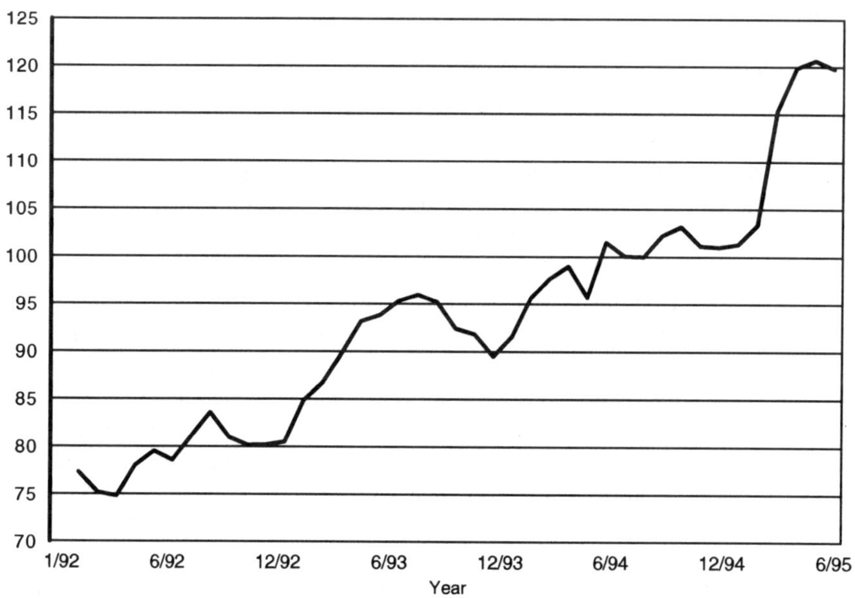

Figure 11.10 Historical Movement of SIMEX US$/JPY Currency Futures

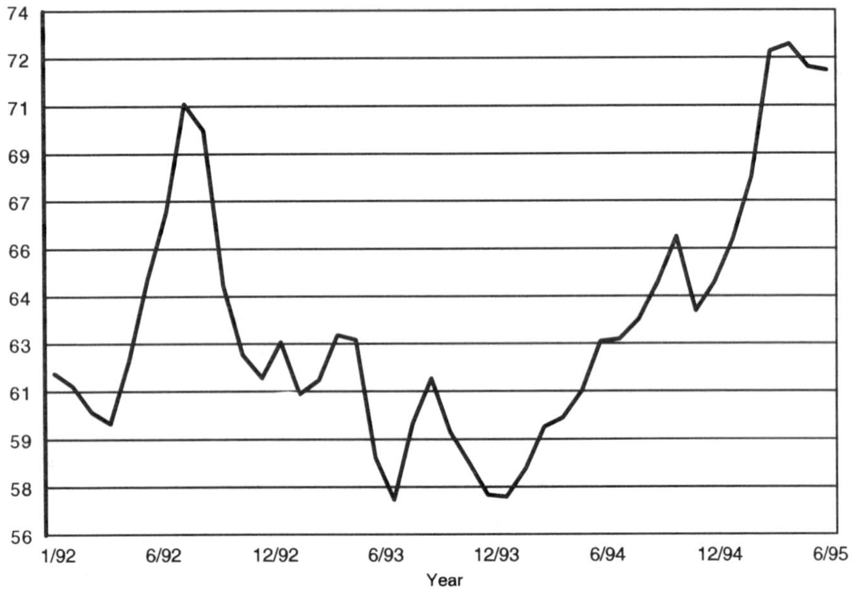

Figure 11.11 Historical Movement of SIMEX US$/DM Currency Futures

Commodity

Commodity Futures/Options/Futures Options

Commodity futures in Singapore are offered via SIMEX and SICOM. SIMEX, which has been the market leader in Singapore primarily as a result of its decision to list and trade offshore financial futures and options, offers contracts on gold and high sulphur fuel oil; it now also trades IPE's Brent crude contract during Asian hours. SICOM, in contrast, offers futures on a variety of rubber products (including three rubber grades and a rubber index), as well as robusta coffee.

SIMEX's gold futures date back to the early 1980s when the Exchange still existed as the Gold Futures Exchange of Singapore; the gold contract is, in fact, the only carryover from SIMEX's predecessor. Despite its longevity, turnover in the gold contract is virtually non-existent: trading volume amounted to 436 contacts in 1993 and a mere 26 contracts in 1994, with no open interest at the end of either year (SIMEX, 1995). Despite the effectively dormant status of the gold future, SIMEX has announced no plans to reconstruct or delist the contract. Table 11.19 provides contract specifications on the gold future while Figure 11.12 illustrates the price movement of the contract since 1992.

Singapore's role as the primary Asian trading centre for energy products has expanded dramatically over the past decade; Singapore is currently active in both listed and OTC energy derivatives (we discuss OTC energy forwards and swaps at

Contract	Gold Futures
Type	Offshore
Exchange	Singapore International Monetary Exchange
Months	February, April, June, October, December
Contract Size	100 troy ounces of gold
Tick Value	US$0.05/oz.
Daily Limit	+/– US$25 against previous day's settlement price, then trading within US$25 band for 30 minutes; thereafter the band expanded to US$50 for the rest of the day. No price limit on the last trading day of expiring contract.
Deliverable Grade	Cash settlement based on London A.M. fixing on the last trading day
Last Trading Day	2nd to last business day of the month preceding the 1st business day of the contract month
Delivery Day	Same as the last trading day
Real-time price data	Bloomberg: GDA <Cmdty>; Reuters: <0#SAU:>; Telerate: 6178

Table 11.19 Contract Specifications for SIMEX Gold Futures

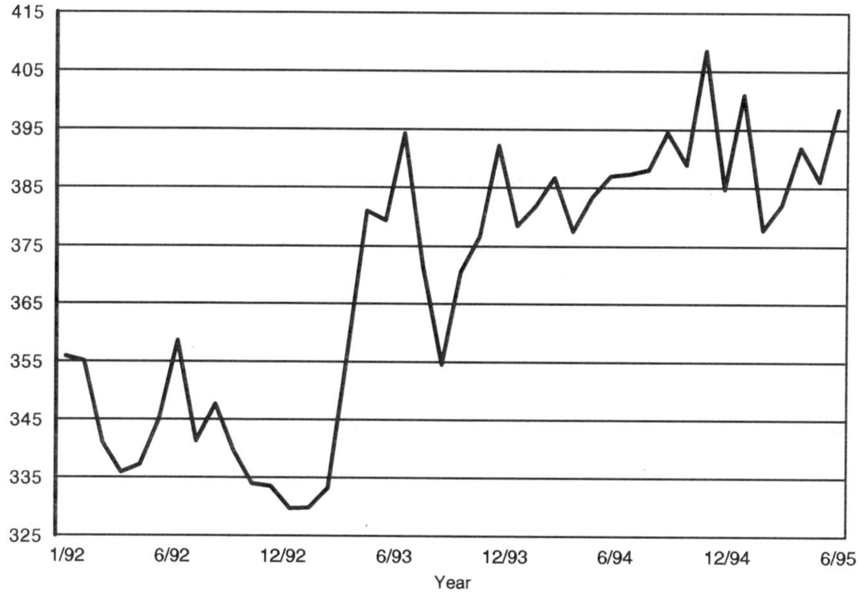

Figure 11.12 Historical Movement of SIMEX Gold Futures

greater length later in the chapter). In listed futures, SIMEX presently offers a contract on high sulphur fuel oil (HSFO) (which it originally introduced in February 1989). Fuel oil, a residual product of crude oil, is used for electricity generation and industrial fuels (including shipping fuel); it can also be converted into middle distillates. Despite significant competition from both the Singapore OTC energy market and energy derivatives listed on NYMEX and IPE, the SIMEX HSFO contract continues to attract a reasonable amount of activity: turnover amounted to 323,006 contracts in 1993 and 171,896 contracts in 1994, with year-end open interest of 7,541 contracts in 1993 and 1,369 contracts in 1994 (SIMEX, 1995). Table 11.20 contains details on the HSFO futures contract, while Figure 11.13 traces the historical price of HSFO futures.

In 1994 SIMEX entered into negotiations with London's IPE regarding listing and trading of the IPE Brent crude futures and options contracts on SIMEX. In March 1995 the two exchanges agreed to list the Brent contracts on SIMEX and in June 1995 regional trading in futures commenced; though trading in Brent options was due to start at the same time, delays have postponed the launch of options trading until 1996. Brent trading through SIMEX now provides Asian participants with access to futures on one of the primary crude benchmarks of the world and expands the trading day for global participants to 18 hours. Clearing and settlement of the crude contract occur directly through SIMEX and positions are mutually offsettable on either exchange. Table 11.21 contains details on the SIMEX/IPE Brent futures contract.

Contract	**High Sulphur Fuel Oil Futures**
Type	Offshore
Exchange	Singapore International Monetary Exchange
Months	Six consecutive months
Contract Size	100 metric tons
Tick Value	US$0.10/ton
Daily Limit	+/– US$10/ton against previous day's settlement price, then trading for 30 minutes within US$10 band; thereafter band is expanded to US$20/ton for 30 minutes, after which price limits are removed. No limit on the spot month.
Deliverable Grade	Cash settlement for small lots (less than ten contracts); for large lots, physical settlement of HSFO with fees and duties paid by seller
Last Trading Day	Last business day of the month preceding the contract month
Delivery Day	Day after 5th business day to the 25th calendar day of the contract month
Real-time price data	Bloomberg: FSA <Cmdty>; Reuters: <0#SFO:>; Telerate: 6180, 8878

Table 11.20 Contract Specifications for SIMEX High Sulphur Fuel Oil Futures

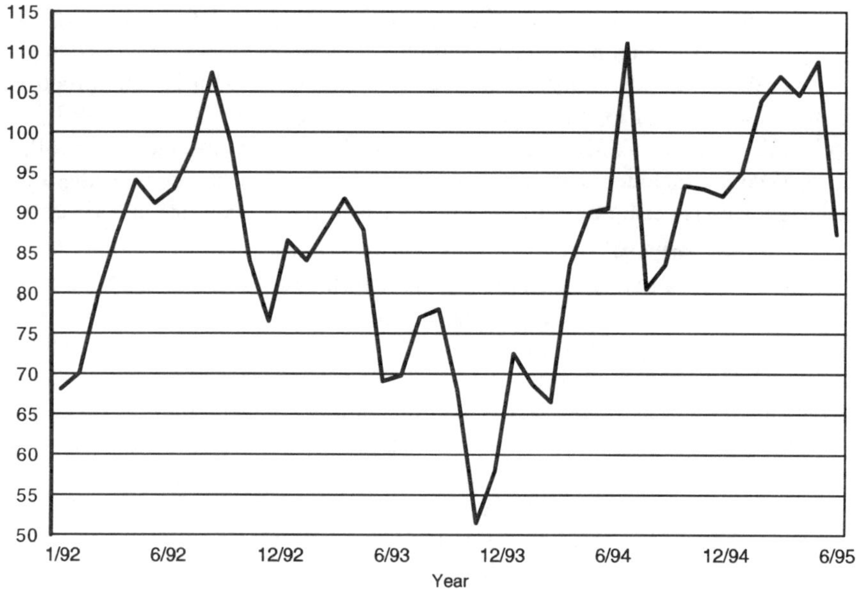

Figure 11.13 Historical Movement of SIMEX High Sulphur Fuel Oil Futures

Contract	**Brent Crude Oil Futures**
Type	Offshore
Exchange	Singapore International Monetary Exchange/International Petroleum Exchange
Months	12 consecutive months following current month
Contract Size	1,000 net barrels
Tick Value	US$10
Daily Limit	No limit
Deliverable Grade	Cash settlement against the Brent Index on the last trading day of the current contract
Last Trading Day	Business day immediately preceding the 15th day prior to the first day of the delivery month
Delivery Day	Day after the last trading day
Real-time price data	Bloomberg: OCA <Cmdty>; Reuters: <0#SCO:>; Telerate: 8878

Table 11.21 Contract Specifications for SIMEX/IPE Brent Crude Oil Futures

In addition to the IPE Brent link, SIMEX and NYMEX signed a letter of intent in 1995 which will place NYMEX's electronic trading system, ACCESS, in Singapore. SIMEX members will be permitted to trade NYMEX energy contracts via ACCESS, with all regional trades cleared through NYMEX; this proposed arrangement is similar to one already in effect between NYMEX and the SFE. Full specifications on the NYMEX energy contracts which will be available via SIMEX during 1996 are included in chapter 2 on Australia. In other energy derivatives the Exchange is considering re-introduction of a gasoil futures contract, a derivative it delisted several years ago.

While SIMEX lists gold and energy products, SICOM deals in agriculturals and softs. Given its history as an exchange focused on rubber, it is not surprising to note that SICOM's primary emphasis at the present time is on rubber futures, including RSS1 (ribbed smoked sheet #1), RSS3 (ribbed smoked sheet #3), TSR20 (technically specified rubber #20) and RCS Index (rubber cash-settled index). Singapore is, in fact, the largest physical rubber trading location in the world, with more than 130 rubber trading companies active in the market; introduction of a comprehensive range of rubber futures over the past few decades (on SICOM's forerunner) has helped enhance the country's role as the world's primary rubber trader. Its geographic location at the centre of Malaysia, Thailand and Indonesia, the top three world rubber producers, has also helped; nearly two-thirds of the world's rubber output is re-exported from, and transhipped through, Singapore. Despite competition from other regional exchanges such as KLCE, TOCOM, ICEB, and KRE, SICOM is emerging as an important global rubber futures exchange.

Since its re-organization in 1992 SICOM has experienced very strong turnover in all three of its physical rubber contracts. Turnover in RSS1 futures reached 697,515 contracts in 1993 and 577,395 contracts in 1994; year-end open interest amounted to 31,750 contracts in 1993 and 20,525 contracts in 1994. Turnover in RSS3 futures (a US dollar-denominated contract) amounted to 419,900 contracts in 1993 and 641,210 contracts in 1994; year-end open interest was 13,795 contracts in 1993 and 19,205 contracts in 1994. Trading volume in TSR20 futures reached 598,520 contracts in 1993 and 528,640 contracts in 1994, with year-end open interest of 20,460 contracts in 1993 and 17,200 contracts in 1994 (SICOM, 1995).

The RCS Index, introduced in August 1993, is a US dollar, cash-settled rubber index based on closing prices of Tokyo and Kobe RSS3 rubber futures; Japan is a major importer of RSS3 and its own futures contracts on RSS3 (traded via TOCOM and KRE) are extremely liquid (note that KRE also features a rubber index future, though the components of its index are broader based than SICOM's and include TSR20, RSS1, RSS3 and SMR (Standard Malaysian Rubber)). Unlike SICOM's physical rubber futures, turnover in rubber index futures has been negligible; total trading volume amounted to 4,400 contracts in 1993 but declined to zero in 1994 (SICOM, 1995). Tables 11.27 through 11.30 provide details on SICOM's rubber contracts. Figures 11.14 to 11.17 illustrate the historical price movement of each SICOM future.

Contract	RSS1 Rubber Futures
Type	Domestic/Offshore
Exchange	Singapore Commodity Exchange
Months	Single months and quarter months, up to 18 months forward
Contract Size	5 metric tons of RSS1 rubber (monthly); 15 metric tons of RSS1 rubber (quarterly)
Tick Value	SGD0.25/kg
Daily Limit	+/– 5% against previous day's settlement price, then 1 hour period where trading must remain within 5% band, after which normal trading resumes. No price limit on the last trading day of the contract month.
Deliverable Grade	Physical settlement of RSS1 rubber (ribbed smoked sheet #1), per International Rubber Quality Standards. Delivery at Singapore, Port Kiang, or Penang
Last Trading Day	Monthly contract: last trading day of the month preceding the contract month; quarterly contract: last trading day of the 4th month preceding the first month of the quarter
Delivery Day	Not later than the 8th business day of the delivery month
Real-time price data	Bloomberg: ROA <Cmdty>; Reuters: <0#SRS:>; Telerate: 40540

Table 11.27 Contract Specifications for SICOM RSS1 Rubber Futures

Contract	RSS3 Rubber Futures
Type	Domestic/Offshore
Exchange	Singapore Commodity Exchange
Months	Single months and quarter months, up to 18 months forward
Contract Size	5 metric tons of RSS3 rubber (monthly); 15 metric tons of RSS3 rubber (quarterly)
Tick Value	US$0.25/kg
Daily Limit	+/– 5% against previous day's settlement price, then 1 hour period where trading must remain within 5% band, after which normal trading resumes. No price limit on the last trading day of contract month.
Deliverable Grade	Physical settlement of RSS3 rubber (ribbed smoked sheet #3), per International Rubber Quality Standards. Delivery at Singapore or Bangkok
Last Trading Day	Monthly contract: last trading day of the month preceding contract month; quarterly contract: last trading day of the 4th month preceding the first month of the quarter
Delivery Day	Not later than the 8th business day of the delivery month
Real-time price data	Bloomberg: RGA <Cmdty>; Reuters: <0#SRU:>; Telerate: 40541

Table 11.28 Contract Specifications for SICOM RSS3 Rubber Futures

Contract	TSR20 Award Rubber Futures
Type	Domestic/Offshore
Exchange	Singapore Commodity Exchange
Months	Single months, quarter months to 18 months forward
Contract Size	20 metric tons of TSR20 rubber (monthly); 60 metric tons of TSR20 rubber (quarterly)
Tick Value	SGD0.25/kg
Daily Limit	+/– 5% against previous day's settlement price, then 1 hour period where trading must remain within 5% band, after which normal trading resumes. No price limit on last trading day of current contract.
Deliverable Grade	Physical settlement via Negotiable Award Certificates related to TSR20 rubber (Technically Specified Rubber #20) of any origin
Last Trading Day	Monthly contract: last trading day of the month preceding the contract month; quarterly contract: last trading day of the 4th month preceding the first month of quarter
Delivery Day	3rd business day of the delivery month
Real-time price data	Bloomberg: REA <Cmdty>; Reuters: <0#STS:>; Telerate: 40542

Table 11.29 Contract Specifications for SICOM TSR20 Award Rubber Futures

Contract	RCS Rubber Index Futures
Type	Offshore
Exchange	Singapore Commodity Exchange
Months	Spot month plus 8 consecutive months
Contract Size	5000 * RCS Rubber Index (which is based on a 2:1 price ratio of TOCOM RSS3 contract and KRE RSS3 contract)
Tick Value	US$0.01/kg
Daily Limit	+/– 5% against previous day's settlement, then 1 hour period where trading must remain within 5% band, after which normal trading resumes. No price limit on current contract month, from 15th trading day onwards.
Deliverable Grade	Cash settlement based on the average of closing prices on the last trading day and four days before the last trading day
Last Trading Day	1st day before TOCOM's and KRE's last trading day
Delivery Day	Same as the last trading day
Real-time price data	Bloomberg: RIA <Cmdty>; Telerate: 40543

Table 11.30 Contract Specifications for SICOM RCS Rubber Index Futures

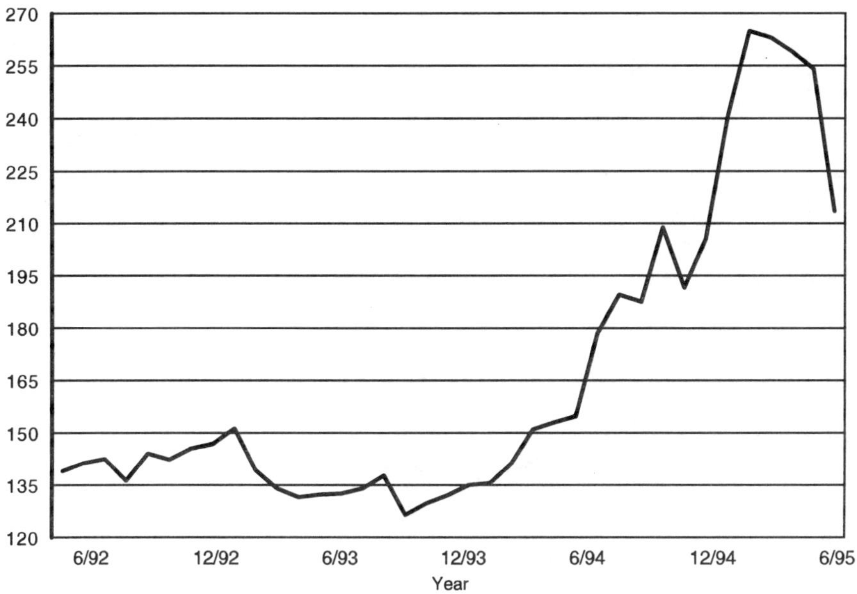

Source: Singapore Commodity Exchange

Figure 11.14 Historical Movement of SICOM RSS1 Rubber Futures

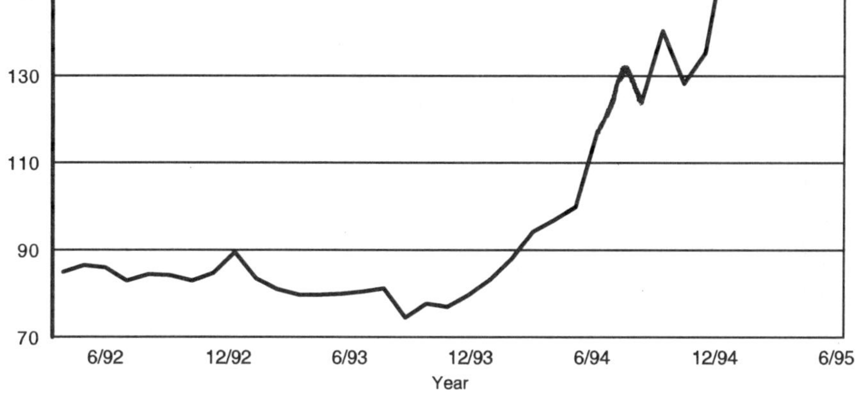

Source: Singapore Commodity Exchange

Figure 11.15 Historical Movement of SICOM RSS3 Rubber Futures

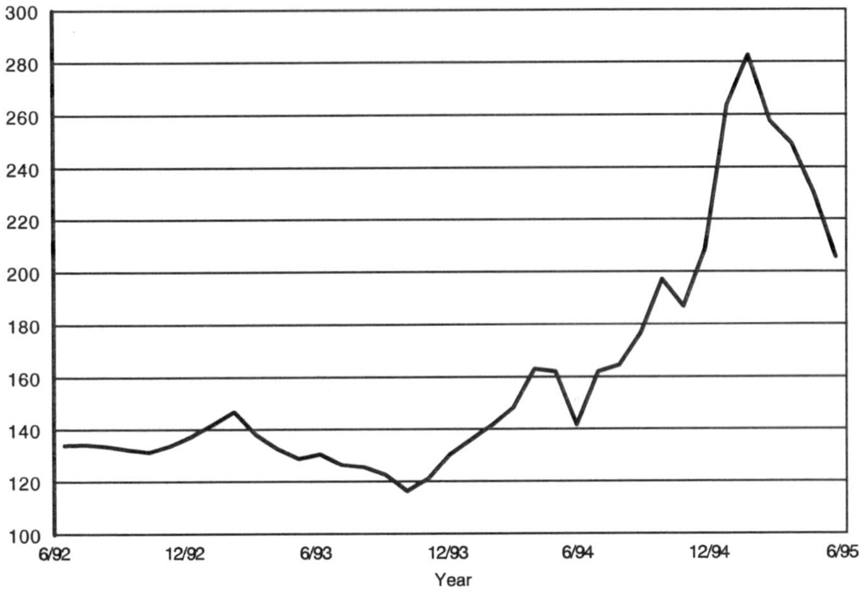

Source: Singapore Commodity Exchange

Figure 11.16 Historical Movement of SICOM TSR20 Rubber Futures

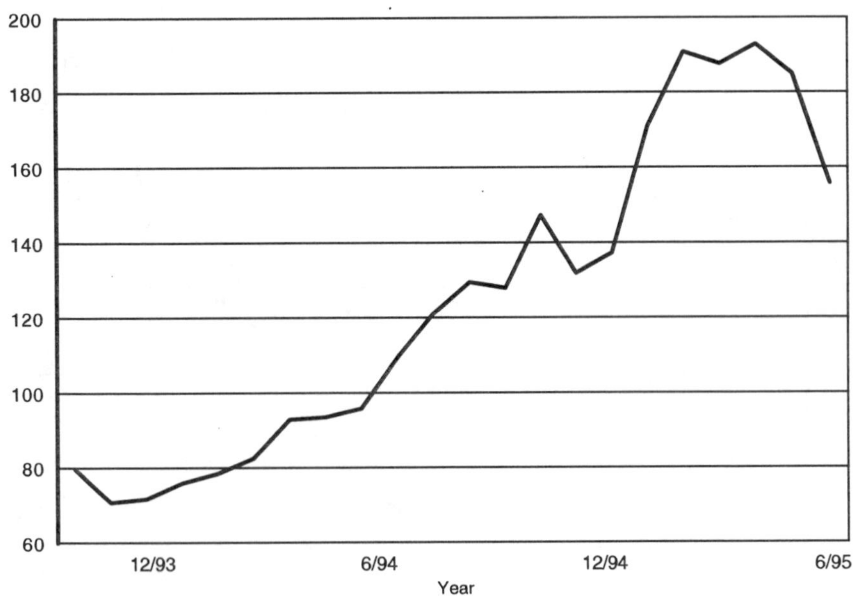

Source: Singapore Commodity Exchange

Figure 11.17 Historical Movement of SICOM RCS Index Futures

Robusta coffee futures, the first non-rubber derivatives offered on SICOM, were introduced in 1995; SICOM's coffee contract is only the fifth internationally accessible coffee future in the world (the others are traded on the London Commodity Exchange (robusta), the Coffee, Sugar and Cocoa Exchange (arabica), MIFE (robusta) and ICEB (robusta)), and is the third to be traded during Asian hours. Design and introduction of the contract coincides with ever-increasing coffee production from Asian nations such as Indonesia and Vietnam (total Asian coffee production in 1994 amounted to 500,000 metric tons, with 50% shipped through Singapore), and ever-increasing consumption of coffee throughout Asia. Coffee roasters in Asia now have at their disposal another regional contract which they can sell against unsold inventory or buy against a forward commitment to deliver; Asian producers, likewise, can hedge forward sales of their robusta production. It should be noted that in order to attract users to the contract, SICOM offered a 50% discount on clearing fees and broker rebates for the first six months of contract trading. Total trading volume during the first six months of operation amounted to 2,440 contracts (SICOM, 1995). Table 11.31 contains specifications on the robusta contract.

Contract	**Robusta Coffee Futures**
Type	Domestic/Offshore
Exchange	Singapore Commodity Exchange
Months	January, March, July, September, November, up to seven odd months
Contract Size	10 metric tons of Singapore Robusta Standard coffee
Tick Value	US$1/ton
Daily Limit	+/– US$300/ton against previous day's settlement price; 1/2 hour during which trading must occur within the band, then all limits removed.
Deliverable Grade	Physical settlement; 10 ton multiples of Singapore Robusta coffee via warrants issued by SICOM nominated warehouses
Last Trading Day	Last business day of the delivery month
Delivery Day	Any trading day of the delivery month or the last trading day of the delivery month
Real-time price data	Bloomberg: RUA <Cmdty>; Reuters: <0#SKD:>; Telerate: 40544

Table 11.31 Contract Specifications for SICOM Robusta Coffee Futures

In order to continue expanding its product line SICOM is presently designing additional commodity contracts on zinc, copper, aluminium and cocoa; preliminary plans call for introduction of the new contracts during 1996.

LISTED/OVER-THE-COUNTER WARRANTS, CONVERTIBLES AND HYBRIDS

Equity

Equity Warrants

Equity warrants in the Singaporean market are available as conventional issuer warrants and third-party covered warrants. Issuer warrants are short- to medium-term derivatives (e.g. one- to five-years) issued in American exercise form by a company on its own shares; exercise of the warrants results in the issuance of new equity by the company. Such warrants, which are normally structured in the ratio of one share per warrant, are listed on, and traded through, the SES; liquidity in warrants of large capitalization blue-chips is generally good. Although predominantly a Singapore dollar-denominated market, the SES also lists and trades warrants issued in foreign currencies, such as the US dollar warrants issued by Jardine Matheson in late 1994 (after Jardine group companies delisted from the Hong Kong bourse in favour of Singapore). As of June 1995, there were over 100 issuer equity warrants outstanding in the local market; Appendix II contains details on all warrants traded as of mid-1995.

The second segment of the Singapore warrant market consists of third-party covered warrants, which are effectively long-term call options issued by financial institutions on a local company's shares; exercise of the warrants results in the re-allocation of existing shares (as opposed to the issuance of new corporate equity). Unlike domestic listed warrants, covered warrants are issued and traded in both the onshore and offshore market. Covered warrants are listed on either the SES or offshore exchanges and may be traded on an exchange or OTC; warrants on Singaporean stocks typically mature between one- and three-years of issue date. Representative offshore covered warrants include Merrill Lynch's Singapore dollar calls on Overseas Union Enterprises (1994), Robert Fleming's US dollar calls on Overseas Chinese Banking Corp (foreign shares) (1995) and Merrill Lynch's US dollar calls on Hotel Properties Ltd (1994). Representative domestic covered warrants include Barclays de Zoete Wedd's Singapore dollar calls on Singapore Airlines (foreign shares) (1995) and Union Bank of Switzerland's Singapore dollar calls on the same stock (1995).

Basket/Index Warrants

While the local market features reasonably active trading of listed single stock warrants through the SES, it does not currently list or trade basket/index warrants. Institutions in the offshore market have, however, developed a range of OTC basket and index warrants tied to groups of domestic stocks and broader Singaporean market indexes. Such warrants typically carry one- to three-year maturities and are either unlisted or listed on overseas exchanges and traded OTC. Representative issues in this category include Swiss Bank Corporation's Deutschmark basket call warrants on a group of eight blue-chip Singaporean stocks (1995), Merrill Lynch's US dollar basket call warrants on a group of Singaporean bank stocks (1994), Merrill Lynch's Singapore dollar basket call warrants on a group of hotel stocks (1994), Société Générale's US dollar index call warrants on the STI (1994), Lehman's US dollar index call warrants on the DBS 50 (1995), and Union Bank of Switzerland's US dollar index call and put warrants on the Singapore 25 Index (1995).

Convertibles

The Singaporean market features a modest amount of domestic convertible bonds; the overall convertible market is still small in size and is very infrequently utilized by larger capitalization companies (e.g Keppel Corporation, Sembawang Maritime). Convertibles in the local market are listed on, and traded through, the SES. Maturities on domestic convertibles are generally under seven years, coupons are low (1% to 5%), and conversion premiums are intermediate (e.g 8% to 10%). Conversion is into domestic shares at a fixed Singapore dollar conversion price.

Domestic companies have not been frequent issuers of offshore convertibles, primarily because they derive their financing needs from retained earnings, conventional bank financing and, to a lesser degree, conventional domestic fixed and floating rate bond issuance. Nonetheless, several local issuers have tapped the Eurodollar convertible market in the past; indeed, Singaporean companies such as Development Bank of Singapore and Keppel Corporation were among the first in Southeast Asia to access the offshore market, floating bonds as early as the mid-1980s. Singaporean Eurodollar convertibles are listed on offshore exchanges and are traded on an OTC basis; the bonds are convertible into local shares at a fixed Singapore dollar conversion price. Offshore deals in the market carry long maturities (in excess of ten years), low coupons (3% to 5%) and low conversion premiums (5%). Appendix III contains details on domestic and offshore Singaporean convertibles.

Index-linked Notes

Index-linked notes, which are most often structured as short- or medium-term securities (e.g. one- to five-years) with embedded long call options (and occasionally long put options or short put options), are issued periodically by foreign financial institutions as a means of providing investors with exposure to Singaporean indexes, primarily the benchmark STI. Notes referencing baskets of Singapore stocks (or even single stocks) are also available, though far less common. Linked notes are floated in the offshore market and may be unlisted and placed privately or listed on an overseas exchange and traded OTC. Despite the general availability of such instruments, overall activity is small in comparison with that found in other Asia Pacific nations (e.g. Hong Kong, Japan, Australia).

Fixed Income

Fixed Income Warrants

The domestic Singapore market does not trade fixed income warrants based on local bonds (e.g. Singapore government bonds), primarily because investor demand is negligible and the overall fixed income market is still in the developing stages. In addition, the MAS's overall posture on domestic derivatives is extremely conservative (particularly with regard to onshore structures used for speculative purposes).

Currency

Currency Warrants

The domestic market does not list or trade currency warrants related to the Singapore dollar, primarily as a result of the MAS's negative view on developing local derivatives for speculative purposes. Financial institutions in the offshore OTC market, however, float very occasional issues of Singapore dollar currency warrants. Such derivatives are listed on overseas exchanges (or remain unlisted) and are traded on an OTC basis; maturities tend to be short-term, extending from one to two years. Overall activity in this market is still extremely limited.

Commodity

Commodity Warrants

Listed commodity warrants referencing domestic indicators are not presently traded in Singapore or in the offshore market.

OVER-THE-COUNTER FORWARDS, SWAPS AND OPTIONS

Equity

Equity Forwards/Swaps

The market for OTC equity forwards and swaps based on individual Singaporean equities is limited. Although outright equity forwards are available (primarily as short-term transactions to two years), equity swaps exchanging a floating rate flow for appreciation or depreciation in the value of an individual stock are very rare. More active are OTC equity options, index options and index swaps, as discussed below.

Equity Options

OTC puts and calls on Singaporean stocks are bought and sold on a routine basis by foreign institutions with equity derivative capabilities. The OTC equity option market has proven successful primarily because it offers institutions flexibility in customizing options with respect to target stock, maturity, notional, strike, and so on; though any potential combination of parameters is possible, most options tend to be vanilla American or European style derivatives with maturities ranging from several months to three years, exercisable into cash or physical. As discussed above, the listed equity option market is effectively dormant at the current time and presents the OTC market with little competition. The listed equity warrant market, in contrast, is far more active and exists as a competitor to the OTC market; the warrant market, however, is primarily a trading forum offering investors liquidity, while the OTC market provides investors with customized hedge or speculative positions. As is common with OTC structures in general, OTC equity options are exercised, closed out or permitted to expire; they are not traded in the secondary market.

Basket/Index Forwards/Swaps

OTC index forwards and swaps referencing Singaporean indexes or baskets of stocks are executed with some frequency, almost exclusively in the offshore market. The primary focus is on one- to three-year index swaps which exchange a floating rate flow for appreciation (and occasionally depreciation) in an underlying domestic equity index (primarily the STI or DBS 50); such swaps are the equivalent of an institution purchasing a medium-term option and paying premium in deferred form. Numerous other combinations of index forwards and swaps are available, e.g. collars, spreads and so on. In addition to index-based transactions, basket forwards and swaps are structured in a similar fashion by combining a number of related domestic equities into a single reference basket.

Basket/Index Options

Offshore OTC index options are bought and sold on a variety of local indexes, including the STI and the DBS 50. The same institutions active in OTC equity options and index swaps are also active in the OTC index options market, creating customized transactions for offshore and domestic institutions. Absence of listed futures or options on local indexes has made OTC structures reasonably popular with those seeking to manage, or gain, exposure to the broader Singaporean market. Basket options are also available and most often structured by combining a number of related industry shares into a single basket (e.g. bank baskets, hotel baskets, property baskets and so on). While virtually any type of basket or index option can be created, most tend to be short- to intermediate-term (e.g. three month to three year), American or European derivatives, exercisable into cash settlement. Note that there is a very small market for exotic index options (e.g. barriers, digitals, Asians); demand for such derivatives is, however, still very limited.

Fixed Income

Fixed Income Forwards/Swaps

Although the fixed income derivative market is relatively new, FRAs and swaps based on Singapore dollar interest rates are becoming more actively traded, with interbank participants and market-makers executing two-way flow for both clients and proprietary books. Since the MAS discourages the use of domestic derivatives unless related to hedging of economic exposures, one must presume that a great deal of the activity executed onshore is related to domestic hedging; activity executed offshore may be for either hedging or speculating. Though the domestic fixed income derivative market is developing it still faces a series of challenges which it will need to overcome as it seeks to expand. Specifically, the market continues to be impacted by: (a) lack of an established short-term floating rate benchmark for valuing floating rate segments of IRSs; (b) lack of a robust government yield curve to provide the market with additional swap pricing information; and (c) lack of easily accessible and liquid fixed income securities for hedging swap positions.

Singapore dollar FRAs, generally structured to reference the interest rates implied by FX forwards, are technically quoted to five years, though most transactions are executed with final maturities under 12 months; a small amount of FRAs (primarily those executed onshore) are structured to reference Singapore dollar SIBOR, the domestic interbank rate. There is no standard interbank dealing size and bid-offer spreads are still very wide as a result of illiquidity and rate volatility.

The domestic IRS market presently distinguishes between onshore and offshore transactions, primarily because the market does not feature an established, and tradeable, short-term benchmark rate. Onshore swaps are normally quoted as fixed Singapore dollars (semi-annual, on an Actual/365-day basis) against Singapore dollar SIBOR. Although a small amount of business is executed onshore, Singapore dollar SIBOR has not developed as the floating benchmark of choice in local IRSs, primarily because the rate is not readily tradeable or easy for swap market-makers to duplicate (leading to problems in hedging and managing cash rolls). As a result of these complications an alternate offshore rate has developed in the form of the Singapore dollar swap offer rate (SOR). The SOR (also used for pricing local currency IRSs in Thailand, Malaysia and Indonesia) provides institutions with a floating rate benchmark accessible and tradeable without restriction and makes pricing and hedging of swaps simpler. Quoting convention for offshore swaps is fixed Singapore dollars (semi-annual, on an Actual/365-day basis) against the Singapore dollar SOR, which is the rate derived from borrowing US dollars and converting into Singapore dollars of the same maturity through the FX forward market; SOR uses the offer side of FX swap rates to swap out of US dollars and into Singapore dollars. SOR is calculated on a daily basis in Singapore through the average of spot and forward point quotes from various domestic and international banks, for maturities of one, three, six and 12 months; the quotes are carried on Telerate page 44178.

The presence of bank market-makers and the development of SOR have led to the establishment of fairly active turnover in domestic onshore/offshore IRSs; recent estimates suggest that SGD42 mln (US$30 mln) is executed on a daily basis in interbank parcels of SGD14 mln (US$10 mln). IRSs are quite active to five years and quotes to seven, and even ten, years are not uncommon (though such swaps tend to be related to very specific asset/liability hedging). Bid-offer spreads for short- and intermediate-term IRSs range from 15 to 20 basis points under normal market conditions, though the relative immaturity and illiquidity of the market still causes considerable variability in spreads. Figure 11.18 illustrates a benchmark Singapore IRS curve (fixed Singapore dollars against six month SOR) from mid-1995.

Although swap turnover is increasing, dealers and market-makers are still faced with hedging challenges. The most liquid (though not always accessible) hedges are found in the short-end of the curve, and include deposits, forward FX and CDs; in the medium- and long-term sectors of the curve buying/selling government bonds for swap hedge purposes is still inefficient and expensive, which creates difficulties in managing term exposures. Future growth of the swap market will depend, in part, on the development of additional liquidity and efficiency in the government bond market.

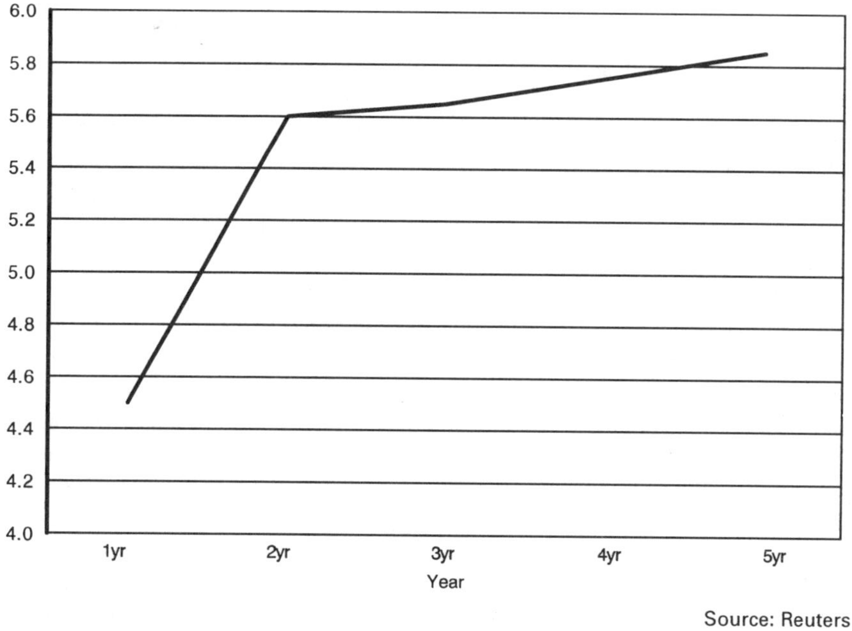

Figure 11.18 Representative Singapore Dollar IRS Curve

Fixed Income Options

The Singapore dollar fixed income option market is in varying stages of development. Although established government bond benchmarks currently exist, OTC bond options written on such securities are rare; as indicated above, MAS actively discourages speculative derivatives transacted on local instruments.

Singapore dollar caps and floors, in contrast, are somewhat more common. Caps and floors to three years are executed with some frequency, though overall deal size is still small; greater liquidity exists in the market for one and two year caps/floors. Caps and floors are structured to reference either the rates implied by FX forwards or, in certain instances, Singapore dollar SIBOR. Swaptions are very expensive to execute though parties do, on occasion, seek to gain protection or exposure through such derivatives. Given the relative infancy of the fixed income option market no standard interbank conventions on dealing size or bid-offer spreads have developed. Future growth in all fixed income options will depend on the development of an accepted floating rate benchmark and the expansion of Singapore dollar forwards and swaps. It should be noted that trading in fixed income options generates scrutiny by the MAS; the regulatory authorities demand particularly comprehensive reporting of open positions and risks.

Currency

Currency Forwards/Swaps

Singapore features growing currency forward and swap markets. Singapore dollar FX forwards are actively quoted and executed to six months and transactions to 12 months are not uncommon, though liquidity is far lower; deals to three years are transacted on occasion. Forwards are generally dealt in parcels of SGD7 mln to SGD14 mln (US$5MM–US$10MM) and the market is dominated by interbank players; as with spot trading, most activity occurs in the onshore, rather than the offshore, market. Figure 11.19 illustrates the historical movement of three- and 12-month forward SGD/US$.

The Singapore dollar CCS market is reasonably active, particularly for very short-term CCSs with full exchange of principal; deals in the six-month to two-year sector are very common and liquidity is quite good, with weekly volume of approximately SGD112 mln to SGD140 mln (US$80 mln to US$100 mln), primarily between onshore counterparties; the offshore market is far less active, dealing only SGD28 mln (US$20 mln) on a periodic basis. Note that the substantial CCS activity onshore, and the negligible activity offshore, is consistent with overall trading in the spot and forward markets, which is concentrated onshore. Though most activity in Singapore dollar CCSs takes places in shorter maturities, ready quotes are available in the two- to five-year sector and deals to seven years are not uncommon (though such transactions tend to be generated by very specific asset or liability hedging). Quoting convention in the local market is fixed Singapore dollars (semi-annual, on

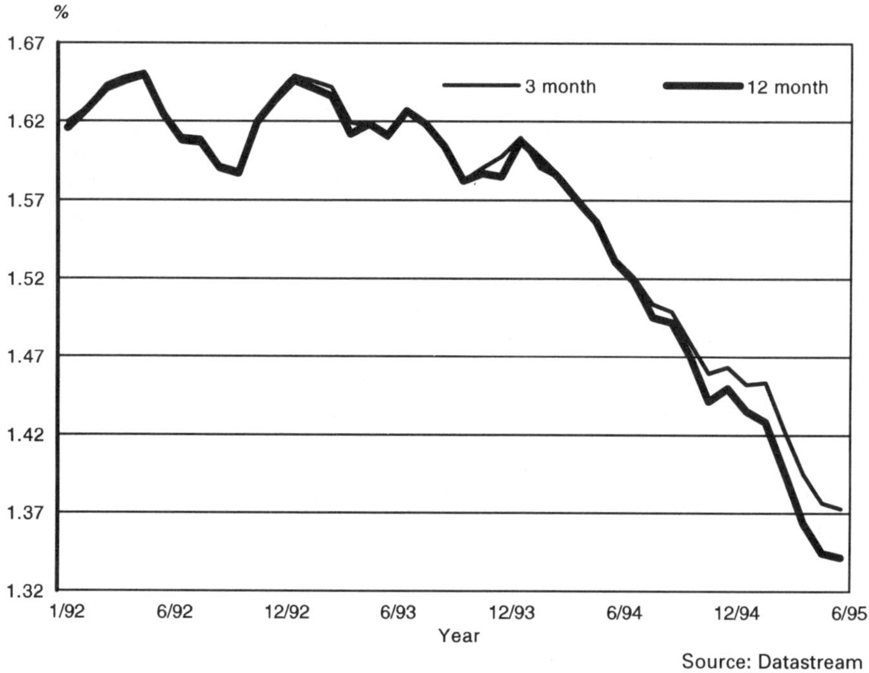

Figure 11.19 Historical Movement of Three- and 12-month SGD/US$ Forwards

an Actual/365-day basis) against six month US$ LIBOR flat. Bid-offer spreads on Singapore dollar CCSs range from 15 to 25 basis points across the curve, to five years; by way of comparison JPY/US$ CCSs, the most liquid in Asia Pacific, trade at spreads of 7–8 basis points throughout the curve.

Currency Options

Given the reasonable liquidity evident in spot/forward Singapore dollars and short-term Singapore dollar CCS's, it is not surprising to note that overall activity in Singapore dollar OTC FX options is on the rise. Vanilla currency options to 12 months are increasingly common and executed in standard interbank size of SGD14 mln (US$10 mln); quotes are typically given in volatility terms, with a one point bid-offer spread taken under normal market conditions. As with local currency derivatives the market exists primarily onshore, with very little activity occurring offshore. Note that there is no real market for exotic options involving the Singapore dollar, though certain institutions are known to arrange ad hoc transactions. In line with the MAS scrutiny detailed above, comprehensive reporting of FX options risk is required on a continuous basis.

Commodity

Commodity Forwards/Swaps

Singapore has been an established centre for trading of spot, forward and swap contracts on energy products for a number of years. Its geographic location at the centre of Southeast Asia, its reputation as a first-class shipping destination with top port facilities, its substantial storage facilities (it is the world's largest fuel oil bunkering centre), its substantial refining capabilities (it is the world's third largest oil refining centre, processing 1.3 mln barrels/day), together with its experience as a financial trading centre have all contributed to the establishment of an active OTC energy derivative market. Singapore is, in fact, the third largest trading centre for OTC energy products after New York and London, and it attracts participation of Asia Pacific energy producers (e.g. oil companies) and consumers (e.g. downstream refiners, electricity authorities). As is common with virtually all the derivatives we have discussed in this chapter, the local OTC energy derivative market is based strictly on offshore products; as a small nation state, Singapore produces no energy products of its own and, as such, can provide no domestic energy references.

Singapore's energy derivative market is centred on both light and heavy oil products. Spot, forward and swap transactions are executed in a variety of Asian and Australian crudes, and in products cracked out of such crudes. Among the crudes traded are those from Indonesia (including Minas, Arun, Attaka, Belida, Cinta, Duri, Handil, Kakap, Lalang and Widuri), Australia (Challis, Jackson Blend, Cooper Basin, Gippsland, Griffin, Jabiru, Skua and Thevenard), China (Nanhai Light, Shengli, Weizhou, Daqing) and Malaysia (Tapis, Dulang and Labuan). Tapis, a light, low sulphur oil, is the current Asian benchmark (though it has not yet established itself firmly on an international scale); the price of Tapis (particularly forward Tapis) tends to track the price of both IPE Brent futures and NYMEX light sweet crude futures (generally based on West Texas Intermediate, though other deliverables are tenderable). Various other sweet Asia Pacific crudes are often priced as a spread to Tapis; in addition, most regional crude paper swaps (discussed below) are based on Tapis (Note: Asian crudes may also be priced to Dubai, Brent or the APPI Index). Figure 11.20 illustrates the price movement (in US$/bbl) of forward Tapis against the two major global crude futures benchmarks, IPE Brent and NYMEX light sweet crude.

In addition to crudes, Singapore also trades a variety of light products, middle distillates and residuals which are obtained during the crude refining process. Light products include high octane 95 and 97 RON (research octane number) gasolines (which normally represent 5%–10% of a crude's yield), and naphtha, which is often cracked into ethylene. Naphtha normally accounts for 5%–15% of a barrel of crude and is widely used in Europe and Japan as feedstock for petrochemicals. The middle distillates include a range of kerosenes (5%–10% of crude) which are often used for jet fuel; Singapore trades jet kerosene rather actively. Heavier middle distillates include gasoil and heating oil (25%–35% of crude), which are used for space

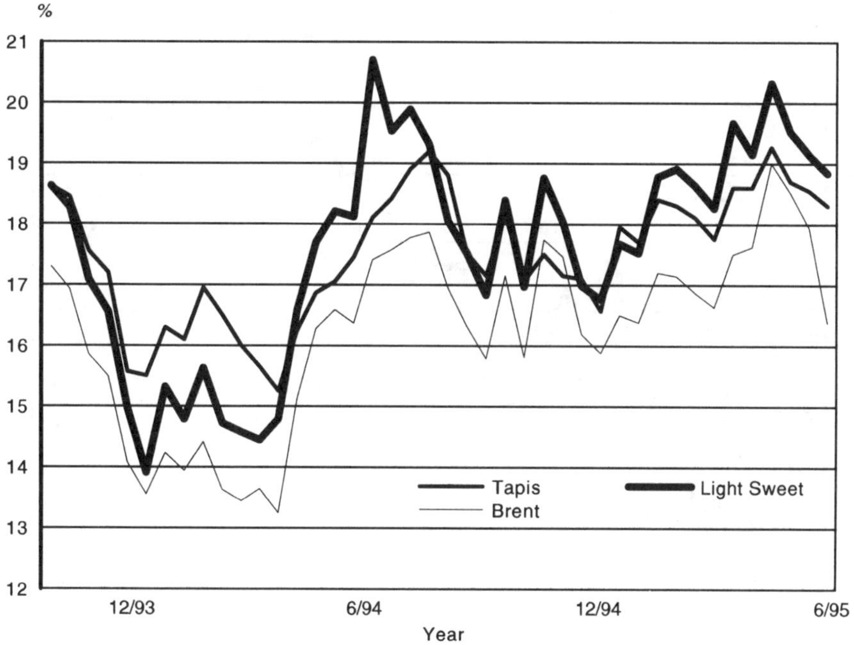

Figure 11.20 Historical Movement of Forward Tapis Against IPE and NYMEX Futures

heating and diesel fuel; certain gasoils can also be used in place of naphtha, if the latter is too expensive based on current market conditions. Residual products (which comprise the balance of a barrel of crude) include fuel oil, bunker fuel and low sulphur wax residue, among other products. Residuals, which are heavy products, are used for electricity generation and industrial fuels; certain fuel oils can be cracked into middle distillates, particularly if their sulphur content is low. Singapore is an active trader of fuel oil and high sulphur fuel oil (180 and 360 centistoke viscosity); as mentioned above, SIMEX also trades high sulphur fuel oil futures. Figure 11.21 illustrates the historical price movement (in US$/ton) of front-month forward Singapore fuel oil against near month SIMEX fuel oil futures.

The most active forward and swap trading in Singapore is centred on crude (primarily Tapis), naphtha (petrochemical grade with a minimum of 65% paraffins), jet kerosene (grade DERD 2494), gasoline (95 or 97 octane, 0.15 grams of lead/liter), and high sulphur fuel oil (maximum 3.5% sulphur, 380 centistoke viscosity). Local forward trading occurs in both the first and second forward months (in contrast to European energy forwards, which trade to the fourth month, and US energy forwards, which trade to the twelfth month). Prices in Singapore are quoted free on board (f.o.b.) (e.g. cargo, insurance and freight costs are not included) on the basis of US dollars per barrel (except fuel oil, which is quoted on the basis of US dollars per ton)(note: Japanese prices are generally quoted c & f, or inclusive of cargo and freight costs – an adjustment must therefore be made when comparing Singaporean

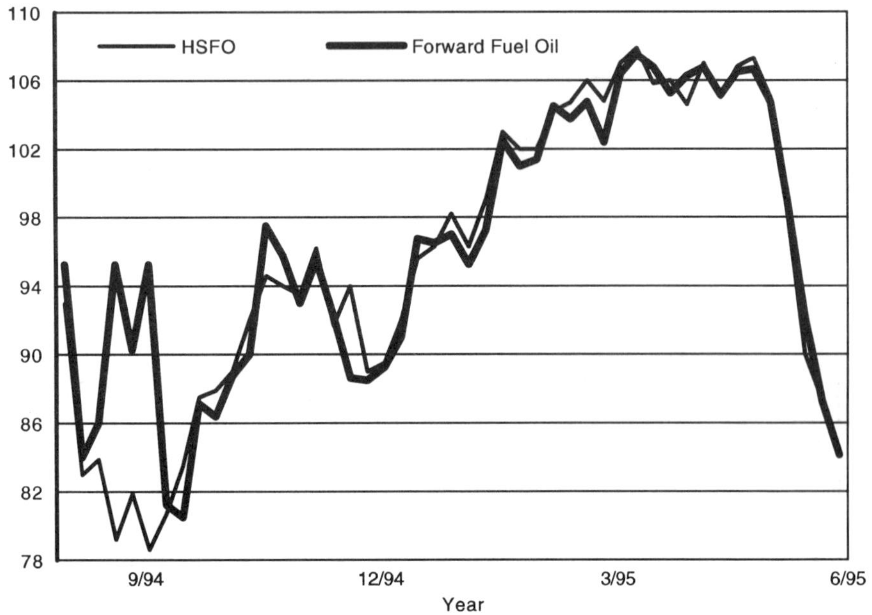

Figure 11.21 Historical Movement of Singapore Forward Fuel Oil and SIMEX HSFO Futures

and Japanese prices). Forward trading results in either physical delivery of underlying energy products or, if structured as a 'paper' transaction, net cash settlement.

The market for 'paper' forwards and swaps is quite active. A paper swap, as the name suggests, involves no physical delivery of the underlying energy product – the transaction occurs strictly on paper. An institution enters into a paper swap by setting the reference commodity, volume, maturity and fixed price. At the conclusion of the transaction (e.g. at maturity), the fixed price indicated under the paper swap is compared with the average level of a floating index (where the averaging period is set in advance by both parties) and a payment is made in one direction or another, depending on the current market value of the transaction. Paper swaps are often used for hedging in the physical market. For instance, an institution may wish to become part of a chain of participants who buy and sell the same cargo of energy products (so-called 'open spec' cargoes). If a trader sells short a cargo of forward delivery fuel oil he becomes part of the chain; to the extent the cash market is also short fuel oil, the chain will remain incomplete and the trader will be forced to deliver a cargo which is not available. That will necessitate covering in the spot market, which could create a loss if the spot market is more expensive. By entering into a paper swap prior to executing a chain transaction the trader will be able to defray all (or a portion) or any loss which may result from an incomplete chain. Singapore paper swaps are actively quoted and traded on crude, naphtha, fuel oil, jet fuel, gasoil and gasoline.

In addition to paper swaps, some participants also trade the spread between particular swaps (e.g. not unlike trading crack spreads in US and European energy markets). In the Singapore market, the most active spread trading occurs between the mean of gasoline swaps and naphtha swaps, the mean of jet kerosene swaps and Tapis swaps, and the mean of jet kerosene swaps and gasoil swaps, all to two months forward. There is also a less actively traded spread between Singapore gasoil and IPE gasoil swaps. Figures 11.22 and 11.23 illustrate the historical price movement (in US dollars) of gasoline/naphtha and jet kerosene/gasoil spreads for both one- and two-month forward swaps.

Recent indicative Singapore paper swap quotes are provided in Table 11.32.

Product	Month	Bid/Offer**
Paper Naphtha	1 month forward	US$19.20–.50
Paper Gas 95RON	1 month forward	US$22.40–.80
Paper Jet/Gasoil*	1 month forward	+15/25 cents
Paper Jet/Gasoil*	2 months forward	+15/25 cents
Paper Gasoil	1 month forward	US$22.25–.45
Paper Fuel oil	1 month forward	US$107.75–$108
Paper Fuel oil	2 months forward	US$105.75–$106

Source: Reuters, April 1995
* against the mean
** US$/barrel except fuel oil, which is US$/ton

Table 11.32 Representative Singapore Paper Swap Quotes

Commodity Options

While the market for OTC commodity forwards is very active, as described above, the market for OTC commodity options is more limited. Although option transactions are executed by institutions operating in Singapore, most target non-Singaporean clients and non-Singapore commodity references; energy options, based on various products described above, are occasionally structured by financial institutions for energy producers or consumers.

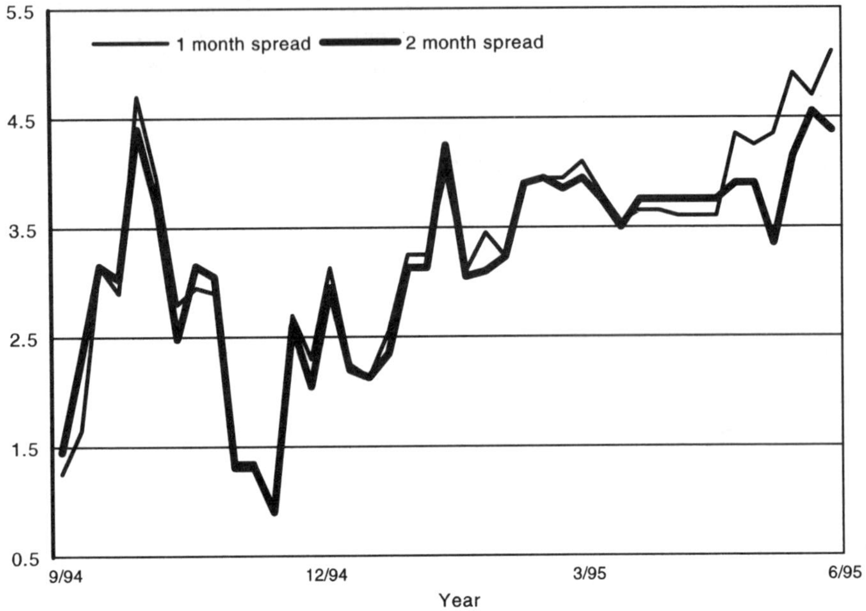

Figure 11.22 Historical Movement of Gasoline/Naphtha Paper Swap Spread

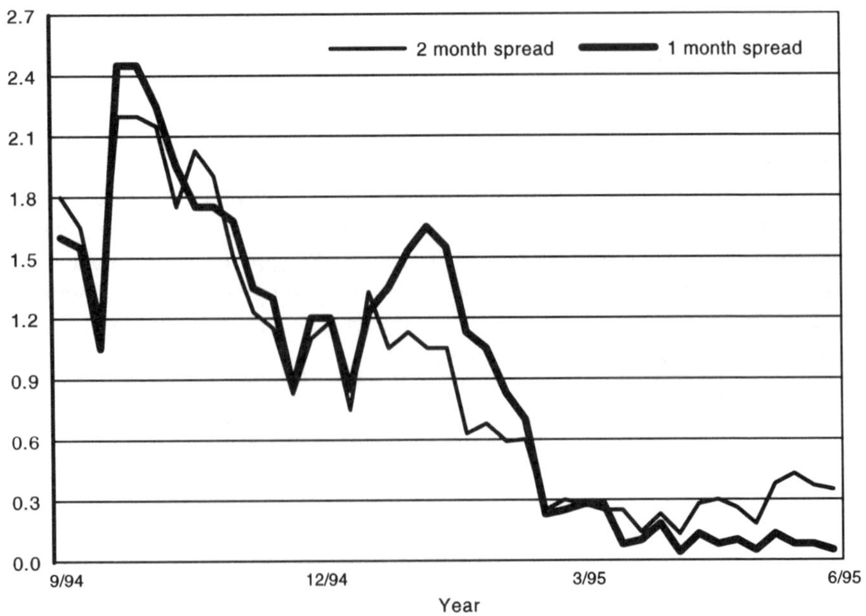

Figure 11.23 Historical Movement of Jet Kerosene/Gasoil Paper Swap Spreads

LOCAL REGULATORY/LEGAL TREATMENT OF DERIVATIVES

The regulatory and legal framework in Singapore is geared primarily toward listed derivatives, since such instruments have been the focal point of the local financial centre for the past two decades. The primary regulatory legislation governing futures contracts is contained in the Futures Trading Act (FTA). Under the FTA, a futures contract is defined to be a contract between two parties, traded through an approved exchange, which is either deliverable or non-deliverable; futures options are considered a sub-set of this definition and are included under the FTA. Underlying instruments which futures (or futures options) may reference include equity indexes, interest rates, currencies and gold. The FTA does not cover futures referencing soft/agricultural commodities, such as coffee and rubber (which are traded on SICOM); in fact, SIMEX is presently the only exchange approved under the FTA (SICOM is supervised by the Singapore Trade Development Board, a statutory body set up by the Singapore Parliament). FTA regulations are applied equally to futures brokers and their representatives futures pool operators and their representatives, and futures trading advisors and their representatives. Licenses are granted to approved brokers, advisors and representatives in accordance with rules established under the FTA. Enforcement and interpretation of the FTA is most often handled by the MAS.

Following the Barings scandal of 1995 (where fraudulent overtrading in SIMEX (and Japanese) Nikkei, JGB and Euroyen futures caused a massive loss and forced the bank to be acquired by another international institution), the Government of Singapore moved quickly to tighten regulations in order to prevent a recurrence of a similar event. The Parliament passed certain amendments to the FTA designed to enhance regulatory control over futures trading in Singapore via the Futures Trading (Amendment) Bill. The amendments were created to give MAS more supervisory authority over SIMEX, and called for: closer oversight and regulation over brokers; individual licensing of futures brokers by the MAS on an annual basis; approval by the MAS of all new contracts listed on SIMEX or a subsidiary of SIMEX; formation of an advisory panel to provide additional consultation and protection; creation of a fidelity compensation fund to cover possible future losses sustained by retail investors (e.g. SIMEX will place 10% of its annual profit into the fund, which will provide investors with compensation of up to S$100,000, or 75% of the loss); ability by the MAS to force the dismissal of external auditors who fail to bring to light problems with controls or reporting; segregation between dealing and back office functions in member firms; higher level of supervision and vigilance by parent firms over their Singapore subsidiaries; regulating the electronic trading system; and strengthening of the internal SIMEX supervisory function.

OTC derivatives in the Singapore market are governed by MAS Regulation 621, which covers internationalization of the Singapore dollar and rates. As indicated above, the MAS's general stance (which is reflected in Regulation 621) is to discourage OTC derivatives transacted on the local currency or interest rates, unless such transactions are deemed to be for legitimate hedging purposes, or provide some direct economic benefit to Singapore as a whole.

LOCAL ACCOUNTING PRACTICES FOR DERIVATIVES

Singaporean authorities have put forth general accounting rules which must be followed for the reporting of derivative exposures; unlike certain other Asia Pacific nations, such rules do not differentiate between derivatives used for hedging or speculating purposes. Gains or losses arising from swaps are amortized over the life of the contract and are included in the income statement. Forward foreign exchange contracts are revalued in Singapore dollars at the rate in existence on balance sheet date, with unrealized gains or losses taken to the income statement in that period.

PROSPECTS FOR THE LOCAL DERIVATIVE MARKET

Summarized below are near-term (one- to three-year) and medium-term (three- to five-year) prospects for Singaporean derivatives.

Near-term:

- Expanded turnover in key SIMEX financial futures/options (e.g. Eurodollars, Euroyen, Nikkei 225, JGBs) as more regional participants are attracted to the deep liquidity and low transactions costs offered by the Exchange.
- Restructuring or abandonment of SIMEX futures which feature no volume or open interest (e.g. gold futures, MSCI Hong Kong Index futures); potential restructuring of SES equity options, and/or liberalization of current rules on short-selling and market-making to promote greater liquidity.
- Greater turnover and liquidity in SICOM rubber futures as the Exchange moves to become the dominant rubber trading location in Southeast Asia (e.g. ahead of both KLCE and ICEB).
- Introduction of new commodity futures contracts on SICOM (e.g. copper, aluminium, cocoa, zinc).
- Continued growth in domestic IRS's and CCS's as a short-term floating rate benchmark is developed and domestic financing needs expand; gradual deepening of liquidity along the yield curve.
- Significant growth in OTC energy forward/swap trading as nations in the Asia Pacific region continue to utilize increasing amounts of energy in their industrial bases.

Medium-term:

- Greater activity in domestic OTC equity derivatives as the underlying cash market becomes more liquid and onshore/offshore investors continue to participate in the market.
- Gradual expansion in liquidity for domestic fixed income options as the underlying swap and forward markets become more liquid, pricing tools improve and demand increases.

Exchange	**Contract**	**1993 Volume (contracts)**	**1994 Volume (contracts)**
SES	Equity options	15,000	4,000
SICOM	RSS1 rubber futures	697,515	577,395
	RSS3 rubber futures	419,900	641,210
	TSR20 rubber futures	598,520	528,640
	RCS rubber index futures	4,400	0
	Robusta coffee futures	n/l*	n/l*
SIMEX	Nikkei 225 index futures	5,100,000	5,800,000
	Nikkei 300 index futures	n/l*	n/l*
	MSCI HK index futures	66,000	500
	Nikkei 225 index futures options	897,000	1,490,000
	Nikkei 300 index futures options	n/l*	n/l*
	Eurodollar futures	5,350,000	8,690,000
	Euroyen futures	3,530,000	6,820,000
	Euromark futures	23,127	231,068
	Eurodollar futures options	6,525	13,545
	Euroyen futures options	57,395	126,280
	JGB futures	29,254	443,564
	JGB futures options	n/l*	39,808
	US$/JPY deferred currency futures	13,182	68,605
	US$/DM deferred currency futures	26,298	131,210
	US$/JPY currency futures#	0	0
	US$/DM currency futures#	0	0
	GBP/US$ currency futures#	0	0
	Gold futures	436	26
	HS Fuel Oil futures	323,006	171,896
	Brent Crude futures	n/l*	n/l*

* n/l: contract not yet listed, #: contract delisted in 1995

Table 11.33 Summary of 1993/1994 Listed Futures and Options Turnover

	Overall Liquidity	Liquid/ Maximum Maturity	Interbank dealing size	Average bid-offer spread
Equity/Index Swaps	fair	12 mos/3 yrs	n/a	n/a
Equity/Index Options	fair	6–12 mos/3 yrs	n/a	n/a
Interest Rate Swaps	fair	5 yrs/10 yrs	US$10–U$30 mln	15–20 bps
Interest Rate Options	poor	1–2 yrs/3 yrs	none	varies
Currency Swaps	fair	1–3 yrs/7 yrs	US$10–US$20 mln	15–25 bps
Currency Options	fair	3–12 mos/2 yrs	US$10 mln	1 pt

Table 11.34 Summary of Domestic OTC Derivatives

12: South Korea

FINANCIAL MARKET OVERVIEW

South Korea's equity, fixed income and currency markets are substantial in size but remain very tightly regulated; the controls currently in place, which apply to both domestic and offshore institutions, have detracted from overall liquidity in key financial instruments. In the equity market overseas investment in local stocks can only be accomplished by obtaining qualified foreign investor (QFI) status; free foreign access to Korean stocks is not yet a reality. In the fixed income market, though the country is in the process of widespread interest rate deregulation which will be completed by 1997, many local money and bond market instruments must still adhere to government dictated interest rates; in addition, foreign investment in local bonds is still extremely restricted. In the foreign exchange market, though regulatory changes are underway which will eventually lead to full convertibility of the Korean won, restrictions on foreign currency trading have dampened liquidity in spot and forward FX. As a result of strict controls impacting liquidity in key financial instruments, the market for local derivatives based on such instruments is still underdeveloped.

Korea's equity market has been in existence since 1956 when the country's first exchange, the Daehan Stock Exchange (DSE), was founded. The DSE was reorganized as a joint-stock company in 1962 and became a non-profit government entity in 1963, at which time it was renamed the Korea Stock Exchange (KSE). The Exchange was reorganized into its present membership structure in 1988 and stands as the country's sole equity trading forum at the present time. Unlike other Asia Pacific stock markets, the Korean market has managed to sustain a record of steady growth in listings, trading volume and market capitalization over the past decade. The value of the equity market increased steadily throughout the 1991–94 period as a result of buoyant equity prices, privatizations and secondary placements; total capitalization reached US$192 bln in 1994, ranking the market as the sixth largest of Asia Pacific's 13 equity markets. Figure 12.1 below illustrates the historical movement of the benchmark Korea Composite Stock Price Index (KOSPI) while Table 12.1 provides details on the nature and size of the Korean equity market (note that a new market capitalization index, the KOSPI 200, has recently been developed for use in index derivatives (as discussed at greater length below); it is likely to replace the KOSPI as the country's primary market index over time).

Figure 12.1 Historical Price Movement of Korea Composite Stock Price Index

Year*	**Market Capitalization (US$ bln)**	**Trading Value (US$ bln)**	**Listed Companies (#)**
1994	191.8	286.1	699
1993	139.4	211.7	693
1992	107.5	116.1	688
1991	96.4	85.5	686
1990	110.5	75.9	669

* to December of each year; Source: IFC, 1995

	1/92–6/95 Annualized Return	**1/92–6/95 Total Return**
Korea Composite Stock Price Index	8.11%	29.68%

Table 12.1 Domestic Equity Market Indicators

As indicated above, foreign investor access to Korean equities is very strictly controlled. Present restrictions on foreign shareholdings (once approved as a QFI) include a 15% ceiling for all foreign investment in any Korean company (12% in any state company) and a 3% ceiling for any single foreign investor in any Korean company; once the ceilings are reached foreign investors can only trade shares among themselves on an OTC basis, generally at a substantial premium to domestic shares.

As indicated above, the local fixed income market is substantial in size but very strictly regulated. The country's sovereign and private sector debt market is the second largest in Asia (after Japan), but is still subject to interest rate controls. Although Korean authorities have outlined a series of interest rate deregulation measures to be taken between 1995 and the end of 1997, at which time all interest rates will be market-determined, a number of key rates are still set by the government. Regulation has been detrimental to the establishment of fixed and floating rate benchmarks, and the absence of such benchmarks has impacted the development of domestic derivatives. As discussed below, the forward FX, interest rate swap, currency swap and currency option markets have all been negatively affected by the absence of market-driven interest rate benchmarks.

The domestic sovereign debt market is comprised of a broad range of instruments which are issued for very specific purposes. Short-maturity instruments (to one year) include Treasury Bills and Monetary Stabilization Bonds (MSBs) which are used primarily for short-term liquidity management. Intermediate- and long-term instruments (one- to 20-years) include Foreign Exchange Fund Stabilization Bonds (used to stabilize the value of the currency), Grain Management Fund Bonds (used to stabilize the price of grain), National Housing Bonds (used to fund housing development), National Investment Bonds (used to finance special capital projects), public corporation bonds (used by public utility corporations to fund their operations), municipal bonds (used by municipalities to fund their operations), and financial debentures (used by banks to fund lending to specific sectors of the economy); financial debentures are sub-divided into industrial debentures, long-term credit debentures, housing debentures, foreign exchange finance debentures, export-import debentures, and small/medium industry debentures. Total sovereign fixed income outstandings amounted to KRW77 tln (US$100 bln) at the end of 1994. The private sector money market includes commercial paper, certificates of deposit (CDs) and bankers' acceptances; all securities mature in under one year. The private sector bond market features substantial issuance of fixed and floating rate corporate bonds, bonds-with-warrants and convertible bonds; private sector bonds carry maturities extending from one- to ten-years, though most issuance occurs in the five-year sector. Total private sector outstandings reached KRW46.2 tln (US$60.1 bln) at the end of 1994 (World Bank, 1995; Banks, 1994).

Although Korea does not yet have established market-determined interest rate benchmarks, it does feature certain domestic interest rate indicators which are increasingly used as financial references; these include the Korean interbank deposit rate (the borrowing cost for banks in the institutional deposit market), the CD rate (the borrowing cost for banks in the retail and institutional CD market), the MSB yield (the one-year borrowing cost of the government) and the prime rate (the borrowing cost for prime Korean corporations). Table 12.2 below contains details on payment frequency, compounding frequency and day count convention for key domestic interest rates.

Rate	**Payment Frequency**	**Compounding Frequency**	**Day Count Convention**
Interbank Dep.	–	–	Actual/365
Won CD	semi-annual	semi-annual	Actual/365
MSB	semi-annual	semi-annual	Actual/365
Prime	semi-annual	semi-annual	Actual/365

Table 12.2 Domestic Interest Rate Summary

The Korean won (KRW) is a non-convertible, semi-floating currency operating under the market average rate (MAR) system. The MAR system was introduced in March 1990 as a means of moving from a rigid multi-currency basket peg to a market-determined rate. Under the MAR the value of the won can fluctuate within a set band on a daily basis. The band was originally set at +/– 0.4% against the previous day's close, but has been increased four times since 1990 and currently stands at +/– 1.5%. The overall Korean currency market is broadly divided into the interbank and customer markets. The customer market is faced with very strict controls which has limited opportunities for expansion. The interbank market, in contrast, is somewhat more active and has increased in size and liquidity as certain deregulation measures have been implemented (as discussed below). Virtually all interbank trading in the won flows through the Korea Financial Telecommunications Centre (KFTC), which acts as an interbank broker; direct bank-to-bank dealing accounts for only 3% of spot, forward and derivative volume, and is related primarily to trading of the won against non-US dollar currencies (KEB, 1994). The fact that all interbank business flows through the KFTC has been cited as a constraint to growth in the currency market; the possibility of ending the KFTC's monopoly by establishing additional commercial FX brokers is presently being considered. Average daily turnover in the spot market (which under Korean market convention is for transaction value on trade date as well as trade date plus one day) is KRW1.54 tln (US$2 bln), up from KRW154 bln (US$200 mln) in 1990 (ERG, 1995). Typical dealing size in the interbank spot market is KRW2.3 bln to KRW3.8 bln (US$3 mln to US$5 mln), though parcels of KRW15.4 bln (US$20 mln) are not uncommon; spot bid-offer spreads are KRW0.10/US$ under normal market conditions.

Deregulation of the won has occurred in various stages over the past few years but is not yet complete. In October 1993 the authorities liberalized the documentary requirement imposed on spot and forward currency trades. Prior to 1993, resident buyers and sellers of spot won were required to submit documentation to the central bank immediately after trade execution; the requirement was abolished and documentation is no longer needed. Residents engaged in forward FX transactions must still submit documentation for transactions in excess of US$3MM but now have up to 45 days to complete and submit all paperwork. Despite these changes, the overall won FX market is still relatively modest in size; additional reforms planned for 1995 (first stage), 1996–97 (second stage) and 1998–99 (third stage) are designed to boost market size and liquidity. First stage reforms call for complete elimination of documentary requirements and the establishment of commercial brokers. Second stage reforms centre on expanding FX position limits for domestic and foreign banks (current limits are overall overbought at a maximum 50% of equity, spot oversold at 2% of equity) and promoting offshore financing of domestic banks. Third stage reforms call for the elimination of all FX position limits which will result in free trading of won against foreign currencies. Full convertibility of the currency may follow after third stage reforms have been enacted. Figure 12.2 below highlights the movement of spot KRW/US$.

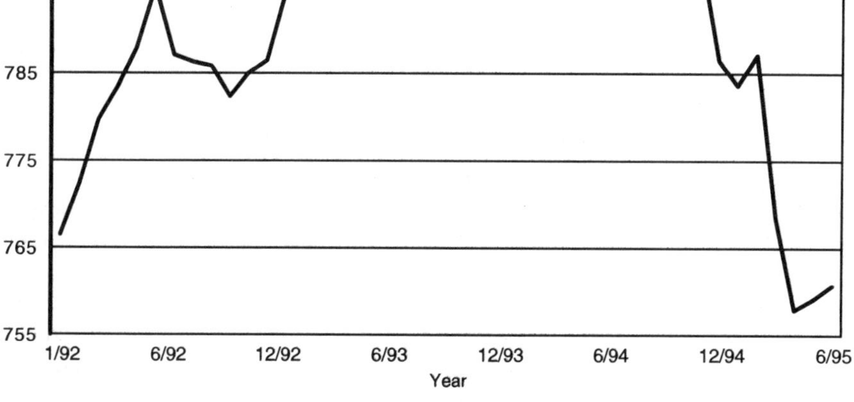

Figure 12.2 Historical Movement of Spot KRW/US$

DERIVATIVE MARKETS AND PRODUCTS

LISTED DERIVATIVE EXCHANGES

Korea's listed derivative effort is presently concentrated on domestic convertible bonds and domestic equity warrants. Both derivative securities are listed on, and traded through, the country's main exchange, the KSE. Although the KSE's primary focus is on equity trading, listing and trading of public sector bonds, corporate bonds (including convertibles), and equity warrants remains an important component of its overall business. Trading of all cash and derivative securities occurs electronically, through the Exchange's SMATS trading system, on an order-driven basis; clearing and settlement occurs on a 'regular way' basis, the second business day after trade date, through a separate company known as the Korea Securities Depository. As discussed at greater length below, KSE is due to expand its role in derivatives in the near term through the introduction of domestic futures.

Korea does not yet feature its own futures exchange or futures contracts, though it has already established a preliminary futures programme which will lead to full futures trading by early 1996. The country's original plans called for establishment of separate exchanges for commodity futures and financial futures. Such an approach, however, appears to have been abandoned in favour of a combined exchange which will list and trade all Korean futures. One major reason for the decision to introduce trading in a combined fashion is related to reorganization within the government itself. In early 1995 the Economic Planning Board and the Ministry of Finance were merged into a single entity, known as the Ministry of Finance and Economy (MOFE); as a combined entity, the new Ministry will have the power to regulate all aspects of combined futures trading. Although individual jurisdiction for commodity futures may remain with separate ministries (e.g. primary agricultural products under the Ministry of Agriculture, Forestry and Fisheries, energy products under the Ministry of International Trade, and so on), the MOFE will maintain overall jurisdiction over domestic commodity futures and financial futures.

The current focus of the Korean futures programme is on stock index derivatives. The authorities have already released information regarding the design and trading of domestic stock index futures; introduction of the contract is planned for early 1996, with 'paper trading' already underway in 1995. In 1990, the KSE appointed the Korea Securities Institute (KSI) to study the viability of listed financial derivatives in the Korean marketplace. The KSI's study recommended development of an index futures contract, followed by stock options and interest rate futures. The KSE went on to study the matter further and established the following guidelines in 1993: any futures created in Korea should be traded on the KSE under the existing regulatory framework (e.g. no new exchange and no new regulatory framework should be created specifically for futures); all futures trades should be cleared and settled via the Korea Securities Depository; all futures should flow through an execution system which is distinct from the one used by the KSE for equity trading; and a new market value-weighted index should be the focal point of the new index futures contract. At the present time it appears that the KSE will be the trading forum for the country's futures. Whether futures will be traded on a new dedicated exchange in the medium-term has been the subject of some debate, and at least one proposal has been put forth for the creation of a new exchange, the Korean Financial Futures Exchange (KOFFEX).

Trading in commodity futures is expected to follow trading in financial futures and options. In 1990 the Office of Supply (OSROK) eased restrictions previously imposed on domestic companies using offshore futures contracts to hedge commodity price exposures. Since the easing of restrictions Korean companies have been permitted to hedge positions through use of virtually all global listed commodity futures, and many have become active users of futures on energy, metals and agricultural goods; Korean firms actively use crude oil, gasoline, aluminium, copper, gold, silver, raw silk, cattle, poultry, soybean, rice and wheat futures to hedge production, deliveries, imports or exports. Given the substantial amount of commodity price hedging being undertaken by Korean companies offshore, the authorities have determined that introduction of select commodity contracts in the onshore market is a logical progression. OSROK and the MOFE have indicated that the creation of local commodity futures will favour commodities with: (a) high price volatility; (b) annual marketing turnover in excess of KRW100 bln (US$130 mln); and (c) active use by a broad spectrum of importers, exporters, producers, retailers and consumers (e.g. so that no special interests are considered). Timing of the introduction of commodity futures has not yet been determined, but is expected to follow index futures and equity options. Table 12.3 highlights Korea's sole listed derivative exchange and instruments.

Exchange	Primary Derivatives
Korea Stock Exchange (KSE)	Convertible bonds; issuer equity warrants; index futures (proposed)

Table 12.3 Listed Derivative Exchanges

LISTED FUTURES AND OPTIONS

Equity

Equity Futures/Options

The domestic market does not presently feature listed equity options, though such derivatives are expected to form the second stage of products offered on the KSE (once index futures are introduced). There are no short- or intermediate-term plans to introduce equity futures.

Index Futures/Options/Futures Options

Although KSE is still in the final stages of establishing its listed derivative programme it has already provided information on its planned domestic stock index contract, tentatively scheduled for launch in early 1996 (institutions began 'paper trading' the contract as part of the testing phase in mid-1995). The KSE will trade stock index futures based on the Korea Stock Price Index (KOSPI) 200, a market capitalization-weighted index comprised of the 200 largest Korean stocks; the index represents approximately 70% of Korea's equity market capitalization. The proposed future will be a cash-settled contract, valued at KRW500,000 times the index, offered on a quarterly cycle with quotes on four contracts at any time; liquidity is likely to be centred primarily in the front month contract.

Stock index futures orders will be input directly by members into remote terminals linked to the KSE's futures trading system; trades will be routed through, and cleared by, the Futures Market Automated Trading System. Contracts will be traded on an individual auction basis via single price order matching. Interestingly, there will be no difference in margins for hedgers, speculators or spreaders; in addition, position limits for foreign and domestic participants will be identical (despite the existence of foreign investment restrictions, as detailed above). Note that along with outright daily price limits to control directional price movement the regulators are also considering imposing a limit on the maximum daily differential between the cash index and the futures price; such a limit (to be set at 3% to 5%), essentially places a cap on the maximum amount of permissible basis risk. The proposed specifications of the KOSPI 200 index future are detailed in Table 12.4.

Contract	**Korea Stock Price Index 200 Index Futures**
Type	Domestic
Exchange	Korea Stock Exchange
Months	March, June, September, December
Contract Size	KRW500,000 * KOSPI 200 Index
Tick Value	0.05 points when index is below 100 0.10 points when index is above 100
Daily Limit	4 points when index is below 100 6 points when index is between 101 and 150 8 points when index is between 151 and 200 10 points when index is above 200
Deliverable Instrument	Cash settlement
Last Trading Day	2nd Thursday of the delivery month or day preceding if such day is a holiday
Delivery Day	Same as the last trading day
Real-time price data	To be determined

Table 12.4 Contract Specifications for KSE Korea Stock Price Index 200 Index Futures (Proposed)

KOSPI index options are expected to be introduced in the medium-term, once futures have established sufficiently liquidity.

Fixed Income

Deposit Futures/Options/Futures Options

The Korean market does not presently feature deposit futures or options. Such futures are not contemplated as part of the country's new programme, primarily because the market features no robust short-term deposit benchmark at the present time. Second stage focus in listed fixed income derivatives is being placed on long-term interest rate futures where institutional demand is higher and price risk is greater.

Interest Rate Futures/Options/Futures Options

The Korean market does not presently feature interest rate futures or options, though such derivatives have been cited as a priority for Korea's local futures programme once it is operational. Given the substantial size of the Korean sovereign and private sector fixed income market (e.g. US$160 bln), together with the country's programme of interest rate deregulation, need for such derivatives is likely to be apparent in the near term. Early efforts will be centred on identifying the appropriate futures reference security so that issues related to pricing, deliverability and so on, can be resolved.

Currency

Currency Futures/Options/Futures Options

Korea does not presently feature currency futures or options. It is unlikely to introduce such contracts in the near term as the immediate focus of its listed derivatives programme is on stock index futures, equity options, bond futures and commodity futures. The presence of strict currency controls would, in any event, make creation of a domestic currency contract meaningless; development of G10 currency contracts would also be questionable, as such would face extreme competition from contracts already listed on other Asia Pacific exchanges (e.g. MIFE, TIFFE, SIMEX, HKFE).

Commodity

Commodity Futures/Options/Futures Options

Although Korea does not presently list or trade domestic commodity futures or options, introduction of such derivatives is a near-term priority under the domestic futures programme. The need for domestic listing of commodity contracts appears quite clear given Korea's role as a major importer and exporter of commodities and finished goods. Potential commodity futures contracts are expected to be based on energy, metals and agricultural products; most references are likely to be drawn from international commodity prices or rates since Korea is not a significant commodity producer and has no major commodity references of its own.

LISTED/OVER-THE-COUNTER WARRANTS, CONVERTIBLES AND HYBRIDS

Equity

Equity Warrants

Korean equity warrants are available in three different forms, including listed domestic issuer equity warrants, listed offshore issuer equity warrants and OTC offshore covered equity warrants.

The domestic market features a modest amount of equity warrants which are listed on, and traded through, the KSE; equity warrants, with maturities ranging from one-to-five years, are generally attached to domestic won bond issues and are then stripped and traded separately. Exercise of the warrants results in the issuance of new equity by the corporation floating the bond-with-warrant package. Most major blue-chip Korean corporations, and numerous smaller capitalization companies, have accessed the domestic warrant market through detachable bond-with-warrant packages.

In addition to domestic equity warrants, Korean companies are active issuers of offshore bonds-with-warrants, in either the domestic Swiss franc market or offshore Eurodollar market. As with domestic equity warrants, offshore warrants are normally detached from the original bonds and traded separately; exercise of the derivatives results in the issuance of new equity by the underlying Korean issuer. Warrants in the Swiss market may be listed on one of the Swiss exchanges or may remain unlisted, while those in the Eurodollar market are generally listed on an offshore exchange (e.g. Luxembourg Stock Exchange); most secondary trading of Swiss and Eurodollar warrants occurs on an OTC basis. Issues in both markets carry maturities ranging from one- to five-years (with occasional issues extending beyond five years) and are floated in a variety of currencies (i.e. US dollars, Deutschmarks, Swiss francs). Appendix II contains a summary listing of offshore Korean warrants.

Issues of covered third-party OTC warrants on Korean equities (which result in the re-allocation of existing shares rather the issuance of new equity, as in the domestic and offshore issuer warrants described above), have been extremely rare to date. While foreign financial institutions routinely write covered call warrants on many individual stocks in other Asia Pacific markets, their activity in the Korean market has been negligible, primarily because of limited investor demand for Korean single stock warrants and the presence of restrictions on foreign access to local shares. The few issues which are floated are either unlisted or listed on offshore exchanges and traded on an OTC basis; maturities range from one- to two-years. A representative issue in this category is Bankers Trust's US dollar call warrants on Hyundai (1994). As foreign investment restrictions are eased and the overall market liberalizes, covered call warrants on Korean stocks may become more popular.

Basket/Index Warrants

The domestic market does not currently list or trade basket or index warrants. Institutions in the offshore market, however, float index warrants based primarily on the broad Korean market (rather than narrower baskets of individual stocks). Although periodic, one- to three-year, covered warrants are written on Korean indexes (e.g. Lehman Brothers' US dollar index call warrants on the KOSPI (1994), JP Morgan's US dollar index call warrants on the KOSPI (1994) and Bankers Trust's four tranche US dollar index call warrants on the KOSPI (1994)), overall activity has remained subdued as a result of restrictions imposed on foreign institutions. The inability freely to buy and sell underlying equities, together with the current lack of index futures, has made it difficult for warrant sellers to manage risk positions in an efficient manner. As the local stock market becomes more accessible to foreign investors, and once KOSPI 200 index futures are available via the KSE, it is likely that additional covered index and basket warrant issues will be floated.

Convertibles

Korea features a small domestic convertible bond market which has been in existence since 1963, when Ssangyong Cement floated the first local won-denominated issue. Domestic convertibles have historically failed to attract a great deal of attention in the local market, primarily because issuers have relied on more familiar fixed rate bonds and bank loans to meet financing needs. In recent years, however, issuance has increased and won convertibles are now a more significant element of local funding. During 1992, KRW146 bln (US$190 mln) of won convertibles were issued; by 1993 that figure had risen to KRW398 bln (US$515 mln) and by 1994 full year issuance was estimated at KRW2 tln (US$2.6 bln) (Banks, 1994). Local convertibles are issued with maturities ranging from two- to ten-years; all issues are listed on the KSE and most trading occurs directly on the Exchange (though a certain amount of OTC broker-to-broker trading is also evident). Bonds are typically issued with low coupons and intermediate conversion premiums. It is interesting to note that, although foreign investors are still prohibited from investing freely in the local fixed income market (until 1997, when restrictions will be lifted), they have been permitted, as of mid-1994, to invest in domestic convertible bonds issued by small and medium companies. Foreign investor holdings in a single issue must still be less than 30% of the total (with no single investor holding more than 5%); before any purchases can occur investors must register with the Securities Supervisory Board and obtain a bond investment registration card, and must open relevant local bank accounts. Foreign investors cannot yet buy or sell domestic convertible bonds floated by Korean chaebols (i.e. large industrial conglomerates such as Hyundai, Samsung and LG).

Along with domestic convertibles, Korean companies frequently raise funds through the issuance of offshore convertibles. The first Korean Eurodollar convertible was issued by Samsung Electronics in 1985 and dozens of bonds have been floated in the offshore Eurodollar and domestic Swiss franc markets since that time. The issuance of all offshore convertibles must be approved in advance by the Korean Securities and Exchange Commission and the Securities Supervisory Board, who limit approval of offshore financings to those related to initial overseas investment, overseas expansion, importing of capital goods and so on.

When the country's first offshore convertibles were floated in the mid-1980s the very strict prohibition on foreign ownership of local shares led secondary convertibles to trade with conversion premiums in excess of 100%; the gradual deregulation of investment restrictions has brought conversion premiums down substantially. Most activity by Korean issuers has been in the Eurodollar market, by corporations such as Ssangyong Oil, Daewoo Corporation, Daewoo Electronics, Jinro, Shinwon Corporation and others. In 1990, total issuance amounted to US$150 mln, in 1991 it increased to US$429 mln, in 1992 it receded to US$188 mln, and in 1993 it recovered to US$338 mln; 1994 issuance reached US$688 mln. Korean issues in the Eurodollar market are floated with maturities of ten- to 15-years; bonds are typically listed on offshore exchanges and trade on a bearer basis in the OTC market. The preferred structures are very low coupon issues (1% to 2%) with initial conversion premiums of approximately 10%; conversion is into an issuer's domestic shares at a won conversion price. In addition to the Eurodollar market, select Korean companies (e.g Yukong) have also floated public or private bonds in the domestic Swiss market. Public deals are listed on, and traded through, the Swiss exchanges, while private deals are unlisted and traded OTC. In comparison with the Eurodollar market, maturities on Swiss issues are much shorter, generally no more than five years. Swiss bonds are floated with both investor puts and issuer (or provisional) calls; the puts permit the investor to put the bonds back to the issuer, while the calls permit the issuer to call the bond, after a non-call period (typically one-half the life of the bond). It should be noted that although Korean regulations presently restrict foreign investor access to equities, offshore convertible bonds are not included in the foreign ownership limits. Appendix III contains details on Korean convertible bonds.

Index-linked Notes

The domestic market does not list or trade index-linked notes tied to the value of the broad Korean equity market. Institutions in the offshore market structure periodic issues of index-linked notes (primarily one- to three-years in maturity with embedded long calls or puts), but overall activity has been very limited. Offshore notes, which reference either the KOSPI or smaller baskets of local stocks, are generally structured as private placements and are not actively traded.

Fixed Income

Fixed Income Warrants

Although the local fixed income market is substantial in size, there have been no listed or OTC fixed income warrants referencing local bonds issued to date.

Currency

Currency Warrants

Institutions in the domestic and offshore markets have not issued listed or OTC warrants pegged to the Korean won, primarily as a result of the currency restrictions presently in place.

Commodity

Commodity Warrants

There have been no listed or OTC commodity warrants referencing domestic commodity indicators issued to date.

OVER-THE-COUNTER FORWARDS, SWAPS AND OPTIONS

Equity

Equity Forwards/Swaps

The domestic market does not currently feature OTC equity forwards or swaps. Institutions in the offshore OTC market buy and sell a very small amount of short- or intermediate-term equity forwards (to three years) on individual Korean equities. The market for equity swaps (e.g. swaps which exchange a floating rate flow for appreciation or depreciation in a single stock) is dormant. Overall activity remains subdued as a result of both limited investor demand and foreign investor restrictions. The restricted access to domestic equities makes it difficult for foreign institutions to manage risks generated by the sale or purchase of equity derivatives, including equity forwards and swaps (as well as equity/index forwards, swaps and options, discussed below); liberalization of investment restrictions should promote additional activity over time.

Equity Options

The domestic market does not feature OTC equity options, though foreign institutions operating in the offshore market periodically execute puts and calls on individual Korean equities. Such options may be customized for clients with regard to target equity, maturity, strike and exercise type, but are generally cash-settled European or American options with maturities of up to 12 months. OTC options are illiquid on a secondary basis as transactions expire without value, are closed out with the arranging bank, or are exercised into cash settlement; resales to third parties do not occur. As with other Korean OTC equity derivatives, overall activity remains very modest for the reasons cited immediately above.

Basket/Index Forwards/Swaps

While the domestic market features no OTC basket or index forwards/swaps, institutions in the offshore market create index forwards and swaps (with maturities ranging from one- to three-years) on a periodic basis. Foreign financial institutions generally sell swaps with embedded calls (or puts), providing investors with appreciation (or depreciation) in an index such as the KOSPI; in exchange for the potential upside (or downside), investors most often pay premium in the form of a periodic floating rate flow. Overall activity in index swaps is still comparatively small, primarily because dealer management of risk positions is challenging (given limited access to equities and the absence of index futures). Basket forwards and swaps structured in a similar fashion are also available, though overall volume is negligible. Note that introduction of KSE's KOSPI futures is likely to present challenges and opportunities for the OTC index forward/swap market. Index futures are likely to challenge vanilla OTC index forwards/swaps for market share as futures can be employed to create similar, or identical, risk/payoff profiles, often at a lower cost. At the same time the availability of index futures will make dealer management of OTC risk positions simpler, fostering potential growth in the market. As with other OTC equity derivatives, further market liberalization is also likely to generate additional demand for basket and index forwards/swaps.

Basket/Index Options

The domestic market features no OTC basket or index options. Despite the absence of domestic options, foreign financial institutions operating in the offshore market are modestly active in buying and selling OTC basket/index puts and calls, primarily in the form of cash-settled vanilla options with maturities to 12 months. There is presently no market for exotic Korean basket/index options. Although overall activity is still rather limited for many of the reasons indicated above, volumes are expected to increase as accessibility to the underlying equity market improves and index futures are introduced.

Fixed Income

Fixed Income Forwards/Swaps

Local interest rate derivatives, including forwards and swaps, are very new to the Korean marketplace; there is, as yet, no legitimate, liquid won interest rate derivative market. Since interest rate deregulation is still in its initial stages (though it will eventually reach the point where all rates are determined by market forces), overall activity in local fixed income derivatives is still negligible. The market continues to be impacted by: (a) lack of an accepted short-term interest rate benchmark to value floating rate segments of IRSs; (b) lack of a true government yield curve to supply the swap market with pricing information; and (c) lack of standard, and liquid, government bonds to hedge swap portfolios (recall from earlier in the chapter that the local bond market is large, but extremely fragmented). In addition, foreign institutions with derivative capabilities/technologies are not presently permitted to transact in onshore swaps or forwards. Until these barriers are overcome, the domestic market is likely to remain modest in both size and liquidity.

Local interest rate derivatives can be divided into onshore and offshore transactions. The market for onshore won IRSs is based on fixed won (semi-annual, on an Actual/365-day basis) against either short-term won certificate of deposit (CD) rates or won commercial paper (CP) rates, with 90- or 180-day reset periods. Since the local CP market is quite active and liquid, CP rates are often used as a proxy floating rate benchmark against fixed rates in a swap. Most onshore activity is limited to maturities of two- and three-years, though transactions to five years occur on a periodic basis; there is no established interbank dealing size at present and bid-offer spreads remain wide and rather unpredictable. Onshore forwards referencing CP or CD rates are only modestly active, to a maximum of 12 months. The offshore IRS market quotes fixed won (semi-annual, on an Actual/365-day basis) against the interest rates implicit in KRW/US$ FX forwards (in a manner similar to the process utilized through the Singapore swap offer rate (SOR) for other Southeast Asian currencies, as mentioned at several points in this text); offshore swaps generally reference 90- or 180-day forward FX points to generate a floating rate indicator. Activity in the offshore market is still very limited and concentrated in maturities of one- to three-years; there is no standard interbank dealing size yet and, as in the onshore market, bid-offer spreads are both wide and volatile.

Table 12.5 traces the growth of both FRAs and IRSs since 1990, and includes both Korean won interest rate derivatives and foreign currency interest rate derivatives transacted in Korea (KEB, 1994). The figures reveal that overall activity in the market is still extremely limited.

Fixed Income Options

There is, at present, no domestic market for fixed income options, for many of the reasons cited in the section immediately above. Bond options, swaptions, caps and floors based on local rates are unlikely to develop until the market establishes a firm

US$ mln	1990	1991	1992	1993	6/1994
FRAs	1030.0	838.0	545.0	389.0	3049.0
IRSs	1390.0	5803.0	3022.0	1942.0	2098.0

Table 12.5 Notional Value of Interest Rate Derivatives Transacted in Korea

floating-rate benchmark and experiences further growth in underlying won forwards and swaps.

Currency

Currency Forwards/Swaps

The market for OTC FX forwards involving the won is growing in size but is still concentrated in very short maturity transactions. Won forwards, which extend from one day after spot settlement to 180 days, are used by domestic and foreign banks to hedge out currency exposures or take a speculative view on currency movements. The forward market is very liquid in the one-day to one-week tenors, but is reasonably illiquid beyond one-week. Typical interbank forward trades are in the range of KRW 2.3 bln to KRW3.8 bln (US$3 mln to US$5 mln), with a maximum of KRW7.7 bln (US$10 mln) possible without moving the market; average weekly won forward volume amounted to KRW77 bln (US$100 mln) in 1994 (ERG, 1995). Bid offer spreads range from KRW2/US$ for short-term forwards to KRW4–8/US$ for six month forwards and KRW15–20/US$ for 12 month forwards (the reader will recall from the beginning of the chapter that spreads for spot trades are KRW0.10/US$ under normal market conditions). Interbank dealers do not currently quote two-way markets; most quote either a bid or an offer. As a means of promoting greater liquidity in the forward market (particularly in longer tenors), the KFTC announced in mid-1995 that it will begin broking two-way spot/forward FX swaps on a daily basis; deals will mature between one-day and one-year after spot settlement.

In addition to standard onshore OTC forwards, there is a growing offshore market for non-deliverable forwards (NDFs) (also known as dollar-settled exchange agreements). Under an NDF, an institution enters into a forward won transaction and, at maturity, cash-settles the market value of the forward in US dollars (rather than physically settling won and dollars). Such structures provide hedging protection or speculative opportunity without the need for dealing in physical currencies (and the attendant restrictions which apply).

The market for currency swaps transacted within Korea is still underdeveloped; there is no liquid currency swap market at present. Long-term cross currency forwards are arranged on a very specific basis and the market is driven primarily by exporter or importer flows requiring currency cover. Current regulations stipulate that currency swaps by domestic institutions must be for hedging foreign currency assets or liabilities, or reducing financing costs for funding executed offshore. In addition to long-term FX swaps, CCSs based on fixed won (semi-annual, on an Actual/365-day basis) against six-month US$ LIBOR are available, but activity is limited and restricted to the two- and three-year sector. There is no standard inter-bank dealing size and bid-offer spreads are still variable. There is a modest market for offshore swaps of won against US dollars which are executed without physical movement of currencies, simply net settlement of profit or loss in US dollars (similar to the NDFs discussed above). Despite the still-modest level of turnover, statistics released by the Bank of Korea indicate gradual growth in the market: total notional outstandings of both types of currency swaps (e.g. won/foreign currency and foreign currency/foreign currency) increased from KRW1.79 tln (US$2.22 bln) in 1992, to KRW1.19 tln (US$1.54 bln) in 1993 and KRW1.54 tln (US$2.03 bln) through the first six months of 1994 (KEB, 1994).

Currency Options

Korea's onshore OTC won currency option market is still in its infancy, having only been formally approved by the authorities in late 1994. At present domestic institutions are permitted to sell OTC currency options (won versus foreign currency, or foreign currency versus foreign currency) when such sales are matched with options purchases and the premium paid is equal to or greater than the premium received (e.g. the authorities want to discourage the practice of selling options as a means of generating upfront premium income). Virtually all options carry maturities of one- to six-months, though certain 12-month deals are executed on occasion. The lack of a deep forward FX market beyond the very short maturities (along with the absence of a floating interest rate benchmark) has made pricing of won options somewhat subjective, which has been detrimental to the broader expansion of the market. While the market is slowly increasing in size, overall activity is likely to remain subdued until currency and interest rate deregulation is complete and associated cash markets develop more fully. Note that the offshore market features a small amount of non-deliverable currency options structured in the same fashion as the NDFs described above.

Commodity

Commodity Forwards/Swaps

Although the Korean market does not feature an OTC commodity derivative capability, local institutions with exposures to commodity prices engage in offshore OTC forwards and swaps with international institutions. Prior to 1990, Korean institutions were prohibited from entering into OTC commodity forwards or swaps with offshore institutions to hedge their commodity price risk (with the exception of energy importers who were allowed to enter into OTC energy derivatives under the assumption that Korea, as a major importer of energy products, should be able to protect itself from volatile energy prices). In early 1990, however, the MOFE removed all restrictions, enabling local companies to transact commodity derivatives in the offshore market with maturities out to five years. In announcing removal of the restrictions, the MOFE released a list of 22 approved commodities on which local companies may buy or sell OTC derivatives; the list includes corn, wheat, soybeans, coffee, cocoa, cotton, rubber, gold, silver, copper, aluminium, zinc, nickel and lead, in addition to oil and oil-related products. Note that all references for commodity forwards and swaps used by Korean companies are based on offshore prices, rates or indexes.

Commodity Options

At the present time there is no local or OTC market for commodity options referencing local commodity indicators. While Korean institutions are users of OTC commodity options (primarily to hedge energy exposures), such structures reference overseas, as opposed to local, commodities.

LOCAL REGULATORY/LEGAL TREATMENT OF DERIVATIVES

Korea's basic regulatory framework was created through the 1962 Securities and Exchange Law (SEL), which set forth rudimentary guidelines related to the securities industry as it existed in the early 1960s. In 1976 an amendment to the SEL resulted in the creation of the Securities and Exchange Commission (SEC), a new supervisory agency charged with overseeing the securities markets. Establishment of the Securities Supervisory Board (SSB) followed shortly thereafter; the SEC and SSB have been the two primary regulators of the Korean market since the 1970s. The SEC has authority over securities market policies, and has broad powers to make decisions on securities markets and to administer the SEL. The SSB, an agency and enforcement arm of the MOFE, is concerned primarily with regulating listed companies. It should be noted that the MOFE retains ultimate regulatory power in Korea, and is capable of repealing or suspending resolutions put forth by the SEC. Korea's primary exchange, the KSE is a self-regulated entity.

As indicated at the beginning of the chapter, Korea is on the verge of establishing its futures programme. Legislative and regulatory aspects of the effort are contained in two key documents, the Commodity Futures Transactions Law (governing listed commodity derivatives) and the Financial Futures Transaction Law (governing listed financial derivatives); the two documents will be combined into a draft Futures Transaction Law and will be presented to the Korean National Assembly in early 1996.

LOCAL ACCOUNTING PRACTICES FOR DERIVATIVES

Despite the fact that activity involving local derivatives is still quite modest, the relatively active derivative business transacted by Korean institutions offshore has led the Korean accounting authorities to develop specific accounting treatment for derivatives under Korean Generally Accepted Accounting Principles (KGAAP). All institutions active in derivatives are required to provide notes in their financial statements regarding their off-balance sheet foreign currency and interest rate derivative exposures; foreign currency contracts are defined to include currency futures, forward FX, FX options and CCSs, while interest rate contracts are defined to include deposit/interest rate futures, forwards/FRAs, IRSs and interest rate options. Under KGAAP all foreign currency and interest rate contracts, regardless of underlying currency, must be converted into Korean won at the forward rate defined (or implied) in the contract. In the absence of any specific conversion rate, the mid-market spot rate is used to value the contracts. Unrealized gains or losses generated by the conversion are not posted to the income statement for the period but are carried forward until the period reflecting the maturity of the derivative. Gains or losses generated by currency or interest rate contracts (whether for hedging or trading purposes) are reflected in the income statement when they are settled (e.g. when the gains or losses are realized). CCS fees and currency option premium are deferred as pre-paid expenses or unearned income and are recognized over the life of the transaction. Interest paid or received prior to maturity is deferred as pre-paid expense or unearned interest income and recognized over the life of the transaction.

PROSPECTS FOR THE LOCAL DERIVATIVE MARKET

Summarized below are the near-term (one- to three-year) and medium-term (three- to five-year) prospects for Korean domestic derivatives.

Near-term:

- Introduction of KOSPI Index futures on the KSE. Planning, design and introduction of bond futures and select commodity futures once index futures have been successfully launched.
- Gradual expansion of IRSs as interest rate deregulation progresses, a short-term benchmark floating rate is established and domestic financing opportunities grow.
- Gradual expansion of CCSs and other currency derivatives as the authorities continue to deregulate the Korean won, and as offshore funding opportunities (and associated swap hedges) increase.
- Continued growth in OTC equity derivatives (including OTC forwards, swaps, options and warrants) as the cash equity market expands, foreign investor access to equities is deregulated and KOSPI futures are introduced.

- Expansion of domestic and offshore convertible bond issuance as domestic corporations continue to require additional sources of funding.

Medium-term:

- Introduction of KOSPI index options and listed equity options.
- Expansion of the domestic IRS market as interest rate deregulation is completed, domestic financing needs grow and foreign institution access to the domestic fixed income and swap market is liberalized; gradual lengthening of swap maturities into the intermediate- and long-term sectors of the curve.
- Early development of domestic fixed income options as interest rate deregulation is completed, foreign derivative technologies are imported and the underlying won swap and forward markets mature.
- Deepening of the OTC equity derivative market as foreign investor derivative technology is transferred, KOSPI futures achieve critical mass and listed index/equity options are introduced.

	Overall Liquidity	**Liquid/ Maximum Maturity**	**Interbank dealing size**	**Average bid-offer spread**
Equity/Index Swaps	poor	12 mos/2–3 yrsP	n/a	n/a
Equity/Index Options	poor	3–12 mos/2–3 yrs	n/a	n/a
Interest Rate Swaps	poor	2–3 yrs/5 yrs	none	varies
Interest Rate Options	non-existent	n/a	n/a	n/a
Currency Swaps	poor	2–3 yrs/3 yrs	none	varies
Currency Options	poor	1–6 mos/12 mos	none	varies

Table 12.6 Summary of Domestic OTC Derivatives

13: Taiwan

FINANCIAL MARKET OVERVIEW

Taiwan's financial markets are large in size and comprehensive in nature, but still limited in liquidity. The domestic equity, fixed income and currency markets are substantial on a primary basis but strict regulations on foreign investment and currency convertibility have impacted secondary activity. This, in turn, has slowed the creation of local derivatives, most of which are in the very preliminary stages of development. As deregulation generates more active secondary participation and the primary markets continue expanding, further domestic derivative innovation and participation is anticipated.

Although informal trading of securities began in Taiwan in the 1950s, the first steps toward the development of the local securities market came in 1960 when the government created the Securities and Exchange Commission (SEC). The SEC was initially charged with co-ordinating primary issuance and secondary trading activities in the local market, and did so until 1961, when the Taiwan Stock Exchange (TwSE) was formed; the TwSE has existed as the country's sole equity trading centre since that time.

The domestic stock market reached a peak in the late 1980s as equity purchases by local retail and institutional investors soared. After the intense speculation of the late 1980s the market dropped to new lows in 1992, but has been in recovery since that time. The primary market has expanded dramatically since 1992 as a result of recovering stock prices, initial public offerings and secondary equity flotations; total capitalization of US$251.5 bln at the end of 1994 ranks the market as the fourth largest of Asia Pacific's 13 markets. Figure 13.1 illustrates the historical trend of the benchmark TwSE Weighted Index, while Table 13.1 contains details on the size and nature of the local equity market.

It should be noted that offshore investors have historically been constrained from investing directly in the market unless approved as qualified foreign institutional investors (QFIIs); even with QFII status investment ceilings put in place have made participation onerous and restrictive. During late 1994 and early 1995 the government began loosening the restrictions on QFII investment and the outlook for greater foreign participation in the future now appears likely; increasing foreign investor access to equities should lead to greater activity in local equity derivatives, as discussed later in the chapter. The recent changes in foreign investor rules include an increase of the foreign investor ceiling from US$7.5 bln to 12% of market capitalization (or approximately US$28 bln as of mid-1995), an increase in the maximum permissible foreign stake in any single company from 10% to 12%, and an increase in the maximum permissible stake by a single foreign investor in any single company from 5% to 6%. Discussions on further deregulation of QFII ceilings are presently underway.

Year*	Market Capitalization (US$ bln)	Trading Value (US$ bln)	Listed Companies (#)
1994	247.3	711.3	313
1993	195.2	346.4	285
1992	101.1	240.7	256
1991	124.8	365.2	221
1990	100.7	715.0	199

* to December of each year; Source: IFC, 1995

	1/92–6/95 Annualized Return*	1/92–6/95 Total Return*
Taiwan Stock Exchange Weighted Index	1.56%	5.28%

* dividends reinvested in index

Table 13.1 Domestic Equity Market Indicators

Taiwan features a well-established fixed income market which has been growing as the country's infrastructure development plan has been enacted. Infrastructure spending has required a substantial amount of funding and a significant portion has come from the issuance of long-term domestic securities, primarily government bonds; future issuance is a virtual certainty as the country continues to fund pubic works projects. The short-end of the sovereign fixed income curve (to one year) consists of treasury bills (also known as Class A bills) used for deficit financing, and central bank bills (also known as Class B bills) used for open market operations; central bank bills are issued with far greater frequency as Taiwan has enjoyed fiscal surpluses for many years and has not required short-term deficit financing. Short-term private sector funding is accessed through commercial paper, certificates of deposit and bankers' acceptances, all of which are actively used by private corporations and financial institutions. Total outstanding short-term sovereign and private sector instruments amounted to NT$1.24 tln (US$45.2 bln) at the end of 1994 (CBC, 1995, Banks, 1994). The medium- and long-term sector of the fixed income market is dominated by Taiwan government bonds, which are fixed rate obligations with maturities ranging from two- to 15-years; government bonds form the single largest component of the local debt market

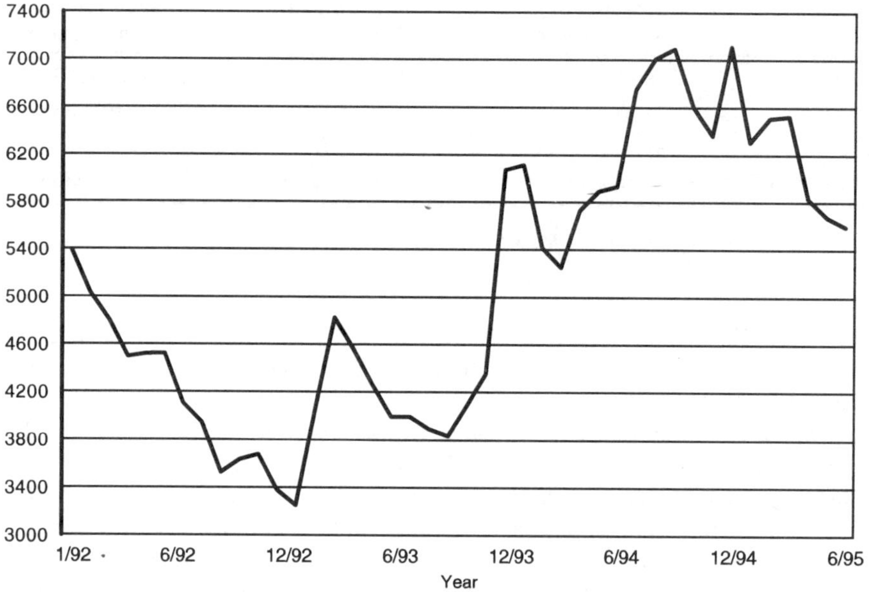

Figure 13.1 Historical Movement of Taiwan Stock Exchange Weighted Index

and represent the primary mechanism for financing domestic infrastructure projects. In addition to government bonds, the sovereign market also includes municipal bonds, provincial bonds, and state enterprise bonds. Total outstanding sovereign bonds amounted to NT$874 bln (US$31.9 bln) at the end of 1994 (primarily in the form of government bonds). Private sector debt instruments are available as fixed rate bonds, exchangeable bonds and convertible bonds, with maturities ranging from two- to ten-years; unlike the sovereign market, the private sector bond market is still in its infancy, with just NT$46.6 bln (US$1.7 bln) in securities outstanding at the end of 1994.

The key interest rates in the local fixed income market include treasury bill yields (the short-term borrowing cost of the government), domestic commercial paper (CP) rates (the borrowing costs for corporations through the short-term paper market), domestic certificate of deposit (CD) rates (the borrowing costs for banks in the domestic deposit market), and government bond yields (the intermediate and long-term borrowing costs of the government). Table 13.2 contains payment frequency, compounding frequency and day count conventions for key domestic interest rates.

The New Taiwan dollar (NT$) is a non-convertible, managed float currency. Taiwan initially moved to floating foreign exchange rates in 1978; rates remained rather stable until 1986, when the country's substantial current account and trade surpluses led to sharp appreciation of the New Taiwan dollar against other trading

Rate	Payment Frequency	Compounding Frequency	Day Count Convention
Bills	–	–	Actual/365
CP	–	–	Actual/365
CDs	semi-annual	semi-annual	Actual/360
Gov't bonds	semi-annual	semi-annual	Actual/365

Table 13.2 Domestic Interest Rate Summary

currencies. This continued until 1989, when Taiwan's key trade indicators deteriorated slightly; the currency has generally been stable since 1989, trading in a range of NT$3/US$.

The New Taiwan dollar is still subject to rather severe restrictions, primarily because the Central Bank of China (CBC) and the Ministry of Finance (MOF) are reluctant to permit instability in the local currency. Under the present structure the MOF implements foreign exchange policy while the CBC manages foreign exchange reserves, the currency and the money supply. Non-trade related transactions (either outward or inward) are limited in size to NT$137 mln (US$5 mln); QFIIs (who receive such designation from the CBC after an application process) must still apply to the central bank for approval on inward and outward currency remittances. Overall foreign exchange trading volume is low, primarily because foreign banks are prohibited from dealing freely in the market. Purchases and sales of New Taiwan dollars must be transacted through local banks or the Taipei Forex Institute (TPFI), the country's sole interbank broker. TPFI deals with 35 local banks and 35 foreign banks, making two-way prices in New Taiwan dollars against various reserve currencies. Average daily spot volume in the onshore market is NT$4.1 bln (US$150 mln); total interbank spot FX turnover amounted to NT$761 bln (US$27.86 bln) in 1993 and NT$1.07 tln (US$37.43 bln) in 1994 (ROC, 1995). Maximum dealing size in the interbank market is NT$136 mln (US$5 mln), though more than two thirds of all trades executed are between NT$27.4 mln and NT$54.8 mln (US$1 mln and US$2 mln); bid-offer spreads for transactions range from NT$0.01/US$ to NT$0.10/US$, depending on market conditions. Note that the TPFI is required to enforce position limit regulations on behalf of the CBC; the limits presently include a maximum NT$164.4 mln (US$6 mln) oversold position and a NT$548 mln (US$20 mln) overbought position, both on an overnight basis. Figure 13.2 highlights the historical movement of spot NT$/US$.

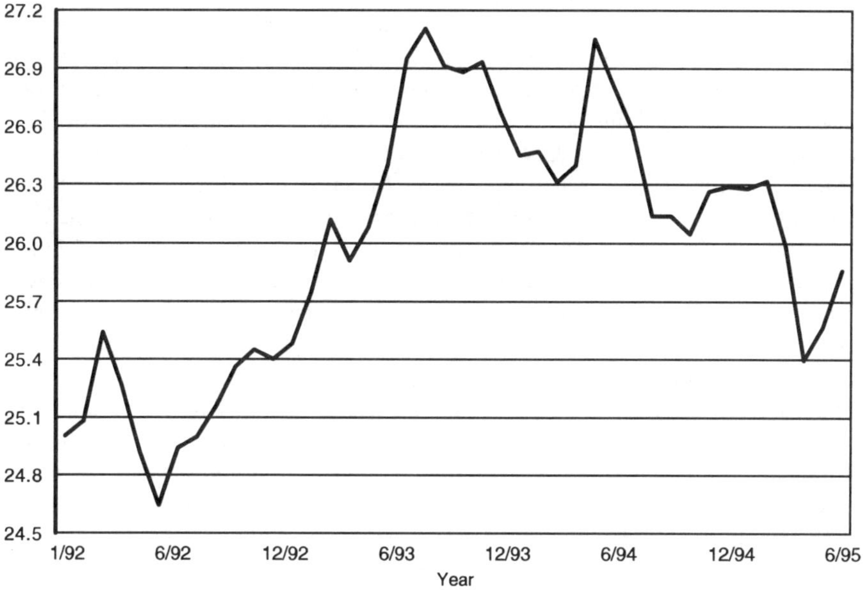

Figure 13.2 Historical Movement of Spot NT$/US$

DERIVATIVE MARKETS AND PRODUCTS

LISTED DERIVATIVE EXCHANGES

The TwSE, discussed above, is the only listed derivative exchange operating in Taiwan at the present time. The TwSE lists and trades domestic Taiwanese convertible and exchangeable bonds, the country's only listed derivatives. Trading of all TwSE securities (i.e. equities, bonds, convertible bonds, exchangeable bonds) occurs via an automated trading system which matches orders by price and time; all clearing occurs through a separate subsidiary known as the Taiwan Securities Central Depository (TSCD).

The creation of a domestic futures exchange is presently under comprehensive and detailed discussion in Taiwan. In the early 1990s the Taiwanese authorities recognized the need to develop a local futures market to support listing and trading of stock index futures, equity options and interest rate futures, and began planning for the creation of such an exchange (the need for such derivatives has become even more pronounced in the mid-1990s as the country's primary and secondary equity and debt markets expand in size and liquidity, and deregulation of equity investment and currency convertibility restrictions proceeds at a rapid pace). Recognizing the potential of, and need for, such a forum, the Government drafted a three phase approach for the introduction of futures trading in Taiwan. The first phase, related to offshore trading of futures and options by Taiwanese individuals and institutions, was implemented in 1993. The Legislative Yuan of 1993 passed the Foreign Futures and Trading Law of January 1993, which outlines the methods by which local investors can access foreign futures exchanges for the purpose of hedging or speculating; the Law contains detailed procedures on executing offshore futures transactions and specific contracts which may be bought or sold. The second phase, which is currently underway, calls for modification of Taiwan's Securities and Exchange Law (SEL) to permit the establishment of a derivatives market which will list a variety of contracts. Modification of the SEL requires legalization of derivatives trading, preparation of rules for the clearing and settling of trades, and development of a trading system; changes to the SEL will be submitted for consideration by the Legislative Yuan in 1995 or 1996. The third phase, to be completed after modification of the SEL and approval of the planned exchange and contracts, calls for establishment of an exchange through the passage of the Domestic Futures and Trading Law by the Legislative Yuan. At the conclusion of the third phase Taiwan will be in a position to trade its own futures contracts. The first stage of the futures programme will focus on index futures and bond futures and the second stage will focus on equity options and other derivatives. Precise timing of the third phase is still unknown, but is expected to occur in late 1996 or early 1997. Table 13.3 highlights Taiwan's sole derivative exchange and its products.

Exchange	**Primary Derivatives**
Taiwan Stock Exchange (TwSE)	Convertible bonds; exchangeable bonds

Table 13.3 Listed Derivative Exchanges

LISTED FUTURES AND OPTIONS

Equity

Equity Futures/Options

The Taiwanese equity market does not presently feature listed equity futures or options. Although there are no immediate plans to introduce either derivative to the local market, listing of equity options is expected as a second stage of Taiwan's proposed futures exchange.

Index Futures/Options/Futures Options

The creation of stock index futures will be the initial focus of Taiwan's domestic futures exchange once it is operational. Though precise timing of such derivatives will depend, in large part, on passage of the Domestic Futures and Trading Law, officials have already stated that stock index futures will be the first priority of the exchange. No contract details have yet been released and no information on a potential index reference has yet been announced.

Fixed Income

Deposit Futures/Options/Futures Options

The local market features no deposit-related derivatives at the present time. Near-term plans for Taiwan's proposed futures exchange do not call for introduction of such instruments, primarily because the country has no established short-term benchmark floating rate.

Interest Rate Futures/Options/Futures Options

The local market features no interest rate-related derivatives at this time. Nonetheless, interest rate futures are expected to be a first stage priority for Taiwan's local exchange once it is established. Given the substantial size of the government bond market (i.e. over US$30 bln) and the significant primary and secondary growth which is presently occurring, introduction of interest rate futures will be important for both hedgers and speculators. Development of such futures should be feasible given the existence of continuous, and significant, government bond issuance in maturities of two- to 15-years (with substantial issuance in the five- and seven-year maturities); to the extent the exchange elects to create a deliverable contract it will have a steady supply of bonds which can be used to deliver against open positions. Introduction of bond options or bond futures options may follow at a later date.

Currency

Currency Futures/Options/Futures Options

Taiwan features no listed currency derivatives at the present time. Such derivatives are not presently contemplated as part of the government's planned futures exchange, primarily because the New Taiwan dollar is subject to strict exchange controls. Deregulation of the currency market, which is likely to take longer than deregulation of the equity and bond markets, may ultimately lead to the consideration of currency futures and options.

Commodity

Commodity Futures/Options/Futures Options

Taiwan features no commodity futures at the present time, and has announced no plans to introduce such derivatives on its planned exchange.

LISTED/OVER-THE-COUNTER WARRANTS, CONVERTIBLES AND HYBRIDS

Equity

Equity Warrants

Although the domestic market features no issuer or covered equity warrants at the present time, foreign financial institutions operating in the offshore market float periodic covered warrants referencing individual Taiwanese stocks. Offshore American or European single stock warrants are typically unlisted, or listed on offshore exchanges, and traded OTC; most warrants carry maturities of one- to three-years and are denominated in foreign currencies (and not the New Taiwan dollar). Unlike other Asian markets, overall activity in Taiwanese single stock warrants is still negligible, primarily because foreign access to local equities is restrictive (i.e. investors must be approved as QFIIs in order to deal in domestic shares).

Basket/Index Warrants

The local Taiwanese market does not presently feature trading of listed or OTC basket or index warrants. Certain institutions in the offshore market, however, float periodic OTC warrants related to baskets of Taiwanese stocks or broader domestic market indexes. Such warrants are unlisted or listed on international exchanges and traded on an OTC basis. Warrants may be American or European exercise and typically carry maturities of one- to three-years. Representative Taiwan basket warrants include Union Bank of Switzerland's 12-month dual currency (US dollar, Swiss franc) basket call warrants linked to a group of five Taiwanese financial institution stocks (1994) and Citibank's Deutschmark basket put and call warrants on a weighted group of ten Taiwanese blue-chip stocks (1994). Representative index warrants include Citibank's US dollar index call warrants on the Citibank Taiwan Index (1995), Bankers Trust's US dollar index call warrants on the Taiwan Weighted Index (1995), Nomura's US dollar index call warrants on the NRI-AP Taiwan Index (1995), Morgan Stanley's Taiwanese 'opals' (optimized portfolios as listed securities), which are warrants on an index of 32 stocks tied to the MSCI Taiwan Index (with maximum tracking error of 2.5%)(1994) and Bankers Trust's five-tranche US dollar index call warrants on the Taiwan Index (1995). Several other offshore basket/index warrants have been executed over the past two years; as the market liberalizes further, additional issues are expected.

Convertibles

The domestic market features two listed equity-linked derivative securities, exchangeable bonds and convertible bonds. Exchangeable bonds and convertible bonds are similar in providing conversion of an underlying fixed income instrument into equity should a certain conversion level be attained. Exchangeable bonds, however, are convertible into the shares of a company other than the issuer of the bond; convertible bonds are convertible into the shares of the bond issuer itself. Taiwanese convertibles and exchangeables are listed on the TSE, though most secondary trading occurs on an OTC basis between brokers. The instruments generally carry intermediate maturities of three- to seven-years (though certain bonds extend as far as ten-years), intermediate coupons of 4% to 7%, and conversion premiums of 10% to 15%. At the end of 1994 there were 17 issuers of domestic convertible and exchangeable bonds, including Sampo (with two issues), Teco Electric & Machinery, Kolin, KPT Industries, Cheng Loong, Long Chen Paper, Tung Ho Steel, United Micro Electronics, Mitac International, Goldsun Development, Pacific Construction, Mercuries and Associates, Delta Electronic, Yue-Loong Motor, Shin Kong Synthetic Fibre and Acer Computer; Yuen Foong Yu Paper issued an exchangeable bond convertible into the shares of Chang Hwa Paper, a 12%-owned affiliate.

Although Taiwan features its own domestic exchangeable and convertible securities, various local companies utilize the offshore convertible market to raise funds. Taiwanese corporations have been accessing the international convertible market since 1989, when Yuen Foong Yu Paper launched the inaugural Taiwanese Euroconvertible issue. Given restrictions imposed on foreign ownership of local shares, the bond traded at a very high conversion premium (in excess of 50%); this is identical to early convertible trading in Korea (where foreign investors are faced with similar equity investment restrictions). Following the initial bond flotations of 1989 issuance declined as the domestic stock market fell. When issuance restarted in 1991, companies such as Pacific Electric, Tung Ho Steel, Acer, Walsin Lihwa, U-Ming Marine and Pacific Construction floated bonds in both the Eurodollar and domestic Swiss franc markets; by the beginning of 1995 total outstanding Taiwanese offshore convertibles amounted to US$4.23 bln, including US$3.5 bln issued in US dollars and US$730 mln equivalent issued in Swiss francs (Liu, 1995).

Bonds floated by Taiwanese companies in the Eurodollar market carry maturities of ten- to 15-years and are listed on overseas exchanges and traded OTC. Bonds floated in the Swiss franc market carry maturities of under five years, and are issued on either a public basis (listed and traded on Swiss stock exchanges) or a private basis (unlisted and traded on an OTC basis). Offshore Taiwanese convertibles are typically floated with intermediate coupons (3% to 7%) and intermediate conversion premiums (10% to 15%), though certain Swiss franc deals are issued with very low coupons (1% to 2%). Appendix III contains details on all domestic and offshore Taiwanese convertible bonds.

It should be noted that overseas investors holding offshore convertibles issued by Taiwanese corporations were granted permission to convert bonds into GDRs (global depository receipts) in December 1994. In February 1995 the Taiwanese SEC took the additional step of permitting offshore investors to convert their holdings into local shares (through special entitlement certificates, a process which takes several days to complete). The SEC authorization was formally approved by the Taiwanese government in June 1995. Prior to these changes, various local issuers were forced to redeem maturing bonds outright, as the ban on offshore conversion prohibited all overseas investors from converting bonds into equity. As part of the removal of the ban on conversion the CBC has also liberalized several other foreign investment restrictions, as discussed at the beginning of the chapter.

Index-linked Notes

The domestic market features no index-linked notes (e.g. bonds with coupons or principal redemption tied to the appreciation or depreciation of the local stock market). Institutions in the offshore OTC market occasionally float such issues, providing foreign investors with an indirect means of participating in the local equity market. Offshore index-linked notes (with embedded long calls or puts) are issued as unlisted private placement securities or public listed securities; trading of the latter occurs in limited fashion on an OTC basis. Most notes carry short- to intermediate maturities of one- to five-years; returns generated from such securities are generally payable in foreign currencies, to neutralize investors from the effect of local currency movements. Despite the availability of certain index-linked notes, overall issuance is still very limited.

Fixed Income

Fixed Income Warrants

Although Taiwan features a growing fixed income market, it does not currently list fixed income warrants based on its government, provincial or municipal bonds. Domestic or offshore OTC warrants referencing Taiwanese bonds have not been executed either, primarily because investor demand for such derivatives is non-existent.

Currency

Currency Warrants

Given the severe restrictions placed on trading of the local currency, the domestic market does not list or trade New Taiwan dollar currency warrants. Institutions in the offshore market, however, issue certain New Taiwan dollar currency warrants on a periodic basis. Such warrants generally mature in one- to three-years and are either unlisted or listed on offshore exchanges; trading is strictly on an OTC basis. One representative issue in this category is Salomon Brothers' two-year New Taiwan dollar call warrants, denominated in US dollars, with valuation pegged to the level of the New Taiwan dollar (1994); the warrant is structured on a cash-settlement basis so there is no physical delivery of currencies upon exercise.

Commodity

Commodity Warrants

The local and offshore markets do not presently list or trade commodity warrants related to Taiwanese commodity indicators.

OVER-THE-COUNTER FORWARDS, SWAPS AND OPTIONS

Equity

Equity Forwards/Swaps

The market for domestic and offshore OTC equity forwards and swaps is only modestly active at the present time, primarily because foreign investor access to local shares is restrictive; lack of foreign access results in complications for offshore financial institutions attempting to manage risks generated by such transactions (as well as equity, basket and index options, mentioned below). Certain foreign banks (particularly those approved as QFIIs) execute short- to medium-term OTC equity forwards in the offshore market on occasion, but overall volumes are thin. Until there is complete access to the local equity market it is likely that activity in most OTC equity derivatives will remain subdued.

Equity Options

The domestic market features no OTC equity options at the present time. Institutions in the offshore market have been only moderately active in offering OTC options (primarily in the form of six- to 12-month, cash-settled American or European derivatives on larger blue-chip domestic equities), for the same reasons cited above (i.e. rigid foreign investor restrictions). Greater activity by offshore institutions is likely to occur following investment deregulation.

Basket/Index Forwards/Swaps

The market for domestic and offshore OTC basket/index forwards and swaps (based primarily on the exchange of a floating rate for appreciation or depreciation in a basket of domestic stocks, or a broader index such as the TwSE Weighted Index) has been only modestly active for the same reasons cited directly above; although certain foreign banks structure short- to intermediate-term basket and index transactions (not unlike the basket/index warrants detailed above), overall volume has been very limited. As with other equity derivatives, Taiwanese OTC index derivatives are likely to expand as foreign investor restrictions are loosened. This segment of the market is also likely to grow once the country introduces its own stock index futures; listed index futures will make it simpler for institutions to manage risks generated by buying or selling OTC index swaps and forwards.

Basket/Index Options

As with the other equity derivatives mentioned above, overall activity in the basket and index options market has been very modest, and is concentrated strictly offshore. Though virtually any type of basket or index option can be structured, the most common transactions (in what is still a very thinly traded market) are vanilla European or American options maturing in under 12-months, tied to either a broad market index or a group of Taiwanese stocks; settlement is generally on a cash basis, as delivery or acceptance of shares is problematic due to foreign investor restrictions. Note that there is presently no market for Taiwanese exotic basket/index options. As investor access to local shares improves (and as local stock index futures are launched), additional basket and index option activity is likely.

Fixed Income

Fixed Income Forwards/Swaps

The market for domestic OTC fixed income forwards and swaps is in the very early stages of development. The overall size and liquidity of the market is still constrained by a number of factors, including: (a) lack of an accepted short-term benchmark which can be used to value the floating component of domestic IRSs (or forwards); (b) lack of a robust yield curve which can provide the market with additional pricing references for IRSs; and (c) lack of reliable swap hedges as a result of modest (albeit growing) liquidity in government bonds. Overcoming these challenges will be the key to future expansion in the domestic swap market.

The only local institutions currently permitted to enter into either domestic or offshore derivatives are corporations and banks (dealing only for their own accounts, not on behalf of clients); securities firms are barred from entering into such transactions. The primary users of domestic and offshore derivatives are the offshore banking units (OBUs) of Taiwanese commercial banks.

Although the domestic forward/IRS market is still small there is very modest activity in three-, six- and 12-month forwards which reference domestic commercial paper (CP) rates (for onshore transactions) or interest rates implied by FX forwards (for offshore transactions); the domestic CP rate is a reasonably well established (though not universally utilized) floating rate benchmark quoted in maturities of 30, 60, 90, 180 and 360 days. Swaps in the onshore market are quoted as fixed New Taiwan dollars (semi-annual, on an Actual/365-day basis) against the domestic CP rate, primarily to two- and three-years; five-year maturities are quoted but dealing is still rare. There is no established interbank dealing size at present and bid-offer spreads are wide and variable due to illiquidity and interest rate volatility. Swaps in the offshore market are quoted as fixed New Taiwan dollars (semi-annual, on an Actual/365-day basis) against the interest rates implicit in three- or six-month FX forwards (not unlike the more formalized Singapore swap offer rate utilized in several Southeast Asian nations, as discussed at several points in this text); offshore swap activity occurs primarily in the one- to three-year sector. Given the immaturity of the market there is no standard interbank dealing size and no consistent bid-offer spread. As with the onshore market, the offshore market is very thinly traded, but is expected to expand as financial deregulation is implemented and the challenges cited above are overcome.

Fixed Income Options

An onshore market for domestic fixed income options does not presently exist, though certain *ad hoc* caps and floors are arranged on occasion in the offshore market, based on the rates implied by FX forwards. Development of the onshore cap and floor market will require establishment of a widely accepted floating-rate benchmark, along with development of a liquid domestic forward and IRS market. There is currently no market for domestic swaptions, and demand for bond options based on Taiwanese government bonds is not meaningful.

Currency

Currency Forwards/Swaps

Since foreign exchange restrictions have dampened overall turnover in the local spot market (to a modest US$150 mln per day (versus US$2 bln to US$4 bln per day in each of Thailand, Malaysia, Indonesia and Singapore)), it is not surprising to note that turnover in OTC New Taiwan dollar forwards is also very thin: total FX forward volume was NT$31.8 bln (US$1.16 bln) in 1993 and NT$35 bln (US$1.28 bln) in 1994; volume in the FX swap market was NT$88.3 bln (US$3.22 bln) in 1993 and NT$180 bln (US$6.56 bln) in 1994 (ROC, 1995). Bid-offer spreads on short-term forwards are approximately NT$0.50/US$ under normal market conditions and maximum maturities extend to six months. In addition to a thinly traded spot market, another fundamental reason for low turnover in forwards is attributable to central bank directives requiring all forwards to be backed by appropriate trade documents, and for a 3% cash, non-interest bearing, deposit to accompany all forwards with maturities of 180 days; counterparties entering into such forwards are only permitted to roll positions once, suggesting a maximum forward cover period of 360 days. The clear aim is to ensure that all forwards are related specifically to trade transactions; the CBC's tolerance for speculation involving the New Taiwan dollar is low. Despite such restrictions, the CBC is presently reviewing the acceptability of permitting forward FX trades on more liberal terms, when such trades are for clear hedging purposes or when they involve movement of investment flows into, or out of, the country. In early 1995 the Finance Bureau of the CBC extended permission to select domestic and foreign banks operating in Taiwan to enter into forwards (and short-term currency swaps) with third parties when such transactions are for purposes of facilitating investment flows related to government-approved investments, dividends, commissions and royalties; the maximum term for such forwards is limited to six months, and proper documentary evidence must still be presented by banks. Maturity extensions to 12 months are considered by the CBC on a special basis in cases where government investments are involved.

In addition to conventional onshore currency forwards, the market also features onshore and offshore non-deliverable forwards (NDFs), also known as dollar-settled exchange agreements. NDFs permit institutions to gain or manage exposure based on the movement of forward NT$/US$, without the need to settle in physical; at the conclusion of a transaction the net market value of the contract is simply settled in US dollars. It should be noted that, while institutions in the offshore market have been executing NDFs for several years, the CBC granted permission for such contracts to be executed onshore (between domestic and foreign banks) in July 1995; Taiwan is the first country with a non-convertible currency to officially permit onshore NDFs. Onshore and offshore NDF activity is concentrated primarily in transactions to six months.

Onshore cross currency swaps involving the New Taiwan dollar are not currently permissible under guidelines established by the CBC (with the exception of short-term currency swaps related to currency flows arising from government investments, dividends, royalties and commissions, as discussed above). Short-term offshore CCS transactions to 12 months are arranged periodically by certain foreign banks; these deals are generally quoted as fixed New Taiwan dollars against US$ LIBOR flat, with no physical settlement of currency on either a coupon or initial/final basis (similar to NDFs, discussed immediately above); they may also be quoted as fixed New Taiwan dollars against fixed US dollars (effectively long-term FX contracts). Overall depth and activity in the offshore swap market is extremely limited and there is no standard bid-offer spread or interbank dealing size at the current time. Until the domestic currency is freely convertible and the CBC loosens documentary and reporting requirements, it is likely that overall CCS trading volume will remain negligible.

Currency Options

CBC regulations prohibit buying or selling of currency options on the New Taiwan dollar at the present time. Short-term offshore option transactions (to 12 months) referencing the New Taiwan dollar (but with no physical settlement of currencies) are executed by foreign institutions, but overall volume is still minimal. As one might expect, there is no market for exotic New Taiwan dollar FX options at the present time. Activity in currency options is likely to remain negligible until the CBC removes its onshore restrictions on purchases and sales of domestic currency options and until currency convertibility occurs.

Commodity

Commodity Forwards/Swaps

The local market does not currently trade in OTC commodity forwards or swaps. Although certain domestic corporations obtain hedging cover from the offshore OTC market (particularly with regard to energy-based products), such hedges reference major international benchmarks, not local Taiwanese benchmarks.

Commodity Options

As with commodity forwards and swaps, the market for commodity options is limited strictly to occasional hedging cover of international commodity exposures (e.g energy products) by domestic corporations.

LOCAL REGULATORY/LEGAL TREATMENT OF DERIVATIVES

Taiwan's primary financial regulators include the Securities and Exchange Commission (SEC), the CBC and the Ministry of Finance (MOF); in addition to regulatory oversight, the CBC and MOF also play broader roles in the management of monetary policy and the domestic financial system. Regulation of financial institutions, exchanges and instruments (including derivatives), is managed by the SEC, a Taiwanese authority controlled by the Ministry of Finance. Although the SEC has been in existence since 1960, the Securities and Exchange Law (SEL) enacted in 1968 to regulate securities dealers and securities exchanges granted the SEC the power to regulate the domestic securities and futures industry. In addition to regulation of public offerings and flotation of securities, the SEC's mandate also includes oversight of all futures business, the approval of commodities for offshore futures trading, and the authorization of all exchanges; the SEC will also have direct regulatory responsibility for the Taiwan's futures exchange when it is created. The SEC and MOF are also specifically responsible for OTC derivatives based on the New Taiwan dollar, including forwards, IRSs, and interest rate options. The CBC, in contrast, is responsible for regulating FX derivatives, including foreign currency FRAs and IRSs, CCSs, FX swaps, OTC FX options, commodity swaps and dual currency deposits; these derivatives are based almost exclusively on offshore currencies.

As a means of gaining additional control over growing activity in both local and offshore derivatives (and in response to the derivatives losses sustained by a local bank, Overseas Chinese Bank, amounting to a minimum of US$20 mln (and a potential maximum of US$60 mln)), the SEC imposed new reporting requirements on OBUs, the primary transactors of derivatives. The 40 Taiwan-based OBUs are required to submit regular reports to the regulatory authorities regarding their derivative exposures, including the nature of the products, the size of exposures and recent trading activity. The SEC has also called for greater involvement by bank boards in the management of derivatives activities, and for the implementation of comprehensive risk management, accounting and control systems.

LOCAL ACCOUNTING PRACTICES FOR DERIVATIVES

Given the underdeveloped nature of the local derivative market it is not surprising to note that Taiwan features no defined accounting procedures for derivatives at the present time. The absence of firm guidelines has led larger and more sophisticated institutions to adopt certain international practices related to market value and accrual accounting (as outlined in chapters 2 and 4, for example).

PROSPECTS FOR THE LOCAL DERIVATIVE MARKET

Summarized below are the near-term (one- to three-year) and medium-term (three- to five-year) prospects for Taiwanese domestic derivatives.

Near-term:

- Establishment of a domestic futures exchange and commencement of trading in index futures, equity options and bond futures (possibly on a deliverable basis).
- Gradual expansion of OTC equity derivatives as foreign investor restrictions are loosened, foreign derivative technologies are imported and index futures are introduced.
- Gradual increase in IRS liquidity as a short-term floating rate benchmark is developed, the overall yield curve becomes more robust, and domestic private sector debt financing opportunities expand.
- Very gradual increase in CCS and currency derivative activity as the authorities continue liberalizing currency restrictions.
- Initial development of fixed income options.

Medium-term:

- Further strengthening of turnover and liquidity in IRSs and forwards and lengthening of domestic swap maturities as the overall market matures.
- Expansion of CCSs and other currency derivatives as currency deregulation continues.
- Further growth in OTC equity derivatives as the domestic equity market continues expanding, foreign participation increases and listed index derivatives achieve critical mass.

	Overall Liquidity	Liquid/ Maximum Maturity	Interbank dealing size	Average bid-offer spread
Equity/Index Swaps	poor	12 mos/12 mos	n/a	n/a
Equity/Index Options	poor	12 mos/12 mos	n/a	n/a
Interest Rate Swaps	poor	2–3 yrs/5 yrs	none	varies
Interest Rate Options	non-existent	n/a	n/a	n/a
Currency Swaps	poor	12 mos/12 mos	none	varies
Currency Options	poor	12 mos/12 mos	none	varies

Table 13.4 Summary of Domestic OTC Derivatives

14: Thailand

FINANCIAL MARKET OVERVIEW

Thailand's financial markets are in the early stages of diversification and expansion. The local equity market is reasonably large on a primary basis but is often illiquid on a secondary basis, particularly in smaller capitalization stocks. The fixed income market is impacted by lack of government bond issuance, which has slowed development of the domestic private sector bond and swap markets. As a result of limitations in Thailand's cash markets, the country's derivative market is still in the first stages of development; despite current limitations, however, the financial authorities have various initiatives underway designed to enhance local derivative capabilities over the coming years.

The origin of the Thai stock market dates back to 1962 when private investors created the Bangkok Stock Exchange (BSE), the country's first formal trading forum. The BSE traded in equities (and debentures) until the early 1970s, when it was disbanded as a result of inactivity. In 1974 the Thai government passed legislation creating a new trading centre, the Securities Exchange of Thailand, and formal trading of equities began on the Securities Exchange in 1975; the Exchange was renamed in the latter part of the 1980s and is known now as the Stock Exchange of Thailand (SET). Note that the country's second equity trading forum, the Bangkok Stock Dealing Centre (BSDC) began operations in late 1995; BSDC is an electronic-trading forum for smaller-capitalization OTC stocks.

The Thai equity market has grown in size and scope over the past few years as strong returns have attracted the attention of both domestic and offshore investors. The bull market of 1993, which drove a number of Southeast Asian markets to new peaks (and which was fuelled primarily by foreign investors seeking attractive returns in local emerging markets), boosted the Thai market considerably; foreign investment in Thailand rose eight-fold between 1992 and 1993 and helped move the benchmark SET Index to record highs. Overall market capitalization doubled to US$130 bln between 1992 and 1993; while most of the increase in capitalization was due to higher equity prices a portion was attributable to the initial public offering of Telecom Asia, which added approximately US$13.6 bln of capital to the market. Though domestic equities receded from their 1993 peak just 12 months later, the Thai market remains one of the most vibrant in Asia Pacific; 1994 market capitalization of US$131.5 bln ranks it as the eighth largest of Asia Pacific's 13 markets. Figure 14.1 below illustrates the price movement of the benchmark SET Index since 1992 while Table 14.1 contains key indicators regarding the Thai equity market.

Note that foreign ownership of Thai equities is generally limited to 49% of a company's outstanding shares (20% for commercial banks or finance companies); once the foreign quota is reached, offshore investors are only permitted to purchase foreign shares through the SET's Foreign Board, generally at a substantial premium to domestic shares.

Year*	Market Capitalization (US$ bln)	Trading Value (US$ bln)	Listed Companies (#)
1994	131.5	80.2	389
1993	130.5	86.9	347
1992	58.2	72.0	305
1991	35.8	30.1	276
1990	23.9	22.9	214

* to December of each year; Source: IFC, 1995

	1/92-6/95 Annualized Return*	1/92-6/95 Total Return*
Stock Exchange of Thailand Index	20.58%	86.55%

* dividends reinvested in index

Table 14.1 Domestic Equity Market Indicators

The Thai fixed income market remains relatively small in comparison with other Asia Pacific debt markets. The short-end of the Thai market is based primarily on private sector certificates of deposit (CDs) and bills of exchange, although the Thai government floated a small issue of short-term Treasury bills in mid-1995 to absorb liquidity in the market (the size and frequency of future issues has not yet been determined). Total outstanding CDs and bills of exchange amounted to THB54 bln (US$2.2 bln) at the end of 1994. Government issuance is largely absent from the intermediate- and long-term sectors of the market. Although the government has floated medium-term coupon and investment bonds in the past, it ceased such issuance in 1990 following several years of budget surpluses; total outstandings have been on the decline as maturing bonds have not been replaced with new bonds. Secondary liquidity in such securities is negligible primarily because existing supply is held by commercial banks to meet reserve requirements. The sole

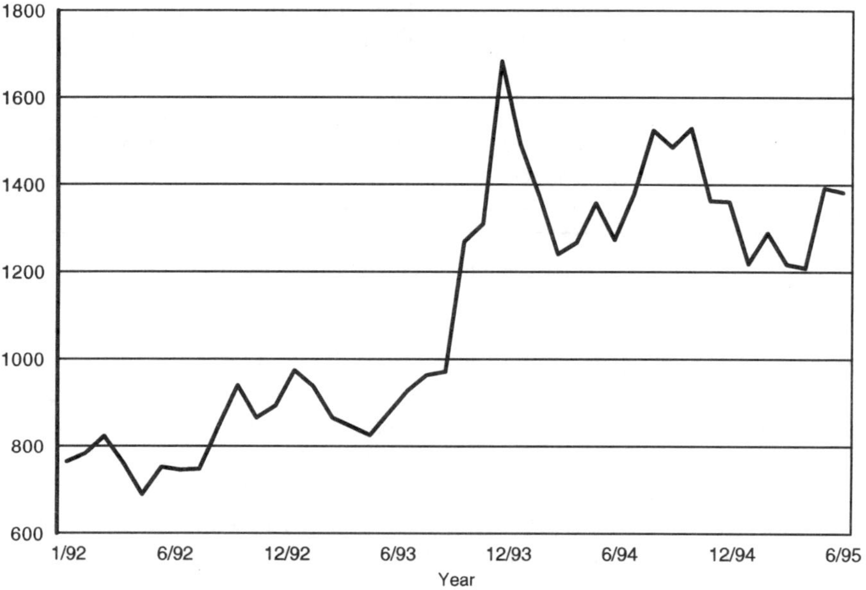

Figure 14.1 Historical Movement of the Stock Exchange of Thailand Index

quasi-sovereign issuance in the Thai market has come from state enterprises; certain state bonds are issued with the full backing of the Thai government while others are floated without explicit government support. Total outstanding government and state enterprise bonds amounted to THB388.7 bln (US$15.8 bln) at the end of 1994. The absence of strong sovereign bond benchmarks has made the development of a private sector bond market more challenging, as ready pricing references normally available through sovereign issues have been lacking. Despite this drawback, issuance of domestic private sector bonds (including fixed rate bonds, convertible bonds and bonds-with-warrants, with maturities ranging from two- to ten-years) has been increasing gradually; total outstandings amounted to just under THB172.2 bln (US$7 bln) in December 1994 (Paisley, 1995).

The key interest rates in the domestic Thai fixed income market include Bangkok Interbank Offered Rate (BIBOR) (the borrowing cost for financial institutions in the domestic interbank market), bill of exchange yields (the borrowing cost for institutions in the short-term bill market), Thai baht fixed CD rates (the medium-term borrowing cost for banks in the CD market), minimum lending rate (MLR) (the borrowing cost for prime corporate customers) and Thai baht interest rate swap rates (the rate for transacting baht interest rate swaps in the interbank market). Table 14.2 contains relevant details on the payment frequency, compounding frequency and day count convention of these domestic rates.

Rate	Payment Frequency	Compounding Frequency	Day Count Convention
BIBOR	–	–	Actual/365
Bills	–	–	Actual/365
CDs	annual	annual	Actual/365
MLR	semi-annual	semi-annual	Actual/365
Swaps	semi-annual	semi-annual	Actual/365

Table 14.2 Domestic Interest Rate Summary

The Thai baht (THB) is a freely convertible currency administered on a managed float basis against a basket of currencies of Thailand's major trading partners. Although the exact composition of the basket is not disclosed by the Bank of Thailand (BOT, the country's central bank), most participants in the market estimate the portfolio to be approximately 80% US dollars, 15% yen, and 5% Deutschmarks. Trading in the Thai baht has been particularly active during the past two years as the relative stability of the currency, together with high local interest rates, has encouraged offshore institutions to purchase baht, sell the underlying components of the basket, and retain the interest differential between the two components; this 'carry trade' has generated 300 to 600 basis points of reasonably low risk earnings in recent years. Trading of baht continues to be most liquid offshore;

Figure 14.2 Historical Movement of Spot THB/US$

approximately THB86 bln to THB98 bln (US$3.5 bln to US$4 bln) is traded in the offshore market on a daily basis, compared with only THB7.4 bln (US$300 mln) traded in the onshore market (Paisley and Woodcock, 1995). Average interbank dealing size in the offshore market is THB50 mln to THB123 mln (US$2 mln to US$5 mln), though THB500 mln to THB740 mln (US$20 mln to US$30 mln) can be executed without moving the market; bid-offer spreads are THB0.01/US$ under normal market conditions. Figure 14.2 traces the historical movement of the spot THB/US$ rate.

DERIVATIVE MARKETS AND PRODUCTS

LISTED DERIVATIVE EXCHANGES

Thailand's only existing listed derivative exchange is the Stock Exchange of Thailand (SET), the country's primary equity trading forum. Although equity trading continues to be the Exchange's main focus it has added derivative securities, in the form of issuer equity warrants and convertible bonds, to its listing over the past three years. Trading in all SET instruments (including equity warrants and convertibles) is accomplished on an electronic basis through ASSET, the SET's computerized trading system.

Thailand does not feature a futures exchange at the present time, though the Thai financial authorities are in the very preliminary stages of establishing such a forum; precise timing for the creation of a national futures exchange remains uncertain but is expected to occur in late 1996 or early 1997. In 1994 the Securities and Exchange Commission (SEC) authorized a study on the development of a Thai futures market; the results of the study, together with accompanying discussions between relevant financial authorities, led to the creation of draft legislation on the development of a local futures market (note that final legislation will be considered by the Thai Parliament once establishment of an exchange is closer to fruition). According to reports from the SEC the focus of the local futures market, once operational, will be on both financial and commodity futures; whether both will be traded on the same exchange has not yet been determined, though there is some indication that they may be traded on two separate exchanges (this appears more likely following an announcement in mid-1995 that the SEC will be responsible for financial futures and the Ministry of Commerce (MOC) will be responsible for commodities and commodity futures). The initial focus of the financial futures market is expected to be on stock index futures (perhaps based on the benchmark SET Index or the new SET 50 Index), followed by short-term deposit futures (perhaps referencing BIBOR) and currency futures (including US$/THB, DM/THB, and JPY/THB). Creation of a long-term bond future is unlikely in the near term, primarily because the Thai government has not actively issued government bonds since 1990 and the lack of supply would make creation of such a contract meaningless. Commodity-related futures are expected to be based on rubber and rice, two of the countries main agricultural exports. No further details on the proposed futures market have been released. Table 14.3 highlights the derivatives traded on Thailand's sole derivative exchange, SET.

Exchange	Primary Derivatives
Stock Exchange of Thailand (SET)	Issuer equity warrants; convertible debentures

Table 14.3 Listed Derivative Exchanges

LISTED FUTURES AND OPTIONS

Equity

Equity Futures/Options

The Thai domestic market does not presently feature listed equity futures or equity options; neither has been selected as a first stage priority for the country's new futures programme, though listed equity options are likely to be considered over the medium-term.

Index Futures/Options/Futures Options

As indicated above, the creation of a stock index futures contract remains a top priority for the Thai financial authorities. Such a contract is likely to be the first listed future in Thailand, though key details such as contract specifications and precise timing of introduction are unknown. Very preliminary details point to the creation of a new index, the SET 50 Index, as a first step in the development of an index contract; the SET 50 Index, comprised of the 50 largest Thai blue-chip stocks, is expected to be introduced at the end of 1995 or beginning of 1996 and may become the reference for the country's index future.

Fixed Income

Deposit Futures/Options/Futures Options

Thailand features no deposit-related futures or options at the present time but introduction of a deposit future is an initial priority for the country's futures programme. Although BIBOR has not yet become the accepted floating-rate benchmark of the country, it is gradually growing in importance and is likely to be the reference for local deposit futures.

Interest Rate Futures/Options/Futures Options

Thailand features no interest rate-related derivatives at the present time and is unlikely to introduce such contracts even after its futures exchange is created, primarily as a result of declining government bond supply. Institutions needing to hedge domestic interest rate exposures must currently utilize the OTC baht forward/IRS markets to obtain cover (as discussed later in the chapter).

Currency

Currency Futures/Options/Futures Options

The Thai market features no currency futures or options at the present time, though development of currency futures based on the primary components of the currency basket (i.e. US$/THB, DM/THB and JPY/THB) has been cited as a first stage priority once the country's futures exchange is operational. Until currency futures are introduced, institutions seeking baht currency exposure or cover must continue to use the OTC forward/CCS and options markets.

Commodity

Commodity Futures/Options/Futures Options

The need for Thai commodity futures has been specifically recognized by the MOC which has indicated that introduction of listed futures to help control or hedge price risk of key Thai agricultural commodities is a priority for the country. Although the MOC has specifically supported the creation of the an agricultural commodity exchange known as the Futures Commodity Market (FCM), it is uncertain whether the FCM will be created as a separate commodity futures centre or whether all futures (i.e. financial and commodity) will be concentrated on a single exchange. The focus of the commodity futures effort, regardless of exchange, will be geared towards rubber and rice, two of Thailand's chief agricultural exports. Preliminary discussions have focused on the development of a rubber futures contract based on ribbed smoked rubber sheets (RSS); RSS3, which is the US dollar benchmark rubber grade of Thailand, is the most likely candidate (note that RSS3 futures are already traded in the region through ICEB (as a forward), SICOM, TOCOM, KRE and certain Chinese exchanges). Rice futures are likely to be based on one or both of Thai white rice and Thai unmilled rice; there are presently rice contracts traded on various Chinese exchanges but no regional contracts which are accessible by offshore participants. In addition to rubber and rice, there are more distant plans to introduce futures on corn and tapioca, two other significant agricultural commodities of Thailand; such contracts would be introduced as a second stage in the development of commodity futures.

LISTED/OVER-THE-COUNTER WARRANTS, CONVERTIBLES AND HYBRIDS

Equity

Equity Warrants

Thailand currently features issuer equity warrants, which are listed and traded domestically, and covered equity warrants, which are listed offshore and traded OTC. The listed Thai equity warrant market dates back to February 1990 when Bangkok Bank of Commerce issued a warrant on its own shares; the warrant was listed on the SET and was converted into shares in 1992. Additional warrants followed from 1993 onwards by blue-chip companies such as Thai Farmers Bank, Land and House, Siam City Bank, Finance One and Christiani and Nielsen; such listings generated increased investor interest in warrants and promoted greater liquidity across all issues.

Issuance of warrants must be in accordance with procedures established by the Exchange; such procedures are monitored on an ongoing basis by the Thai Securities and Exchange Commission. Current regulations stipulate that warrants must only be issued by public companies which have been listed on the Exchange for more than one year and have more than 250 shareholders. Warrants must be structured as baht-denominated, American exercise derivatives, maturing between one- and five-years of issue date (note that the authorities are studying the introduction of ten-year warrants); the resulting equity allocation cannot account for more than 30% of an institutions paid-in capital (note: an early warrant issue for Star Block accounted for 67% of the firm's paid-in capital and caused difficulties for both issuer and investors). Although there are no specific leverage constraints defined by the SET all current issues are levered between one and seven times. As of June 1995 there were 28 equity warrants listed on, and traded through, the SET. Appendix II contains details on all warrants traded in the domestic market.

In addition to domestic issuer warrants, financial institutions in the offshore market routinely float covered third-party, equity warrants referencing Thai stocks. Such derivatives result in the re-allocation of equity from the seller to the buyer of the warrant upon exercise, rather than the flotation of new corporate equity by the underlying company. Offshore covered warrants typically carry maturities of one- to two- years and are floated in a variety of foreign currencies (and generally not in baht); issues are either unlisted or listed on offshore exchanges and traded on an OTC basis. One representative issue in this category is Bankers Trust's call warrant on Bangkok Bank (1994).

Basket/Index Warrants

The domestic market does not feature listed basket or index warrants. Despite the absence of domestic activity, institutions operating in the offshore market are active issuers of OTC warrants which reference groups of Thai stocks or the broader Thai market. Third-party covered warrants are either unlisted or listed on overseas exchanges and are traded on an OTC basis; most derivatives are denominated in foreign currencies and carry maturities ranging from one- to three-years. Representative index warrants include Lehman's US dollar index call warrants on the SET (1995), Bankers Trust's US dollar index call warrants on the SET (1995) and Barings' US dollar index call warrants and capped call warrants on the Bangkok Index (1994). Representative basket warrants include Merrill Lynch's US dollar basket call warrants on a group of Thai bank stocks (1994), Credit Lynonnais' US dollar basket call warrants on a diversified group of five blue-chip Thai stocks (1995) and SBC Warburg's US dollar basket call warrants on a group of 50 Thai stocks (the warrants are sold as 'basket performance certificates') (1995).

Convertibles

Thailand features issuance of convertible bonds in both the domestic and offshore markets. Domestic convertibles, referred to locally as convertible debentures, are still a new form of financing in the local market. In 1993, the first year such securities were offered, three issues worth THB690 mln (US$28 mln) were floated; this was followed by a further seven issues worth THB5.1 bln (US$207 mln) in 1994, and three issues worth THB6 bln (US$244 mln) in the first half of 1995 (SEC, 1995).

Although domestic convertible debentures are relatively new to the Thai market they are already beginning to attract the attention of investors and issuers, as evidenced by the rapid growth in outstandings. All domestic convertibles are listed on the SET, though many trade on an OTC basis. Bonds may be floated on either a secured or unsecured basis and carry maturities ranging from three- to seven-years; coupons are typically 50 to 150 basis points below those on standard fixed rate corporate bonds.

In addition to domestic convertibles, Thai companies are active issuers of offshore convertibles in both the Eurodollar and domestic Swiss franc markets. The inaugural offshore Thai convertible issue came in April 1993 when Land and House floated a small US$60 mln bond; this was followed by 16 issues worth US$1.57 bln in 1993 (from companies such as Dhana Siam, Bangkok Bank, Finance One and Sino Thai Engineering). Total issuance in 1994 included nine bonds worth US$900 mln (SEC, 1995). Thai issues launched in the Eurodollar market generally carry long maturities (i.e. ten years and over), intermediate coupons (3% to 5%) and intermediate premiums (10% to 15%). All Eurodollar securities are listed in bearer form on overseas exchanges and trade on an OTC basis. In addition to the Eurodollar market, certain Thai companies have floated bonds in the domestic Swiss franc market, either on a public or private placement basis; public bonds are listed and traded on the Swiss exchanges while private bonds are unlisted and traded OTC. Public and private bonds typically carry maturities of less than five years; conversion premiums in the Swiss market remain about the same as those in the Eurodollar market, though coupons on Swiss deals tend to be lower. Swiss franc convertibles are issued with both investor puts and issuer calls, enabling investors to put bonds to issuers and issuers to call bonds from investors (once a certain market price has been exceeded, and after an initial non-call period has passed). Note that both Eurodollar and Swiss franc bonds are ultimately convertible into the shares of the Thai issuer at a baht conversion price. Appendix III contains details on all Thai convertible bond issues.

Index-linked Notes

Although the market for Thai index-linked notes is very small (and concentrated exclusively offshore), periodic issues are floated on an OTC basis by foreign financial institutions. Such notes, with maturities ranging from one- to five-years, are generally linked to the key SET index and provide investors with enhanced returns (via higher coupons or greater principal redemption) based on appreciation (or depreciation) in the underlying Thai equity market; this structure effectively provides investors with long-dated calls (or puts) on the Thai market. Index-linked notes are typically denominated in foreign currencies (and not in baht); most securities are held until maturity and are only rarely traded on a secondary basis.

Fixed Income

Fixed Income Warrants

There have been no domestic or OTC Thai fixed income warrant issues floated in the market to date, primarily because investor demand for such derivatives is non-existent.

Currency

Currency Warrants

The domestic market does not presently list or trade currency warrants. Activity in the offshore currency warrant market has been subdued as well, primarily because the THB/US$ rate has displayed a history of stability and low volatility (with the exception of early 1995, as discussed below); lack of volatility makes warrants unappealing to investors.

Commodity

Commodity Warrants

The local and offshore markets do not feature warrants which reference Thai commodity prices or indicators.

OVER-THE-COUNTER FORWARDS, SWAPS AND OPTIONS

Equity

Equity Forwards/Swaps

The market for OTC Thai equity forwards is moderately active, primarily in forwards on blue-chip stocks; though long-term forwards of two- and three-years are available, most volume is centred in shorter-term forwards to six- and 12-months. The market for equity swaps (e.g. swaps which exchange deferred premium (in the form of a floating rate flow) for appreciation or depreciation in a given equity) is considerably smaller; more common are OTC index options, equity options and index swaps, discussed below.

Equity Options

In the absence of domestic listed equity options a market for offshore OTC equity options has developed. Foreign financial institutions routinely buy and sell puts and calls on Thai equities, providing investors with customized positions referencing specific Thai stocks. Although virtually any type of equity option can be created in the OTC market, the most common structures involve vanilla European or American puts and calls with maturities of six- to 12-months, exercisable into cash settlement (though physical settlement of shares is possible). Though hedging of equity options is made challenging by a ban on onshore short-selling and restrictions imposed on offshore ownership of domestic shares (and the need occasionally to deal in more expensive foreign shares), overall access to the market is sufficiently flexible to permit active business. Secondary liquidity in OTC equity options is negligible as a result of the customized nature of the transactions; positions are exercised, closed out with the arranging bank or permitted to expire (resales to third parties are non-existent).

Basket/Index Forwards/Swaps

The onshore and offshore OTC market for Thai basket/index forwards and swaps is reasonably active to five years. Foreign financial institutions often execute transactions which provide clients with upside or downside exposure to the broad Thai market (or sector-specific baskets) in exchange for deferred premium in the form of floating rate flows (often US$ LIBOR); these structures are equivalent to clients purchasing medium-term OTC basket/index calls or puts. Numerous other structures are available, including purchases of call swaps and sales of higher strike call swaps (capping potential returns from index appreciation), or purchases of call swaps and sales of put swaps (providing index appreciation but requiring payment of index depreciation); such structures permit a reduction (or possible elimination) of premium payments. Swaps with embedded exotics (e.g. barriers, Asians), which provide institutions with more specific risk or return payoffs, are also available though far less prevalent.

Basket/Index Options

In the absence of listed index options, the market for offshore OTC index options has become reasonably popular; foreign financial institutions have been active primarily in buying and selling vanilla OTC index options on the SET. Typical options are six- to 12-months in tenor, with American or European exercise into cash settlement. Basket options, written on groups of Thai stocks (e.g. property baskets, bank baskets, construction baskets and so on) are written under similar terms. Exotic structures, such as outperformance options, barrier options and quanto options are also available, though much less common. As with OTC equity options, there is no secondary market for OTC basket/index options (e.g. transactions are either exercised, closed out with the arranging bank or allowed to expire).

Fixed Income

Fixed Income Forwards/Swaps

Although the market for Thai baht interest rate forwards and swaps is still modest in size, increasing two-way onshore flow has spurred growth in products and liquidity, and has permitted gradual lengthening of transaction maturity. As with any developing market, however, the Thai forward and swap market is still faced with various challenges, including: (a) lack of an established short-term floating-rate benchmark to provide uniform valuation of the floating-rate component of IRSs; (b) absence of a government bond yield curve to provide the market with swap pricing information; and (c) lack of government bond supply for hedging of swap positions. All three hurdles must be overcome if the Thai fixed income derivative market is to progress to a more advanced stage.

The baht FRA market, which is based on BIBOR (for onshore transactions), and the interest rates implied by FX forwards (for offshore transactions), is only moderately active, primarily to 12 months (though long-term deals to three years are executed on occasion); given the infancy of the market there is no standard interbank dealing size at the present time. Although flows are gradually increasing, the small size of the market and the volatility of domestic rates means bid-offer spreads are still very wide (e.g. 40 basis points under normal market conditions) and often quite variable. Until broader development of a local floating-rate benchmark occurs (as discussed below), it is likely that spreads will remain wide and overall volumes limited.

The Thai IRS market, which has become significantly more active over the past few years, is still faced with pricing challenges and hedging difficulties. Participants in the local market must contend with the lack of a uniform floating-rate benchmark which can be set against fixed baht rates in domestic swaps. The absence of a robust domestic benchmark means the market distinguishes between onshore and offshore rates. In the onshore market, floating rate references are available in BIBOR (the local interbank rate), minimum lending rate (MLR, a semi-floating rate applied to prime corporate customers) and commercial bill of exchange yields. While certain swaps in the onshore market quote fixed baht rates (semi-annual, on an Actual/365-day basis) against BIBOR, others are executed against the MLR, while still others are set against commercial bills. Under a typical transaction a local bank may lend funds to a prime corporate at MLR; the corporate may then enter into a swap paying fixed baht against receipt of MLR in order to lock in funding costs. The swap bank, in turn, may enter into a basis swap of MLR against BIBOR to carry MLR/BIBOR basis risk rather than fixed/floating risk. The primary difficulty with MLR, BIBOR and bill yields is that they are not readily tradeable and, as such, present market-makers with pricing and hedging difficulties.

Lack of a broadly accepted domestic benchmark has led to the development of the Singapore-based baht swap offer rate (SOR), an offshore floating rate reference (which is also used to price local currency IRSs in the Indonesian, Malaysian and Singaporean markets). Many institutions have commenced using the baht SOR, which is simply the rate derived from borrowing in US dollars and converting into Thai baht of equal tenor through the forward FX market; the SOR utilizes the offer side of the FX swap rate to swap out of dollars and into baht. SOR quotes, carried on Telerate page 44178, are available in one-, three-, six- and 12-month maturities. Offshore swaps are thus quoted as fixed baht (semi-annual, on an Actual/365-day basis) against baht SOR (typically on a six-month reset basis).

The market for onshore and offshore swaps is most liquid in the one- and two-year sector, though swaps of three- and five-years are reasonably common; swaps to seven years are executed on occasion but tend to be related to very specific asset or liability hedging. Average dealing in the market is limited to two or three transactions per week, with an average size of THB246 mln (US$10 mln) each. Bid-offer spreads for fixed baht swaps against the SOR average 15–20 basis points throughout the curve; however, the relative illiquidity of the market, the volatility of baht rates, and occasional supply and demand imbalances (i.e. a market heavily driven by liability-based transactions) can cause spreads to widen. Figure 14.3 below highlights a representative yield curve from mid-1995 (fixed baht against six-month baht SOR).

In addition to the lack of a uniform floating rate benchmark, participants in the Thai market are faced with swap hedging challenges. While in most emerging derivative markets hedging of swap books can be difficult, in Thailand such hedging is made particularly complex by the relatively small supply of fixed income instruments in the market; those which are available are often illiquid. As indicated at the beginning of this chapter, the Thai bond market is still small compared with other Asian markets and lack of regular government issuance means dealers have extremely limited access to government securities to hedge their books. The only practical hedging solution for dealers is to use money market instruments such as

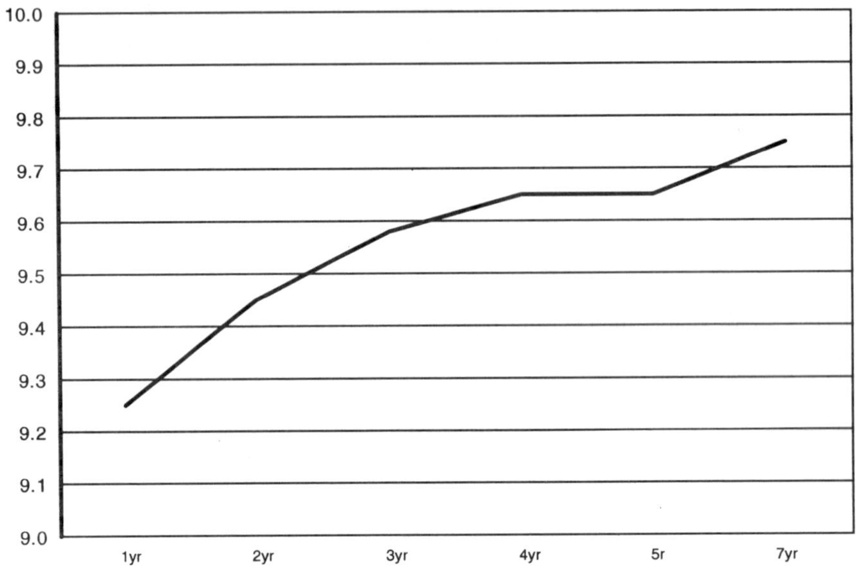

Figure 14.3 Representative Baht IRS Curve

deposits and forward foreign exchange (i.e. the rates implied in the forwards) or to lay swaps off with other dealers; the latter is still a difficult task as the market is occasionally one-sided and volumes are still limited. Growth in the domestic swap market is likely to remain somewhat constrained until hedging supply improves (i.e. more state enterprise and corporate bonds, more two-way swap flow).

Fixed Income Options

The market for baht fixed income options, like the IRS market described above, is developing very gradually. Baht caps and floors, which reference either BIBOR or the rates implicit in FX forwards, are active primarily to three years (though quotes to five years can be obtained). Given the immaturity of the market, there is no standard interbank dealing size and bid-offer spreads (quoted in volatility terms) are still wide and rather erratic. Baht receiver and payer swaptions are available but can be very expensive and, as such, are not particularly common. Overall growth in baht caps, floors and swaptions is likely to remain restrained until an onshore floating rate benchmark is established and there is greater activity in underlying baht forwards and swaps. A proper bond option market has not yet developed, primarily because there are very few government bonds outstanding in the market (and none which would be considered true benchmarks); an OTC bond option market based on government bonds is unlikely to develop in the near-term.

Currency

Currency Forwards/Swaps

The market for OTC baht currency forwards and swaps has been expanding over the past few years. The currency forward market presently features good liquidity in deals to 12 months; long-term FX forwards are also available to five years, though these tend to be far less liquid. Bid-offer spreads range from THB0.08/US$ for three-month forwards to THB0.15/US$ for six-month forwards and THB0.30/US$ for one-year forwards. Standard interbank dealing size is THB245 mln to THB370 mln (US$10 mln to US$15 mln).

The Thai baht CCS market has grown rapidly over the past five years as issuers, investors and importers/exporters have sought to hedge liabilities, assets and offshore currency receipts. The cross currency swap market of baht against US dollars is most active in the one- to three-year sector, but is quoted with increasing frequency to five- and seven-years; structured deals to ten years are also known to occur. Standard dealing size in currency swaps is THB245 mln to THB370 mln (US$10 mln to US$15 mln), and there is now a fairly consistent flow of THB290 mln to THB740 mln (US$20 mln to US$30 mln) executed on a daily basis. Standard baht CCSs are quoted as fixed baht (semi-annual, on an Actual/365-day basis) against US$ LIBOR flat. Typical bid-offer spreads on baht CCSs are 20 basis points, though relative instability in the currency during the first quarter of 1995 caused short-term spreads to widen out to 35–40 basis points. Given the relative illiquidity of the THB/US$ CCS market, bid-offer spreads are considerably higher than those found in liquid and developed CCS markets (e.g. the JPY/US$ market features reasonably constant 7–8 basis point bid-offer spreads across the curve). Table 14.3 displays the range of spreads in evidence under normal market conditions. Figure 14.4. traces the historical movement of the fixed baht/US$ LIBOR swap curve while Figure 14.5 traces the movement of key two-, three- and five-year CCS rates.

Maturity	Bid-Offer Spreads
1 year	20–30 bps
2 year	20–30 bps
3 year	20–30 bps
4 year	20–30 bps
5 year	30–40 bps

Table 14.3 THB/US$ CCS Bid-Offer Spreads

It should be noted that, unlike certain other Asia Pacific markets (e.g. Australia, Japan, Hong Kong), there is no currency basis swap market (e.g. BIBOR against US$ LIBOR), as no single floating Thai benchmark has been firmly established.

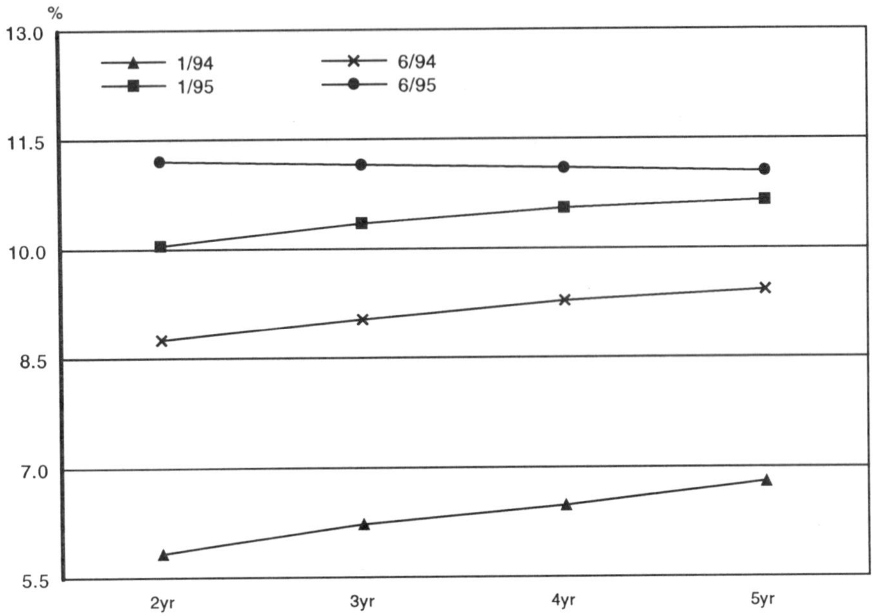

Figure 14.4 Historical Movement of THB/US$ CCS Curves

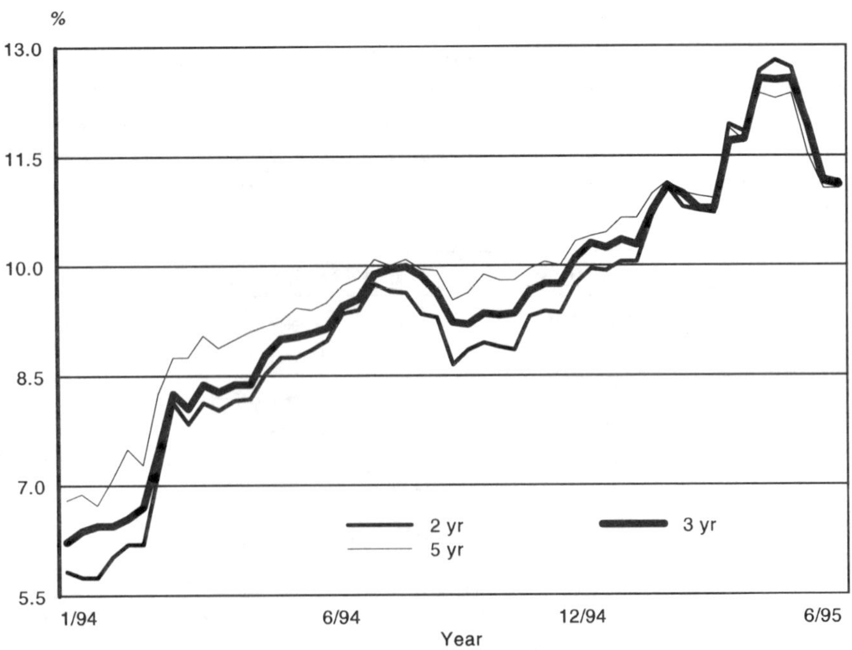

Figure 14.5 Historical Movement of Key THB/US$ CCS Rates

Currency Options

Overall activity in the OTC baht currency option market has expanded considerably in recent years as domestic and foreign institutions have employed options to generate attractive investment returns or hedge specific currency exposures. The market is active primarily in the one- to 12-month sector where standard interbank dealing size is THB245 mln (US$10 mln). Baht options are quoted in volatility terms; given the historically low volatility of the baht as a result of its link to the dollar, yen and Deutschmark, quotes for 12-month options have generally been in the range of 2 to 4 points, with bid-offer spreads of 1 to 2 points, depending on market conditions. In late 1994 and early 1995 volatility on baht options increased to 6 to 8 points as the Mexican peso devaluation (and ensuing crisis) caused instability in several Southeast Asian currencies, including the baht; volatility quotes also increased as a result of significant demand by Thai exporters for US$ put/THB call options (in order to hedge 75% of US dollar receivables, under a mandatory government ruling). With renewed stability in the currency and declining demand for hedges, it is possible volatility quotes will return to more 'normal' (i.e. historic) levels.

In addition to conventional options, a number of institutional investors actively purchase baht basket options. Such options replicate the strategy often employed in the spot and forward markets, which calls for purchasing baht and shorting the components of the basket (dollars, yen, Deutschmarks) in order to take advantage of the substantial carry (and low currency volatility) which has existed. Exotic baht currency options, such as barriers, lookbacks and Asians, are also executed on occasion but overall activity is still very modest.

Commodity

Commodity Forwards/Swaps

Thailand features an informal market for OTC commodity forwards based on two of its major exports, rice and rubber (note that it also features more modest forward trading in tapioca, copra and corn). Unlike Indonesia (which features standardized forward contracts through ICEB), most OTC forward trading in Thailand is based on independently negotiated transactions between buyer and seller. The forward market is active primarily to six months and virtually all transactions result in physical delivery or acceptance of underlying agricultural commodities. As the country moves to introduce commodity futures (e.g. through FCM), the same hedging protection currently available through the informal forward market will be available through standard futures contracts. Note that in addition to domestic agricultural forwards, local companies seeking hedging cover for energy and base metals occasionally execute forwards/swaps through the offshore OTC market.

Commodity Options

The domestic market does not currently feature commodity options based on domestic commodity references.

LOCAL REGULATORY/LEGAL TREATMENT OF DERIVATIVES

Laws and regulations related to securities and derivatives are set forth in the Securities and Exchange Act of 1992 (SEC Act). Under the original SEC Act, a new regulator, the Securities and Exchange Commission (SEC), was given authority to supervise all securities trading in Thailand, including primary activity related to equities, convertible bonds, warrants and debentures; secondary market activity in such instruments is carried out by the SET, a self-regulating entity. In addition, the Act references and recognizes futures and options (under Section 218) but separate legislation, including amendments to the Act, will be required prior to the formal introduction of listed futures or options. There are currently no specific domestic regulations or laws regarding OTC derivatives.

In mid-March 1995 the Bank of Thailand established certain parameters designed to ensure institutions have appropriate risk-management control over their derivative activities. Specifically, the BOT has established compulsory reporting of derivatives portfolios and requires all banks to provide information on their risk management processes, including responsibilities of managers responsible for trading, details on risk control of foreign exchange and derivatives, information on the accounting system used for trading and derivatives, and the nature of the internal audit process as related to derivatives. The BOT directives apply equally to foreign and local commercial banks operating in Thailand.

LOCAL ACCOUNTING PRACTICES FOR DERIVATIVES

Given the developing nature of Thailand's local derivative market, it is not surprising that comprehensive accounting policies for derivatives have not been developed. Under present rules all general financial statements must be prepared in accordance with the standards established by the voluntary Thai accounting organization, ICAAT. ICAAT draws guidance primarily from International Accounting Standards and US Generally Accepted Accounting Principles, though it occasionally creates more specific rules of its own. Where no ICAAT standards have been established institutions are expected to utilize rules set forth by International Accounting Standards. ICAAT has not released a specific circular related to accounting treatment of derivative hedging or trading positions and, as such, most local participants active in derivatives (e.g. banks) follow International Accounting Standards. For derivatives employed as hedge transactions, the accrual method of accounting is generally utilized, where gains or losses from derivatives are accrued over the life of the transaction. If derivatives are employed for trading or speculative purposes, positions are revalued on a daily basis, with differences between contracted value and market value posted to the income statement immediately. It should be noted that in the case of foreign exchange derivatives (primarily foreign currency swaps, options and forwards), certain Thai financial institutions value the derivatives on balance date based on spot, rather than forward, rates, and post resulting unrealized gains or losses to the income statement; again, there is no specific treatment for currency derivatives.

PROSPECTS FOR THE LOCAL DERIVATIVE MARKET

Summarized below are the near-term (one- to three-year) and medium-term (three- to five-year) prospects for Thai domestic derivatives.

Near-term:

- Introduction of a futures exchange to trade financial futures (index, currency, deposit) and commodity futures (rice, rubber); no introduction of bond futures due to a of lack of government bond supply.
- Further growth in listed equity warrants as the domestic equity market expands and small/large companies continue to require capital for expansion.
- Expansion of OTC equity derivative products as foreign investor restrictions are loosened and onshore short-selling of equities becomes permissible.
- Meaningful growth in IRS activity and liquidity as a floating rate benchmark is established and becomes widely accepted, and as growing domestic financing needs lead to greater swap opportunities; hedging will be aided by more balanced two-way swap flow. Lengthening of the swap curve as the overall market matures.
- Gradual increase in fixed income options turnover for many of the reasons outlined above.
- Expansion in currency derivatives as overall trading in baht becomes more liquid and offshore funding opportunities increase.

Medium-term:

- Introduction of index options, equity options and 'second stage' commodity futures.
- Greater liquidity in OTC equity derivatives as index futures become actively traded (and permit easier management of risk positions).
- Deepening of IRSs as two-way flows permit further warehousing of risk; extension of maturities and narrowing of bid-offer spreads as the market matures.

	Overall Liquidity	Liquid/ Maximum Maturity	Interbank dealing size	Average bid-offer spread
Equity/Index Swaps	fair	1–3 yrs/5 yrs	n/a	n/a
Equity/Index Options	fair	12 mos/2–3 yrs	n/a	n/a
Interest Rate Swaps	fair	1–2 yrs/7 yrs	US$10 mln	15–20bps
Interest Rate Options	poor	1–3 yrs/5 yrs	none	varies
Currency Swaps	fair	1–3 yrs/7 yrs	US$10–15 mln	20–30bps
Currency Options	fair	1–12 mos/12 mos	US$10 mln	1–2 pts

Table 14.4 Summary of Domestic OTC Derivatives

Appendix I

LISTED DERIVATIVE EXCHANGE CONTACTS

Australia

Australian Stock Exchange
8th Floor, 20 Bond Street, Sydney, NSW 2000, Australia
Tel: 612-227-0000 Fax: 612-235-0056

ASX Derivatives
Same as Australian Stock Exchange

Sydney Futures Exchange
30-32 Grosvenor Street, Sydney, NSW 2000, Australia
Tel: 612-256-0555 Fax: 612-256-0666

China

Beijing Commodity Exchange
Chenuyn Building, 8 Beichen East Road, Chaoyang District, Beijing, People's Republic of China
Tel: 86-1-492-6688 Fax: 86-1-493-3183

Changchun United Commodity Exchange
80 Stalin Street, Changchun, People's Republic of China
Tel: 86-431-895-7396 Fax: 86-431-895-7392

China Commodity Futures Exchange of Hainan
8/F, Huaneng Building, Haikou, Hainan Province, People's Republic of China
Tel: 86-898-670-0107 Fax: 86-898-670-0099

China Zhengzhou Commodity Exchange
20 Huanyuan Road, Zhengzhou, People's Republic of China
Tel: 86-371-594-5421 Fax: 86-371-594-5424

Dalian Commodity Exchange
38 Da Lian Xi, Yuan District, Sheng Li Road, Dalian, People's Republic of China
Tel: 86-411-364-5110 Fax: 86-411-364-5244

Guangdong United Futures Exchange
JingXing Hotel, 91 LinHe West Road, Guangzhou, People's Republic of China
Tel: 86-20-750-9653 Fax: 86-20-750-9654

Nanfang Non-ferrous Metals Exchange
154 Guang Fu Yi Road, Huang Qi, Nan Hai City, Guangdong,
People's Republic of China
Tel: 86-750-500-3939 Fax: 86-750-500-8999

Nanjing Petroleum Exchange
3/F, Jinagsu Convention Centre, 22 Xuan Wu Men, Nanjing,
People's Republic of China
Tel: 86-25-336-4999 Fax: 86-25-336-4333

Shanghai Cereals and Oils Exchange
1455 Shanghai Nan Su Zhou Road, Shanghai, People's Republic of China
Tel: 86-21-253-3663 Fax: 86-21-217-2390

Shanghai Commodity Exchange
38 Caobao Road, 3rd Fl, Huaxia Hotel, Shanghai, People's Republic of China
Tel: 86-21-482-0908 Fax: 86-21-472-7986

Shanghai Metals Exchange
2250 Shanghai Zhon Shan North Road, Shanghai, People's Republic of China
Tel: 86-21-257-7719 Fax: 86-21-257-7717

Shanghai Stock Exchange
15 Huang Pu Road, Shanghai, People's Republic of China
Tel: 86-21-306-8888 Fax: 86-21-306-3076

Shenyang Commodity Exchange
38 Shenyang He Pin District, Cai Ta Road, Shenyang, People's Republic of China
Tel: 86-24-390-4386 Fax: 86-24-390-4392

Shenzhen Metal and United Futures Exchange

1/F, Block B, Zhongjian Overseas Decoration Building, Hua Fu Road, Shenzhen, People's Republic of China
Tel: 86-755-334-3502 Fax: 86-755-334-3505

Shenzhen Stock Exchange

203 Shangbu Industrial Area, Shenzhen, People's Republic of China
Tel: 86-755-320-3431 Fax: 86-755-320-3505

Suzhou Commodity Exchange

128 Suzhou Shan Xiang Road, Suzhou, People's Republic of China
Tel: 86-512-829-9275 Fax: 86-512-828-5090

Tianjin United Futures Exchange

3rd Fl, Block B, Longmen Building, Tianjin, People's Republic of China
Tel: 86-22-446-5613 Fax: 86-22-446-5579

Hong Kong

Hong Kong Futures Exchange

6/F Asia Pacific Finance Tower, Citibank Plaza, 3 Garden Road, Central, Hong Kong
Tel: 852-2842-9333 Fax: 852-2810-5089

Stock Exchange of Hong Kong

1/F, Exchange Square 1 and 2, Central, Hong Kong
Tel: 852-2522-1122 Fax: 852-2810-4475

India

Bombay Stock Exchange

Phiroze Jeejeebhoy Towers, Dalal Street, Bombay, India 400 001
Tel: 91-22-265-5860 Fax: 91-22-265-8121

Over-the-Counter Exchange of India

92 Makers Towers F, Cuffe Parade, Bombay, India 400 005
Tel: 91-22-218-8164 Fax: 91-22-218-8012

Indonesia

Indonesian Commodity Exchange Board, Gedung Burasa, Jalan Medan Merdeka Selatan, Jakarta 10110, Indonesia
Tel: 62-21-344-1921 Fax: 62-21-380-4426

Jakarta Stock Exchange

14 Jalan Medan Merdeka Selatan, Jakarta 10110, Indonesia
Tel: 62-21-386-2464 Fax: 62-21-380-1841

Japan

Hokkaido Grain Exchange

3 Odori Nishi, 5-chome, Chuo-ku, Sapporo 060, Japan
Tel: 81-11-221-9131 Fax: 81-11-221-4964

Kanmon Commodity Exchange

1-5 Nabe-cho, Shimonoseki 750, Japan
Tel: 81-832-31-1313 Fax: 81-832-23-1947

Kansai Agricultural Exchange

1-10-14 Azawa, Nishi-ku, Osaka 550, Japan
Tel: 816-531-7931 Fax: 816-541-9343

Kobe Raw Silk Exchange

126 Higashi-machi, Chuo-ku, Kobe 650, Japan
Tel: 81-78-331-7141 Fax: 81-78-331-7145

Kobe Rubber Exchange

49 Harima-cho, Chuo-ku, Kobe 650, Japan
Tel: 81-78-331-4211 Fax: 81-78-332-1622

Maebashi Dried Cocoon Exchange

1-49-1 Furuichi-machi, Maebashi 371, Japan
Tel: 81-272-52-1401 Fax: 81-272-51-8270

Nagoya Grain and Sugar Exchange

2-3-2 Meieki-minami, Nakamura-ku, Nagoya 450, Japan
Tel: 81-52-571-8161 Fax: 81-52-581-4653

Nagoya Stock Exchange
3-17 Sakae, 3-chome, Naka-ku, Nagoya 460, Japan
Tel: 81-52-262-3172 Fax: 81-52-241-1527

Nagoya Textile Exchange
3-2-15 Nishiki, Naka-ku, Nagoya 460, Japan
Tel: 81-52-951-2171 Fax: 81-52-961-6407

Osaka Stock Exchange
8-16 Kitahama, 1-chome, Chuo-ku, Osaka 541, Japan
Tel: 816-229-8643 Fax: 816-231-2639

Osaka Textile Exchange
2-5-28, Kyutaro-machi, Chuo-ku, Osaka 541, Japan
Tel: 816-253-0031 Fax: 816-253-0034

Tokyo Commodity Exchange
1-10-8 Nihonbashi, Horidome-cho, Chuo-ku, Tokyo 103, Japan
Tel: 813-3661-9191 Fax: 813-3661-7568

Tokyo Grain Exchange
1-12-5 Kakigara-cho, Nihonbashi, Chuo-ku, Tokyo 103, Japan
Tel: 813-3668-9311 Fax: 813-3668-9566

Tokyo International Financial Futures Exchange
1-3-1 Marunouchi, Chiyoda-ku, Tokyo 100, Japan
Tel: 813-5223-2400 Fax: 813-5223-2450

Tokyo Stock Exchange
2-1 Nihonbashi, Kabuto-cho, Chuo-ku, Tokyo 103, Japan
Tel: 813-3666-0141 Fax: 813-3663-0625

Toyohashi Dried Cocoon Exchange
2-52 Ekimae-odori, Toyohashi-shi, Aichi-ken 40, Japan
Tel: 81-532-526-231 Fax: 81-532-552-017

Yokohama Raw Silk Exchange
1 Yamashita-cho, Naka-ku, Yokohama 236, Japan
Tel: 81-45-641-1341 Fax: 81-45-641-1346

Malaysia

Kuala Lumpur Commodity Exchange
Citypoint, Dayabumi Complex, Jalan Sultan, Hisahmuddin, 50740 Kuala Lumpur, Malaysia
Tel: 60-3-293-6822 Fax: 60-3-274-2215

Kuala Lumpur Stock Exchange
Exchange Square, Jalan Sematan, Damansara Heights, 50490 Kuala Lumpur, Malaysia
Tel: 60-3-254-6433 Fax: 60-3-255-7463

New Zealand

New Zealand Futures and Options Exchange
10th Floor, Finance Centre, 191 Queen Street, Auckland 1, New Zealand
Tel: 64-9-309-8308 Fax: 64-9-309-8817

New Zealand Stock Exchange
8th Floor Caltex Tower, 286-292 Lambton Quay, Wellington, New Zealand
Tel: 64-4-472-7599 Fax: 64-4-473-1470

Philippines

Manila International Futures Exchange
7th Floor, Producers Bank Centre, Paseo de Roxas, Makati, Metro Manila, Philippines
Tel: 63-2-818-5496 Fax: 63-2-818-5529

Philippine Stock Exchange
PSE Centre, Exchange Road, Pasig, Metro Manila, Philippines
Tel: 63-2-636-0122 Fax: 63-2-634-5920

Singapore

Singapore Commodity Exchange
111 North Bridge Road, No 23-04/05, Peninsula Plaza, Singapore 0617
Tel: 65-338-5600 Fax: 65-338-9640

Singapore International Monetary Exchange
1 Raffles Place, No 07-00, OUB Centre, Singapore 0104
Tel: 65-535-7382 Fax: 65-535-7282

Stock Exchange of Singapore
20 Cecil Street, No 26-01/08, The Exchange, Singapore 0104
Tel: 65-535-3788 Fax: 65-535-6994

South Korea

Korea Stock Exchange
33 Yoido-dong, Youngdeungpo-gu, Seoul 150-010, Korea
Tel: 82-2-780-2271 Fax: 82-2-786-0263

Taiwan

Taiwan Stock Exchange
Floors 2-10, City Building, 85 Yen Ping South Road, Taipei, Taiwan
Tel: 886-2311-4020 Fax: 886-2375-3669

Thailand

Stock Exchange of Thailand
132 Sinthon Building, Wireless Road, Bangkok 10500, Thailand
Tel: 66-2-254-0960 Fax: 66-2-263-2746

Appendix II

ASIA PACIFIC DOMESTIC AND OFFSHORE WARRANT ISSUES

Highlighted below are summary details on listed Asia Pacific equity and index warrants as of mid-1995.

AUSTRALIA

Issuer	Amount (000s)	Issue Date	Expiry Date	Shs/ Wrnt	Currency Shs/Wrnt
Al Engineering	8,250	4/95	10/98	1	A$/A$
Alkane Explor	36,011	10/93	6/96	1	A$/A$
Alliegance Min	1,000	10/93	11/96	1	A$/A$
All Ords Index-s	500	3/95	2/97	10	A$/CHF
All Ords Index-s	500	3/95	2/97	10	A$/CHF
Anaconda Nickel	30,000	3/94	12/95	1	A$/A$
Anglo Aust Res	12,880	11/93	9/96	1	A$/A$
Aquarius Expl	62,601	8/92	6/97	1	A$/A$
Arboyne NL	46,281	2/93	12/95	1	A$/A$
Associated Gold	87,897	10/93	1/97	1	A$/A$
Atlas Pacific	16,668	1/94	6/97	1	A$/A$
Atlas Pacific	16,668	6/94	6/97	1	A$/A$
Audax Res	29,151	7/94	7/96	1	A$/A$
Aurifex Mining	1,407	1/95	10/99	1	A$/A$
Australian Dev	19,926	10/92	12/95	1	A$/A$
Australian Gold	71,506	7/94	12/96	1	A$/A$
Australian Over	19,632	3/94	2/96	1	A$/A$
Australian United	56,670	8/93	5/98	1	A$/A$
Auto Logistics	11,915	2/94	12/97	1	A$/A$
Bamboo Gold	62,013	12/93	11/98	1	A$/A$
Barron Enterp	4,260	12/94	11/97	1	A$/A$
Biotech Intl	2,447	6/92	12/95	1	A$/A$
Black Hill Min	155,347	4/93	12/97	1	A$/A$

AUSTRALIA (continued)

Issuer	Amount (000s)	Issue Date	Expiry Date	Shs/ Wrnt	Currency Shs/Wrnt
Black Mountain	16,000	4/95	3/97	1	A$/A$
Bligh Oil & Min	18,763	12/94	12/96	1	A$/A$
Border Gold	40,708	5/93	9/96	1	A$/A$
Britannia Gold	26,000	1/94	12/96	1	A$/A$
Broken Hill Prop	2,500	11/93	9/96	1	A$/A$
Browns Creek	15,688	6/93	1/97	1	A$/A$
Callina NL	17,887	11/92	12/95	1	A$/A$
Cambrian Res	1	1/93	12/96	1	A$/A$
Camelot Res	29,667	12/94	9/99	1	A$/A$
Carrington Eq	1,651	6/93	6/98	1	A$/A$
CCI Hldg	4,604	1/93	11/95	1	A$/A$
Centamin	40,501	12/93	6/97	1	A$/A$
Centenary Intl	85,934	12/93	4/96	1	A$/A$
Centennial Coal	4,823	8/94	6/99	1	A$/A$
Chardon Ind	3,000	2/95	11/97	1	A$/A$
Charter Pac	11,518	12/92	11/97	1	A$/A$
Charters	25,303	12/93	12/96	1	A$/A$
Cityview Inv	8,000	7/94	6/96	1	A$/A$
Claim Minerals	21,216	8/94	3/99	1	A$/A$
Cluff Res	72,940	11/93	6/98	1	A$/A$
Cloncurry Min	4,014	2/93	4/96	1	A$/A$
Coldstream	822	4/92	12/96	1	A$/A$
Coldstream	1,736	1/95	8/98	1	A$/A$
Colonial Res	11,159	2/94	8/95	1	A$/A$
Comet Gold	7,500	3/94	6/96	1	A$/A$
Consex	1	7/92	3/97	1	A$/A$
Cons Prop Inv	3,200	12/94	12/97	1	A$/A$
Coplex Res	1,000	6/94	7/95	1	A$/A$
Copperfield Gold	28,025	8/94	6/96	1	A$/A$
Cornwall Res	53,488	1/94	9/98	1	A$/A$
Crest Res	15,000	2/94	2/97	1	A$/A$
Cumnock Coal	6,043	12/93	3/96	1	A$/A$
Dioro Expl	31,093	7/92	5/97	1	A$/A$
Divers United	22,500	12/91	11/96	1	A$/A$
Dollar Swe	6,240	12/94	12/95	1	A$/A$
Duketon Gold	1	5/93	1/97	1	A$/A$
East Coast	19,463	12/94	6/99	1	A$/A$
Environ Solution	15,638	7/94	5/96	1	A$/A$
Federation Res	3,241	1/95	3/97	1	A$/A$

AUSTRALIA (continued)

Issuer	Amount (000s)	Issue Date	Expiry Date	Shs/ Wrnt	Currency Shs/Wrnt
Fimston Mining	37,000	5/92	12/96	1	A$/A$
Finders Gold	22,665	4/93	12/97	1	A$/A$
First Res Dev	20,200	12/94	12/97	1	A$/A$
Franked Inc	34,107	6/94	11/97	1	A$/A$
Gemcor	25,315	11/93	9/98	1	A$/A$
Gen Gold Res	10,300	2/94	10/95	1	A$/A$
Geographe Res	10,878	11/93	12/95	1	A$/A$
Ghana Gold	35,000	6/94	6/97	1	A$/A$
Gindalbie Gold	20,000	4/94	1/98	1	A$/A$
Gold and Min	77,288	8/93	11/96	1	A$/A$
Golden Plateau	30,634	6/93	6/96	1	A$/A$
Gold Mines	85,788	12/94	12/98	1	A$/A$
Gold Partners	17,182	6/94	6/96	1	A$/A$
Goldstream Min	10,445	10/94	11/98	1	A$/A$
Growth Res	1	4/94	11/98	1	A$/A$
Gwalia Cons	23,824	11/90	11/95	1	A$/A$
Hampton Hill	16,000	5/94	1/98	1	A$/A$
Huntley Inv	20,521	1/94	8/96	1	A$/A$
Indus Inv	27,278	7/94	7/99	1	A$/A$
Inovax	2,246	5/94	11/96	1	A$/A$
Interchrome	38,719	3/94	9/98	1	A$/A$
Intercontinental	165,289	2/91	6/98	1	A$/A$
Intermin Res	12,405	10/93	9/98	1	A$/A$
Intl Equities	17,204	3/93	12/96	1	A$/A$
Intl Mineral	12,000	7/94	1/96	1	A$/A$
ISR Group	15,164	4/94	7/95	1	A$/A$
Jardine Strat	113,061	4/95	5/98	1	A$/A$
Jervois Mining	31,601	10/93	6/97	1	A$/A$
JF Asia	13,064	5/94	12/95	1	A$/A$
JF China	35,176	10/93	1/97	1	A$/A$
Kakadu Res	28,092	1/91	5/97	1	A$/A$
Kanowna Lights	13,500	5/94	12/98	1	A$/A$
Kalgoorlie Res	160,616	9/93	5/98	1	A$/A$
Kilkenny Gold	30,000	9/94	1/99	1	A$/A$
Kimberley Diary	6,000	1/94	11/98	1	A$/A$
Kingstream Res	8,997	1/94	11/98	1	A$/A$
Kiwi Gold	38,800	12/93	1/96	1	A$/A$
KKR Res	16,431	11/93	7/98	1	A$/A$
Laverton Gold	56,020	9/94	6/97	1	A$/A$

AUSTRALIA (continued)

Issuer	Amount (000s)	Issue Date	Expiry Date	Shs/ Wrnt	Currency Shs/Wrnt
Leader Res	15,528	5/94	6/97	1	A$/A$
Lone Star Expl	26,844	12/93	7/97	1	A$/A$
Long Homes	20,078	1/94	12/96	1	A$/A$
Lynas Gold	30,592	7/94	6/99	1	A$/A$
Magnet Group	258,607	12/93	6/98	1	A$/A$
Majestic Res	40,944	11/91	9/96	1	A$/A$
Maple Oil	10,269	7/94	7/96	1	A$/A$
Markwell Pac	1,072	2/94	12/96	1	A$/A$
Matlock Min	84,451	1/92	1/96	1	A$/A$
Med Research	10,122	5/91	3/96	1	A$/A$
Media Tech	23,169	6/94	11/98	1	A$/A$
Meekatharra Min	12,023	5/93	12/95	1	A$/A$
Menzies Gold	2,315	8/94	3/96	1	A$/A$
Menzies Gold	5,215	12/93	3/96	1	A$/A$
Merritt Min	12,700	10/93	12/97	1	A$/A$
Metex Res	6,245	12/93	1/97	1	A$/A$
Micromedial	3,000	8/93	6/96	1	A$/A$
Mineral Comm	13,668	8/93	12/95	1	A$/A$
Moonstone Diam	12,500	11/93	10/96	1	A$/A$
Mosaic Oil	33,750	5/94	12/95	1	A$/A$
Mosaix Tech	887	12/94	11/97	1	A$/A$
Mount Grace	25,000	3/94	3/96	1	A$/A$
Multistack Int	1	2/93	9/95	1	A$/A$
Murchison Hldg	5,949	5/94	3/97	1	A$/A$
National Inv	9,793	6/94	5/99	1	A$/A$
Newsnet	3,333	4/95	12/98	1	A$/A$
Nine Network	1	6/91	9/95	1	A$/A$
NMFM Asia	20,000	5/94	3/98	1	A$/A$
Noble Res	60,049	6/92	5/96	1	A$/A$
Normandy Min	145,960	5/91	5/96	1	A$/A$
Norminco	500	8/93	12/97	1	A$/A$
North Star Res	33,851	12/93	11/98	1	A$/A$
Norvet	14,000	8/94	11/98	1	A$/A$
Ocean Res	1,189	12/94	3/96	1	A$/A$
Ocean Res	16,860	9/93	6/98	1	A$/A$
OKA Motor	6,000	12/94	3/96	1	A$/A$
Pac Res	30,023	9/94	12/97	1	A$/A$
Panorama Res	12,000	3/94	1/98	1	A$/A$
Parmelia Res	14,033	12/92	10/95	1	A$/A$

AUSTRALIA (continued)

Issuer	Amount (000s)	Issue Date	Expiry Date	Shs/ Wrnt	Currency Shs/Wrnt
Peregrine Res	95,920	6/93	1/97	1	A$/A$
Peter Lehman	7,360	8/93	11/97	1	A$/A$
Pilabara Min	26,420	2/94	6/98	1	A$/A$
Pima Min	50,929	2/92	12/95	1	A$/A$
Pinnacle Min	18,999	7/94	6/98	1	A$/A$
Pirie Capital	12,355	10/94	6/99	1	A$/A$
Platinum Cap	50,000	6/94	7/96	1	A$/A$
Platsearch	7,032	2/94	3/96	1	A$/A$
Plenty River	196,449	1/94	11/98	1	A$/A$
Plumbing World	1,608	10/92	2/96	1	A$/A$
Port Douglas	11,425	7/94	3/99	1	A$/A$
Precious Metal	18,107	12/93	6/96	1	A$/A$
Prima Res	10,000	6/94	6/97	1	A$/A$
Probe Res	68,969	2/94	2/97	1	A$/A$
Quest Invest	23,044	4/94	3/97	1	A$/A$
Ramsgate Res	34,025	8/93	6/98	1	A$/A$
Red River	27,752	1/91	12/97	1	A$/A$
Reef Mining	26,500	4/94	3/97	1	A$/A$
Reefton Mining	22,500	1/94	9/96	1	A$/A$
Resource & Ind	22,580	12/94	6/99	1	A$/A$
Rhodes Min	69,442	3/94	1/98	1	A$/A$
River House	18,750	3/93	10/97	1	A$/A$
Riverina Gold	11,748	11/93	6/96	1	A$/A$
Roehamption Res	13,500	12/94	12/97	1	A$/A$
Sabre Group	5,500	7/94	4/99	1	A$/A$
Scitec	20,218	12/93	11/95	1	A$/A$
Sedimentary	17,663	6/93	4/96	1	A$/A$
Sentry Invest	40,780	5/94	12/98	1	A$/A$
Skansen Hldg	2,362	8/93	8/96	1	A$/A$
Spectrum Network	1,651	6/93	6/98	1	A$/A$
Speedy Wheels	7,440	7/94	6/98	1	A$/A$
Spencer Gulf	244	11/94	11/96	1	A$/A$
Stirling Res	15,494	12/93	10/97	1	A$/A$
Strat Ind	44,442	5/94	3/96	1	A$/A$
Strategic Min	70,778	6/93	6/97	1	A$/A$
Strike Mining	18,750	5/94	3/99	1	A$/A$
Striker Res	36,882	9/93	6/97	1	A$/A$
Summit Gold	16,000	4/94	7/95	1	A$/A$
Sunbase China	175,275	11/91	6/96	1	A$/A$

AUSTRALIA (continued)

Issuer	Amount (000s)	Issue Date	Expiry Date	Shs/ Wrnt	Currency Shs/Wrnt
Sydney Oil	25,110	11/94	6/99	1	A$/A$
Taiga Minerals	10,698	5/93	3/98	1	A$/A$
Taipan Res	10,000	11/93	8/96	1	A$/A$
Target Res	34,681	3/95	10/97	1	A$/A$
Tempo Service	18,875	6/94	7/98	1	A$/A$
Tiger Inv	25,000	5/94	1/99	1	A$/A$
Tindals Gold	60,529	7/94	12/98	1	A$/A$
Transcom	131,394	1/92	12/95	1	A$/A$
Trans Global	95,734	10/93	5/98	1	A$/A$
Trans Global	216,885	12/93	5/98	1	A$/A$
Triton Res	12,955	10/91	7/96	1	A$/A$
TTL Corp	2,050	5/93	10/95	1	A$/A$
Union Mining	48,056	12/93	12/96	1	A$/A$
Unitel Corp	3,233	3/95	7/97	1	A$/A$
Valiant Cons	20,404	5/93	8/97	1	A$/A$
Vincent	1,200	7/94	12/96	1	A$/A$
Waraluck	21,220	7/93	6/96	1	A$/A$
Welcome Str	28,933	3/94	2/97	1	A$/A$
Wells Gold	21,600	7/94	6/98	1	A$/A$
West Aust New	26,900	5/94	6/99	1	A$/A$
Western Mining	15,000	8/94	3/96	1	A$/A$
Western Mining	102,350	2/94	9/97	1	A$/A$
West Gold Res	171,114	12/94	12/97	1	A$/A$
Whitechurch	10,090	1/94	6/96	1	A$/A$
Zanex	116,685	6/93	3/97	1	A$/A$
Zephyr Mineral	20,536	5/94	6/96	1	A$/A$

s-Swiss listed

HONG KONG

Issuer	Amount (000s)	Issue Date	Expiry Date	Shs/ Wrnt	Currency Shs/Wrnt
Alco Hldg	72,000	11/92	11/95	1	HK$/HK$
All Pantron	18,210	4/94	4/96	1	HK$/HK$
Allan Intl	56,000	8/91	7/95	1	HK$/HK$
Amoy Prop	400,000	4/95	6/96	0.1	HK$/HK$
Applied Intl	139,657	1/95	12/99	1	HK$/HK$

HONG KONG (continued)

Issuer	Amount (000s)	Issue Date	Expiry Date	Shs/ Wrnt	Currency Shs/Wrnt
Asia Commercial	106,457	8/93	8/96	1	HK$/HK$
Asia Orient	27,540,400	8/94	12/95	1	HK$/HK$
AWT World	34,000	2/93	12/95	1	HK$/HK$
Baltrans Hldg	39,998	5/92	7/95	2	HK$/HK$
Bank East Asia*	100,000	1/94	1/96	0.13	HK$/HK$
Bank East Asia	100,000	6/95	8/96	0.1	HK$/HK$
Cap Asia	82,125	9/93	10/96	1	HK$/HK$
Cathay Inv	11,322	10/92	9/95	1	HK$/HK$
Century City	81,161	9/94	12/96	1	HK$/HK$
Century City	162,322	9/94	12/95	1	HK$/HK$
Chaifa Hold	40,800	2/94	3/97	1	HK$/HK$
Champion Tec	99,999	8/92	7/95	2	HK$/HK$
Cheeful Hold	63,900	4/94	4/96	1	HK$/HK$
Cheung Kong*	300,000	6/94	1/96	0.1	HK$/HK$
Cheung Kong	350,000	2/92	7/95	0.1	HK$/HK$
Cheung Kong	125,000	3/95	2/97	0.1	HK$/HK$
Cheung Kong*	75,000	9/94	3/96	0.1	HK$/HK$
Chevalier Intl	142,517	10/94	9/97	1	HK$/HK$
Chi Cheung	35,551	6/93	6/96	1	HK$/HK$
China Aerospace	186,050	12/93	12/95	1	HK$/HK$
China Everbright	156,000	4/94	3/96	1	HK$/HK$
China Food	53,299	2/92	12/95	1.21	HK$/HK$
China Invest	62,325	7/94	6/96	0.2	HK$/HK$
China Light	30,000	3/93	2/96	0.1	HK$/HK$
China Light*	50,000	6/95	8/96	0.1	HK$/HK$
China Light*	1,750	5/94	1/96	0.1	HK$/HK$
China Merchants	20,000	7/93	6/96	1	HK$/HK$
China Overseas	655,980	8/92	8/95	1	HK$/HK$
China Pharma	120,000	6/94	12/96	1	HK$/HK$
China Strategic	63,000	9/92	8/97	1.03	HK$/HK$
Chinese Estate	124,169	10/87	12/95	0.79	HK$/HK$
Chuang China	104,140	10/94	6/96	1	HK$/HK$
Chuang China	22,950	3/92	12/95	0.31	HK$/HK$
Chuangs Intl	204,487	1/95	3/96	1	HK$/HK$
Chun Wo Hldg	308,000	3/93	3/96	1	HK$/HK$
Chung Tai	60,000	9/92	7/95	1	HK$/HK$
CIL Hldg	57,760	7/93	7/96	1	HK$/HK$
CITIC Pacific*	200,000	8/94	2/96	0.1	HK$/HK$
CITIC Pacific	40,000	2/94	8/95	1	HK$/HK$

HONG KONG (continued)

Issuer	Amount (000s)	Issue Date	Expiry Date	Shs/ Wrnt	Currency Shs/Wrnt
CITIC Pacific*	95,000	6/95	6/96	0.1	HK$/HK$
CITIC Pacific	40,000	8/93	10/95	0.1	HK$/HK$
Climax Intl	80,000	3/92	12/95	1	HK$/HK$
Companion Bldg*	46,000	9/93	9/96	1.2	HK$/HK$
Cons Elec Power	350,000	10/94	9/96	0.1	HK$/HK$
Culturecom	219,310	12/93	12/96	1	HK$/HK$
Dah Bang	40,000	7/94	7/97	1	HK$/HK$
Dah Hwa Intl	33,600	8/94	7/97	1	HK$/HK$
Dairy Farm*	20,000	8/92	8/95	1	US$/HK$
Dao Heng	200,000	2/94	1/96	0.1	HK$/HK$
Dharmala Hldg	96,000	10/93	6/96	1	HK$/HK$
Dickson Cons	61,600	12/92	12/95	1	HK$/HK$
Dransfield Hldg	46	4/93	12/95	1	HK$/HK$
Dynamic Hldg	2,500	1/94	12/96	1	HK$/HK$
Egana Intl	192,000	6/93	6/96	1	HK$/HK$
Emperor Int'l	71,854	4/92	8/95	0.13	HK$/HK$
Emperor Int'l	61,608	6/94	8/97	1	HK$/HK$
Englong Intl	21,582	3/92	3/97	1	HK$/HK$
Essential En	111,485	3/92	12/95	1.1	HK$/HK$
Fairyoung Hldg	63,168	11/94	6/96	1	HK$/HK$
Far East Hotel	94,833	2/94	3/96	1	HK$/HK$
First Asia	88,686	9/94	9/95	1	HK$/HK$
Fourseas Travel	160,000	10/92	9/95	1	HK$/HK$
Frankie Dom	1,000	4/94	6/97	1	HK$/HK$
Fung Cheung	80,000	4/91	9/95	1	HK$/HK$
Gold Face	90,000	5/94	3/96	1	HK$/HK$
Gold Lion	73,000	9/93	7/95	1	HK$/HK$
Gold Lion	73,000	8/93	7/96	1	HK$/HK$
Gold Peak In	41,186	1092	10/95	1	HK$/HK$
Govett Asia	7,500	4/93	12/98	1	HK$/HK$
Great Wall Ent	83,647	8/93	3/96	1	HK$/HK$
Group Sense	160,000	1/93	12/95	1	HK$/HK$
Guangdong Intl*	400,000	10/94	3/96	0.1	HK$/HK$
Hang Lung	150,000	2/94	7/95	0.1	HK$/HK$
Hang Lung	500	12/94	10/97	1	HK$/HK$
Hang Seng	100,000	1/94	1/96	0.1	HK$/HK$
Hang Seng	50,000	4/95	5/96	0.1	HK$/HK$
Hang Seng*	100,000	8/94	1/96	0.1	HK$/HK$
Hang Seng*	6,000	8/94	1/96	0.1	HK$/HK$

HONG KONG (continued)

Issuer	Amount (000s)	Issue Date	Expiry Date	Shs/ Wrnt	Currency Shs/Wrnt
Harbour Ring	270,900	8/94	7/97	1	HK$/HK$
HB Int'l	22,500	5/94	5/97	1	HK$/HK$
Henderson	100,000	3/95	8/96	0.1	HK$/HK$
Henderson*	200	11/93	11/95	0.1	HK$/HK$
Henderson*	300,000	6/95	8/96	0.1	HK$/HK$
Henderson*	750,000	9.94	1/96	0.1	HK$/HK$
Henderson	256,483	12/94	3/96	1	HK$/HK$
HK30 Index-g	5,000	2/95	5/96	0.2	HK$/DM
HK30 Index-g#	5,000	2/95	5/96	0.2	HK$/DM
HK30 Index-g	5,000	2/95	8/96	0.2	HK$/DM
HK30 Index-g#	5,000	2/95	8/96	0.2	HK$/DM
HK30 Index-g#	5,000	2/95	2/97	0.2	HK$/DM
HK30 Index-g	5,000	2/95	2/97	0.2	HK$/DM
HK30 Index-us	2,600	10/93	10/95	2	HK$/US$
HK30 Index-us#	2,400	10/93	10/95	2	HK$/US$
HK30 Index-us#	1,500	12/93	6/96	3	HK$/US$
HK30 Index-us	1,000	12/93	6/96	3	HK$/US$
HK30 Index-us	1,600	12.93	12/95	1	HK$/US$
HK30 Index-us	1,150	11/93	11/95	10	HK$/US$
HK30 Index-us	6,000	10/93	11/96	2	HK$/US$
HK30 Index-us#	6,300	1/94	1/96	3.03	HK$/US$
HK30 Index-us	6,300	1/94	1/96	3.03	HK$/US$
HK30 Index-us#	2,400	2/94	8/96	3	HK$/US$
Hoi Sing Hldg	43,600	2/92	3/96	1	HK$/HK$
Hong Kong China	186,024	11/92	9/95	1	HK$/HK$
Hong Kong China	50,000	3/94	1/96	1.44	HK$/HK$
Hong Kong China	60,000	12/93	11/95	1.44	HK$/HK$
Hong Kong China	170,000	5/95	6/96	0.1	HK$/HK$
Hong Kong China	169,426	5/94	12/95	1.44	HK$/HK$
Hong Kong Dly	23,319	5/93	12/95	1	HK$/HK$
Hong Kong Eng*	250,000	3/94	3/96	0.1	HK$/HK$
Hong Kong Eng	80,000	6/95	11/96	0.1	HK$/HK$
Hong Kong Ferry	220,979	7/94	6/96	1	HK$/HK$
Hong Kong Mac	49,237	12/92	12/95	0.6	HK$/HK$
Hong Kong Land*	350,000	1/94	1/96	0.1	HK$/HK$
Hong Kong Pkvw	106,905	10/94	12/96	1	HK$/HK$
Hong Kong Tel*	450,000	12/93	11/95	0.1	HK$/HK$
Hong Kong Tel	192,184	9/90	10/95	1	HK$/HK$
Hong Kong Tel*	100,000	3/94	1/96	0.1	HK$/HK$

HONG KONG (continued)

Issuer	Amount (000s)	Issue Date	Expiry Date	Shs/ Wrnt	Currency Shs/Wrnt
Hong Kong Tel*	200,000	6/94	11/95	0.1	HK$/HK$
Hong Kong Tel*	500,000	7/94	12/95	0.1	HK$/HK$
Hop Hing Hldg	70,276	11/94	12/97	1	HK$/HK$
Hopewell	750,000	4/95	4/96	0.1	HK$/HK$
Hopewell*	200,000	8/94	1/96	1	HK$/HK$
Hopewell*	250,000	9/93	9/95	0.1	HK$/HK$
HSBC Hldg*	300,000	3/94	2/96	0.1	HK$/HK$
HSBC Hldg*	140	1/94	1/96	0.1	HK$/HK$
HSBC Hldg*	50,000	3/95	2/97	0.1	HK$/HK$
HSBC Hldg*	100,000	6/94	12/95	0.1	HK$/HK$
HSBC Hldg*	250,000	3/94	1/96	0.1	HK$/HK$
HSBC Hldg*	50,000	6/95	6/96	0.1	HK$/HK$
HSBC Hldg*	100,000	6/94	12/95	0.1	HK$/HK$
HSBC Hldg	1,000	9/93	8/95	0.1	HK$/HK$
HS Index	40,000	4/95	2/97	100	HK$/HK$
HS Index	10,000	1/94	11/95	100	HK$/HK$
Hutchison*	200,000	6/94	11/95	0.1	HK$/HK$
Hutchison*	50,000	4/95	3/96	0.1	HK$/HK$
Hutchison	250,000	12/93	12/95	0.1	HK$/HK$
Hutchison*	30	7/93	7/95	1	HK$/HK$
Hutchison	300,000	6/95	4/97	0.1	HK$/HK$
Hutchison*	60,000	4/95	6/96	0.1	HK$/HK$
Hutchison	300,000	6/95	4/97	0.1	HK$/HK$
Hutchison-I	30	2/95	2/96	1	HK$/HK$
Hysan Dev*	20,000	10/93	9/95	1	HK$/HK$
Hysan Dev	100,000	4/94	9/95	0.1	HK$/HK$
Hysan Dev	1,500	5/91	12/95	1	HK$/HK$
Ideal Pac	1	10/94	9/97	1	HK$/HK$
Indesen Ind	49,981	8/92	7/95	1	HK$/HK$
Innovative Ind	49,981	9/92	3/96	1	HK$/HK$
Interform	15,000	5/94	4/97	1	HK$/HK$
Jinhui Hold	101,654	10/93	12/95	1	HK$/HK$
JF Indonesia	9,994	12/92	12/95	1	HK$/HK$
Keng Fong	2,500	12/93	12/95	1	HK$/HK$
Kingmaker	1	10/94	6/97	1	HK$/HK$
Kosonic Intl	76,000	3/93	2/96	1	HK$/HK$
KTP Hldg	1	4/92	12/96	1	HK$/HK$
Lafe Intl	27,043	7/89	7/96	1	HK$/HK$
Leading Spir	42,002	3/94	6/96	1	HK$/HK$

HONG KONG (continued)

Issuer	Amount (000s)	Issue Date	Expiry Date	Shs/ Wrnt	Currency Shs/Wrnt
Leefung Asco	48,440	1/92	12/95	1.1	HK$/HK$
Linkful Intl	120,000	3/93	3/96	1	HK$/HK$
Lucky Man	39,088	5/93	12/96	1	HK$/HK$
Luks Intd	120,658	8/93	6/96	1	HK$/HK$
Magnum Intl	80,000	12/92	11/95	1	HK$/HK$
Magnum Intl	41,001	1/95	2/98	1	HK$/HK$
Mandarin Dra	92,720	10/93	12/96	1	HK$/HK$
Mansion Hldg	45,000	7/92	7/95	1	HK$/HK$
Mei Ah Intl	50,000	10/93	10/96	1	HK$/HK$
Min Xin Hldg	59,409	4/94	12/96	1	HK$/HK$
Morning Star	61,311	9/93	9/96	1	HK$/HK$
Nam Pei Hong	22,419	11/91	10/96	1.01	HK$/HK$
Nam Hing Hldg	70,156	2/95	12/96	1	HK$/HK$
New World Dev	200,000	3/94	2/96	0.1	HK$/HK$
New World Dev	56,612	4/93	4/96	1	HK$/HK$
New World Dev	200,000	3/94	2/96	0.1	HK$/HK$
New World Dev	120,000	3/95	3/96	0.1	HK$/HK$
Ngai Lik Ind	65,999	9/92	9/95	1	HK$/HK$
Ocean Info	59,549	9/94	9/96	1	HK$/HK$
Onfem Hldg	54,509	9/94	8/97	1	HK$/HK$
Oriental Metal	1	12/94	12/96	1	HK$/HK$
Pac Andes	1	10/94	9/97	1	HK$/HK$
Paliburg Dev	300,000	1/95	12/96	1	HK$/HK$
Paliburg Dev	150,000	1/95	12/97	1	HK$/HK$
Paramount	46,867	1/93	12/95	1	HK$/HK$
Paul Y ITC	152,200	9/93	9/95	1	HK$/HK$
Pearl Oriental	250,000	1/94	12/96	1	HK$/HK$
Perfectech	32,000	10/92	12/95	1	HK$/HK$
Pico Far East	258,100	2/94	4/96	1	HK$/HK$
Prod Art Tech	128,817	5/95	9/96	1	HK$/HK$
QPL Intl	82,582	4/94	2/96	1	HK$/HK$
Rhine Hldg	56,000	4/91	12/96	1	HK$/HK$
Rivera	253,574	3/94	1/97	1	HK$/HK$
Rockapetta	60,000	2/94	2/97	1	HK$/HK$
SAS Dragon	48,000	10/94	9/96	1	HK$/HK$
Sea Hold	174,972	12/87	12/08	2.39	HK$/HK$
Seapower Res	243,262	9/93	9/96	1	HK$/HK$
Seaunion	468,043	9/94	12/95	1	HK$/HK$
Shang Intl	64,900	9/93	12/95	1	HK$/HK$

HONG KONG (continued)

Issuer	Amount (000s)	Issue Date	Expiry Date	Shs/ Wrnt	Currency Shs/Wrnt
Shang Intl	10,000	1/94	11/96	1	HK$/HK$
Sharp Brave	337,500	10/92	9/95	1	HK$/HK$
Shell Elec	70,780	4/94	3/96	1	HK$/HK$
Shougang Tech	54,360	3/91	12/95	1	HK$/HK$
Shun Cheong	260,000	10/92	9/95	1	HK$/HK$
Shun Shing	2,500	1/94	2/96	1	HK$/HK$
Singamas Con	76,000	7/95	6/97	1	HK$/HK$
Sino Land	190,255	1/93	10/97	1.2	HK$/HK$
Sino Land	180,713	6/91	12/95	1.1	HK$/HK$
S.Megga Intl	87,357	12/91	12/96	1	HK$/HK$
South China Br	80,000	7/93	7/95	1	HK$/HK$
South China Br	80,000	7/93	7/95	1	HK$/HK$
Stone Elect	120,000	3/93	3/96	1	HK$/HK$
Star Enter	56,000	7/94	9/95	1	HK$/HK$
Star Paging	95,656	8/94	12/96	1	HK$/HK$
Starlight Ind	101,391	9/93	7/95	0.31	HK$/HK$
Styland Hldg	102,243	3/92	12/96	1	HK$/HK$
Sun Fook Kong	159,221	7/94	6/99	1	HK$/HK$
Sun Hung Kai	65,000	4/95	6/96	0.1	HK$/HK$
Sun Hung Kai	150,000	10/94	3/96	0.1	HK$/HK$
Sun Hung Kai	40,000	6/95	6/96	0.1	HK$/HK$
Sun Hung Kai*	100,000	6/94	1/96	0.1	HK$/HK$
Swire Pacific	100,000	4/94	4/96	0.1	HK$/HK$
Swire Pacific	13,000	6/94	11/95	0.1	HK$/HK$
Swire Pacific	300,000	2/94	1/96	0.1	HK$/HK$
Swire Pacific	80,000	2/95	3/96	0.1	HK$/HK$
Tak Hsin Hldg	60,000	2/93	2/96	1	HK$/HK$
Tak Wing Inv	22,911	11/94	10/96	1	HK$/HK$
Tem Fat Hing	182,733	10/92	10/95	1	HK$/HK$
Tian An China	175,363	1/94	1/96	1	HK$/HK$
Top Glory	183,022	1/91	11/95	1	HK$/HK$
Truly Intl	40,220	9/94	8/96	1	HK$/HK$
Tsim Sha Tsui	111,034	1/93	10/97	1	HK$/HK$
Tung Fong	89,042	12/91	11/96	1	HK$/HK$
Universal Ap	1,418,625	5/94	12/96	1	HK$/HK$
Uniworld Hldg	2,207,990	10/94	10/95	1	HK$/HK$
Van Shung	49,334	2/94	2/96	1	HK$/HK$
Vincent Int	38,788	9/93	9/95	1	HK$/HK$
Vtech Hldg	9,311	4/92	9/96	1	HK$/HK$

HONG KONG (continued)

Issuer	Amount (000s)	Issue Date	Expiry Date	Shs/ Wrnt	Currency Shs/Wrnt
Wah Nam Group	192,508	4/94	5/96	1	HK$/HK$
Wai Kee Hldg	125,036	10/94	12/96	1	HK$/HK$
Wanon Intl	52,800	4/93	3/96	1	HK$/HK$
Wharf Hldg	100,000	4/95	7/96	0.1	HK$/HK$
Wharf Hldg*	180,000	2/94	7/95	0.1	HK$/HK$
Wharf Hldg*	200,000	2/94	8/95	0.1	HK$/HK$
Wheelock	50,000	1/94	12/95	1	HK$/HK$
Wheelock*	30,000	10/93	10/95	1	HK$/HK$
Winfoong Inv	114,879	5/93	5/98	1	HK$/HK$
Wing Fai Int'l	77,600	10/94	10/97	1	HK$/HK$
World House	1,000	8/93	12/95	1	HK$/HK$
Yau Lee Hldg	150,952	8/91	8/96	1.02	HK$/HK$
Yeebo Intl	91,410	10/94	8/96	1	HK$/HK$
Yiu Wing Int	48,494	2/95	3/96	1	HK$/HK$
Yiu Wing Int	115,415	2/95	3/97	1	HK$/HK$
Yugang Intl	25,000	11/93	10/96	1	HK$/HK$

put, * covered, us-US listed, g-German listed, l-Luxembourg listed

INDIA

Issuer	Amount (000s)	Issue Date	Expiry Date	Shs/ Wrnt	Currency Shs/Wrnt
Bombay Dyeing-l	500	1/94	12/95	1	IRP/US$
CESC-l	1	4/94	4/96	1	IRP/US$
Hindalco Ind-s	1	11/93	11/95	1	IRP/CHF
Hindalco Ind-l	1	11/93	11/95	1	IRP/US$
Hindustan Dev-l	1	11/94	9/96	1	IRP/US$
ITC-l	500	10/93	11/95	1	IRP/US$
Tata Engineer-l	500	7/94	3/96	1	IRP/US$

l-Luxembourg listed, s-Swiss listed

JAPAN

Issuer	Amount (000s)	Issue Date	Expiry Date	Shs/ Wrnt	Currency Shs/Wrnt
Aderans-s	70	8/93	8/97	39.4	JPY/CHF
Advantest-s	20	7/91	7/95	100	JPY/CHF
AG Ajikawa-s	25	9/93	9/97	91.2	JPY/CHF
Aichi Toke-s	60	10/93	10/97	100	JPY/CHF
Aigan-s	65	7/93	7/97	37.4	JPY/CHF
Akebono Br-s	150	8/93	7/97	119	JPY/CHF
Akebono Br-s	115	7/91	7/95	100	JPY/CHF
Akiyama-s	75	10/93	10/97	46.9	JPY/CHF
Almetax-s	100	2/94	2/98	57.6	JPY/CHF
Alpine Elec-s	11	12/91	12/95	466	JPY/US$
Alpine Elec	11	12/91	12/95	466	JPY/US$
Aoki Intl-s	300	6/93	6/97	17.4	JPY/CHF
Apollo Elec-s	18	5/91	5/96	100	JPY/CHF
Arab Oil-s	40	9/91	9/95	115	JPY/US$
Arab Oil	40	9/91	9/95	115	JPY/US$
Asahi Glass-s	74	6/91	6/98	590	JPY/US$
Asahi Glass	74	6/91	6/98	590	JPY/US$
Asahipen-s	80	10/93	10/97	109	JPY/CHF
Asakawagum-s	50	7/91	8/95	100	JPY/CHF
Autobacs-s	20	3/92	3/96	87.9	JPY/US$
Autobacs	20	2/95	2/99	56.2	JPY/US$
Autobacs	20	3/92	3/96	87.9	JPY/US$
Bandai Co-s	50	10/93	11/97	162	JPY/US$
Bandai Co	50	10/93	11/97	162	JPY/US$
Best Denki-s	32	5/93	5/97	370	JPY/US$
Best Denki	32	5/93	5/97	370	JPY/US$
Bunka Shut	20	3/94	3/98	667	JPY/US$
C Cube Co-s	34	2/92	2/96	118	JPY/CHF
C Cube Co-s	25	4/93	4/98	102	JPY/CHF
Canon Sale-s	360	10/92	10/96	54.2	JPY/CHF
Canon Sale-s	450	10/93	11/97	27.3	JPY/CHF
Casio Comp-s	50	11/91	11/95	479	JPY/US$
Casio Comp-s	70	2/93	3/97	642	JPY/US$
Casio Comp	50	11/91	11/95	479	JPY/US$
Casio Comp	70	2/93	3/97	642	JPY/US$
Chiyoda Co-s	54	9/92	10/96	316	JPY/US$
Chiyoda Co	54	9/92	10/96	316	JPY/US$
Chubu Eng-s	35	8/93	8/97	46.9	JPY/CHF
Chubu Seki-s	40	3/94	2/98	45	JPY/CHF

JAPAN (continued)

Issuer	Amount (000s)	Issue Date	Expiry Date	Shs/ Wrnt	Currency Shs/Wrnt
Chubu Steel-g	100	7/91	7/95	48.7	JPY/DM
Chubu Steel-s	100	7/91	7/95	48.7	JPY/DM
Chugai Pharm	44	5/93	5/97	353	JPY/US$
Chugai Pharm-s	44	5/93	5/97	353	JPY/US$
Chugoku Ma-s	70	10/92	10/96	158	JPY/CHF
Chuo Wool-g	30	12/91	10/95	66.1	JPY/DM
Citizen Watch-s	1	10/92	10/96	92.8	JPY/DM
Citizen Watch-g	1	10/92	10/96	92.8	JPY/DM
Citizen Watch	40	10/92	10/96	683	JPY/US$
Citizen Watch-s	40	10/92	10/96	683	JPY/US$
CKD Corp-s	70	12/93	11/97	98.7	JPY/CHF
Cleanup Co-s	50	11/93	12/97	41	JPY/CHF
Cleanup Co	14	11/93	12/97	307	JPY/US$
Cleanup Co	14	11/93	12/97	307	JPY/US$
Cosmo Oil-l	60	3/94	3/98	606	JPY/US$
Cosmo Oil	60	3/94	3/98	606	JPY/US$
Credit Sai-s	30	4/91	4/96	306	JPY/US$
Credit Sai	30	4/91	4/96	306	JPY/US$
Dai-ichi Hotel-s	33	6/91	6/96	100	JPY/CHF
Dai-ichi Pharm-s	200	4/93	4/97	43.2	JPY/CHF
Daicel Chem-s	40	8/91	8/95	1167	JPY/US$
Daicel Chem	40	8/91	8/95	1168	JPY/US$
Daido Hoxan-s	200	7/93	8/97	109	JPY/CHF
Daido Steel-s	44	7/91	7/96	1232	JPY/US$
Daido Steel-s	112	9/91	9/98	100	JPY/CHF
Daido Steel	40	7/93	7/97	943	JPY/US$
Daido Steel	44	7/91	7/96	1232	JPY/US$
Daido Steel-s	40	7/93	7/97	943	JPY/US$
Daiho Cons-s	70	3/94	2/98	74.9	JPY/CHF
Daiken Corp-g	150	7/91	7/95	94	JPY/DM
Daiken Corp-s	150	7/91	7/95	94	JPY/DM
Daiko Denc-s	55	1/92	2/96	43.3	JPY/CHF
Dainic Col-s	100	6/93	6/97	85.4	JPY/CHF
Dainippon Sh-s	55	3/94	3/98	77.7	JPY/CHF
Daio Paper	20	3/95	2/99	489	JPY/US$
Daishinku Co-s	60	3/92	3/96	79	JPY/DM
Daishinku Co-g	60	3/92	3/96	79	JPY/DM
Daishinku Co-s	100	8/95	8/99	66	JPY/CHF
Daito Gyo-s	25	9/92	10/96	265	JPY/CHF

JAPAN (continued)

Issuer	Amount (000s)	Issue Date	Expiry Date	Shs/ Wrnt	Currency Shs/Wrnt
Daito Kogyo-s	92	9/91	9/95	100	JPY/CHF
Daito Seiki-g	40	7/91	8/95	23	JPY/DM
Daiwa Danchi-g	150	2/92	2/96	91.9	JPY/DM
Daiwa Danchi-s	150	2/92	2/96	91.9	JPY/DM
Daiwa House-g	400	5/91	4/96	39.3	JPY/DM
Daiwa House-s	300	11/92	11/96	62.2	JPY/CHF
Daiwa House-s	70	4/91	4/96	327	JPY/US$
Daiwa House-s	400	5/91	4/96	39.3	JPY/DM
Daiwa House-s	60	11/92	11/96	444	JPY/US$
Daiwa House	60	11/92	11/96	442	JPY/US$
Daiwa House	60	10/93	10/97	333	JPY/US$
Daiwa House	70	4/91	4/96	327	JPY/US$
Daiwa Ind-s	50	10/92	11/96	98.8	JPY/CHF
Daiwa Ind-s	70	7/95	7/99	84.8	JPY/CHF
Daiwa Ind	10	11/93	11/97	464	JPY/US$
Daiwa Kosh-s	34	9/91	9/95	438	JPY/US$
Daiwa Kosh	34	9/91	9/95	438	JPY/US$
Daiwa Kosh	40	6/93	6/97	401	JPY/US$
Daiwa Kosh-s	40	6/93	6/97	401	JPY/US$
Daiwa Rak	17	6/93	6/97	222	JPY/US$
Daiwa Sei-s	40	2/93	3/98	110	JPY/CHF
Denki Kogy-s	30	3/94	3/98	52	JPY/CHF
Denyo Co	10	1/94	1/98	371	JPY/US$
Domy Co-s	35	12/93	12/97	75.1	JPY/CHF
Dowa Mining-l	26	11/93	12/97	1283	JPY/US$
Dowa Mining-s	24	1/92	1/96	1304	JPY/US$
Dowa Mining-s	24	3/93	3/97	1064	JPY/US$
Dowa Mining-s	20	11/92	11/96	1218	JPY/US$
Dowa Mining-s	26	12/93	12/97	1276	JPY/US$
Dowa Mining	24	1/92	1/96	1304	JPY/US$
Dowa Mining	20	11/92	11/96	1218	JPY/US$
Dowa Mining	24	3/93	3/97	1064	JPY/US$
Dowa Mining	26	11/93	12/97	1284	JPY/US$
Dowa Mining	20	3/95	2/99	992	JPY/US$
Ebara-g	160	3/94	3/98	39.6	JPY/DM
Ebara-s	30	3/92	3/96	413	JPY/US$
Ebara	30	3/92	3/96	413	JPY/US$
Eidensha Co-g	60	2/92	2/96	64.6	JPY/DM
Eidensha Co	12	9/93	8/97	393	JPY/US$

JAPAN (continued)

Issuer	Amount (000s)	Issue Date	Expiry Date	Shs/ Wrnt	Currency Shs/Wrnt
Eidensha Co-s	60	2/92	2/96	64.6	JPY/DM
Enplas Co-s	30	8/92	8/96	42.4	JPY/CHF
Ezaki Glico-s	100	9/94	9/98	69.6	JPY/CHF
Exedy Corp-s	70	2/94	2/98	51.2	JPY/CHF
Footwork Con-s	40	2/94	1/98	33.8	JPY/CHF
Footwork Int-s	48	10/90	9/95	100	JPY/CHF
Footwork Int-g	60	2/92	3/96	64.7	JPY/DM
Footwork Int-s	60	3/92	3/96	64.7	JPY/DM
FP Corp-s	90	10/93	10/97	23.4	JPY/CHF
Fudo Const-s	100	4/93	4/97	115	JPY/CHF
Fuji Co-s	39	6/91	6/98	115	JPY/CHF
Fuji Ph-s	50	9/94	9/98	64	JPY/CHF
Fuji Oil-s	20	9/91	9/95	688	JPY/US$
Fuji Oil	20	9/91	9/95	688	JPY/US$
Fuji Seiko-s	20	10/90	11/95	106	JPY/CHF
Fuji Seiko-s	35	3/92	4/96	104	JPY/CHF
Fuji Univa-s	25	6/93	6/97	98.9	JPY/CHF
Fujikura-s	40	2/91	2/98	698	JPY/US$
Fujikura-s	100	12/91	12/98	119	JPY/CHF
Fujikura	40	2/91	2/98	698	JPY/US$
Fujisawa Phar-g	150	6/91	6/96	45.8	JPY/DM
Fujisawa Phar-s	150	6/91	6/96	45.8	JPY/DM
Fujitec-s	100	11/93	10/97	60	JPY/CHF
Fujitec-s	12	11/93	10/97	445	JPY/US$
Fujitec	12	10/93	10/97	445	JPY/US$
Fujitsu-s	256	6/91	6/98	100	JPY/CHF
Furukawa-s	147	7/90	8/95	135	JPY/CHF
Furukawa	20	8/91	8/95	883	JPY/US$
Gastec Ser-s	60	10/94	9/98	106	JPY/CHF
Godo Steel-s	20	2/93	2/97	643	JPY/US$
Godo Steel	20	2/93	2/97	643	JPY/US$
Goldwin-s	100	1/92	1/96	94	JPY/CHF
Goldwin-s	40	3/93	3/97	82.5	JPY/CHF
Goldwin-s	300	7/94	7/98	55	JPY/CHF
Gourmet-s	17	7/91	7/95	120	JPY/CHF
Gunze	26	5/92	4/96	1133	JPY/US$
Gunze-s	26	4/92	4/96	1132	JPY/US$
Hac Kimisawa-g	50	2/92	2/96	50.3	JPY/DM
Hac Kimisawa-s	50	2/92	2/96	1	JPY/DM

JAPAN (continued)

Issuer	Amount (000s)	Issue Date	Expiry Date	Shs/ Wrnt	Currency Shs/Wrnt
Haneda-s	25	12/92	12/96	177	JPY/CHF
Hankyu Corp-s	50	1/91	2/98	1085	JPY/US$
Hankyu Corp	50	1/91	2/98	1085	JPY/US$
Hankyu Dep-s	40	3/91	3/96	445	JPY/US$
Hankyu Dep	40	3/91	3/96	445	JPY/US$
Hanwa Co-s	72	1/92	2/96	514	JPY/US$
Hanwa Co	71	1/92	2/96	514	JPY/US$
Harashin-s	35	2/94	2/98	69.3	JPY/CHF
Harima-s	34	7/91	7/95	100	JPY/CHF
Haseko Co	50	11/89	12/95	598	JPY/JPY
Heiwa Paper-s	35	10/93	10/97	47.3	JPY/CHF
Heiwado-s	200	11/93	10/97	35.7	JPY/CHF
Hibiya Eng-s	50	11/92	11/96	117	JPY/CHF
Hitachi In-s	100	3/92	3/96	56	JPY/CHF
Hitachi Zo-s	40	3/94	3/98	930	JPY/US$
Hitachi Zo	40	3/94	3/98	930	JPY/US$
Hokkaido Can-s	20	8/91	9/95	417	JPY/US$
Hokkaido Can	20	8/91	9/95	417	JPY/US$
Hokkaido Gas-s	50	3/92	4/96	185	JPY/CHF
Hokkaido Gas-s	100	7/93	8/97	116	JPY/CHF
Hokuetsu Ind-s	30	10/90	11/95	100	JPY/CHF
Hokuetsu Paper-g	130	2/92	2/97	103	JPY/DM
Hokuetsu Paper-s	120	11/91	11/95	119	JPY/CHF
Hokuetsu Paper-s	130	2/93	2/97	103	JPY/DM
Hokuetsu Paper	14	3/94	3/98	614	JPY/US$
Home Wide-s	30	2/93	2/97	80.5	JPY/CHF
Home Wide-s	50	3/94	2/98	41.6	JPY/CHF
Honen Corp-s	10	12/92	12/96	955	JPY/US$
Honen Corp	10	12/92	12/96	955	JPY/US$
Hosiden-s	20	10/91	10/95	371	JPY/US$
Hosiden	20	10/91	10/95	371	JPY/US$
Hosokawa Mic	20	2/92	2/96	139	JPY/US$
Hosokawa Mic-s	20	2/92	2/96	139	JPY/US$
Hotel New Otani-s	50	11/91	12/95	134	JPY/CHF
Ibiden Co-s	150	10/93	10/97	83.2	JPY/CHF
Ichida-s	22	7/91	8/95	100	JPY/CHF
Ihara Chem-s	40	3/94	3/98	82.8	JPY/CHF
Ishihara-s	24	9/91	9/95	1372	JPY/US$
Ishihara	24	9/91	9/95	1372	JPY/US$

JAPAN (continued)

Issuer	Amount (000s)	Issue Date	Expiry Date	Shs/ Wrnt	Currency Shs/Wrnt
Ishizuka-s	99	9/90	10/95	100	JPY/CHF
Itochu Fuel-s	20	1/92	2/96	678	JPY/US$
Itochu Fuel	20	1/92	2/96	677	JPY/US$
Itochu Fuel	30	2/94	2/98	533	JPY/US$
Iwatani-s	196	6/91	6/98	104	JPY/CHF
Iwatani-s	200	9/92	9/96	145	JPY/CHF
Izumiya Co	10	1/87	2/97	528	JPY/JPY
Japan Brid-s	55	11/93	12/97	133	JPY/CHF
Japan Radio-s	30	3/92	3/96	290	JPY/US$
Japan Radio-s	150	3/94	3/98	36.6	JPY/CHF
Japan Radio	30	3/92	3/96	290	JPY/US$
Japan Radio	40	3/94	3/98	260	JPY/US$
Japan Steel-s	30	7/92	7/96	154	JPY/CHF
Japan Steel-s	30	7/91	7/95	1048	JPY/US$
Japan Steel	30	7/91	7/95	1048	JPY/US$
Japan Sto Ba-s	20	8/91	8/95	872	JPY/US$
Japan Sto Ba	20	8/91	8/95	872	JPY/US$
Japan Tran-s	100	6/93	6/97	86.5	JPY/CHF
JDC Corp	28	6/93	6/97	774	JPY/US$
JDC Corp-s	28	6/93	6/97	774	JPY/US$
JGC Corp-s	20	7/91	8/95	525	JPY/US$
JGC Corp-s	20	7/91	8/95	618	JPY/ECU
JGC Corp	20	7/91	8/95	525	JPY/US$
Juel Verit-s	30	3/94	3/98	88.3	JPY/CHF
Kaga Elec-s	14	7/91	7/95	100	JPY/CHF
Kaigen-s	30	2/94	2/98	68.9	JPY/CHF
Kameda Sei-s	16	11/91	12/95	100	JPY/CHF
Kamigumi-g	300	9/92	9/96	91.7	JPY/DM
Kamigumi-g	450	12/93	12/97	54	JPY/DM
Kamigumi-s	300	4/93	4/97	71.4	JPY/CHF
Kamigumi-s	450	12/93	12/97	54	JPY/DM
Kamigumi-s	300	9/92	9/96	91.7	JPY/DM
Kanamoto-s	60	8/93	8/97	37.8	JPY/CHF
Kansai Sup-s	60	10/92	10/96	86.6	JPY/CHF
Kasai Kogyo-g	44	9/93	9/97	120	JPY/DM
Kasumi Co	20	9/93	9/97	435	JPY/US$
Katokichi	38	9/93	9/97	161	JPY/US$
Katsum Const-s	20	9/92	9/96	160	JPY/CHF
Kawasaki Eng-s	59	12/90	12/95	160	JPY/CHF

JAPAN (continued)

Issuer	Amount (000s)	Issue Date	Expiry Date	Shs/ Wrnt	Currency Shs/Wrnt
Kawasaki Eng-s	100	12/91	12/96	109	JPY/CHF
Kawasaki Heavy-s	72	8/91	8/95	1383	JPY/US$
Kawasaki Heavy	72	8/91	8/95	1383	JPY/US$
Kawasumi Lab-g	65	9/93	9/97	25.4	JPY/DM
Kawasumi Lab-s	65	9/93	9/97	25.4	JPY/DM
Keihin Elec-s	100	10/92	10/96	232	JPY/CHF
Keihin Elec-l	50	9/93	8/97	709	JPY/US$
Keihin Elec	50	9/93	8/97	709	JPY/US$
Keisei Ele-s	40	4/93	3/97	533	JPY/US$
Keisei Ele	40	4/93	3/97	533	JPY/US$
Keisei Ele	50	3/94	3/98	553	JPY/US$
Keityo Co-s	20	7/91	7/95	272	JPY/US$
Keiyo Co-s	80	10/92	10/96	62.9	JPY/CHF
Keiyo Co-g	100	7/93	7/97	30.2	JPY/DM
Keiyo Co-s	100	7/93	7/97	30.2	JPY/DM
Keiyo Co	20	7/91	7/95	272	JPY/US$
Keiyo Teito-s	200	1/93	1/97	169	JPY/CHF
Kibun Food-s	25	3/94	2/98	161	JPY/CHF
Kikusui-s	35	3/94	3/98	55.1	JPY/CHF
King Co-s	60	11/93	12/97	101	JPY/CHF
Kinki Nippon-s	300	3/94	3/01	86.2	JPY/CHF
Kinki Sharyo-s	70	6/91	6/96	106	JPY/CHF
Kissei Pha-s	20	11/92	10/96	193	JPY/US$
Kissei Pha	20	11/92	10/96	193	JPY/US$
Kissei Pha	20	2/94	1/98	115	JPY/US$
Kitakei-s	25	7/95	8/99	83.8	JPY/CHF
Kitano Con-s	150	6/93	6/97	66.6	JPY/CHF
Kobayashi-s	40	11/91	11/95	117	JPY/CHF
Kobe Elec-s	90	4/92	5/96	144	JPY/CHF
Kobe Elec-s	90	4/93	5/97	110	JPY/CHF
Kobe Steel-s	74	6/91	6/96	1333	JPY/US$
Kobe Steel	74	6/91	6/96	1333	JPY/US$
Kokune Con-s	45	3/93	3/97	154	JPY/CHF
Komatsu Seir-s	20	7/91	7/95	455	JPY/US$
Komatsu Seir	20	7/91	7/95	455	JPY/US$
Konami Co-s	142	7/91	7/95	11	JPY/CHF
Kubota Corp-s	150	8/94	8/98	101	JPY/CHF
Kumagai-s	72	8/91	8/95	975	JPY/US$
Kuraray-s	100	7/92	8/96	102	JPY/CHF

JAPAN (continued)

Issuer	Amount (000s)	Issue Date	Expiry Date	Shs/ Wrnt	Currency Shs/Wrnt
Kuraray-s	300	4/93	5/97	68.5	JPY/CHF
Kuraray-s	30	7/92	8/96	678	JPY/US$
Kuraray-s	100	5/91	6/96	111	JPY/CHF
Kuraray	20	2/95	1/99	485	JPY/US$
Kuraray	30	7/92	8/96	678	JPY/US$
Kuraray	40	1/94	1/98	525	JPY/US$
Kurita Water-s	20	8/91	8/95	283	JPY/US$
Kurita Water	20	8/91	8/95	283	JPY/US$
KYC Machine-s	50	3/92	3/96	71.7	JPY/CHF
Kyocera-s	1000	8/95	2/97	1	JPY/CHF
Kyocera	100	1/94	1/98	87.8	JPY/US$
Kyokutu-s	23	2/93	2/97	172	JPY/CHF
Kyoritsu-s	37	10/91	9/95	100	JPY/CHF
Kyoto Tool-s	25	3/93	2/97	103	JPY/CHF
Lecien Corp-s	56	10/91	10/95	103	JPY/CHF
Limit Ind-s	31	11/90	12/95	100	JPY/CHF
Lintec-s	14	10/93	9/97	285	JPY/CHF
Lion Corp	20	12/92	12/96	1080	JPY/US$
Lion Corp-g	150	12/93	12/97	112	JPY/DM
Lion Corp-s	20	12/92	12/96	1080	JPY/US$
Lion Corp-s	150	12/93	12/97	112	JPY/DM
Lion Corp-s	100	6/95	6/99	148	JPY/CHF
Lintec	14	9/93	9/97	285	JPY/US$
Longchamp-s	39	7/91	8/95	100	JPY/CHF
Maeda Corp-s	40	2/93	2/97	736	JPY/US$
Maeda Corp	40	3/94	2/98	429	JPY/US$
Maeda Corp	40	2/93	2/97	736	JPY/US$
Magara Const-s	60	12/91	12/95	104	JPY/CHF
Marudai-s	150	1/92	2/96	81.8	JPY/CHF
Marudai Food-g	150	2/92	2/96	81	JPY/DM
Marutomi Grp-g	70	7/91	8/95	13.9	JPY/DM
Marutomi Grp-g	90	3/92	4/96	15.9	JPY/DM
Marutomi Grp-s	70	7/91	8/95	79.4	JPY/DM
Marutomi Grp-s	90	3/92	4/96	15.9	JPY/DM
Maruwn-s	45	6/92	6/96	120	JPY/CHF
Maruwn-s	45	6/93	6/97	82.1	JPY/CHF
Maruzen-s	16	10/91	10/95	699	JPY/ECU
Maruzen-s	30	7/93	7/97	684	JPY/US$
Maruzen	30	7/93	7/97	684	JPY/US$

JAPAN (continued)

Issuer	Amount (000s)	Issue Date	Expiry Date	Shs/ Wrnt	Currency Shs/Wrnt
Matsuo Bri-s	35	10/92	10/96	131	JPY/CHF
Matsuo Bri-s	50	11/93	12/97	86.7	JPY/CHF
Matsush Elec-s	60	12/92	12/96	675	JPY/US$
Matsush Elec	40	8/91	9/95	546	JPY/US$
Matsush Elec	60	12/92	12/96	675	JPY/US$
Meiko Cons-s	22	8/91	8/95	100	JPY/CHF
Meisei Ind-s	100	3/95	2/99	90.6	JPY/CHF
Meisei Ind-s	33	6/91	7/96	106	JPY/CHF
Meisei Ind-s	50	8/92	8/96	104	JPY/CHF
Meisei Ind-s	100	11/93	12/97	60.7	JPY/CHF
Meitec-s	22	7/91	7/95	139	JPY/US$
Meitec	22	7/91	7/95	172	JPY/US$
Meitetsu-s	20	4/93	4/97	118	JPY/CHF
Meitetsu-s	50	5/94	5/98	83.6	JPY/CHF
Metalart-s	30	8/91	8/95	125	JPY/CHF
Metalart-s	20	3/94	2/98	179	JPY/CHF
Mikasa Coc-s	26	6/91	7/96	100	JPY/CHF
Minolta-g	200	4/91	4/98	102	JPY/DM
Minolta-s	200	4/91	4/98	102	JPY/DM
Misawa Cer-s	25	12/94	12/98	88	JPY/CHF
Misawa Home-s	29	12/91	11/95	423	JPY/US$
Misawa Home-s	150	3/95	3/99	78	JPY/CHF
Misawa Home	28	12/91	11/95	423	JPY/US$
Misawa Home-s	150	10/94	10/98	84.2	JPY/CHF
Mitsuba El-s	65	3/94	3/98	87.3	JPY/CHF
Mitsubishi Ca-s	26	7/91	8/95	830	JPY/US$
Mitsubishi Ca	26	7/91	8/95	830	JPY/US$
Mitsubishi Ch-s	60	7/91	8/95	1394	JPY/US$
Mitsubishi Ch	60	7/91	8/95	1394	JPY/US$
Mitsubishi El-g	200	4/91	4/98	99.6	JPY/DM
Mitsubishi El-s	200	4/91	4/98	99/6	JPY/DM
Mitsubishi Hv-s*	65	8/88	6/95	50	JPY/CHF
Mitsubishi Kak-s	100	8/94	8/98	61.9	JPY/CHF
Mitsubishi Mat-s	60	10/91	10/95	1272	JPY/ECU
Mitsubishi Oil-g	250	7/91	7/95	82.7	JPY/DM
Mitsubishi Oil-s	300	11/92	11/96	100	JPY/CHF
Mitsubishi Oil-s	46	7/92	7/96	754	JPY/USD
Mitsubishi Oil-s	30	7/91	7/95	759	JPY/CHF
Mitsubishi Oil-s*	6	8/95	8/98	520	JPY/US$

JAPAN (continued)

Issuer	Amount (000s)	Issue Date	Expiry Date	Shs/ Wrnt	Currency Shs/Wrnt
Mitsubishi Oil-s	40	7/93	7/97	545	JPY/US$
Mitsubishi Oil	46	7/92	7/96	753	JPY/US$
Mitsubishi Oil	40	7/93	7/97	545	JPY/US$
Mitsubishi Oil	30	7/91	7/95	759	JPY/US$
Mitsubishi Oil	50	3/94	3/98	535	JPY/US$
Mitsui Eng	76	1/92	1/96	1179	JPY/US$
Mitsui Eng-s	76	1/92	1/96	1179	JPY/US$
Mitsui Eng-s	400	4/93	3/97	1504	JPY/CHF
Mitsui Gre-s	30	9/93	9/97	38.1	JPY/CHF
Mitsui Min-s*	36	12/91	12/95	606	JPY/FRF
Mitsui Toa-s	60	2/90	1/98	773	JPY/US$
Mitsui Toa	60	2/90	1/98	773	JPY/US$
Miura Print-s	30	8/93	7/97	79.4	JPY/DM
Miura Print-g	30	8/93	7/97	79.4	JPY/DM
Miyaji Iron-s	54	8/90	8/95	101	JPY/CHF
Miyaji Iron-s	30	9/92	9/96	184	JPY/CHF
Miyaji Iron-s	40	3/94	3/98	101	JPY/CHF
Miyaji Iron-s	40	3/95	3/99	150	JPY/CHF
Mizuno-s	14	8/91	7/95	529	JPY/ECU
Moonbat-s	47	6/91	6/96	100	JPY/CHF
Morinaga-s	16	10/91	10/95	1071	JPY/ECU
Mr Max Co-g	100	7/91	7/95	42.4	JPY/DM
Mr Max Co-s	100	7/91	7/95	42.4	JPY/DM
Mr Max Co-s	220	3/94	2/98	27.3	JPY/CHF
Nagahori-s	33	9/91	8/95	100	JPY/CHF
Nagahori-s	45	11/93	12/97	82.1	JPY/CHF
Nagoya Rail-s	30	1/93	1/97	1426	JPY/US$
Nagoya Rail	30	1/93	1/97	1426	JPY/US$
Naigai-s	20	7/91	7/95	507	JPY/US$
Naigai	20	7/91	7/95	507	JPY/US$
Nakai Co-s	18	7/91	6/96	110	JPY/CHF
Nakai Co-s	50	3/94	3/98	40/5	JPY/CHF
Nakano Co	15	3/92	3/96	803	JPY/US$
Nakao Co-s	15	3/92	3/96	730	JPY/US$
Nakayama	24	7/91	7/96	501	JPY/US$
Nankai Con-s	45	8/93	8/97	128	JPY/CHF
Nankai Elec-s	60	4/92	4/96	945	JPY/US$
Nankai El	60	4/92	4/96	945	JPY/US$
Nankai El	60	12/93	12/97	715	JPY/US$

JAPAN (continued)

Issuer	Amount (000s)	Issue Date	Expiry Date	Shs/ Wrnt	Currency Shs/Wrnt
Narasaki-s	400	7/94	7/98	116	JPY/CHF
Narasaki-s	65	8/90	9/95	100	JPY/CHF
Neutren-s	40	9/92	9/96	135	JPY/CHF
NGK Ins-s	60	7/93	7/97	484	JPY/US$
NGK Ins	60	7/93	7/97	484	JPY/US$
NGK Spark-s	40	12/92	12/96	744	JPY/US$
NGK Spark	40	12/92	12/96	744	JPY/US$
NGK Spark	50	1/94	1/98	492	JPY/US$
Nichias-s	100	11/91	12/95	156	JPY/CHF
Nichias-s	150	11/93	11/97	146	JPY/CHF
Nichiha-s	50	3/94	3/98	42.4	JPY/CHF
Nichii Co-g	400	5/93	5/97	45.3	JPY/DM
Nichii Co-s	300	5/93	5/97	50	JPY/CHF
Nichii Co-s	400	5/93	5/97	45.3	JPY/DM
Nichirei Co-g	130	6/91	6/96	99.6	JPY/DM
Nichirei Co-s	130	6/91	6/96	99.6	JPY/DM
Nichirei Co	20	6/91	6/98	879	JPY/US$
Nihon Intl-s	58	8/91	8/95	100	JPY/CHF
Nihon Koden-s	40	1/92	1/96	83.5	JPY/CHF
Nihon Koden-s	70	3/93	3/97	54.4	JPY/CHF
Nihon Mata-s	75	12/93	12/97	112	JPY/CHF
Nihon Noh-s	60	4/92	5/96	97.3	JPY/CHF
Nihon Noh-s	70	10/93	11/97	65.8	JPY/CHF
Nikkei 225-l#	1,500	3/95	3/96	1	JPY/JPY
Nikkei 225-l#	1,500	3/95	3/96	1	JPY/JPY
Nikkei 225-l	3,000	9/95	12/96	1	JPY/JPY
Nikkei 225-l	2,000	3/95	3/96	1.68	JPY/JPY
Nikkei 225-l	2,000	3/95	3/96	1.68	JPY/JPY
Nikkei 225-l	2,000	3/95	3/96	1.68	JPY/JPY
Nikkei 225-l	2,000	3/95	3/96	1.68	JPY/JPY
Nikkei 225-l	2,000	3/95	3/96	1.68	JPY/JPY
Nikkei 225-l	2,000	3/95	3/96	1.68	JPY/JPY
Nikkei 225-l	2,000	3/95	3/96	1.68	JPY/JPY
Nikkei 225-g	10,000	7/95	3/97	0.1	JPY/DM
Nikkei 225-g#	10,000	7/95	3/97	0.1	JPY/DM
Nikkei 225-g#	2,000	5/95	11/96	0.1	JPY/DM
Nikkei 225-g	2,000	5/95	11/96	0.1	JPY/DM
Nikkei 225-g#	2,000	5/95	11/96	0.1	JPY/DM
Nikkei 225-g	10,000	7/95	3/97	0.1	JPY/DM

JAPAN (continued)

Issuer	Amount (000s)	Issue Date	Expiry Date	Shs/ Wrnt	Currency Shs/Wrnt
Nikkei 225-g#	10,000	7/95	3/97	0.1	JPY/DM
Nikkei 225-g	2,000	5/95	11/96	0.1	JPY/DM
Nikkei 225-g	10,000	7/95	3/97	0.1	JPY/DM
Nikkei 225-g#	2,000	5/95	11/96	0.1	JPY/DM
Nikkei 225-g#	10,000	7/95	3/97	0.1	JPY/DM
Nikkei 225-g	2,000	5/95	11/96	0.1	JPY/DM
Nikkei 225-g	10,000	7/95	3/97	0.1	JPY/DM
Nikkei 225-g#	10,000	7/95	3/97	0.1	JPY/DM
Nikkei 225-s	1,000	8/95	3/97	1	JPY/CHF
Nikkei 225-s	1,000	8/95	3/97	1	JPY/CHF
Nikkei 225-s	1,000	8/95	3/97	1	JPY/CHF
Nikkei 225-s#	1,000	8/95	3/97	1	JPY/CHF
Nikkei 225-s#	1,000	8/95	3/97	1	JPY/CHF
Nikkei 225-s	1,000	4/95	4/99	10	JPY/CHF
Nikkei 225-s	1,000	4/95	10/96	10	JPY/CHF
Nikkei 225-s#	1,000	4/95	4/96	10	JPY/CHF
Nikkei 225-s#	1,000	4/95	10/96	10	JPY/CHF
Nikkei 225-s	1,000	4/95	3/96	1	JPY/CHF
Nikkei 225-s	1,000	4/95	3/96	1	JPY/CHF
Nikkei 225-s	3,000	8/95	1/96	1	JPY/CHF
Nikkei 225-s	1,000	4/95	3/96	1	JPY/CHF
Nikkei 225-s#	1,000	4/95	3/96	1	JPY/CHF
Nikkei 225-s	500	4/95	10/96	1	JPY/CHF
Nikkei 225-s	500	4/95	10/96	1	JPY/CHF
Nikkei 225-s	500	4/95	10/96	1	JPY/CHF
Nikkei 225-s#	500	4/95	10/96	1	JPY/CHF
Nikkei 225-s#	500	4/95	10/96	1	JPY/CHF
Nikkei 225-s#	500	4/95	10/96	1	JPY/CHF
Nikkei 225-s	10,000	5/95	5/96	1	JPY/CHF
Nikkei 300-l	50,000	3/95	2/96	1	JPY/JPY
Nikkei 300-l	50,000	3/95	2/96	1	JPY/JPY
Nikkei 300-l	50,000	3/95	2/96	1	JPY/JPY
Nikkei 300-l	50,000	3/95	8/96	1	JPY/JPY
Nikkei 300-l	20,000	3/95	8/96	1	JPY/JPY
Nikkei 300-l	20,000	3/95	8/96	1	JPY/JPY
Nikkei 300-l	20,000	3/95	8/96	1	JPY/JPY
Nikkei 300-l	20,000	3/95	8/96	1	JPY/JPY
Nikkei 300-l	20,000	3/95	2/96	1	JPY/JPY
Nikkei 300-l	50,000	3/95	8/96	1	JPY/JPY

JAPAN (continued)

Issuer	Amount (000s)	Issue Date	Expiry Date	Shs/ Wrnt	Currency Shs/Wrnt
Nikkei 300-I	20,000	3/95	2/96	1	JPY/JPY
Nikkei 300-I	50,000	3/95	8/96	1	JPY/JPY
Nikkei 300-I	50,000	10/94	7/95	1	JPY/JPY
Nikkei 300-I	700	5/94	6/96	100	JPY/US$
Nikkei 300-I	700	5/94	6/97	100	JPY/US$
Nikkei 300-I	700	5/94	6/97	100	JPY/US$
Nikkei 300-I#	700	5/94	6/97	100	JPY/US$
Nikkei 300-I#	700	5/94	6/96	100	JPY/US$
Nikkei 300-I	5,000	11/93	10/95	50	JPY/US$
Nikkei 300-I	5,000	11/93	10/95	50	JPY/US$
Nikkei 300-I	5,000	11/93	10/95	50	JPY/US$
Nikkei 300-I	20,000	7/94	11/95	1	JPY/JPY
Nikkei 300-I	5,000	11/93	10/95	50	JPY/US$
Nikkei 300-I	5,000	11/93	10/95	50	JPY/US$
Nikkei 300-I	5,000	11/93	10/95	50	JPY/US$
Nikkei 300-I	20,000	7/94	11/95	1	JPY/JPY
Nikkei 300-I#	5,000	11/93	10/95	50	JPY/US$
Nikkei 300-I#	5,000	11/93	10/95	50	JPY/US$
Nikkei 300-I#	5,000	11/93	10/95	50	JPY/US$
Nikkei 300-I	20,000	7/94	11/95	1	JPY/JPY
Nikkei 300-I	20,000	7/94	11/95	1	JPY/JPY
Nikkei 300-g#	1,000	3/95	6/96	1	JPY/DM
Nikkei 300-g#	1,000	6/94	6/96	10	JPY/DM
Nikkei 300-g	1,000	3/95	6/96	1	JPY/DM
Nikkei 300-g	1,000	6/94	6/96	10	JPY/DM
Nikkei 300-g	10,000	6/94	6/96	10	JPY/DM
Nikkei 300-g#	1,000	6/94	6/96	10	JPY/DM
Nikkei 300-g	3,000	5/94	12/95	0.1	JPY/DM
Nikkei 300-g#	3,000	5/94	12/95	0.1	JPY/DM
Nikkei 300-g	500	5/94	12/95	0.01	JPY/DM
Nikkei 300-g#	500	5/94	12/95	0.01	JPY/DM
Nikkei 300-g	500	5/94	12/95	0.01	JPY/DM
Nikkei 300-g#	500	5/94	12/95	0.01	JPY/DM
Nikkei 300-g	500	5/94	12/95	0.01	JPY/DM
Nikkei 300-g#	500	5/94	12/95	0.01	JPY/DM
Nikkei 300-g	1,000	3/95	6/96	1	JPY/DM
Nikkei 300-g#	1,000	3/95	6/96	1	JPY/DM
Nikkei 300-g	1,000	3/95	6/96	1	JPY/DM
Nikkei 300-g#	1,000	3/95	6/96	1	JPY/DM

JAPAN (continued)

Issuer	Amount (000s)	Issue Date	Expiry Date	Shs/ Wrnt	Currency Shs/Wrnt
Nikkei 300-g	1,000	3/95	12/96	1	JPY/DM
Nikkei 300-g#	1,000	3/95	12/96	1	JPY/DM
Nikkei 300-s	8,000	8/95	8/96	1	JPY/CHF
Nikkei 300-s#	1,500	5/94	5/96	10	JPY/CHF
Nikkei 300-s#	1,500	5/94	5/96	10	JPY/CHF
Nikkei 300-s#	1,500	5/94	5/96	10	JPY/CHF
Nikkei 300-s	1,500	5/94	5/96	10	JPY/CHF
Nikkei 300-s	1,500	5/94	5/96	10	JPY/CHF
Nikkei 300-s#	500	5/94	6/96	10	JPY/CHF
Nikkei 300-s	500	5/94	6/96	10	JPY/CHF
Nikkei 300-s#	1,500	5/94	5/96	0.1	JPY/CHF
Nikkei 300-s	2,500	5/94	12/95	1	JPY/CHF
Nikkei 300-s	1,000	2/95	12/96	10	JPY/CHF
Nikkei 300-s#	1,000	2/95	12/96	10	JPY/CHF
Nikken Chem-g	150	12/93	12/97	76	JPY/DM
Nikkei Chem-s	150	12/93	12/97	76	JPY/DM
Nippei Toy-s	95	2/91	2/96	100	JPY/CHF
Nippon Cer-s	70	7/93	7/97	27.9	JPY/CHF
Nippon Chem-s	100	10/91	10/95	70	JPY/CHF
Nippon Com-s	12	9/90	12/96	1228	JPY/US$
Nippon Com	20	3/94	2/98	350	JPY/US$
Nippon Com	12	12/92	12/96	1228	JPY/US$
Nippon Com	20	3/95	3/99	393	JPY/US$
Nippon Densan-s	65	7/91	7/95	10.5	JPY/CHF
Nippon Dents-s	40	8/91	8/95	100	JPY/CHF
Nippon Dents-s	40	8/94	8/98	74.9	JPY/CHF
Nippon Denwa-s	35	1/93	1/97	158	JPY/CHF
Nippon Flo-s	100	7/92	7/96	150	JPY/CHF
Nippon Hi-s	60	12/93	12/97	56.5	JPY/CHF
Nippon Kas-s	132	9/90	10/95	100	JPY/CHF
Nippon Kos-s	12	4/92	4/96	1918	JPY/US$
Nippon Kos	12	4/92	4/96	1918	JPY/US$
Nippon Meas-s	62	8/91	8/95	110	JPY/CHF
Nippon Meas-s	200	7/92	7/96	57.4	JPY/CHF
Nippon Meas-s	300	3/93	3/97	49.8	JPY/CHF
Nippon Met-s	130	11/91	12/95	155	JPY/CHF
Nippon Pillar-s	25	2/92	3/96	153	JPY/CHF
Nippon Pillar-s	20	3/94	3/98	124	JPY/CHF
Nippon Piston-s	50	9/90	9/96	217	JPY/CHF

JAPAN (continued)

Issuer	Amount (000s)	Issue Date	Expiry Date	Shs/ Wrnt	Currency Shs/Wrnt
Nippon Piston-s	60	3/94	3/98	152	JPY/CHF
Nippon Piston-s	60	3/95	3/99	180	JPY/CHF
Nippon She-s	44	8/91	8/95	1173	JPY/US$
Nippon She	44	8/91	8/95	1173	JPY/US$
Nippon Shin-s	50	10/94	10/98	65.2	JPY/CHF
Nippon Sig-s	42	9/91	9/95	100	JPY/CHF
Nippon Sta-s	20	7/91	8/95	775	JPY/US$
Nippon Syn-s	20	4/92	4/96	1212	JPY/US$
Nippon Syn	20	4/92	4/96	1212	JPY/US$
Nippon Type-s	50	9/92	9/96	117	JPY/CHF
Nippon Yus-s	300	10/89	12/96	100	JPY/CHF
Nippon Yus-s	228	12/89	12/96	100	JPY/US$
Nippon Yus	20	4/93	3/97	1109	JPY/US$
Nishikawa-s	55	2/93	2/00	37.6	JPY/CHF
Nishimatsu-s	30	12/92	12/96	579	JPY/US$
Nishimatsu	30	12/92	12/96	579	JPY/US$
Nishimoto-s	30	2/94	2/98	44	JPY/CHF
Nishio Ren	12	3/94	2/98	196	JPY/US$
Nissan Chem-s	100	7/94	7/98	99	JPY/CHF
Nissen Co-g	190	3/94	2/98	17.8	JPY/DM
Nissen Co-g	50	10/92	11/96	70.8	JPY/DM
Nisshin St-s	72	4/91	4/96	210	JPY/US$
Nisshin St	72	4/91	4/96	210	JPY/US$
Nisshinbo-s	20	2/92	3/96	754	JPY/ECU
Nissho Co	26	9/93	10/97	356	JPY/US$
Nissho Co-s	46	7/91	7/95	133	JPY/CHF
Nissho Co-s	26	9/93	10/97	324	JPY/US$
Nitori Co-s	80	2/94	2/98	27.5	JPY/CHF
NOF Corp-s	40	6/93	6/97	94	JPY/CHF
NOF Corp-s	20	6/93	6/97	684	JPY/US$
NOF Corp	20	6/93	6/97	684	JPY/US$
Nohmi Bosai-g	70	3/92	3/96	65	JPY/DM
Nohmi Bosai-s	70	3/92	3/93	65	JPY/DM
Obayashi-s	72	7/91	8/95	690	JPY/US$
Obayashi-s	100	11/91	11/95	51	JPY/CHF
Obayashi	72	7/91	8/95	690	JPY/US$
Ohba Co-s	40	9/93	9/97	41.5	JPY/CHF
Ohki Const-s	60	12/92	12/96	135	JPY/CHF
Ohki Const-s	10	3/94	3/98	742	JPY/US$

JAPAN (continued)

Issuer	Amount (000s)	Issue Date	Expiry Date	Shs/ Wrnt	Currency Shs/Wrnt
Ohtsu Tire-s	50	10/92	10/96	238	JPY/CHF
Ohtsu Tire-g	75	6/91	7/95	146	JPY/DM
Ohtsu Tire-s	75	6/91	7/95	146	JPY/DM
Okamoto Mach-s	53	7/91	8/95	100	JPY/CHF
Okura-s	20	1/92	1/96	875	JPY/US$
Okura	20	1/92	1/96	875	JPY/US$
Oliver Co-s	50	7/93	7/97	47.3	JPY/CHF
Olympus-s	80	12/92	12/96	568	JPY/US$
Olympus	80	12/92	12/96	568	JPY/US$
Onward Kash	40	3/92	3/96	575	JPY/US$
Onward Kash	40	4/92	3/96	575	JPY/CHF
Optec Dai-s	20	2/92	2/96	1102	JPY/US$
Optec Dai	20	2/92	2/96	1102	JPY/US$
Osaka Bearing-s	20	2/92	2/96	165	JPY/CHF
Osaka Bearing-s	25	2/95	2/99	149	JPY/CHF
Osaka Cem-s	20	7/91	7/95	1362	JPY/US$
Osaka Cem	20	7/91	7/95	1362	JPY/US$
Osaka Diam-s	35	3/92	4/96	147	JPY/CHF
Osaka Stad-	400	7/94	7/98	43.3	JPY/CHF
Osaka Uoichi-g	100	2/92	3/96	101	JPY/DM
Osaka Uoichi-s	100	2/92	3/96	101	JPY/DM
Osaki Ele-s	80	8/93	8/97	72.7	JPY/CHF
Pac Metals-s	202	7/91	7/96	100	JPY/CHF
Parco-g	100	4/92	4/96	76	JPY/DM
Parco-s	100	4/92	4/96	76	JPY/DM
Parco	22	8/95	7/99	509	JPY/US$
Penta Ocean-s	40	7/92	7/96	933	JPY/US$
Penta Ocean	40	7/92	7/96	933	JPY/US$
Pokka Corp-g	90	10/92	11/96	59.6	JPY/DM
Pokka Corp-s	61	2/91	2/96	105	JPY/CHF
Pokka Corp-s	90	10/92	11/96	56.8	JPY/DM
Prima Meat-g	60	9/91	9/95	133	JPY/DM
Prima Meat-s	60	9/91	9/95	134	JPY/DM
Rasa Inds-s	40	11/93	12/97	134	JPY/CHF
Renown-s*	73	8/90	8/97	101	JPY/CHF
Renown Look-s	70	5/91	5/96	45.5	JPY/DM
Rhythm Wat-s	100	9/92	9/96	1477	JPY/US$
Rhythm Wat	10,000	9/92	9/96	1477	JPY/US$
Riken Corp-s	130	11/93	11/97	157	JPY/CHF

JAPAN (continued)

Issuer	Amount (000s)	Issue Date	Expiry Date	Shs/ Wrnt	Currency Shs/Wrnt
Riken Vinyl-s	100	10/93	10/97	72.5	JPY/CHF
Riken Vinyl-s	78	7/91	8/95	100	JPY/CHF
Rio Chain-s	70	9/93	8/97	35.1	JPY/CHF
Rio Chain-s	16	7/91	7/95	100	JPY/CHF
Rock Field-s	30	3/94	3/98	39/8	JPY/CHF
Rohm-s	250	11/93	11/97	24	JPY/CHF
Rokko Butter-s	20	10/93	10/97	125	JPY/CHF
Ryobi-g	20	9/88	9/95	512	JPY/DM
Ryobi	20	3/93	3/98	1052	JPY/US$
Ryobi-s	20	3/93	3/98	1052	JPY/CHF
Ryoden Trdg-s	20	12/91	12/95	583	JPY/US$
Ryoden Trdg	20	12/91	12/95	583	JPY/US$
Ryosan	20	7/91	7/95	183	JPY/US$
Sagami Chn-s	40	5/93	5/97	37.4	JPY/CHF
Sagami Co-g	60	3/92	3/96	98.6	JPY/DM
Sagami Co-s	60	3/92	3/96	98.6	JPY/DM
Saibu Gas-s	100	12/91	12/95	223	JPY/CHF
Sakai Chem-s	20	8/91	8/95	943	JPY/US$
Sakai Chem	20	8/91	8/95	943	JPY/US$
Sakurada-s	40	8/93	8/97	72.3	JPY/CHF
San-ai Oil-s	75	3/94	3/98	85	JPY/CHF
Sanken Elec-s	100	10/91	10/95	95.1	JPY/CHF
Sankyo Alum-g	120,000	6/91	7/95	56.1	JPY/DM
Sankyo Alum-s	120,000	6/91	7/95	56.1	JPY/DM
Sankyo Alum-s	40	7/91	7/95	513	JPY/US$
Sankyo Alum	40	7/91	7/95	513	JPY/US$
Sansei Yus-s	25,000	3/93	3/00	67.1	JPY/CHF
Sansin Elec-s	90	3/95	3/99	74.9	JPY/CHF
Sansin Elec-s	42	11/92	12/96	98.2	JPY/CHF
Sanwa Shutter-s	52	12/91	12/95	570	JPY/US$
Sanwa Shutter	52	12/91	12/95	570	JPY/US$
Sanwa Shutter	60	2/94	1/98	589	JPY/US$
Sanyo Denki-s	56	7/90	7/95	100	JPY/CHF
Sanyo Elec-s	70	4/93	4/97	151	JPY/CHF
Sanyo Elec-s	65	3/94	3/98	154	JPY/CHF
Sapporo Brew-g	200	11/93	11/97	66.9	JPY/DM
Sapporo Brew-s	200	11/93	11/97	75.9	JPY/CHF
Sapporo Brew	40	6/94	6/98	530	JPY/US$
Sata Const-s	20	9/92	9/96	104	JPY/CHF

JAPAN (continued)

Issuer	Amount (000s)	Issue Date	Expiry Date	Shs/ Wrnt	Currency Shs/Wrnt
Seika Corp	20	2/93	2/97	900	JPY/US$
Seikitokyu-s	110	3/93	3/97	123	JPY/CHF
Seino Tran-s	96	7/93	7/97	316	JPY/US$
Seino Tran	96	7/93	7/97	316	JPY/US$
Seiren-s	20	11/91	11/95	515	JPY/US$
Seiren	20	11/91	11/95	515	JPY/US$
Sekisui Ho-s	200	1/93	1/97	89.3	JPY/CHF
Sekisui Ho-s	40	6/91	6/96	528	JPY/US$
Sekisui Ho-s	40	1/93	1/97	644	JPY/US$
Sekisui Ho-s	250	8/94	8/98	85.3	JPY/CHF
Sekisui Ho	40	1/93	1/97	644	JPY/US$
Sekisui Ho	40	6/91	6/96	528	JPY/US$
Sekisui Jus-g	70	10/91	11/95	39.2	JPY/DM
Sekisui Jus-s	100	12/92	12/96	55.7	JPY/CHF
Sekisui Jus-s	70	10/91	11/95	39.1	JPY/DM
Sekisui Plas-g	100	2/92	3/96	105	JPY/DM
Sekisui Plas-s	100	2/92	3/96	105	JPY/DM
Senko Co-s	130	11/93	12/97	109	JPY/CHF
Senko Co-s	20	8/91	8/95	873	JPY/US$
Senko Co	20	8/91	8/95	873	JPY/US$
Senshukai-s	20	7/91	7/95	307	JPY/US$
Senshukai	20	7/91	7/95	307	JPY/US$
Sharp Corp-s	500	12/92	12/96	92.6	JPY/CHF
Sharp Corp-s	700	3/94	3/98	43	JPY/CHF
Shibu Ware-s	16	1/93	1/97	948	JPY/US$
Shibu Ware	16	1/93	1/97	948	JPY/US$
Shibaura Eng-s	70	9/90	9/95	100	JPY/CHF
Shimadzu-s	30	8/91	8/95	991	JPY/US$
Shimadzu	30	8/91	8/95	991	JPY/US$
Shimano-s	20	3/92	3/96	469	JPY/ECU
Shina Fuel-s	37	7/91	7/95	110	JPY/CHF
Shina Fuel-s	37	7/91	7/96	110	JPY/CHF
Shina Fuel-s	14	9/92	8/96	1122	JPY/ECU
Shina Fuel	30	9/93	9/97	448	JPY/US$
Shindengen-s	77	7/91	7/95	100	JPY/CHF
Shinko Elec-s	160	6/93	6/97	21	JPY/CHF
Shinko Kogyo-s	35	11/90	12/95	100	JPY/CHF
Shinko Kogyo-s	60	11/91	11/96	56.5	JPY/CHF
Shinko Shoji	12	8/95	7/99	333	JPY/US$

JAPAN (continued)

Issuer	Amount (000s)	Issue Date	Expiry Date	Shs/ Wrnt	Currency Shs/Wrnt
Shinko Shoji	12	8/95	7/99	333	JPY/US$
Shinko Wire-g	60	4/92	4/96	209	JPY/DM
Shinko Wire-s	60	4/92	4/96	209	JPY/DM
Shinobu-s	40	10/92	10/96	68.6	JPY/CHF
Shinsho Corp-g	90	11/91	12/95	155	JPY/DM
Shinsho Corp-s	90	11/91	12/95	155	JPY/DM
Shiroki-s	18	7/91	7/95	1194	JPY/US$
Shiroki	18	7/91	7/95	1194	JPY/US$
Shiseido-s	100	2/93	1/97	64.2	JPY/CHF
Shiseido-s	40	1/93	1/97	479	JPY/US$
Shiseido	40	1/93	1/97	479	JPY/US$
Shizuki El-s	50	6/91	7/96	100	JPY/CHF
Sho bond-s	80	1/92	1/96	50.2	JPY/CHF
Shochiku-s	20	7/92	7/96	588	JPY/US$
Shochiku	20	7/92	7/96	588	JPY/US$
Shofu-s	35	10/94	11/98	64.6	JPY/CHF
Showa Alum-g	130	2/92	1/96	122	JPY/DM
Showa Alum-s	130	2/92	1/96	122	JPY/DM
Showa Elec-s	24	7/91	7/95	940	JPY/US$
Showa Elec-s	30	10/92	10/96	1017	JPY/US$
Showa Elec	24	7/91	7/95	940	JPY/US$
Showa Elec	30	10/92	10/96	1017	JPY/US$
Showa High-g	50	3/92	3/96	72.6	JPY/DM
Showa High-s	100	10/93	10/97	48.7	JPY/CHF
Showa High-s	50	3/92	3/96	72.6	JPY/DM
Showa Sang-s	32	9/92	9/97	1089	JPY/US$
Showa Sang	32	9/92	9/97	1089	JPY/US$
SMC Corp-s	20	7/91	7/95	128	JPY/US$
SMC Corp	20	7/91	7/95	128	JPY/US$
Snow Brand-g	200	1/92	1/96	110	JPY/DM
Snow Brand-s	200	8/93	7/97	87	JPY/CHF
Snow Brand-s	200	3/92	1/96	110	JPY/DM
SNT Corp-s	35	4/92	4/96	94	JPY/CHF
SNT Corp-s	45	11/93	11/97	79.7	JPY/CHF
Sokkia Co-s	80	4/93	4/97	49	JPY/CHF
Sokkia Co-s	24	10/90	10/95	110	JPY/CHF
Suminoe-g	100	10/91	10/95	116	JPY/DM
Suminoe-s	100	11/91	10/95	117	JPY/DM
Sumit Osaka	30	2/92	2/96	1221	JPY/US$

JAPAN (continued)

Issuer	Amount (000s)	Issue Date	Expiry Date	Shs/ Wrnt	Currency Shs/Wrnt
Sumit Osaka-s	20	8/91	7/95	1022	JPY/US$
Sumit Osaka-s	40	7/93	7/97	879	JPY/US$
Sumit Osaka	20	8/91	7/95	1022	JPY/US$
Sumit Osaka	20	8/93	7/97	879	JPY/US$
Sumit Osaka-s	30	2/92	2/96	1221	JPY/US$
Sumitomo Chem-g	250	5/91	5/98	165	JPY/DM
Sumitomo Chem-s	250	5/91	5/98	165	JPY/DM
Sumitomo Elec	50	7/91	7/99	711	JPY/JPY
Sumitomo H-s	34	3/92	2/96	1127	JPY/US$
Sumitomo H	34	3/92	2/96	1127	JPY/US$
Sumitomo L-s	160	7/91	7/98	101	JPY/CHF
Sumitomo L-s	85	12/91	12/95	176	JPY/CHF
Sumitomo M-s	60	4/91	5/96	535	JPY/US$
Sumitomo M-s	80	12/92	12/97	939	JPY/US$
Sumitomo M	60	4/91	5/96	535	JPY/US$
Sumitomo M	20	8/91	8/95	1550	JPY/US$
Sumitomo M	80	12/92	12/97	939	JPY/US$
Sumitomo Re-s	200	12/92	12/96	105	JPY/CHF
Sumitomo Re-s	20	7/91	7/96	1073	JPY/US$
Sumitomo Re	20	7/91	7/96	1073	JPY/US$
Sun Wave-s	20	10/91	10/95	397	JPY/US$
Sun Wave	20	10/91	10/95	397	JPY/US$
Suncall-s	30	10/91	11/95	91.8	JPY/CHF
Sunx-s	19	7/91	8/95	100	JPY/CHF
Super Daiei-s	27	8/94	7/98	43.7	JPY/CHF
Suzutan-s	20	10/91	10/95	299	JPY/US$
Suzutan	20	10/91	10/95	299	JPY/US$
SXL Corp-g	125	12/91	11/95	71.7	JPY/DM
SXL Corp-s	200	3/95	2/99	82.9	JPY/CHF
SXL Corp-s	16	2/93	2/97	757	JPY/US$
SXL Corp-s	125	12/91	11/95	71.7	JPY/DM
SXL Corp	16	2/93	2/97	757	JPY/US$
SXL Corp	40	2/94	2/98	393	JPY/US$
Tachi Co-g	65	3/92	3/96	73.3	JPY/DM
Tachi Co-s	65	3/92	3/96	73.3	JPY/DM
Taisei Pre-s	20	3/92	3/96	98.6	JPY/US$
Taisei Pre	20	3/92	3/96	98/6	JPY/US$
Taiyo Kag-s	60	10/92	10/96	68.4	JPY/CHF
Takada Kik-s	35	12/92	12/96	85	JPY/CHF

JAPAN (continued)

Issuer	Amount (000s)	Issue Date	Expiry Date	Shs/ Wrnt	Currency Shs/Wrnt
Takara Stand-s	100	11/92	11/96	88/2	JPY/CHF
Takara Stand-g	150	2/94	1/98	46.8	JPY/DM
Takashimaya-s	56	6/91	7/98	100	JPY/CHF
Takashimaya-s	54	7/91	7/96	447	JPY/US$
Takashimaya	54	7/91	7/96	447	JPY/US$
Taki Chem-s	35	11/93	12/97	138	JPY/CHF
Takiron-s	13	4/92	4/96	1119	JPY/US$
Takiron	13	4/92	4/96	1119	JPY/US$
Tamura Co-s	14	12/91	12/95	968	JPY/US$
Tamura Co	14	12/91	12/95	968	JPY/US$
Tasaki Shi-s	34	5/91	5/98	126	JPY/CHF
Tasaki Shi-s	20	11/93	12/97	455	JPY/US$
Tasaki Shi	20	11/93	12/97	455	JPY/US$
Tateyama-s	40	7/91	8/95	102	JPY/CHF
Tateyama-s	20	10/92	10/96	518	JPY/US$
Tateyama	20	10/92	10/96	518	JPY/US$
Teijin Sei	20	7/91	7/96	763	JPY/US$
Teijin Sei-s	20	7/91	7/96	763	JPY/CHF
Tenmaya St-s	18	6/91	7/95	100	JPY/CHF
Teraoka Seis-g	40	7/91	7/95	53.4	JPY/DM
Teraoka Seis-s	40	7/91	7/95	53.4	JPY/DM
Teraoka Seis	6	3/94	2/98	537	JPY/US$
Tesac Co-s	60	2/92	2/96	160	JPY/CHF
Tigers Pol-s	22	5/91	6/96	100	JPY/CHF
Toa Corp-s	50	10/92	10/96	142	JPY/CHF
Toa Corp-s	62	9/91	10/95	100	JPY/CHF
Toa Corp-s	20	7/91	7/95	979	JPY/US$
Toa Corp-s	50	2/94	2/98	104	JPY/CHF
Toa Corp-s	30	2/93	2/97	867	JPY/US$
Toa Corp	20	7/91	7/95	979	JPY/US$
Toa Corp	30	2/93	2/97	867	JPY/US$
Toa Corp	30	3/94	3/98	728	JPY/US$
Toa Steel-s	32	7/91	7/96	447	JPY/US$
Toa Steel-s	52	10/92	10/97	504	JPY/US$
Toa Steel	32	7/91	7/96	447	JPY/US$
Toa Steel	52	10/92	10/97	504	JPY/US$
Toagosei-s	20	6/92	5/96	1103	JPY/US$
Toagosei	20	6/92	5/96	1103	JPY/US$
Tobu Rail-s	200	6/93	6/97	87.6	JPY/CHF

JAPAN (continued)

Issuer	Amount (000s)	Issue Date	Expiry Date	Shs/ Wrnt	Currency Shs/Wrnt
Tobu Rail-s	60	8/91	7/95	986	JPY/US$
Tobu Rail	60	8/91	7/95	986	JPY/US$
Tobu Rail	80	3/94	3/98	761	JPY/US$
Tobu Store	13	1/93	1/97	877	JPY/US$
Toho Real	10	7/93	6/97	576	JPY/US$
Toho Real-s	10	7/93	6/97	576	JPY/US$
Toho Store-s	60	1/94	1/98	88.1	JPY/CHF
Tobu Store-s	13	1/93	1/97	877	JPY/US$
Toho Rayon-s	96	8/91	8/95	100	JPY/CHF
Toho Zinc-s	11	9/91	9/95	1031	JPY/US$
Toho Zinc	11	9/91	9/95	1031	JPY/US$
Toho Zinc	24	10/93	10/97	893	JPY/US$
Tokimec-s	10	10/91	10/95	656	JPY/US$
Tokimec	10	10/91	10/95	656	JPY/US$
Toko Inc-s	60	7/91	7/95	100	JPY/CHF
Tokyo Buhin-s	51	9/91	9/95	100	JPY/CHF
Tokyo Elec-s	60	7/91	7/95	208	JPY/US$
Tokyo Elec	60	7/91	7/95	208	JPY/US$
Tokyo Sang-s	45	5/93	4/97	66.2	JPY/CHF
Tokyo Tanabe-s	50	8/94	9/98	82	JPY/CHF
Tokyo Tekko-g	180	10/92	11/97	47.4	JPY/DM
Tokyo Tekko-s	53	7/91	7/96	100	JPY/CHF
Tokyo Tekko-s	180	10/92	11/97	47.3	JPY/DM
Tokyu Con	36	1/93	1/97	1464	JPY/US$
Tokyu Con-s	180	11/92	11/97	47.4	JPY/CHF
Tokyu Hotel-s	24	7/91	7/95	538	JPY/US$
Tokyu Hotel	24	7/91	7/95	538	JPY/US$
Tokyu Recr-s	55	8/92	8/96	132	JPY/CHF
Tokyu Store-s	160	3/94	2/98	80.4	JPY/CHF
Toli Corp-s	80	8/91	8/95	88.3	JPY/DM
Toli Corp-g	80	8/91	8/95	88.3	JPY/DM
Tomiya App-s	20	8/92	9/96	146	JPY/CHF
Tomiya App-s	40	1/94	2/98	39.9	JPY/CHF
Tomoe Corp-s	25	3/92	3/96	90.6	JPY/CHF
Tomoe Corp-s	70	2/94	2/98	63	JPY/CHF
Tomoku Co	14	11/92	12/96	1320	JPY/US$
Tomoku Co	20	3/94	3/98	681	JPY/US$
Tonami Trad-s	100	2/94	1/98	91	JPY/CHF
Topy Ind-s	20	8/91	8/95	1333	JPY/US$

JAPAN (continued)

Issuer	Amount (000s)	Issue Date	Expiry Date	Shs/ Wrnt	Currency Shs/Wrnt
Topy Ind	20	8/91	8/95	1333	JPY/US$
Torigoe-s	25	7/95	6/99	174	JPY/CHF
Torishima-g	80	6/94	6/98	55	JPY/DM
Toshiba-s	20	7/91	7/96	497	JPY/US$
Toshiba	20	7/91	7/96	497	JPY/US$
Tosho Prince-s	80	10/92	10/96	146	JPY/CHF
Tostem Co-s	30	8/90	8/97	126	JPY/US$
Tostem Co	30	8/90	8/97	126	JPY/US$
Totetsu-s	40	2/92	3/96	74	JPY/CHF
Toyo Chem-s	45	2/95	1/99	128	JPY/CHF
Toyo Chem-s	25	12/92	12/96	200	JPY/CHF
Toyo Const-s	20	5/91	5/96	851	JPY/US$
Toyo Const-s	100	2/93	2/97	160	JPY/CHF
Toyo Const	20	5/91	5/96	851	JPY/US$
Toyo Eng-s	40	4/93	3/97	709	JPY/US$
Toyo Eng	40	4/93	3/97	709	JPY/US$
Toyo Kanetsu-s	20	8/92	8/96	1279	JPY/US$
Toyo Kanetsu	20	8/92	8/96	1279	JPY/US$
Toyo Radiat-s	50	11/90	11/97	100	JPY/CHF
Toyo Shutter-g	70	7/91	8/95	37.2	JPY/DM
Toyo Shutter-s	100	9/92	9/96	93.7	JPY/CHF
Toyo Shutter-s	70	8/91	8/95	690	JPY/DM
Toyo Shutter-s	120	3/94	3/98	65	JPY/CHF
Toyo Suisan	40	9/92	10/96	406	JPY/US$
Toyo Suisan-s	40	10/92	10/96	406	JPY/US$
Trans Cosm	20	8/93	8/97	134	JPY/US$
Tsubak Min-s	35	6/93	6/97	84.8	JPY/CHF
Tsukamoto-s	35	6/93	6/97	95.5	JPY/CHF
Tsurukame-s	30	2/94	1/98	97.6	JPY/CHF
Tsurumi	10	11/92	11/96	524	JPY/US$
Tsurumi-s	10	11/92	11/96	524	JPY/US$
Tsutsunaka-s	20	7/91	7/95	461	JPY/US$
Tsutsunaka	20	7/91	7/95	461	JPY/US$
Tsuzuki Den-s	70	10/91	11/95	59.7	JPY/CHF
Ube Indus-s	176	7/91	6/96	100	JPY/CHF
UniCharm-s	100	9/91	10/95	74.6	JPY/CHF
Uniden-s	150	3/93	2/97	43.7	JPY/CHF
Uniden	32	3/94	3/98	141	JPY/US$
Wakachiku-s	150	11/93	11/97	160	JPY/CHF

JAPAN (continued)

Issuer	Amount (000s)	Issue Date	Expiry Date	Shs/ Wrnt	Currency Shs/Wrnt
Wakita	20	9/93	8/97	240	JPY/US$
Yahagi Const-g	100	10/91	10/95	72.7	JPY/DM
Yaizu Sui-s	25	6/93	6/97	41.5	JPY/CHF
Yamaichi	8	6/86	6/96	747	JPY/US$
Yamanouchi Ph	40	4/93	4/97	222	JPY/US$
Yamatake-s	20	2/93	2/97	480	JPY/CHF
Yamatake	20	2/93	2/97	480	JPY/US$
Yamato Int-s	65	1/91	2/96	105	JPY/CHF
Yamato Int-s	65	1/91	2/96	105	JPY/CHF
Yamato Set-s	40	10/92	9/96	100	JPY/CHF
Yamazen Corp-g	140	5/91	5/96	69.7	JPY/DM
Yamazen Corp-s	60	5/92	6/97	113	JPY/CHF
Yamazen Corp-s	60	6/92	6/97	113	JPY/DM
Yaohan Jap	20	12/92	12/96	463	JPY/US$
Yaohan Jap-s	20	12/92	12/96	463	JPY/US$
Yodogawa	60	12/93	12/97	853	JPY/US$
Yokogama Br-s	100	7/94	7/98	46.5	JPY/CHF
Yokohama R	24	11/92	11/96	1275	JPY/US$
Yokohama R-s	36	12/92	11/96	1213	JPY/CHF
Yonekyu Co-s	25	9/92	9/96	92.8	JPY/CHF
Yotai Refrig-s	30	11/91	11/95	120	JPY/CHF
Yuasa Trad-s	100	8/92	9/96	173	JPY/CHF
Yuasa Trad-s	130	12/93	12/97	152	JPY/CHF
Zenchiku-s	10	2/93	2/97	1411	JPY/US$
Zenchiku	10	2/93	2/97	1411	JPY/US$
Zuken Inc-g	150	10/92	10/96	27.1	JPY/DM
Zuken Inc-s	150	10/92	10/96	27.1	JPY/DM
Xebio-s	70	8/92	8/96	53.8	JPY/CHF

* covered, # put, l-Luxembourg listed, s-Swiss listed, g-German listed; balance domestic/broker's broker

MALAYSIA

Issuer	Amount (000s)	Issue Date	Expiry Date	Shs/ Wrnt	Currency Shs/Wrnt
Actacorp	18,860	6/94	12/98	1	MYR/MYR
Affin Hldg	102,056	5/95	11/99	1	MYR/MYR
Alum Co of Mal	10,000	8/91	7/96	1	MYR/MYR

MALAYSIA (continued)

Issuer	Amount (000s)	Issue Date	Expiry Date	Shs/ Wrnt	Currency Shs/Wrnt
Antah Hldg	75,361	12/94	8/99	1	MYR/MYR
Aokam Perdana	43,020	10/92	4/97	1	MYR/MYR
Apex Equity	24,760	7/94	6/98	1	MYR/MYR
Bandar Raya	145,000	6/93	9/97	1	MYR/MYR
Bandar Raya-si	145	6/93	9/97	1	MYR/SGD
Bejaya Leisure	150,000	4/94	4/99	1	MYR/MYR
Berjaya Singer	75,000	9/93	9/95	1	MYR/MYR
Bolton Prop	45,490	10/92	6/96	1	MYR/MYR
Bolton Prop-si	45,500	9/92	6/96	1	MYR/SGD
Buildcon	16,791	12/94	12/99	1	MYR/MYR
CHG Ind	22,500	9/94	6/99	1	MYR/MYR
Commerce Asset	76,487	1/94	6/98	1	MYR/MYR
Daibochi P&P	9,688	10/93	1/99	1	MYR/MYR
DCB Hldg	195,077	1/95	12/99	1	MYR/MYR
Gamuda	31,032	3/95	1/00	1	MYR/MYR
Genting-I*	5,000	7/93	7/95	1	MYR/US$
Genting-I*	5,000	10/93	10/95	1	MYR/US$
George Kent	16,875	10/94	1/99	1	MYR/SGD
George Kent	16,875	10/94	1/99	1	MYR/MYR
Hexza Corp	35,810	1/93	1/98	1	MYR/MYR
Hexza Corp-si	36,000	1/93	1/98	1	MYR/SGD
IGB Corp	233,400	12/93	12/98	1	MYR/MYR
IGB Corp-si	233,400	12/93	1/98	1	MYR/SGD
IOI Corp	185,450	7/91	10/95	1	MYR/MYR
IOI Corp	50,510	5/94	5/98	1	MYR/MYR
IOI Corp-si	185,400	5/91	10/95	1	MYR/SGD
Juan Kuang	12,000	4/95	4/99	1	MYR/MYR
Johan Hldg	92,081	7/94	1/99	1	MYR/MYR
Kedah Cement	124,755	5/93	11/95	1	MYR/MYR
Kelanamas Ind	57,000	6/93	2/99	1	MYR/MYR
Kim Hin Ind	20,000	7/94	7/98	1	MYR/MYR
Kian Joo Can	15,423,429	2/95	5/99	1	MYR/MY
KLSE Index-I	1,000	3/95	3/96	5	MYR/US$
KLSE Index-I	1,000	3/95	3/96	5	MYR/US$
KLSE Index-I	1,000	3/95	3/97	5	MYR/US$
KLSE Index-I#	500	7/93	7/95	1	MYR/US$
KLSE Index-I	1,000	3/95	3/97	5	MYR/US$
KLSE Index-I	500	7/93	7/95	1	MYR/US$
Kulim	94,406	4/94	1/99	1	MYR/MYR

MALAYSIA (continued)

Issuer	Amount (000s)	Issue Date	Expiry Date	Shs/ Wrnt	Currency Shs/Wrnt
Kwong Onn Ind	25,456	1/94	11/98	1	MYR/MYR
Larut Const	65,439	2/95	1/00	1	MYR/MYR
Lien Hoe	85,700	9/93	8/97	1	MYR/MYR
Lien Hoe-si	85,700	9/93	8/97	1	MYR/SGD
Leong Hup Hldg	14,488	6/94	9/99	1	MYR/MYR
Malayan Bank	10,000	5/95	11/96	1	MYR/MYR
Malaysian Gen	30,064	3/95	8/99	1	MYR/MYR
Malaya Glass	12,450	1/94	9/98	1	MYR/MYR
Malaysia Ind	108,000	12/94	11/97	1	MYR/MYR
Malaysian Re	82,300	6/93	5/97	1	MYR/MYR
Malaysian Re-si	82,500	1/93	5/97	1	MYR/SGD
MBF Hldg	116,000	10/92	8/96	1	MYR/MYR
MBF Hldg-si	116,000	9/92	8/96	1	MYR/SGD
MCB Hldg	55,000	3/94	5/99	1	MYR/MYR
Metroplex	185,970	3/93	11/98	1	MYR/MYR
Metroplex-si	185,970	11/93	11/98	1	MYR/SGD
Multi Purpose	150,206	5/94	11/98	1	MYR/MYR
MWE Hldg	67,243	8/94	2/99	1	MYR/MYR
Nanyang Press	17,420	5/93	7/98	1	MYR/MYR
OSK Hldg	30,000	4/94	3/99	1	MYR/MYR
Paramount	33,000	10/92	8/96	1	MYR/MYR
Petronas Dagang	120,000	2/94	2/99	1	MYR/MYR
Pernas Intl	186,406	4/95	1/00	1	MYR/MYR
Pilecon Eng	67,530	7/94	7/99	1	MYR/MYR
Sungei Way	27,420	10/92	8/97	1	MYR/MYR
Sungei Way	21,175	3/94	6/99	1	MYR/MYR
Sungei Way-si	28,300	9/92	8/97	1	MYR/SGD
Siah Bros	17,100	11/93	2/99	1	MYR/MYR
Sriwani Hldg	42,080	1/95	11/99	1	MYR/MYR
Taiping Const	138,333	9/93	9/98	1	MYR/MYR
TA Ent	60,000	2/94	11/98	1	MYR/MYR
Tiong Nam Trans	8,500	11/94	5/99	1	MYR/MYR
Tongkah Hldg	32,400	7/94	5/99	1	MYR/MYR
UMW Hldg	30,734	4/95	1/00	1	MYR/MYR
Uniphoenix	69,550	7/91	12/97	1	MYR/MYR
Uniphoenix-si	69,500	1/93	12/97	1	MYR/SGD
Uniphone Tel	34,900	11/94	9/99	1	MYR/MYR
Worldwide Hldg	79,900	5/94	9/99	1	MYR/MYR

MALAYSIA (continued)

Issuer	Amount (000s)	Issue Date	Expiry Date	Shs/ Wrnt	Currency Shs/Wrnt
Wing Tiek	17,250	10/94	1/99	1	MYR/MYR
YTL Corp	90,371	8/93	8/97	1	MYR/MYR

* covered, # put, l-Luxembourg listed, si-Singapore listed, all others domestic

NEW ZEALAND

Issuer	Amount (000s)	Issue Date	Expiry Date	Shs/ Wrnt	Currency Shs/Wrnt
Direct Capital	17,000	9/94	6/97	1	NZ$/NZ$
Heritage Mining	24,750	6/95	3/00	1	NZ$/NZ$
Iddison Group	3,750	10/94	9/97	1	NZ$/NZ$
Max Resources	17,000	2/95	7/99	1	NZ$/NZ$
NMFM Asia	75,000	5/94	3/98	1	NZ$/NZ$
Templeton	8,023	12/94	9/04	1	NZ$/NZ$

SINGAPORE

Issuer	Amount (000s)	Issue Date	Expiry Date	Shs/ Wrnt	Currency Shs/Wrnt
Amcol Hldg	5,200	12/92	5/98	1	SGD/SGD
Apollo Entertain	34,200	12/93	1/99	1	SGD/SGD
Asiamatrix	4,400	1/94	12/96	1	SGD/SGD
Carnaudmetal	21,000	12/93	12/98	1	SGD/SGD
Centerpoint	134,900	5/92	4/97	1	SGD/SGD
City Development	60,900	9/93	7/98	1	SGD/SGD
Clipsal	9,100	9/93	8/98	1	US$/US$
DBS50 Index-I	1,000	3/95	3/96	5	SGD/SGD
DBS50 Index-I	1,000	3/95	3/97	5	SGD/SGD
DBS Land*	40,000	4/95	9/96	1	SGD/SGD
First Capital	81,600	6/92	5/97	1	SGD/SGD
Fraser & Neave	35,300	4/93	5/98	1	SGD/SGD
Fraser & Neave*	6,000	12/93	12/95	1	SGD/SGD
GK Goh	66,221	3/95	2/00	1	SGD/SGD
Goldtron	54,450	12/93	12/98	1	SGD/SGD

SINGAPORE (continued)

Issuer	Amount (000s)	Issue Date	Expiry Date	Shs/ Wrnt	Currency Shs/Wrnt
Hai Sun Hup	69,575	8/92	2/97	1	SGD/SGD
Haw Par Bros	32,900	8/93	6/98	1	SGD/SGD
Hong Fok Co	13,600	10/92	9/97	1	SGD/SGD
Hong Kong Land	50,000	3/95	3/97	1	US$/US$
Hong Leong Fin	44,800	9/93	11/98	1	SGD/SGD
Hour Glass	19,200	10/92	12/95	1	SGD/SGD
Inter Roller	675	7/95	7/00	1	SGD/SGD
Jack Chia	48,447	3/95	1/00	1	SGD/SGD
Jardine Ma	150,000	11/94	10/96	0.1	US$/US$
Jardine Strat	118,060	5/95	5/98	1	US$/US$
Jaya Hldg	13,900	9/93	8/98	1	SGD/SGD
Keppel Corp	109,168	9/92	6/97	1	SGD/SGD
Keppel Finance	49,300	4/91	2/96	1	SGD/SGD
Kim Eng Hldg	48,400	1/94	2/97	1	SGD/SGD
L&M Group	36,900	12/93	1/99	1	SGD/SGD
Low Keng Huat	36,000	3/95	2/00	1	SGD/SGD
OCBC	33,700	3/92	7/95	1	SGD/SGD
OCBC*	100,000	6/95	11/96	0.1	SGD/SGD
Overseas Union	49,600	8/93	7/98	1	SGD/SGD
Parkway Hldg	6,000	11/91	11/96	1	SGD/SGD
Parkway Hldg	70,100	11/93	10/98	1	SGD/SGD
Provisions	500	10/93	10/98	1	SGD/SGD
QAF	125,600	11/93	11/98	1	SGD/SGD
Shangri-la Hotel	22,500	11/92	11/97	1	SGD/SGD
Singapore Inv	10,800	9/93	12/98	1	SGD/SGD
Singapura Bl	12,770	2/94	2/98	1	SGD/SGD
Singatronics	565,000	1/89	1/96	1	SGD/SGD
Straits Steam	81,000	5/91	6/96	1	SGD/SGD
Tat Lee Bank	17,300	8/92	8/97	1	SGD/SGD
Tat Lee Bank	45,900	9/93	8/98	1	SGD/SGD
Tat Lee Finance	18,000	12/93	1/99	1	SGD/SGD
Tuan Sing	141,700	2/93	1/98	1	SGD/SGD
United Engineer	77,100	11/94	11/98	1	SGD/SGD
United Ind	281,600	9/93	8/98	1	SGD/SGD
United Int'l	33,000	7/90	6/95	1	SGD/SGD
United Overseas	88,800	6/92	6/97	1	SGD/SGD
United Overseas	71,500	5/92	6/97	1	SGD/SGD
Van Der Horst	31,400	8/92	8/98	1	SGD/SGD

* covered, l-Luxembourg listed

SOUTH KOREA

Issuer	Amount (000s)	Issue Date	Expiry Date	Shs/ Wrnt	Currency Shs/Wrnt
Daewoo Corp-l	1	11/91	11/96	112	KRW/US$
Daewoo Corp-s	1	11/91	11/96	224	KRW/US$
Hansol Paper-l	5	5/94	5/97	159.93	KRW/US$
Kia Motors-l	1	2/95	2/00	2221	KRW/US$
Sam Yang-l	8	5/93	3/98	134.76	KRW/US$
Yukong-s	15,000	7/91	6/96	140.54	KRW/US$
Yukong-s	120	7/95	6/99	20.22	KRW/US$
Yukong-l	15,000	7/91	6/96	140.54	KRW/US$

l-Luxembourg listed, s-Swiss listed

THAILAND

Issuer	Amount (000s)	Issue Date	Expiry Date	Shs/ Wrnt	Currency Shs/Wrnt
Asia Hotel	12,000	2/94	11/96	1	THB/THB
Banpu Co	6,000	3/94	11/98	1	THB/THB
Christiani & Niel	13,500	12/93	9/98	1.77	THB/THB
Dhana Siam Fin	5,000	12/93	10/98	3.62	THB/THB
Ekachart Fin	15,750	10/94	5/99	1	THB/THB
Finance One	24,000	6/94	3/99	2.75	THB/THB
Finance One B	24,000	6/94	3/99	2.75	THB/THB
First Pac Land	20,500	6/93	11/95	1.43	THB/THB
General Fin	5,000	3/94	12/98	2.30	THB/THB
General Fin B	5,000	3/94	12/98	2.30	THB/THB
Industrial Fin	60,000	3/94	11/97	1.19	THB/THB
Land & House	10,000	6/93	2/98	1	THB/THB
MK Real Estate	12,000	10/94	12/98	1	THB/THB
Nakornthon Bank	24,060	3/94	11/97	1	THB/THB
National Publish	12,000	3/95	10/99	1	THB/THB
One Multiple	8,310	11/92	7/95	1	THB/THB
Prop Perfect	8,000	12/94	7/99	1.01	THB/THB
Pizza Co	7,500	11/94	9/99	1	THB/THB
Quality House	13,600	2/95	10/99	1.39	THB/THB
Siam City Bank	22,194	12/94	10/99	1	THB/THB
Supalai Publish	5,125	3/95	12/99	1	THB/THB
Swedish Motor	3,600	3/94	12/99	1.94	THB/THB
Thai Farmers Bank	75,000	12/94	10/99	1	THB/THB
Thai German	22,500	10/94	4/99	1	THB/THB

THAILAND (continued)

Issuer	Amount (000s)	Issue Date	Expiry Date	Shs/ Wrnt	Currency Shs/Wrnt
Thai Modern	4,480	1/95	8/99	1	THB/THB
Tipco Asphalt	4,000	6/94	12/98	3.63	THB/THB
United Finance	9,100	3/95	11/99	1	THB/THB

Appendix III

ASIA PACIFIC DOMESTIC AND OFFSHORE CONVERTIBLES

Highlighted below are summary details on offshore and Asia Pacific convertibles as of mid-1995.

AUSTRALIA

Issuer	Amount (mln)	Domestic/ Offshore	Coupon (%)	Maturity
Adelaide Bank	A$40.7	D	11.50	2002
Adelaide Bright	A$57.9	D	11.00	perp
Amcor	A$150.5	D	6.50	perp
Amcor	A$100	O	9.00	perp
Amcor	A$93.6	D	9.00	perp
Ampol Exp	A$74.9	D	8.00	1998
ANI	A$54.3	D	10.00	1996
Aust Found	A$55.7	D	9.00	2002
Barrier Hldg	A$13.7	D	11.00	1996
Bendigo Bk	A$30.1	D	10.50	2000
BTR Nylex	A$630	D	9.00	perp
Burns Philp	US$100	O	5.50	2004
Century Drill	A$4.8	D	10.20	1999
Challenge Bk	A$67.5	D	float	1998
Clutha Ltd	A$36	D	9.50	2003
Cons Mfg	A$6.6	D	9.00	1997
CSR	A$1.2	D	8.00	1997
Futuris Corp	A$75.6	D	7.50	2000
Gold Mines Kal.	US$65	O	7.50	2000
Hancock Gore	A$4	D	12.25	perp
Ipoh Garden	A$33	D	10.00	1999
Kalamazoo Hldg	A$11.3	D	13.50	1998
Kern Corp	A$64.5	D	9.00	1997
Lend Lease	US$200	O	4.75	2003

AUSTRALIA (continued)

Issuer	Amount (mln)	Domestic/ Offshore	Coupon (%)	Maturity
Macraes Min	A$76.7	D	7.00	1998
MIM Hldg	US$125	O	6.50	1997
MIM Hldg	A$125	D	9.75	1997
Pac Dunlop	US$75	O	6.75	1997
Pac Dunlop	US$65	O	7.00	1996
Pac Hydro	A$9.5	D	10.00	1997
Parbury Ltd	A$20.3	D	10.00	1997
Payce Cons	A$6	D	12.00	1997
Pioneer Con	A$175	D	9.50	1998
QCT Res	A$66.4	D	12.00	perp
Renison Gold	A$52	D	8.00	1996
Ridley Corp	A$24.5	D	10.00	1996
SA Brewing	US$60	O	7.50	1998
South Cross	A$1.6	D	14.75	1996
Telecasters	A$11.3	D	8.50	1998
TNT	A$175	D	9.00	1998

CHINA

Issuer	Amount (mln)	Domestic/ Offshore	Coupon (%)	Maturity
China Southern	US$45	O	5.25	2000
Guandong Inv	US$72	O	4.50	1998
Guangzhou Inv	US$90	O	4.50	1998

HONG KONG

Issuer	Amount (mln)	Domestic/ Offshore	Coupon (%)	Maturity
Applied Intl	US$75	O	5.25	2000
Amoy Prop	US$300	O	5.50	perp
China Overseas	US$143.7	O	4.25	1998
China Travel	US$143.7	O	4.25	1998
Daido Concrete	CHF16.7	O	1.50	1999
Daido Concrete	CHF11	O	3.00	1997
Dickson Const	DM22	O	3.00	1996
Fountain Set	US$38	O	2.50	2001
Gold Lion	US$50	O	4.88	1999

HONG KONG (continued)

Issuer	Amount (mln)	Domestic/ Offshore	Coupon (%)	Maturity
HKCB Bank	CHF65	O	1.63	1999
HK China Treas	US$120	O	2.00	1999
HK Shang Hotel	US$175	O	5.00	2001
HK Resorts	US$100	O	4.75	2000
Hon Kwok Land	US$50	O	4.88	2000
Hysan Dev	US$175	O	6.75	2000
Jinhui Fin	US$50	O	2.50	1997
Johnson Elec	US$150	O	4.50	2000
Kumagai Gumi HK	US$115	O	4.88	1998
Lai Fung	US$150	O	5.50	1998
Lippo Land	US$100	O	1.25	2000
New World Dev	US$300	O	4.38	2000
Pac Concord	US$125	O	4.75	1998
Paul Y ITC	US$100	O	5.00	2001
Peregrine Fin	US$200	O	4.50	2000
Regal Hotels	US$125	O	5.25	2008
Rhine Hldg	CHF30	O	2.00	1998
Ryoden Dev	US$50	O	3.00	1998
Shangri-la Asia	US$258.7	O	2.88	2000
Shougang Conc	US$183	O	4.50	1998
Shougang Grand	US$100	O	1.50	1998
Sino Land	US$200	O	5.00	2000
S. Megga	US$47.5	O	2.50	2002
Stelux	CHF125	O	1.75	2001
Wharf Hldg	US$402.5	O	5.00	2000

INDIA

Issuer	Amount (mln)	Domestic/ Offshore	Coupon (%)	Maturity
Anargam Fin*	IRP21	D	16.00	2000
Arihant Thread*	IRP30.1	D	16.00	2001
Armour Poly*	IRP4	D	14.00	2000
Ashok Leyland*	IRP201.9	D	14.00	1998
Atlas Cycle*	IRP9.9	D	15.00	2001
Auto Corp Goa*	IRP8.1	D	17.00	2001
Ballarpur Ind	US$35	O	4.00	1999
Bausch India	IRP3.7*	D	14.00	1999

INDIA (continued)

Issuer	Amount (mln)	Domestic/ Offshore	Coupon (%)	Maturity
Bell Ceramics*	IPR6.4	D	16.00	1999
Bharat Vijay*	IRP8.3	D	16.50	2002
Can Fin Homes*	IRP26.2	D	14.00	1999
Carborundum*	IRP35.4	D	15.00	2001
Ceat*	IRP110.3	D	15.00	2002
Chambal Fert*	IRP424	D	15.00	2001
Cosmo Film#	IRP17.9	D	15.00	2000
DCM Shriram*	IRP34.5	D	15.00	2001
DCW*	IRP31.5	D	16.50	1999
Deccan Cem*	IRP8.7	D	15.00	2000
Dharamsi Chem*	IRP12	D	16.00	1999
Drillco Hertel*	IRP4.5	D	16.00	2001
EID Parry*	IRP133.5	D	15.00	2002
Electrosteel*	IRP25.2	D	15.00	2001
Elgi Equip*	IRP7.5	D	16.00	2002
Ennore Found*	IRP6.8	D	15.00	2001
Essar Gujarat	US$65	O	5.50	1998
Essar Shipping*	IRP185.1	D	16.50	2002
Flex Food*	IRP6.4	D	16.00	2001
Flex Ind*	IRP39.3	D	17.50	2002
Ganesh Benz*	IRP5.6	D	17.00	1998
German Rem*	IRP6.2	D	15.00	2002
Gov't India**	IRP3000	D	12.75	1998
Gujarat Ambuja	US$75	O	3.50	1999
Gujarat Ind	IRP24	D	12.50	2001
Herbertsons*	IRP10.8	D	15.00	2000
Herdilla Uni*	IRP18	D	12.50	2001
Hero Honda*	IRP19.4	D	15.00	2002
Hindustan Dev*	IRP300.2	D	14.00	1999
Hindustan San*	IRP20.7	D	15.00	2002
Hyderabad Ind*	IRP20	D	15.00	2002
ICICI	US$200	O	2.50	2000
Indian Organic*	IRP25	D	15.00	2000
Indian Petro*	IRP251	D	16.00	2001
Indian Seam*	IRP63	D	15.00	2001
Intl Comp*	IRP6	D	12.50	2002
Ion Exchange*	IRP13.2	D	15.00	2001
Jain Irrig*	IRP45.3	D	15.00	2000
Jayant Vit*	IRP4.7	D	15.00	2000

INDIA (continued)

Issuer	Amount (mln)	Domestic/ Offshore	Coupon (%)	Maturity
Jayaswals Neco*	IRP12	D	15.00	2000
Jindal Drill*	IRP20	D	16.50	2001
Jindal Iron*	IRP42.6	D	12.50	2000
Jindal Strips	US$55	O	4.25	1999
Jindal Strips*	IRP267	D	12.00	1997
JK Ind*	IRP175.5	D	15.00	2002
KG Denim*	IRP43.6	D	17.00	2000
Kolhapur St*	IRP0.3	D	15.00	1999
Kotak Mah*	IRP15.5	D	14.00	2001
Kothari Ind*	IRP18.9	D	16.00	2000
Kothari Sugar*	IRP13.6	D	16.00	2000
Kumar Cotex#	IRP25.2	D	16.00	1997
Lakshmi Mills*	IRP6.3	D	15.00	2000
LG Balakrish*	IRP6.7	D	16.00	2002
Lupin Chem*	IRP45.6	D	12.50	2003
Lupin Lab*	IRP186.5	D	16.00	1999
Madhusudan Ind*	IRP15	D	15.00	2001
Mahavir Spin*	IRP112.6	D	14.00	1999
Mahindra Ugine*	IRP12.1	D	12.50	1997
Modi Mirrlee*	IRP11.2	D	14.00	2001
Monica Elec*	IRP11.7	D	14.00	2000
Montarri Le*	IRP11.9	D	14.00	2001
Murudeshwar Ce*	IRP16.2	D	16.00	2001
Nagarjuna Fert*	IRP221.1	D	16.00	2001
Natco Labs*	IRP5.6	D	17.50	2000
Network*	IRP8.4	D	15.00	2000
Nicholas Piram*	IRP16.3	D	12.50	2002
Nippon Denro	US$125	O	3.00	2001
Novopan India*	IRP2.4	D	16.00	2000
Orient Press*	IRP15	D	14.50	2001
Orissa Lamps*	IRP8.8	D	16.00	2002
Pampasar Dist*	IRP3.25	D	16.50	2000
Pennar Alum*	IRP56.5	D	16.00	2001
Piramal Spin*	IRP9.1	D	17.00	2001
Ponni Sugar*	IRP22.1	D	16.00	2000
Raashi Fert*	IRP8.8	D	16.00	2001
Rajasthan Pet*	IRP8.2	D	15.00	2001
Rama News*	IRP110	D	16.00	2001
Ranbaxy Lab*	IRP43	D	12.50	1999

INDIA (continued)

Issuer	Amount (mln)	Domestic/ Offshore	Coupon (%)	Maturity
Rane Brake*	IRP8.9	D	16.00	2001
Reliance Ind	US$140	O	3.50	1999
Reliance Ind*	IRP478.8	D	12.50	2002
Reliance Poly#	IRP375	D	16.00	1999
Reliance Poly#	IRP400	D	16.00	1999
Sabero Org*	IRP8.6	D	16.00	2001
Saurashtra Cem*	IRP83.9	D	18.00	2001
SCICI	US$100	O	3.50	2004
Shanthi Gear*	IRP4.6	D	17.00	2000
Sharada Prod*	IRP39.4	D	17.00	2001
Shri Ishar Stl*	IRP25.8	D	15.00	2002
Siltap Chem*	IRP6.1	D	15.00	1996
Siyaram Silk*	IRP15.4	D	16.00	2002
Somany Pilk*	IRP17.5	D	15.00	2000
Special Steel*	IRP89.7	D	14.00	2000
Stand Ind*	IRP32.5	D	17.50	2000
Sterlite Ind	US$100	O	3.50	1999
Straw Prod*	IRP23.2	D	14.00	2001
Supreme Ind*	IRP81	D	15.00	2000
Supreme Petr*	IRP87.7	D	16.00	2002
Tata Chemicals*	IRP80.5	D	12.50	2001
Tata Chemicals*	IRP225	D	12.50	2001
Tata Electric*	IRP212	D	14.00	2002
Tata Electric*	IRP212	D	14.00	2002
Tata Iron	US$100	O	2.25	1999
Tata Vashisti*	IRP25.4	D	14.00	2001
Thapar Milk#	IRP7.4	D	14.00	1996
Thirani Chem*	IRP4.1	D	14.00	2001
Timex Watches*	IRP56	D	12.50	2002
Tri Sure India*	IRP23.2	D	14.00	2002
Triveni Eng*	IRP23.6	D	14.00	2000
Tube Inv*	IRP32.1	D	15.00	2001
Udaipur Phos*	IRP4.6	D	16.00	1999
Uniglobe Gly*	IRP140.5	D	16.00	1999
United Phosph*	IRP78.1	D	17.00	2000
Vardhman Spin*	IRP50.1	D	14.00	2001
Videocon#	IRP240	D	10.00	2000
Vijay Fire#	IRP3.4	D	14.00	1995

INDIA (continued)

Issuer	Amount (mln)	Domestic/ Offshore	Coupon (%)	Maturity
Vikas Hybrids*	IRP7.3	D	16.00	2000
Woolworth Ind*	IRP31.7	D	12.50	2001

* Partly convertible debenture, ** zero-coupon convertible debenture, # fully convertible debenture; ## IRP in crore (1 crore = IRP10,000)

INDONESIA

Issuer	Amount (mln)	Domestic/ Offshore	Coupon (%)	Maturity
Astra Intl	US$125	O	6.75	2000
Eka Gunatam	US$45	O	4.00	1997
Indorama	CHF40	O	1.75	2000
Indorama	CHF60	O	4.50	1997
Indorayon	US$60	O	7.00	2006
Indorayon	US$60	O	5.50	2002
Indorayon	CHF60	O	4.75	1997
Surya Citra	US$30	O	4.00	1997
Tjiwi Kimia	US$40	O	0.00	1997
Tjiwi Kimia	CHF50	O	5.00	1997
Tjiwi Kimia	US$75	O	7.25	2001

JAPAN

Issuer	Amount (mln)	Domestic/ Offshore	Coupon (%)	Maturity
Aderans	CHF100	O	0.87	1998
Aderans	JPY970	D	1.80	1997
Aisan	JPY5,000	D	2.10	1995
Aisan Seiki	JPY30,000	D	1.90	1998
Aisan Seiki	JPY30,000	D	2.00	2004
Aisan Seiki	JPY20,000	D	2.10	1996
Ajinomoto	JPY70,000	D	1.40	1997
Ajinomoto	JPY50,000	D	1.90	2002
Ajinomoto	JPY30,000	D	3.20	1997
Alinco	CHF45	O	0.62	1998
Almetax	CHF25	O	1.00	1997
Alp Elec	JPY50,000	D	2.00	2002

JAPAN (continued)

Issuer	Amount (mln)	Domestic/ Offshore	Coupon (%)	Maturity
Amada Co	JPY30,000	D	2.10	1997
Amada Co	JPY30,000	D	2.30	2001
Amada Co	US$30	O	5.50	1997
Amada Met	JPY20,000	D	1.60	1999
Amada Met	JPY10,000	D	1.70	1997
Aoki Corp	JPY15,000	D	2.00	2000
Aoki Corp	JPY15,000	D	2.00	2003
Aoki Corp	JPY30,000	D	2.30	2001
Aoki Corp	JPY30,000	D	2.30	2004
Aoki Corp	JPY12,000	D	5.30	1996
Aoki Corp	JPY20,000	D	5.40	1997
Aoki Corp	JPY20,000	D	5.50	1998
Asahi Bank	JPY15,000	D	1.40	1996
Asahi Bank	JPY15,000	D	1.40	1996
Asahi Bank	US$100	O	1.75	2002
Asahi Brew	JPY20,000	D	0.90	2001
Asahi Brew	JPY20,000	D	0.95	2002
Asahi Brew	JPY40,000	D	1.00	2003
Asahi Brew	JPY30,000	D	2.00	1995
Asahi Brew	JPY20,000	D	2.10	1997
Asahi Brew	JPY20,000	D	2.50	2001
Asahi Brew	JPY35,000	D	6.20	1996
Asahi Brew	JPY15,000	D	6.40	1998
Asahi Chem	JPY80,000	D	1.50	1999
Asahi Chem	JPY50,000	D	1.70	2003
Asahi Chem	JPY10,000	D	2.30	1997
Asahi Chem	JPY30,000	D	3.00	1995
Ashikaga Bk	US$50	O	2.12	2002
Ashimori Ind	JPY6,000	D	2.30	1996
Ashimori Ind	JPY4,000	D	3.80	1996
Atsugi Motor	JPY5,000	D	3.70	1995
Bandai Logic	CHF20	O	0.62	1998
Bank of Fuku	JPY20,000	D	1.50	1996
Bank of Tokyo	JPY20,000	D	1.30	1995
Bank of Tokyo	US$100	O	3.38	2004
Bank of Tokyo	JPY50,000	D	3.75	2003
Bank of Tokyo	JPY50,000	D	4.25	perp
Bank of Tokyo	JPY20,000	D	6.10	1997
Bank of Tokyo	JPY20,000	D	6.20	1998

JAPAN (continued)

Issuer	Amount (mln)	Domestic/ Offshore	Coupon (%)	Maturity
Bank of Yoko	JPY15,000	D	1.50	1996
Bank of Yoko	US$100	O	2.38	2001
Cabin Co	JPY10,000	D	1.90	1997
Cabin Co	JPY10,000	D	4.20	2001
Canon	JPY30,000	D	1.00	2002
Canon	JPY30,000	D	1.20	2005
Canon	JPY40,000	D	1.30	2008
Canon	US$100	O	3.00	2000
Canon	US$50	O	5.50	1996
Canon	US$50	O	6.75	1995
Casio Comp	JPY25,000	D	1.90	2004
Casio Comp	JPY15,000	D	2.90	1998
Casio Comp	US$100	O	3.00	2000
Catena	JPY10,000	D	2.20	2004
Catena	CHF40	O	3.62	1997
Catena	CHF80	O	4.62	1996
Cesar	CHF100	O	0.13	1998
Cesar	CHF100	O	0.75	1998
Cesar	JPY4,500	D	2.60	1996
Chino Co	JPY3,000	D	2.40	1997
Chiyoda Co	JPY10,000	D	4.25	1998
Citizen	US$50	O	3.00	2000
Cosmo Oil	JPY30,000	D	1.10	2005
Cosmo Oil	JPY40,000	D	3.40	2000
Cosmo Oil	JPY48,000	D	4.40	2000
Cowboy Co	JPY10,000	D	3.00	2002
Daidoh	JPY7,000	D	1.90	1999
Daidoh	JPY4,000	D	3.90	1996
Daiei	JPY20,000	D	1.60	1999
Daiei	JPY20,000	D	1.60	2002
Daiichi Co	JPY10,000	D	1.70	1996
Daiho Const	JPY5,000	D	1.00	2001
Daiho Const	JPY5,000	D	2.20	1996
Daiken Corp	JPY10,000	D	2.10	2002
Daimaru	JPY30,000	D	1.70	1999
Damiaru	JPY20,000	D	2.40	2004
Daimei Tel	JPY8,000	D	1.70	2002
Daimei Tel	JPY8,000	D	1.80	2009
Daimei Tel	JPY4,000	D	1.90	1997

JAPAN (continued)

Issuer	Amount (mln)	Domestic/ Offshore	Coupon (%)	Maturity
Dainippon Pr	JPY15,000	D	1.50	1997
Dainippon Pr	JPY25,000	D	1.50	2002
Dainippon Pr	JPY20,000	D	1.80	2000
Dainippon Pr	JPY30,000	D	1.80	2003
Dainippon Pr	JPY20,000	D	1.90	1996
Dainippon Sc	JPY20,000	D	3.40	1995
Daiwa House	JPY30,000	D	0.80	1998
Daiwa House	JPY15,000	D	2.00	1996
Daiwa House	JPY15,000	D	2.00	1998
Daiwa House	JPY30,000	D	2.00	2001
Daiwa Sec	JPY20,000	D	1.20	1995
Daiwa Sec	JPY20,000	D	1.30	1997
Daiwa Sec	JPY10,000	D	1.40	1996
Daiwa Sec	JPY30,000	D	1.40	1998
Daiwa Sec	JPY40,000	D	1.40	2000
Daiwa Sec	JPY40,000	D	1.40	2003
Daiwa Sec	JPY20,000	D	1.50	1997
Daiwa Sec	JPY20,000	D	1.50	1999
Daiwa Sec	JPY20,000	D	1.50	2002
Daiwa Sec	JPY10,000	D	1.90	1996
Daiwa Sec	JPY10,000	D	1.90	1998
Daiwa Sec	US$50	O	5.50	1995
Daiwa Sec	US$60	O	5.50	1998
DKB	JPY20,000	D	1.10	01995
DKB	US$100	O	2.75	2001
DKB	DM200	O	2.87	1996
DKB	US$300	O	3.87	2004
Dynic Co	JPY4,000	D	2.70	1998
Eighteen Bk	JPY10,000	D	1.70	1999
Eighteen Bk	JPY18,000	D	2.00	2003
Ezaki Glico	JPY15,000	D	1.30	2004
Ezaki Glico	JPY8,000	D	1.80	1996
Fanuc	JPY20,000	D	1.87	1995
Fanuc	US$80	O	3.75	1998
Fuji Elec	JPY30,000	D	5.30	1996
Fuji Elec	US$30	O	5.50	1996
Fujikura	JPY10,000	D	2.00	2003
Fujikura	JPY10,000	D	2.00	2004
Fujikura	JPY10,000	D	2.40	2002

JAPAN (continued)

Issuer	Amount (mln)	Domestic/ Offshore	Coupon (%)	Maturity
Fujikura	JPY14,000	D	4.00	2001
Fujita Corp	JPY30,000	D	1.70	1999
Fujita Corp	JPY30,000	D	1.80	2002
Fujita Corp	JPY30,000	D	2.10	1999
Fujitsu	JPY40,000	D	1.30	1998
Fujitsu	JPY40,000	D	1.40	2004
Fujitsu	JPY40,000	D	1.90	2002
Fujitsu	JPY40,000	D	1.95	2003
Fujitsu	JPY20,000	D	2.00	2004
Fujitsu	US$180	O	3.00	1999
Fujitsu	JPY35,000	D	4.30	1995
Fujitsu	US$80	O	5.50	1996
Fukuoka Sogo	US$50	O	1.62	2002
Fuji Bank	US$200	O	1.75	2002
Fuji Bank	US$100	O	2.75	2000
Fuji Heavy	JPY40,000	D	1.80	2003
Fuji Heavy	US$50	O	3.00	2000
Fuji Oil	JPY10,000	D	1.90	1996
Fuji Oil	JPY20,000	D	2.30	2004
Futaba Corp	JPY10,000	D	1.60	1997
Godo Steel	JPY15,000	D	2.60	2002
Gourmet Kine	JPY5,000	D	1.70	2000
Gunma Bank	JPY20,000	D	1.70	1997
Gunma Bank	US$50	O	2.13	2002
Hankyu Dep	JPY10,000	D	1.90	1997
Hankyu Dep	JPY15,000	D	2.00	2000
Haseko Corp	JPY15,000	D	2.10	1997
Haseko Corp	JPY15,000	D	2.10	2002
Haseko Corp	JPY40,000	D	2.30	2001
Haseko Corp	JPY40,000	D	2.30	2004
Haseko Corp	JPY10,000	D	2.40	1998
Heiwa Real	JPY20,000	D	1.70	1996
Heiwa Real	JPY10,000	D	2.50	2002
Heiwado Co	JPY10,000	D	1.90	1999
Heiwado Co	JPY15,000	D	1.90	2002
Heiwado Co	JPY8,000	D	2.00	1996
Hirose Elec	JPY10,000	D	1.70	2003
Hitachi AIC	JPY4,000	D	4.70	1998
Hitachi Cable	JPY15,000	D	1.40	1997

JAPAN (continued)

Issuer	Amount (mln)	Domestic/ Offshore	Coupon (%)	Maturity
Hitachi Cable	US$60	O	1.75	2002
Hitachi Cable	JPY8,000	D	1.80	2002
Hitachi Cred	JPY15,000	D	1.80	2004
Hitachi Cred	US$40	O	5.00	1996
Hitachi Max	US$70	O	1.50	2003
Hitachi Max	US$30	O	4.75	1997
Hitachi Trans	JPY10,000	D	2.25	2002
Hitachi Zos	JPY30,000	D	1.40	2001
Hitachi Zos	JPY20,000	D	3.20	2002
Hogy Medical	US$50	O	2.75	1997
Hokkaido Bk	JPY15,000	D	1.90	2003
Hokkaido Bk	US$30	O	2.13	2002
Hokkaido Tak	US$100	O	1.75	2002
Hokuriku Bank	US$100	O	1.50	2002
Hokuriku Bank	US$100	O	3.13	2003
Hokuriku Elec	JPY4,000	D	2.40	2002
Hokushin Co	JPY7,000	D	1.00	2003
Hokushin Co	JPY4,000	D	1.20	2003
Hokushin Co	JPY2,500	D	2.40	1998
Hokushin Co	JPY4,000	D	2.70	2002
Hokushin Co	JPY4,000	D	4.40	1999
Honda Motor	US$100	O	5.25	1998
Honda Motor	US$80	O	5.50	1997
House Food	JPY15,000	D	1.50	1999
House Food	JPY15,000	D	1.80	2002
House Food	JPY10,000	D	2.20	1996
Ichikawa Wool	JPY4,000	D	2.50	1998
Ichikoh Ind	JPY4,000	D	4.00	1995
Iino Kaiun	JPY13,000	D	4.90	2000
Inageya	JPY6,000	D	2.00	1997
Isetan	JPY20,000	D	1.70	2002
Isetan	JPY10,000	D	2.20	1998
Isetan	JPY10,000	D	2.20	2001
Itoham Food	JPY20,000	D	1.80	2003
Itoham Food	JPY10,000	D	2.30	1999
Itoman	JPY20,000	D	1.70	1996
Itoman	JPY10,000	D	1.80	1998
Itoman	JPY15,000	D	2.40	1996
Ito-yokado	JPY30,000	D	1.80	2002

JAPAN (continued)

Issuer	Amount (mln)	Domestic/ Offshore	Coupon (%)	Maturity
Ito-yokado	JPY30,000	D	3.20	1995
Iwaki Co	JPY3,000	D	2.30	1995
Izumi Co	JPY10,000	D	1.70	2002
Izumi Co	JPY10,000	D	2.30	1998
Izumi Co	JPY10,000	D	4.50	2001
Izumiya	JPY30,000	D	0.80	1999
Izumiya	JPY30,000	D	1.70	2003
Izutsuya	JPY5,000	D	2.60	1997
Jaccs Co	JPY18,000	D	0.80	2001
Jaccs Co	US$25	O	5.50	1996
Japan Aircrf	JPY5,000	D	2.50	1997
Japan Aviat	US$40	O	3.00	2000
Japan Pulp	JPY20,000	D	1.70	2002
Japan Pulp	JPY18,000	D	2.30	2004
Japan Trans	JPY9,000	D	2.30	2003
Japan Vilene	JPY5,000	D	2.00	1997
Japan Vilene	JPY5,000	D	2.10	2003
JCR Pharm	CHF50	O	0.62	1998
JDC Corp	JPY10,000	D	1.80	1998
JDC Corp	JPY10,000	D	1.90	2001
JDC Corp	JPY5,000	D	2.60	1996
Joyo Bk	JPY20,000	D	1.60	1997
Jusco	JPY25,000	D	1.20	2001
Jusco	JPY15,000	D	1.30	1997
Jusco	JPY25,000	D	1.40	2003
Jusco	GBP10	O	8.00	1996
JVC Corp	JPY30,000	D	1.40	1999
JVC Corp	JPY30,000	D	1.50	2005
JVC Corp	US$100	O	5.00	1997
Kagome	JPY15,000	D	1.80	1999
Kagome	JPY10,000	D	2.00	1996
Kajima Corp	JPY15,000	D	1.50	1997
Kajima Corp	JPY15,000	D	1.60	2001
Kajima Corp	JPY20,000	D	2.10	1998
Kaken Pharm	JPY20,000	D	1.00	2003
Kaken Pharm	JPY10,000	D	2.70	2002
Kanro Corp	JPY3,000	D	2.00	1995
Kanto Bio	CHF65	O	0.62	1998
Kanto Bio	CHF39	O	3.75	1997

JAPAN (continued)

Issuer	Amount (mln)	Domestic/ Offshore	Coupon (%)	Maturity
Kasumi	JPY7,000	D	0.90	2002
Kasumi	CHF40	O	1.25	1999
Kasumi	JPY5,000	D	2.50	1997
Kato Denki	CHF25	O	0.25	1998
Kato Denki	CHF50	O	1.00	1997
Kato Denki	CHF50	O	1.37	1999
Katokichi	JPY10,000	D	1.80	1996
Katokichi	JPY5,000	D	1.80	1996
Katokichi	JPY15,000	D	3.70	1999
Kawachiya	JPY3,000	D	1.30	2001
Kayaba Ind	JPY6,000	D	4.30	1995
Keihan Elec	JPY20,000	D	1.00	2003
Keihan Elec	JPY7,000	D	3.40	1998
Keihin Seiki	JPY4,500	D	2.30	1995
Kinki Elec	JPY14,000	D	1.60	2003
Kinki Elec	JPY15,000	D	1.90	2004
Kinki Sogo	US$50	O	2.87	2003
Kirin Brew	JPY50,000	D	1.30	1997
Kisoji Co	JPY5,000	D	1.70	2000
Kitano	JPY5,000	D	2.20	1996
Koa Fire	JPY30,000	D	0.50	1999
Koa Fire	US$70	O	1.75	2002
Koa Fire	JPY10,000	D	2.00	2002
Koito Mfg	JPY10,000	D	2.40	1996
Kokuyo Co	JPY20,000	D	1.90	2002
Kyowa Exeo	JPY15,000	D	1.00	2004
Kyowa Exeo	JPY10,000	D	1.70	1997
Kumagai Gumi	JPY40,000	D	2.80	1997
Kumagai Gumi	US$115	O	4.62	1998
Kuraray Co	JPY10,000	D	1.00	2003
Kuraray Co	JPY15,000	D	1.80	2003
Kuraray Co	JPY15,000	D	2.20	2002
Kuraray Co	JPY10,000	D	3.30	1997
Kyushu Denki	JPY10,000	D	2.30	1997
Life Co	US$25	O	6.00	1996
LTCB	JPY20,000	D	1.20	1995
LTCB	US$200	O	1.75	2002
Maeda Road	JPY20,000	D	1.70	1998
Maeda Road	JPY12,000	D	2.20	1996

JAPAN (continued)

Issuer	Amount (mln)	Domestic/ Offshore	Coupon (%)	Maturity
Marubeni	JPY20,000	D	1.80	1995
Marubeni	JPY30,000	D	1.90	1997
Marubeni	JPY30,000	D	2.00	2000
Marubeni	JPY25,000	D	2.10	1996
Marubeni	JPY25,000	D	2.10	2001
Maruetsu	JPY8,000	D	2.10	2002
Marui Co	JPY60,000	D	1.40	2003
Marui Co	US$100	O	3.50	1999
Marui Co	US$50	O	6.00	1996
Marui Co	JPY70,000	D	6.10	1999
Maruyoshi	CHF40	O	0.62	1998
Matsush Comm	JPY30,000	D	1.50	1996
Matsush El Wk	JPY80,000	D	1.00	2005
Matsush El Wk	JPY100,000	D	1.30	1998
Matsush El Wk	JPY80,000	D	1.50	2003
Mtasush El Wk	JPY50,000	D	2.00	2001
Matsush El Wk	JPY50,000	D	2.70	2002
Matsush El Wk	JPY35,000	D	3.30	1995
Matsush El Wk	JPY55,000	D	4.30	2000
Matsush El Wk	US$100	O	7.50	1995
Mazda Motor	JPY100,000	D	1.70	1998
Mazda Motor	US$100	O	3.00	2000
Mazda Motor	JPY80,000	D	6.50	1999
Mikuni Co	JPY5,000	D	2.60	1997
Minebea	JPY18,000	D	3.60	1995
Minebea	US$80	O	5.50	1998
Minolta	DM200	O	0.00	1997
Minola	US$40	O	5.00	1996
Mitani Corp	JPY3,000	D	2.00	1996
Mitsubishi Bk	JPY20,000	D	1.20	1995
Mitsubishi Bk	US$300	O	1.75	2002
Mitsubishi Bk	US$100	O	2.87	2000
Mitsubishi Co	JPY30,000	D	1.60	1996
Mitsubishi Bk	US$300	O	3.50	2004
Mitsubishi El	JPY70,000	D	1.30	1997
Mitsubishi El	JPY130,000	D	1.40	1999
Mitsubishi El	JPY80,000	D	2.00	2003
Mitsubishi El	US$100	O	2.87	2000
Mitsubishi El	US$100	O	5.25	1998

JAPAN (continued)

Issuer	Amount (mln)	Domestic/ Offshore	Coupon (%)	Maturity
Mitsubishi El	US$80	O	5.75	1996
Mitsubishi Hv	JPY100,000	D	2.10	2001
Mitsubishi Hv	US$100	O	4.75	1999
Mitsubishi Ra	JPY30,000	D	1.70	1999
Mitsubishi Ra	JPY10,000	D	1.80	2003
Mitsubishi Tr	US$100	O	1.75	2002
Mitsubishi Tr	US$100	O	2.50	2001
Mitsubishi Tr	US$100	O	3.25	2003
Mitsui Co	JPY100,000	D	1.05	2009
Mitsui Co	JPY50,000	D	1.40	1997
Mitsui Co	JPY100,000	D	1.40	1999
Mitsui Co	JPY50,000	D	1.50	2003
Mitsui Trust	JPY40,000	D	1.30	1996
Mitsui Trust	JPY40,000	D	1.40	1998
Mitsui Trust	US$100	O	2.37	2001
Mitsukoshi	JPY20,000	D	1.70	2000
Mitsukoshi	JPY20,000	D	1.70	2003
Mitsukoshi	JPY30,000	D	5.70	1997
Miura Print	JPY2,500	D	2.30	1996
Miura Print	JPY5,000	D	5.5	01996
Mizuno	JPY5,000	D	1.80	1997
Mizuno	JPY5,000	D	1.90	2003
Mizuno	JPY20,000	D	2.10	1998
Mizuno	JPY3,000	D	2.30	1997
Morinaga	JPY10,000	D	1.60	1999
Morinaga	JPY10,000	D	2.00	2001
Morinaga	JPY10,000	D	2.50	2002
Morinaga	JPY10,000	D	2.70	2002
Morinaga	JPY10,000	D	3.50	1996
Morinaga	JPY20,000	D	1.00	2001
Morinaga	JPY15,000	D	1.70	1995
Morozoff	JPY2,000	D	2.10	1996
Murata	JPY40,000	D	1.80	2002
Musashino Bk	JPY10,000	D	2.00	1997
Nakabayashi	JPY8,000	D	1.40	2002
Nakabayashi	JPY10,000	D	2.00	1997
Nakagawa Mu	JPY3,000	D	2.20	1997
Nakamuraya	JPY5,000	D	2.20	2002
Nakamuraya	JPY5,000	D	2.60	1996

JAPAN (continued)

Issuer	Amount (mln)	Domestic/ Offshore	Coupon (%)	Maturity
Namco	JPY27,500	D	0.00	1997
Namco	JPY10,000	D	0.80	2001
Namco	JPY15,000	D	0.90	2003
Namco	JPY15,000	D	4.70	1998
Namura Ship	JPY7,000	D	1.00	2001
Namura Ship	JPY7,000	D	3.80	1996
Nat'l House	JPY30,000	D	1.60	1999
Nat'l House	JPY15,000	D	2.20	1998
Nat'l House	JPY10,000	D	2.40	1996
Nat'l House	JPY15,000	D	2.40	2002
NEC Corp	CHF500	O	1.00	1999
NEC Corp	JPY30,000	D	1.70	1999
NEC Corp	JPY100,000	D	1.80	2002
NEC Corp	JPY40,000	D	1.90	2001
NEC Corp	JPY120,000	D	1.90	2004
NEC Corp	JPY60,000	D	2.10	1998
NEC Corp	US$150	O	2.87	2000
NEC Corp	US$80	O	5.25	1997
NEC Corp	GBP30	O	5.75	1996
NEC Systems	CHF130	O	1.13	1997
Nichicon Co	JPY10,000	D	1.80	1996
Nichicon Co	JPY8,000	D	2.10	1999
Nichiei Con	JPY10,000	D	1.40	1997
Nichiei Con	JPY10,000	D	1.50	1999
Nichiei Con	JPY10,000	D	1.70	2002
Nichiei Con	JPY10,000	D	1.80	1997
Nichiei Con	JPY10,000	D	1.90	2005
Nichii Co	JPY30,000	D	1.20	1996
Nichii Co	JPY30,000	D	1.20	1997
Nichii Co	JPY20,000	D	1.30	1998
Nichii Co	JPY15,000	D	1.50	1997
Nichii Co	JPY10,000	D	1.60	2000
Nichii Co	JPY10,000	D	1.60	2003
Nichii Co	JPY20,000	D	1.80	2000
Nichii Co	JPY20,000	D	1.80	2003
Nichii Co	JPY20,000	D	2.20	1999
Nichirei Corp	JPY10,000	D	1.70	1997
Nichirei Corp	JPY10,000	D	1.80	2003
Nichirei Corp	JPY10,000	D	2.30	1997

JAPAN (continued)

Issuer	Amount (mln)	Domestic/ Offshore	Coupon (%)	Maturity
Nichirei Corp	JPY10,000	D	4.90	1996
Nichirei Corp	JPY10,000	D	5.00	1997
Nichiwa San	JPY3,500	D	1.50	2001
NIFCO	JPY15,000	D	2.10	2004
NIFCO	JPY15,000	D	2.30	2008
NIFCO	JPY7,000	D	3.60	1995
Nihon Kogyo	CHF55	O	0.75	1998
Nihon Matai	JPY4,000	D	2.50	1998
Nippon Cable	JPY7,000	D	2.30	1997
Nippon Chem	JPY10,000	D	2.30	2002
Nippon Col	JPY10,000	D	2.10	1996
Nippon Denso	JPY100,000	D	1.20	1997
Nippon Denso	JPY40,000	D	1.40	1999
Nippon Denso	JPY60,000	D	1.60	2002
Nippon Denso	JPY30,000	D	4.10	1998
Nippon Hodo	JPY10,000	D	2.20	1999
Nippon Koei	JPY10,000	D	1.90	1997
Nippon Koei	JPY10,000	D	4.10	2001
Nippon Konpo	JPY8,000	D	2.30	1997
Nippon Konpo	JPY4,000	D	3.70	1996
Nippon Konpo	JPY10,000	D	4.10	1999
Nippon Meat	JPY10,000	D	1.80	1997
Nippon Meat	JPY10,000	D	1.90	2003
Nippon Meat	JPY8,000	D	2.00	1999
Nippon Oil	JPY70,000	D	1.50	1999
Nippon Oil	JPY70,000	D	1.60	2005
Nippon Oil	JPY30,000	D	1.70	2000
Nippon Oil	JPY50,000	D	1.70	2003
Nippon Oil	JPY25,000	D	2.10	1996
Nippon Oil	JPY25,000	D	2.10	2001
Nippon Oil	JPY50,000	D	2.80	2000
Nippon Oil	US$70	O	3.00	2000
Nippon Oil	US$50	O	3.25	1999
Nippon Oil	US$50	O	5.50	1998
Nippon Road	JPY20,000	D	1.80	1999
Nippon Road	JPY10,000	D	2.40	1997
Nippon Seiko	JPY20,000	D	1.50	1999
Nippon Seiko	JPY20,000	D	1.60	2005
Nippon Seiko	JPY15,000	D	2.40	1998

JAPAN (continued)

Issuer	Amount (mln)	Domestic/ Offshore	Coupon (%)	Maturity
Nippon Seiko	JPY22,500	D	2.40	2001
Nippon Seiko	US$70	O	3.25	1999
Nippon Suisan	US$30	O	3.25	1995
Nippon Suisan	JPY8,000	D	3.60	1995
Nippon Tel	JPY7,000	D	2.10	1997
Nippon Yus	CHF50	O	4.87	1996
Nishi Nipp	US$70	O	2.87	2003
Nissan Motor	JPY100,000	D	1.60	2003
Nissan Motor	US$100	O	5.75	1998
Nissan Motor	GBP50	O	6.00	1996
Nisseki House	JPY9,000	D	1.00	2001
Nisseki House	JPY7,000	D	2.00	1996
Nisseki House	CHF110	O	2.00	1999
Nisseki House	CHF65	O	3.75	1997
Nisseki House	CHF50	O	4.75	1996
Nisshinbo	JPY30,000	D	1.70	1999
Nisshinbo	JPY20,000	D	2.10	1997
Nisshin Flour	JPY20,000	D	1.80	2003
Nissho Iwai	US$40	O	8.00	1996
Nissin Food	JPY10,000	D	3.10	1996
Nissin Sugar	JPY5,000	D	2.60	1997
Nitto Denko	JPY15,000	D	2.20	1999
Nitto Denko	JPY25,000	D	3.90	2001
Nitto Denko	US$40	O	5.75	1996
Nitto Seiko	JPY3,000	D	2.70	1996
Nitto Seiko	JPY4,000	D	4.80	1998
Nittoc Const	JPY3,000	D	2.60	1997
Odakyu Elec	JPY20,000	D	1.50	1998
Odakyu Elec	JPY30,000	D	1.60	2002
Odakyu Elec	JPY10,000	D	4.20	1998
Odakyu Elec	JPY30,000	D	4.90	1997
ODD Corp	JPY5,000	D	2.20	1997
Ohbayashi	JPY10,000	D	1.50	1998
Ohbayashi	JPY10,000	D	1.60	2001
Ohbayashi	JPY10,000	D	1.60	2004
Ohbayashi	JPY20,000	D	2.10	1999
Ohbayashi	JPY20,000	D	2.10	2002
Okayel El	JPY3,000	D	2.50	1998
Okumura Co	US$30	O	5.75	1997

JAPAN (continued)

Issuer	Amount (mln)	Domestic/ Offshore	Coupon (%)	Maturity
Olympic Corp	JPY5,000	D	1.00	1999
Olympic Corp	JPY5,000	D	1.25	1998
Olympic Sport	JPY5,000	D	1.75	1997
Olympus Opt	US$40	O	6.75	1997
Omron	JPY30,000	D	1.70	2004
Omron	US$150	O	2.62	2002
Onward Ka	JPY10,000	D	2.20	1999
Orient Corp	JPY20,000	D	1.90	1997
Orient Corp	JPY25,000	D	1.90	1999
Orient Corp	JPY25,000	D	1.90	2002
Orient Corp	US$60	O	5.25	1997
Orient Corp	GBP15	O	8.00	1995
Oriental Ye	JPY3,000	D	2.10	2003
Orix	JPY8,000	D	1.30	1996
Orix	GBP10	O	8.00	1995
Osaki Elec	JPY6,000	D	2.60	2002
Osaki Elec	CHF50	O	4.00	1995
OSG Mfg	JPY8,000	D	5.20	1996
QP Corp	JPY10,000	D	0.80	2001
QP Corp	JPY20,000	D	1.00	2005
QP Corp	JPY10,000	D	1.90	1996
QP Corp	JPY10,000	D	2.00	2002
Rengo Co	JPY10,000	D	1.90	1998
Rengo Co	JPY10,000	D	2.00	2004
Rengo Co	JPY10,000	D	2.30	2003
Rengo Co	JPY8,000	D	3.80	1999
Rengo Co	JPY10,000	D	3.90	2001
Rengo Co	JPY15,000	D	6.50	1997
Ricoh	JPY40,000	D	1.50	2002
Ricoh	JPY30,000	D	1.80	2002
Ricoh	JPY30,000	D	1.90	1998
Riso Kagaku	JPY18,000	D	1.50	2009
Riso Kagaku	JPY7,000	D	1.62	1998
Riso Kagaku	JPY10,000	D	1.87	2002
Riso Kagaku	JPY10,000	D	2.50	1998
Riso Kagaku	JPY5,000	D	4.50	1999
Riso Kagaku	CHF30	O	5.50	1995
Royal Co	JPY18,000	D	1.80	1997
Royal Co	US$70	O	2.62	2001

JAPAN (continued)

Issuer	Amount (mln)	Domestic/ Offshore	Coupon (%)	Maturity
Royal Co	US$40	O	3.00	1999
Ryobi Co	JPY15,000	D	2.80	2002
Sakahi Hvy	US$15	O	5.75	1996
Sakura Bank	US$120	O	1.75	2002
Sakura Bank	US$100	O	2.62	2001
Sakura Bank	US$200	O	2.62	2003
Sakura Bank	JPY100,000	D	5.40	1996
San-ai Oil	JPY5,000	D	1.60	2005
San-ai Oil	JPY8,000	D	1.80	2007
San-ai Oil	JPY5,000	D	2.10	1999
San-ai Oil	JPY5,000	D	2.20	2001
San-ai Oil	CHF100	O	4.00	1995
Sankyo Seiki	JPY10,000	D	6.20	1997
Sanraku	JPY15,000	D	2.00	2002
Sanraku	JPY20,000	D	2.00	2004
Sanrio	JPY10,000	D	1.80	1996
Sanyo Elec	JPY10,000	D	1.60	2002
Sanyo Elec	JPY20,000	D	1.40	1996
Sanyo Elec	JPY20,000	D	1.50	1998
Sanyo Elec	JPY20,000	D	1.60	1996
Sanyo Elec	JPY60,000	D	1.60	2004
Sanyo Elec	US$100	O	3.50	1999
Sanwa Bank	JPY15,000	D	1.60	1995
Sanwa Bank	US$300	O	1.75	2002
Sanwa Bank	US$100	O	2.75	2000
Sapporo Br	JPY20,000	D	1.20	2009
Sapporo Br	JPY40,000	D	1.37	2000
Sapporo Br	JPY30,000	D	1.60	1997
Sapporo Br	JPY30,000	D	1.80	2002
Secom Co	JPY10,000	D	1.40	1996
Secom Co	JPY10,000	D	1.50	1998
Secom Co	JPY10,000	D	1.60	2002
Secom Co	JPY10,000	D	1.60	2004
Secom Co	JPY10,000	D	2.00	1996
Secom Co	JPY10,000	D	4.40	1996
Sega Ent	JPY35,000	D	0.00	1996
Sega Ent	JPY20,000	D	0.000	1999
Sega Ent	JPY100,000	D	0.55	2000
Sega Ent	JPY20,000	D	3.90	1995

JAPAN (continued)

Issuer	Amount (mln)	Domestic/ Offshore	Coupon (%)	Maturity
Seikagaku	CHF130	O	0.12	1998
Seikagaku	JPY4,000	D	2.50	1997
Seikagaku	JPY4,000	D	2.70	2000
Seiyo Food	US$25	O	3.25	2000
Seiyo Food	JPY10,000	D	5.10	1997
Seiyo Food	JPY7,000	D	5.20	1998
Seiyu Stores	US$15	O	7.25	1996
Sekisui House	JPY50,000	D	0.80	2001
Sekisui House	JPY50,000	D	0.90	2003
Sekisui House	JPY20,000	D	1.50	1997
Sekisui House	JPY20,000	D	1.60	1996
Sekisui House	JPY30,000	D	1.60	2000
Sekisui House	JPY30,000	D	1.60	2003
Sekisui House	JPY50,000	D	1.70	2002
Sekisui House	JPY20,000	D	2.40	2000
Sekisui House	JPY20,000	D	2.50	2002
Sekisui House	JPY25,000	D	4.60	1997
Sekisui House	JPY25,000	D	4.70	1998
Sekisui House	JPY25,000	D	4.80	1999
Shikoku Coca	JPY6,500	D	2.40	2002
Shimac	JPY5,000	D	3.60	1995
Shimano	JPY15,000	D	2.00	1998
Shimano	JPY3,000	D	2.60	1999
Shin-Etsu Ch	JPY40,000	D	1.30	1999
Shin-Etsu Ch	JPY25,000	D	2.00	1998
Shin-Etsu Ch	JPY15,000	D	2.10	1997
Shin-Etsu Ch	US$30	O	3.00	2000
Shin-Etsu Po	JPY5,000	D	2.40	1999
Shin Kobe El	JPY8,000	D	4.40	2001
Shin Meiwa	JPY10,000	D	2.20	2003
Shin Meiwa	JPY15,000	D	2.40	2004
Shin Meiwa	JPY6,000	D	2.70	1996
Shin Meiwa	JPY18,000	D	4.70	2000
Shinko Elec	JPY15,000	D	2.40	2000
Shinko Elec	JPY10,000	D	4.50	1995
Shinko Wire	JPY7,000	D	1.40	2002
Shinko Wire	JPY5,000	D	1.70	2000
Shinnihon	JPY5,000	D	1.90	2000
Showa Air	JPY7,000	D	2.00	1997

JAPAN (continued)

Issuer	Amount (mln)	Domestic/ Offshore	Coupon (%)	Maturity
Showa Air	JPY7,000	D	2.30	2002
Showa Air	JPY12,000	D	4.40	1999
Showa Corp	JPY10,000	D	1.70	2000
Showa Corp	JPY6,000	D	2.00	1998
Showa Corp	JPY4,000	D	2.70	1996
Showa Sangyo	JPY10,000	D	2.30	2002
Skylark	JPY20,000	D	1/60	1996
Snow Brand	JPY10,000	D	1.60	2000
Snow Brand	JPY10,000	D	1.70	2000
Snow Brand	JPY10,000	D	1.70	2002
Snow Brand	JPY10,000	D	1.70	2003
Snow Brand	JPY5,000	D	2.40	1997
Snow Brand	JPY5,000	D	2.40	1999
Sony	JPY92,000	D	1.40	2003
Sony	JPY300,000	D	1.40	2005
Sony	JPY75,000	D	1.50	2002
Sony	JPY300,000	D	2.00	2000
Sony	US$50	O	6.00	1997
Sotetsu Ros	JPY5,000	D	1.00	2003
Sotetsu Ros	JPY5,000	D	2.00	1999
Sotetsu Ros	JPY4,000	D	2.30	1997
Sotetsu Ros	JPY3,000	D	2.30	1998
Sotetsu Ros	JPY6,000	D	6.30	1997
SRL	JPY3,880	D	4.00	1999
Star Mfg	US$50	O	3.50	2000
Star Mfg	US$150	O	4.00	1998
Sugimura War	JPY4,000	D	0.90	2001
Sumitomo Bk	US$120	O	2.75	2000
Sumitomo Bk	US$300	O	3.13	2004
Sumitomo Ch	JPY10,000	D	1.40	1996
Sumitomo Ch	JPY20,000	D	1.50	1998
Sumitomo Ch	JPY20,000	D	1.60	1997
Sumitomo Ch	JPY20,000	D	1.70	2003
Sumitomo Ch	JPY10,000	D	4.60	1998
Sumitomo Ch	JPY10,000	D	4.70	1999
Sumitomo Ch	JPY10,000	D	4.70	2000
Sumitomo Co	JPY50,000	D	1.40	1998
Sumitomo Co	JPY50,000	D	1.50	2004
Sumitomo Co	JPY20,000	D	1.60	2002

JAPAN (continued)

Issuer	Amount (mln)	Domestic/ Offshore	Coupon (%)	Maturity
Sumitomo Den	JPY3,000	D	2.10	1997
Sumitomo Met	JPY100,000	D	1.60	2004
Sumitomo Met	US$50	O	5.25	1996
Sumitomo Met	US$50	O	7.00	1995
Sumitomo Spc	US$50	O	3.00	2000
Sumitomo Tr	US$100	O	1.75	2002
Sumitomo Tr	US$150	O	2.50	2001
Sumiya Co	JPY3,000	D	2.60	2002
SuntelCo	JPY6,000	D	1.90	1995
Suzuki	JPY3,000	D	2.10	2003
SXL Corp	JPY20,000	D	0.90	2001
SXL Corp	JPY10,000	D	2.40	2003
SXL Corp	JPY5,000	D	2.60	1996
SXL Corp	JPY10,000	D	2.50	2000
SXL Corp	JPY15,000	D	2.70	2002
SXL Corp	JPY12,500	D	6.20	1997
Tada Corp	CHF50	O	6.75	1996
Taisei Corp	JPY50,000	D	2.20	1998
Taisei Road	JPY10,000	D	1.70	2002
Taisei Road	JPY5,000	D	3.90	1995
Taiyo	JPY15,000	D	2.50	2002
Taiyo Yuden	US$50	O	3.25	2000
Takara	JPY10,000	D	1.62	1998
Takara	JPY5,000	D	2.30	1996
Takara	JPY5,000	D	2.40	1998
Takara	JPY3,000	D	4.20	1995
Takeda Chenm	JPY30,000	D	1.90	1998
Tasaki Shin	JPY10,000	D	1.50	2003
Tasaki Shin	JPY7,000	D	1.70	2000
Tasaki Shin	JPY6,000	D	1.90	1996
TDK Corp	JPY30,000	D	1.40	1996
Teijin	JPY30,000	D	1.60	2002
Teijin	JPY20,000	D	3.20	1997
Tochigi Fuji	JPY3,500	D	2.10	1997
Toenec Co	JPY10,000	D	1.00	2004
Toenec Co	JPY5,000	D	1.10	2006
Toenec Co	JPY13,000	D	4.50	1998
Toho Rayon	JPY8,000	D	2.40	1999
Tohoku Tel	JPY2,000	D	2.20	1997

JAPAN (continued)

Issuer	Amount (mln)	Domestic/ Offshore	Coupon (%)	Maturity
Tohoku Tel	JPY2,500	D	4.50	1999
Tokai Bank	JPY20,000	D	1.30	1995
Tokai Bank	JPY30,000	D	1.40	1997
Tokai Bank	US$100	O	2.37	2001
Tokai Corp	JPY10,000	D	1.30	2004
Tokai Corp	JPY10,000	D	2.00	1999
Tokai Corp	JPY8,000	D	2.20	2003
Tokai Rika	JPY10,000	D	2.00	1998
Tokai Rika	JPY8,000	D	2.20	1996
Tokai Rika	JPY10,000	D	4.80	1997
Tokai Senko	JPY3,000	D	2.30	1996
Tokatsu Food	JPY5,000	D	1.20	2001
Tokin Corp	JPY10,000	D	1.50	2002
Tokin Corp	JPY6,500	D	6.30	1997
Tokyo Nissan	JPY10,000	D	2.40	1998
Tokyo Style	JPY15,000	D	2.10	1997
Tokyu Dept	US$25	O	5.75	1996
Tomoku	JPY10,000	D	1.70	2000
Tomoku	JPY7,000	D	1.90	1997
Tomoku	JPY4,000	D	2.90	1996
Tomoku	JPY10,000	D	5.40	1997
Toppan Print	JPY15,000	D	1.20	1997
Toppan Print	JPY35,000	D	1.40	2005
Toppan Print	JPY30,000	D	1.90	2001
Toppan Print	JPY20,000	D	3.00	1997
Toray Ind	JPY30,000	D	1.70	2002
Toshiba Cer	JPY15,000	D	2.30	1998
Toshiba Cer	US$50	O	3.00	2000
Toshoku	CHF400	O	0.12	1997
Toshoku	CHF299	O	4.00	1996
Totenko	JPY3,000	D	4.40	1995
Toyo Menka	US$20	O	7.75	1996
Toyo Suisan	JPY15,000	D	3.90	1999
Toyo Trust	JPY35,000	D	1.40	1996
Toyo Trust	US$100	O	1.75	2002
Toyo Umpanki	JPY5,000	D	2.20	1999
Toyo Umpanki	JPY5,000	D	2.70	2002
Toyoda Gos	JPY15,000	D	2.00	1997
Toyoda Gos	JPY11,000	D	4.70	1997

JAPAN (continued)

Issuer	Amount (mln)	Domestic/ Offshore	Coupon (%)	Maturity
Toyota	JPY300,000	D	1.20	1998
Toyota	JPY200,000	D	1.70	1996
Toyota AB	JPY12,000	D	2.40	1998
Tsugami Corp	US$20	O	3.25	2000
Tsuken Corp	CHf40	O	0.75	1998
Ube Indus	JPY30,000	D	1.80	1998
Ube Indus	CHF200	O	4.75	1996
Uehara	JPY4,000	D	2.40	1997
Wel Mart	CHF30	O	0.62	1998
Yakult Hon	JPY15,000	D	1.70	2003
Yakult Hon	JPY10,000	D	2.10	1999
Yamanouchi	JPY30,000	D	0.00	1999
Yamanouchi	JPY40,000	D	0.25	2014
Yamanouchi	JPY15,000	D	1.50	2002
Yamanouchi	JPY30,000	D	1.62	2000
Yamanouchi	JPY20,000	D	2.70	2000
Yamanouchi	US$50	O	2.75	2000
Yamanouchi	JPY10,000	D	2.90	1997
Yamato Trans	JPY40,000	D	1.20	2009
Yamato Trans	JPY50,000	D	1.70	2002
Yamato Trans	US$40	O	3.00	2000
Yamato Trans	JPY35,000	D	3.90	2001
Yaskawa El	JPY20,000	D	1.80	1999
Yaskawa El	JPY8,000	D	4.10	1996
Yasuda Tr	US$100	O	1.75	2002
Yasuda Tr	US$100	O	2.37	2001
Yasuda Tr	US$100	O	10.50	1995
Yodogawa St	JPY10,000	D	4.80	1996
Yokohama Rei	JPY4,500	D	2.00	1996
York Benim	JPY10,000	D	1.80	1997

MALAYSIA

Issuer	Amount (mln)	Domestic/ Offshore	Coupon (%)	Maturity
Aokam Perdama	US$135	O	3.50	2004
AMMB Hldg*	MYR424	D	7.50	1999
Arab Mal Corp*	MYR143.9	D	5.00	1997
Arab Mal Dev*	MYR145.6	D	5.50	2002

MALAYSIA (continued)

Issuer	Amount (mln)	Domestic/ Offshore	Coupon (%)	Maturity
Arab Mal Corp*	MYR411.6	D	5.00	2002
Arab Mal Fin*	MYR202.8	D	7.50	1999
Berjaya*	MYR30	D	6.00	1998
Commerce Asset	US$120	O	1.75	2004
Dunlop Estate*	MYR310	D	10.00	1996
Far East Asset*	MYR390.9	D	9.00	1997
IGB Corp*	MYR30.1	D	1.00	1995
IJM Corp*	MYR7.7	D	7.00	1997
KFC Corp*	MYR22	D	7.00	1995
Land & General	US$100	O	4.50	2004
Renong	US$225	O	2.50	2005
Renong	US$150	O	2.00	2005
Renong*	MYR623.5	D	3.00	1996
TRI	US$200	O	0.00	2004
TRI	US$175	O	2.75	2004
Telekom Mal	US$350	O	4.00	2004
United Eng*	MYR270.9	D	4.00	1999
United Eng	US$230	O	2.00	2004
Worldwide Hld*	MYR20	D	6.00	1998
YTL Corp*	US$50	O	0.00	2002

* CULS

NEW ZEALAND

Issuer	Amount (mln)	Domestic/ Offshore	Coupon (%)	Maturity
Arthur Barnes	NZ$3.1	D	8.00	1996
Brierley Inv	NZ$350	D	9.00	1998
Carter Holt	CHF100	O	3.13	1997
DB Group	NZ$106	D	7.00	1996
Fletcher Chall	NZ$250	D	0.00	2000
Fletcher Chall	NZ$250	D	10.00	2005
Nat Gas Corp	NZ$280	D	10.50	1997
Seabil NZ	NZ$91.5	D	9.00	1999
St Lukes Group	NZ$223	D	8.80	2004

Note: a series of seven Fletcher Challenge and 13 Brierley Investment convertible capital notes are also listed on the NZSE; total outstandings are negligible, however, so they have not included in the table above.

PHILIPPINES

Issuer	Amount (mln)	Domestic/ Offshore	Coupon (%)	Maturity
Ayala Corp	US$100	O	3.00	2000
Bacnotan	US$55	O	5.50	2004
Benpres Hldg	US$44.3	O	4.20	Perp
EEI Corp	CHF30	O	3.50	2000
Filinvest	US$100	O	3.75	2004
Intl Container	US$20	O	6.00	2000
Intl Container	US$60	O	5.00	2001
JG Summit	US$300	O	3.50	2003
Metrobank	US$100	O	2.75	2000

SINGAPORE

Issuer	Amount (mln)	Domestic/ Offshore	Coupon (%)	Maturity
Amcol Hldg	SGD70	D	5.50	1999
Dairy Farm	US$208.9	O	6.50	perp
HK Land	US$410	O	4.00	2001
Jardine Strat	US$601.5	O	7.50	perp
Jaya Hldg	SGD20.9	D	3.00	1998
Keppel Corp	SGD109	D	1.50	1997
Keppel Corp	US$75	O	2.75	1997
Keppel Corp	US$75	O	4.00	1997
Sembawang Mar	SGD70	D	1.50	1998

SOUTH KOREA

Issuer	Amount (mln)	Domestic/ Offshore	Coupon (%)	Maturity
Anam Ind	CHF50	O	6.00	1996
Asia Motors	US$70	O	4.00	1996
Cheil Food	US$30	O	3.00	2006
Daechang Ind	US$15	O	0.13	2008
Daeduck Elec	US$20	O	0.25	2004
Daewoo Corp	US$75	O	0.00	2004
Daewoo Corp	US$50	O	0.25	2008
Daewoo Corp	CHF50	O	0.38	2000
Daewoo Corp	CHF75	O	3.25	1997
Daewoo Elec	CHF50	O	0.38	1999

SOUTH KOREA (continued)

Issuer	Amount (mln)	Domestic/ Offshore	Coupon (%)	Maturity
Daewoo Elec	CHF50	O	0.38	2000
Daewoo Elec	US$70	O	2.25	2008
Daewoo Elec	US$50	O	3.50	2007
Daewoo Heavy	US$40	O	3.00	2001
Daewoo Metal	US$15	O	0.25	2004
Daewoo Prec	CHF15	O	0.38	2000
Daewoo Tel	US$50	O	3.50	2006
Dae Ryung	CHF23	O	0.00	1998
Dai Yan Metal	US$20	O	0.25	2002
Dong a Pharm	US$25	O	3.13	2006
Dong ah Const	US$50	O	1.25	2004
Dong ah Const	CHF75	O	3.25	1997
Dong Yang Tin	CHF10	O	0.25	2000
Doosan Const	CHF15	O	0.25	1999
Goldstar	US$70	O	3.25	2006
Haitai Confect	CHF45	O	0.25	1999
Han Yang Chem	US$56	O	3.25	2006
Hanbo Steel	US$45	O	1.50	2009
Hanil Cement	US$15.5	O	0.25	2004
Hansol Paper	CHF23	O	0.38	2000
Hansung Ent	CHF11	O	0.25	2000
Hanyang Chem	US$56	O	3.25	2006
HS Chemical	US$10	O	0.38	2000
Hung Chang	CHF20	O	0.25	2000
Hyundai Metal	US$15	O	0.38	2009
Inkel Corp	US$20	O	0.75	2003
Jindo Corp	CHF25	O	6.00	1996
Jinro Corp	US$30	O	0.25	2009
Jinro Corp	CHF21.5	O	4.00	1996
Kangwon Ind	US$40	O	3.13	2006
Keyang Elec	CHF16	O	0.25	2000
Kia Precision	US$18	O	0.50	2009
Kia Steel	US$26	O	3.50	2007
Kohap	CHF20	O	0.38	2000
Kohap	CHF40	O	0.63	1999
Kolon Ind	US$50	O	0.25	2004
Kolon Int	US$20	O	1.00	2008
Korea Computer	CHF32	O	0.25	1999
Korea Green	US$10	O	0.25	2009

SOUTH KOREA (continued)

Issuer	Amount (mln)	Domestic/ Offshore	Coupon (%)	Maturity
Korea Tungsten	US$8	O	0.25	2002
Kum Kang Trdg	US$15	O	0.25	2004
Kumho Const	US$20	O	0.25	2009
Kunyoung Co	CHF25	O	0.75	1999
Miwon Co	US$30	O	1.75	2005
Newmax	CHF12	O	0.25	2000
Nong Shim	CHF15	O	0.68	2000
Onyang Pulp	CHF25	O	0.25	1999
Orion Elec	US$50.5	O	0.50	2009
Saehan Media	CHF15	O	0.38	2000
Saehan Media	US$30	O	1.75	2003
Samick Music	US$30	O	1.00	2004
Sammi Steel	US$70	O	4.00	1996
Samsung Disp	US$30	O	0.50	2002
Samsung Elec	CHF70	O	0.25	2000
Samsung Heavy	US$50	O	0.50	2009
Shin Sung	CHF20	O	1.00	1999
Shinwon Corp	US$18	O	0.50	2008
Ssangyong Cem	US$70	O	3.00	2005
Ssangyong Oil	US$50	O	3.00	2004
Ssangyong Oil	US$150	O	3.75	2008
STC Corp	US$30	O	1.25	2004
Sungshin Cem	US$12	O	3.50	2007
Sunkyong Ind	US$40	O	1.50	2005
Sunkyong Ltd	CHF75	O	4.75	1996
Taeil Media	CHF36	O	0.50	1998
Taeil Media	US$10.5	O	0.75	2009
Tailim Pkg	CHF16	O	0.25	2000
Tongyang Cement	CHF20	O	0.38	2000
Tongyang Nylon	US$30	O	3.25	2005
Tri Gem	US$30	O	3.50	1996
Woo Sung Con	CHF40	O	1.00	1999
Youngone Co	CHF15	O	0.50	1999
Young Poong	CHF16	O	0.50	1998
Yukong	CHF70	O	1.00	1998
Yukong	CHF20	O	3.00	2001

TAIWAN

Issuer	Amount (mln)	Domestic/ Offshore	Coupon (%)	Maturity
Acer	US$45	O	4.00	2001
ADI Corp	CHF60	O	0.50	1998
Cheng Loong	US$60	O	2.50	2001
Cheng Loong	NT$750	D	6.00	1996
Chia Hsin Cem	US$65	O	4.00	2002
Chung Hwa Pulp	NT$700	D	6.00	1996
Chuntex Elec	CHF60	O	2.00	2000
Delta Elec	NT$500	D	4.00	2001
Eagle Hldg	CHF55	O	0.50	1999
Ever Fortune	CHF40	O	2.00	2001
Far East Dep	US$75	O	3.00	2001
Far East Text	US$50	O	4.00	2006
Feng An Metal	CHF40	O	3.25	1999
Formosa Chem	US$250	O	1.75	2001
Goldsun Dev	NT$600	D	5.50	1996
Great Wall Ent	CHF30	O	0.75	1999
Kinpo Elec	US$40	O	3.00	2001
Kolin	NT$1,000	D	6.00	1996
KPT Ind	NT$350	D	5.75	1996
Long Chen	NT$500	D	3.50	2004
Mercuries	NT$600	D	4.00	2001
Microtek	US$29	O	3.50	2001
Mitak	NT$450	D	5.50	1996
Nan Ya Plastic	US$350	O	1.75	2001
Ornatube Ent	CHF37	O	1.68	2000
Pacific Const	CHF60	O	2.13	1998
Pacific Const	NT$1,200	D	5.75	1997
Pacific Elec	US$65	O	3.75	2001
President Ent	US$100	O	0.00	2001
Ruentex Const	CHF72.5	O	2.00	2001
Sampo Corp	US$50	O	2.68	2001
Sampo Corp	NT$350	D	6.00	1995
Sampo Corp	NT500	D	5.00	1996
Shinkong Synth	NT$1,000	D	5.75	1998
Sincere Navig	US$36	O	3.75	2003
Taiwan Kolin	JPY4,000	O	2.87	2000
Teco Elec	US$100	O	2.75	2004
Teco Elec	NT$600	D	3.75	2001
Tung Ho Steel	US$40	O	4.00	2001

TAIWAN (continued)

Issuer	Amount (mln)	Domestic/ Offshore	Coupon (%)	Maturity
Tung Ho Steel	NT$1,000	D	4.25	1998
U-Ming Marine	US$90	O	1.50	2001
United Micro	US$160	O	1.25	2004
United Micro	NT$1,500	D	3.50	2004
Walsin Lihwa	US$75	O	3.25	2004
Walsin Lihwa	US$60	O	3.00	2002
Yangming Mar	US$160	O	2.00	2001
Yieh Hsing	CHF70	O	2.00	2000
Yieh Loong	CHF80	O	2.00	2000
Yue Loong	NT$1,000	D	4.25	1997
Yuen Fong Yu	US$100	O	2.00	1999

THAILAND

Issuer	Amount (mln)	Domestic/ Offshore	Coupon (%)	Maturity
Asia Credit	US$100	O	3.75	2003
Alphatec Elec	US$45	O	4.00	1999
Bangkok Bank	US$400	O	3.25	2004
Bangkok Land	CHF400	O	3.125	2001
Bangkok Land	CHF50	O	4.50	1997
Bangkok Land	US$150	O	4.50	2003
Bank of Asia	US$75	O	3.75	2004
Banpu Coal	US$80	O	3.50	2004
CMIC Fin	US$50	O	3.50	2003
Dhana Siam	US$45	O	4.00	2003
Finance One	US$75	O	5.75	2003
Hemeraj Land	US$60	O	3.50	2003
Intl Engineer	THB1,200	D	4.00*	2000
Juldis Dev	US$60	O	4.25	2003
Kiatnakin Fin	US$60	O	4.00	2003
Krisda Mahan	THB640	D	6.00	1999
Land & House	US$60	O	5.00	2003
Loxley	US$85	O	3.50	2005
MDX Public	US$80	O	4.75	2003
NTS Steel	CHF80	O	1.00	2000
NTS Steel	US$100	O	4.00	2008

THAILAND (continued)

Issuer	Amount (mln)	Domestic/ Offshore	Coupon (%)	Maturity
One Hldg	THB950	D	6.50	2000
Phatra Than	US$175	O	3.50	2003
Robinson Dept	US$40	O	4.25	2004
Robinson Dept	US$50	O	3.25	2000
Sahaviriya St	US$105	O	3.50	2005
Siam Comm Bk	US$160	O	3.25	2004
Siam Syntech	US$40	O	4.50	2002
Sino Thai Eng	US$80	O	1.75	2003
Somprasong Land	US$80	O	3.875	2004
Tanayong	US$130	O	3.50	2004
Thai Cen Chem	US$60	O	3.75	2003
Union Asia Fin	US$75	O	3.375	2003
Wall St Fin	US$55	O	3.75	2004
Wattachak	US$80	O	3.50	2003

* step-up by 1% p.a.

Appendix IV

ASIA PACIFIC FUTURES/OPTIONS TRADED ON INTERNATIONAL EXCHANGES

Summarized below is a listing of 'Asia-related' futures and options (e.g. those which reference Asia Pacific prices, rates or indexes) which are traded on international futures exchanges.

Index

Contract	**Nikkei 225 Index Futures**
Type	Offshore
Exchange	Chicago Mercantile Exchange
Months	March, June, September, December
Contract Size	US$5 * Nikkei 225 Index
Tick Value	US$25/contract
Daily Limit	+/– 1,000 points against previous settlement price if index is under 20,000
	+/– 1,500 points against previous settlement price if index is between 20,005 and 30,000
	+/– 2,000 points against previous settlement price if index is over 30,005
Deliverable Instrument	Cash settlement
Last Trading Day	1st business day preceding the contract delivery day
Delivery Day	2nd Friday of the contract month
Real-time price data	Bloomberg: NXA <Cmdty>; Reuters: <0#NK:>; Telerate: 631

Contract	Options on Nikkei 225 Index Futures
Type	Offshore
Exchange	Chicago Mercantile Exchange
Months	Two consecutive months plus three quarterly months from March, June, September, December cycle
Contract Size	1 Nikkei 225 Index future
Tick Value	US$25/contract
Daily Limit	No price limits except trading is suspended if underlying futures contract is limit bid or offered
Deliverable Instrument	Physical settlement into underlying futures contract
Last Trading Day	Same as exercise day
Exercise Day	American exercise – any business day up to, and including, the expiry day for futures
Real-time price data	Bloomberg: NXA <Cmdty> OMON; Reuters: <0#NKmy+>; Telerate: 36616-23

Contract	Japan Index Options
Type	Offshore
Exchange	American Stock Exchange
Months	Three near-term months plus five additional months
Contract Size	US$100 * Japan Index
Tick Value	US$6.25 for options under US$3
	US$12.50 for all others
Daily Limit	No limit
Deliverable Instrument	Cash settlement
Last Trading Day	Penultimate business day prior to expiration
Exercise Day	European exercise – Saturday after the 3rd Friday of the expiration month only
Real-time price data	Bloomberg: JPN <Index> OMON; Reuters:<0#JPN*.A>
Other	Japan Index is based on 210 actively traded stocks from the TSE

Contract	Hong Kong Option Index
Type	Offshore
Exchange	American Stock Exchange
Months	Three near-term months plus two successive months from March, June, September, December cycle (also available as long-term options with 36 month expiry)
Contract Size	US$100 * Hong Kong Option Index
Tick Value	US$6.25 for options under US$3
	US$12.50 for all others
Daily Limit	No limit
Deliverable Instrument	Cash settlement
Last Trading Day	Penultimate business day prior to expiration
Exercise Day	European exercise – Saturday after the 3rd Friday of the expiration month only
Real-time price data	Bloomberg: HKO <Index> OMON, HKL <Index> OMON; Reuters: <0#HKO*.A>
Other	Hong Kong Option Index is based on 30 actively traded stocks from the SEHK

Contract	Nikkei 300 Index Options
Type	Offshore
Exchange	Chicago Board Options Exchange
Months	Two near-term months plus two months from the March, June, September, December cycle (also available as long-term options with 36 month expiry)
Contract Size	US$300 * Nikkei 300 Index
Tick Value	US$6.25 for options under US$3
	US$12.50 for all others
Daily Limit	No limit
Deliverable Instrument	Cash settlement
Last Trading Day	Business day preceding the day on which settlement value is determined
Exercise Day	European exercise – last business day of the contract month only
Real-time price data	Bloomberg: NIK <Index> OMON, NIKL <Index> OMON; Reuters: <0#NIK*.W>

Interest Rate

Contract	Ten-year Japanese Government Bond Futures
Type	Offshore
Exchange	London International Financial Futures Exchange
Months	March, June, September, December
Contract Size	JPY100 mln
Tick Value	JPY10,000/contract
Daily Limit	+/– 2 points against previous TSE close; no limits on last hour of trading
Deliverable Instrument	Cash settlement
Last Trading Day	One business day prior to the TSE's last trading day
Delivery Day	Business day following the last trading day
Real-time price data	Bloomberg: N A <Cmdty>; Reuters: <0#FYB:>; Telerate: 994

Currency

Contract	A$/US$ Currency Futures
Type	Offshore
Exchange	Chicago Mercantile Exchange
Months	January, March, April, June, July, September, October, December plus spot month
Contract Size	A$100,000
Tick Value	US$10/contract
Daily Limit	+/– US$2,000 per contract against previous day's settlement price for 15 minutes, then expanded price limits of US$3,000, US$6,000, US$9,000, US$12,000, each for 15 minute intervals
Deliverable Instrument	Physical settlement in the country of issuance at a bank designated by the clearinghouse
Last Trading Day	2nd business day immediately preceding the 3rd Wednesday of the contract month
Delivery Day	3rd Wednesday of the contract month
Real-time price data	Bloomberg: ATA <Cmdty>; Reuters: <0#AD:>; Telerate: 915

Note: contract also available through Globex

Contract	Options on A$/US$ Currency Futures
Type	Offshore
Exchange	Chicago Mercantile Exchange
Months	March, June, September, December, plus one short-dated contract and two contract months not in March–December cycle
Contract Size	1 A$/US$ currency future
Tick Value	US$10/contract
Daily Limit	No price limits but option trading ceases when futures price limits are reached
Deliverable Instrument	Physical settlement into underlying futures contract
Last Trading Day	Long-dated: 2nd Friday immediately preceding the 3rd Wednesday of the contract month; short-dated: 1st Friday succeeding the 3rd Wednesday of the contract month. For both: preceding business day if a holiday
Exercise Day	American exercise – any business day up to, and including, the last trading day
Real-time price data	Bloomberg: ATA <Cmdty> OMON; Reuters: <0#ADmy+>; Telerate: 8486-89

Note: contract also available through Globex

Contract	US$/JPY Currency Futures
Type	Offshore
Exchange	Chicago Mercantile Exchange
Months	January, March, April, June, July, September, October, December plus spot month
Contract Size	JPY12,500,000
Tick Value	US$12.50/contract
Daily Limit	+/– US$2,500 per contract against previous day's settlement price for 15 minutes, then expanded price limits of US$3,750, US$7,500, US$11,250, US$15,000, each for 15 minute intervals
Deliverable Instrument	Physical settlement in the country of issuance at a bank designated by the clearinghouse
Last Trading Day	2nd business day immediately preceding the 3rd Wednesday of the contract month
Delivery Day	3rd Wednesday of the contract month
Real-time price data	Bloomberg: JYA <Cmdty>; Reuters: <0#JY:>; Telerate: 914

Note: contract also available through Globex

Contract	Options on US$/JPY Currency Futures
Type	Offshore
Exchange	Chicago Mercantile Exchange
Months	March, June, September, December, plus one short dated contract and two contract months not in March-December cycle
Contract Size	1 US$/JPY currency future
Tick Value	US$12.50/contract
Daily Limit	No price limits but option trading ceases when futures price limits are reached
Deliverable Instrument	Physical settlement into underlying futures contract
Last Trading Day	Long-dated: 2nd Friday immediately preceding the 3rd Wednesday of the contract month; short-dated: 1st Friday succeeding the 3rd Wednesday of the contract month. For both: preceding business day if a holiday
Exercise Day	American exercise – any business day up to, and including, the last trading day
Real-time price data	Bloomberg: JYA <Cmdty> OMON; Reuters: <0#JYmy+>; Telerate: 9229-32

Note: contract also available through Globex

Contract	JPY/US$ Rolling Spot Currency Futures
Type	Offshore
Exchange	Chicago Mercantile Exchange
Months	March, June, September, December
Contract Size	US$250,000
Tick Value	JPY2,500/contract
Daily Limit	No limit
Deliverable Instrument	Physical settlement in the country of issuance at a bank designated by the clearinghouse
Last Trading Day	2nd business day immediately preceding the 3rd Wednesday of the contract month; if a holiday in Chicago or NY, closest business day
Delivery Day	3rd Wednesday of the contract month
Real-time price data	Bloomberg: RYA <Cmdty>; Telerate: 633
Other	Instead of delivery, participants can maintain position by rolling over to next business day; open positions are charged relevant swap points from spot/next quotes

Note: contract also available through Globex

Contract	**JPY/US$ Currency Forward Futures**
Type	Offshore
Exchange	Chicago Mercantile Exchange
Months	12 consecutive months plus four additional months in March, June, September, December cycle
Contract Size	One JPY/US$ rolling spot future
Tick Value	JPY625/contract
Daily Limit	No limit
Deliverable Instrument	Physical settlement into underlying futures contract
Last Trading Day	2nd business day immediately preceding the 3rd Wednesday of the contract month
Delivery Day	3rd Wednesday of the contract month
Real-time price data	Bloomberg: JYA <Cmdty>; Telerate: 9247
Other	Instead of delivery, participants can maintain position by rolling over to next business day; open positions are charged relevant swap points from spot/next quotes

Note: contract also available through Globex

Contract	**DM/JPY Currency Futures**
Type	Offshore
Exchange	Chicago Mercantile Exchange
Months	January, March, April, June, July
Contract Size	DM125,000
Tick Value	JPY1,250/contract
Daily Limit	+/– JPY1.50/DM against previous day's settlement price for 15 minutes
Deliverable Instrument	Physical settlement in the country of issuance at a bank designated by the clearinghouse
Last Trading Day	2nd business day immediately preceding the 3rd Wednesday of the contract month
Delivery Day	3rd Wednesday of the contract month
Real-time price data	Bloomberg: DJA <Cmdty>; Reuters: <0#DJ:>; Telerate: 634

Note: contract also available through Globex

Contract	Options on DM/JPY Currency Futures
Type	Offshore
Exchange	Chicago Mercantile Exchange
Months	March, June, September, December, plus one short dated contract and two contract months not in March-December cycle
Contract Size	1 DM/JPY currency future
Tick Value	JPY1,250/contract
Daily Limit	No price limits but option trading ceases when futures price limits are reached
Deliverable Instrument	Physical settlement into underlying futures contract
Last Trading Day	Long-dated: 2nd Friday immediately preceding the 3rd Wednesday of the contract month; short-dated: 1st Friday succeeding the 3rd Wednesday of the contract month. For both: preceding business day if a holiday
Exercise Day	American exercise – any business day up to, and including, the last trading day
Real-time price data	Bloomberg: DJA <Cmdty> OMON; Reuters: <0#DJmy+>; Telerate: 26173

Note: contract also available through Globex

Note: As of this writing, A$/US$ rolling spot currency futures, A$/US$ rolling spot currency futures options, and US$/JPY rolling spot currency futures options have been approved by the US regulatory authorities but have not yet been listed on the CME.

Contract	A$/US$ Currency Futures
Type	Offshore
Exchange	MidAmerica Commodity Exchange
Months	March, June, September, December
Contract Size	A$50,000
Tick Value	US$5
Daily Limit	No limit
Deliverable Instrument	Physical settlement of currencies; notice of delivery must be given to the clearinghouse
Last Trading Day	2nd business day immediately preceding the 3rd Wednesday of the contract month; if a holiday in Chicago or New York, on preceding business day
Delivery Day	3rd Wednesday of the contract month; if not a business day in Chicago or country of home currency, the next business day
Real-time price data	Bloomberg: XAA <Cmdty>

Contract	US$/JPY Currency Futures
Type	Offshore
Exchange	MidAmerica Commodity Exchange
Months	March, June, September, December
Contract Size	JPY6,250,000
Tick Value	US$6.25
Daily Limit	No limit
Deliverable Instrument	Physical settlement of currencies; notice of delivery must be given to the clearinghouse
Last Trading Day	2nd business day immediately preceding the 3rd Wednesday of the contract month; if a holiday in Chicago or New York, on preceding business day
Delivery Day	3rd Wednesday of the contract month; if not a business day in Chicago or country of home currency, the next business day
Real-time price data	Bloomberg: XJA <Cmdty>; Reuters: <0#XJ:>

Contract	A$/US$ Currency Futures
Type	Offshore
Exchange	Philadelphia Board of Trade
Months	March, June, September, December plus two near months
Contract Size	A$100,000
Tick Value	US$10
Daily Limit	No limit
Deliverable Instrument	Physical settlement of currencies
Last Trading Day	Friday before the 3rd Wednesday of the contract month
Delivery Day	3rd Wednesday of the contract month
Real-time price data	Bloomberg: ZAA <Cmdty>

Contract	**US$/JPY Currency Futures**
Type	Offshore
Exchange	Philadelphia Board of Trade
Months	March, June, September, December plus two near months
Contract Size	JPY12,500,000
Tick Value	US$12.50
Daily Limit	No limit
Deliverable Instrument	Physical settlement of currencies
Last Trading Day	Friday before the 3rd Wednesday of the contract month
Delivery Day	3rd Wednesday of the contract month
Real-time price data	Bloomberg: ZJA <Cmdty>; Telerate: 8467

Contract	**US$/JPY Currency Futures**
Type	Offshore
Exchange	Financial Instrument Exchange
Months	March, June, September, December
Contract Size	JPY12,500,000
Tick Value	US$12.50
Daily Limit	No limit
Deliverable Instrument	Physical settlement of currencies
Last Trading Day	Two business days prior to the 3rd Wednesday of the contract month
Delivery Day	3rd Wednesday of the contract month
Real-time price data	Bloomberg: YYA <Cmdty>

Contract	DM/JPY Currency Futures
Type	Offshore
Exchange	Financial Instrument Exchange
Months	March, June, September, December
Contract Size	DM125,000
Tick Value	JPY1,250
Daily Limit	No limit
Deliverable Instrument	Physical settlement of currencies
Last Trading Day	Two business days prior to the 3rd Wednesday of the contract month
Delivery Day	3rd Wednesday of the contract month
Real-time price data	Bloomberg: JXA <Cmdty>

Contract	Options on DM/JPY Currency Futures
Type	Offshore
Exchange	Financial Instrument Exchange
Months	March, June, September, December plus two near months
Contract Size	1 DM/JPY currency future
Tick Value	JPY1,250
Daily Limit	No limit
Deliverable Instrument	Physical settlement into underlying futures contract
Last Trading Day	Two business days prior to the last trading day in futures
Exercise Day	American exercise – any business day up to, and including, the last trading day
Real-time price data	Bloomberg: JXA <Cmdty> OMON

REFERENCES

Areddy, J., 'Stock futures to make debut in Hong Kong', *Asian Wall Street Journal*, 1995, 16 February, p. 14.

Andersen, A., (1993), *Asia Pacific Capital Markets* (London: EIU).

Asahi Evening News, 'Sydney exchange plans to be Asia hub', 18 January, 1995, p. 10.

Asiamoney, 'SFE equity derivatives', May 1994, pp. 46–9.

Asiamoney, 'Looking offshore for inspiration', September 1994, pp. 29–36.

Asian Wall Street Journal, 'Manila bourse plans to list bonds, warrants', 28 December, 1994, p. 18.

Asian Wall Street Journal, 'Chinese futures exchange plans to open market for foreigners', 20 January, 1995, p. 18.

Asian Wall Street Journal, 'Hong Kong prepares to launch futures contracts on 8 currencies', 9 February, 1995, p. 13.

Asian Wall Street Journal, 'China orders state enterprises to clear plans on futures trading', 15 February, 1995, p. 20.

Asian Wall Street Journal, 'Thai official calls for derivatives measures', 22 February, 1995, p. 18.

Asian Wall Street Journal, 'Hong Kong, Thailand increase scrutiny of derivatives activities', 9 March, 1995, p. 21.

Asian Wall Street Journal, 'IPE, SIMEX plan joint trading of Brent crude futures by June', 30 March, 1995, p. 16.

Asian Wall Street Journal, 'Shanghai defers starts of trading in forward currency contracts', 9 April, 1995, p. 15.

Asian Wall Street Journal, 'Two Sinar Mas subsidiaries begin recovery from derivatives losses', 31 May, 1995, p. 11.

Asian Wall Street Journal, 'Regulators in China approve constitutions, rules for exchanges', 31 May, 1995, p. 13.

Asian Wall Street Journal, 'Taiwan alters its policy on forward contracts', 6 July, 1995, p. 20.

ASX Derivatives, 'Information Memorandum', June 1995.

Austin, B., 'China to standardize futures exchanges, curb speculation in 1995', *Bloomberg Business News*, 16 December, 1994.

Austin, B., 'China's national foreign exchange trading centre tops $66.4 bln', *Bloomberg Business News*, 24 April, 1994.

Australian Financial Markets Association (1994), *Australian Financial Markets Report 1994*, (Sydney: Australian Financial Markets Association).

Australian Financial Review, 'Derivatives Survey', 30 January, 1995, pp. 37–51.

Australian Stock Exchange (1995), *Fact Book* (Sydney: Australian Stock Exchange).

Bajpai, R., 'India okays options, but the market is not quite ready for it', *Bloomberg Business News*, 30 January, 1995.

Bajpai, R., 'Indian stocks tumble on disappointment over new trading rules', *Bloomberg Business News*, 28 July, 1995.

Balan, A., 'Berjaya Industrial denies liability for derivatives loss', *Business Times*, 29 December, 1994.

Bank Negara Malaysia (1994), *Money and Banking in Malaysia, (4th ed.)* (Kuala Lumpur: Bank Negara Malaysia).

Bank of Japan (1994), *Quarterly Bulletin, August* (Tokyo: Bank of Japan).

Bank of Japan (1995), *Quarterly Bulletin, February* (Tokyo: Bank of Japan).

Bank of Thailand (1994), *Quarter Bulletin, December* (Bangkok: Bank of Thailand).

Banks, E. (1994), *Emerging Asian Fixed Income Markets* (London: Macmillan Press).

Becker, J., 'Wild gambling fever grips China's futures markets', *South China Morning Post*, 18 June, 1995, p. 15.

Beidleman, C., ed. (1992), *Cross Currency Swaps* (Homewood, Illinois: Business One Irwin).

Bernama News Agency, 'Malaysia yet to issue tax rulings for swap transactions', 10 June, 1995.

Botsford, C., 'Exotic currencies', *Asia Risk Manager*, February 1995, pp. 25–28.

Bremner, B., 'China suspends rice, oil futures in market clean-up bid', *Bloomberg Business News*, 25 October, 1994.

Buckley, J., ed. (1989), *Guide to World Commodity Markets, (6th ed.)* (London: Kogan Page).

Business Times, 'Indonesia prepares bill for commodity futures trading', 30 January, 1993.

Business Times, 'RAS to launch new rubber futures contract', 28 August, 1993.

Business Times, 'Singapore product swaps market sees rising liquidity', 14 October, 1993.

Business Times, 'Singapore: Options trading outlook gloomy', 14 September, 1994.

Chan, C., 'Market trade returns for Shanghai bond futures', *South China Morning Post*, 11 March, 1995, p. 1.

Chau, F., 'HK Futures Exchange hopes to rescue HIBOR contract', *Reuter Textline*, 3 May, 1991.

Chia, W., 'Modernland will be first to issue warrants in Indonesia', *Reuters News Service*, 27 October, 1994.

China Securities Bulletin, 6 June, 1994, p. 5.

China Securities Bulletin, 27 July, 1994, p. 3.

China Securities Bulletin, 24 November, 1994, p. 2.

China Securities Bulletin, 20 December, 1994, p. 2.

China Securities Bulletin, 16 January, 1995, p. 1

China Securities Bulletin, 18 January, 1995, p. 1.

China Securities Bulletin, 23 January, 1995, p. 3.

Choudhury, S.P. , 'From A to Z in Asia', *Risk*, April 1995, pp. 41–5.

Choudhury, S.P. , 'Derivatives still in demand', *Risk*, July 1995, pp. 7–9.

Clubley, S. (1989), *Trading in Oil Futures* (New York: Nichols Publishing).

Connolly, K. and Philips G. (1992), *Japanese Warrant Markets* (London: Macmillan Press).

Coogan, P., 'HK Futures Exchange shifts to a new era', *Financial Times*, 27 April, 1994, pp. 21–22.

Cooper, G., 'Blossom time', *Risk*, November 1993, pp. 22–6.

Cooper, G., 'Tokyo in transition', *Risk*, July 1994, pp. 29–33.

Das, S. (1994), *Swaps and Financial Derivatives, (2nd ed.)* (Sydney: Law Book Company).

Dattel, E. (1994), *The Sun That Never Rose* (Chicago: Probus).

David, P., 'Bank Negara Malaysia's guidelines on financial derivatives', *Capital Asia*, 7 April, 1995.

Derivatives Week, 'Dealers look to India for booming derivatives mart', 16 January, 1995.

Derivatives Week, 'Hong Kong Exchange plans futures on Chinese shares', 23 January, 1995.

Din, D., 'Derivative products in Malaysia', *Asia Risk Manager*, September 1994, pp. 36–7.

Elms, D., 'Rationale of ratios', *Risk*, August 1995, pp. 24–31.

Elton, E., and Gruber M. (1990), *Japanese Capital Markets* (New York: Harper & Row).

Energy Risk, 'The war for Singapore', December 1994, p. 2.

Euromoney Research Guides, *Emerging Currencies*, June 1995.

Euromoney Supplement, *Indonesia's stockmarket: The bourse of tomorrow?*, August 1995.

Euromoney Supplement, *Thailand: Blueprint for the 21st Century*, August 1995.

Fabozzi, F. (ed.), (1990), *Japanese Bond Markets* (Chicago: Probus).

Falloon, W., 'Fighting for futures', *Risk*, August 1994, pp. 16–22.

Far Eastern Economic Review, 'Futures shock', 16 March, 1995, pp. 60–70.

Fluendy, S., 'Buoyant year sets scene for extra futures products deals', *South China Morning Post*, 27 December, 1994, p. 2.

Fluendy, S., and Fung N., 'Debt paper futures next in line', *South China Morning Post*, 25 April, 1995, p. 14.

Foo, C.P. , 'Investors swing back to futures', *South China Morning Post*, 28 March, 1995, p. 4.

Ford, M., 'Bank Bali applies for offer of rights issue with warrants', *Bloomberg Business News*, 23 May, 1995.

Foreign Exchange Letter, 'Currency snapshot: Taiwan', 16 January , 1995, p. 8.

Freris, A. (1991), *The Financial Markets of Hong Kong* (London: Routledge).

Fung, N., 'Guidelines to be set on trading of derivatives', *South China Morning Post*, 23 December, 1994, p. 1.

Fung, N., 'Exchange Fund broadens scope with derivatives', *South China Morning Post*, 27 December, 1994, p. 1.

Fung, N., 'Insurance firms to get derivatives guidelines', *South China Morning Post*, 16 March, 1995, p. 2.

Futures Industry, 'Top 20 futures contracts worldwide', February 1995, p. 10.

Goldsmith, B., 'Australia wool contract starts new era in futures', *Reuter Textline*, 9 March, 1995.

Gopalakrishnan, R., 'India pressed to end ban on futures', *Reuters New Service*, 13 May, 1992.

Grossman, W., 'China: Rebuilding the futures industry', *Futures Industry*, February 1995, p. 17.

Halesworth, P., 'Sinar Mas firms' earnings reflect derivative losses of US$69 mln', *Asian Wall Street Journal*, 2 May, 1995, p. 4.

Hannam, P. , 'Hong Kong exchanges fight over share futures contracts', *Bloomberg Business News*, October 25, 1994.

Hastings, W., 'London leads global currency market', *Asian Wall Street Journal*. 20 September, 1995, p. 1.

Hendry, S., 'China coddles bonds while punishing futures', *Bloomberg Business News*, 24 June, 1994.

Hendry, S., 'Shanghai brokerage says other firms had bond losses', *Bloomberg Business News*, 27 February, 1995.

Hendry, S., 'Chinese securities watchdog acts against bond futures violators', *Bloomberg Business News*, 1 April, 1995.

Hewett, G., 'Exchange gives details of new currency futures', *South China Morning Post*, 2 March, 1995, p. 3.

Hill, S., 'Australian banks' derivatives risk is A$50bln, central bank says', *Bloomberg Business News*, 15 September, 1994.

Hills, Q., 'The potential for ASEAN derivatives market growth', *Asia Risk Manager*, September 1994, pp. 10–12.

Hirsh, M., 'Why Japan won't change', *Institutional Investor*, 11 September, 1994, pp. 57–69.

Hokkaido Grain Exchange, 'Information Memorandum', June 1995.

Hong Kong Futures Exchange, 'Information Memorandum', March 1995.

Hong Kong Monetary Authority, 'Bilateral netting under the capital adequacy framework', *Quarterly Bulletin*, May 1995, pp. 27–30.

Hong Kong Monetary Authority, 'Use of interest rate swaps in the management of the Exchange Fund', *Quarterly Bulletin*, May 1995, pp. 27–30.

Howell, M., 'Hong Kong Stock Exchange to begin options market next August', *Bloomberg Business News*, 10 October, 1994.

Hwong, T., 'Hong Kong Stock Exchange allows listing of call spread warrants', *Bloomberg Business News*, 9 June, 1994.

Hwong, T. and Austin B., 'Hong Kong's new China share index may spawn derivatives', *Bloomberg Business News*, 5 August, 1994.

Indonesian Commodity Exchange Board, 'Information Memorandum', June 1995.

International Finance Corporation (1995), *Emerging Stockmarket Factbook* (Washington DC: IFC).

International Financing Review, 'Swaps still booming', 11 February, 1995, p. 103.

International Financing Review, 'Futures for Honkers', 11 February, 1995, p. 105.

International Financing Review, 'Warrants back in fashion in Asia', 11 February, 1995, p. 108.

International Securities Institute (1994), *Handbook on Financial Futures and Traded Options in Asia* (Hong Kong: ISI).

International Securities Institute (1994), *Asian Stockmarket Factbook 1994/1995* (Hong Kong: ISI).

Jakarta Stock Exchange, 'Information Memorandum', June 1995.

Japan Securities Research Institute (1992), *Capital Markets and Financial Services in Japan: Regulation and Practice* (Tokyo: JSRI).

Jay, P. (ed.) (1994), *Asia Pacific Securities Handbook* (Hong Kong: Philip Jay).

Jay, P. (ed.) (1994), *China Securities Handbook* (Hong Kong: Philip Jay).

Jiarathanakul, S., 'Development of Thai Warrants', *Asia Risk Manager*, January 1995, pp. 44–7.

Kahn, J., 'Regulator gets new chief as China tightens security', *Asian Wall Street Journal,* 7 March, 1995, p. 1.

Kanmon Commodity Exchange, 'Information Memorandum', June 1995.

Kansai Agricultural Commodities Exchange (1995), *Guide to trading at the KANEX*, (Osaka: KANEX).

Kaufman, P. (1984), *Handbook of Futures Markets* (New York: John Wiley).

Kennedy, S., 'Derivative disasters unlikely in Hong Kong', *South China Morning Post*, 27 December, 1994, p. 2.

Khandeparkar, U., 'India's BSE takes first step toward futures trade', *Reuter News Service*, 24 May, 1994.

Kobe Raw Silk Exchange, 'Information Memorandum', March 1995.

Kobe Rubber Exchange, 'Information Memorandum', January 1995.

Korea Economic Daily, 'Commodity and financial futures market merge starting next year,' 6 January, 1995.

Korea Exchange Bank (1994), *Quarterly Review, Third Quarter* (Seoul: Korea Exchange Bank).

Korea Stock Exchange (1995), *Outline of Korean Stock Price Index Futures* (Seoul: Korea Stock Exchange).

Kuala Lumpur Commodity Exchange, 'Information Memorandum', June 1995.

Kuala Lumpur Options and Financial Futures Exchange, 'Information Memorandum', August 1995.

Kumakura, T., 'Malaysia said to allow trading of warrants on listed stocks', *Bloomberg Business News*, 7 December, 1994.

Lam, A., 'HK likely to see flood of call spread warrants', *Reuter Textline*, 9 June, 1994.

Lap Lam, W., 'Firms told to avoid futures trading', *South China Morning Post*, 11 March, 1995, p. 7.

Lee, P. , 'Futures on stocks: Is this the right way forward?' *Securities Journal*, December 1994, pp. 4–6.

Lee, Y.H., 'Singapore rubber futures brokers face tough times', *Reuters News Service*, 11 February, 1993.

Lim, S.N., 'HK bourse plans to trade options from August', *Reuters News Service*, 24 November, 1994.

Liu, J., 'Foreigners allowed to convert Taiwan convertibles', *Reuters News Service*, 15 February, 1995.

Locke, J., 'Getting to know the bear', *Risk*, April 1994, pp. 56–60.

Locke, J., 'Home and away', *Risk*, September 1994, pp. 11–14.

Lopez, L., 'BAPEPAM warns Indonesian listed firms on derivatives', *Bloomberg Business News*, 6 December, 1994.

Maebashi Dried Cocoon Exchange, 'Information Memorandum', June 1995.

Mahumud, E., 'Establishing the KLFM', *Asia Risk Manager*, May 1995, pp. 36–9.

Manila International Futures Exchange (1995), *Guide to Futures Exchange*, (Manila: MIFE).

Mark, J. and Brauchli, M., 'Barings débacle spurs reform in Singapore', *Asian Wall Street Journal*, 1 March, 1995, p. 1.

McNab, D., 'Accounting for interest rate swaps', *Asia Risk Manager*, January 1995, pp. 51–4.

Montagnon, P. and Mallet, V., 'Thailand aims to set up futures exchange', *Financial Times*, 4 November, 1994.

Moshavi, S., 'Indian stocks rise on plan to start options trading', *Bloomberg Business News*, 30 January, 1995.

Nagoya Grain and Sugar Exchange, 'Information Memorandum', June 1995.

Nagoya Stock Exchange, 'Information Memorandum', March 1995.

Nagoya Textile Exchange, 'Information Memorandum', June 1995.

New Zealand Futures and Options Exchange, 'Information Memorandum', March 1995.

Osaka Stock Exchange, 'Information Memorandum', December 1994.

Osaka Stock Exchange, 'Information Memorandum', June 1995.

Osaka Textile Exchange, 'Information Memorandum', March 1995.

Paisley, E. and Woodcock, N., 'Southeast Asia's currencies come of age', *Institutional Investor*, February 1995, pp. 38–47.

Park, K. and Schoenfeld, S. (1992), *The Pacific Rim Futures and Options Markets* (Chicago: Probus).

Rattanaik, S. (ed.) (1993), *Corporate Finance/Treasury Managers Yearbook 1993* (London: Euromoney).

Redmayne, J. (1994), *Convertibles: An International Perspective* (London: Euromoney).

Rees, M., 'Philadelphia Exchange's currency options to trade in Hong Kong', *Bloomberg Business News*, 16 March, 1995.

Republic of China (1995), *Financial Statistics Monthly, Taiwan District* (Taipei: Central Bank of China).

Reserve Bank of New Zealand (1995), *Reserve Bank Bulletin, March Quarter* (Wellington: Reserve Bank of New Zealand).

Reuters News Service, 'Australia introduces exchange traded warrants', 11 January, 1991.

Reuters News Service, 'HK bourse issues new rules on covered warrants', 3 November, 1992.

Reuters News Service, 'Financial futures, options marts to open soon', 1 April, 1994.

Reuters News Service, 'Thailand aims to set up commodity futures exchange', 5 August, 1994.

Reuters News Service, 'India report on commodity futures due out soon', 22 September, 1994.

Reuters News Service, 'Japan MOF eases rules on yen interest rate swaps', 14 October, 1994.

Reuters News Service, 'Text of Indian statement ending ban on options', 27 January, 1995.

Reuters News Service, 'Korea derivative trading volume', 23 February, 1995.

Reuters News Service, 'Korea draws up safeguards for index futures', 2 March, 1995.

Reuters News Service, 'Great loss in interest swaps – Nippon Sanso', 29 March, 1995.

Reuters News Service, 'Malaysia to introduce options on palm oil futures', 3 April, 1995.

Reyes, A., 'Under new names derivatives still pushed in Manila', *Bloomberg Business News*, 23 March, 1995.

Riley, I., 'Development of the Hong Kong Futures Exchange', *Asia Risk Manager*, January 1995, pp. 4–7.

Roche, J. (1993), *Commodity-linked Derivatives* (London: IFR).

Sathirathaya, M., 'Development of exotic swaps in Asia', *Asia Risk Manager*, February 1995, pp. 17–18.

Schwartz, R. and Smith, C. (1990), *The Handbook of Currency and Interest Rate Risk Management* (New York: NYIF).

Scott, A. and Dunnett B., 'TPI Polene ponders action in UBS Dispute', *Asian Wall Street Journal*, 9 March, 1995, p. 11.

Securities and Exchange Commission of Thailand, 'Securities offerings information memorandum', 7 July, 1995.

Segal, P. , 'Singapore to trade futures on Hong Kong stocks', *Bloomberg Business News*, 27 October, 1994.

Segal, P. , 'Debate rages in Hong Kong over stock futures', *Bloomberg Business News*, 12 December, 1994.

Sharma, S., 'India launches cross currency options', *Reuters News Service*, 27 January, 1994.

Silverman, G., 'Accidents will happen', *Far Eastern Economic Review*, 16 March, 1995, pp. 60–70.

Singapore Commodity Exchange, 'Information Memorandum', June 1995.

Singapore International Monetary Exchange, 'Information Memorandum', March 1995.

South China Morning Post, 'T-bond futures turnover soars to 2,800bln yuan', 23 January, 1995, p. 4.

South China Morning Post, 'FEC to allow currency forward trades', 9 March, 1995, p. 6.

South China Morning Post, 'CSRC sets standards for futures', 20 June, 1995, p. 12.

Sydney Futures Exchange, 'Information Memorandum', June 1995.

Takagi, S. (1993), *Japanese Capital Markets* (Cambridge: Blackwell).

Tokyo Commodity Exchange, 'Historical review', April 1995.

Tokyo Grain Exchange, 'Information Memorandum', June 1995.

Tokyo International Financial Futures Exchange, 'Monthly statistics report, 1995' (TIFFE: Tokyo).

Tokyo Stock Exchange (1994), *Fact Book 1994* (Tokyo: TSE).

Tokyo Stock Exchange, 'Information Memorandum', June 1995.

Toyohashi Dried Cocoon Exchange, 'Information Memorandum', June 1995.

Viner, A. (1987), *Inside Japan's Financial Markets* (London: Economist Publications).

Yokohama Raw Silk Exchange, 'Information Memorandum', March 1995.

World Bank (1994), *China: Internal market development and regulation* (Washington D.C.: World Bank).

World Bank (1995), *The Emerging Asian Bond Market* (Washington D.C.: World Bank).

Wyatt, S., 'Positive signals for futures', *Australian Financial Review*, 31 October, 1994, p. 66.

Zubulake, L. (1991), *The Complete Guide to Convertible Securities Worldwide* (New York: John Wiley).

Index of Listed Derivatives by Exchange

Australia

though NYMEX link

China

Beijing Commodity Exchange

Changchun United Futures Exchange

China Commodity Futures Exchange of Hainan

Hong Kong

Indonesia

Japan

Singapore

South Korea

Index of Listed Futures and Options by Category

Equity Futures

Equity Options

Index Futures

Index Options/Futures Options

Deposit Futures

Deposit Options/Futures Options

Interest Rate Futures

Interest Rate Options/Futures Options

Currency Futures

Currency Options/Futures Options

Commodity Futures (Agriculturals/Softs)

Commodity Options/Futures Options (Agriculturals/Softs)

Commodity Futures (Energy)

Commodity Options/Futures Options (Energy)

None available

Through the NYMEX link. Contracts also expected to be available on the Singapore International Monetary Exchange

Commodity Futures (Metals)

Commodity Options/Futures Options (Metals)

None available

Commodity Futures (Precious Metals)

Commodity Options/Futures Options (Precious Metals)

None available

Commodity Futures (Other)

Commodity Options/Futures Options (Other)

None available

General Index